LIFE OF JOHN COLERIDGE PATTESON

By Charlotte Mary Yonge

PREFACE.

There are of course peculiar advantages as well as disadvantages in endeavouring to write the life of one recently departed. On the one hand, the remembrances connected with him are far fresher; his contemporaries can be consulted, and much can be made matter of certainty, for which a few years would have made it necessary to trust to hearsay or probable conjecture. On the other, there is necessarily much more reserve; nor are the results of the actions, nor even their comparative importance, so clearly discernible as when there has been time to ripen the fruit.

These latter drawbacks are doubled when the subject of the biography has passed away in comparatively early life: when the persons with whom his life is chiefly interwoven are still in full activity; and when he has only lived to sow his seed in many waters, and has barely gathered any portion of his harvest.

Thus what I have written of Bishop Patteson, far more what I have copied of his letters, is necessarily only partial, although his nearest relations and closest friends have most kindly permitted the full use of all that could build up a complete idea of the man as he was. Many letters relate to home and family matters, such as it would be useless and impertinent to divulge; and yet it is necessary to mention that these exist, because without them we might not know how deep was the lonely man's interest and sympathy in all that concerned his kindred and friends. Other letters only repeat the narrative or the reflections given elsewhere; and of these, it has seemed best only to print that which appeared to have the fullest or the clearest expression. In general, the story is best told in letters to the home party; while thoughts are generally best expressed in the correspondence with Sir John Taylor Coleridge, to whom the Nephew seems to have written with a kind of unconscious carefulness of diction. There is as voluminous a correspondence with the Brother, and letters to many Cousins; but as these either repeat the same adventures or else are purely domestic, they have been little brought forward, except where any gap occurred in the correspondence which has formed the staple material.

Letters upon the unhappy Maori war have been purposely omitted; and, as far as possible, such criticisms on living personages as it seemed fair towards the writer to omit. Criticisms upon their publications are of course a different thing. My desire has been to give enough expression of Bishop Patteson's opinions upon Church and State affairs, to represent his manner of thinking, without transcribing every detail of remarks, which were often made upon an imperfect report, and were, in fact, only written down, instead of spoken and forgotten, because correspondence served him instead of conversation.

I think I have represented fairly, for I have done my best faithfully to select passages giving his mind even where it does not coincide completely with my own opinions; being quite convinced that not only should a biographer never attempt either to twist or conceal the sentiments of the subject, but that either to apologise for, or as it were to argue with them, is vain in both senses of the word.

The real disadvantage of the work is my own very slight personal acquaintance with the externals of the man, and my ignorance of the scenes in which the chief part of his life was passed. There are those who would have been far more qualified in these respects than myself, and, above all, in that full and sympathetic masculine grasp of a man's powerful mind, which is necessarily denied to me. But these fittest of all being withheld by causes which are too well known to need mention, I could only endeavour to fulfil the work as best I might; trusting that these unavoidable deficiencies may be supplied, partly by Coleridge Patteson's own habit of writing unreservedly, so that he speaks for himself, and partly by the very full notes and records with which his friends have kindly supplied me, portraying him from their point of view; so that I could really trust that little more was needed than ordinary judgment in connecting and selecting. Nor until the work is less fresh from my hand will it be possible to judge whether I have in any way been allowed to succeed in my earnest hope and endeavour to bring the statue out of the block, and as it were to carve the figure of the Saint for his niche among those who have given themselves soul and body to God's Work.

It has been an almost solemn work of anxiety, as well as one of love. May I only have succeeded in causing these letters and descriptions to leave a true and definite impression of the man and of his example!

Let me here record my obligations for materials—I need hardly say to the immediate family and relations—for, in truth, I act chiefly as their amanuensis; but likewise to the Bishop of Lichfield, Bishop Abraham.

Lady Martin, the Rev. B. T. Dudley, the Rev. E. Codrington, and Captain Tilly, for their valuable aid—the two first mentioned by correction and revision, the others by contributions such as could only be supplied by eye-witnesses and fellow-workers. Many others I must thank for kindly supplying me with letters.

CHARLOTTE MARY YONGE. ELDERFIELD, September 19, 1873.

CHAPTER I. CHILDHOOD AT HOME AND AT SCHOOL, 1827-1838.

So much of a man's cast of character depends upon his home and parentage, that no biography can be complete which does not look back at least as far as the lives of the father and mother, from whom the disposition is sure to be in part inherited, and by whom it must often be formed. Indeed, the happiest natures are generally those which have enjoyed the full benefit of parental training without dictation, and have been led, but not forced, into the way in which they should go.

Therefore it will not be irrelevant to dwell on the career of the father whose name, though still of great weight in his own profession, may not be equally known to the younger generation who have grown up since the words 'Mr. Justice Patteson' were of frequent occurrence in law reports.

John Patteson, father of the subject of the present memoir, was son to a clergyman of a Norfolk family, and was born at Coney Weston, on February 11, 1790. He was educated at Eton, and there formed more than one friendship, which not only lasted throughout his life, but extended beyond his own generation. Sport and study flourished alike among such lads as these; and while they were taught by Dr. Groodall to delight in the peculiarly elegant and accurate scholarship which was the characteristic of the highest education of their day, their boyhood and youth were full of the unstained mirth that gives such radiance to recollections of the past, and often causes the loyalty of affectionate association to be handed on to succeeding generations. The thorough Etonian impress, with all that it involved, was of no small account in his life, as well as in that of his son.

The elder John Patteson was a colleger, and passed on to King's College, Cambridge, whence, in 1813, he came to London to study law. In 1816 he opened his chambers as a special pleader, and on February 23, 1818, was married to his cousin, Elizabeth Lee, after a long engagement. The next year, 1819, he was called to the Bar, and began to go the Northern circuit. On April 3, 1820, Mrs. Patteson died, leaving one daughter, Joanna Elizabeth. Four years later, on April 22, 1824, Mr. Patteson married Frances Duke Coleridge, sister of his friend and fellow-barrister, John Taylor Coleridge. This lady, whose name to all who remember her calls up a fair and sweet memory of all that was good, bright, and beloved, was the daughter of James Coleridge, of Heath's Court, Ottery St. Mary, Devon, Colonel of the South Devon Volunteers. He was the eldest of the numerous family of the Rev. John Coleridge, Master of Ottery St. Mary School, and the poet, Samuel Taylor Coleridge, was the youngest.

The strong family affection that existed between all Colonel Coleridge's children, and concentrated itself upon the only sister among them, made marriage with her an adoption into a group that could not fail to exercise a strong influence on all connected with it, and the ties of kindred will be found throughout this memoir to have had peculiar force.

John Coleridge Patteson, his mother's second child and eldest son, was born at No. 9, Grower Street, Bedford Square, on the 1st of April, 1827, and baptized on the 8th. Besides the elder half-sister already mentioned, another sister, Frances Sophia Coleridge, a year older than, and one brother, James Henry, nearly two years younger than Coleridge, made up the family.

Three years later, in 1830, Mr. Patteson was raised to the Bench, at the unusually early age of forty.

It is probable that there never was a period when the Judicial Bench could reckon a larger number of men distinguished not only for legal ability but for the highest culture and for the substantial qualities that command confidence and respect. The middle of the nineteenth century was a time when England might well be proud of her Judges.

There was much in the habits of the Bench and Bar to lead to close and friendly intimacy, especially on the circuits. When legal etiquette forbade the use of any public conveyance, and junior barristers shared post-chaises, while the leaders travelled in their own carriages, all spent a good deal of time together, and it was not unusual for ladies to go a great part of the circuit with their husbands, especially when it lay in the direction of their own neighbourhood. The Judges' families often accompanied them, especially at the summer assize, and thus there grew up close associations between their children, which made their intimacy almost like that of relationship. Almost all, too, lived in near neighbourhood in those parts of London that now are comparatively deserted, but which were then the especial abodes of lawyers, namely, those adjacent to Bedford Square, where the gardens were the daily resort of their children, all playing together and knowing one another with that familiarity that childhood only gives.

'Sir John Patteson's contemporaries have nearly all, one by one, passed away,' writes one of them, Sir John Taylor Coleridge. 'He has left few, if any, literary monuments to record what his intellectual powers were; and even in our common profession the ordinary course and practice are so changed, that I doubt whether many lawyers are now familiar with his masterly judgments; but I feel that I speak the truth when I describe him as a man of singularly strong common sense, of great acuteness, truthfulness, and integrity of judgment. These were great judicial qualities, and to these he added much simplicity and geniality of temper and manners; and all these were crowned by a firm, unhesitating, devout belief in the doctrines of our faith, which issued in strictness to himself and the warmest, gentlest charity to his fellow-creatures. The result was what you might expect. Altogether it would be hard to say whether you would characterise him as a man unusually popular or unusually respected.'

Such was the character of Mr. Justice Patteson, a character built upon the deep, solid groundwork of religion, such as would now be called that of a sound Churchman of the old school, thoroughly devout and scrupulous in observance, ruling his family and household on a principle felt throughout, making a conscience of all his and their ways, though promoting to the utmost all innocent enjoyment of pleasure, mirth, or gaiety. Indeed, all who can look back on him or on his home remember an unusual amount of kindly genial cheerfulness, fun, merriment, and freedom, i.e. that obedient freedom which is the most perfect kind of liberty.

Though this was in great part the effect of having such a head of the family, the details of management could not but chiefly depend upon the mother, and Lady Patteson was equally loved for her tenderness and respected for her firmness. 'She was, indeed,' writes her brother, 'a sweet and pious person, of the most affectionate, loving disposition, without a grain of selfishness, and of the stoutest adherence to principle and duty. Her tendency was to deal with her children fondly, but this never interfered with good training and discipline. What she felt right, she insisted on, at whatever pain to herself.'

She had to deal with strong characters. Coleridge, or Coley, to give him the abbreviation by which he was known not only through childhood but through life, was a fair little fellow, with bright deep-blue eyes, inheriting much of his nature from her and her family, but not by any means a model boy. He was, indeed, deeply and warmly affectionate, but troublesome through outbreaks of will and temper, showing all the ordinary instinct of trying how far the authorities for the time being will endure resistance; sufficiently indolent of mind to use his excellent abilities to save exertion of intellect; passionate to kicking and screaming pitch, and at times showing the doggedness which is such a trial of patience to the parent. To this Lady Patteson 'never yielded; the thing was to be done, the point given up, the temper subdued, the mother to be obeyed, and all this upon a principle sooner understood than parents suppose.'

There were countless instances of the little boy's sharp, stormy gusts of passion, and his mother's steady refusal to listen to his 'I will be good' until she saw that he was really sorry for the scratch or pinch which he had given, or the angry word he had spoken; and she never waited in vain, for the sorrow was very real, and generally ended in 'Do you think God can forgive me?' When Fanny's love of teasing had exasperated Coley into stabbing her arm with a pencil, their mother had resolution enough to decree that no provocation could excuse 'such unmanliness' in a boy, and inflicted a whipping which cost the girl more tears than her brother, who was full of the utmost grief a child could feel for the offence. No fault was lightly passed over; not that punishment was inflicted for every misdemeanour, but it was always noticed, and the children were shown with grave gentleness where they were wrong; or when there was a squabble among them, the mother's question, 'Who will give up?' generally produced a chorus of 'I! I! I!' Withal 'mamma' was the very life of all the fun, and play, and jokes, enjoying all with spirits and merriment like the little ones' own, and delighting in the exchange of caresses and tender epithets. Thus affection and generosity grew up almost spontaneously towards one another and all the world.

On this disposition was grafted that which was the one leading characteristic of Coley's life, namely, a reverent and religious spirit, which seems from the first to have been at work, slowly and surely subduing inherent defects, and raising him, step by step, from grace to grace.

Five years old is in many cases an age of a good deal of thought. The intelligence is free from the misapprehensions and misty perceptions of infancy; the first course of physical experiments is over, freedom of speech and motion have been attained, and yet there has not set in that burst of animal growth and spirits that often seems to swamp the deeper nature throughout boyhood. By this age Coley was able to read, and on his birthday he received from his father the Bible which was used at his consecration as Bishop twenty-seven years later.

He had an earnest wish to be a clergyman, because he thought saying the Absolution to people must make them so happy, 'a belief he must have gleaned from his Prayer-book for himself, since the doctrine was not in those days made prominent.' The purpose was fostered by his mother. 'She delighted in it, and encouraged it in him. No thought of a family being to be made, and of Coley being the eldest son, ever interfered for a moment. That he should be a good servant at God's altar was to her above all price.'

Of course, however, this was without pressing the thought on him. He grew on, with the purpose accepted but not discussed, except from time to time a half-playful, half-grave reference to himself as a future clergyman.

Reverence was strongly implanted in him. His old nurse (still his sister's valued servant) remembers the little seven years old boy, after saying his own prayers at her knee, standing opposite to his little brother, admonishing him to attention with 'Think, Jemmy; think.' In fact, devoutness seems to have been natural to him. It appears to have been the first strongly traceable feature in him, and to have gradually subdued his faults one by one.

Who can tell how far this was fostered by those old-fashioned habits of strictness which it is the present habit to view as repellent? Every morning, immediately after breakfast, Lady Patteson read the Psalms and Lessons for the day with the four children, and after these a portion of some book of religious instruction, such as 'Horne on the Psalms' or 'Daubeny on the Catechism.' The ensuing studies were in charge of Miss Neill, the governess, and the life-long friend of her pupils; but the mother made the religious instruction her individual care, and thus upheld its pre-eminence. Sunday was likewise kept distinct in reading, teaching, employment, and whole tone of conversation, and the effect was assuredly not that weariness which such observance is often supposed to produce, but rather lasting benefit and happy associations. Coley really enjoyed Bible-reading, and entered into explanations, and even then often picked up a passage in the sermons he heard at St. Giles's-in-the-Fields from the Rev. J. Endell Tyler, and would give his home-oracles no peace till they had made it as clear to his comprehension as was possible.

The love of his home may be gathered from the fact that his letters have been preserved in an unbroken series, beginning from a country visit in 1834, after a slight attack of scarlet fever, written in the round-hand of a boy of seven years old, and finished off with the big Roman capitals FINIS, AMEN, and ending with the uncompleted sheets, bearing as their last date September 19, 1871.

The boy's first school was at Ottery St. Mary, in Devonshire, of which his great-grandfather and great-uncle had both been head-masters.

There was much to make Ottery homelike to Coley, for his grandparents lived at Heath's Court, close to the church, and in the manor-house near at hand their third son, Francis George Coleridge, a solicitor, whose three boys were near contemporaries of Coley, and two of them already in the school.

From first to last his letters to his parents show no symptom of carelessness; they are full of ease and confidence, outpourings of whatever interested him, whether small or great, but always respectful as well as affectionate, and written with care and pains, being evidently his very best; nor does the good old formula, 'Your affectionate and dutiful son,' ever fail or ever produce stiffness.

The shrinking from rough companions, and the desire to be with the homelike relatives around, proved a temptation, and the little boy was guilty of making false excuses to obtain leave of absence. We cannot refrain from giving his letter of penitence, chiefly for the sake of the good sense and kindness of his uncle's treatment:—

'April 26, 1836.

'My dear Papa,—I am very sorry for having told so many falsehoods, which Uncle Frank has told mamma of. I am very sorry for having done so many bad things, I mean falsehoods, and I heartily beg your pardon; and Uncle Frank says that he thinks, if I stay, in a month's time Mr. Cornish will begin to trust me again. Uncle Frank to-day had me into his house and told me to reflect upon what I had done. He also lectured me in the Bible, and asked me different questions about it. He told me that if I ever told another falsehood he should that instant march into the school and ask Mr. Cornish to strip and birch me; and if I followed the same course I did now and did not amend it, if the birching did not do, he should not let me go home for the holidays; but I will not catch the birching...

'So believe me your dear Son,
'J. C. PATTESON.'
On the flap of the letter 'Uncle Frank' writes to the mother:—

'My dear Fanny,—I had Coley in my room to-day, and talked to him seriously about his misdeeds, and I hope good has been done. But I could scarcely keep my countenance grave when he began to reduce by calculation the exact number of fibs he had told. He did not think it was more than two or three at the utmost: and when I brought him to book, I had much to do to prevent the feeling that the sin consisted in telling many lies. However the dear boy's confession was as free as could be expected, and I have impressed on his mind the meanness, cowardice, and wickedness of the habit, and what it will end in here and hereafter. He has promised that he will never offend in future in like manner, and I really believe that his desire to be away from the school and at ease among his friends induced him to trump up the invitations, &c., to Mr. Cornish, in which consisted his first fibs. I shall watch him closely, as I would my own child; and Cornish has done wisely, I think, by giving the proper punishment of confining him to the school-court, &c., and not letting him go to his friends for some time. The dear boy is so affectionate, and has so much to work on, that there is no fear of him; only these things must be looked after promptly, and he must learn practically (before his reason and religion operate) that he gains nothing by a lie... He is very well, and wins one's heart in a moment...

'Ever your affectionate Brother,
'F. G. C.'
The management was effectual, and the penitence real, for this fault never recurred, nor is the boy's conduct ever again censured, though the half-yearly reports often lament his want of zeal and exertion. Coley was sufficiently forward to begin Greek on his first arrival at Ottery, and always held a fair place for his years, but throughout his school career his character was not that of an idle but of an uninterested boy, who preferred play to work, needed all his conscience to make him industrious, and then was easily satisfied with his performances; naturally comparing them with those of other boys, instead of doing his own utmost, and giving himself full credit for the diligence he thought he had used. For it must be remembered that it was a real, not an ideal nature; not a perfect character, but one full of the elements of growth.

A childish, childlike boy, he was now, and for many years longer, intensely fond of all kinds of games and sports, in which his light active form, great agility, and high spirit made him excel. Cricket, riding, running-races, all the school amusements were his delight; fireworks for the 5th of November sparkle with ecstasy through his letters, and he was a capital dancer in the Christmas parties at his London home. He had likewise the courage and patience sure to be needed by an active lad. While at Ottery he silently bore the pain of a broken collar-bone for three weeks, and when the accident was brought to light by his mother's embrace, he only said that 'he did not like to make a fuss.'

Consideration for others, kindness, and sweetness of nature were always his leading characteristics, making him much beloved by all his companions, and an excellent guardian and example to his little brother, who soon joined him at Ottery. Indeed, the love between these two brothers was so deep, quiet, and fervid, that it is hard to dwell on it while 'one is taken and the other left.' It was at this time a rough buffeting, boyish affection, but it was also a love that made separation pain and grief, and on the part of the elder, it showed itself in careful protection from all harm or bullying, and there was a strong underlying current of tenderness, most endearing to all concerned with the boys, whether masters, relations, friends, or servants.

CHAPTER II. BOYHOOD AT ETON. 1838—1845.

After the Christmas holidays of 1837-8, when Coley Patteson was nearly eleven years old, he was sent to Eton, that most beautifully situated of public schools, whose delightful playing fields, noble trees, broad river, and exquisite view of Windsor Castle give it a peculiar charm, joining the venerable grandeur of age to the freshness and life of youth, so as to rivet the affections in no common degree.

It was during the head-mastership of Dr. Hawtrey that Patteson became, in schoolboy phrase, an Eton fellow, being boarded in the house of his uncle, the Rev. Edward Coleridge, one of the most popular and successful Eton masters. Several of his cousins were also in this house, with other boys who became friends of his whole life, and he was thoroughly happy there, although in these early days he still felt each departure from home severely, and seldom failed to write a mournful letter after the holidays. There is one, quite pathetic in its simplicity, telling his mother how he could not say his prayers nor fall asleep on his first night till he had resolutely put away the handkerchief that seemed for some reason a special link with home. It illustrates what all who remember him say, how thoroughly a childlike being he still was, though a well-grown, manly, high-spirited boy, quite able to take care of himself, keep his place, and hold his own.

He was placed in the lower remove of the fourth form, which was then 'up to' the Rev. Charles Old Goodford, i.e. that was he who taught the division so called in school.

The boy was evidently well prepared, for he was often captain of his division, and his letters frequently tell of successes of this kind, while they anticipate 'Montem.'

That of 1838 was a brilliant one, for Queen Victoria, then only nineteen, and her first year of sovereignty not yet accomplished, came from the Castle to be driven in an open carriage to Salt Hill and bestow her Royal contribution.

In the throng little Patteson was pressed up so close to the Royal carriage that he became entangled in the wheel, and was on the point of being dragged under it, when the Queen, with ready presence of mind, held out her hand: he grasped it, and was able to regain his feet in safety, but did not recover his perceptions enough to make any sign of gratitude before the carriage passed on. He had all a boy's shyness about the adventure; but perhaps it served to quicken the personal loyalty which is an unfailing characteristic of 'Eton fellows.'

The Royal custom of the Sunday afternoon parade on the terrace of Windsor Castle for the benefit of the gazing public afforded a fine opportunity for cultivating this sentiment, and Coley sends an amusingly minute description of her Majesty's dress, evidently studied for his mother's benefit, even to the pink tips of her four long ostrich feathers, and calling to mind Chalon's water-colours of the Queen in her early youth. He finishes the description with a quaint little bit of moralising. 'It certainly is very beautiful with two bands playing on a calm, blessed Sunday evening, with the Queen of England and all her retinue walking about. It gives you an idea of the Majesty of God, who could in one short second turn it all into confusion. There is nothing to me more beautiful than the raising one's eyes to Heaven, and thinking with adoration who made this scene, and who could unmake it again.'

A few days later the record is of a very different scene, namely, Windsor Fair, when the Eton boys used to imagine they had a prescriptive right to make a riot and revel in the charms of misrule.

'On the second day the Eton fellows always make an immense row. So at the signal, when a thing was acting, the boys rushed in and pulled down the curtain, and commenced the row. I am happy to say I was not there. There were a great many soldiers there, and they all took our part. The alarm was given, and the police came. Then there was such a rush at the police. Some of them tumbled over, and the rest were half-knocked down. At last they took in custody three of our boys, upon which every boy that was there (amounting to about 450) was summoned. They burst open the door, knocked down the police, and rescued our boys. Meantime the boys kept on shying rotten eggs and crackers, and there was nothing but righting and rushing.'

A startling description! But this was nothing to the wild pranks that lived in the traditions of the elder generation; and in a few years more the boys were debarred from the mischievous licence of the fair.

Coley had now been nearly a year at Eton, and had proceeded through the lower and middle removes of the fourth form, when, on November 23, he achieved the success of which he thus writes:—

'Rejoice! I was sent up for good yesterday at eleven o'clock school. I do not know what copy of verses for yet, but directly I do, I will send you a copy.... Goodford, when I took my ticket to be signed (for I was obliged to get Goodford, Abraham, and my tutor to sign it), said, "I will sign it most willingly," and then kept on stroking my hand, and said, "I congratulate you most heartily, and am very glad of it." I am the only one who is sent up; which is a good thing for me, as it will give me forty or fifty good marks in trials. I am so splitting with joy you cannot think, because now I have given you some proof that I have been lately sapping and doing pretty well. Do not, think that I am praising myself, for I am pretty nearly beside myself, you may suppose.'

One of his cousins adds, on the same sheet: 'I must tell you it is very difficult to be sent up in the upper fourth form, and still more so in the middle remove.'

The subject of the Latin verses which obtained this distinction was a wreath or garland, and there must have been something remarkable in them, for Mr. Abraham preserved a copy of them for many years. There was something in the sweetness and docility of the boy, and in the expression of his calm, gentle face, that always greatly interested the masters and made them rejoice in his success; and among his comrades he was a universal favourite. His brother joined him at Eton during the ensuing year, when the Queen's wedding afforded the boys another glimpse of Royal festivity. Their tumultuous loyalty and audacity appear in Coley's letter:—

'In college, stretching from Hexter's to Mother Spier's was a magnificent representation of the Parthenon: there were three pillars, and a great thing like this (a not over-successful sketch of a pediment), with the Eton and Royal arms in the middle, and "Gratulatur Etona Victoria et Alberto" It cost £150, and there were 5,000 lamps hung on it. Throughout the whole day we all of us wore large white bridal favours and white gloves. Towards evening the clods got on Long Walk Wall; and as gentle means would not do, we were under the necessity of knocking some over, when the rest soon jumped off. However, F—— and myself declared we would go right into the quadrangle of the Castle, so we went into the middle of the road and formed a line. Soon a rocket (the signal that the Queen was at Slough) was let off, and then some Life Guards came galloping along, and one of them ran almost over me, and actually trod on F——'s toe, which put him into dreadful pain for some time. Then came the Queen's carriage, and I thought college would have tumbled down with the row. The cheering was really tremendous. The whole 550 fellows all at once roared away. The Queen and Consort nodding and bowing, smiling, &c. Then F—— and I made a rush to get up behind the Queen's carriage, but a dragoon with his horse almost knocked us over. So we ran by the side as well as we could, but the crowd was so immensely thick, we could not get on as quick as the Queen. We rushed along, knocking clean over all the clods we could, and rushing against the rest, and finally F—— and myself were the only Eton fellows that got into the quadrangle. As we got there, the Queen's carriage was going away. You may fancy that we were rather hot, running the whole way up to the Castle, besides the exertion of knocking over the clods and knocking at doors as we passed; but I was so happy.'

Such is bliss at twelve years old!

The first half-year of 1839 had brought Patteson into the Remove, that large division of the school intermediate between the fourth and fifth forms. The work was harder, and his diligence somewhat relaxed. In fact, the Coley of this period and of a good while later had more heart for play than work. Cricket, bathing, and boating were his delight; and though his school-work was conscientiously accomplished, it did not interest him; and when he imagined himself to have been working hard and well, it was a thunderbolt to him to find, at the end of the half-year, that a great deal more had been expected of him by his tutor. It shows how candid and sweet his nature was, that, just as when he was a little fellow at Ottery, his penitent letter should contain the rebuke he had received, without resentment against anyone but himself:—

'Aunt has just called me down into the drawing-room and shown me my character. I am stupefied at it; it is so shocking just when I most wanted a good one on account of mamma's health. I am ashamed to say that I can offer not the slightest excuse; my conduct on this occasion has been very bad. I expect a severe reproof from you, and pray do not send me any money, nor grant me the slightest [favour?]. Whilst ....., who has very little ability (uncle says), is, by plodding on, getting credit, I, who (my tutor says) have abilities, am wickedly neglecting and offending both my heavenly and earthly Father by my bad use of them. Aunt called me into the drawing-room, and very kindly showed me the excessive foolishness of my conduct; but from this very moment I am determined that I will not lose a moment, and we will see what the next three weeks will produce.'

Poor little fellow! his language is so strong that it is almost a surprise to find that he was reproaching himself for no more heinous fault than not having worked up to the full extent of his powers! He kept his promise of diligence, and never again incurred reproof, but was sent up for good again in November. His career through the school was above the average, though not attaining to what was expected from his capabilities; but the development of his nature was slow, and therefore perhaps ultimately the more complete, and as yet study for its own sake did not interest him; indeed, his mind was singularly devoid of pleasure in classical subjects, though so alert in other directions.

He was growing into the regular tastes of the refined, fastidious Eton boy; wrote of the cut of his first tail-coat that 'this is really an important thing;' and had grown choice in the adorning of his room and the binding of his books, though he never let these tastes bring him into debt or extravagance. His turn for art and music began to show itself, and the anthems at St. George's Chapel on the Sunday afternoons gave him great delight; and in Eton Chapel, a contemporary says, 'I well remember how he used to sing the Psalms with the little turns at the end of the verses, which I envied his being able to do.' Nor was this mere love of music, but devotion. Coley had daily regular readings of the Bible in his room with his brother, cousins, and a friend or two; but the boys were so shy about it that they kept an open Shakespeare on the table, with an open drawer below, in which the Bible was placed, and which was shut at the sound of a hand on the door.

Hitherto No. 33 Bedford Square had been the only home of the Patteson family. The long vacations were spent sometimes with the Judge's relations in the Eastern counties, sometimes with Lady Patteson's in the West. Landwith Rectory, in Cornwall, was the home of her eldest brother, Dr. James Coleridge, whose daughter Sophia was always like an elder sister to her children, and the Vicarage of St. Mary Church, then a wild, beautiful seaside village, though now almost a suburb of Torquay, was held by her cousin, George May Coleridge; and here the brothers and sisters climbed the rocks, boated, fished, and ran exquisitely wild in the summer holidays. Christmas was spent with the Judge's mother at Ipswich, amongst numerous cousins, with great merriment and enjoyment such as were never forgotten.

Colonel Coleridge had died in 1836, his widow in her daughter's house in 1838, and Heath's Court had become the property of Mr. Justice Coleridge, who always came thither with his family as soon as the circuit was over. In 1841, Feniton Court, about two miles and a half from thence, was purchased by Judge Patteson, much to the delight of his children. It was a roomy, cheerful, pleasantly-situated house, with a piece of water in the grounds, the right of shooting over a couple of farms, and all that could render boy life happy.

Feniton was a thorough home, and already Coley's vision was, 'When I am vicar of Feniton, which I look forward to, but with a very distant hope, I should of all things like Fanny to keep house for me till I am married;' and again, when relating some joke with his cousins about the law-papers, of the Squire of Feniton, he adds: 'But the Squire of Feniton will be a clergyman.'

Whether this were jest or earnest, this year, 1841, brought the dawn of his future life. It was in that year that the Rev. George Augustus Selwyn was appointed to the diocese of New Zealand. Mrs. Selwyn's parents had always been intimate with the Patteson family, and the curacy which Mr. Selwyn had held up to this time was at Windsor, so that the old Etonian tie of brotherhood was drawn closer by daily intercourse. Indeed, it was from the first understood that Eton, with the wealth that her children enjoyed in such large measure, should furnish 'nerves and sinews' to the war which her son was about to wage with the darkness of heathenism, thus turning the minds of the boys to something beyond either their studies or their sports.

On October 31, the Rev. Samuel Wilberforce, then Archdeacon of Surrey, and since Bishop of Oxford and of Winchester, preached in the morning at New Windsor parish church, and the newly-made Bishop of New Zealand in the afternoon. Coley was far more affected than he then had power to express. He says: 'I heard Archdeacon Wilberforce in the morning, and the Bishop in the evening, though I was forced to stand all the time. It was beautiful when he talked of his going out to found a church, and then to die neglected and forgotten. All the people burst out crying, he was so very much beloved by his parishioners. He spoke of his perils, and putting his trust in God; and then, when, he had finished, I think I never heard anything like the sensation, a kind of feeling that if it had not been on so sacred a spot, all would have exclaimed "God bless him!"'

The text of this memorable sermon was, 'Thine heart shall be enlarged, because the abundance of the sea shall be converted unto thee, the forces also of the Gentiles shall come unto thee.' (Is. lx. 5.) Many years later we shall find a reference to this, the watchword of the young hearer's life.

The Archdeacon's sermon was from John xvii. 20, 21: 'Neither pray I for these alone, but for them also which shall believe on Me through their word; that they all may be One, as Thou, Father, art in Me, and I in Thee, that they also may be

One in Us: that the world may believe that Thou hast sent Me.' And here again we find one of the watchwords of Coley's life, for nothing so dwelt with him and so sustained him as the sense of unity, whether with these at home in England, or with those in the inner home of the Saints. When the sermon concluded with the words, 'As we are giving of our best, as our Church is giving of her best, in sending forth from her own bosom these cherished and chosen sons, so let there go forth from every one of us a consenting offering; let us give this day largely, in a spirit of self-sacrifice, as Christian men, to Christ our Lord, and He will graciously accept and bless the offerings that we make'—the preacher could little guess that among the lads who stood in the aisle was one in whom was forming the purpose of offering his very self also.

For at that time Coleridge Patteson was receiving impressions that became the seed of his future purpose, and the eyes of his spirit were seeing greater things than the Vicarage of Feniton. Indeed, the subject was not entirely new to him, for Edward Coleridge was always deeply interested in missions, and had done his best to spread the like feeling, often employing the willing services of his pupils in copying letters from Australia, Newfoundland, &c.

When the Bishop of New Zealand came to take leave, he said, half in earnest, half in playfulness, 'Lady Patteson, will you give me Coley?' She started, but did not say no; and when, independently of this, her son told her that it was his greatest wish to go with the Bishop, she replied that if he kept that wish when he grew up he should have her blessing and consent.

But there was no further mention of the subject. The sisters knew what had passed, but it was not spoken of to his father till long after, when the wish had become purpose. Meantime the boy's natural development put these visions into the background. He was going on with ordinary work and play, enjoying the pageantry of the christening of the Prince of Wales, and cheering himself hoarse and half-frantic when the King of Prussia came to see the school; then on his father's birthday writing with a 'hand quite trembling with delight' to announce what he knew would be the most welcome of birthday presents, namely, the news that he had been 'sent up' for a very good copy of seventy-nine verses, 'all longs, on Napoleon e Seylhia profugus, passage of Beresina, and so forth.' His Latin verses were his strong point, and from this time forward he was frequently sent up, in all twenty-five times, an almost unprecedented number.

In fact he was entering on a fresh stage of life, from the little boy to the lad, and the period was marked by his Confirmation on May 26, 1842. Here is his account both of it and of his first Communion. The soberness and old-fashioned simplicity of expression are worth remarking as tokens of the quietly dutiful tone of mind, full of reverence and sincere desire to do right, and resting in the consciousness of that desire, while steadily advancing towards higher things than he then understood. It was a life and character where advancement with each fresh imparting of spiritual grace can be traced more easily than usual.

It is observable too that the boy's own earnestness and seriousness of mind seem to have to him supplied the apparent lack of external aids to devotional feeling, though the Confirmation was conducted in the brief, formal, wholesale manner which some in after-life have confessed to have been a disappointment and a drawback after their preparation and anticipation:—

'You will know that I have been confirmed to-day, and I dare say you all thought of me. The ceremony was performed by the Bishop of Lincoln, and I hope that I have truly considered the great duty and responsibility I have taken upon myself, and have prayed for strength to support me in the execution of all those duties. I shall of course receive the Sacrament the first time I have an opportunity, and I trust worthily. I think there must have been 200 confirmed. The Bishop gave us a very good charge afterwards, recommending us all to take pattern by the self-denial and true devotion of the Bishop of New Zealand, on whom he spoke for a long-while. The whole ceremony was performed with the greatest decorum, and in the retiring and coming up of the different sets there was very little noise, and not the slightest confusion. I went up with the first set, and the Bishop came round and put his hands on the heads of the whole set (about forty), and then going into the middle pronounced the prayer. The responses were all made very audibly, and everyone seemed to be impressed with a proper feeling of the holiness and seriousness of the ceremony. After all the boys had been confirmed about seven other people were confirmed, of whom two were quite as much as thirty, I should think.'

'June 5.

'I have just returned from receiving the Holy Sacrament in Chapel. I received it from Hawtrey and Okes, but there were three other ministers besides. There was a large attendance, seventy or eighty or more Eton boys alone. I used the little book that mamma sent me, and found the little directions and observations very useful. I do truly hope and believe that I received it worthily... It struck me more than ever (although I had often read it before) as being such a particularly impressive and beautiful service. I never saw anything conducted with greater decorum. Not a single fellow spoke except at the responses, which were well and audibly made, and really every fellow seemed to be really impressed with the awfulness of the ceremony, and the great wickedness of not piously receiving it, I do not know whether there will be another Sacrament here before the holidays, or whether I shall receive it with you at Feniton next time.'

No doubt the whole family (except the yet unconfirmed younger brother) did so receive it in the summer holidays, the last that were to be spent in the full joy of an unbroken household circle, and, as has been already said, one of unusual warmth and kindliness, binding closely into it all who were connected therewith. Each governess became a dear friend; the servants were deeply attached, and for the most part fixtures; and one, the nurse already mentioned, says she never recollects a time when Master Coley had to leave Feniton for London without his offering the servants to take charge of their messages or parcels. All dependents and poor people, in fact whatever came under Judge Patteson's genial, broad-hearted influence, were treated with the like kindness, and everything alive about the place seemed full of happiness and affection.

The centre of this bright home had always been the mother, fervently loved by all who came in contact with her, fragile in health, and only going through her duties and exertions so cheerily by the quiet fortitude of a brave woman. In the course of this year, 1842, some severe spasmodic attacks made her family anxious; and as the railway communication was still incomplete, so that the journey to London was a great fatigue to an invalid, her desire to spend Christmas in Devonshire led to her remaining there with her daughters, when her husband returned to London on the commencement of term.

He had been gone little more than a fortnight when, on November 17, a more severe attack came on; and though she was soon relieved from it, she never entirely rallied, and was firmly convinced that this was 'the beginning of the end.' Her husband was summoned home, Judge Coleridge taking a double portion of his work to set him at liberty, and the truth began to dawn on the poor boys at Eton. 'Do you really mean that there is anything so very, very dreadful to fear?' is Coley's cry in his note one day, and the next, 'Oh, Papa, you cannot mean that we may never, unless we come down to Feniton, see mamma again. I cannot bear the thought of it. I trust most earnestly that it is not the case. Do not hide anything from me, it would make me more wretched afterwards. If it shall (which I trust in His infinite mercy it will not) please Almighty God to take our dearest mamma unto Himself, may He give us grace to bear with fortitude and resolution the dreadful loss, and may we learn to live with such holiness here that we may hereafter be united for ever in Heaven.' This letter is marked twice over 'Only for Papa,' but the precaution was needless, for Lady Patteson was accustoming all those about her to speak freely and naturally of what she felt to be approaching. Her eldest brother, Dr. Coleridge, was greatly comforting her by his ministrations, and her sons were sent for; but as she did not ask for them, it was thought best that they should remain at their Uncle Frank's, at Ottery, until, on the evening of Sunday, the 27th, a great change took place, making it evident that the end was drawing near.

The sufferer was told that the boys were come, and was asked if she would see them. She was delighted, and they came in, restraining their grief while she kissed and blessed them, and then, throwing her arms round their father, thanked him for having brought her darling boys for her to see once more. It was not long before she became unconscious; and though all the family were watching and praying round her, she showed no further sign of recognition, as she gradually and tranquilly fell asleep in the course of the night.

To his cousin, Mrs. Martyn, Coley wrote the following letter just after the funeral:—

'We only came down from our rooms to go to church, and directly the beautiful service was over we went upstairs again. I need not tell you what we then felt, and now do feel. It is a very dreadful loss to us all; but we have been taught by that dear mother, who has been now taken from us, that it is not fit to grieve for those who die in the Lord, "for they rest from their labours." She is now, we may safely trust, a blessed saint in Heaven, far removed from all cares and anxieties; and, instead of spending our time in useless tears and wicked repinings, we should rather learn to imitate her example and virtues, that, when we die, we may sleep in Him as our hope is this our sister doth, and may be finally united with her in

Heaven. Yesterday was a day of great trial to us all: I felt when I was standing by the grave as if I must have burst.

'Dear Papa bears up beautifully, and is a pattern of submission to us all. We are much more happy than you could suppose, for, thank God, we are certain she is happy, far happier than she could be on earth. She said once, "I wonder I wish to leave my dearest John and the children, and this sweet place, but yet I do wish it" so lively was her faith and trust in the merits of her Saviour.'

A deep and permanent impression was left upon the boy's mind, as will be seen by his frequent references to what he had then witnessed; but for the present he was thought to be less depressed than the others, and recovered his natural tone of spirits sooner than his brother and sisters. The whole family spent their mournful Christmas at Thorverton Rectory, with Dr. and Mrs. Coleridge and their daughter Fanny, their chief comforters and fellow-sufferers; and then returned to London. The Judge's eldest daughter, Joanna, who had always been entirely one with the rest, had to take her place at the head of the household. In her own words, 'It was trying for a lad of fifteen and a half, but he was very good, and allowed me to take the command in a way that few boys would nave done.'

'It has struck me as remarkable that friends and relations have again and again spoken of different incidents as 'turning-points' in Coley's life. If he had literally turned at them all, his would have been a most revolving career; but I believe the fact to have been that he never turned at all, for his face was always set the right way, but that each of these was a point of impulse setting him more vigorously on his way, and stirring up his faithful will. Such moments were those of admission to religious ordinances, to him no dead letters but true receptions of grace; and he likewise found incitements in sorrows, in failures, in reproofs. Everything sank deeply, and his mind was already assuming the introspective character that it had throughout the period of growth and formation. One of his Eton companions, four years younger, has since spoken of the remarkable impression of inwardness Patteson made on him even at this time, saying that whenever he was taken by surprise he seemed to be only ruminating till he spoke or was spoken to, and then there was an instant return to the outer world and ready attention to whatever was in hand.

The spring found him of course in the full tide of Eton interests. The sixth and upper fifth forms, to the latter of which he had by this time attained, may contend in the public examination for the Newcastle scholarship, just before the Easter holidays, and it is a great testimony to a boy's ability and industry if his name appears among the nine select for their excellence. This time, 1843, Coley, who was scarcely sixteen, had of course but little chance, but he had the pleasure of announcing that his great friend, Edmund Bastard, a young Devonshire squire, was among the 'select,' and he says of himself: 'You will, as I said before, feel satisfied that I did my best, but it was an unlucky examination for me. It has done me a great deal of good in one way. It has enabled me to see where I am particularly deficient, viz. general knowledge of history, and a thorough acquaintance with Greek and Roman customs, law courts and expressions, and Greek and Roman writers. I do not find myself wanting in making out a stiff bit of Greek or Latin if I have time, but I must read History chiefly this year, and then I hope to be selected next time. My tutor is not at all disappointed in me.'

This spring, 1843, Patteson became one of the Eleven, a perilously engrossing position for one who, though never slurring nor neglecting his studies, did not enjoy anything so much as the cricket-field. However, there the weight of his character, backed by his popularity and proficiency in all games and exercises, began to be a telling influence.

On November 2, 1843, when the anniversary of his mother's death was coming round, he writes to his eldest sister:—

'I had not indeed forgotten this time twelvemonth, and especially that awful Sunday night when we stood round dear mamma's bed in such misery. I never supposed at that time that we could ever be happy and merry again, but yet it has been so with me; and though very often the recollection of that night has come upon me, and the whole scene in its misery has passed before me, I hope I have never forgotten, that though a loss to us, it was a gain to her, and we ought rather to be thankful than sorrowful.... By the bye, I do not really want a book-case much, and you gave me the "Irish Stories," and I have not yet been sent up. I would rather not have a present, unless the Doctor means to give me an exercise. Do not lay this down to pride; but you know I was not sent up last half, and if this passes, a blank again, I do not deserve any fresh presents.'

This piece of self-discipline was crowned by joyous notices of being 'sent up for good' and 'for play' in the next half; when also occurs a letter showing a spirit of submission to a restriction not fully understood:—

'Tuesday evening.

'My dearest Father,—Hearing that "Israel in Egypt" was to be performed at Exeter Hall on Friday night, I went and asked my tutor whether he had any objection to my running up that night to hear it, and coming back the next morning, quite early at six. My tutor said that, without any absurd feelings on the matter, he should not think himself of going to such a thing in Lent. "It was not," he said, "certainly like going to the play, or any of those sort of places," but he did not like the idea of going at all. Do you think that there was any harm in the wish?

'I do not ask because I wish you to write and say I may go, but because I wish to learn whether my asking at all was wrong. Even if you have no objection, I certainly shall not go, because for such a trifling thing to act in opposition to my tutor, even with your consent, would be very foolish.

'...Good-bye, my dearest Father. God bless you, says your affectionate and dutiful Son,

'J. C. P.'

This year, 1844, the name of Patteson appeared among the 'select.' 'I shall expect a jolly holiday for my reward,' he merrily says, when announcing it to his sisters. He had begun to join the Debating Society at Eton, and for a while was the president. One of the other members says, 'His speeches were singularly free from the bombast and incongruous matter with which Eton orators from fifteen to eighteen are apt to interlard their declamations. He spoke concisely, always to the point, and with great fluency and readiness. A reputation for good sense and judgment made his authority of great weight in the school, and his independent spirit led him to choose, amongst his most intimate friends and associates, two collegers, who ultimately became Newcastle scholars and medallists.

'That the most popular oppidan of his day should have utterly ignored the supposed inferiority of the less wealthy section of the school, and looked on worth and high character as none the worse for being clothed in a coarse serge gown, is a fact seemingly trivial to ordinary readers, but very noticeable to Eton men. As a rank and file collegian myself, and well remembering the Jew and Samaritan state that prevailed between oppidans and collegers, I remember with pride that Patteson did so much to level the distinctions that worked so mischievously to the school. His cheerfulness and goodness were the surest guarantee for good order amongst his schoolfellows. There was no Puritanism in him, he was up to any fun, sung his song at a cricket or foot-ball dinner as joyfully as the youngest of the party; but if mirth sank into coarseness and ribaldry, that instant Patteson's conduct was fearless and uncompromising....'

Here follows an account of an incident which occurred at the dinner annually given by the eleven of cricket and the eight of the boats at the hotel at Slough.

A custom had arisen among some of the boys of singing offensive songs on these occasions, and Coley, who, as second of the eleven, stood in the position of one of the entertainers, gave notice beforehand that he was not going to tolerate anything of the sort. One of the boys, however, began to sing something objectionable. Coley called out, 'If that does not stop, I shall leave the room;' and as no notice was taken, he actually went away with a few other brave lads. He afterwards found that, as he said, 'fellows who could not understand such feelings thought him affected;' and he felt himself obliged to send word to the captain, that unless an apology was made, he should leave the eleven—no small sacrifice, considering what cricket was to him; but the gentlemanlike and proper feeling of the better style of boys prevailed, and the eleven knew their own interests too well to part with him, so the apology was made, and he retained his position. The affair came to the knowledge of two of the masters, Mr. Dupuis and Mr. Abraham, and they gratified their warm sense of approbation by giving Patteson a bat, though he never knew the reason why, as we shall see in one of his last letters to one of the donors.

His prowess at cricket must be described in the words of his cousin, Arthur Duke Coleridge, who was at this time in college: 'He was by common consent one of the best, if not the best, of the cricketers of the school. The second year of his appearance at Lord's Cricket Ground was the most memorable, as far as his actual services were concerned, of all the matches he played against Harrow and Winchester. He was sent in first in the Harrow match; the bowling was steady and straight, but Patteson's defence was admirable. He scored fifty runs, in which there was but one four, and by steady play completely broke the neck of the bowling. Eton won the match easily, Patteson making a brilliant catch at point, when the last Harrow man retired. Full of confidence, Eton began the Winchester match. Victory for a long time seemed a certainty for Eton; but Kidding, the

Winchester captain, played an uphill game so fiercely that the bowling had to be repeatedly changed. Our eleven were disorganised, and the captain had so plainly lost heart, that Patteson resolved on urging him to discontinue his change of bowling, and begin afresh with the regular bowlers. The captain allowed Patteson to have his way, and the game, though closely contested, was saved. His powers of defence were indeed remarkable. I saw the famous professional cricketer Lillywhite play once at Eton in his time, and becoming almost irritated at the stubbornness and tenacity with which Coley held his wicket. After scoring twenty and odd times in the first, and forty in the second innings, (not out), Lillywhite said, 'Mr. Patteson, I should like to bowl to you on Lord's Ground, and it would be different.' 'Oh, of course,' modestly answered Coley; 'I know you would have me out directly there.'

The next cricket season this champion was disabled by a severe sprain of the wrist, needing leeches, splints, and London advice. It was when fixing a day for coming up to town on this account that he mentioned the occurrence of the previous year in a letter to his father:—

'I have a great object in shirking the oppidan dinner. I not only hate the idea of paying a sovereign for a dinner, but last year, at the cricket dinner, I had a great row, which I might possibly incur another time, and I wish very much to avoid.'

Then, after briefly stating what had passed, he adds: 'At this dinner, where the captain of the boats manages it, I should be his guest, and therefore any similar act of mine would make matters worse. You can therefore see why I wish Tuesday to be the day for my coming up.'

The sprain prevented his playing in the matches at Lord's that summer, though he was well enough to be reckoned on as a substitute in case any of the actual players had been disabled. Possibly his accident was good for his studies, for this was a year of much progress and success; and though only seventeen, he had two offers of tutorship for the holidays, from Mr. Dugdale and the Marchioness of Bath. The question where his university life was to be spent began to come forward. Studentships at Christchurch were then in the gift of the Canons, and a nomination would have been given him by Dr. Pusey if he had not been too young to begin to reside, so that it was thought better that he should wait and go up for the Balliol scholarship in the autumn.

In the October of 1844 he describes to his eldest sister the reception of King Louis Philippe at Eton, accompanied by the Queen, Prince Albert, and the Duke of Wellington:

'The King wore a white great coat, and looked a regular jolly old fellow. He has white frizzle hair and large white whiskers. The former, I suspect, is a wig. The cheering was tremendous, but behind the royal carriage the cheers were always redoubled where the old Duke, the especial favourite hero, rode. When they got off their horses in the schoolyard, the Duke being by some mistake behindhand, was regularly hustled in the crowd, with no attendant near him.

'I was the first to perceive him, and springing forward, pushed back the fellows on each side, who did not know whom they were tumbling against, and, taking off my hat, cheered with might and main. The crowd hearing the cheer, turned round, and then there was the most glorious sight I ever saw. The whole school encircled the Duke, who stood entirely alone in the middle for a minute or two, and I rather think we did cheer him. At last, giving about one touch to his hat, he began to move on, saying, "Get on, boys, get on." I never saw such enthusiasm here; the masters rushed into the crowd round him, waving their caps, and shouting like any of us. As for myself, I was half-mad and roared myself hoarse in about five minutes. The King and Prince kept their hats off the whole time, incessantly bowing, and the King speaking. He walked arm-in-arm with the Queen, who looked well and very much pleased. The Duke walked with that Grand Duchess whose name you may see in the papers, for I can't spell it.'

Very characteristic this both of Eton's enthusiasm for the hero, and of the hero's undemonstrative way of receiving it, which must have somewhat surprised his foreign companions.

A week or two later, in November 1844, came the competition for the Balliol scholarship, but Coley was not successful. On the Saturday he writes:—

'The scholarship was decided last night; Smith, a Rugby man, got the first, and Grant, a Harrow man, the second.... I saw the Master afterwards; he said, "I cannot congratulate you on success, Mr. Patteson, but you have done yourself great credit, and passed a very respectable examination. I shall be happy to allow you to enter without a future examination, as we are all quite satisfied of your competency." He said that I had better come up to matriculate next term, but should not have another examination. We were in about nine hours a day, three hours in the evening; I thought the papers very hard; we had no Latin elegiacs or lyrics, which was rather a bore for the Eton lot. I am very glad I have been up now, but I confess it was the longest week I ever recollect. I feel quite seedy after a whole week without exercise.... The very first paper, the Latin Essay (for which we were in six hours), was the worst of all my papers, and must have given the examiners an unfavourable impression to start with. The rest of my papers, with the exception of the Greek prose and the critical paper, I did very fairly, I think.'

A greater disappointment than this was, however, in store for Coley. He failed in attaining a place among the 'select,' at his last examination for the Newcastle, in the spring of 1845. Before the list was given out he had written to his father that the Divinity papers were far too easy, with no opportunity for a pretty good scholar to show his knowledge, 'the ridicule of every one of the masters,' but the other papers very difficult.

'Altogether,' he adds, 'the scholarship has been to me unsatisfactory. I had worked hard at Greek prose, had translated and re-translated a good deal of Xenophon, Plato, and some Demosthenes, yet to my disappointment we had no paper of Greek prose, a thing that I believe never occurred before, and which is generally believed to test a boy's knowledge well. My Iambics were good, I expect, though not without two bad faults. In fact, I cannot look back upon a single paper, except my Latin prose, without a multitude of oversights and faults presenting themselves to me... I almost dread the giving out of the select. Think if my name was not there. It is some consolation that Hawtrey, yesterday, in giving me an exercise for good, asked how I liked the examination. Upon my saying, "It was not such a one as I expected, and that I had done badly," he said "That is not at all what I hear," but this cannot go for much... I want exercise very badly, and my head is very thick and stupid, as I fear this last paper must show the examiners.'

The omission of Patteson's name from among the select was a great mortification, not only to himself but his father, though the Judge kindly wrote:—

'Do not distress yourself about this unfortunate failure as to the Newcastle. We cannot always command our best exertions when we want to do so, and you were not able on this occasion to bring forward all you knew. It was not from idleness or want of attention to school business. Work on regularly, and you will do well at Oxford. I have a line from your tutor, who seems to think that it was in Juvenal, Cicero and Livy, and in Iambics, that the faults principally were. I cannot say that I am not disappointed; but I know so well the uncertainty of examinations and how much depends on the sort of papers put, and on the spirits and feeling one is in, that I am never surprised at such results, and I do not blame you at all.' Those who knew Coley best agree in thinking that this reverse took great effect in rousing his energies. This failure evidently made him take himself to task, for in the summer he writes to his father:—

There are things which have occurred during my stay at Eton which cannot but make me blame myself. I mean principally a want of continuous industry. I have perhaps for one half or two (for instance, last Easter half) worked hard, but I have not been continuously improving, and adding knowledge to knowledge, half by half. I feel it now, because I am sure that I know very little more than I did at Easter. One thing I am improved in, which is writing themes; and you will be pleased to know that Hawtrey has again given me the School Theme prize, worth 5L., which counts for another sent up exercise.'

In reply, the Judge, on July 22, wrote in the midst of the circuit, from Stafford, a letter that might well do a son's heart good:—

'I rejoice in your finale, and shall be glad to see the exercise. You have gone through Eton with great credit and reputation as a scholar, and what is of more consequence, with perfect character as to truth and conduct in every way. This can only be accounted for by the assistance of the good Spirit of God first stirred up in you by the instructions of your clear mother, than whom a more excellent human being never existed. I pray God that this assistance may continue through life, and keep you always in the same good course.'

A few days more and the boy's departure from the enthusiastically loved school had taken place, together with his final exploits as captain in the cricket-field, where too he formed an acquaintance with Mr. C. S. Roundell, the captain of the Harrow eleven, which ripened into a lifelong friendship.

'You may suppose,' writes Coley, 'that I was really very miserable at leaving Eton. I did not, I assure you, without thanking God for the many advantages I have there enjoyed and praying for His forgiveness for my sin in neglecting so many. We began our match with Harrow yesterday, by going in first; we got 261 runs by tremendous hitting, Harrow 32, and followed up and got 55: Eton thus winning in one innings by 176 runs, the most decided beating ever known at cricket.'

So ended Coleridge Patteson's school life, not reaching to all he saw that it might have been; but unstained, noble, happy, honourable, and full of excellent training for the future man. No sting was left to poison the fail-memory of youth; but many a friendship had been formed on foundations of esteem, sympathy, and kindness which endured through life, standing all tests of separation and difference.

CHAPTER III. UNDERGRADUATE LIFE AT BALLIOL AND JOURNEYS ON THE CONTINENT.
1845—1852.

University life is apt to exert a strong influence upon a man's career. It comes at the age at which there is probably the most susceptibility to new impressions. The physical growth is over, and the almost exclusive craving for exercise and sport is lessening; there is more voluntary inclination to intellectual application, and the mind begins to get fair play. There is also a certain liberty of choice as to the course to be taken and the persons who shall become guides, and this renders the pupilage a more willing and congenial connection than that of the schoolboy: nor is there so wide a distance in age and habits between tutor and pupil as between master and scholar.

Thus it is that there are few more influential persons in the country than leading University men, for the impress they leave is on the flower of English youth, at the very time of life when thought has come, but action is not yet required. At the same time the whole genius loti, the venerable buildings with their traditions, the eminence secured by intellect and industry, the pride that is taken in the past and its great men, first as belonging to the University, and next to the individual college, all give the members thereof a sense of a dignity to keep up and of honour to maintain, and a certainty of appreciation and fellow-feeling from the society with which they are connected.

The Oxford of Patteson's day was yet untouched by the hand of reformation. The Colleges were following or eluding the statutes of their founders, according to the use that had sprung up, but there had been a great quickening into activity of intellect, and the religious influences were almost at their strongest. It was true that the master mind had been lost to the Church of England, but the men whom he and his companions had helped to form were the leaders among the tutors, and the youths who were growing up under them were forming plans of life, which many have nobly carried out, of unselfish duty and devotion in their several stations.

Balliol had, under the mastership of Dr. Jenkyns, attained preeminence for success in the schools, and for the high standard required of its members, who formed 'the most delightful society, the very focus of the most stimulating life of the University,' within those unpretending walls, not yet revivified and enlarged.

Here Coleridge Patteson came to reside in the Michaelmas term of 1845; beginning with another attempt for the scholarship, in which he was again unsuccessful, being bracketed immediately after the fourth with another Etonian, namely, Mr. Hornby, the future head-master, His friend, Edmund Bastard, several of his relations, and numerous friends had preceded him; and he wrote to his sister Fanny:—

'You cannot think what a nice set of acquaintance I am gradually slipping into. Palmer and myself take regular familiar walks; and Riddell, another fellow who is the pet of the College, came up the other evening and sat with me, and I breakfast with them, and dine, &c. The only inconvenience attaching itself to such a number of men is, that I have to give several parties, and as I meant to get them over before Lent, I have been coming out rather strong in that line lately, as the pastry-cook's bill for desserts will show in good time.

'I have been asked to play cricket in the University eleven, and have declined, though not without a little struggle, but cricket here, especially to play in such matches as against Cambridge, &c., entails almost necessarily idleness and expense.'

The struggle was hardly a little one to a youth whose fame in the cricket field stood so high, and who was never happy or healthy without strong bodily exercise. Nor had he outgrown his taste for this particular sport. Professor Edwin Palmer (alluded to above) describes him as at this time 'a thorough public schoolboy, with a full capacity for enjoying undergraduate society and undergraduate amusements, though with so fond a recollection of Eton that to some of us he hardly seemed to appreciate Oxford sufficiently.'

Again, Mr. Roundell (his late adversary at Lord's) says: 'He was a reluctant and half-interested sojourner was ever looking back to the playing-fields of Eton, or forward to the more congenial sphere of a country parish.' So it was his prime pleasure and glory that he thus denied himself, though not with total abstinence, for he played occasionally. I remember hearing of a match at Ottery, where he was one of an eleven of Coleridge kith and kin against the rest of Devon. His reputation in the field was such that, many years later, when he chanced to be at Melbourne at the same time with the champion English eleven, one of the most noted professional cricketers, meeting him in the street, addressed him confidentially, 'I know, sir, the Bishop of Melbourne does not approve of cricket for clergymen in public, but if you would meet me in private at five o'clock to-morrow morning, and let me give you a few balls, it would be a great satisfaction!'

Some resolution thus was required to prevent cricket from becoming a tyrant, as so often befalls those whose skill renders them valuable. Tennis became Coley's chief recreation, enabling him to work off his superfluous energy at the expense of far less time than cricket matches require, and in this, as in everything active, he soon excelled.

As to the desserts upon which the young men in turn were spending a good deal out of mere custom, harmlessly enough, but unnecessarily; as soon as the distress of the potato famine in Ireland became known, Patteson said, 'I am not at all for giving up these pleasant meetings, but why not give up the dessert?' So the agreement was made that the cost should for the present be made over to the 'Irish fund.'

Another friend of this period, now well known as Principal Shairp of St. Andrews', was then in the last year of a five years' residence. He has been kind enough to favour me with the following effective sketch of Coley as an undergraduate:—

'Patteson as he was at Oxford, comes back to me, as the representative of the very best kind of Etonian, with much good that he had got from Eton, with something better, not to be got at Eton or any other school. He had those pleasant manners and that perfect ease in dealing with men and with the world which are the inheritance of Eton, without the least tincture of worldliness. I remember well the look he then had, his countenance massive for one so young, with good sense and good feeling, in fact, full of character. For it was character more than special ability which marked him out from others, and made him, wherever he was, whether in cricket in which he excelled, or in graver things, a centre round which others gathered. The impression he left on me was of quiet, gentle strength and entire purity, a heart that loved all things true and honest and pure, and that would always be found on the side of these. We did not know, probably he did not know himself, the fire of devotion that lay within him, but that was soon to kindle and make him what he afterwards became.'

In truth he was taking deep interest in the religious movement, though in the quiet unexcited way of those to whom such doctrines were only the filling out of the teachings of their childhood. He was present at that sermon on the 'Entire Absolution of the Penitent,' with which, on the Fourth Sunday after Epiphany, 1846, Dr. Pusey broke his enforced silence of three years.

The same evening Coley wrote to his sister Fanny:—

'I have just returned from University sermon, where I have been listening with great delight to Pusey's sermon on the Keys for nearly two hours. His immense benevolence beams through the extreme power of his arguments, and the great research of his inquiry into all the primitive writings is a most extraordinary matter, and as for the humility and prayerful spirit in which it was composed, you fancied he must have been on his knees the whole time he was writing it. I went early to Christ Church, where it was preached, and, after pushing through such a crowd as usually blocks up the entrance into Exeter Hall, I found on getting into the Cathedral that every seat was occupied. However, standing to hear such a man was no great exertion, and I never was so interested before. It will probably be printed, so that you will have no occasion for any remarks of mine. It is sufficient that he preached the doctrine to my mind in an invincible manner.' The letter has a postscript—'Easter vacation will be from three weeks to a month. Hurrah! say I; now a precious deal more glad am I to leave Oxford for the holidays than Eton, though Feniton is better than either.'

Even in the last undergraduate year, the preference for Eton remained as strong as ever. Coley intended to remain at Oxford to read for honours through great part of the Long vacation; and after refreshing himself with a run to Eton, he wrote:—

'Now for a very disagreeable contrast, but still I shall find great interest in my work as I go on, and reading books for the second or third time is light work compared to the first stodge at them. I am, however, behindhand with my work, in spite of not having wasted much time here.... I really don't see my way through the mass of work before me, and half repent having to go up for class.

'...I went to the opera on Tuesday, but was too much taken up by Eton to rave about it, though Grisi's singing and acting were out and out; but, in sober earnest, I think if one was to look out simply for one's own selfish pleasure in this world, staying at Eton in the summer is paradise. I certainly have not been more happy, if so happy, for years, and they need no convincing there of my doting attachment to the place. I go down to Eton on Election Saturday and Sunday for my last enjoyment of it this year; but if I am well and nourishing in the summer of 1849, and all goes right with me, it is one of the jolliest prospects of my emancipation from the schools to think of a month at Eton. Oh! it's hard work reading for it, I can tell you.'

Thus Coley Patteson's work throughout his undergraduate three years was, so to speak, against the grain, though it was more diligent and determined than it had been at Eton. He viewed this as the least satisfactory period of his life, and probably it was that in which he was doing the most violence to his likings. It struck those who had known him at Eton that he had 'shaken off the easy-going, comfortable, half-sluggish habit of mind' attributed to him there, and to be earnestly preparing for the future work of life. His continued interest in Missions was shown by his assisting to collect subscriptions for the Society for the Propagation of the Gospel. In fact, his charm of manner, and his way of taking for granted that people meant to do what they ought, made him a good collector, and he had had a good deal of practice at Eton in keeping up the boys to the subscription for the stained glass of the east window of the Chapel which they had undertaken to give.

That Long vacation of study was a great effort, and he felt it tedious and irksome, all the more from a weakness that affected his eyelids, and, though it did not injure his sight, often rendered reading and writing painful. Slight ailments concurred with other troubles and vexations to depress his spirits; and besides these outward matters, he seems to have had a sense of not coming up to his ideal. His standard was pitched higher than that of most men: his nature was prone to introspection, and his constitutional inertness rendered it so difficult for him to live up to his own views, that he was continually dissatisfied with himself; and this, in spite of his sweet unselfish temper, gave his manner at home an irritability, and among strangers a reserve—the very reverse of the joyous merry nature which used to delight in balls, parties, and gaieties.

Though an ardent friend, he became disinclined to enter into general society; nor was the distaste ever entirely overcome, though he never failed to please by the charm alike of natural manner and of Christian courtesy; the same spirit of gentleness and kindness very soon prevailed in subduing, even in family life, any manifestation of the tender points of a growing character.

In the autumn of 1849, he obtained a second class in the school of Literae humaniores, a place that fairly represented his abilities as compared with those of others. When the compulsory period of study was at an end, his affection for Oxford and enjoyment of all that it afforded increased considerably, though he never seems to have loved the University quite as well as Eton.

As he intended to take Holy Orders, he did not give up his residence there; but his first use of his leisure was to take a journey on the Continent with his brother and Mr. Hornby. It was then that, as he afterwards wrote, his real education began, partly from the opening of his mind by the wonders of nature and art, and partly from the development of his genius for philology. Aptitude for language had already shown itself when his sister Fanny had given him some German lessons; and even on his first halt at Cologne, he received the compliment, 'Sie sprechen Deutsch wohl' and he found himself talking to a German on one side and a Frenchman on the other.

His letters throughout his foreign travels are more copious than ever, but are chiefly minute descriptions of what he saw, such as would weary the reader who does not want a guide-book even full of individuality. Yet they cannot be passed by without noticing how he fulfilled the duty of study and endeavour at appreciation which everyone owes to great works of art, instead of turning aside with shallow conceit if he do not enter into them at first sight.

After the wonders of Vienna and the mines of Salzburg, the mountain scenery of the Tyrol was an unspeakable pleasure, which tries to express itself in many closely written pages. Crossing into Italy by the Stelvio Pass, a sharp but passing fit of illness detained Coley at Como for a day, and caused him to call in an Italian doctor, who treated him on the starvation system, administered no medicines, and would take no fee. The next day Coley was in condition to go on to Milan, where his first impression of the Cathedral was, as so often happens, almost of bewilderment. He did not at first like the Lombardo-Gothic style, but he studied it carefully, and filled his letter with measurements and numbers, though confessing that no part pleased him so much as the pinnacles terminating in statues, 'each one a very beautiful martyr's memorial.' Two more visits of several hours, however, brought the untutored eye to a sense of the harmony of proportion, and the surpassing beauty of the carvings and sculpture.

It did not need so much study to enjoy Lionardo da Vinci's great fresco, of which he wrote long and elaborately, and, altogether, Milan afforded him very great delight and was a new world to him. It was the farthest limit of his travels on this occasion. The party returned by way of Geneva; and Coley, alone with four guides, attempted the Col du Geant. Then following is his account of the danger in which he found himself:—

'On Monday at 4.15 A.M. we started from the Montanvert, with our alpenstocks, plenty of ropes, and a hatchet to cut steps in the ice. We walked quickly over the Mer de Glace, and in about three hours came to the difficult part. I had no conception of what it would be. We had to ascend perpendicular walls of ice, 30, 40, 50 feet high, by little holes which we cut with the hatchet, and to climb over places not a foot broad, with enormous crevasses on each side. I was determined not to give in, and said not a word, but I thought that no one had a right to expose himself to such danger if known beforehand. After about three hours spent in this way, (during which I made but one slip, when I slid about twelve feet down a crevasse, but providentially did not lose my head, and saved myself by catching at a broken ridge of ice, rising up in the crevasse, round which I threw my leg and worked my way up it astride), got to the region of snow, and here the danger was of falling into hidden crevasses. We all five fastened ourselves to one another with ropes. I went in the middle, Couttet in front, then Payot. Most unluckily the weather began to cloud over, and soon a sharp hailstorm began, with every indication of a fog. We went very cautiously over the snow for about three hours, sinking every now and then up to our middles, but only once in a crevasse, when Couttet suddenly fell, singing out "Tirez! tirez!" but he was pulled out instantly. We had now reached the top, but the fog was so dense that I could scarcely see 30 feet before me, and the crevasses and mountains of snow looming close round us looked awful. At this moment the guides asked me if I must make the passage. I said instantly that I wanted to do so, but that I would sooner return at once than endanger the lives of any of them. They told me there was certainly great danger, they had lost their way, but were unwilling to give up. For an hour and a half we beat about in the fog, among the crevasses, trying every way to find the pass, which is very narrow, wet to the skin, and in constant peril; but we knew that the descent on the Chamouni side is far more difficult than that on the Courmayeur side. At last all the guides agreed that it was impossible to find the way, said the storm was increasing, and that our only chance was to return at once. So we did, but the fearful difficulties of the descent I shall never forget. Even in the finest weather they reckon it very difficult, but yesterday we could not see the way, we were numbed with intense cold, and dispirited from being forced to return.

In many places the hail and sleet had washed out the traces we trusted as guides. After about four hours, we had passed the most dangerous part, and in another hour we were safely upon the Mer de Glace, which we hailed with delight: Couttet, who reached the point of safety first, jumping on the firm ice and shouting to me "Il n'y a plus de danger, Monsieur." Here we took off the ropes, and drank some more brandy, and then went as hard as we could, jumping across crevasses, which two days before I should have thought awkward, as if they were cart ruts. We reached Chamouni at 8.30 P.M., having been sixteen and a quarter hours without resting. I was not at all tired; the guides thanked me for having given so little trouble, and declared I had gone as well as themselves. Indeed I was providentially unusually clear-headed and cool, and it was not till the danger was over that I felt my nerves give way. There was a good deal of anxiety about us at Chamouni, as it was one of the worst days ever seen here. Hornby had taken all my clothes to Geneva, so I put on a suit of the landlord's, and had some tea, and at 11 P.M. went to bed, not forgetting, you may be sure, to thank God most fervently for this merciful protection, as on the ice I did many times with all my heart.

'On reviewing coolly, to-day, the places over which we passed, and which I shall never forget, I remember seven such as I trust never again to see a man attempt to climb. The state of the ice and crevasses is always shifting, so that the next person who makes the ascent may find a comparatively easy path. We had other dangers too, such as this: twice the guides said to me, "Ne parlez pas ici, Monsieur, et allez vite," the fear being of an ice avalanche falling on us, and we heard the rocks and ice which are detached by the wet falling all about. The view from the top, if the day is fine, is about the most magnificent in the Alps; and as in that case I should have descended easily on the other side, the excursion would not have been so difficult. I hope you will not think I have been very foolish; I did not at all think it would be so dangerous, nor was it possible to foresee the bad weather. My curiosity to see some of the difficulties of an excursion in the Alps is fully satisfied.'

After this adventure, the party broke up, James Patteson returning home with Mr. Hornby, while Coley, who hoped to obtain a Fellowship at Merton, and wished in the meantime to learn German thoroughly in order to study Hebrew by the light of German scholarship, repaired to Dresden for the purpose; revelling, by the way, on the pictures and glass at Munich, descriptions of which fill three or four letters. He remained a month at Dresden, reading for an hour a day with a German master, and spending many hours besides in study, recreating himself with German newspapers at the cafe where he dined, and going to the play in the evening to hear colloquialisms. The picture galleries were his daily enjoyment, and he declared the Madonna di San Sisto fully equal to his anticipations. There is that about the head of the Virgin which I believe one sees in no other picture, a dignity and beauty with a mixture of timidity quite indescribable.'

Returning home for Christmas, Coley started again in January 1851, in charge of a pupil, the son of Lord John Thynne, with whom he was to go through Italy. The journey was made by sea from Marseilles to Naples, where the old regime was still in force. Shakespeare and Humboldt were seized; and after several hours' detention on the score of the suspicious nature of his literature, Mr. Patteson was asked for a bribe.

The climate was in itself a great charm to one always painfully susceptible to cold; and, after duly dwelling on the marvels of Vesuvius and Pompeii, the travellers went on to Rome. There the sculptures were Coley's first delight, and he had the advantage of hints from Gibson on the theory of his admiration, such as suited his love of analysis. He poured forth descriptions of statues and pictures in his letters: sometimes apologising.—'You must put up with a very stupid and unintelligible sermon on art. The genius loci would move the very stones to preach on such a theme. Again: The worst is, that I ought to have months instead of days to see Rome in. I economise my time pretty well; but yet I find every night that I can only do a little of what I propose in the morning; and as for my Italian, an hour and a half a day is on an average more than I give to it. I suffer a good deal from weakness in the eyes; it prevents my working at night with comfort. I have a master every other day. I tried to draw, but it hurt me so much after looking about all day that I despair of doing anything, though I don't abandon the idea altogether.'

There are many letters on the religious state of Rome. The apparently direct supplications to the Saints, the stories told in sermons of desperate sinners—saved through some lingering observance paid to the Blessed Virgin, and the alleged abuse of the Confessional, shocked Patteson greatly, and therewith he connected the flagrant evils of the political condition of Rome at that time, and arrived at conclusions strongly adverse to Roman Catholicism as such, though he retained uninjured the Catholic tone of his mind.

It was art which was the special attraction to Coley of all the many spells of old Rome. He spent much time in the galleries, and studied 'modern painters' with an earnestness that makes Ruskinism pervade his letters.

At Florence, Coley wrote as usual at much length of the galleries, where the Madonna del Cardellino seems to have been what delighted him most. He did not greatly enter into Michel Angelo's works, and perhaps hardly did their religious spirit full justice under the somewhat exclusive influence of Fra Angelico and Francia, with the Euskinese interpretation. The delight was indescribable. He says: — 'But I have written again and again on this favourite theme, and I forget that it is difficult for you to understand what I write, or the great change that has taken place in me, without seeing the original works. No one can see them and be unchanged. I never had such enjoyment.' His birthday presents were spent on a copy of the beloved Madonna del Cardellino, of which he says:—'though it does not reach anything like the intensity of feeling of the original, is still a very excellent painting, and will always help to excite in my imagination, and I hope to convey to you, some faint image of the exceeding beauty of this most beautiful of all paintings.'

Readers chiefly interested in the subsequent career of the missionary would feel interrupted by the overflowing notes on painting, sculpture and architecture which fill the correspondence, yet without them, it is scarcely possible to realise the young man's intense enthusiasm for the Beautiful, especially for spiritual beauty, and thus how great was the sacrifice of going to regions where all these delights were unknown and unattainable. He went on to Venice, where he met a letter which gave a new course to his thoughts, for it informed him that the deafness, which had long been growing on his father had now become an obstacle to the performance of his duties as a Judge, and announcing his intention of retiring.

In the fulness of his heart he wrote:—

'Venice, Hotel de la Villa: May 2, 1851.

'My dearest Father,—I have not been in Venice an hour yet, but little did I expect to find such news waiting for me as is contained in Jem's letter, and I can lose no time in answering it. It is indeed a heavy trial for you, that, in addition to many years of constant annoyance from your deafness, you should be obliged now, in the full vigour of your mind, and with the advantage of your experience, to give up a profession you so thoroughly delight in. I don't deny that I have often contemplated the possibility of such a thing; and I had some conversation with Uncle John last winter in consequence of my fancying your deafness was on the increase, though the girls did not perceive it; I hope with all my heart I was wrong. I told him what I know you feel, that, painful as it will be to you to retire from the

Bench, if any dissatisfaction was expressed at your not hearing sufficiently what passed, you would choose rather to give up your seat than to go on under such circumstances. His answer, I remember, was that it was most difficult to know what to do, because it was no use concealing the fact that your infirmity did interfere with the working of the Court more or less, on Circuit especially, and at other times when witnesses were examined, but that your knowledge of law was so invaluable that it was difficult to see how this latter advantage could fail to outweigh the former defect; and everybody knew that they can't find a lawyer to fill your place, though another man might do the ordinary circuit work with greater comfort to the Bar; though therefore nobody is so painstaking and so little liable to make mistakes, yet to people in general and in the whole, another man would seem to do the work nearly as well, and would do his work, as far as his knowledge and conscientiousness went, with more ease;—this was something like the substance of what passed then, and you may suppose that since that time I have thought more about the possibility of your retirement; but as I know how very much you will feel giving up an occupation in which you take a regular pride, I do feel very sorry, and wish I was at home to do anything that could be done now. I know well enough that you are the last man in the world to make a display of your feelings, and that you look upon this as a trial, and bear it as one, just as you have with such great patience and submission (and dear Joan too,) always quietly borne your deafness; but I am sure you must, and do feel this very much, and, added to Granny's illness, you must be a sad party at home. I feel as if it were very selfish to be in this beautiful city, and to have been spending so much money at Florence. Neither did Joan, in her last letter, nor has Jem now, mentioned whether you received two letters from Florence, the first of which gave some description of my vetturino journey from Rome to Florence. I little thought when I was enjoying myself so very much there, that all this was passing at home.... Your influence in the Privy Council (where I conclude they will offer you a seat) might be so good on very important questions, and it would be an occupation for you; and I have always hoped that, if it should please God you should retire while still in the prime of life for work, you would publish some great legal book, which should for ever be a record of your knowledge on these subjects. However it may be, the retrospect of upwards of twenty years spent on the Bench with the complete respect and admiration of all your friends, is no slight thing to fall back upon: and I trust that this fresh trial will turn to your good, and even happiness here, as we may trust with safety it will hereafter.

'Ever your very affectionate and dutiful Son,
  '**JOHN COLERIDGE PATTESON.**'

In this winter of 1852, Mr. Justice Patteson's final decision to retire was made and acted upon. The Judge delighted in no occupation so much as the pursuit of law, and therefore distrusted his own opinion as to the moment when his infirmity should absolutely unfit him for sitting in Court. He had begged a friend to tell him the moment that the impediment became serious; and this, with some hesitation, was done. The intimation was thankfully received, and, after due consideration, carried out.

On January 29, 1852, after twenty-two years on the Bench, and at the age of sixty-two, Mr. Justice Patteson wrote his letter of resignation to Lord Truro, then Lord Chancellor, petitioning for the usual pension. It was replied to in terms of warm and sincere regret; and on the 2nd of February, Sir John Patteson was nominated to the Privy Council, as a member of the Judicial Committee; where the business was chiefly conducted in writing, and he could act with comparatively little obstacle from his deafness.

On February 10, 1852, he took his leave of the Bar. The Court of Queen's Bench was crowded with barristers, who rose while the Attorney-General, Sir Alexander Cockburn, made an address expressive of the universal heartfelt feeling of respect and admiration with which the retiring Judge was regarded.

John Patteson's reply, read with a voice broken by emotion, is so touching in its manly simplicity and humility that a paragraph or two may well be quoted:—

'Mine,' he said, 'is one of the many instances which I know that a public man without pre-eminent abilities, if he will but exert such as it has pleased God to bestow on him honestly and industriously, and without ostentation, is sure to receive public approbation fully commensurate with, and generally much beyond, his real merits; and I thank God if I shall be found not to have fallen entirely short in the use of those talents which He has entrusted to me.' Then, after some words on the misfortune that necessitated his withdrawal, he continued, 'I am aware that on some, and I fear too many, occasions I have given way to complaints and impatient expressions towards the Bar and the witnesses in Court, as if they were to blame when, in truth, it was my own deficiency; and heartily sorry have I been and am for such want of control over myself. I have striven against its recurrence earnestly, though not always successfully. My brethren on the Bench, and you, and the public, have been very kind and indulgent to me; the recollection of which will remain with, and be a great solace to me for the rest of my life.

'And now, gentlemen, I bid you farewell most affectionately. I wish you many years of health and happiness, of success and honour in your liberal profession; the duties of which have been and are and I trust ever will be performed, not only with the greatest zeal, learning, and ability, but with the highest honour and integrity, and a deep sense of responsibility to God and to man, and which being so performed, are, in my humble judgment, eminently conducive, under the blessing of God, to maintain the just prerogative of the Crown, and the true right, liberties, and happiness of the people.'

He then rose from the Judges' seat, and bowed his farewell to the assembly, who stood respectful and silent, except for some suppressed tokens of emotion, for in truth to many the parting was from an old familiar and much trusted friend.

Private letters poured in, expressive of deep regret, esteem, and affection, and not only were gratefully read at the time, but became to the family valuable memorials of the heartfelt appreciation gained by a high-minded and upright course of life, and evidences that their father had done that which is perhaps the best thing that it is permitted to man to do here below, namely, 'served God in his generation.'

CHAPTER IV. FELLOWSHIP OF MERTON. 1852—1854.

In the summer of 1852 Coleridge Patteson stood for a fellowship of Merton, obtained it, and moved into rooms there. Every college has a distinctive character; and Merton, if not actually the eldest, is at least one of the oldest foundations at Oxford, and is one of the most unchanged in outward aspect. There is a peculiar charm in the beauty and seclusion of the quadrangle, in the library, still mediaeval even to the fittings; and the church is above all impressive in the extraordinary loveliness of the early decorated architecture, and the space and loftiness of the choir. The whole, pre-eminently among the colleges, gives the sense of having been unaltered for five hundred years, yet still full of life and vigour.

Coley attached himself to Merton, though he never looked to permanent residence there. The Curacy in the immediate neighbourhood of his home was awaiting him, as soon as he should be ordained; but though his purpose was unchanged and he was of full age for Holy Orders, he wished for another year of preparation, so as to be able to study both Hebrew and theology more thoroughly than would be possible when pastoral labour should have begun. What he had already seen of Dresden convinced him that he could there learn Hebrew more thoroughly and more cheaply than at home, and to this he intended to devote the Long Vacation of 1852, without returning to Feniton. There the family were settling themselves, having given up the house in Bedford Square, since James Patteson had chambers in King's Bench Walk, where the ex-Judge could be with him when needed in London. There had some notion of the whole family profiting by Sir John's emancipation to take a journey on the Continent, and the failure of the scheme elicited the following letter:—

'Merton: June 18.

'My dearest Fan,—I can, to a certain extent, sympathise with you thoroughly upon this occasion; the mere disappointment at not seeing so many interesting places and things is a sharp one, but in your instance this is much increased by the real benefit you hoped to derive from a warmer climate; and no wonder that the disappearance of your hopes coupled with bodily illness makes you low and uncomfortable. The weather too is trying to mind and body, and though you try as usual to shake off the sense of depression which affects you, your letter is certainly sad, and written like the letter of one in weak health. Well, we shall see each other, please GOD, at Christmas now. That is better than passing nearly or quite a year away from each other; and some other time I hope you will be able to go to Italy, and enjoy all the wonders there, though a tour for health's sake cannot be too soon. It is never too soon to get rid of an ailment....

'I find that I am getting to know the undergraduates here, which is what I wanted to do; it is my only chance of being of any use. True, that I have to do it at the expense of two half-days' cricketing, which I have quite ceased to care about, but I know that when I went up to Balliol, I was glad when a Fellow played with us. It was a guarantee for orderly conduct, and as I say, it gives me an opportunity of knowing men. I hope to leave London for Dresden on Monday week; Arthur is gone thither, as I find out from Jem, and I hope the scheme will answer. If I find I can't work, from my eyes, or anything else, preventing me, I shall come home, but I have no reason to expect any such thing. My best love to Joan and all friends.

'Your loving Brother,
'J. C. PATTESON.'

The 'Arthur' here mentioned was the youngest son of Mr. Frank Coleridge, and became Coley's companion at Dresden, where he was studying German. He writes:—

'Patteson spoke German fluently, and wrote German correctly. He had studied the language assiduously for about two years previously, and so successfully that whilst we were at Dresden, he was enabled to dispense with a teacher and make his assistance little more than nominal. Occasionally he wrote a German exercise, but rather as an amusement than a discipline, and merely with the view of enlarging his German vocabulary. I remember his writing an elaborate description of Feniton Court, and imagining the place to be surrounded with trees belonging to all sorts of climates. The result was very amusing to ourselves, and added to the writer's stock of words on particular subjects. When our master Schier appeared, the conversation was led by a palpable ambuscade to the topic which had been made the subject of Patteson's exercise, and conversation helped to strengthen memory. After looking over a few of Patteson's German exercises, Mr. Schier found so little to correct, in the way of grammatical errors, that these studies were almost relinquished, and gave way to Arabic and Hebrew. Before we left Dresden, Patteson had read large portions of the Koran; and, with the aid of Hurwitz's Grammar and Bernhard's Guide to Hebrew Students, books familiar to Cambridge men, he was soon able to read the Psalms in the original. I remember the admiration and despair I felt in witnessing Patteson's progress, and the wonder expressed by his teacher in his pupil's gift of rapid acquirement. We had some excellent introductions; amongst others, to Dr. ——, a famous theologian, with whom Patteson was fond of discussing the system and organisation of the Church in Saxony. Up to the time of his leaving England he was constantly using Olshausen's Commentary on the New Testament, a book he was as thoroughly versed in as Archbishop Trench himself. I think that he consulted no other books in his study of the Gospels, but Olshausen and Bengel's Gnomon.

'In our pleasures at Dresden there was a mixture of the utile with the dulce. Our constant visits to the theatre were strong incentives to a preparatory study of the plays of Goethe, Schiller, and Lessing. What noble acting we saw in that Dresden theatre!

'With regard to the opera, I have never seen Weber or Meyerbeer's works given so perfectly and conscientiously as at Dresden. Patteson's chief delight was the Midsummer Night's Dream, with Mendelssohn's music. He had a tuneful baritone voice and a correct ear for music. We hired a piano for our sitting-room; and, though I failed to induce him to cultivate his voice, and join me in taking lessons, he sang some of Mendelssohn's Lieder very pleasingly, and knew most of the bass music from the Messiah by heart. He began to play a few scales on the piano, and hoped to surprise his sisters on his return to England by playing chants, but the Arabic and Hebrew studies proved too absorbing; he grudged the time, and thought the result disproportioned to the sacrifice.

'In our daily walks we talked constantly of Church matters. Some sharp and sad experiences in the loss of more than one of his Eton and Oxford friends, who had abandoned the Church of England, failed to shake his confidence in the Church he was to serve so faithfully and to die for so gloriously. His faith and daily practice seem to me a protest and warning against the folly, if not the falsehood, of extremes. Moderation, quiet consistency of life, and unswerving loyalty to a faith which had been the joy and comfort of his dear mother, whose loveable nature he inherited and reflected, a blameless life and unfailing charity enabled him when the time came to live a life of incessant toil, and face a martyr's death. I remember the present Bishop of Carlisle inciting Cambridge undergraduates to become, by virtue of earnestness, gentleness, and toleration, "guides not judges, lights not firebrands." He drew a perfect description of Patteson, who came more completely up to that ideal than anyone I ever knew. Here was a man capable of the purest and most tender friendship, with an exquisite appreciation of all that is noblest in life, and he was ready to give up all, and content to lead the forlorn hope of Christianity, and perish in the front ranks of the noble army. "And having been a little tried he shall be greatly rewarded, for God proved him, and found him worthy for Himself."'

I have given this letter almost entire, because it shows the impression Coley made on one, little his junior, in the intimate associations of cousin, neighbour, and schoolfellow, as well as travelling companion.

This year seems to have been a marked stage of development. He was now twenty-five, and the boyish distaste for mental exertion which had so long rendered study an effort of duty had passed into full scholarly enjoyment. The individuality and originality of his mind had begun to awaken, and influenced probably by the German atmosphere of thought in which he was working, were giving him that strong metaphysical bent which characterised his tone through life, and became apparent in his sermons when he addressed an educated audience.

Here is a letter to his eldest sister: 'The weather has been better suited for work, and I feel pretty well satisfied with my Hebrew. What makes it so difficult is principally this, that as it is an Oriental language, it is entirely different in structure, and in its inflections, &c., from any language I ever came across. I can't fall back upon anything already learnt to help me; but I see my way pretty clear now, and shall soon have little more than a knowledge of the meaning of the words to learn, which is only a matter of patience, and can be learnt with a good dictionary and practice. A real complete knowledge of the grammar is of course the great thing.

'The great Dresden fair, called the Vogelschiesser, is going on; it began last Sunday and ends next Sunday. About half a mile from the town there is a very large meadow by the river, where a small town of booths, tents, &c., is erected, and where shooting at targets with wooden darts, sham railway-trains and riding-horses, confectionery of every kind, beer of every name, strength, and colour, pipes, cigars, toys, gambling, organ-grinding, fiddling, dancing, &c., goes on incessantly. The great attraction, however, is the shooting at the bird, which occupies the attention of every Saxon, and is looked upon as the consummation of human invention and physical science. A great pole, nearly 80 feet high, is erected with a wooden bird, about the size of a turkey, at the top; to hit this with a crossbow from a regular stand, about 50 feet from the foot of the pole, is the highest ambition of this great people. The accompaniments are rich in the extreme: cannon firing, drums rolling, for a successful shot, the shooting society, who exist only for the sole honour and glory of hacking this bird to pieces, the presence of the King, I think to-day, and the intense interest taken in the amusement by the whole population; certainly the Germans are satisfied with less than any people I ever saw (barring two things, smoke and beer, in which they are insatiable). I went out to see it all, but it rather bored me after an hour or so. Tom F—— and I threw some dice for a pair of braces for Arthur, which we presented in due form; and we had some shots at the targets—mine were eminently unsuccessful.

'Last night we had a great treat. Emil Devrient, who has been acting in London, you know, came back, and acted Marquis Posa in "Don Carlos." The play acts very much better than it reads. Schiller certainly has great dramatic genius; only I agree with Goethe that there is always a longing for exhibiting cruelty in its most monstrous form, and refinement of cruelty and depravity overstepping almost the natural conditions of humanity. I always thought Iago about the most awful character in Shakspeare; but Schiller's Philip II. is something beyond even this, without perhaps so much necessity for the exhibition of this absolute delight in evil. It is long since I have been so excited in a theatre. I was three rows from the stage, heard and understood everything, and was so completely carried away by the grandeur and intense feeling of Devrient (who was well supported by the Don Carlos), that I had some difficulty to keep quiet, and feel to-day rather odd, shaken, as it were, from such a strain upon the feelings.'

Here is a letter, enclosed within one to his sister Fanny on September 9, written on a scrap of paper. The apologetic tone of confession is amusing:—

'My dearest Father,—I have not before told you that I have been at work for just three weeks upon a new subject; reading, however, Hebrew every day almost for three hours as well. Schier is not a great Hebraist; and I found the language in one sense easier than I expected, so that with good grammar and dictionary I can quite get on by myself, reading an easy part of the Bible (historical books, e.g.) at the rate of about twenty-five verses an hour. Well, I began to think that I ought to use the opportunities that Dresden affords. I know that Hebrew is not a rich language; that many words occur only once, and consequently have an arbitrary meaning attached to them, unless they can be illustrated from cognate languages. Now I have a taste for these things, and have in three weeks progressed so far in my new study as to feel sure I shall make it useful; and so I tell you without fear I am working at Arabic. I hope you won't think it silly. It is very hard, and for ten days was as hard work as I ever had in my life. I think I have learnt enough to see my way now, and this morning read the first chapter of Genesis in three-quarters of an hour. It is rich, beyond all comparison, in inflexions; and the difficulty arises from the extreme multiplicity of all its forms: e.g. each verb having not only active, middle, and passive voices, but the primitive active having not less than thirty-five derivative forms and the passive thirteen. The "noun of action,"—infinitive with article (to akonein) of the Greek—is again different for each voice or form; and the primitive can take any of twenty-two forms, which are not compounded according to any rule. Again, there are twenty-eight sets of irregular plurals, which are quite arbitrary. No grammarian has ever given any explanation about them. All mere matters of memory. The very alphabet shows the richness of the language. There are twenty-nine letters, besides vowel points; and each letter is written in four different ways, so that it is different when isolated, when in the beginning, middle, or end of a word. It took me some hours to learn them. In very many respects, it is closely allied to the Hebrew, so that everybody who writes Hebrew grammars and lexicons necessarily has much to do with Arabic; and a knowledge of it may be of great use in clearing up difficulties in the Bible. My year in Oxford will enable me to go on with it, for in three weeks more I hope to be able to go on alone. To-morrow I begin the Koran. My lessons will not in all exceed 31; and I really should have gone on, perhaps, not much faster with Hebrew if I had worked it exclusively; and it is hard to read so many hours at one thing: and I may say, now without doubt, that I have laid the foundation for a study of Oriental languages, if I have time and opportunity that may be fairly given to them. Think what one hour a day is, and the pleasure to me is very great, and I feel that I have a knack rather (if I may say so) of laying hold of these things. Don't mention it to anyone.'

There the fragment breaks off; and in a letter of August 29 there occurs this reply to a message from his eldest sister:—

'Thank dear Joan for her caution: I know I need it sadly, especially now when I am at work upon somewhat out-of-the-way subjects, and feel the danger of forgetting that if I mistake the means for the end, and feel gratified with the mere intellectual amusement, I am doing very wrong, even when I am working very hard at very difficult matters. I like these things, I must confess, and the time is so well adapted to work here, and now that the weather is cool I can secure every day a good long time to myself.' In the enclosed letter he announces that he shall leave Dresden in another three weeks. He says:—

'We have had a steady working time of it here; and as I know some members of the family rather discourage these Continental flights, I just sum up the advantages thereof. Being naturally endowed with a love of music, the probability is, that when you, Clara, and Miss Horsley are together in the house, as soon as a Lied or Sonata began, away would go my books, or at all events my thoughts. You know well that the piano goes at all hours, and always in the morning at home. Then riding, walking with Father, long sitting after dinner, &c. do not improve the chances for reading. In fact, you know that what with visitors from without, friends within, parties, &c., I should have had very little reading in the vacation, and that not through my own fault—not a Stilbehen in the house could protect me from music. Here I make my own time, and last week my eyes were troublesome. I walked twice every day, exactly at the hour when I most wanted it; and without nonsense, I may say that I have in two months done really a great deal more than I could have done at home even with masters. This all applies to Arthur just as much. He has read German exclusively most of the time, and knows as well as I do that it is not possible to work at home. If I could go on just as well as with Mendelssohn ringing in my ears, it would be different, but I can't. You remember how pleasant, but how very idle, last vacation was, and especially the last six weeks of it!'

Then, after much about family matters, commissions, and little gifts which he was collecting for all at home—

I should like to get something for everybody, but that is not possible. Luckily, my lessons are less expensive than I expected, and, considering the work, wonderfully cheap. I make good progress, I can say; but the difficulty is great enough to discourage any but a real "grinder" at such work. I have written a scrap for Father, and you will see that I am working away pretty well. I have finished my introductory book, consisting of forty-one fables; and though difficulties present themselves always to really good scholars from time to time, the Bible is not one of the hardest books, not so hard, e.g. as the Koran. Now I can at any future time, if the opportunity comes, go on with these things, and I hope find them really useful. I know you like to hear what I am doing; but be sure to keep it all quiet, let no one know but Father and Joan. You might carelessly tell it to anyone in fun, and I don't wish it to be known. Especially don't let any of the family know. Time enough if I live out my Oxford year, and have really mastered the matter pretty well. Remember this is taken up with a view to elucidate and explain what is so very hard in Hebrew. Hebrew is to be the Hauptsache, this the Hulfsmittel, or some day I hope one of several such helps. It is very important to accustom one's mind to the Denk and Anschauungswerk of the Orientals, which is so different from that of Europeans or their language. How hard are the metaphors of the Bible for this reason!'

There is something in all these long apologies and strenuous desire for secrecy about these Arabic studies that reminds one that the character was a self-conscious introspective one, always striving for humility, and dreading to be thought presumptuous. A simpler nature, if devoid of craving for home sympathy, would never have mentioned the new study at all; or if equally open-hearted, would have let the mention of it among home friends take its chance, without troubling himself as to their possible comments. Indeed, it is curious to observe how elaborate he was at this period about all his concerns, meditating over the cause of whatever affected him. It was a form of growth; and dropped off when the time of action arrived, and his character had shaped itself. It must be remembered, too, that his habit of pouring out all his reflections and feelings to his sisters, and their preservation of his letters, have left much more on record of these personal speculations than is common.

His father made a much simpler matter of the Arabic matter, in the following characteristic letter:—

'Feniton Court: September 14, 1852,

'My dearest Coley,—So far from thinking you wrong in learning Arabic, I feel sure that you are quite right. However, we shall keep your secret, and not say anything about it. I am heartily glad that you should acquire languages, modern as well as ancient. You know I have often pressed the former on your and Jem's notice, from myself feeling my deficiency and regret at it. I can well understand that Arabic, and I should suppose Syriac also, must be of the greatest use towards a true understanding of much of the Old Testament: a great deal of which is doubtless not understood by those who understand only our translation, or even the Septuagint, which I suspect to have many passages far from a faithful vehicle of the meaning of the original. I was greatly delighted with your theological letter, so to speak, as well as with the first, and look to have some jolly conversations with you on such subjects.

'We have many more partridges than our neighbours, and Jem shoots uncommonly well. Three double shots yesterday. I shoot worse than usual; and cannot walk without much fatigue and frequent pain, so that I shall not be able to work enough to get much sport. I got through the Mary Church affair very well—that is, not making a fool of myself—and if I did not do much good, I think I did no harm. The Bishop of Exeter [Phillpotts] is mightily pleased, and wrote me a letter to that effect. Of course I cannot tell you what I said, it would be too long, nor are you likely to see it. It was fully inserted in "Woolmer," and from him copied into the "Guardian."

'I live in hopes to see you well and hearty at Oxford on the 14th of October, till when, adieu, God bless you.

'Your affectionate Father,

'J. PATTESON.'

The interview with the Bishop of Sydney never took place, for the excellent Bishop Broughton arrived with health shattered by his attendance on the sufferers from fever in the ship which brought him from St. Thomas, and he did not long survive his landing.

The 'Mary Church affair' here referred to was the laying the foundation-stone of the Church, built or restored, it is hard to say which, on the lines of the former one, and preserving the old tower, at St. Mary Church, near Torquay. Though the death of the Rev. Gr. M. Coleridge had broken one tie with the place, it continued to be much beloved by the Patteson family, and Sir John had taken so much share in the church-building work as to be asked to be the layer of the corner-stone. The speech he made at the ensuing luncheon excited much attention and the sisters took care that their brother should not miss reading it. The stay at Dresden was drawing to an end; and he was preparing to return through Berlin, intending to go direct to Oxford and reside there till the summer, when he meant to seek ordination and enter on the Curacy at Alfington. He says to his sister Joanna:—

'It is a long time to pass without seeing you, but I hope, if it please God that we all live on together, that it will be long before such another interval occurs. I have not grown out of an occasional fit of home sickness yet; and on these occasions

Arthur and I talk incessantly about domestic matters, and indulge our fancies in conjecturing what you are all doing, and so forth. I followed Joan and Clara's trip, step by step, from the Den at Teignmouth to St. Mary Church, Oddiscombe, Rabbicombe, Anstey's Cave, Meadfoot, &c. How I remember every inch of the dear old places! Better than the mud banks at Felixstowe, are they not, Clara? I shall keep always the scrap from the "Guardian" with Father's speech. I don't think I remember any speech on a similar occasion so thoroughly good, and so likely to do good. Plain, sensible, and manly, no question of words and unimportant differences of opinion; no cant, high or low, just like himself. I pray I may have but a tenth part of his honesty and freedom from prejudice and party spirit. It may come, under God's blessing, if a man's mind is earnestly set on the truth; but the danger is of setting up your own exclusive standard of truth, moral and intellectual. Father certainly is more free from it than any man we ever knew. He tells me in his letter that the Bishop of Sydney is coming home to consult people in England about Synodical Action, &c., and that he is going to meet him and explain to him certain difficulties and mistakes into which he has fallen with regard to administering the Oath of Abjuration and the like matters. How few people, comparatively, know the influence Father exercises in this way behind the scenes, as it were. His intimacy with so many of the Bishops, too, makes his position really of very great importance. I don't want to magnify, but the more I think of him, and know how very few men they are that command such general respect, and bear such a character with all men for uprightness and singleness of purpose, it is very difficult to know how his place could be supplied when we throw his legal knowledge over and above into the scale. I hope he will write: I am quite certain that his opinion will exercise a great influence on very many people. Such a speech as this at Mary Church embodies exactly the sense of a considerable number of the most prudent and most able men of the country, and his position and character give it extra weight, and that would be so equally with his book as with his speech. How delightful it will be to have him at Oxford. He means to come in time for dinner on the 14th, and go away on the 16th; but if he likes it, he will, I daresay, stop now and then on his way to town and back. Jem will not be back in town when he goes up for the Judicial Committee work, so he will be rather solitary there, won't he. I am not, however, sure about the number of weeks Jem must reside to keep his term....'

The enjoyment of the last few days at Dresden 'was much marred by a heavy cold, caught by going to see an admirable representation of 'Egmont,' the last of these theatrical treats so highly appreciated. The journey to Berlin, before the cold was shaken off, resulted in an attack of illness; and he was so heavy and uncomfortable as to be unable to avail himself of his opportunities of interesting introductions.

He returned to his rooms at Merton direct from Germany. Like many men who have come back to Oxford at a riper age than that of undergraduate life, he now entered into the higher privileges and enjoyments of the University, the studies, friendships, and influences, as early youth sometimes fails to do. He was felt by his Oxford friends to have greatly developed since his Balliol terms had been over and the Eton boy left behind. Study was no longer a toil and conscientious effort. It had become a prime pleasure; and men wondered to find the plodding, accurate, but unenthusiastic student of three years back, a linguist and philologist of no common power and attainment. Mr. Roundell says, 'He had become quite another person. Self-cultivation had done much for him. Literature and art had opened his mind and enlarged his interests and sympathies. The moral and spiritual forces of the man were now vivified, refined, and strengthened by the awakening of his intellectual and esthetic nature.'

Ever reaching forward, however, he was on his guard against, as he said, making the means the end. Languages were his pleasure, but a pleasure held in check as only subservient to his preparation for the ministry. He did not mean to use them to the acquirement of academical honour nor promotion, nor did he even rest in the intellectual delight of investigation; he intended them only as keys to the better appreciation of the Scriptures and of the doctrines of the Church, unaware as yet that the gift he was cultivating would be of inestimable value in far distant regions.

In February, while Sir John Patteson was in London, his son James was the cause of much alarm, owing to a mistake by which he swallowed an embrocation containing a large amount of laudanum. Prompt measures, however, prevented any ill effects; and all danger was over before the letter was sent off which informed Coley of what had happened; but the bare idea of the peril was a great shock to one of such warm affections, and so deeply attached to his only brother. He wrote the two following letters to his father and sisters on the first impulse on the receipt of the intelligence:—

'Shrove Tuesday.

'My dearest Father,—I believe I speak truly when I say that I never in my life felt so thoroughly thankful and grateful to God for His great mercy as I did this morning, on reading of dear Jem's danger and safety. He is less accustomed to talk about his feelings than I am, in which I see his superiority, but partly because our tastes are in several respects different, chiefly because of his exceeding amiability and unselfishness. I am sure we love each other very dearly. Ever since his illness at Geneva, I have from time to time contemplated the utter blank, the real feeling of loss, which anything happening to him would bring with it, and the having it brought home close to me in this way quite upset me, as it well might. I pray God that no ill effects may follow, and from what you say I apprehend none. I have often thought that it is much better when two brothers propose to themselves different objects in life, and pursue them with tastes dissimilar on unimportant matters. They act better upon one another; just as I look to Jem, as I have more than once told him, to give me a hint when he sees a want of common sense in anything I take up, because I know I act a good deal from impulse, and take an interest in many things which are perhaps not worth the time I spend on them. It is a mercy that I hope I shall never forget, never cease to be thankful for. Many and many a time, if it please God, I shall look to him in difficulties, and remember how nearly once he was lost to me. I can get away with the greatest ease for a few days on Thursday if desirable, and perhaps old Jem will feel low after this, when you have left him. I think this very likely, from what I know of him, and if you think it too, without asking him if he would like it, I will come up for some other reason. You will not go, I know, unless he is perfectly well; but he might, and I think would, like to have some one with him just at first. Let me know what you think.

'Good-bye, my dearest father.

'Ever your affectionate and dutiful son,

'J. C. PATTESON.'

'Merton, Shrove Tuesday.

'My dearest Joan and Fan,—How we must all have united this morning in pouring out our thanks to God for His great mercy! You will not suspect me of being wanting in love to you, if I say that the contemplation of what might have happened presented such a scene of desolation, such a void, that it would have required all the strength I possess to turn to God in resignation and submission to His will. I have often, very often, thought of that illness at Geneva, but this brought it home to me, perhaps closer still; and I hope I shall never cease to be mindful of, and thankful for, this special providence. Father seems pretty confident that all mischief is prevented; and Jem wrote six hours after he took the laudanum, and had then felt no drowsiness to speak of, and Dr. Watson said there was no fear of anything happening after two hours had elapsed.

'I should like to join with you in showing our gratitude by some deed of charity, or whatever you think right. Something that without any show might be a thank-offering to God for His signal act of mercy.

'Ever your loving Brother,

'J. C. PATTESON.

'5.30. I wrote this quite early this morning. I can hardly think yet what it all means. Now, I feel only a sense of some very heavy affliction removed. Poor dear Father, and all of us! what should we have been without him!'

A letter to the brother himself was written under the same impulse, even more tenderly affectionate, but so deep and intimate, that it would almost be treason to give it to the world. The next letter was written soon after the alarm had passed, but is undated:—

'My dear Fan,—Yesterday I was unluckily too seedy with headache to go on the ice, and this morning I have been skating for half an hour, but the ice is spoilt. Very jolly it is to be twisting and turning about once more. I thought of writing to old Jem to come down for it, as I should think the frost is not severe enough to freeze any but the shallow water of the floods, but it was not good enough to reward him for the trouble of coming so far.

'The constant sense of his preservation from that great danger really prevents my feeling so acutely perhaps as I ought to do the distress of others. I really think I ought to be less cheerful and happy than I feel myself to be. I had a pleasant little talk with Dr. Pusey on Monday: he was recommending me two or three books for Hebrew reading, but they would be of no use to me yet; the language is difficult to advance far into, and you know my shallow way of catching a thing at first rather quickly perhaps, but only superficially. I find my interest increasing greatly in philological studies. One language helps another very much; and the beautiful way in which the words, ideas, and the whole structure indeed, of language pervades whole families, and even the different families, (e.g., the Indo-Germanic and Semitic races,) is not only interesting, but very useful. I wish I had made myself a better Greek and Latin scholar, but unfortunately I used to hate classics. What desperate uphill work it was to read them, a regular exercise of self-denial every morning! Now I like it beyond any study, except Divinity proper, and I try to make up for lost time. There are admirable books in my possession which facilitate the acquisition of critical scholarship very much, and I work at these, principally applying it to New Test. Greek, LXX, &c. But my real education began, I think, with my first foreign trip. It seems as if there was not time for all this, for I have Hebrew, Arabic, &c., to go on with (though this is a slow process), Pearson, Hooker, Blunt on the Reformation (a mere sketch which I read in a day or two at odd times), Commentaries, Trench's Books on Parables and Miracles, which are in my room at home, and would in parts interest you; he is a writer of good common sense, and a well-read man. But I of course want to be reading history as well, and that involves a good deal; physical geography, geology, &c., yet one things helps another very much. I don't work quite as methodically as I ought; and I much want some one to discuss matters with relating to what I read. I don't say all this, I am sure you know, as if I wanted to make out that I am working at grand subjects. I know exceeding little of any one of them, so little history, e.g., that a school girl could expose my ignorance directly, but I like to know what we are doing among ourselves, and we all get to know each other better thereby. I felt so much of late with regard to Jem, that a natural reserve prevents so often members even of the same family from communicating freely to each other their opinions, business, habits of life, experiences of sympathy, approval, disapproval, and the like; and when one member is gone, then it is felt how much more closely such a habit of dealing with each other would have taught us to know him.... Nothing tests one's knowledge so well as questions and answers upon what we have read, stating difficulties, arguments which we can't understand, &c., to each other. Ladies who have no profession to prepare for, in spite of a very large correspondence and numerous household duties, may (in addition to their parochial work as curates!) take up a real course of reading and go into it thoroughly; and this gives girls not only employment for the time, but gives the mind power to seize every other subject presented to it. If you are quite alone, your reading is apt to become desultory. I find it useful to take once or twice a week a walk with Riddell of Balliol, and go through a certain period of Old Testament history; it makes me get it up, and then between us we hammer out so many more explanations of difficult passages than, at all events, I should do by myself. He is, moreover, about the best Greek scholar here, which is a great help to me. You have no idea of the light that such accurate scholarship as his throws upon many disputed passages in the Bible, e.g., "Wisdom is justified of her children," where the Greek preposition probably gives the key to the whole meaning, and many such. So you see, dear old Fan, that the want of some one to pour out this to, for it sounds fearfully pedantic, I confess, has drawn upon you this grievous infliction.

'My kindest love to Father and dear Joan,
'Ever your loving
'J. C. P.'

Fanny Patteson answered with arguments on the other duties which hindered her from entering on the course of deep study which he had been recommending. He replies:—

'Feb. 25, 1853.

'My dearest Fan,—I must answer your very sensible well-written letter at once, because on our system of mutual explanation, there are two or three things I wish to notice in it. First, I never meant that anything should supersede duties which I am well aware you practise with real use to yourself and those about you, e.g., the kindness and sympathy shown to friends, and generally due observance of all social relations. Second, I quite believe that the practical application of what is already known, teaching, going about among the poor, is of far more consequence than the acquisition of knowledge, which, of course, for its own sake is worth nothing. Third, I think you perfectly right in keeping up music, singing, all the common amusements of a country life; of course I do, for indeed what I said did not apply to Joan or you, except so far as this, that we all know probably a great deal of which each one is separately ignorant, and the free communication of this to one another is desirable, I think.

'My own temptation consists perhaps chiefly in the love of reading for its own sake. I do honestly think that for a considerable time past I have read, I believe, nothing which I do not expect to be of real use, for I have no taste naturally for novels, &c. (without, however, wishing to deny that there may be novels which teach a real insight into character). Barring "I Promessi Sposi" which I take up very seldom when tired, I have not read one for ages: I must except "Old Mortality," read last Vacation at Feniton; but I can't deny that I like the study of languages for its own sake, though I apply my little experience in it wholly to the interpretation of the Bible. I like improving my scholarship, it is true, but I can say honestly that it is used to read the Greek Testament with greater accuracy: so of the Hebrew, Syriac, Arabic. I feel, I confess, sometimes that it is nice, &c., to know several languages, but I try to drive away any such thoughts, and it is quite astonishing how, after a few weeks, a study which would suggest ideas of an unusual course of reading becomes so familiar that I never think of myself when pursuing it, e.g., I don't think that after two hours' grind at Arabic the stupid wrong feeling of its being an out-of-the-way study comes upon me now, it is getting quite natural. It comes out though when I talk or write perhaps with another, but I must try and get over it.

'I believe it to be a good thing to break off any work once or twice a day in the middle of any reading, for meditating a little while and for prayer. This is more easily done at College than elsewhere; and is, I hope, a preventive against such thoughts. Then, as I jog on I see how very little I know, what an immense deal I have to learn to become ordinarily well acquainted with these things. I am in that state of mind, perhaps, when Ecclesiastes (which I am now reading) puts my own case exactly before me. I think, What's the good of it all? And the answer comes, it may be very good properly used, or very mischievous if abused. I do indeed look forward to active parochial work: I think I shall be very happy so employed, and I often try to anticipate the time in thought, and feel with perfect sincerity that nothing is so useful or so full of comfort as the consciousness of trying to fulfil the daily duties of my situation. Here of course I need do nothing; I mean there is nothing to prevent my sitting all day in an arm-chair and reading "Pickwick.".... One word about the way languages help me, that you may not think what I am doing harder than it really is. These three bear the same kind of relation to each other (or rather say these five, Arabic, Syriac, Hebrew, Chaldee, Ethiopia; but of the last I know nothing whatever, and of Chaldee only so much as that it is a dialect of Hebrew in the same character, and consequently anyone who knows Hebrew knows something about it), as German to English, e.g., Bahlom (Arab.), Beel (Syr.), Baal (Heb.), are the same word, as you can see, only written in different characters, and all mean "a lord," so Baal, Beelzebub, or Baalzebeb. Baal Peor, which means, literally, "the Lord of the ravine," viz., the idol worshipped at the Pass in the wilderness. Consequently, in reading any one of these languages, the same word keeps on occurring in all; and the chief use is of course that often a word which occurs only once or twice in Hebrew perhaps is in common use in the others, and so its meaning is fixed. Add to all this, that the Syriac version of the New Testament was made (as all agree) early in the second century, if not at the end of the first, and thus is the very best exponent of the New Testament where the Greek is doubtful; and the additional fact, that though a mixture of Chaldee and Syriac was the language of Palestine in our Lord's time, yet He certainly sometimes spoke what is now our Syriac (e.g., Talitha cumi, &c.), and the importance of it is apparent. Surely to read the language that our Blessed Lord himself used is no small profit as well as delight.

'So I think we may each go on in our several pursuits, each helping each, and each trying to do so without a foolish affectation of learning.

'My best love to dear Father and Joan,

'Ever your affectionate Brother,

'J. C. P.'

Fenelon has said that in a certain stage of piety there is much of self, and Coley was evidently in that stage. His own figure was the primary object before his eyes, neither indulged, nor admired, but criticised, repressed, and by his very best efforts thrust aside, whenever he was conscious that his self-contemplation was self-complacency. Still it was in his nature to behold it, and discuss it, and thus to conquer and outgrow the study in time, while leaving many observations upon self-culture and self-training, that will no doubt become deeply valued as the result of the practical experience of one who so truly mastered that obtrusive self.

Patteson was one of the most decided workers for the admission of improvements and reduction of abuses within his own college, with which each Oxford foundation was endeavouring to forestall compulsory reformation by a University Commission. Mr. Roundell says:—

'His early years as Fellow of Merton coincided with the period of active reform at Oxford which followed upon the Report of the Commission in 1852. What part did the future Missionary Bishop take in that great movement? One who worked with him at that time—a time when University reform was as unfashionable as it is now fashionable—well remembers. He threw himself into the work with hearty zeal; he supported every liberal proposal. To his loyal fidelity and solid common sense is largely due the success with which the reform of Merton was carried out. And yet in those first days of college reform the only sure and constant nucleus of the floating-Liberal majority consisted of Patteson and one other. Whatever others did, those two were always on the same side. And so, somehow, owing no doubt to the general enlightenment which distinguished the senior Fellows of Merton under the old regime—an enlightenment unquestionably due to the predominance in that College of the lay non-resident element—the new reforming spirit found itself in the ascendency. It is to the honour of Patteson, and equally to the honour of the older Fellows of the College at that time, that so great an inroad upon old traditions should have been made with such an entire absence of provocation on the one side, or of irritation on the other. But Patteson, with all his reforming zeal, was also a high-bred gentleman. He remembered what was due to others as well as to himself. His bearing was one of respect for authority, of deference towards those who were his superiors in age. He knew how to differ. He showed towards others the considerate courtesy which others in return so abundantly showed towards him. And this generous forbearance of the seniors had its reward. It entailed upon the juniors a reciprocity of respect. It was felt by them at the time to be an additional incentive to moderation, to sobriety, to desistance from extreme views. The result was that the work got done, and what was done left no heartburnings behind.

'Yet it would be delusive to pretend to claim Bishop Patteson as a Liberal in the political sense of the word. He was no such thing. If anything, his instincts, especially in Church matters, drew him the other way. But those who knew the man, like those who have seen the Ammergau Play, would as soon think of fastening upon that a sectarian character, as of fixing him with party names. His was a catholic mind. What distinguished him was his open-mindedness, his essential goodness, his singleness and simplicity of aim. He was a just man, and singularly free from perturbations of self, of temper, or of nerves. You did not care to ask what he would call himself. You felt what he was, that you were in the presence of a man too pure for party, of one in whose presence ordinary party distinctions almost ceased to have a meaning. Such a man could scarcely be on the wrong side. Both the purity of his nature and the rectitude of his judgment would have kept him straight.'

Coley remained at Merton until the Long Vacation of 1853; when his Oxford life terminated, though not his connection with the University, for he retained his Fellowship until his death, and the friendships he had formed both at Balliol and Merton remained unbroken.

CHAPTER V. THE CURACY AT ALFINGTON. 1853-1855.

Preparation for ordination had become Patteson's immediate object. As has been already said, his work was marked out. There was a hamlet of the parish of Ottery St. Mary, at a considerable distance from the church and town, and named Alfington.

Some time previously, the family of Sir John Kennaway had provided the place with a school, which afterwards passed into the hands of Mr. Justice Coleridge, who, in 1849, there built the small church of St. James, with parsonage, school, and house, on a rising ground overlooking the valley of Honiton, almost immediately opposite to Feniton; and, at the same time, took on himself the expenses of the curacy and school, for the vicar of the parish, the Rev. Dr. Cornish, formerly master of Ottery School.

The first curate of Alfington was Judge Coleridge's son Henry, the well-known author of the beautiful Life of St. Francis Xavier. On his leaving our communion, it was his father's wish that Coleridge Patteson should take the cure; and, until his ordination, it was committed temporarily to other hands, in especial to the Rev. Henry Gardiner, who was much beloved there. In the spring of 1853, he had a long and dangerous illness, when Coley came to nurse him, and became so much attached to him, that his influence and unconscious training became of great importance. The church was served by such clerical friends as could give their assistance on Sunday, and the pastoral care, attention to the school, cottage visiting, &c., became the employment of the candidate for Holy Orders, who thus began his work under the direction of his disabled friend.

A letter to his sister shows how he plunged into the drudgery of the parish, doing that which always cost him most, namely, administering rebukes; so that it was no wonder that he wrote with a sort of elation at having lashed himself up to the point of giving a thorough warning:—

'Feniton: July 19, 1853.

'My dearest Fan,—I am going to Thorverton to-day to stay till Thursday. Gardiner came downstairs on Sunday, and again yesterday, and is making very rapid strides towards perfect recovery. He even went out yesterday for a few minutes. So I don't mind leaving him in the least; and indeed he is going to Sidmouth himself, probably at the end of the week. I have seen him every day without one exception, and have learnt a very great deal from him. He has studied very closely school work, condition of the labourer, boys' homes, best method of dispensing charity, &c., and on all these points his advice has been really invaluable. I feel now that I am quite to all intents working the district. People ask me about their children coming to school. I know almost all the people in the village, and a good many out of it, and begin to understand, in a very small way, what a clergyman's life is. A mixture of sorrow and pleasure indeed! There are many very sad cases of hypocrisy, filthiness, and wickedness (as I suppose there are in every district); and yesterday I had a very hard-working and in one case most painful day.

'Some people had asked me to take their boy, three years and a half old, to school—a wretched pair, with a little savage for a son. I said I would speak to

Miss Wilkins, and put plainly before her the character of parents and child. However, she wished to have him, and I knew it was so far well to get the boy away from home. But such a scene ensued! The boy was really like a little savage; kicked, dashed his head against the wall, and at length, with his nose bleeding violently, exhausted with his violence, fell asleep. Next day, he is so bad, he is sent home; when the mother drives him back to school, cursing and swearing, telling Miss Wilkins she may kill him if she pleases! Unluckily, I was not in school.

'Yesterday he was in school and more quiet, but did not kneel down at prayers, and seemed like a little beast beginning to be tamed. So, after school, I called him to me, and putting him before my knees asked him some questions very kindly: "Did he know who God was? Had he never been taught to kneel down and say his prayers? Of course he had not, but it gave me the proper opportunity of speaking to his parents. So having now considered the matter for two or three days previously, having ascertained all the facts about the people, after an hour among some others in the village, I went right into their cottage, and luckily found father and mother and grandmother at home, besides one or two more (who are lodgers) in a room adjoining, with the door open. 'I am come to talk to you about William,' I began, whereupon I saw the woman turn quite red. However, I spoke for about ten minutes slowly and very quietly, without any appearance (as I believe) of anger or passion at all, but yet speaking my mind quite plainly. "I had no idea any child could be so neglected. Did they suppose the school was a place where any parent might send a child merely to get it out of the way (of course they do, you know, most of them)? Was it possible that a child could be made good as if by magic there, when it learns nothing but wicked words at home? Do you think you can or ought to get rid of the duties you owe your child? Do you suppose that God will not require from you an account of the way you have behaved towards him, you who have never taught him to know who God is, what God is, what is prayer, what is the church, who have taught that little mouth, which God created for praise and blessings, to curse and blaspheme? I know that many children do and say wicked things, but it is in most cases owing to the neglect of their parents, who do not speak kindly to their children, and do what they can to keep them out of temptation, but this is a different case. Your boy is not fit to come into the company of little Christians! Awful as it is to think of, he is already, at his early age, the very dread of the parents who live near you."

'They had not a word to say, not a syllable beyond the objection which I had already met, that other children were bad too. I did not say what I might have said with truth, because it is only from Gardiner's report, not from my own knowledge —viz., that neither father nor mother ever come to church, and that their house is the centre of evil to the young people of the village.

'"Now," I said, in conclusion, "I fully meant to send back your boy, and tell you I would examine him six months hence, to see if he was fit to be brought into the school, but as I do trust he may behave better, and that this may be the means of recovering him from this sad state, I shall take him still, unless he behaves again very badly. But remember this—this is the turning point in the boy's life, and all, humanly speaking, depends on the example you set him. What an awful thing it would be, if it pleased God to take him away from you now, and a fit of measles, scarlatina, or any such illness, may do it any day! Remember that you are responsible to a very great extent for your child; that unless it sees you watchful over your thoughts, words, and actions; unless it sees you regular and devout in prayer at home (I don't believe they ever think of such a thing—God forgive me, if I am wrong); unless it sees you habitually in your place in God's house, you are not doing your duty to yourselves or your child, you are not laying up any hope or comfort whatever for the day of your sickness and death. Now I hope you clearly understand me. I have spoken plainly—exactly what I think, and what I mean to act upon. You know now the sort of person you have to deal with. Good morning,"—and thereupon I marched out, amazed at my own pluck, and heartily glad that I had said what I wished, and felt I ought to say.

'But I need hardly tell you that this left me in a state of no slight excitement, and that I should be much comforted by hearing what you and Father and Joan think of my behaviour.

'Meanwhile, there are some very nice people; I dearly love some of the boys and girls; and I do pray that this plan of a boys' home may save some from contamination. I, seated with Sanders last night, found him and his wife very hearty about it. I have only mentioned it to three people, but I rather wish it to be talked about a little now, that they may be curious, &c., to know exactly what I mean to do. The two cottages, with plenty of room for the Fley's family and eight boys, with half an acre of garden at £11. 5s. the year. I shall of course begin with only one or two boys—the thing may not answer at all; but everyone, Gardiner, several farmers, and two or three others, quite poor, in different places, all say it must work well, with God's blessing. I do not really wish to be scheming away, working a favourite hobby, &c., but I do believe this to be absolutely essential. The profligacy and impurity of the poor is beyond all belief. Every mother of a family answers (I mean every honest respectable mother of a family): "Oh sir, God will bless such a work, and it is for want of this that so much misery and wretchedness abound." I believe that for a year or so it will exhaust most of my money, but then it is one of the best uses to which I can apply it; for my theory is, that help and assistance is wanted in this way, and I would wish to make most of these things self-supporting. Half an acre more of garden, thoroughly well worked, will yield an astonishing return, and I look to Mary as a person of really economical habits. It is a great relief to have poured all this out. It is no easy task that I am preparing for myself. I know that I fully expect to be very much disappointed, but I am determined to try it. I am determined to try and make the people see that I am not going to give way to everybody that asks; but that I am going to set on foot and help on all useful industrial schemes of every kind, for people of every age. I am hard at work, studying spade husbandry, inspectors' reports of industrial schools, &c. I am glad you are all so happy. I am so busy. Best love to all.

'Your loving

'J. C. P.'

Coley was thus already serving a vigorous apprenticeship in pastoral work, while preparing himself for receiving deacon's orders. It was a trying time both to his family and himself, for, as before said, his standard was very high, and his own strong habit of self-contemplation made his dissatisfaction with himself manifest in his manner to those nearest to him. He was always gentle and unselfish; not showing temper, but unhappiness.

Here are letters showing a good deal of his state of mind: the first only dated 'Saturday evening,' but evidently written about this time, in reply to the cautions with which his sister had replied to the above letter of eager plans of improvement.

'My dearest Fan,—Your letter has just reached me from Honiton, and I have read it with very great interest. I liked it better on a second perusal of it, which showed in itself that I wanted it, for it is quite true that I require to be reminded of the only true principle upon which one ought to work; and I allow quite willingly that I trace interested motives—e.g., love of self-approval or applause in actions where such feelings ought least of all to enter. I certainly did feel pleased with myself for speaking plainly to those people, and I often find myself indulging the notion that I am going to be a very hard-working clergyman, with a remedy for all the evils of the age, &c. If I was to hunt about for an excuse, I might perhaps find one, by saying that I am in that state of mind which attends always, I suppose, the anticipation of any great crisis in a person's life; sometimes hard work and hard thought, sometimes (though alas! very seldom) a real sense of the very awful responsibility of ministering in the Church, sometimes a less natural urging of the mind to contemplate and realise this responsibility. I was for some time reading Wilberforce's new book, and this involved an examination of the question in other writers; but lately I have laid all controversial works aside almost entirely, and have been reading Pearson, Bull, and the Apostolical Fathers, Clement and Ignatius. I shall probably read Justin Martyr's Apologies, and some treatises of Tertullian before next month is over. I have read some part already. There is such a very strong practical element in these very early writings that they ought to soothe and calm the mind; but I cannot honestly conceal the fact that the theological interest for the most part outweighs the practical teaching.

'My light reading is of a new and very amusing and interesting character—viz., books on school economy, management of school farms, allotments, the modern dairy, spade husbandry, agricultural chemistry. K, W, F, C, and G, and I have great talks; and as they all agree with me, I think them capital judges.

'I don't think at all that my present state of mind is quite natural. You quite repeat my own words when you say it is transitory. A calm undisturbed spirit of prayer and peace and contentment is a great gift of God, and to be waited for with patience. The motto of "The Christian Year" is very beautiful. I sent the roses on Tuesday. My best love to dear Father and Joan.

'Ever your loving Brother,
'J. C. P.'

These words 'love of self-approval' perfectly analysed that snare of Coley's early life, against which he so endeavoured to guard—not self-conceit, but love of self-approval.

So the Easter week drew on, and during it he writes to his cousin:—

'Friday, Wallis Lodgings, Exeter: September, 1853.

'My dear Sophy,—We have had a good examination, I think; perhaps rather harder than I expected. Woolecombe and Chancellor Harrington spoke to me this morning, thanking me for my papers, and telling me to read the Gospel at the Ordination.

'I did feel very nervous last Sunday and Monday, and the Ember Prayer in the morning (when I was at Ottery) fairly upset me, but I don't think anybody saw it; now, I am thankful to say, I am very well, and feel thoroughly happy. I shall be nervous, no doubt, on Sunday, and especially at reading the Gospel, but not I think so nervous as to break down or do anything foolish; so when you know I am reading—for you won't hear me, if you are in the stalls, don't distress yourself about me.

'I can't tell what it was that upset me so on Sunday and Monday—thinking of dear Mamma and how she had wished for this, the overwhelming kindness of everybody about me, dear Father's simple words of very affectionate comfort and advice.

'But I walked into Exeter, and on the way got quite calm, and so I have been ever since. It is not strange that the realising the near approach of what I have for years wished for, and looked forward to, should at times come upon me with such force that I seem scarcely master of myself; but it is only excitement of feeling, and ought, I know, to be repressed, not for a moment to be entertained as a test of one's religious state, being by no means a desirable thing. I am very glad the examination is over. I did not worry myself about it, but it was rather hard work, and now I have my time to myself for quiet thought and meditation.

'Ever, dear Sophy, your affectionate Cousin,

'J. C. PATTESON.'

The next evening he writes:—

'Saturday, 5.45 P.M.

'My dearest Father,—I must write my last letter as a layman to you. I can't tell you the hundredth part of the thoughts that have been passing through my mind this week. There has been no return of the excitement that I experienced last Sunday and Monday, and I have been very happy and well.

'To-day my eyes are not comfortable, from I know not what cause, but as all the work for them is over, it does not matter so much. I am glad to have had a quiet time for reflection. Indeed, I do not enough realise my great unworthiness and sinfulness, and the awful nature of the work I am undertaking. I pray God very earnestly for the great grace of humility, which I so sadly need: and for a spirit of earnest prayer, that I may be preserved from putting trust in myself, and may know and forget myself in my office and work. I never could be fit for such work, I know that, and yet I am very thankful that the time for it has come. I do not feel excited, yet I am somewhat nervous because it requires an effort to meditate steadily. I have thought so much of my early life, of dearest Mamma. What a snare it seems, so full of transitory earthly plans and pursuits; such a want of earnestness of purpose and steady performance of duty! God grant my life as a clergyman may be more innocent to myself, and more useful to others! Tell dear Joan the gown came this morning. My kind love to her, Fan, and Jem.

'Ever, my dearest Father,

'Your affectionate and dutiful Son,

'J. C. PATTESON.'

On the ensuing day, Sunday, September 14, 1853, John Coleridge Patteson received the Diaconate at the hands of the venerable Bishop Phillpotts, in Exeter Cathedral. His being selected to read the Gospel was the proof of his superiority in the examination—no wonder, considering the two additional years that he had spent in preparation, and the deep study and searchings of heart of the last few months.

He was established in a small house at Alfington—the usual habitation of the Curate. And of his first sermon there, his uncle, Sir John Coleridge, gives the following touching description from his diary:—

'October 23, 1853.—Yesterday morning Arthur and I went to Alfington Church, to be present at Coley's first sermon. I don't know when I have been so much delighted and affected. His manner of saying the prayers was exceedingly good: his voice very sweet and musical; without seeming loud, it was fully audible, and gave assurance of more power if needed: his manner quite unaffected, but sweet and devout. His sermon was a very sound and good one, beautifully delivered; perhaps in the early parts, from the very sweetness of his voice, and the very rapid delivery of his words, a little more variety of intonation would have helped in conveying his meaning more distinctly to those who formed the bulk of his congregation. But when he came to personal parts this was not needed. He made a kind allusion to me, very affecting to me; and when I was in this mood, and he came to the personal parts, touching himself and his new congregation, what he knew he ought to be to them and to do for them, what they should do for themselves, and earnestly besought their prayers, I was completely overcome, and weeping profusely.

Fanny Patteson and Arthur Coleridge were sitting with the Judge, and were equally overcome. When the service was over, and the congregation dispersed, Coley joined these three in the porch, holding out his hands, taking theirs and shedding tears, and they with him—tears of warm emotion too deep for words. He was evidently surprised at the effect produced. In fact, on looking at the sermon, it does not seem to have been in itself remarkable, but as his cousin Arthur says: 'I suppose the deep spirituality of the man, and the love we bore him for years, touched the emotional part of us.' The text was significant: 'We preach not ourselves, but Christ Jesus the Lord; and ourselves your servants for Jesus' sake' (2 Cor. iv. 5).

The services that the newly-ordained Deacon undertook were the ordinary Sunday ones, and Wednesday and Friday Matins and Litany, Saints'-day prayers and lecture, and an Advent and Lent Evensong and lecture on Wednesdays and Fridays. These last had that great popularity which attends late services. Dr. Cornish used to come on one Sunday in the month to celebrate the Holy Communion (which is given weekly in the mother Church); and when Mr.

Grardiner was able to be at Sidmouth, recovering from his illness, he used to come over on the second Sunday in the month for the same purpose; and the next Lent, the Matins were daily, and followed by a lecture.

At this time Patteson's constitutional shrinking from general society was in full force, and he also had that dislike to 'speaking to' people in the way of censure, which so often goes with tender and refined natures, however strong; so that if his housekeeper needed a reproof, he would make his sister administer it, and creep out of reach himself; but this was one of the deficiencies with which he was struggling all his life, and fortunately it is a fact that the most effective lectures usually come from those to whom they cost the most.

This was the hardest part of his ministry. Where kindness and attention were needed, nothing could be more spontaneous, sweet, or winning than his ways. One of his parishioners, a farmer's daughter, writes:—

'Our personal knowledge of him began some months before his Ordination, owing, I suppose, to Mr. Gardiner's severe illness; and as he was very much respected, Mr. Patteson's attentions won from the first our admiration and gratitude, which went on and on until it deepened into that love which I do not think could have been surpassed by the Galatians for their beloved St. Paul, which he records in his Epistle to them (chap. iv. 15). All were waiting for him at his Ordination, and a happy delusion seemed to have come over the minds of most, if not all, that he was as completely ours as if he had been ordained expressly for us.'

It was not his own feeling, for he knew that when his apprenticeship should be past, the place was too small, and the work too easy, for a man in full force and vigour, though for the sake of his father he was glad to accept it for the present, to train himself in the work, and to have full time for study; but he at that time looked to remaining in England during his father's lifetime, and perhaps transferring himself to Manchester, Liverpool, London, or some large city, where there was need of mission work among the neglected.

His father was on the City of London Charter Commission, and was in London from November to February, the daughters joining him there, but there was no lack of friends around Alfington. Indeed it was in the midst of an absolute clan of Coleridges, and in Buckerell parish, at Deerpark, that great old soldier, Lord Seaton, was spending the few years that passed between his Commissioner-ship in the Ionian Isles and his Commandership in Ireland.

He was connected with the Coleridges through the Yonge family, and the young people were all on familiar cousinly terms. Coley was much liked by him; and often joined in the rides through the lanes and to the hills with him and his daughters, when there were many conversations of much interest, as there could not fail to be with a man who had never held a government without doing his utmost to promote God's work in the Church and for education; who had, moreover, strong opinions derived from experience of the Red Indians in Upper Canada—namely, that to reclaim the young, and educate them was the only hope of making Christianity take root in any fresh nation.

It was at Deerpark, at a dinner in the late autumn of this year 1853, that I saw

Coley Patteson for the second and last time. I had seen him before in a visit of three days that I made at Feniton with my parents in the September of 1844, when he was an Eton boy, full of high spirits and merriment. I remember then, on the Sunday, that he and I accompanied our two fathers on a walk to the afternoon service at Ottery, and that on the way he began to show something of his inner self, and talked of his mother and her pleasure in Feniton; but it began to rain, and I stayed for the night at Heaths Court, so that our acquaintance ceased for that time. It was not a formal party at Deerpark, and the evening was chiefly spent in playing at games, thread paper verses and the like, in which Coley took his part with spirit. If I had guessed what he was to be, I should have observed him more; but though, in after years, our intercourse in letters makes us feel intimate with one another, these two brief meetings comprise the whole of my personal acquaintance with one in whom I then only saw a young clergyman with his heart in his work.

Perhaps this is the best place to mention his personal appearance, as the portrait at the beginning of this volume was taken not more than a year later.

He was tall and of a large powerful frame, broad in the chest and shoulders, and with small neat hands and feet, with more of sheer muscular strength and power of endurance than of healthiness, so that though seldom breaking down and capable of undergoing a great deal of fatigue and exertion, he was often slightly ailing, and was very sensitive to cold. His complexion was very dark, and there was a strongly marked line between the cheeks and mouth, the corners of which drooped when at rest, so that it was a countenance peculiarly difficult to photograph successfully. The most striking feature was his eyes, which were of a very dark clear blue, full of an unusually deep earnest, and so to speak, inward, yet far away expression. His smile was remarkably bright, sweet and affectionate, like a gleam of sunshine, and was one element of his great attractiveness. So was his voice, which had the rich full sweetness inherited from his mother's family, and which always excited a winning influence over the hearers. Thus, though not a handsome man, he was more than commonly engaging, exciting the warmest affection in all who were concerned with him, and giving in return an immense amount of interest and sympathy, which only became intensified to old friends while it expanded towards new ones. Here is a letter to his father, undated, but written not long after his settling down at Alfington. After expressing his regret that his voice had been inaudible to his sister Joanna at a Friday evening service, he proceeds:—

'I did not speak very loud, because I don't think I could do so and at the same time keep my mind at work and thoughts collected. Anything which is so unnatural and unusual as to make me conscious of myself in a peculiar manner would prevent, I fear, my getting on with my oration at all.

'I am glad you think I could not have acted otherwise with E——. I quite expect ere long to find something going on which may call for my interference, and I specially guarded myself on this point. It is distinctly understood that I shall speak to him quite plainly whenever and wherever I think it necessary to do so. I do not suppose it very likely that he can go on long without my being forced to take some step; but I really feel so very unequal to expressing a decided opinion upon the great question of Bible readers, that I am certainly glad I have not taken up a hostile position hastily. As a matter of fact, he reads in very few cottages in my district; tracts he distributes almost everywhere.

'Now I see of course the distinction between a man making it his business to read the Bible and neighbours dropping in occasionally to read a chapter to one who is unable to read, but where you are distinctly told that the wish is most decidedly to support the clergyman, and answers not unsatisfactory are given upon main points, what difference remains between the two cases I have put that can furnish matter for fair argument, with a man from education, &c., disposed to take a different view of the whole question? Add to this, that I cannot appeal to the universal practice of the clergy. "Why," might it be said, "do you, as a clergyman find a difficulty where Mr. H. finds none? You are, after all, acting on your own private opinion, though you lay claim to authority for it." I cannot successfully appeal to the distinctive teaching of our Church, clear and manifest as it is, for the very words I think conclusive contain no such evidence for him, and so on ad infinitum. Besides, to speak quite what I feel at present, though only so perhaps because my view is necessarily unformed, the natural order of things in such a district as this seems to be: gain the affections of the people by gentleness and showing real interest in their welfare, spiritual and temporal; show them in the Bible such teaching as the Church considers necessary (but not as yet upon the authority of the Church, or at least not so expressed to them); lead them gradually to the acknowledgment of such truths as these: that Christ did found a society called the Church, and appoint to certain persons whom he sent the Ministry of reconciliation; that if we have no guide but mere opinion, there will be thousands of conflicting opinions in the world even among good men, whereas Truth can be but one, and that practically this is found to be so; that it is no argument to say, that the Spirit so operated as to enlighten the reason of each individual to this extent, viz., that it may compose a Creed for him or herself; that the Spirit acts now in the ordinary, though not less real and heavenly manner; and that the infinite divisions among sectaries proves the fact to be as I state it.

'Thus I imagine the want of that external and visible Church will be felt as necessary to fix the Creeds pasa katadike.

'But to reverse this process, to cram positive teaching down their throats upon the authority of the Church before they know what the Church is, or feel the need of any power outside (so to speak) their own minds to guide them, does seem to me in a place like this (humanly speaking) suicidal. I cannot, of course, tell how much preparatory teaching they have received, but I must judge from what I see and hear, and deal accordingly in each cottage. Some few there are to whom I can speak, as to Church people in the real sense of the word, but these are as two or three in a hundred.

'One line to say whether you think me right or wrong, would be a great comfort to me. I feel no tendency to latitudinarianism, but only to see much good in systems unrecognised by your very highflyers. I believe that the Church teaching is represented in an unfavourable, often offensive, light to many of our poor, because they hear words and see things which find no response in their hearts; because they are told, ordered almost, to believe things the propriety of believing which they do not recognise; because the existence of wants is implied when they have never been felt, and a system for supplying them introduced which finds no room in the understanding or affections of the patient.

'But you know, dear Father, what I mean, without more dusky attempts at explaining myself.

'Do not many High Churchmen want a little more "experimental religion" in Bishop Jebb's sense of the terms: not a religion of the feelings, but a religion brought home to the heart, and truly felt so as to prohibit any systematic criticism of the feelings?

'I am late this week with my sermons, I have not begun either of them, and may have one to-morrow evening if my voice will do its part. I write very long washy concerns, and find it difficult to do otherwise, for it is a good pull upon me week after week, and latterly I have not been able to read very much. I shall look out two or three that I think fair specimens, and ask you by-and-by to run your eye over them, that you may point out the defects.

'My ignorance of the Bible astonishes me, though not so much as it ought to do. I purpose, D.V., to commence a thorough study of the original texts. I must try to become something of a scholar, at all events, to make any progress in the work. I sometimes hope that, in spite of my many backslidings and broken resolutions, some move is taking place within, where most it is wanted; but I live here so quietly, that I have little (comparatively) food for some special faults. Good-bye, my dear Father,

'Your affectionate and dutiful Son,

'**J. C. P.**'

'Some move taking place within!' It is impossible not to pause and observe how as Confirmation and Communion had almost palpably strengthened the boy's struggles with his inherent faults, so the grace conferred with the Deacon's orders is now felt to be lifting him higher, and enabling him to see further than he has yet seen.

Sermons were, however, never Patteson's forte. Though his pen flowed so freely in letters, and he could pour out his heart extemporaneously with great depth, fervour and simplicity, his sermons were laboured and metaphysical, as if he had taken too much pains with them as it were, and he could not speak to the abstract, as he could to the individual, or when he saw the effect of his words. It was perhaps owing to the defective system which threw two sermons a week upon a young deacon at a time when his mind was working through such an experimental course of study and thought. Yet his people, who had learnt to believe in little but preaching, would not have come to prayers alone; and the extemporary addresses, in which he would probably have been much more successful, would have seemed to him at his age and at that period—twenty years back—too presumptuous to be attempted, at any rate till he had better learnt his ground. How his system would have succeeded, we cannot tell. The nature of the peasantry of the county he had to deal with is, to be quick-witted, argumentative, and ready of retort; open to religious impressions, but with much of self-opinion and conceit, and not much reverence, and often less conscientious in matters of honesty and morality than denser rustics of less apparent piety. The Church had for a long-period been at a peculiarly low ebb in the county, and there is not a neighbourhood which has not traditions of incredibly ignorant, careless and underbred—if not dissipated—clergy; and though there were grand exceptions, they were only respected as men; faith in the whole system, as a system, was destroyed. Bishop Phillpotts, coming down on such elements as these, was, in spite of his soundness of faith and grand trenchant force of character, better as a warrior than as a shepherd, and the controversial and political sides of his character, though invaluable to the Church, did not recommend him to the affections of the people of his diocese, who could not understand the points of the debate, and wanted the direct evidence of spirituality which they could appreciate.

The cholera of 1832 had been especially terrible in the unwholesome precincts of the Devonshire seaports, and the effect was a great craving for religion. The Church was in no condition to avail herself of it; in fact, she would have viewed it with distrust as excitement. Primitive Methodism and Plymouth Brethrenism supplied the void, gave opportunities of prayer, and gratified the quickened longing for devotion; and therewith arose that association of the Church with deadness and of Dissent with life, which infected even the most carefully tended villages, and with which Patteson was doing his best to contend at Alfington. The stage of gaining the people's affection and confidence, and of quickening their religious life, he had attained; and the further work of teaching them that the Church alone gives security of saving union with Christ, was yet to come when his inward call led him elsewhere.

On the 12th of December he says:—

'Yesterday was a very happy day; Gardiner came to help me and he administered the Holy Communion to twenty-seven or twenty-eight of my own people. This is nearly double the average before I came, and two regular attendants are prevented by sickness from being at Church. I trust I have not urged the necessity of communicating unwisely upon them. I preach on it once a month, as you know, and in almost every sermon allude to it, and where occasion offers, speak about it to individuals at home; but I try to put before them the great awfulness of it as well as the danger of neglecting it, and I warn them against coming without feeling really satisfied from what I read to them, and they read in the Bible concerning it. Six came yesterday for the first time.... Old William (seventy-five years of age), who has never been a communicant, volunteered on Thursday to come, if I thought it right. He is, and always has been (I am told), a thoroughly respectable, sober, industrious man, regular at Church once a day; and I went to his cottage with a ticket in my pocket to urge him to consider the danger of going on as if content with what he did and without striving to press onwards, &c. But, after a long conversation on other matters, he said; "I should like, Sir, to come to the Sacrament, if you have no objection;" and very happy and thankful I felt, for I had prayed very earnestly that this old man might be led thither by God's grace, and now it was done without any urging on my part, beyond what he heard in

Church and what I had said to his daughter about him.'

The next of his letters is occupied with the pecuniary affairs of his lodging house for farm boys, and the obtaining of ground where they might grow vegetables for their own use.

In February his family returned home, and his sister Fanny thus speaks of him to a friend:—

'He does not look well; and at first we were quite uneasy, for his eyes were heavy and puffed, but he is much better, and confesses that dinners and evenings here do him good, though he quite denies the starving, and Mrs. Knowles also. She says he gets over anxious in mind, and was completely chilled the week he sat in the hall. No doubt his house is still both cold and damp, and the Church the same, and therefore the labour of reading and preaching is very great. We are by degrees interesting him in our winter life, having heard all his performances and plans; and he is very glad to have us back, though much too busy to have missed us when we were away. Now he has daily morning service, with a lecture; and if it lasts, the impression he has made is really extraordinary. We may well pray that he should not be vain of his works. There are men whose whole lives seem changed, if I am to believe what I hear.'

Such was the young Deacon's early success. With an affectionate brother close at hand, and friends within easy reach, his Fellowship preserving his connection with Oxford, his father's and brother's profession with London, in fact, all England could offer; and he would easily have it in his power to take fresh holidays on the Continent and enjoy those delights of scenery, architecture, art and music, which he loved with an appreciation and enthusiasm that could easily have become an absorbing passion. Who could have a smoother, easier, pleasanter career open to him than the Rev. John Coleridge Patteson at six and twenty?

Yet even then, the wish breathed to his mother, at fourteen, that he might devote himself to the cause of the heathen, lay deep in his heart; although for the present, he was, as it were, waiting to see what God would have him do, whether his duty to his father required him to remain at hand, or whether he might be called to minister in some great English manufacturing town.

Early in 1854, it became known that the Bishop of New Zealand and Mrs. Selwyn were about to spend a year in England. Coley's aspirations to mission work were renewed. The thoughts excited by the sermons he had heard at Eton twelve years previously grew in force. He remembered his mother's promise of her blessing, and seriously considered of offering himself to assist in the work in the Southern Hemisphere. He discussed the matter seriously with his friend, Mr. Gardiner, who was strongly of opinion that the scheme ought not to be entertained during his father's lifetime. He acquiesced; but if his heart and mind were convinced, his soul and spirit were not, and the yearnings for the forefront of the battle were not quenched, though there was no slackening of zeal over the present little flock, to make them suspect that he had a thought beyond.

Old ties of friendship already mentioned made the Bishop and Mrs. Selwyn promise to spend a few days at Feniton; and on the 19th of August the New Zealand guests arrived at Feniton. After joining in the family welcome, Coley went apart, and gave way to a great burst of tears, due, perhaps, not so much to disappointed ardour, as to the fervent emotion excited by the actual presence of a hero of the Church Militant, who had so long been the object of deep silent enthusiasm. The next morning, Coley walked from Alfington to breakfast at home, and afterwards went into the garden with the Bishop, who led him to talk freely of his present work in all its details. By-and-by the question arose, Did it satisfy him?

Yes, the being near his father satisfied him that it was right for the present, but at some future time, he hoped to do more, go perhaps to some great manufacturing town, or, as he could not help going on to say, what he should like would be to go out as a missionary, only the thought of his father withheld him.

'But,' replied the Bishop, 'if you think about doing a thing of that sort, it should not be put off till you are getting on in life. It should be done with your full strength and vigour.'

Then followed an endeavour on both sides to ascertain whether the inclination was a real earnest desire, or only fancy for the romance of mission work. The test might be whether he were willing to go wherever he might be sent, or only where he was most interested. Coley replied, that he was willing to work anywhere, adding that his sister Fanny could testify whether his desire were a real one of long standing or the mere outcome of a fit of enthusiasm.

Therewith they separated, and Coley, going straight to Fanny, told her what had passed: 'I could not help it,' he said:—'I told the Bishop of my wish.'

'You ought to put it to my father, that he may decide it,' she answered; 'he is so great a man that he ought not to be deprived of the crown of the sacrifice if he be willing to make it.'

So Coley repaired to his father, and confessed his long cherished wish, and how it had come forth to the Bishop. Sir John was manifestly startled; but at once said: 'You have done quite right to speak to me, and not to wait. It is my first impulse to say No, but that would be very selfish.'

Coley explained that he was 'driven to speak;' he declared himself not dissatisfied with his present position, nor he hoped, impatient. If his staying at home were decided upon, he would cheerfully work on there without disappointment or imagining his wishes thwarted. He would leave the decision entirely in the hands of his father and the Bishop.

Luncheon brought the whole family together; and Sir John, making room for his younger daughter beside him, said, 'Fan, did you know this about Coley?'

She answered that she had some idea, but no more could pass till the meal was ended; when her father went into another room, and she followed him. The great grief broke out in the exclamation: 'I can't let him go;' but even as the words were uttered, they were caught back, as it were, with—'God forbid I should stop him.'

The subject could not be pursued, for the Bishop was public property among the friends and neighbours, and the rest of the day was bestowed upon them. He preached on the Sunday at Alfington, where the people thronged to hear him, little thinking of the consequences of his visit.

Not till afterwards were the Bishop and the father alone together, when Sir John brought the subject forward. The Bishop has since said that what struck him most was the calm balancing of arguments, like a true Christian Judge. Sir John spoke of the great comfort he had in this son, cut off as he was by his infirmity from so much of society, and enjoying the young man's coming in to talk about his work. He dwelt on all with entire absence of excitement, and added: 'But there, what right have I to stand in his way? How do I know that I may live another year?'

And as the conversation ended, 'Mind!' he said; 'I give him wholly, not with any thought of seeing him again. I will not have him thinking he must come home again to see me.'

That resolution was the cause of much peace of mind to both father and son. After family prayers that Sunday night, when all the rest had gone upstairs, the Bishop detained the young man, and told him the result of the conversation, then added: 'Now, my dear Coley, having ascertained your own state of mind and having spoken at length to your father and your family, I can no longer hesitate, as far as you recognise any power to call on my part, to invite you most distinctly to the work.'

The reply was full acceptance.

Then taking his hand, the Bishop said, 'God bless you, my dear Coley! It is a great comfort to me to have you for a friend and companion.'

Such was the outward and such the inward vocation to the Deacon now within a month of the Priesthood. Was it not an evident call from Him by whom the whole Church is governed and sanctified? And surely the noble old man, who forced himself not to withhold 'his son, his firstborn son,' received his crown from Him who said: 'With blessing I will bless thee.'

And he wrote to his brother:—

'August 21.

'My dear old Jem,—I have news for you of an unexpected and startling kind; about myself: and I am afraid that it will cause you some pain to hear what I am to tell you. You must know that for years I have felt a strong leaning toward missionary work, and though my proceedings at Alfington and even the fact of going thither might seem to militate against such a notion, yet the feeling has been continually present to me, and constantly exercising an increasing influence over me. I trust I have not taken an enthusiastic or romantic view of things; my own firm hope and trust is that I have decided upon calm deliberate conviction, and it is some proof of this, that Fanny and Joan have already guessed my state of mind, and months ago anticipated what has now taken place.... And so, dear Jem, you must help them all to bear what will of course be a great trial. This is my trial also; for it is hard to bear the thought that I may be giving unnecessary pain and causing distress without really having considered sufficiently the whole matter. But then I think God does not call now by an open vision; this thought has been for years working in my mind: it was His providence that brought me into contact with the Bishop in times past, and has led me to speak now. I cannot doubt this. I feel sure that if I was alone in the world I should go; the only question that remains is, "am I bound to stay for my dear Father's sake, or for the sake of you all?" and this has been answered for me by Father and the Bishop. And now, my dear Jem, think well over my character, sift it thoroughly, and try to see what there is which may have induced me to act wrongly in a matter of so much consequence. This is the kindest thing you can do; for we ought to take every precaution not to make a mistake before it is too late. Speak out quite plainly; do tell me distinctly as far as you can see them my prevailing faults, what they were in boyhood at Eton, and at College. It may help me to contemplate more clearly and truly the prospect before me. We shall have many opportunities, I trust, of discussing all this by-and-by. I shall tell Uncle John, because some arrangements must be made about Alfington as soon as may be. My tutor knows something about it already; it will soon be known to more. But do not suppose that I imagine myself better qualified for this work than hundreds of others more earnest, and infinitely more unselfish, and practically good; but I have received an invitation to a peculiar work, which is not offered to many others. We must all look onwards: we must try to think of this world as but a short moment in our existence; our real life and home is beyond the grave. On September 24th I hope to be ordained Priest; think of me and pray for me, my dear old fellow, that God will give me more of your own unselfishness and care and interest for others, and teach me to act not according to my own will and pleasure, but solely with a view to His honour and glory. God bless you, my dear old Jem, my dear, dear brother.

'Your most loving brother,

'J. C. P.

From that moment the matter was treated as fixed; and only three days later, the intention was announced to the relations at Thorverton.

This is the letter to the little fatherless cousin, Paulina Martyn, who had always been devoted to Coley, and whom he loved with a triple portion of the affection children always gained from him. She was only eight years old, but had the precocity of solitary children much attended to by their elders:—

'Feniton: August 24, 1854.

'My darling Pena,—I am going to tell you a secret, and I am afraid it is one which will make you feel very sorry for a little while. Do you remember my talking to you one day after breakfast rather gravely, and telling you afterwards it was my first sermon to you? Well, my darling, I was trying to hint to you that you must not expect to go on very long in this world without troubles and trials, and that the use of them is to make us think more about God and about Heaven, and to remember that our real and unchangeable happiness is not to be found in this world, but in the next. It was rather strange for me to say all this to a bright happy good child like you, and I told you that you ought to be bright and happy, and to thank God for making you so. It is never right for us to try to make ourselves sad and grieve. Good people and good children are cheerful and happy, although they may have plenty of trials and troubles. You see how quietly and patiently Mamma and Grandpapa and Grandmamma take all their trouble about dear Aunty; that is a good lesson for us all. And now, my darling, I will tell you my secret. I am going to sail at Christmas, if I live so long, a great way from England, right to the other end of the world, with the good Bishop of New Zealand. I dare say you know where to find it on the globe. Clergymen are wanted out there to make known the

Word of God to the poor ignorant people, and for many reasons it is thought right that I should go. So after Christmas you will not see me again for a very long time, perhaps never in this world; but I shall write to you very often, and send you ferns and seeds, and tell you about the Norfolk Island pines, and you must write to me, and tell me all about yourself, and always think of me, and pray for me, as one who loves you dearly with all his heart, and will never cease to pray God that the purity and innocence of your childhood may accompany you all through your life and make you a blessing (as you are now, my darling) to your dear mother and all who know you.

'Ever your most affectionate,

'J. C. PATTESON.'

To the child's mother the words are:—

'I pray God that I may have chosen aright, and that if I have acted from sudden impulse too much, from love of display, or from desire to raise some interest about myself, or from any other selfish and unholy motive, it may be mercifully forgiven.

'Now, at all events, I must pray that with a single honest desire for God's glory, I may look straight onwards towards the mark. I must forget what is behind, I must not lose time in analysing my state of mind to see how, during years past, this wish has worked itself out. I trust the wish is from God, and now I must forget myself, and think only of the work whereunto I am called. But it is hard to flesh and blood to think of the pain I am causing my dear dear Father, and the pain I am causing to others outside my own circle here. But they are all satisfied that I am doing what is right, and it would surprise you, although you know them so well, to hear the calmness with which we talk about outfits.'

A heavy grief was even now on the family. The beloved, 'Uncle Frank,' so often affectionately mentioned, had been failing for some time. He had taken a journey abroad, with one of his daughters, in hopes of refreshment and invigoration, but the fatigue and excitement were more than he could bear; he returned home, and took to his bed. He suffered no pain, and was in a heavenly state of mind indeed, a most blessed death-bed, most suggestive of comfort and peace to all who survive as a most evident proof of what the close of life may be, if only 'that life is spent faithfully in doing our duty to God'—as Patteson wrote to his old friend, Miss Neill.

'And now one word about myself, which at such a time I should not obtrude upon you, but that the visit of the Bishop of New Zealand made it necessary for me to speak.

'I am going with him to work, if all is well, at the Antipodes, believing that the growing desire for missionary work, which for years has been striving within me, ought no longer to be resisted, and trusting that I am not mistaken in supposing that this is the line of duty that God has marked out for me.

'You may be sure that all this is done with the full consent and approbation of my dear Father. He and the Bishop had a great deal of conversation about it, and I left it entirely for them to determine. That it will be a great trial to us all at Christmas when we sail, I cannot conceal from myself; it is so great a separation that I cannot expect ever to see my dear Father, perhaps not any of those I love best, again in this world. But if you all know that I am doing, or trying to do, what is right, you will all be happy about me; and what has just been taking place at the Manor House teaches us to look, on a little to a blessed meeting in a better place soon. It is from no dissatisfaction at my present position, that I am induced to take this step. I have been very happy at Alfington; and I hope to be ordained Priest, on the 24th of September, with a calm mind. I trust I am not following any sudden hasty impulse, but obeying a real call to a real work, and (in the midst of much self-seeking and other alloy) not wholly without a sincere desire to labour for the honour and glory of God.'

With this purpose full in view, Coleridge Patteson received Ordination as a Priest in the ensuing Ember Week, again at the hands of Bishop Phillpotts, in Exeter Cathedral; where a beautiful marble pulpit is to commemorate the fact.

The wrench from home and friends could not but be terrible. The sisters, indeed, were so far prepared that they had been aware from the first of his wish and his mother's reception of it, and when they told their Father, he was pleased and comforted; for truly he was upheld by the strength of willing sacrifice. Those were likewise sustained who felt the spirit of missionary enterprise and sympathy, which was at that time so strongly infused into the Church; but the shock was severe to many, and especially to the brother who had been devoted to Coley from their earliest infancy, and among his relations the grief was great.

As to the district of Alfington, the distress was extreme. The people had viewed Mr. Patteson as their exclusive property, and could not forgive the Bishop of New Zealand for, as they imagined, tempting him away. 'Ah! Sir,' was the schoolmistress's answer to some warm words from Mr. Justice Coleridge in praise of Bishop Selwyn, 'he may be—no doubt he is—a very good man. I only wish he had kept his hands off Alfington.' 'It would not be easy,' says the parishioner from whom I have already quoted, 'to describe the intense sorrow in view of separation. Mr. Patteson did all he could to assure us that it was his own will and act, consequent upon the conviction that it was God's will that he should go, and to exonerate the Bishop, but for some time he was regarded as the immediate cause of our loss; and he never knew half the hard things said of him by the same people who, when they heard he was coming, and would preach on the Sunday, did their utmost to make themselves and their children look their very best.'

Indeed, the affectionate writer seems to have shared the poor people's feeling that they had thus festally received a sort of traitor with designs upon their pastor. She goes on to tell of his ministrations to her mother, whose death-bed was the first he attended as a Priest.

It would be impossible for me to say all he was to her. Not long before her death, when he had just left the room, she said, 'I have not felt any pain or weakness whilst Mr. Patteson has been here.' I was not always present during his visits to her, and I think their closer communings were only known to Him above, but their effects were discernible in that deep confidence in him on her part, and that lasting impression on him, for you will remember, in his letter last April, he goes back in memory to that time, and calls it—'a solemn scene in my early ministry.' Solemn, indeed, it was to us all that last night of her life upon earth. He was with her from about the middle of the day on Monday until about four o'clock on Tuesday morning; when, after commending her soul to God, he closed her eyes with his own hands, and taking out his watch, told us the hour and moment of her departure. He then went home and apprised Miss Wilkins of her death in these words: 'My soul fleeth unto the LORD before the morning watch, I say before the morning watch,' and at the earliest dawn of day, the villagers were made aware that she had passed away by the tolling bell, and tolled by him. This was not the only death during his ministry among us; but it was the first occasion where he gave the Communion of the Sick, also when he read the Burial Service. Cases of rejoicing with those that rejoiced as well as of weeping with those that wept, the child and the aged seemed alike to appreciate his goodness. In him were combined those qualities which could inspire with deep reverence and entire confidence. Many, many are or will be the stars in the crown of his rejoicing, and some owe to him under God, their deeper work of grace in the heart and their quickening in the divine life.'

A remarkable testimony is this to the impression remaining after the lapse of sixteen years from a ministry extending over no more than seventeen months. 'Our Mr. Patteson' the people called him to the last.

Yet, in the face of all this grief, the parting till death, the work broken off, the life cut short midway, the profusion of needs at home for able ministers, is it to be regretted that Coleridge Patteson devoted himself to the more remote fields abroad? I think we shall find that his judgment was right. Alfington might love him dearly, but the numbers were too small to afford full scope for his powers, and he would have experienced the trials of cramped and unemployed energies had he remained there beyond his apprenticeship. Nor were his gifts, so far as can be judged, exactly those most requisite for work in large towns. He could deal with individuals better than with masses, and his metaphysical mind, coupled with the curious difficulty he had in writing to an unrealised public, either in sermons or reports, might have rendered him less effective than men of less ability. He avoided, moreover, the temptations, pain, and sting of the intellectual warfare within the bosom of the Church, and served her cause more effectually on her borders than he could in her home turmoils. His great and peculiar gifts of languages, seconded by his capacity for navigation, enabled him to be the builder up of the Melanesian Church in so remarkable a manner that one can hardly suppose but that he was marked out for it, and these endowments would have found no scope in an ordinary career. Above all, no man can safely refuse the call to obey the higher leadings of grace. If he deny them, he will probably fall below that which he was before, and lose 'even that which he seemeth to have.'

A few days later, he wrote to his cousin Arthur Coleridge an expression of his feelings regarding the step he had taken in the midst of the pain it was costing to others:—

'Feniton: November 11, 9 A.M.

'My dear Arthur,—Your letter was very acceptable because I am, I confess, in that state of mind occasionally when the assurance of my being right, coming from another, tends to strengthen my own conviction.

'I do not really doubt as I believe; and yet, knowing my want of consideration for others, and many other thoughts which naturally prevent my exercising a clear sound judgment on a matter affecting myself, I sometimes (when I have had a conversation, it throws me back upon analysing my own conduct) feel inclined to go over the whole process again, and that is somewhat trying.

'On the other hand, I am almost strangely free from excitement. I live on exactly as I did before: and even when alone with Father, talk just as I used to talk, have nothing more to tell him, not knowing how to make a better use of these last quiet evenings.

'By-and-by I shall wish I had done otherwise, perhaps, but I do not know now, that I have anything specially requiring our consideration: we talk about family matters, the movements in the theological and political world, &c., very little about ourselves.

'One of all others I delight to think of for the music's sake, and far more for the glorious thought that it conveys. "Then shall the righteous," not indeed that I dare apply it to myself (as you know), but it helps one on, teaches what we may be, what our two dear parents are, and somehow the intervening, space becomes smaller as the eye is fixed steadily on the glory beyond.

'God bless you, my dear fellow.

'Ever your affectionate

'J. C. P.'

The Mission party intended to sail immediately after Christmas in the 'Southern Cross,' the schooner which was being built at Blackwall for voyages among the Melanesian isles. In expectation of this, Patteson went up to London in the beginning of December, when the admirable crayon likeness was taken by Mr. Richmond, an engraving from which is here given. He then took his last leave of his uncle, and of the cousins who had been so dear to him ever since the old days of daily meeting in childhood; and Miss Neill, then a permanent invalid, notes down: 'On December 13, I had the happiness of receiving the Holy Communion from dear Coley Patteson, and the following morning I parted from him, as I fear, for ever. God bless and prosper him, and guard him in all the dangers he will encounter!' He wrote thus soon after his return:—

'Feniton: December 22, 1854.

'My dear Miss Neill,—I began a note to you a day or two ago, but I could not go on with it, for I have had so very much to do in church and out of it, parochializing, writing sermons, &c. It makes some little difference in point of time whether I am living here or at Alfington, and so the walking about from one house to another is not so convenient for writing letters as for thinking over sermons.

'I need not tell you what a real happiness and comfort it is to me to have been with you again and to have talked so long with you, and most of all to have received the Communion with you. It is a blessed thought that no interval of space or time can interrupt that Communion of the Spirit, and that we are one in Him, though working in different corners of the Lord's field.

'I want to look you out a little book or two; and Fanny has told you that if ever my picture is photographed, I have particularly desired them to send you a copy with my love. Your cross I have now round my neck, and I shall always wear it; it will hang there with a locket containing locks of hair of my dear Father and Mother, the girls, and Jem.

'You will be glad to hear that they all seem cheerful and hearty. Fan is not well, but I do not see that she is depressed or unhappy. In fact, the terrible events of the war prove a lesson to all, and they feel, I suppose, that it might be far worse, and that so long as I am doing my duty, there is no cause for sorrow.

'Still there will be seasons of loneliness and sadness, and it seems to me as if it always was so in the case of all the people of whom we read in the Bible. Our Lord distinctly taught His disciples to expect it to be so, and even experienced this sorrow of heart Himself, filling up the full measure of His cup of bitterness. So I don't learn that I ought exactly to wish it to be otherwise, so much is said in the Bible about being made partaker of His, sufferings, only I pray that it may please God to bear me up in the midst of it. I must repeat that your example is constantly before me, as a witness to the power that God gives of enduring pain and sickness. It is indeed, and great comfort it gives me. He is not indeed keeping you still in the world without giving you a work to do, and enabling you from your bed of sickness to influence strongly a circle of friends.

'God bless you for all your kindness to me, and watchfulness over me as a child, for your daily thought of me and prayers for me, and may He grant that I may wear your precious gift not only on but in my heart.

'Always your very affectionate

'J. C. PATTESON.

'P.S.—I do not expect to sail for three weeks; this morning I had a line about the ship, and they say that she cannot be ready for a fortnight.'

On Christmas-day, he was presented with a Bible subscribed for by the whole Alfington population. Here is a sentence from his letter of acknowledgment:—

'If these poor needy souls can, from love to a fellow creature whom they have known but a few months, deny themselves their very crumb of bread to show their affection, what should be our conduct to Him from whom we have received all things, and to whom we owe our life, strength, and all that we possess?'

The farewell service was said by one of these poor old people to be like a great funeral. Sexagesima Sunday was Sir John's sixty-sixth birthday, and it was spent in expectation that it would be the last of the whole party at home, for on the Monday Sir John was obliged to go to London for a meeting of the Judicial Committee. The two notes his son wrote during his absence are, perhaps to prove good spirits, full of the delights of skating, which were afforded by the exceptionally severe frost of February 1855, which came opportunely to regale with this favourite pastime one who would never tread on solid ice again. He wrote with zest of the large merry party of cousins skating together, of the dismay of the old housekeeper when he skimmed her in a chair over the ice, sighing out, in her terror, 'My dear man, don't ye go so fast,' with all manner of endearing expressions—of the little boys to whom he threw nuts to be scrambled for, and of his own plunge through the thinner ice, when, regardless of drenched garments, he went on with the sport to the last, and came home with clothes frozen as stiff as a board.

He was not gone when his father and brother came home on the twenty-sixth, prepared to go with him to Southampton.

The note to his cousin Arthur written at this time thus ends: 'We worked together once at Dresden. Whatever we have acquired in the way of accomplishments, languages, love of art and music, everything brings us into contact with somebody, and gives us the power of influencing them for good, and all to the glory of God.'

Many were touched when, on the first Sunday in Lent, as Sir John Patteson was wont to assist in Church by reading the Lessons, it fell to him to pronounce the blessing of God upon the patriarch for his willing surrender of his son.

After all, the 'Southern Cross' was detected in leaking again, and as she was so small that the Mission party would have been most inconveniently crowded for so long a voyage, the Bishop was at length persuaded to relinquish his intention of sailing in her, and passages were taken for himself, Mrs. Selwyn, Mr. Patteson, and another clergyman, in the 'Duke of Portland,' which did not sail till the end of March, when Patteson was to meet her at Gravesend.

Thus he did not depart till the 25th. 'I leave home this morning I may say, for it has struck midnight,' he wrote to Miss Neill. 'I bear with me to the world's end your cross, and the memory of one who is bearing with great and long-tried patience the cross that God has laid upon her.'

He chose to walk to the coach that would take him to join the railway at Cullompton. The last kisses were exchanged at the door, and the sisters watched him out of sight, then saw that their father was not standing with them. They consulted for a moment, and then one of them silently looked into his sitting room, and saw him with his little Bible, and their hearts were comforted concerning him. After that family prayers were never read without a clause for Missionaries, 'especially the absent member of this family.'

He went up to his brother's chambers in London, whence a note was sent home the next day to his father:—

'I write one line to-night to tell you that I am, thank God, calm and even cheerful. I stayed a few minutes in the churchyard after I left you, picked a few primrose buds from dear mamma's grave, and then walked on.

'At intervals I felt a return of strong violent emotion, but I soon became calm; I read most of the way up, and felt surprised that I could master my own feelings so much.

'How much I owe to the cheerful calm composure which you all showed this morning! I know it must have cost you all a great effort. It spared me a great one.'

On the 27th the brothers went on board the 'Duke of Portland,' and surveyed the cabins, looking in at the wild scene of confusion sure to be presented by an emigrant ship on the last day in harbour. A long letter, with a minute description of the ship and the arrangements ends with: 'I have every blessing and comfort. Not one is wanting. I am not in any excitement, I think, certainly I do not believe myself to be in such a state as to involve a reaction of feeling. Of course if I am seedy at sea for a few days I shall feel low-spirited also most likely, and miss you all more in consequence. But that does not go below the surface. Beneath is calm tranquil peace of mind.'

On the 28th the two brothers joined the large number of friends who went down with the Mission party, among them Mr. Edward Coleridge.

Parting notes were written from on board to all the most beloved; to little Paulina, of bright hopes, to Miss Neill of her cross; to Arthur the German greeting, 'Lebe wohl, doch nicht auf Ewigkeit,'—to Mr. Justice Coleridge:—

'March 28, 1855.

'My dear Uncle,—One line more to thank you for all your love and to pray for the blessing of God upon you and yours now and for ever.

'We sail to-day. Such letters from home, full of calm, patient, cheerful resignation to his will. Wonderfully has God supported us through this trial. My kind love to Arthur. Always, my dear Uncle, Your affectionate, grateful Nephew,

'JOHN COLERIDGE PATTESON.'

Perhaps the frame of mind in which Coley left England can best be gathered from the following extract from a letter to his father from his uncle Edward:—

'While on board I had a good deal of quiet talk with him, and was fully confirmed by his manner and words, of that which I did not doubt before, that the surrender of self, which he has made, has been put into his heart by God's Holy Spirit, and that all his impulses for good are based on the firm foundation of trust in God, and a due appreciation of his mortal, as well as professional condition. I never saw a hand set on the plough stead with more firmness, yet entire modesty, or with an eye and heart less turned backwards on the world behind. I know you do not in any way repine at what you have allowed him to do; and I feel sure that ere long you will see cause to bless God not only for having given you such a son, but also for having put it into his heart so to devote himself to that particular work in the Great Vineyard.'

About 5 P.M. the 'Duke of Portland' swung round with the tide, strangers were ordered on shore, Coleridge and James Patteson said their last farewells, and while the younger brother went home by the night-train to carry the final greetings to his father and sisters, the ship weighed anchor and the voyage was begun.

CHAPTER VI. THE VOYAGE AND FIRST YEAR. 1855-1856.

When the See of New Zealand was first formed, Archbishop Howley committed to the care of the first Bishop the multitudinous islands scattered in the South Pacific. The technical bounds of the diocese were not defined; but matters were to a certain degree simplified by Bishop Selwyn's resolution only to deal with totally heathen isles, and whatever superiority the authorised chief pastor might rightfully claim, not to confuse the minds of the heathen by the sight of variations among Christians, and thus never to preach in any place already occupied by Missions, a resolution from which he only once departed, in the case of a group apparently relinquished by its first teachers. This cut off all the properly called Polynesian isles, whose inhabitants are of the Malay type, and had been the objects of care to the London Mission, ever since the time of John Williams; also the Fiji Islands; and a few which had been taken in hand by a Scottish Presbyterian Mission; but the groups which seem to form the third fringe round the north-eastern curve of Australia, the New Hebrides, Banks Islands, and Solomon Isles, were almost entirely open ground, with their population called Melanesian or Black Islanders, from their having much of the Negro in their composition and complexion. These were regarded as less quick but more steady than the Polynesian race, with somewhat the same difference of character as there is between the Teuton and the Kelt. The reputation of cannibalism hung about many of the islands, and there was no doubt of boats' crews having been lost among them, but in most cases there had been outrage to provoke reprisals.

These islands had as yet been little visited, except by Captain Cook, their first discoverer, and isolated Spanish exploring expeditions; but of late whalers and sandal wood traders, both English and American, had been finding their way among them, and too often acting as irresponsible adventurous men of a low class are apt to do towards those whom they regard as an inferior race.

Mission work had hardly reached this region. It was in attempting it that John Williams had met his death at Erromango, one of the New Hebrides; but one of his best institutions had been a school in one of the Samoan or Navigators' Islands, in which were educated young men of the native races to be sent to the isles to prepare the way for white men. Very nobly had these Samoan pupils carried out his intentions, braving dislike, disease and death in the islands to which they were appointed, and having the more to endure because they came without the prestige of a white man. Moreover, the language was no easier to them than to him, as their native speech is entirely different from the Melanesian; which is besides broken into such an extraordinary number of different dialects, varying from one village to another in an island not twenty miles long, that a missionary declared that the people must have come straight from the Tower of Babel, and gone on dividing their speech ever since. Just at the time of the formation of the See of New Zealand, the excitement caused at home by Williams's death had subsided, and the London Mission's funds were at so low an ebb that, so far from extending their work, they had been obliged to let some of it fall into abeyance.

All this came to the knowledge of the Bishop of New Zealand while he was occupied with the cares of his first seven years in his more immediate diocese, and in 1848, he made a voyage of inspection in H.M.S. 'Dido.' He then perceived that to attempt the conversion of this host of isles of tropical climate through a resident English clergyman in each, would be impossible, besides which he knew that no Church takes root without native clergy, and he therefore intended bringing boys to New Zealand, and there educating them to become teachers to their countrymen. He had lately established, near Auckland, for the sons of the colonists, St. John's College, which in 1850 was placed under the Reverend Charles John Abraham, the former Eton master, who had joined the Bishop to act as Archdeacon and assist in the scheme of education; and here it was planned that the young Melanesians should be trained.

The Bishop possessed a little schooner of twenty-two tons, the 'Undine,' in which he was accustomed to make his expeditions along the coast; and in August 1849, he set forth in her, with a crew of four, without a weapon of any sort, to 'launch out into the deep, and let down his nets for a draught.' Captain Erskine of H.M.S. 'Havannah' readily undertook to afford him any assistance practicable, and they were to cruise in company, the 'Undine' serving as a pilot boat or tender on coasts where the only guide was 'a few rough sketches collected from small trading vessels.'

They met near Tanna, but not before the Bishop had been in Dillon's Bay, on the island of Erromango, the scene of Williams's murder, and had allowed some of the natives to come on board his vessel as a first step towards friendly intercourse. The plan agreed on by the Bishop and the Captain was to go as far north as Vate, and return by way of the Loyalty Isles, which fringe the east coast of New Caledonia, to touch at that large island, and then visit the Island of Pines, at its extreme south point, and there enquire into a massacre said to have taken place. This was effected, and in each place the natives showed themselves friendly. From New Caledonia the Bishop brought away a pupil named Dallup, and at two of the Loyalty Islands, Nengone or Mare, and Lifu, where Samoan teachers had excited a great desire for farther instruction, boys eagerly begged to go with him, and two were taken from each, in especial Siapo, a young Nengone chief eighteen or nineteen years old, of very pleasing aspect, and with those dignified princely manners which rank is almost sure to give. The first thing done with such lads when they came on board was to make clothes for them, and when they saw the needle employed in their service, they were almost sure to beg to be taught the art, and most of them soon became wonderfully dexterous in it.

On the Island of Pines, so called from the tower-like masses of the Norfolk pine on the shores, was at that time the French Bishop of New Caledonia, the Oul, as the natives called him and his countrymen, for whom they had little love. After an interview between the two bishops, the 'Undine' returned to New Zealand, where the native boys were brought to St. John's College. The system of education there combined agricultural labour and printing with study, and the authorities and the boys shared according to their strength in both, for there was nothing more prominent in the Bishop's plan than that the coloured man was not to be treated as a mere hewer of wood and drawer of water, but, as a Maori once expressed the idea: 'Gentleman—gentleman thought nothing that ought to be done at all too mean for him; pig-gentleman never worked.' The whole community, including the ladies and their guests, dined together in hall.

The five boys behaved well, Siapo being a leader in all that was good, and made advances in Christian knowledge; but it was one of the Bishop's principles that none of them should be baptized till he had proved whether his faith were strong enough to resist the trial of a return to his native home and heathen friends. The climate of New Zealand is far too chilly for these inhabitants of tropical regions, and it was absolutely necessary to return them to their homes during the winter quarter from June to August. The scheme therefore was to touch at their islands, drop them there, proceed then further on the voyage, and then, returning the same way, resume them, if they were willing to come under instruction for baptism and return to the college. In the lack of a common language, Bishop Selwyn hoped to make them all learn English, and only communicate with one another in that.

The 'Undine,' not being large enough for the purpose, was exchanged for the 'Border Maid;' and in the course of the next three years an annual voyage was made, and boys to the number of from twelve to fourteen brought home. Siapo of Nengone was by far the most promising scholar. He was a strong influence, when at home, on behalf of the Samoan teachers, and assisted in the building of a round chapel, smoothly floored, and plastered with coral lime. In 1852 he was baptized, together with three of his friends, in this chapel, in his own island, by the Bishop, in the presence of a thousand persons, and received the name of George. When the 'Border Maid' returned, though he was convalescent from a severe illness, he not only begged that he might come back, but that the young girl to whom he was betrothed might be taken to New Zealand to be trained in Christian ways. Ready consent was given, and the little Wabisane, and her companion Wasitutru (Little Chattering Bird), were brought on board, and arrayed in petticoats fashioned by the Bishop's own hands, from his own counterpane, with white skirts above, embellished with a bow of scarlet ribbon, the only piece of finery to be found in the 'Border Maid.' The Rev. William Nihill had spent the period of this trip at Nengone, and had become deeply interested in the people. The island was then thought likely to become a centre whence to work on adjacent places; but to the grief and disappointment of all, George Siapo did not live through the summer at St. John's. He had never recovered his illness at home, and rapidly declined; but his faith burnt brighter as his frame became weaker, and his heart was set on the conversion of his native country. He warmly begged Mr. Nihill to return thither, and recommended him to the protection of his friends, and he wished his own brother to become scholar at St. John's. His whole demeanour was that of a devoted Christian, and when he died, in the January of the year 1853, he might be regarded as the firstfruits of the Melanesian Church. Since Mr. Nihill was about to return to Nengone, and there was a certain leaven of Christianity in the place, the girls were not subjected to the probation of a return before baptism, but were christened Caroline and Sarah, after Mrs. Abraham and Mrs. Selwyn.

Another very satisfactory pupil was little Umao. An English sailor in a dreadful state of disease had been left behind by a whaler at Erromango, where the little Umao, a mere boy, had attached himself to him, and waited on him with the utmost care and patience, though meeting with no return but blows and rough words. The man moved to Tanna, where there are mineral springs highly esteemed by the natives, and when the 'Border Maid' touched there, in 1851, he was found in a terrible condition, but with the little fellow faithfully attending him. The Englishman was carried to Sydney, and left in the hospital there; but Umao begged not to be sent home, for he said his parents cruelly ill-used him and his brothers, and set them to watch the fire all night to keep off evil spirits; so, when New Zealand became too cold for him, he was sent to winter at the London Society's station in Anaiteum. His sweet friendly nature expanded under Christian training, but his health failed, and in the course of the voyage of 1853 he became so ill that his baptism was hastened, and he shortly after died in the Bishop's arms.

Two more boys, cousins, from Lifu, also died. There never was any suspicion or displeasure shown among the relatives of these youths. Their own habits were frightfully unhealthy; they were not a long-lived people, and there was often great mortality among them, and though they were grieved at the loss of their sons, they never seemed distrustful or ungrateful. But it was evident that, even in the summer months, the climate of New Zealand was trying to these tropical constitutions, and as it was just then determined that Norfolk Island should no longer be the penal abode of the doubly convicted felons of Botany Bay, but should instead become the home of the descendants of the mutineers of the 'Bounty' who had outgrown Pitcairn's Island, the Bishop cast his eyes upon it as the place most likely to agree alike with English and Melanesian constitutions, and therefore eminently fitted for the place of instruction.

The expenses of the voyages in the 'Border Maid' had been met partly by the Eton Association, and partly by another association at Sydney, where a warm interest in these attempts had been excited and maintained by the yearly visits of Bishop Selwyn, who usually visited Australia while the lads were wintering at their homes. But the 'Border Maid' was superannuated, nor had she ever been perfectly fitted for the purpose; and when, in 1853, the Bishop was obliged to come to England to take measures for dividing his diocese, he also hoped to obtain permission to establish a Melanesian school on Norfolk Island, and to obtain the means of building a schooner yacht, small enough to be navigated in the narrow, shallow creeks separating the clustered islets, and yet capacious enough for the numerous passengers. In the meantime Mr. Nihill went to Nengone with his wife and child. His lungs were much affected, but he hoped that the climate would prolong his power of working among the Christian community, who heartily loved and trusted him.

Other fellow-labourers the Bishop hoped to obtain at home, though it was his principle never to solicit men to come with him, only to take those who offered themselves; but all the particulars of the above narration had been known to Coley Patteson through the Bishop's correspondence with Mr. Edward Coleridge, as well as by the yearly report put forth by the Eton Association, and this no doubt served to keep up in his heart the flame that had burnt unseen for so many years, and to determine its direction, though he put himself unreservedly at the Bishop's disposal, to work wherever he might be sent.

The means for the mission ship 'Southern Cross' were raised. She was built at Blackwall by Messrs. Wigram, and, after all the delays, sailed on the very same day as the 'Duke of Portland.'

Meantime here are a few extracts from Patteson's journal-letter during the voyage. Sea-sickness was very slightly disabling with him; he was up and about in a short time, and on the 8th of April was writing:—

'What a day this has been to me, the twenty-eighth anniversary of my baptism to begin with, and then Easter Day spent at sea!

'April 20th, lat, 4° N., long. 25° W.—Rather hot. It is very fine to see all the stars of the heavens almost rise and pass overhead and set—Great Bear and Southern Cross shining as in rivalry of each other, and both hemispheres showing forth all their glory. Only the Polar Star, that shines straight above you, is gone below our horizon; and One alone knows how much toil, and perhaps sorrow, there may be in store for me before I see it again. But there is and will be much happiness and comfort also, for indeed I have great peace of mind, and a firm conviction that I am doing what is right; a feeling that God is directing and ordering the course of my life, and whenever I take the only true view of the business of life, I am happy and cheerful.

'May 10.—It is, I find, quite settled, and was indeed always, that I am to go always with the Bishop, roving about the Melanesian department, so that for some years, if I live, I shall be generally six months at sea. And not little to my delight, I find that the six winter months (i.e. your summer months) are the ones that we shall spend in sailing about the islands within or near the tropics, so that I shall have little more shivering limbs or blue hands, though I may feel in the long run the effect of a migratory swallow-like life. But the sea itself is a perpetual tonic, and when I am thoroughly accustomed to a sea life, I think I shall be better almost on board ship.'

This seems the place for Bishop Selwyn's impression, as written to a friend at this very time. 'Coley Patteson is a treasure which I humbly set down as a Divine recompense for our own boys*. He is a good fellow, and the tone of his mind is one which I can thoroughly enjoy, content with the 'to aei' present, yet always aiming at a brighter and better future.'

*(Footnote: Left at home for education.)

'June 18.—You must think of us at 8 P.M. on Sundays—just at 8.20 A.M. before you come down to prayers. The Bishop has a service in the College chapel; then, after all the "runners" (clergy who have district chapels) have returned, chanting Psalms, and reading collects, which bear especially on the subject of unity, introducing the special Communion thanksgiving for Whitsunday, and the Sanctus, and the Prayer for Unity in the Accession Service. I feel that it must be an impressive and very happy way of ending the Sunday, and you will be at Sunday prayers at the other end of the world praying with us.

'July 3.—Still at sea. As soon as we rounded the North Cape on Friday, June 29, a contrary wind sprang up, and we have been beating about, tacking between North Cape and Cape Brett ever since. Fine sunny weather and light winds, but always from the south. To me it is a matter of entire indifference; I am quite ready to go ashore, but do not mind a few more days at sea. The climate is delightful, thermometer on deck 55° to 60°, and such glorious sunsets! There is really something peculiar in the delicacy of the colours here—faint pink and blue, and such an idea of distance is given by the great transparency of the air. It is full moon too now, and I walk the deck from eleven to twelve every night with no great-coat, thinking about you all and my future work. Last night the Bishop was with me, and told me definitely about my occupation for the time to come. All day we have been slowly, very slowly, passing along from the north headland of the Bay of Islands to Cape Brett, and along the land south of it. A fine coast it is, full of fine harbours and creeks, the bay itself like a large Torbay, only bolder. Due south of us is the Bream headland, then the Barrier Islands. We are only about a mile from the shore, and refreshing it is to look at it; but as yet we have seen no beach; the rock runs right into the sea. Such bustle and excitement on board! emigrants getting their things ready, carpenters making the old "Duke" look smart, sailors scrubbing, but no painting going on, to our extreme delight. It is so calm, quite as smooth as a small lake; indeed there is less perceptible motion than I have felt on the Lake of Como. No backs, no bones aching, though here I speak for others more than for myself, for the Bishop began his talk last night by saying, "One great point is decided, that you are a good sailor. So far you are qualified for Melanesia."'

To this may be added that Patteson had been farther preparing for this work by a diligent study of the Maori language, and likewise of navigation; and what an instructor he had in the knowledge of the coasts may be gathered from the fact that an old sea captain living at Kohimarama sent a note to St. John's College stating that he was sure that the Bishop had come, for he knew every vessel that had ever come into Auckland harbour, and was sure this barque had never been there before; yet she had come in the night through all the intricate passages, and was rounding the heads without a pilot on board. He therefore concluded that the Bishop must be on board, as there was no other man that could have taken command of her at such a time, and brought her into that harbour.

The Bishop and Mrs. Selwyn went on shore as soon as possible; Patteson waited till the next day. Indeed he wrote on July 5 that he was in no hurry to land, since he knew no one in the whole neighbourhood but Archdeacon Abraham. Then he describes the aspect of Auckland from the sea:—

'It looks much like a small sea-side town, but not so substantially built, nor does it convey the same idea of comfort and wealth; rude warehouses, &c., being mixed up with private houses on the beach. The town already extends to a distance of perhaps half a mile on each side of this cove, on which the principal part of it is built. Just in the centre of the cove stands the Wesleyan chapel. On the rising ground on the east of the cove is the Roman Catholic chapel, and on the west side is St. Paul's Church, an Early English stone building, looking really ecclesiastical and homelike. The College, at a distance of about five miles from the town, on some higher ground, northwest of it, is reached from the harbour by a boat ascending a creek to within a mile of the buildings, so that we shall not go into the town at all when we land. By water too will be our shortest, at all events our quickest way from the college to the town.

'July 9, St. John's College.—Though we reached harbour on July 5, and landed the next day, I have scarcely found a minute to write a line. Imagine my feelings as I touched land and jumped ashore at a creek under Judge Martin's house, in the presence of Rota Waitoa, the only native clergyman in the diocese; Levi, who is perhaps to be ordained, and four or five other natives. Tena ra fa koe e ho a? "How are you, my friends?" (the common New Zealand greeting), said I as I shook hands with them one by one. We walked up from the beach to the house. Roses in full flower, and mimosa with a delicate golden flower, and various other shrubs and flowers in full bloom. Midwinter, recollect. The fragrance of the air, the singing of the birds, the fresh smell (it was raining a little and the grass was steaming) were delicious, as you may suppose. Here I was, all at once, carrying up baggage, Maoris before and behind, and everything new and strange, and yet I felt as if it were all right and natural. The Bishop and Mrs. Selwyn had landed the day before, and we were heartily welcomed. Mr. Martin took me into his study. "I am thankful to see you as a fresh labourer among us here; a man of your name needs no introduction to a lawyer." Nothing could exceed his kindness. He began talking of at once.

'We dined at about 12.30. Clean mutton chops, potatoes and pumpkin (very good indeed), jam pudding, bread, and plenty of water (beer I refused). It did taste so good, I am quite ashamed of thinking about it. About two o'clock I started with the Bishop for the College, nearly six miles from Auckland.

'The Bishop is at a kind of collegiate establishment on the outskirts of Auckland, where Mr. Kissling, a clergyman, is the resident, and thither I go on Wednesday, to live till October 1, when we start, please God, in the "Southern Cross" for the cruise around New Zealand. Here, at Mr. Kissling's, I shall have work with Maoris, learning each day, I trust, to speak more correctly and fluently. Young men for teachers, and it may be for clergymen, will form at once my companions and my pupils, a good proportion of them being nearly or quite of my own age. I am to be constantly at the Judge's, running in and out, working on Sundays anywhere as I may be sent. So much for myself.

'The College is really all that is necessary for a thoroughly good and complete place of education; the hall all lined with kauri pine wood, a large handsome room, collegiate, capable of holding two hundred persons; the school-room, eighty feet long, with admirable arrangements for holding classes separately. There are two very cosy rooms, which belong to the Bishop and Mrs. Selwyn respectively, in one of which I am now sitting.... On the walls are hanging about certain tokens of Melanesia in the shape of gourds, calabashes, &c., such as I shall send you one day; a spade on one side, just as a common horse halter hanging from Abraham's bookshelf, betokens colonial life. Our rooms are quite large enough, bigger than my room at Feniton, but no furniture, of course, beyond a bedstead, a table for writing, and an old bookcase; but it is never cold enough to care about furniture... I clean, of course, my room in part, make my bed, help to clear away things after meals, &c., and am quite accustomed to do without servants for anything but cooking. There is a weaving room, which used to be well worked, a printing press (from C. M. S.) which has done some good work, and is now at work again—English, Maori, Greek and Hebrew types. Separate groups of buildings, which once were filled with lads from different Melanesian isles—farm buildings, barns, &c. Last of all, the little chapel of kauri wood, stained desk, like the inside of a really good ecclesiastical building in England, porch S.W. angle, a semicircular apse at the west, containing a large handsome stone font, open seats of course. The east end very simple, semicircular apse, small windows all full of stained glass, raised one step, no rails, the Bishop's chair on the north side, bench on the south. Here my eye and my mind rested contentedly and peacefully. The little chapel, holding about seventy persons, is already dear to me. I preached in it last night at the seven o'clock service. We chanted the Unity Psalms CXXII, CXXIII, CXXIV, and CL, heartily, all joining to a dear old double chant in parts. I felt my heart very full as I spoke to them of the blessedness of prayer and spiritual communion. I was at Tamaki in the morning, where I read prayers, the Archdeacon preaching. A little stone church, very rude and simple, but singing again good, and congregation of fifty-one, attentive. At Panmure, about three miles off, in the afternoon, a tiny wooden church—where Abraham took all the duty. In the evening, in the chapel, he read prayers, and I preached to about thirty-five or forty people. We left the chapel just as you were getting ready for breakfast, and so passed my first Sunday in New Zealand. To-day I have had hard work; I walked with Abraham to Auckland—six miles of rough work, I promise you, except the two last.

I believe it was in the course of this walk that Patteson experimented on his Maori, a native whom they visited, and who presently turned upon the Archdeacon, and demanded, 'Why do you not speak like Te Pattihana?' Such a compliment has seldom been paid on so early an attempt at colloquialism in a new language. Journal continues:—

'Lugged down boxes, big empty ones, from the Judge's house to the beach. Went with the Bishop to the old ship, packed up books, brought away all our things almost, helped to pack them in a cart and drag, and then walked back to the College, which I reached in the dark at 7.30. It is delightful to see the delight of the natives when they see the Bishop. "E—h te Pikopa!" and then they all come round him like children, laughing and talking. Two common men we met on Friday from Rotoma, 150 miles off, who said that their tribe had heard that the Queen of England had taken away his salary, and they had been having subscriptions for him every Sunday. They are of various shades of colour, some light brown, some nearly black, and some so tattooed all over that you can't tell what colour they are. I was talking to-day to the best of my power with a native teacher upon whose face I could not see one spot as big as a shilling that was not tattooed, beautifully done in a regular pattern, one side corresponding to the other. Each tribe, as it is said (I know not how truly), has a pattern of its own; so they wear their coats-of-arms on their faces, that is all. The young Christian natives are not tattooed at all, and I have been to-day with Sydney, whose father was the great fighting man of Honghi (miscalled Shanghi) who was presented to George IV. This young man's father helped to exterminate a whole tribe who lived on a part of the College property (as it is now), and he is said to be perhaps the first New Zealander who was baptized as an infant. I find it hard to understand them; they speak very indistinctly—not fast, but their voices are thick in general. I hope to learn a good deal before October. My first letter from the ends of the world tells of my peace of mind, of one sound and hearty in body, and, I thank God, happy, calm, and cheerful in spirit.'

'July 11, 1855; St. John's College, Auckland.

'My dear Fan,—I do not doubt that I am where I ought to be; I do think and trust that God has given me this work to do; but I need earnest prayers for strength that I may do it. It is no light work to be suddenly transplanted from a quiet little country district, where every one knew me, and the prestige of dear Father's life and your active usefulness among the people made everything smooth for me, to a work exceeding in magnitude anything that falls to the lot of an ordinary parish priest in England—in a strange land, among a strange race of men, in a newly forming and worldly society, with no old familiar notions and customs to keep the machine moving; and then to be made acquainted with such a mass of information respecting Church government and discipline, educational schemes, conduct of clergy and teachers, etc., etc. It is well that I am hearty and sound in health, or I should be regularly overwhelmed with it. Two texts I think of constantly: "Whatsoever thy hand findeth to do, do it with thy might." "Sufficient for the day," etc. I hardly dare look forward to what my work may be on earth; I cannot see my way; but I feel sure that He is ordering it all, and I try to look on beyond the earth, when at length, by God's mercy, we may all find rest.

'That I have been so well in body and so cheerful in mind ever since I left home —I mean cheerful on the whole, not without seasons of sadness, but so mercifully strengthened at all times—must, I think, without any foolish enthusiasm, be remembered by me as a special act of God's goodness and mercy. I was not the least weary of the sea. Another month or two would have made very little difference to me, I think. I am very fond of it, and I think of my voyages to come without any degree of dread from that cause, and I have no reason to expect any great discomfort from any other. I have my whole stock of lemon syrup and lime juice, so that the salt meat on the "Southern Cross" will be counteracted in that way; and going round those islands we shall be ashore every few days. But what most surprises me is this: that when I am alone, as here at night in a great (for it is large) cheerless, lonely room, as I should have thought it once; though I can't help thinking of my own comforts at home, and all dear faces around me, though I feel my whole heart swelling with love to you all, still I am not at all sad or gloomy, or cast down. This does surprise me: I did not think it would or could be so. I have indeed prayed for it, but I had not faith to believe that my prayer would be so granted. The fact itself is most certain. I have at Alfington, when alone of an evening, experienced a greater sense of loneliness than I have once done out here. Of this hitherto I feel no doubt: it may be otherwise any day of course; and to what else can I attribute this fact, in all soberness of mind, but to the mercy of God in strengthening me for my work? Much of it may be the effect of a splendid climate upon my physique, that is true; for indeed to find flowers in full blossom, green meadows, hot suns, birds singing, etc., in midwinter, with a cool, steady breeze from the sea invigorating me all the while, is no doubt just what I require; but to-day we have a north-easter, which answers to your south-west wind, with pouring rain, and yet my spirits are not going down with the barometer. All the same, the said barometer will probably soon recover himself; for I believe these heavy storms seldom last long. There is no fire in the room where I sit, which is the Bishop's room when he is here; no fire-place indeed, as it opens into Mrs. Selwyn's room. The thermometer is 58°, and it is midwinter.'

To Miss Neill, on the same day, after repeating his conviction that he was in the right place, he says:—

'I have written to them at home what I ought not perhaps to have said of myself, but that it will give them comfort—that from all sides my being here as the Bishop's companion is hailed as likely to produce very beneficial results. But I must assure you that I fully know how your love for me and much too high opinion of me makes you fancy that I could be of use at home. But we must not, even taking this view, send our refuse men to the colonies. Newly forming societies must be moulded by men of energy, and power, and high character; in fact, churches must be organised, the Gospel must be preached by men of earnest zeal for God's glory in the salvation of souls. To lower the standard of Christian life by exhibiting a feeble faint glimmering instead of a burning shining light is to stamp upon the native mind a false impression, it may be for ever.

'Remember, we have no ancient customs nor time-hallowed usages to make up for personal indifference and apathy; we have no momentum to carry on the machine. We have to start it, and give it the first impulse, under the guidance of the Spirit of God; and oh! if it takes a wrong direction at first, who can calculate the evil that must follow? It is easy to steer a vessel in smooth water, with a fair breeze; but how are you to keep her head straight in a rolling sea with no way on her?'

This letter, with two or three more, went by the first mail after his arrival. From that time he generally kept a journal-letter, and addressed it to one or other of his innermost home circle; while the arrival of each post from home produced a whole sheaf of answers, and comments on what was told, by each correspondent, of family, political or Church matters. Sometimes the letter is so full of the subject of immediate interest as absolutely to leave no room for personal details of his own actual life, and this became more the case as the residence in New Zealand or Norfolk Island lost its novelty, while it never absorbed him so as to narrow his interests. He never missed a mail in writing to his father and sisters, and a letter to his brother was equally regular, but these latter were generally too much concerned with James's own individual life to be as fully given as the other letters, which were in fact a diary of facts, thoughts, and impressions.

'July 12, St. Stephen's, Mr. Kissling's School-house.—You know I am to live here when not on the "Southern Cross," or journeying in the Bush; so I must describe, first, the place itself, then my room in it. The house is a large one-storied building of wood, no staircase in it, but only a succession of rooms.... There are at present fourteen or sixteen girls in the school, boarding here, besides Rota, who is a native deacon, spending a month here; Levi, who is preparing for ordination, and three other men. The house stands on table-land about four hundred yards from the sea, commanding glorious views of the harbour, sea, and islands, which form groups close round the coast. It is Church property all round, and the site of a future cathedral is within a stone's throw of it.... Now for my room. Plenty large enough to begin with, not less than sixteen feet long by twelve wide, and at least eleven high, all wood, not papered or painted, which I like much, as the kauri is a darkish grained wood; no carpet of course, but I am writing now at 10 P.M., with no fire, and quite warm. The east side of the room is one great window, latticed, in a wooden frame; outside it a verandah, and such a beautiful view of the harbour and bay beyond. I will tell you exactly what I have done to-day since two o'clock, as a sample of my life.

'2 P.M., dinner, roast mutton; my seat between the Bishop and Eota. Fancy the long table with its double row of Maoris. After dinner, away with the Bishop to the hospital, a plain wooden building a mile off, capable of taking in about forty patients in all. I am to visit it regularly when here, taking that work off the parish clergyman's shoulders, and a great comfort it will be. I went through it to-day, and had a long talk with the physician and surgeon, and saw the male patients, two of them natives. One of them is dying, and so I am to be now talking as well as I can, but at all events reading and praying, with this poor fellow, and a great happiness it is to have such a privilege and so on. Came back to tea, very pleasant. After tea made Eota, and Sydney, a young-man who knows English pretty well, sit in my room (N.B., there is but one chair, in which I placed Eota), and then I made them read Maori to me, and read a good deal myself, and then we talked as well as we could. At 6.15, prayers, the whole party of Maoris assembled. Mr. Kissling read the first verse of the chapter (Joshua vi.), and we each read one verse in turn, and then he questioned them for perhaps fifteen minutes. They were very intelligent and answered well, and it was striking to see grown-up men and young women sitting so patiently to be taught. Then the evening service prayers; and so I knelt with these good simple people and prayed with them for the first time. Very much I enjoyed all this. Soon after came supper, a little talking, and now here am I writing to you.

'I wish you could see the tree-ferns; some are quite twenty feet high in the trunk, for trunk it is, and the great broad frond waves over it in a way that would make that child Pena clap her hands with delight. Then the geraniums and roses in blossom, the yellow mimosa flower, the wild moncha, with a white flower, growing everywhere, and the great variety of evergreen trees (none that I have seen being deciduous) make the country very pretty. The great bare volcanic hills, each with its well-defined crater, stand up from among the woodlands, and now from among pastures grazing hundreds of oxen; and this, with the grand sea views, and shipping in the harbour, make a very fine sight.

'July 14.—I write to-night because you will like a line from me on the day when first I have in any way ministered to a native of the country. I was in the hospital to-day, talked a little, and read St. Luke xv. to one, and prayed with another Maori. The latter is dying. He was baptized by the Wesleyans, but is not visited by them, so I do not scruple to go to him. Rota, the native deacon, was with me, and he talked a long while with the poor fellow. It is a great comfort to me to have made a beginning. I did little more than read a few prayers from the Visitation Service, but the man understood me well, so I may be of use, I hope. He has never received the Lord's Supper; but if there is time to prepare him, the Bishop wishes me to administer it to him.

'July 20.—Yesterday in sailed the "Southern Cross" with not a spar carried away or sail lost, perfectly sound, and in a fit state to be off again at once. She left England on the same day that we did, and arrived just a fortnight after us, and this is attributable to her having kept in low latitudes, not going higher than 39°; whereas we were in 51° 30', which diminished the distance and brought us in the way of more favourable winds. I saw from my windows about 9 A.M. a schooner in the distance, and told the Bishop I thought it might be the "Southern Cross" (she has no figure-head and a very straight bow). Through the day, which was very rainy, we kept looking from time to time through our glasses. At 3 P.M. the Bishop came in: "Come along, Coley; I do believe it is the 'Southern Cross.'" So I hurried on waterproofs, knowing that we were in for some mudlarking. Off we went, lugged down a borrowed boat to the water, tide being out. I took one oar, a Maori another, and off we went, Bishop steering. After twenty minutes' pull, or thereabouts, we met her, jumped on board, and then such a broadside of questions and answers. They had a capital passage. Two men who were invalided when they started died on the voyage—one of dysentery, I think—all the rest flourishing, the three women respectable and tidy-looking individuals, and two children very well. After a while the Bishop and I went off to shore, in one of his boats, pulled by two of the crew, Lowestoft fishermen, fine young fellows as you ever saw. Then we bought fresh meat, onions, bread, etc., for them, and so home by 7 P.M. "Mudlarking" very slight on this occasion, only walking over the flat swamp of low-water marsh for a quarter of a mile; but on Tuesday we had a rich scene. Bishop and I went to the "Duke of Portland" and brought off the rest of our things; but it was low-water, so the boats could not come within a long way of the beach, and the custom is for carts to go over the muddy sand, which is tolerably hard, as far into the water as they can, perhaps two and a half or three feet deep when it is quite calm, as it was on Tuesday. Well, in went our cart, which had come from the College, with three valuable horses, while the Bishop and I stood on the edge of the water. Presently one of the horses lost his footing, and then all at once all three slipped up, and the danger was of their struggling violently and hurting themselves. One of those in the shafts had his head under water, too, for a time. Instanter Bishop and I had our coats off, my trousers were rolled over my knees, and in we rushed to the horses. Such a plunging and splashing! but they were all got up safe. This was about 4 P.M., and I was busy about the packages and getting them into the carts, unloading at Mr. Kissling's till past 8; but I did not catch cold. Imagine an English Bishop with attending parson cutting into the water up to their knees to disentangle their cart-horses from the harness in full view of every person on the beach. "This is your first lesson in mudlarking, Coley," was the remark of the Bishop as we laughed over our respective appearance.

'July 21.—I was finishing my sermon for the soldiers to-morrow at 11.30, when Mr. Kissling came in to say that the schooner just come into the harbour was the vessel which had been sent to bring Mr. and Mrs. Nihill from Nengone or Mare Island. He was in very bad health when he went there, and great doubts were entertained as to his coming back. I was deputed to go and see. I ran a good part of the way to the town on to the pier, and there heard that Mr. Nihill was dead. An old acquaintance of Mrs. Nihill was on the pier, so I thought I should be in the way, and came back, told Mrs. Kissling, and went on to the Judge's, and told Mrs. Martin and Mrs. Selwyn. Whilst there we saw a boat land a young lady and child on the beach just below the house, and they sent me down. Pouring with rain here on the beach, taking shelter in a boat-house with her brother, I found this poor young widow; and so, leaning on my arm, she walked up to the house. I just waited to see Mrs. Selwyn throw her arms round her neck, and then walked straight off, feeling that the furious rain and wind chimed in with a violent struggle which was just going on in my own mind. I go through such scenes firmly enough at the time, but when my part is over I feel just like a child, and I found the tears in my eyes; for the universal sympathy which has been expressed by everyone here for the lonely situation of the Nihills at Nengone made me feel almost a personal interest in them. He was a good linguist, and his loss will be severely felt by the Bishop.

'August 14.—I marked out to-day some pretty places for the two wooden houses for the "Southern Cross" sailors at Kohimarama (Focus of Light), a quiet retired spot, with a beautiful sparkling beach, the schooner lying just outside the little bay a third of a mile off. Forty or fifty acres of flat pasturage, but only sixteen properly cleared, and then an amphitheatre of low hills, covered with New Zealand vegetation. I passed fine ferns to-day quite thirty feet in the stem, with great spreading-fronds, like branches of the Norfolk Island pine almost.

'On the 17th of August came the welcome mail from home. "Oh what a delight it is to see your dear handwriting again!" is the cry in the reply. Father's I opened first, and read his letter, stopping often with tears of thankfulness in my eyes to thank God for enabling him not to be over-anxious about me, and for the blessing of knowing that he was as well as usual, and also because his work, so distasteful to him, was drawing to a close. Then I read Fan's, for I had a secret feeling that I should hear most from her about Alfington.'

On the evening of that day he wrote to Fanny. In answer to the expression of the pain, of separation, he says:—

'There is One above who knows what a trial it is to you. For myself, hard as it is, and almost too hard sometimes, yet I have relief in the variety and unceasing-multiplicity of my occupations. Not a moment of any day can I be said to be idle. Literally, I have not yet had a minute to untie my "Guardians;" but for you, with more time for meditating, with no change of scene, with every object that meets you at home and in your daily walks reminding you of me, it must indeed be such a trial as angels love to look upon when it is borne patiently, and with a perfect assurance that God is ordering all things for our good; and so let us struggle on to the end. All good powers are on our side, and we shall meet by the infinite mercy one day when there shall be no separation for ever.

'I read on in your letter till I came to "Dear Coley, it is very hard to live without you,"—and I broke down and cried like a child. I was quite alone out in the fields on a glorious bright day, and it was the relief I had longed for. The few simple words told me the whole story, and I prayed with my whole heart that you might find strength in the hour of sadness. Do (as you say you do) let your natural feelings work; do not force yourself to appear calm, do not get excited if you can help it; but if your mind is oppressed with the thought of my absence, do not try to drive it away by talking about something else, or taking up a book, etc.; follow it out, see what it ends in, trace out the spiritual help and comfort which have already, it may be, resulted from it, the growth of dependence upon God above; meditate upon the real idea of separation, and think of Mamma and Uncle Frank.'

'August 26, 1855, 10.40 P.M.: S. Stephen's, Auckland. 'My dear Arthur,—I am tired with my Sunday work, which is heavy in a colony, but I just begin my note on the anniversary of your dear, dear father's death. How vividly I remember all the circumstances of the last ten days—the peaceful, holy, happy close of a pure and well-spent life! I do so think of him, not a day passing without my mind dwelling on him; I love to find myself calling up the image of his dear face, and my heart is very full when I recollect all his love for me, and the many, many tokens of affection which he used to pour out from his warm, generous, loving heart. I can hardly tell you what an indescribable comfort it is to me now I think of these things, cut off from the society and sympathy of friends and the associations of home; the memory is very active in recalling such scenes, and I almost live in them again. I have very little time for indulging in fancies of any kind now; I begin to get an idea of what work is; but in my walks or at night (if I am awake), I think of dear Mamma and your dear father, and others who are gone before, with unmixed joy and comfort. You may be quite sure that I am not likely to forget anybody or anything connected with home. How I do watch and follow them through the hours of the day or night when we are both awake and at our work! I turn out at 6.45, and think of them at dinner or tea; at 10, I think of them at evening prayers; and by my own bed-time they are in morning church or busied about their different occupations, and I fancy I can almost see them.

'So it goes on, and still I am calm and happy and very well; and I think I am in my place and hope to be made of some use some day. I like the natives in this school very much. The regular wild untamed fellow is not so pleasant at first—dirty, unclothed, always smoking, a mass of blankets, his wigwam sort of place filthy; his food ditto; but then he is probably intelligent, hospitable, and not insensible to the advantage of hearing about religion. It only wants a little practice to overcome one's English feelings about dress, civilisation, etc., and that will soon come.

'But here the men are nice fellows, and the women and girls make capital servants; and so whereas many of the clergy and gentry do not keep a servant (wages being enormous), and ladies like your sisters and mine do the whole work of the housemaid, nursery-maid, and cook (which I have seen and chatted about with them), I, on the contrary, by Miss Maria (a wondrous curly-headed, black-eyed Maori damsel, arrayed in a "smock," weiter nichts), have my room swept, bed made, tub—yes, even in New Zealand—daily filled and emptied, and indeed all the establishment will do anything for me. I did not care about it, as I did all for myself aboard ship; but still I take it with a very good grace.

'In about six weeks I expect we shall sail all round the English settlement of New Zealand, and go to Chatham Island. This will occupy about three months, and the voyage will be about 4,000 miles. Then we start at once, upon our return, for four months in the Bush, among the native villages, on foot. Then, once again taking ship, away for Melanesia. So that, once off, I shall be roving about for nearly a year, and shall, if all goes well, begin the really missionary life.

'It is late, and the post goes to morrow. Good-bye, my dear Arthur; write when you can.

'Ever your affectionate
'**J. C. PATTESON.**'

'August 27.—I have just been interrupted by Mrs. Kissling, who came to ask me to baptize privately the young son of poor Eota, the native deacon, and his wife Terena. Poor fellow! This child was born two or three days after he left this place for Taranaki with the Bishop, so he has not seen his son as yet. He has one boy about four, and has lost three or four others; and now this little one, about three weeks old, seems to be dying. I was almost glad that the first time I baptized a native child, using the native language, should be on Fan's birthday. It was striking to see the unaffected sympathy of the natives here. The poor mother came with the child in her arms to the large room. A table with a white cloth in the centre, and nearly the whole establishment assembled. I doubt if you would have seen in England grown-up men and women more thoroughly in earnest. It was the most comforting private baptism I ever witnessed.

'Henri has been for an hour or more this morning asking me questions which you would seldom hear from farmers or tradesmen at home, showing a real acquaintance with the Bible, and such a desire, hunger and thirst, for knowledge. What was the manna in the wilderness? he began. He thought it was food that angels actually lived upon, and quoted the verse in the Psalm readily, "So man did eat angel's food." So I took him into the whole question of the spiritual body; the various passages, "meats for the belly," etc., our Lord's answer to the Sadducees, and so on to 1 Cor. xv. Very interesting to watch the earnestness of the man and his real pleasure in assenting to the general conclusion expressed in 1 John iii. 2 concerning our ignorance of what we shall be, not implying want of power on God's part to explain, but His divine will in not withdrawing the veil wholly from so great a mystery. "E marama ana," (I see it clearly now): "He mea ngaro!" (a mystery). His mind had wholly passed from the carnal material view of life in heaven, and the idea of food for the support of the spiritual body, and the capacity for receiving the higher truths (as it were) of Christianity showed itself more clearly in the young New Zealander than you would find perhaps in the whole extent of a country parish. I think that when I know the language well enough to catechize freely, it will be far more interesting, and I shall have a far more intelligent set of catechumens, than in England. They seem especially fond of it, ask questions constantly, and will get to the bottom of the thing, and when the catechist is up to the mark and quick and wily in both question and illustration, they get so eager and animated, all answering together, quoting texts, etc. I think that their knowledge of the Bible is in some sense attributable to its being almost the only book printed that they care much about.'

The 11th of September produced another long letter full of home feeling, drawn forth in response to his sister. Here are some extracts:—

'Sometimes I cannot help wishing that I could say all this, but not often. There is One who understands, and in really great trials even, it is well to lean only on Him. But I must write freely. You will not think me moody and downhearted, because I show you that I do miss you, and often feel lonely and shut up in myself. This is exactly what I experience, and I think if I was ill, as you often are, I should break down under it; but God is very merciful to me in keeping me in very good health, so that I am always actively engaged every day, and when night comes I am weary in body, and sleep sound almost always, so that the time passes very rapidly indeed, and I am living in a kind of dream, hardly realizing the fact of my being at half the world's distance from you, but borne on from day to day, I scarcely know how. Indeed, when I do look back upon the past six months, I have abundant cause to be thankful. I never perhaps shall know fully how it is, but somehow, as a matter of fact, I am on the whole cheerful, and always busy and calm in mind. I don't have tumultuous bursts of feeling and overwhelming floods of recollection that sweep right away all composure. Your first letters upset me more than once as I re-read them, but I think of you all habitually with real joy and peace of mind. And I am really happy, not in the sense that happiness presents itself always, or exactly in the way that I used to feel it when with you all, or as I should feel it if I were walking up to the lodge with my whole heart swelling within me. It is much more quiet and subdued, and does not perhaps come and go quite as much; but yet in the midst of all, I half doubt sometimes whether everything about and within me is real. I just move on like a man in a dream, but this again does not make me idle. I don't suppose I ever worked harder, on the whole, than I do now, and I have much anxious work at the Hospital. Such cases, Fan! Only two hours ago, I left a poor sailor, by whose side I had been kneeling near three-quarters of an hour, holding his sinking head and moistening his mouth with wine, the dews of death on his forehead, and his poor emaciated frame heaving like one great pulse at each breath. For four days that he has been there (brought in a dying state from the Merchantman) I have been with him, and yesterday I administered to him the Holy Communion. He had spoken earnestly of his real desire to testify the sincerity of his repentance and faith and love. I have been there daily for nine days, but I cannot always manage it, as it is nearly two miles off. The responsibility is great of dealing with such cases, but I trust that God will pardon all my sad mistakes. I cannot withhold the Bread of Life when I see indications of real sorrow for sin, and the simple readiness to obey the command of Christ, even though there is great ignorance and but little time to train a soul for heaven. I cannot, as you may suppose, prepare for my Sunday work as I ought to do, from want of time. Last Sunday I had three whole services, besides reading the Communion Service and preaching at 11 A.M., and reading Prayers at 5 P.M. I should have preached five times but that I left my sermon at Mr. T.'s, thinking to go back for it.... Mrs. K. gave me an old "Woolmer" the other day, which gladdened my eyes. Little bits of comfort come in, you see, in these ways. Nothing can be kinder than the people here, I mean in Auckland and its neighbourhood—real, simple, hearty kindness. Perhaps the work at Kohimarama is most irksome to me. It is no joke to keep sailors in good humour ashore, and I fear that our presence on board was much needed during the passage out.'

With reference to his sister's reading, he continues:—'Take care of Maurice, Fan; I do not think it too much to say that he is simply and plainly "unsound" on the doctrine of the Atonement; I don't charge him with heresy from his standpoint, but remember that you have not been brought into contact with Quakers, Socinians, &c., and that he may conceive of a way of reconciling metaphysically difficulties which a far inferior but less inquisitive and vorsehender geist pronounces for itself simply contrary to the word of God. There are two Greek prepositions which contain the gist of the whole matter, huper, in behalf of, and anti, instead of, in the place of. Maurice's doctrine goes far to do away with the truth of the last, as applied to the Sacrifice of Christ. I have an exceedingly high regard for him, and respect for his goodness no less than his ability. His position has exposed him to very great difficulties, and therefore, if he is decidedly wrong, it is not for us to judge him. Read his "Kingdom of Christ," and his early books; but he is on very slippery and dangerous ground now. It is indeed a great and noble task to propose to oneself, viz.—to teach that God is our Father, and to expose the false and most unhappy idea that has at times prevailed of representing God as actuated by strong indignation, resentment, &c., against the human race, so that men turned from Him as from some fearful avenging power. This is the worst form of Anthropomorphism, but this is not the Scriptural idea of a just God. We cannot, perhaps, conceive of absolute justice; certainly we are no judges of God's own revealed scheme of reconciling Justice with Law, and so I call Maurice's, to a certain extent, human teaching, more philosophy than religion, more metaphysics than revelation.'

On the 22nd the Ordination took place, and the second Maori deacon was ordained, Levi (or according to Maori pronunciation, Eivata) Ahea, a man of about thirty-eight, whose character had long been tested. Immediately after, the Bishop, Mrs. Selwyn, Mr. Patteson, and the new deacon, set forth on a coasting expedition in the new vessel.

The language of the journal becomes nautical, and strong in praise of the conduct of the little ship, which took the party first to Nelson, where Sunday, the 7th of October, was spent, the Bishop going ashore while Patteson held a service for the sailors on board, first going round to the vessels anchored in the harbour to invite the men's attendance, but without much success. On the 10th he wrote:—

'Already I feel to a certain extent naturalized. I do not think I should despair of qualifying myself in three months for the charge of a native parish. I don't mean that I know the niceties of the language so as to speak it always correctly, but I should be able to communicate with them on ordinary subjects, and to preach and catechize. But, after all, Melanesia is becoming more and more a substantial reality.'

The history of Bishop Selwyn's visitation hardly belongs to Patteson's life; but after one Sunday morning's ministration at Queen Charlotte's Sound, Patteson was thus entreated: 'At 2.30 I was on shore again, and soon surrounded by some thirty or forty natives, with whom I talked a long while about the prospect of a clergyman being settled among them. "We want you! You speak so plainly, we can understand you!"

"'No, I am going to the islands, to the blacks there." (N.B. The Maoris speak of the Blacks with a little touch of contempt.)

"'You are wanted here! Never mind the blacks!"

"'Ought not the Gospel to be preached to them, too? They have no teacher. Is it not right they should be taught as you have been?"

"'Ke rae tika ana. Yes, yes, that is right!'"

The settlements, then new, of Canterbury and Dunedin were visited, and then, the Bishop remaining on shore on other work, the 'Southern Cross' started for the Chatham Isles, gaining high commendation for all the good qualities of which a schooner could be supposed capable.

'It was pretty to see the little, vessel running away from the great broad-backed rollers which rolled over the shore far above. Every now and then she shipped a sea, and once her deck was quite full of water, up to the gunwale nearly.' And as for her future skipper, he says, 'I had plenty of work at navigation. It really is very puzzling at first; so much to remember—currents, compass, variation, sun's declination, equation of time, lee way, &c. But I think I have done my work pretty well up to now, and of course it is a great pleasure as well as a considerable advantage to be able to give out the true and magnetic course of the ship, and to be able from day to day to give out her position.'

The Chatham Islands are dependencies of New Zealand, inhabited by Maoris, and as it has fallen to the lot of few to visit them, here is this extract concerning them:—

'I buried a man there, a retired sea captain who had spent some twenty years of his life in China, and his widow was a Chinese woman, a little dot of a thing, rather nice-looking. She spoke a little English and more Maori. We walked through the Pa to the burial-ground, some twenty natives all dressed in black, i.e. something black about them, and many in a good suit, attending the funeral. Levi had spent the day before (Sunday) with them and had told them about me. As I approached the Pa before the funeral they all raised the native cry of welcome, the "Tangi." I advanced, speaking to them collectively, and then went through the ceremony of shaking hands with each one in order as they stood in a row, saying something, if I could think of it, to each. After the funeral they all (according to native custom) sat down in the open air, round a large cloth on the ground, on which were spread tins of potatoes, fish, pork, &c. The leader came to me and said, "This is the Maori fashion. Come, my friend, and sit with us," and deposited three bottles of beer at my feet, while provisions enough for Dan Lambert were stored around—a sort of Homeric way of honouring me, and perhaps they made a Benjamin of me. However, I had already eaten a mouldy biscuit and had a glass of beer at the house of the Chinawoman, so I only said grace for them, and after talking a little while, I shook hands all round and went off. Their hands, being used as knives and forks, were not a little greasy; but of course one does not think of that.

As I passed the end of the Pa I heard a cry, and saw a very old man with a perfectly white beard, too old to come to the feast, who had crawled out of his hut to see me. He had nothing on but a blanket, and I was sorry I had not known of his being there, that I might have gone to the old gentleman, so we talked and shook hands, and I set off for my eight miles walk back. The whole island is one vast peat field, in many places below in a state of ignition; then the earth crumbles away below and pits are formed, rank with vegetation, splendid soil for potatoes.'

Christmas-day was spent at Wellington, in services on shore, the Christmas dinner eaten on board, but the evening spent at the Governor's in blind man's buff and other games with the children, then evening prayers on board for the crew. The stay at Wellington was altogether enjoyable, and it ended by Mr. Patteson taking the command of the vessel, and returning with Mrs. Selwyn to Auckland, while the Bishop pursued his journey by land, no small proof of the confidence inspired by so recent a mariner. He was sorry to lose the sight of the further visitation, and in his New Year's letter of 1856, written soon after receiving a budget from home, there is one little touch of home sickness:—

'Really it is a fine land, with wonderful facilities for large manufacturing, commercial, and agricultural interests; worth visiting, too, merely for the scenery, but somehow enjoying scenery depends a good deal upon having one's own friends to enjoy it with. One thing I do enjoy thoroughly, and that is the splendid sunsets. I don't remember anywhere to have seen such fine soft golden sunsets; and they are not wanting in variety, for occasionally he goes to bed among red and crimson and purple clouds, with wild scuds flying above, which suggest to me the propriety of turning up my bed and looking out for a good roll in the night. But there is certainly a peculiar transparency in the air which makes the distances look distant indeed.'

This trip, so cheerfully described, was rather a pull on the frame which had yet to become seasoned to the heat of the southern midsummer, and there was a languor about the outward man, the last remnant of the original sluggishness, which, if ever a doubt arose of the fitness of the instrument for the work, awoke it during the voyage. There was depression likewise, in part, no doubt, from the spending the first Christmas away from home and friends, and partly from a secret disappointment at the arrangement which made him for a time acting-master, not to say steward, of the ship, so that he had to live on board of her, and make himself useful on Sundays, according to need, in the churches on shore, a desultory life very trying to him, but which he bore with his usual quiet determination to do obediently and faithfully the duty laid on him, without picking or choosing.

The journal-letters continue on the 17th of January: 'Wrote a Maori sermon this morning, not feeling able yet to preach extempore in the native language, though it is much better to do so as soon as I can. Now I must stick to the vessel again. I have been quite frisky, really, for two days past, and have actually slept on shore, the fourth time since September 24. The sensation is exceedingly pleasant of firm ground underneath and clean water, a basin, &c., to wash in. And yet I almost like coming back to my ship home: it is really very comfortable, and you know I always liked being a good deal alone. I am reading, for lightish reading, the first part of the third volume of Neander's Church History, which is all about Missions. It is the fifth volume in the way his works are usually bound up, and came out in this box the other day. It is very interesting, especially to me now, and it is curious to observe how much the great men insisted upon the necessity of attending to the more secular part of missionary work,—agriculture, fishing, and other means of humanizing the social condition of the heathen among whom they lived. Columbanus and Boniface, and his pupil Gregory, and others (all the German Missionaries, almost) just went on the plan the Bishop wants to work out here.

'2. P.M. I am off to Otaki to see my native parishioners. What different work from calling in at S. W.'s and other good Alfingtonians! The walk will be pleasant, especially as I have been grinding away at navigation all the morning. My stupid head gets puzzled at that kind of work; and yet it is very good for me, just because it requires accuracy.

'29th. Just as I am beginning to get some hold of the Maori, so as to make real use of it, the Island languages are beginning to come into work. I have a curious collection here now—some given by the Judge, who is a great philologist, others belonging to the Bishop—a MS. grammar here, one chapter of St. Mark in another language, four Gospels in a third, a few chapters of Kings with the Lord's Prayer in a fourth, besides Marsden's Malay grammar and lexicon. Mrs. Nihill has given me some few sheets of the Nengone language, and also lent me her husband's MS. grammar. One letter, written (—);, but pronounced a sort of rg in the throat, yet not like an ordinary guttural, she declares took two years to learn. You may fancy I have enough to do, and then all my housekeeping affairs take up a deal of time, for I not only have to order things, but to weigh them out, help to cut out and weigh the meat, &c., and am quite learned in the mysteries of the store-room, which to be sure is a curious place on board ship. I hope you are well suited with a housekeeper: if I were at home I could fearlessly advertise for such a situation. I have passed through the preliminary steps of housemaid and scullerymaid, and now, having taken to serving out stores, am quite qualified for the post, especially after my last performance of making bread, and even a cake.'

This seems to be the right place for the description which the wife of Chief Justice Martin gives of Mr. Patteson at this period. The first meeting, she says, 'was the beginning of an intimate friendship, which has been one of the great blessings of our lives. After a short stay at St. John's College, he came into residence at St. Stephen's native institution, of which Archdeacon Kissling was then the Principal. He learned rapidly to read and speak Maori, and won all hearts there by his gentle unassuming manners. My husband was at that time a great invalid, and as our dear friend was living within five minutes' walk of our house he came in whenever he had a spare half-hour. He used to bring Archer Butler's sermons to read with us, and I well remember the pleasant talks that ensued. The two minds were drawn together by common tasks and habits of thought. Both had great facility in acquiring languages, and interest in all questions of philology. Both were also readers of German writers on Church history and of critical interpretation of the New Testament, and I think it was a help to the younger man to be able to discuss these and kindred subjects with an older and more trained mind. I had heard much of our dear friend before he arrived, and I remember feeling a little disappointed at first, though much drawn to him by his gentle affectionate thoughtfulness and goodness. He said little about his future work. He had come obedient to the call and was quietly waiting to do whatever should be set him to do. As my husband a few months later told Sir John Patteson, there was no sudden flame of enthusiasm which would die down, but a steady fire which would go on burning. To me he talked much of his home. He used to walk beside my pony, and tell me about "his dear father"—how lovingly his voice used to linger over those words!—of the struggle it had been to leave him, of the dreariness of the day of embarkation. Years after he could hardly bear to recall it to mind. I remember his bright look the first day it became certain that we must visit England. "Why, then you will see my dear father, and tell him all about me!" I knew all his people quite well before, and when I went to visit his little parish of Alfington I seemed to recognise each cottage and its humble inmates, so faithfully had he described his old people and haunts.

'One thing that specially impressed me was his reverent appreciation of the good he had gained from older friends. He certainly had not imbibed any of the indifference to the opinion of elders ascribed to the youth of this generation. "Dear old tutor," his uncles, Sir John Coleridge and Dr. Coleridge, to whom he looked up with almost filial reverence, the beloved Uncle Frank, whose holy life and death he dwelt on with a sort of awe, how gratefully and humbly he spoke of the help he had got from them! He was full of enthusiasm about music, painting, and art in general. He would flow on to willing listeners of Mendelssohn and other great composers, and when he found that we hoped to visit Italy he was just as eager about pictures. He owned that both at Dresden and at Rome he had weakened his eyes by constant study of his favourite masters.

'Altogether he gave me the impression of having had a very happy youth and having enjoyed it thoroughly. His Eton and Oxford life, the society of men of thought at his father's house, home interests, foreign travel, art, happy days with his brother Jem in the Tyrol, were all entertained as pleasant memories, and yet he was able without conscious effort or struggle to put them all aside for his work's sake.

'The Bishop kindly gave us a passage to Wellington in the "Southern Cross," and Mr. Patteson went with us in charge of the vessel. We were five days at sea. I used to lie on the deck, and watch with amused interest the struggle going on between his student habits and his practical duties, which were peculiarly distasteful to him. He was never quite well at sea, but was headachy and uncomfortable. He was scrupulously neat and clean, and the dirt and stiffness displeased him—how much we never knew, till he spoke out one day when very ill at our house in 1870. He was not apt at teaching, but he used conscientiously to hear a young lad spell and read daily. He would come up with some book of thought in his hand, and seemed buried in it, till he suddenly would remember he ought to be directing or overlooking in some way. This would happen half a dozen times in an afternoon.

'He shrank at this time from finding fault. It was a positive distress to him. At Wellington we parted. He seemed a little depressed, I remember, as to what use he would be. I said: "Why, you will be the son Timothy! This was after some years of partially failing health, when these feelings had become habitual. I do not think they existed in his earlier voyages so long waited for." His face brightened up at the thought. "Yes, if I can release the Bishop of some of his anxieties, that will be enough."'

No doubt he was depressed at parting with the Chief Justice and Mrs. Martin, who were thoroughly home-like friends, and whose return was then uncertain. His success as a sea-captain however encouraged him, and he wrote as follows on his return:—

'Kohimarama: March 6, 1856.
"Southern Cross."

'My dear Miss Neill,—How kind of you to write to me, and such a nice long letter. It cost you a great effort, I am sure, and much pain, I fear; but I know it was a comfort to you that it was written, and indeed it was a great happiness to me to read it. Oh, these letters! The intense enjoyment of hearing about you all at home, I know no pleasure like it now. Fond as I always was of reading letters and papers, the real happiness of a mail from England now is quite beyond the conception of any but a wanderer in foreign parts. Our mail went out yesterday at 2 P.M., rather unluckily for me, as I only returned from a very rapid and prosperous voyage to Wellington yesterday morning.

'I took the Chief Justice and Mrs. Martin (such dear, excellent people) to Wellington to meet the "Seringa-patam," homeward bound from that port; and I brought back from Wellington the Governor's sick wife and suite. Only absent a fortnight for a voyage of 1,100 miles, including three days' stay at Wellington. The coast of New Zealand is so uncertain, and the corners so many in coasting from Auckland to Wellington, that the usual passage occupies seven or eight days; and when the "Southern Cross" appeared yesterday morning in harbour, I was told by several of the officers and other residents that they feared we had put back from foul weather, or because the Judge could not bear the motion of the vessel. They scarcely thought we could actually have been to Wellington and returned.

'Most thankful am I for such a fine passage, for I had two sets of invalids, the Judge being only now (as we trust) recovering from a severe illness, and Mrs. Martin very weakly; and I felt the responsibility of having the charge of them very much. This was my second trip as "Commodore," the Bishop still being on his land journey; but we expect him in Auckland at the end of the month. As you may suppose, I am getting on with my navigation, take sights, of course, and work out errors of watches, place of ship, &c.; it is pretty and interesting work, and though you know well enough that I have no turn for mathematics, yet this kind of thing is rendered so easy nowadays by the tables that are constructed for nautical purposes, that I do not think I should feel afraid of navigating a ship at all. The "seamanship" is another thing, and that the master of the ship is responsible for.... You ask me, dear Miss Neill, where I am settled. Why, settled, I suppose I am never to be: I am a missionary, you know, not a "stationary." But, however, my home is the "Southern Cross," where I live always in harbour as well as at sea, highly compassionated by all my good friends here, from the Governor downwards, and highly contented myself with the sole possession of a cosy little cabin nicely furnished with table, lots of books, and my dear father's photograph, which is an invaluable treasure and comfort to me. In harbour I live in the cabin. It is hung round with barometers (aneroids), sympie-someters, fixed chest for chronometers, charts, &c. Of course, wherever the "Southern Cross" goes I go too, and I am a most complete skipper. I feel as natural with my quadrant in my hand as of old with a cricket bat. Then I do rather have good salt-water baths, and see glorious sunsets and sunrises, and star-light nights, and the great many-voiced ocean, the winds and waves chiming all night with a solemn sound, lapping against my ear as I lie in my canvas bed, six feet by two and a half, and fall sound asleep and dream of home. Oh! there is much that is really enjoyable in this kind of life; and if the cares of the vessel, management of men, &c., do harass me sometimes, it is very good for me; security from such troubles having been anxiously and selfishly pursued by me at home.

'If it please God to give success to our mission work, I may some day be "settled" (if I live) on some one of the countless islands of the South Pacific, looking after a kind of Protestant Propaganda College for the education of teachers and missionaries from among the islanders, but this is all uncertain.

'Now good-bye, my dear Miss Neill. I never doubt that in all your sufferings God does administer abundant sources of consolation to you. Even my life, so painless and easy, is teaching me that we judge of these things by a relative standard only, and I can conceive of one duly trained and prepared for heaven that many most blessed anticipations of future rest may be vouchsafed in the midst of extreme bodily pain. It is in fact a kind of martyrdom, and truly so when borne patiently for the love of Christ.

'Always, my dear Miss Neill,
'Your very affectionate,
'J. C. PATTESON.'

The Sundays were days of little rest. Clergy were too scarce for one with no fixed cure not to be made available to the utmost, and the undeveloped state of the buildings and of all appliances of devotion fell heavily and coldly on one trained to beauty, both of architecture and music, though perhaps the variety of employment was the chief trial. His Good Friday and Easter Sunday's journal show the sort of work that came on him:—

'Taurarua, Good Friday.—I am tired, for walking about in a hot sun, with a Melanesian kit, as we call them, slung round the neck, with clothes and books, is really fatiguing. Yesterday and to-day are just samples of colonial work. Thursday, 7.30, prayers in chapel; 10.30, Communion service in chapel. Walked two miles to see a parishioner of the Archdeacon's. 1.30, dinner; 2.30, walked to Taurarua, five and a half miles, in a burning sun; walked on to Mr. T.'s and back again, three miles and a half more. 7, tea, wrote a sermon and went to bed. To-day, service and sermon, for 600 soldiers at 9; Communion service and preached at 11. Back to Taurarua after three miles' walk, on to the College, and read prayers at 7. Not much work, it is true, but disjointed, and therefore more fatiguing. I do sometimes long almost for the rest of English life, the quiet evening after the busy day; but I must look on to a peaceful rest by and by; meanwhile work away, and to be sure I have a grand example in the Bishop.

'Easter Day.—I was at Tamaki chapel, a cold, bare, barn-like building of scoria, all this country being of volcanic origin. Fifty persons present perhaps: two or three faint female voices, two or three rough most discordant male voices, all the attempt at singing. No instrument of any kind. The burthen of trying to raise the tone of the whole service to a really rejoicing thankful character wholly, I suppose, upon myself, and I so unequal to it. But the happy blessed services themselves, they gradually absorbed the mind, and withdrew it from all relative and comparative ideas of externals of worship. What a training it is here for the appreciation of the wondrous beauty of our Church services, calming all feeling of excitement and irreverent passionate zeal, and enabling one to give full scope to the joy and glory of one's heart, without, I hope, forgetting to rejoice with reverence and moderation. Here, at Tamaki, you have nothing but the help the services themselves give, and I suppose that is very good for one in reality, though at the time it makes one feel as if something was wanting in the hearty sympathy and support of earnest fellow-worshippers. The College chapel nicely decorated.

'1st Sunday after Easter: Taurarua.—I walked in from the College yesterday afternoon, took the soldiers' service at 9.15 A.M., Communion service and sermon at St. Matthew's at 11, Hospital at 2.30. Preached at St. Paul's at 6 P.M., reminding me of my Sunday's work when I was living at St. Stephen's. It is a comfort to have a Sunday in Auckland occasionally—more like a Sunday, with a real church, and people responding and singing.'

So passed that first year, which many an intending missionary before Patteson has found a crucial test which he has not taken into his calculations. The soreness of the wrench from home is still fresh, and there is no settled or regular work to occupy the mind, while the hardships are exactly of the kind that have not been anticipated, and are most harassing, though unsatisfying to the imagination, and all this when the health is adapting itself to a new climate, and the spirits are least in time, so that the temper is in the most likely condition to feel and resent any apparent slight or unexpected employment. No one knows how many high hopes have sunk, how many intended workers have been turned aside, by this ordeal of the first year.

Patteson, however, was accepting whatever was distasteful as wholesome training in the endurance of hardships, and soon felt the benefit he reaped from it. The fastidiousness of his nature was being conquered, his reluctance to rebuke forced out of being a hindrance, and no doubt the long-sought grace of humility was rendered far more attainable by the obedient fulfilment of these lowly tasks.

CHAPTER VII. THE MELANESIAN ISLES. 1856-1857.

And now, in his twenty-ninth year, after all the unconscious preparation of his education, and the conscious preparation of two years, Coleridge Patteson began the definite work of his life. Bishop Selwyn was to sail with him in the "Southern Cross," making the voyage that had been intermitted during the expedition to England, introducing him to the Islands, and testing his adaptation to the work there. The first point was, however, to be Sydney, with the hope of obtaining leave to use Norfolk Island as the headquarters of the Mission. They meant to touch there, weather permitting, on their way northward.

Ascension Day was always Bishop Selwyn's favourite time for starting, so that the charge might be ringing freshly in his ears and those of his companions, 'Go ye and teach all nations, baptizing them in the name of the Father, and of the Son, and of the Holy Ghost.'

There was morning service and Holy Communion at the little College chapel on the 1st of May, Ascension Day of 1856; then the party went on board, but their first start was only to Coromandel Bay, in order that the Bishop might arrange a dispute with the Maoris, and they then returned to Auckland to take up Mrs. Selwyn. The crew were five in number, and Mr. Leonard Harper, son of the future Bishop of Lyttelton, likewise accompanied them, and relieved Patteson of his onerous duties as steward.

The first adventure was such a storm as the little vessel had never yet encountered. The journal-letter thus describes it:—'On Saturday morning it began to blow from the north-east, and for the first time I experienced a circular gale or hurricane. Mrs. Somerville, I think, somewhere describes the nature of them in her "Physical Geography." The wind veered and hauled about a point or two, but blew from the north-east with great force, till about seven P.M. we could do no more with it and had to lie to. Ask old D. what that means, if you can't understand my description of it. The principle of it is to set two small sails, one fore and one aft, lash the rudder (wheel) amidships, make all snug, put on hatches, batten everything down, and trust to ride out the storm. As the vessel falls away from the wind by the action of one sail, it is brought up to it again by the other-sail. Thus her head is always kept to the wind, and she meets the seas, which if they caught her on the beam or the quarter would very likely send her down at once. About midnight on Saturday the wind suddenly chopped round to W.S.W., so that we were near the focus of the gale; it blew harder and harder till we took down the one sail forward, as the ropes and spars were enough for the wind to act upon. From 1 P.M. to 7 P.M. on Sunday it blew furiously. The whole sea was one drift of foam, and the surface of the water beaten down almost flat by the excessive violence of the wind, which cut off the head of every wave as it strove to raise itself, and carried it in clouds of spray and great masses of water, driving and hurling it against any obstacle, such as our little vessel, with inconceivable fury. As I stood on deck, gasping for breath, my eyes literally unable to keep themselves open, and only by glimpses getting a view of this most grand and terrible sight, it seemed as if a furious snow-storm was raging over a swelling, heaving, dark mass of waters. When anything could be seen beyond the first or second line of waves, the sky and sea appeared to meet in one cataract of rain and spray. A few birds were driving about like spirits of the storm. It was, as Shakspeare calls it, a regular hurly. Add to this the straining of the masts, the creaking of the planks, the shrill whistle of the wind in the ropes and cordage, the occasional crash of a heavy sea as it struck us with a sharp sound, and the rush of water over the decks, down the companion and hatches, that followed, and you have a notion of a gale of wind. And yet this was far from all the wind and sea can do, and we were never in any danger, I believe. That is, an unlucky sea at such a time may be fatal, and if anything about the schooner had been unsound it might have been awkward. At prayers, the Bishop read the prayer to be used in a storm, but I never myself entertained the idea of our being really in peril, nor did I suffer anything like the anxiety that I did when we were rounding Cape Palliser on our way to Wellington with the Judge. Here we had sea room and no fear of driving upon rocks. It is blowing a good deal now, as you see by my writing. I have a small ink-bottle of glass, made like an eel-pot (such as tax-gatherers use), tied to my buttonhole, and with this I can scribble away in almost any sea. Dear me! you could not sit still a minute, even now. I was qualmish on Saturday, and for a minute sick, but pretty comfortable on Sunday, though wearied by the constant pitching and rolling.'

The day after this, namely May 15, the Bishop and Mr. Patteson rowed into Cascade Bay, Norfolk Island, amid a heavy surf, but they saw no cascade, as there had been no rain for a long time; and there were only rocks surmounted by pine trees, no living creature, no landing-place, as they coasted along. At last they saw a smooth-looking rock with an iron staple, and concluding that it was the way of approach, they watched their time, and through the surf which broke over it they leapt on it, and dashed ashore before the returning swell caught them. They walked inland, and met a man, one of twelve convicts who had been left behind to receive the Pitcairners, who had not yet arrived, but were on their way from their original island in H.M.S. 'Juno.' The vegetation and climate struck them as beautiful; there were oranges, lemons, sweet potatoes, and common potatoes, and English vegetables, and the Norfolk Island pine growing to a great height: 'but,' writes Coley, 'it is coarser in the leaf and less symmetrical in shape than I had expected. I thought to have seen the tree of Veitch's nursery garden on a scale three or four times as large, and so I might have done in any of the gardens; but as they grow wild in the forest, they are not so very different from the more common fir tribe.'

They saw one house, but had little time, and getting down to the smooth rock, stood there, barefooted, till the boat could back in between the rollers; the Bishop leapt in at the first, and the boat made off at once, and till it could return, Patteson had to cling to the clamps to hinder himself from being washed off, as six or seven waves broke over him before the boat could come near enough for another spring. These difficulties in landing were one of the recommendations of the island, by isolating the future inhabitants from the demoralising visits of chance vessels.

Then followed some days of great enjoyment of the calm warmth of the semi-tropical winter, chiefly varied by catching a young shark, and contrasting him with his attendant pilot, as the ugliest and prettiest of fish. Patteson used the calm to write (May 30) one of his introspective letters, owning that he felt physical discomfort, and found it hard to banish 'recollections of clean water, dry clothes, and drink not tasting like medicine; but that he most of all missed the perfect unconstrained ease of home conversation.'

Then he continues:—

'But now, don't you see, Fan, how good this is for me? If you think impartially of me, as you recollect me, you will see how soft and indolent I was, how easily I fell into self-indulgent habits, how little I cared to exert myself and try and exercise the influence, etc., a clergyman may be supposed to possess; there was nothing about me to indicate energy, to fit me for working out a scheme and stamping my own mind upon others who came in contact with me. Perhaps there is no one person who can trace any sensible influence to anything I ever did or said.

'Now I don't of course venture to say that this is otherwise now; but I think that this is the best training to make it so. I think that I ought to be gaining strength of purpose, resolution, energy of character, under these circumstances. And observe, what should I be without some such change pressing on me? Just imagine me, such a one as I was at Alfington, alone on an island with twenty-five Melanesian boys, from half as many different islands, to be trained, clothed, brought into orderly habits, &c., the report of our proceedings made in some sort the test of the working of the Mission; and all this to be arranged, ordered, and worked out by me, who found H. B―― and W. P―― a care too great for me.

'Don't you see that I must become very different from what I was—more of a man; to say nothing of the higher and religious side of this question? While then there is much that my carnal self-indulgent nature does not at all like, and while it is always trying to rebel, my better sense and the true voice within tells me that, independently of this particular work requiring such a discipline, the discipline itself is good for the formation of my own character.... Oh! the month of June at Feniton! the rhododendrons, azaleas, and kalmias, the burst of flowers and trees, the song of thrush and blackbird (both unknown to New Zealand). The green meadows and cawing rooks, and church towers and Sunday bells, and the bright sparkling river and leaping trout: and the hedges with primrose and violet (I should like to see a hedge again); and I am afraid I must add the green peas and beans, and various other garden productions, which would make salt pork more palatable! Yes, I should like to see it all again; but it is of the earth after all, and I have the "many-twinkling smile of Ocean," though there is no soft woodland dell to make it more beautiful by its contrast. Well, I have had a happy hour scribbling away, and now to work.'

'I am less distressed now,' he adds, a few days later, in the same strain, 'at the absence of all that is customary in England on these occasions (great festivals), though I dare not say how far the loss of all these privileges produces a bad effect upon my heart and character. One often loses the spirit when the form is withdrawn, and I still sorely long for the worship of God in the beauty of holiness, and my mind reverts to Ottery Church, and college chapels and vast glorious cathedrals.'

On the 10th of June the 'Southern Cross' was in Sydney harbour, and remained there a fortnight, Bishop Barker gladly welcoming the new arrivals, though in general Bishop Selwyn and his Chaplain announced themselves as like the man and woman in the weather-glass, only coming-out by turns, since one or other had to be in charge of the ship; but later an arrangement was made which set them more at liberty. And the churches at Sydney were a great delight to Patteson; the architecture, music, and all the arrangements being like those among which he had been trained.

'A Sunday worth a dozen gales of wind!' he exclaims, 'but you can hardly judge of the effect produced by all the good substantial concomitants of Divine worship upon one who for fourteen months has scarcely seen anything but a small wooden church, with almost all the warmth of devotion resting on himself. I feel roused to the core. ...I felt the blessing of worshipping the Lord with a full heart in the beauty of holiness. A very good organ well played, and my joy was great when we sang the long 78th Psalm to an old chant of itself almost enough to upset me, the congregation singing in parts with heart and voice.'

His exhilaration showed itself in a letter to his little cousin, Paulina Martin:—

"Southern Cross," Sydney Harbour: June 18, 1856.

'My darling Pena,—Are you so anxious to have a letter from me, and do you think I am going to forget all about you? However, you have had long before this two or three letters from me, I hope, and when I write to grandpapa or grandmamma or mamma, you must always take it as if a good deal was meant for you, for I have not quite so much time for writing as you have, I dare say, in spite of music and French and history and geography and all the rest of it. But I do dearly love to write to you when I can, and you must be quite certain that I shall always do so as I have opportunity.

'Don't you ever talk to me about any of your English watering-places and sea-port towns! No one knows anything about what an harbour can be for perfect beauty of earth, air, and sea, for wooded banks and rocky heights, and fine shipping and handsome buildings, and all the bustle and stir of a town of 80,000 inhabitants somehow lost and hidden among gum trees and Norfolk Island pines and parks and gravel walks; and everywhere the magnificent sea view breaking in upon the eye. Don't be angry, darling, for I love Dawlish very much, and would sooner go and sail the "Mary Jane" with you in some dear little basin among the rocks at low tide, and watch all the little crabs and other creatures with long Latin names, than walk about Sydney arm-in-arm with the Bishops of New Zealand and Newcastle, to call on the Governor. But I must say what I think about the natural scenery of places that I visit, and nowhere, even in New Zealand—no, not even in Queen Charlotte's Sound, nor in Banks's Peninsula, have I seen anything so completely beautiful as this harbour—'"heoi ano" "that's enough." The Governor told us yesterday that when he was at Hobart Town, he made the convicts cut a path through one of the deep gullies running down from a mountain 4,500 feet high to the sea. The path was two miles long, and all the way the tree-ferns, between twenty and thirty feet high, formed a natural roof arched and vaulted like the fretted roofs of our Tudor churches and chapels. There is a botanical garden here with a very good collection of all the Australian trees and shrubs, and with many New Zealand and many semi-tropical plants besides. All the English flowers and fruits grow here as well, so that in the warmer months it must look beautiful. It is close to the sea, which runs here in little creeks and bays close up among the public walks and buildings; and as the shore is all rocky and steep at low water, there is no mud or swamp or seaweed, but only clear green water quite deep and always calm and tranquil, because the harbour is so broken up and diversified by innumerable islets, gulfs, &c., that no wind can raise any sea of consequence in it.

'Just now it is winter time—slight frost at night, but no appearance of it after the sun is up; bright hot days, and bracing cold nights, the very perfection of a climate in winter, but in summer very hot. It is so funny to me to see regular stone and brick houses, and shops, and carriages, and cabs, &c., all quite new to me.

'To-night there is a great missionary meeting. Bishops of Sydney, New Zealand, and Newcastle present. Bishop of Newcastle and a Mr. King advocate the cause of the Australian blacks, and the Bishop of New Zealand and unfortunate I have to speechify about Melanesia. What on earth to say I don't know, for of course the Bishop will exhaust the subject before me.

'However, I must try and not be in a great fright; but I would sooner by half be going to have a talk with a parcel of Maoris. Now, you must get Fanny Patteson to tell you all about our voyage from New Zealand, our adventure at Norfolk Island, &c.

'We sail on Monday, 23rd, for Norfolk Island again, as it is in our way to the Solomon group, because we shall get the S.E. trades just about there, and so run away in style to the Solomon Islands, and perhaps farther north still, but that is not probable this time.

'Always, my darling,
'Your affectionate cousin,
'J. C. PATTESON.'

This meeting was called by the Australian Board of Missions to receive information or propositions concerning the missions to the Australians and Melanesians. Bishop Barker of Sydney was in the chair, and the Bishop of Newcastle, who had made one Melanesian cruise in the 'Border Maid,' was likewise present. The room was crowded to excess, and from 900 to 1,000 were certainly present, many more failing to get in. Afterwards Patteson writes to his father:—

'The Bishop of New Zealand, in introducing me to the meeting, spoke before all these people of you and me in a way that almost unnerved me, and I had to speak next. What he said is not reported, or very badly—calling me his dear friend, with his voice quivering—I never saw him more, or so much affected—"I ought to be most thankful to God for giving me so dear a companion, &c." But he spoke so of you, and people here seemed to know of you, coming up to me, and asking about you, after the meeting. The Bishop of Newcastle spoke of you most kindly, and really with very great feeling. An evening I had dreaded ended happily. Before I dined with the three Bishops; last night with Chief Justice Sir Alfred Stephen, and met the trio again, Bishop everywhere speaking of me as one of his family. "No, my boys are not with me; but we have my dear friend Mr. Patteson." Of course all this exhibition of feeling never comes out when we are alone, we know each other too well. And now the romance of Mission work is over, and the real labour is to begin. There has been bad work among the islands lately, but you know in whose hands we are.'

The collections both at the door and on the following Sunday were very large, and a strong warm feeling was excited in Sydney which has never since died away. Mr. Patteson was much beloved there, and always met with kind welcome and ready assistance from all classes. But there was one great disappointment. The Bishop of New Zealand, on formally setting before Sir William Denison, Governor-General of Australia, his plan for making Norfolk Island the site of a school for training Melanesian teachers, and eventually the seat of a bishopric, received a refusal, and was not permitted even to place a chaplain there. Sir William, as he tells us in his published diary, had heard from some quarter or other rumours respecting the Melanesian scholars which made him suppose that their presence might have a bad effect upon the Pitcairners; and repeated that his instructions were that the islanders should be left as much as possible to themselves. The request to be permitted to place Mr. Patteson there was refused on the ground that Norfolk Island belonged to the see of Tasmania, and not to that of New Zealand. But the Bishop of Tasmania could hardly visit it without great inconvenience, and he had therefore placed it under the care of his brother of New Zealand, full in whose track it lay. The matter was referred to the Colonial Secretary, and in the meantime Bishop Selwyn adhered to his purpose of visiting it on leaving Sydney, and though he could not place his chaplain there, leaving Mrs. Selwyn to assist in the work of training the new comers to the novelties of a more temperate climate and a more genial soil than they had known on the torrid rock of Pitcairn's Island.

Accordingly, on the 4th of July, the 'Southern Cross' again approached the island, and finding that the Pitcairners had come, and that their magistrate and Mr. Nobbs, their clergyman, would gladly welcome assistance, the Bishop brought Mrs. Selwyn on shore, and left her there to assist Mr. Nobbs in preparing the entire population to be confirmed on his return. But the Pitcairners have been amply written about, and as Coleridge Patteson's connection with them was only incidental, I shall not dwell on them or their history.

The 'Southern Cross' reached Anaiteum on the 14th of July. This island was occupied by Mr. Inglis and Mr. Greddie, of the Scottish Presbyterian Mission, who had done much towards improving the natives. Small canoes soon began to come off to the vessel, little craft consisting of no more than the trunk of a tree hollowed out, seldom more than a foot broad, and perhaps eighteen inches deep, all with outriggers—namely, a slight wooden frame or raft to balance them, and for the most part containing two men, or sometimes three or four. Before long, not less than fifteen or twenty had come on board, with woolly hair and mahogany skins, generally wearing a small strip of calico, but some without even this. They were small men, but lithe and supple, and walked about the deck quite at ease, chattering in a language no one understood except the words 'Missy Inglis,' as they pointed to a house. Presently another canoe arrived with a Samoan teacher with whom the Bishop could converse, and who said that Mr. Geddie was at Mare. They were soon followed by a whale boat with a Tahitian native teacher, a Futuma man, and a crew of Anaiteans.

'The Futuma man had expended his energies upon his hair, which was elaborately dressed after a fashion that precluded the possibility of any attention being bestowed upon the rest of his person, which was accordingly wholly unencumbered with any clothing. The perfection of this art apparently consisted in gathering up about a dozen hairs and binding them firmly with grass or fine twine of cocoa-nut fibre plastered with coral lime. As the hair grows, the binding is lengthened also, and only about four or five inches are suffered to escape from this confinement, and are then frizzed and curled, like a mop or a poodle's coat. Leonard Harper and I returned in this boat, Tahitian steering, Samoan, Futuman, and Anaiteans making one motley crew. The brisk trade soon carried us to the beach in front of Mr. Inglis's house, and arrived at the reef I rode out pick-a-back on the Samoan, Leonard following on a half-naked Anaitean. We soon found ourselves in the midst of a number of men, women and children, standing round Mr. Inglis at the entrance of his garden. I explained to him the reason of the Bishop's being unable to land, that he alone knew the harbour on the other side of island, and so could not leave the vessel.

'Then, having delivered the boxes and letters we had brought for him from Auckland, we went into his house, gazing with delight at cocoanut trees, bananas, breadfruit trees, citrons, lemons, taro, &c., with bright tropical colouring thrown over all, lighting up the broad leaves and thick foliage of the trees around us.

'The house itself is built, after the fashion of these islands, of wattle plastered with coral lime, the roof thatched with the leaves of the cocoa-nut and pandana; the fences of the garden were made of cane, prettily worked together in a cross pattern; the path neatly kept, and everything looking clean and tidy. We sat down in a small, well-furnished room, and looked out upon the garden, verandah, and groups of men and women standing outside. Presently Mrs. Inglis came into the room, and after some discussion I was persuaded to stay all night, since the schooner could not reach her anchorage before dark, and the next day the water-casks were to be filled.

'An excellent dinner was provided: roast fowl with taro, a nutritious root somewhat like potato, rice and jam, bananas and delicious fruit, bread and Scotch cheese, with glasses of cocoa-nut milk.

'Afterwards he showed us the arrangements for boarding young men and women—twelve of the former, and fourteen of the latter. Nothing could well exceed the cleanliness and order of their houses, sleeping rooms, and cooking rooms. The houses, wattled and plastered, had floors covered with native mats, beds laid upon a raised platform running round the inner room, mats and blankets for covering, and bamboo cane for a pillow. The boys were, some writing, some making twine, some summing, when we went in; the girls just putting on their bonnets, of their own manufacture, for school.

'They learn all household work—cooking, hemming, sewing, &c.; the boys tend the poultry, cows, cultivate taro, make arrowroot, &c. All of them could read fluently, and all looked happy, clean, and healthy. The girls wear their native petticoats of cocoa-nut leaves, with a calico body. Boys wear trousers, and some had shirts, some waistcoats, and a few jackets.

'We walked about a small wood adjoining the house, through which a small fresh-water stream runs. In the wood we saw specimens of the various trees and shrubs, and flowers of the island, including those already noticed in Mr. Inglis's garden, and the breadfruit tree and sugar-cane, and a beautiful bright flower of scarlet colour, a convolvulus, larger than any I had ever seen elsewhere; also a tree bearing a very beautiful yellow flower.

'We then returned to the house, and shortly afterwards went to the church, which is at present used also as the school-house, though the uprights of a larger school-house are already fixed in the ground.

'Men, women, and children to the number of ninety-four had assembled in a large oblong building, wattled and plastered, with open windows on all sides; mats arranged on the floor, and a raised platform or bench running round the building for persons who prefer to sit after the English, instead of the native fashion,

'All that were called upon to read did so fluently; the singing was harsh and nasal enough, but in very good time; their counting very good, and their writing on slates quite equal to the average performance, I am satisfied, of a good English parish school. They listened attentively when Mr. Inglis spoke to them, and when at his request I said a few words, which he translated. The most perfect order and quiet prevailed all the time we were in the school. At the end of the lessons they came forward, and each one shook hands with Leonard Harper and myself, smiling and laughing with their quick intelligent eyes, and apparently pleased to see strangers among them.

'By this time it was dusk, and we went back to the Mission House, and spent a pleasant evening, asking and answering questions about Anaiteum and the world beyond it, until 8 P.M., when the boarders came to prayers, with two or three persons who live about the place. They read the third chapter of St. Matthew's Gospel in turns, verse by verse, and then a prayer from Mr. Inglis followed. At 8.30 we had private family prayers, and at 9 went to bed.

'July 16.—We got up at four, and were soon ready for our walk to the south side of the Island; Mr. Inglis came with us, and ten or twelve natives. For the first half-mile we walked along the beach among cocoa-nut trees, bananas and sugar-canes, the sun, not yet above the horizon, tingeing the light clouds with faint pink and purple lines, the freshness of the early dawn, and the soft breeze playing about us, gladdening at once our eyes and our hearts. Soon we struck off to the south, and passing through taro plantations, began to ascend the slopes of the island. As we walked along we heard the sound of the logs beaten together, summoning the people to attend the various schools planted in every locality, under the management of native teachers, and we had a good opportunity of observing the careful system of irrigation adopted by the natives for the cultivation of the taro plant. Following the course of a small mountain stream, we observed the labour with which the water was brought down from it upon causeways of earth, carried in baskets from very considerable distances; occasionally the water-course is led round the head of various small ravines; at other times the trunk of a tree is hollowed out and converted into an aqueduct; but no pains have been wanting to make provision for the growth of the staple food of the island.'

From this scene of hope and encouragement the 'Southern Cross' sailed on the sixteenth, and passing Erromango, came in sight of Fate, also called Sandwich, a wooded island beautiful beyond description, but with a bad character for cannibalism, and where the Samoan teachers had been murdered. So the approach was cautious, and the vessel kept a mile from the shore, and was soon surrounded with canoes, one of them containing a native who had been instructed in Samoa, and was now acting as teacher.

'The first canoe that came had five men on board. Girdles of beautifully plaited cocoa-nut fibre round their waists were their only clothing, but some had wreaths of flowers and green leaves round their heads, and most of them wore mother-of-pearl shells, beads, &c., round their necks and in their ears. They do not tattoo, but brand their skins. All five came, and presently three more, and then another; but seeing a large double canoe with perhaps twenty men in her coming close, we stood away. Two of our visitors chose to stay, and we have them on board now: Alsoff, a man of perhaps forty-five, and Mospa, a very intelligent young man from whom I am picking up words as fast as I can. F. would have laughed to have seen me rigging them out in calico shirts, buttoning them up. Mospa gave me his wooden comb, which they push through their hair, as you ladies do coral or gold pins at parties. Another fellow whose head was elaborately frizzled and plastered with coral lime, departed with one of my common calico pocket-handkerchiefs with my name in Joan's marking. This is to adorn his head, and for aught I know, is the first, and certainly the best specimen of handwriting in the island. We hope to call at all these islands on our way back from the north, but at present we only dodge a few canoes, &c.

'July 20.—I suppose you like to know all little things, so I tell you that our Fate friends, being presented each with a blanket, just wound themselves up on the cabin floor, one close to Leonard and me, and slept away in style; that I soon taught them to eat with a knife and fork, and to-day have almost succeeded in making them believe that plum pudding (our Sunday dish) is a fine thing.

'July 21.—All day we have been very slowly drifting along the west side of Espiritu Santo. A grand mountainous chain runs along the whole island, the peaks we estimate at 4,000 feet high. This alone is a fine sight—luxuriant vegetation to nearly the top of the peaks, clouds resting upon the summit of the range, from the evaporation caused by the vast amount of vegetable matter.

'As we were lying to, about half-way along the coast, we espied a brig at anchor close on shore. Manned the boat and rowed about two miles to the brig, found it was under the command of a notorious man among the sandal-wood traders for many a dark deed of revenge and unscrupulous retaliation upon the natives. At Nengone he shot three in cold blood who swam off to his ship, because the people of the place were said to be about to attempt to take his vessel. At Mallicolo but lately I fear he killed not less than eight, though here there was some scuffling and provocation. For the Nengone affair he was tried for his life at Sydney, Captain Erskine and the Bishop having much to do with his prosecution. He is now dealing fairly (apparently) with these people, and is certainly on very friendly terms with them. The Bishop has known him many years, and baptized some years ago his only child, a son. We are glad to let these men see that we are about in these seas, watching what they do; and the Bishop said, "Mr. Patteson is come from England on purpose to look after these islands," as much as to say, Now there will be a regular visitation of them, and outrages committed on the natives will probably be discovered.

'Well, on we rowed, half a mile to shore—such a lovely scene. A bend in the coral reef made a beautiful boat harbour, and into it we rowed. Clear as crystal was the water, bright as tropical sun at 2.30 P.M. could make it was the foliage on the shore. Numbers of children and boys were playing in the water or running about on the rocks and sands, and there were several men about, all of course naked, and as they lead an amphibious life they find it very convenient. They work little; breadfruit trees, cocoa-nut trees, and bananas grow naturally, and the yam and taro cultivations are weeded and tended by the women. They have nothing to do but eat, drink, and sleep, and lie on the warm coral rock, and bathe in the surf.

'There was no shyness on the part of the children, dear little fellows from six to ten clustering round me, unable to understand my coat with pockets, and what my socks could be—I seemed to have two or three skins. The men came up and soon shook hands, but did not seem to know the custom. A Nengone man was ashore, and with him I could talk a little. Soon I was walking on shore arm-in-arm with him, stark naked, and he was asking me about Mrs. Nihill and her child. A little boy of the island held the other hand, and so, leaving the boat, we walked inland into the bush to see a native village. Ten minutes' walk brought us to it—cottages all of bamboos tied together with cocoa-nut fibre, thatched with leaves, a ridge-pole and sloping roof on either side reaching to the ground. No upright poles or side-walls; they were quite open at the two ends, perhaps 20, 30, or even 40 feet long; the general appearance clean and healthy. Their food was kept on raised stages as in New Zealand, and they had plenty of earthenware pots and basins, some of good shape, and all apparently strong and serviceable. Large wooden or earthenware platters are used for stirring up and pounding the yams with a heavy wooden pestle, and they have a peculiar way of scraping the yam, on a wooden board roughened like a grater, into a pulp, and then boiling it into a fine dough.

'They have plenty of pigs and dogs, which they eat, and some fowls. Spears I saw none, but bows and arrows. I took a bow out of a man's hand, and then an arrow, and fitted it to the string; he made signs that he shot birds with it. Clubs they have, but as far as I saw only used for killing pigs. There is a good deal of fighting on the island, however. Recollect with reference to all these places, that an island fifty or sixty miles long, one mass of forest with no path, is not like an

English county. It may take months to get an accurate knowledge of one of them; we can only at present judge of the particular spots and bays we touch at. But there is every indication here of friendliness, of a gentle, soft disposition, and I hope we shall take away some of the boys when we return. I never saw children more thoroughly attractive in appearance and manner,—dear little fellows, I longed to bring off some of them. You would have liked to have seen them playing with me, laughing and jumping about. These people don't look half so well when they have any clothes on, they look shabby and gentish; but seeing them on shore, or just coming out of a canoe, all glistening with water, and looking so lithe and free, they look very pleasant to the eye. The colour supplies the place of clothing. The chief and most of the men were unfortunately absent at a great feast held a few miles off, but there were several women and many children.

'We went to their watering place, about a quarter or half a mile from the beach, a picturesque spot in a part of the wood to which the water from the hills is carried in canes of bamboo, supported on cross sticks. The water was very clear and sweet, and one of our little guides soon had a good shower-bath, standing under the shoot and then walking in the sun till in a few minutes his glistening skin was dry again. Coming back we met a man carrying water in cocoa-nut shells, six or eight hanging by strings two feet long at each end of a bamboo cane slung across over his shoulder, nicely balanced and very pretty. One of our party carried perhaps two and a half gallons of water in a bamboo stuffed at the end with grass. About five P.M. we went back to the schooner and made sail for Bauro (San Cristoval).'

At this place there was a great disappointment at first in the non-appearance of William Diddimang, an old baptized scholar at St. John's; and though he came at last, and dined on board, he had evidently so far fallen away as to be unwilling to meet the Bishop. The canoes here were remarkably beautiful, built of several pieces, fastened with a kind of gum. The shape was light and elegant, the thwarts elaborately carved with figures of birds or fish, and the high prow inlaid with mother-of-pearl let into black wood.

As a Sunday at sea was preferable to one among curious visitors who must be entertained, the schooner put out to sea to visit one to two other neighbouring islets, and then to return again to Bauro.

Kennell Island, where she touched on the 27th, proved to be inhabited by Maoris. One man, who swam alone to the vessel, offered the salutation of rubbing noses, New Zealand fashion, and converse could be held in that language. Two more joined him, and spent the night on board in singing a kaka or song of love for their visitors. Next day the island was visited. 'Oh the beauty of the deep clefts in the coral reef, lined with coral, purple, blue, scarlet, green, and white! the little blue fishes, the bright blue starfish, the little land-crabs walking away with other people's shells. But nothing of this can be seen by you; the coral loses its colour, and who can show you the bright line of surf breaking the clear blue of this truly Pacific Ocean, and the tropical sun piercing through masses of foliage which nothing less dazzling could penetrate. Our three friends, with two more men, their wives and children, form the whole population of the south end of the island at all events, perhaps twenty in all. I trod upon and broke flowering-branches of coral that you would have wondered at.'

Bellona likewise had a Maori-speaking population. There was no passage through the reef, so the Bishop and Patteson took off their coats, one took two hatchets and the other two adzes, and with a good header, swam ashore. Walking up the beach, they found a place in the bush with nine beautiful canoes, with nets, and large wooden hooks in them, but at first no people; and they were leaving their presents in the canoes when Patteson spied two men, and advanced to them while the Bishop went back to fetch the goods. After a rubbing of noses and a Maori greeting, the men were reassured, and eleven more came up, one a chief with a spear in his hand. 'I had my straw hat fastened by a ribbon, which my friend coveted, so I let him take it, which he did by putting his adze (my gift) against it, close to my ear, and cutting it, off—not the least occasion to be afraid of them.' A characteristic comment, certainly! But there was no foolhardiness. The Bishop was on the alert, and when presently he saw his companion linger for a moment, a quick 'Come along,' was a reminder that 'this was not the beach at Sidmouth.' The peculiar quickness of eye—verily circumspect, though without the least betrayal of alarm or want of confidence, which was learnt from the need of being always as it were on guard, was soon learnt likewise by Patteson, while the air of suspicion or fear was most carefully avoided. The swim back to the boat was in water 'too warm, but refreshing,' and ended with a dive under the boat for the pure pleasure of the thing.

Then, as before arranged, Bauro was revisited on another part of the coast, where Iri was ready with a welcome, but Diddimang appeared no more. He had returned to native habits, and had made no attempt at teaching, but the visits he had made to New Zealand were not lost, for the Bishop had acquired a knowledge of the language, and it was moreover established in the Bauro mind that a voyage in his ship was safe and desirable. 'This part of Bauro was exceedingly beautiful:—

'Here were coral crags, the masses of forest trees, the creepers literally hundreds of feet long, crawling along and hanging from the cliffs, the cocoa-nut trees and bananas, palms, &c., the dark figures on the edge of the rocks looking down upon us from among the trees, the people assembling on the bright beach—coral dust as it may be called, for it was worn as fine as white sand—cottages among the trees, and a pond of fresh water close by, winding away among the cliffs.'

Here a visit was paid to Iri's boathouse, which contained three exquisite canoes, beautifully inlaid; then to his house, long, low, and open at the ends, like those formerly described, but with low wattled side walls. Along the ridge-pole were ranged twenty-seven skulls, not yet blackened with smoke, and bones were scattered outside, for a fight had recently taken place near at hand. 'In this Golgotha,' the Bishop, using his little book of Bauro words, talked to the people, and plainly told them that the Great God hated wars and cruelty, and such ornaments were horrible in his sight. Iri took it all in good part, and five boys willingly accepted the invitation to New Zealand. One little fellow about eight years old had attached himself to Coley, clinging about his waist with his arms, but he was too young to be taken away. Iri came down to the beach, and waded up to his waist in the water as the boat put off.

In the night Gera, or Guadalcanar, was reached, a fine mountainous island, with a detached reef. Numerous canoes surrounded the vessel, bringing yarns for barter. Fish-hooks were of no account; it was small hatchets that were in request, and the Bauro boys could hold some sort of converse with the people, though theirs was quite another dialect. They were gaily decked out with armlets, frontlets, bracelets, and girdles of shell, and almost all of them wore, not only nose-rings, but plugs of wood or mother-of-pearl in the tip of the nose. One man in particular had a shell eyelet-hole let into his nose, into which he inserted his unicorn decoration. The Bishop amused himself and Coley by saying, as he hung a fishhook on this man's nose-hook, 'Naso suspendis adunco.' Others had six or eight pieces of wood sticking out from either side of the nose, like a cat's whiskers. Two young men were taken from hence, and more would have gone, but it was not thought well to take married men.

The isle of Mara or Malanta had a very shy population, who seemed to live inland, having probably been molested by the warlike Gera men. It had been supposed that there was a second islet here, but the 'Southern Cross' boat's crew found that what had been taken for a strait was only the mouth of a large river, where the casks were filled.

The wondrous beauty of the scene, sea and river alike fringed with the richest foliage, birds flying about (I saw a large blue bird, a parrot, I suppose), fish jumping, the perfectly still water, the mysterious smoke of a fire or two, the call of a man heard in the bush, just enough of novelty to quicken me to the full enjoyment of such a lovely bay as no English eyes save ours have ever seen.'

No communication with the native inhabitants was here accomplished, but at four little flat, cocoanut-covered islets, named after Torres, were the head-quarters of an English dealer in cocoa-nut oil. The native race were Maori-speaking, but their intercourse with sailors had given them a knowledge of the worst part of the English language, and as usual it was mournfully plain how much harm our countrymen instil.

The next group, sighted on the 17th of August, had already a remarkable history, to which Patteson refers in his journal, with no foreboding of the association those reefs and bays were to acquire for him, and far more through him.

Alvaro de Mendana had, in 1567, gone forth from Peru on a voyage of discovery in the Pacific, and had then found, and named, most of the Solomon Isles. Grera and Bauro owed their names of Guadalcanar and San Cristoval to him. In 1594, he obtained permission to found a colony on San Cristoval, and set forth with his wife and four ships. But the Bauro people were spared that grievous misfortune of a Spanish settlement; Mendana missed his way, blundered into the Marquesas first, and then came upon a cluster of islands, one large and beautiful, two small, and one a volcano in full action.

He called the large island Santa Cruz, and fancied the natives of the same race he had seen in Bauro, but they knew nothing of the language he had learnt there, and though courteous at first, presently discharged their arrows. However, he found a beautiful harbour on the other side of the island, and a friendly and dignified old chief called Malope, who in South Sea fashion exchanged names and presents with him. Mendana and his wife Dona Ysabel seem to have wished to be on good terms with the natives, and taught them to sign the cross, and say amigos, and they proceeded to found their intended city, but neither Mendana nor Malope could restrain their followers; there were musket-shots on one side and arrow-shots on the other, and at last, the chief Malope himself fell into the hands of some Spanish soldiers, who murdered him. Mendana punished them with death; but his own health was fast failing, he died in a few weeks, and his widow deserted the intended city, and returned home with the colonists, having probably bequeathed to the island a distrust of white men.

All this was in Patteson's mind, as he shows by his journal, as the lovely scenery of Santa Cruz rose on him. The people came out in canoes with quantities of yams and taro, of which they knew the full value; but the numbers were so large that no 'quiet work' could be done, and there was little to be done but to admire their costume, armlets, necklaces, plates of mother-of-pearl, but no nose ornaments. They had strips of a kind of cloth, woven of reed, and elaborate varieties of head-gear, some plastering their hair white with coral lime, others yellow, others red; others had shaved half the head with no better implement than a sharp shell, and others had produced two lines of bristles, like hogs' manes, on a shaven crown. Their decorations made a great sensation among the Solomon Islanders, who made offers of exchange of necklaces, &c.

In the evening the schooner made for the volcano, about three miles off. It was a magnificent sight—a perfect cone, the base of the mountain and all except the actual cone being under water. The cone was apparently about 2,000 feet high, clouds hanging about it near the top, lurid and fiery, increasing the grandeur of the glow at the summit. Every minute streams of fire, falling from the top or sides, rushed down the mount, so that for a space of perhaps half a mile in breadth the whole cone was always streaked, and sometimes covered with burning-masses of stones, cinders, &c. Bumbling noises were heard only a few times.

'About 7 to 9 A.M. we sailed quite round the island, and saw there that the fiery appearance at night is not actually fire or flame, but caused by hot burning stones and masses of scoria, &c., constantly falling down the sides of the cone, which on the lee side are almost perpendicular. On the weather side are cocoa-nut trees, and one small house, but we could see no people. It was grand to see the great stones leaping and bounding down the sides of the cone, clearing 300 or 400 feet at a jump, and springing up many yards into the air, finally plunging into the sea with a roar, and the splash of the foam and steam combined.

This was on the 12th of August, and here is the ensuing note, how full now of significance, which it would be faithless to term melancholy:—'We then went on to Nukapu, an island completely encircled by a coral reef. The natives soon came off in canoes, and brought breadfruit and cocoa-nuts. They spoke a few words of

Maori, but wore their hair like the people of Santa Cruz, and resembled them in the character of their ornaments and in their general appearance. They had bows and clubs of the same kind, tapa stained with turmeric, armlets, ear-rings and nose-rings of bone and tortoiseshell.'

Returning to Santa Cruz, a large supply of the produce was obtained by barter, but the people were still in such noisy crowds that nothing could be effected beyond these commercial transactions.

Tubua was the next ensuing island, a lovely spot within its encircling ring, over which the Bishop and Patteson waded, and found thirteen men on the beach. Patteson went up to the first, tied a bit of red tape round his head, and made signs that he wanted a cocoa-nut in exchange for a fish-hook. Plenty were forthcoming; but the Bishop, to his companion's surprise, made a sudden sign to come away, and when the boat was regained he said: 'I saw some young men running through the bush with bows and arrows, and these young gentry have not the sense to behave well like their parents.'

Vanikoro was the next stage. This too had its history, encircled as it is with a complete reef of coral, in some parts double. In the year 1785, two French vessels, which were commanded by Count La Perouse, and named 'La Boussole' and 'L'Astrolabe,' had set forth from Brest on a voyage of discovery in the Pacific. They made a most discursive survey of that ocean, from Kamtschatka southwards, and at the end of 1787 were at the Samoan Isles, then unconverted, and where their two boats' crews were massacred, and the boats lost. The ships came to Port Jackson, in Australia, to build fresh boats, left it in February 1788, and were never heard of more. One or two attempts were made to ascertain their fate, but none succeeded till, in 1826, a sandal-wood trader named Dillon found in the possession of a European, who had lived since 1813 in Ticopia, the silver guard of a sword, and ascertained from him that the natives had several articles, such as china, glass, and the handle of a silver fork, which evidently came from a ship. He had been told that these articles had been procured from another isle called Vanikoro, where two large ships had been wrecked.

His intelligence led to the fitting out of a vessel, in which he was sent to ascertain the fate of the Frenchmen, and by the help of the man who had been so long in Ticopia, he was able to examine a Vanikoran chief. It appeared that the two ships had run aground on the parallel reefs. One had sunk at once, and the crew while swimming out had been some of them eaten by the sharks, and others killed by the natives; indeed, there were sixty European skulls in a temple. The other vessel had drifted over the reef, and the crew entrenched themselves on shore, while building another vessel. They went out and foraged for themselves in the taro fields, but they made no friends; they were ship-spirits, with noses two hands long before their faces (their cocked hats). Articles were recovered that placed the fact beyond a doubt, and which were recognised by one of the expedition who had left it in Kamtschatka, the sole survivor. Of the fate of the two-masted vessel built by the shipwrecked crew, nothing was ever discovered.

The Mission party landed here, but saw nobody. They sent a black boy up a tree for cocoa-nuts, and left a tomahawk beneath it as payment. That there were inhabitants somewhere there was horrible proof, for a frightful odour led to search being made, and the New Zealander Hoari turning up the ground, found human bones with flesh hanging to them. A little farther off was a native oven, namely, a pit lined with stones.

This was Patteson's nearest contact with cannibalism, and it left a deep impression of horror.

The Banks group of islands came next—Great Banks Isle, or in the native language Vanua Lava, Valua or Saddle Isle, a long narrow ridge of hills, Mota or Sugarloaf Island, an equally descriptive name; Star Island, and Santa Maria. These places were to become of great importance to the Mission, but little was seen of them at this time—the walls of coral round them were remarkably steep and difficult of access.

Valua had no beach and no canoes, and such swarms of natives clustering upon the cliffs that the Bishop did not think it prudent to land. In Mota, though the coast for the most part rises up in sheer crags, forty or fifty feet above the sea, with a great volcanic cone in the centre, a little cove was found with a good beach, where a number of inhabitants had assembled. They were entirely without clothing or ornament, neither tattooed nor disfigured by betel-nut, and their bright honest faces greatly attracted Patteson, though not a word of their language could be then understood. He wanted to swim ashore among them, but the Bishop would not allow it, lest it should be difficult to escape from the embraces of so many without giving offence. Great numbers swam out to the boat, and canoes brought fruits of all kinds, and bamboos decked with leaves and flowers. 'I crammed native combs in my hair,' says Patteson, 'picked up what words I could, and made up the rest by a grand display of gesticulation.'

At Santa Maria, the next day, there was the like scene around the boat, only the sight of a bit of striped calico caused immense excitement. At other islands it had been unheeded, but here the people were mad to get it, and offered their largest yams for strips of it, and a pair of scarlet braces were purchased for two beautiful bows.

At Vanua Lava, or Great Banks Island, on the 20th, a large canoe with seven men came alongside, three-quarters of a mile from shore. They would not, however, venture on board till Patteson had gone into the water, and placed himself in their canoe, after which they were induced to come on deck, were 'decorated with the order of the tape,' and received axes. No weapon was seen among them, and there was reason to think them the tractable and hopeful race they have since proved.

Bligh Island, the next visited, plainly revealed itself as the cone of an enormous submerged volcano, the water forming a beautiful and extensive bay where numbers of people could be seen. There was a landing and a little trading for yams, and then, after the like intercourse with some of the inhabitants of the cluster of small islets named after Torres, the vessel steered for Espiritu Santo, but wind and time forbade a return to the part previously visited, nor was there time to do more than touch at Aurora, and exchange some fish-hooks for some bows.

At Malicolo, in 1851, the Bishop and his party, while fetching water, had been assailed with stones and arrows, and had only escaped by showing the utmost coolness. There was, therefore, much caution shown in approaching this bay, called Port Sandwich, and the boat stopped outside its breakwater coral reef, where numerous canoes flocked round, the people with their bows and arrows, not attempting to barter. Their faces were painted some red, some black, or yellow. An old chief named Melanbico was recognised by the Bishop, and called by name into the boat. Another old acquaintance named Nipati joined him, and it was considered safe to row into the harbour. The Bishop had learnt a little of the language, and talked to these two, while Patteson examined Nipati's accoutrements—a club, a bow, arrows neatly made, handsomely feathered, and tipped with a deadly poison, tortoiseshell ear-rings, and a very handsome shell armlet covering the arm from the elbow eight or nine inches upward, his face painted red and black. The Bishop read out the list of names he had made on the former visit, and to several the answer was 'dead, or 'shot,' and it appeared that a great mortality had taken place. Large numbers, however, were on the beach, and the Bishop and Patteson landed among them, and conversed with them; but they showed no disposition to trade, and though some of the lads seemed half-disposed to come away with the party, they all changed their minds, and went back again. However, all had behaved well, and one little boy, when offered a fish-hook, at once showed that he had received one already. It was plain that a beginning had been made, which might lead to further results.

Two whales were seen while rowing back to the ship. One—about a third of a mile off—leapt several times fairly out of the water, and fell back on the sea 'with a regular crack,' dashing up the spray in clouds. There was now very little time to spare, as the time of an ordination at Auckland was fixed, and two important visits had yet to be paid, so the two Fate guests were sent ashore in the canoes of some of their friends, and the 'Southern Cross' reached Nengone on the 1st of September. The Bishop had left a boat there some years before, and the Samoan teacher, Mark, who had been Mrs. Nihill's best friend and comforter, came out in it with a joyful party full of welcome. The Bishop and Patteson went ashore, taking with them their two Bauro scholars, to whom the most wonderful sight was a cow, they never having seen any quadruped bigger than a pig. All the native teachers and their wives were assembled, and many of the people, in front of the house where Mr. Nihill had died. They talked of him with touching affection, as they told how diligently he had striven to bring young and old to a knowledge of his God; and they eagerly assisted in planting at his grave a cross, which the Bishop had brought from Auckland for the purpose, and which bore the words: 'I am the Resurrection and the Life.'

The coral lime church and the houses of the teachers among the cocoa-nut trees gave the place a civilised look, and most of the people had some attempt at clothing. Here several passengers were taken in. The two girls, Caroline Wabisane and Sarah Wasitutru, were both married—Caroline to a Maori named Simeona, and Sarah to a man from her own isle called Nawiki. All these and two more men wished to go to St. John's for further instruction, and were taken on board, making up a party of fourteen Melanesians, besides Sarah's baby. 'Mrs. Nihill will be glad to have the women,' writes Coley, 'and I am glad to have the others—not the baby, of course.'

Close quarters indeed, but not for very long, for on the 3rd of September the schooner again put into Norfolk Island, and on the next Sunday Coley was present at the confirmation of the whole population, excepting the younger children, and at the subsequent Communion. Strong hopes were then entertained that the Pitcairners, standing as it were between the English and the islanders, would greatly assist in the work of the Gospel, but this plan was found only capable of being very partially carried out.

Off Norfolk Island, he wrote to his brother an account of the way of life on the voyage, and of the people:—

'They are generally gentle, and seem to cling to one, not with the very independent goodwill of New Zealanders, but with the soft yielding character of the child of the tropics. They are fond, that is the word for them. I have had boys and men in a few minutes after landing, follow me like a dog, holding their hands in mine as a little child does with its nurse.

'My manner of life on board is as I described it before. I eschewed shoes and socks, rather liking to be paddling about all day, when not going on shore, or otherwise employed, which of course made up eight or ten out of the thirteen hours of daylight. When I went ashore (which I did whenever the boat went), then I put on my shoes, and always swam in them, for the coral would cut my feet to pieces. Usual swimming and wading attire—flannel shirt, dark grey trousers, cap or straw hat, shoes, basket round my neck with fish-hooks, or perhaps an adze or two in my hand. I enjoyed the tropical climate very much—really warm always in the water or out of it. On the reefs, when I waded in shallow water, the heat of it was literally unpleasant, more than a tepid bath.'

On the 13th of September, the little missionary vessel came safe into harbour at Auckland, and Coley and his boys—they were considered especially as his—took up their quarters at St. John's College. All through the voyage he had written the journals here followed for the general benefit of his kindred, and at other leisure moments he had written more personal letters. On his sister Fanny's birthday, when the visit to Malicolo was just over, after his birthday wishes, he goes on:—

'And now, how will you be when this reaches Feniton? I think of all your daily occupations,—school, garden, driving, &c.—your Sunday reading, visiting the cottages, &c., and the very thought of it makes me feel like old times. When occasionally I dream, or fall into a kind of trance when awake, and fancy myself walking up from the lodge to the house, and old forms and faces rise up before me, I can scarcely contain the burst of joy and happiness, and then I give a shake and say, "Well, it would be very nice, but look about the horizon, and see how many islands you can count!" and then, instead of thoughts of home for myself, I am tempted to induce others to leave their homes, though I don't really think many men have such a home to leave, or remain so long as I did, one of the home fire-side.

'I have been reading one or two of the German books you sent out. "Friedrich der Grosse" is interesting, but henceforth I don't think I shall have time for aught but a good German novel or two for wet days and jumping seas; or such a theological book as I may send for.'

The effect of the voyage seems to have shown itself in an inflamed leg, which was painful, but not disabled for some time. There was a welcome budget of letters awaiting him,—one from his uncle Dr. Coleridge, to which this is the reply:

'September 15, 1856: St. John's College.

'Your letter of March 26 was awaiting my arrival here. How thankful I am that (as Fan says) in little as in great things God is so good to us. Letters from me arriving on the anniversary of my departure! and all at Thorverton!

'You are clearly right in what you say about my post in the S. X. I did not like it at first, just as a schoolboy does not like going back to school; but that it was good for me I have no doubt; and now see! here I am on shore for seven or eight months, if I live so long—my occupations most interesting, working away with twelve Melanesians at languages, etc., with the highest of all incentives to perseverance, trying to form in them habits of cleanliness, order, decency, etc.

'Last night (Sunday—their first Sunday in New Zealand), after explaining to the Solomon Islands boys, seven in number, the nature of the Lord's Prayer as far as my knowledge of their language would carry me, I thought myself justified in making them kneel down round me, and they uttered with their lips after me (i.e. the five most intelligent) the first words of prayer to their Father in Heaven. I don't venture to say that they understood much—neither does the young child taught at his or her mother's knees—neither do many grown persons perhaps know much about the fulness of the Prayer of Prayers—(these scenes teach me my ignorance, which is one great gain)—yet they knew, I think, that they were praying to some great and mighty one—not an abstraction—a conscious loving Being, a Father, and they know at least the name of His Son, Jesus Christ.

'Their first formula was: "God the Father, God the Son, and God the Holy Ghost, only One God." I can't yet explain that our Blessed Lord came from heaven and died for our sins; neither (as far as human thought may reach) does the power of God's Spirit as yet work in their hearts consciousness of sin, and with that the sense of the need of a Redeemer and Saviour. I asked in my sermon yesterday the prayers of the people for the grace of God's Holy Spirit to touch the hearts and enlighten the understandings of these heathen children of a common Father, and I added that greatly did their teachers need their prayers that God would make them apt to teach, and wise and simple in endeavouring to bring before their minds the things that belong unto their peace. You too, dear Uncle, will think I know of these things, for my trust is great. In this cold climate, 26° or 27° of latitude south of their own island, I have much anxiety about their bodily health, and more about their souls.

'The four youngest, sixteen to eighteen, sleep in my room. One is now on my bed, wrapped up in a great opossum rug, with cold and slight fever; last night his pulse was high, to-day he is better. I have to watch over them like a cat. Think of living till now in a constant temperature of 84°, and being suddenly brought to

56°. New Zealand is too cold for them, and the College is a cold place, wind howling round it now.

'Norfolk Island is the place, and the Pitcairners themselves are most co-operative and hearty; I trust that in another year I may be there.

'Thank you for all your kind wishes on my birthday. I ought to wish to live many years, perhaps, to try and be of use; especially as I am so unfit to go now, or rather I ought not to wish at all. Sometimes I feel almost fainthearted, which is cowardly and forgetful of our calling "to fight manfully under Christ's banner." Ah! my Bishop is indeed a warrior of the Cross. I can't bear the things Sophy said in one of her letters about my having given up.

It seems mock humility to write it; but, dear Uncle, if I am conscious of a life so utterly unlike what all you dear ones fancy it to be, what must it be in the sight of God and His holy angels? What advantages I have always had, and have now! and not a day goes by and I can say I have done my duty. Good-bye, dear dear Uncle.

'Always your affectionate and grateful nephew,

'**J. C. PATTESON.**

'Love to dear Aunt.'

Almost the first experience after settling in at St. John's College was a sharp attack of fever that fell on Kerearua, one of the Bauro lads. Such illnesses, it seemed, were frequent at home and generally fatal. His companion Hirika remarked, 'Kerearua like this in Bauro ah! in a few days he would die; by-and-by we go back to Bauro.' The sick boys were always lodged in Coley's own room to be more quiet and thoroughly nursed. Fastidiousness had been so entirely crushed that he really seemed to take pleasure in the arrangement, speaking with enthusiasm of the patient's obedience and gratitude, and adding, 'He looks quite nice in one of my night-shirts with my plaid counterpane, and the plaid Joan gave me over it, a blanket next to him.'

The Melanesians readily fell into the regular habits of short school, work out of doors, meals in hall and bed-time, and they were allowed a good deal of the free use of their limbs, needful to keep them happy and healthy. Now and then they would be taken into Auckland, as a great treat, to see the soldiers on parade, and of course the mere living with civilization was an immense education to them, besides the direct instruction they received.

The languages of Nengone and Bauro were becoming sufficiently familiar to Mr. Patteson to enable him to understand much of what they said to him. He writes to Miss Neill (October 17):—

'I talk with them about common things, and learn a great deal of their wild savage customs and habits, but I can do but little as yet in the way of real instruction. Some ideas, I trust, they are beginning to acquire concerning our Blessed Lord. Is it not a significant fact that the god worshiped in Gfera, and in one village of Bauro, is the Serpent, the very type of evil? I need not say that these dear boys have won their way to my heart, they are most docile and affectionate. I think some will really, if they live, leave their own island and live with me at Norfolk Island, or here, or wherever my dwelling may be whenever I am not in the "Southern Cross."

'But of course I must not dwell on such notions. If it come to pass that for some years I can retain a hold upon them, they may be instructed sufficiently to make them teachers in their turn to their own people. But all this is in the hands of God. My home journal will tell you particulars of our voyage. Don't believe in the ferocity, &c., of the islanders. When their passions are excited, they do commit fearful deeds, and they are almost universally cannibals, i.e. after a battle there will be always a cannibal feast, not otherwise. But treat them well and prudently, and I apprehend that there is little danger in visiting them, meaning by visiting merely landing on the beach the first time, going perhaps to a native village the next time, sleeping on shore the third, spending ten days the fourth, &c., &c. The language once learnt from the pupils we bring away, all is clear. And now good-bye, my dear Miss Neill. That I think of you and pray for you, you know, and I need not add that I value most highly your prayers for me. When I think of my happiness and good spirits, I must attribute much, very much, to God's goodness in accepting the prayers of my friends.'

After the old custom of telling the home party all his doings, the journal-letter of the 27th of November goes through the teaching to the Bauro boys:—

'I really think they comprehend thus much, that God, who made all things, made man, Adam and Eve, very good and holy; that Adam and Eve sinned, that they did not listen to the word of God, but to the Bad Spirit; that God found them out, though they were afraid and tried to hide (for He sees and knows all things); that He drove them out of the beautiful garden, and said that they must die; that they had two sons, Cain and Abel; that Cain killed his brother, and that all fighting and killing people, and all other sins (I mention all for which I have names) came into the world because of sin; that God and man were far apart, not living near, no peace between them because men were so evil. That God was so good that He loved men all the time, and that He promised to save all men who would believe in His Son Jesus Christ, who was to die for them (for I can't yet express, "was to die that men might not go down to the fire, but live for ever with God "); that by and by He sent a flood and drowned all men except Noah and seven other people, because men would not be good; that afterwards there was a very good man, named Abraham, who believed all about Jesus Christ, and God chose him, and his son Isaac, and his son Jacob, and his twelve sons, to be the fathers of a people called Jews; that those people alone knew about God, and had teachers and praying men: and that they killed lambs and offered them (gave them to God as a sign of Jesus Christ being one day slain and offered to God on a cross) but these very men became wicked too, and at last, when no man knew how to be happy and good, Jesus Christ came down from heaven. His mother was Mary, but He had no father on earth, only God the Father in heaven was His Father: the Holy Ghost made Mary to be mother of Jesus Christ.

'Then I take two books, or anything else, and say, This one is God, and this is man. They are far apart, because man is so bad and God is so good. But Jesus Christ came in the middle between them, and joins them together. He is God and He is Man too; so in(side) Him, God and Man meet, like the meeting of two men in one path; and He says Himself He is the true Way, the only true Path to God and heaven. God was angry with us because we sinned; but Jesus Christ died on the cross, and then God the Father forgave us because Jesus Christ gave His life that we might always live, and not die. By and by He will come to judge us; and He knows what we do, whether we steal and lie, or whether we pray and teach what is good. Men of Bauro and Gera and Santa Cruz don't know that yet, but you do, and you must remember, if you go on doing as they do after you know God's will, you will be sent down to the fire, and not see Jesus Christ, who died that you might live.

'I think that they know all this, and much in the exactly equivalent words. Of course I find difficulty in rendering religious ideas in a language which contains scarcely any words adequate to express them, but I am hopeful enough to believe that they do know so much at all events. How far their hearts are affected, One alone knows. It is indeed but little after they have been with us four months; but till I had them on shore, I could get very little work done. The constant boat work took me away, and anywhere in sight of islands, of course they were on deck in eagerness to see the strange country. Then I could not work with energy while my leg would not let me take exercise. But it is now beginning to be a real pleasure as well as duty to teach both Nengone and Bauro people. Enough of the language to avoid most of the drudgery has been got over, I hope, though not near enough for purposes of 'exact and accurate translation.'

I have given at length this account of Patteson's fundamental teaching, though to some it may seem to savour of the infant school, because in spite of being hampered by imperfect knowledge of the language, he has thrown into it the great principle both of his action and teaching; namely, the restoration of the union of mankind with God through Christ. It never embraced that view of the heathen world which regards it as necessarily under God's displeasure, apart from actual evil, committed in wilful knowledge that it is evil. He held fast to the fact of man having been created in the image of God, and held that whatever good impulses and higher qualities still remained in the heathen, were the remnants of that Image, and to be hailed accordingly. Above all, he realised in his whole life the words to St. Peter: 'What God hath cleansed that call not thou common,' and not undervaluing for a moment Sacramental Grace, viewed human nature, while yet without the offer thereof, as still the object of fatherly and redeeming love, and full of fitful tokens of good coming from the only Giver of life and holiness, and needing to be brought nearer and strengthened by full union and light, instead of being left to be quenched in the surrounding flood of evil. 'And were by nature the children of wrath,' he did not hold to mean that men were objects of God's anger, lying under His deadly displeasure; but rather, children of wild impulse, creatures of passion, swayed resistlessly by their own desires, until made 'children of grace,' and thus obtaining the spiritual power needful to enable them to withstand these passions. An extract from the sermon he had preached at Sydney may perhaps best serve to illustrate his principle:—

'And this love once generated in the heart of man, must needs pass on to his brethren; that principle of life must needs grow and expand with its own inherent energy; the seed must be developed into the tree, and strike its roots deep and wide, and stretch out its branches unto the sea and its boughs unto the rivers. No artificial nor accidental circumstances can confine it, it recognises no human ideas of nationality, or place, or time, but embraces like the dome of heaven all the works of God. And love is the animating principle of all. In every star of the sky, in the sparkling, glittering waves of the sea, in every flower of the field, in every creature of God, most of all in every living soul of man, it adores and blesses the beauty and the love of the great Creator and Preserver of all.

'Viewed indeed from that position which was occupied by ancient philosophers, the existing contrarieties between nations might well appear inexplicable, and intellectual powers might seem to be the exclusive heritage of particular nations. But Christianity leads us to distinguish between the nature of man as he came fresh from the hands of his Creator, and that natural propensity to sin which he has inherited in consequence of his fall from original innocence. It teaches that as God has "made of one blood all nations to dwell together on the face of the whole earth," and has given in virtue of this common origin one common nature destined to be pure and holy and divine, so, by virtue of Redemption and Regeneration, the image of God may be restored in all, and whatever is the result of his depravity therefore may be overcome. And this seems to be the answer to all statements relating to the want of capacity in certain nations of the earth for the reception of Divine Truth, that every man, because he is a man, because he is a partaker of that very nature which has been taken into the Person of the Son of God, may by the grace of God be awakened to the sense of his true life, of his real dignity as a redeemed brother of Christ.

'The spark of heavenly fire may indeed have been all but quenched by the unbridled indulgence of his passions; the natural wickedness of the heart of man may have exhibited itself with greater fearfulness where no laws and customs have introduced restraints against at least the outward expression of vice; but the capacity for the Christian life is there; though overlaid, it may be, with monstrous forms of superstition or cruelty or ignorance, the conscience can still respond to the voice of the Gospel of Truth.'

And one who so entirely believed and acted upon these words found them true. The man who verily treated the lads he had gathered round him with a perfectly genuine sympathy, a love and a self-denial—nay more, an identification of self with them—awoke all that was best in their characters, and met with full response. Enthusiastic partiality of course there was in his estimate of them; but is it not one of the absolute requisites of a good educator to feel that enthusiasm, like the parent for the child? And is it always the blind admiration at which outsiders smile; is it not rather indifference which is blind, and love which sees the truth?

'I would not exchange my position with these lads and young men for anything (he wrote, on December 8, to his uncle, the Eton master). I wish you could see them and know them; I don't think you ever had pupils that could win their way into your heart more effectually than these fellows have attached themselves to me. It is no effort to love them heartily. Gariri, a dear boy from San Cristoval, is standing by me now, at my desk, in amazement at the pace that my pen is going, not knowing that I could write to you, my dear old tutor, for hours together if I had nothing else to do. He is, I suppose, about sixteen, a most loveable boy, gentle, affectionate, with all the tropical softness and kindliness.

'We have seven Solomon Islanders—five from Mata, a village at the north-west of San Cristoval, and two from the south-east point of Guadalcanar, or Gera, a magnificent island about twenty-five or twenty miles to the north-west of San Cristoval. From frequent intercourse they are almost bilingual, a great "lounge" for me, as one language does for both; the structure of the two island tongues is the same, but scarcely any words much alike. However, that is not much odds.

'Then from Nengone, where you remember Mr. Nihill died after eighteen months' residence on the island, we have four men and two women, both married. Of these, two men and both the women have been baptized, some time ago, by the Bishop, in 1852, and one by the London Mission, who now occupy the island. These four I have, with full trust, admitted to the Holy Communion. Mr. Nihill had taught them well, and I am sure they could pass an examination in Scriptural history, simple doctrinal statements, &c., as well as most young English people of the middle class of life. The other two are well taught, and one of them knows a great deal, but, poor fellow, he misconducted himself at Nengone, and hence I cannot recommend him to the Bishop for baptism without much talk about him.

'But I think my love is more poured out upon my Bauro and Gera lads. They are such dear fellows, and I trust that already they begin to know something about religion. Certain it is that they answer readily questions and say with their mouths what amounts almost to a statement of the most important Christian truths. Of course I cannot tell what effect this may have on their hearts. They join in prayer morning and evening, they behave admirably, and really there is nothing in their conduct to find fault with. If it please God that any of them were at some future time to stay again with us, I have great hopes that they may learn enough to become teachers in their own country.

'The Nengone lads are quite in a different position. Their language has been reduced to writing, the Gospel of St. Mark translated, and they can all read a little English, so that at evening prayers we read a verse all round, and then I catechise and expound to them in Nengone.

'I really trust that by God's blessing some real opening into the great Solomon group has been effected. There is every hope that many boys will join us this next voyage. No one can say what may be the result. As yet it is possible to get on without more help, but I do not for a moment doubt that should God really grant not only a wide field of labour, but some such hope of cultivating it, He will send forth plenty of men to share in this work. Men who have some means of their own—£100 a year is enough, or even less—or some aptitude for languages, surely will feel drawn in this direction. It is the happiest life a man can lead, full of enjoyment, physical and mental, exquisite scenery, famous warm climate, lots of bathing, yams and taro and cocoa-nut enough to make an alderman's mouth water, and such loving, gentle people. But of course something depends on the way in which a man looks at these things, and a fine gentleman who can't get on without his servant, and can't put his luggage for four months into a compass of six feet by one-and-a-half, won't like it....

'You know the kind of incidents that occur, so I need not repeat them to you. I have quite learnt to believe that there are no "savages" anywhere, at least among black or coloured people. I'd like to see anyone call my Bauro boys savages! Why, the fellows on the reef that have never seen a white man will wade back to the boat and catch one's arms to prevent one falling into pits among the coral, just like an old nurse looking after her child. This they did at Santa Maria, where we two swam ashore to a party of forty or fifty men, and where our visit was evidently a very agreeable one on both sides, though we did not know one syllable of the language, and then.... But I almost tremble to think of the immense amount of work opening upon one. Whither will it lead? But I seldom find any time for speculations; and oh, my dear tutor, I am as happy as the day is long, though it never seems long to me!.... My dear father writes in great anxiety about the Denison case. Oh dear! what a cause of thankfulness it is to be out of the din of controversy, and to find hundreds of thousands longing for crumbs which are shaken about so roughly in these angry disputes! It isn't High or Low or Broad Church, or any other special name, but the longing desire to forget all distinctions, and to return to a simpler state of things, that seems naturally to result from the very sight of heathen people. Who thinks of anything but this: "They have not heard the Name of the Saviour Who died for them," when he is standing with crowds of naked fellows round him? I can't describe the intense happiness of this life. I suppose trials will come some day, and I almost dread the thought, for I surely shall not be prepared to bear them. I have no trials at all, even of a small kind, to teach me how to bear up under great ones.'

In truth Coleridge Patteson had entered on the happiest period of his life. He had found his vocation, and his affections were fastening themselves upon his black flock, so that, without losing a particle of his home love, the yearnings homewards were appeased, and the fully employed time, and sense of success and capability, left no space for the self-contemplation and self-criticism of his earlier life. He gives amusing sketches of the scenes:—

'The donkey here, a fatally stubborn brute, is an unceasing amusement to my boys. No one of them can retain his seat more than ten minutes, but they all fall like cats on their legs amid cries of laughter. The donkey steers straight for some small scrubby trees, and then kicks and plunges, or else rubs their legs against the sides of the house, and all this time the boys are leaping about the unfortunate fellow who is mounted, and the fun is great.

'Wadrokala, one of the Nengone lads, who had recently made his first communion, became the prominent scholar at this time. He had thought a good deal. One night he said: "I have heard all kinds of words used—faith, repentance, praise, prayer—and I don't clearly understand what is the real great thing, the chief thing of all. They used these words confusedly, and I feel puzzled. Then I read that the Pharisees knew a great deal of the law, and so did the Scribes, and yet they were not good. I am not doing anything good. Now I know something of the Bible, and I can write; and I fear very much, I often feel very much afraid, that I am not good, I am not doing anything good."'

He was talked to, and comforted with hopes of future work; but a day or two later his feelings were unconsciously hurt by being told in joke that he was wearing a shabby pair of trousers to save the good ones to take home to Nengone. His remonstrance was poured out upon a slate:—

'Mr. Patteson, this is my word:—I am unhappy because of the word you said to me that I wished for clothes. I have left my country. I do not seek clothes for the body. What is the use of clothes? Can my spirit be clothed with clothes for the body? Therefore my heart is greatly afraid; but you said I greatly wished for clothes, which I do not care for. One thing only I care for, that I may receive the life for my spirit. Therefore I fear, I confess, and say to you, it is not the thing for the body I want, but the one thing I want is the clothing for the soul, for Jesus Christ's sake, our Lord.'

Soon after a very happy Christmas, Wadrokala and Kainwhat expressed a desire, after a final visit to their native island, to return with Mr. Patteson, and be prepared to be sent as native teachers to any dark land, as the Samoans had come to them.

Wadrokala narrated something of the history of his island, a place with 6,000 inhabitants, with one tribe forming a priestly caste, the head of which was firmly believed by even these Christian Nengonese to possess the power of striking men dead by his curse. Caroline, Kainwhat and Kowine were the children of a terrible old chief named Bula, who had fifty-five wives, and whose power was almost absolute. If anyone offended him, he would send either a priest or one of his sons to kill the man, and bring the corpse, of which the thighs were always reserved for his special eating, the trunk being given to his slaves. If one of his wives offended him, he sent for the high priest, who cursed her—simply said, 'She has died,' and die she did. A young girl who refused to marry him was killed and eaten, or if any person omitted to come into his presence crouching, the penalty was to be devoured; in fact, he seems to have made excuses for executions in order to gratify his appetite for human flesh, which was considered as particularly dainty fare. Everyone dreaded him, and when at last he died a natural death, his chief wife was strangled by her own brother, as a matter of course. Such horrors as these had pretty well ceased by that time, though still many Nengonese were heathen, and the priests were firmly believed to have the power of producing death and disease at will by a curse. Wadrokala, with entire conviction, declared that one of his father's wives had thus been made a cripple for life.

Nengonese had become almost as familiar to Coley as Maori, and his Sundays at this time were decidedly polyglot; since, besides a regular English service at Taranaki, he often took a Maori service, and preached extempore in that tongue, feeling that the people's understanding went along with him; and there were also, in early morning and late evening, prayers, partly in Nengonese, partly in Bauro, at the College chapel, and a sermon, first in one language, and then repeated in the other. The Nengone lads, who had the question of adherence to the London Mission at home, or the Church in New Zealand, put to them, came deliberately to entreat to remain always with Mr. Patteson, saying that they saw that this teaching of the Church was right, and they wished to work in it. It was a difficult point, as the London Mission was reasserting a claim to the Loyalty Isles, and the hopes of making them a point d'appui were vanishing; but these men and their wives could not but be accepted, and Simeona was preparing for baptism. A long letter to Professor Max Muller on the languages will be found in the Appendix. The Bishop of New Zealand thus wrote to Sir John Patteson respecting Coley and his work:—

'Taurarua, Auckland: March 2, 1857.'

'My dear Judge,—Your letter of December 5 made me very happy, by assuring me of the satisfaction which you feel in your son's duties and position. I do indeed most thankfully acknowledge the goodness of God in thus giving me timely aid, when I was pledged to a great work, but without any steady force to carry it on. Coley is, as you say, the right man in the right place, mentally and physically: the multiplicity of languages, which would try most men, is met by his peculiar gift; the heat of the climate suits his constitution; his mild and parental temper makes his black boys cling about him as their natural protector; and his freedom from fastidiousness makes all parts of the work easy to him; for when you have to teach boys how to wash themselves, and to wear clothes for the first time, the romance of missionary work disappears as completely as a great man's heroism before his valet de chambre.

'On Sunday, February 22, we had a native baptism, an adult from Nengone and his infant child. Coley used the Baptismal Service, which he had translated, and preached fluently in the Nengone tongue, as he had done in the morning in New Zealand. The careful study which we had together of the latter on our voyage out will be of great use in many other dialects, and Mrs. Nihill has given him her husband's Nengone manuscripts.

'You know in what direction my wishes tend, viz., that Coley, when he has come to suitable age, and has developed, as I have no doubt he will, a fitness for the work, should be the first island Bishop, upon the foundation, of which you and your brother Judge, and Sir W. Farquhar, are trustees; that Norfolk Island should be the see of the Bishop, because the character of its population, the salubrity of its climate, and its insular position, make it the fittest place for the purpose.

'Your affectionate and grateful friend,

'G. A. NEW ZEALAND.'

By the same mail Patteson himself wrote to Miss Neill:—

'If it please God to give us some few native teachers from Bauro and Grera, not to be sent before, but to go with or follow us (i.e. Bishop and me), in a short time the word of God might be heard in many a grand wild island, resplendent with everything that a tropical climate and primeval forests, etc., can bestow, and thickly populated with an intelligent and, as I imagine, tolerably docile race, of whom some are already "stretching out their hands unto God."

'All these Solomon Islanders here would answer questions about Christianity as well, perhaps, as children of nine or ten years old in England. Some seem to feel that there is a real connection between themselves and what they are taught, and speak of the love of God in giving Jesus Christ to die for them, and say that

God's Holy Spirit alone can enlighten their dark hearts.

'That beautiful image of light and darkness seems common to all nations. The regular word used by the Nengone people, who are far more advanced in Christian knowledge and practice, for all heathen places is "the dark lands."

'On Sunday week, February 22, we had a deeply interesting service in the College chapel at 7.15 P.M., just as the English world was beginning its Sunday. Simeona and his infant boy of four weeks and three days old were baptized. The College chapel was nicely lighted, font decorated simply. I read the service in Nengone, having had all hands at work setting the types and printing on Friday and Saturday. The Bishop took the part of the service which immediately precedes the actual baptism, and baptized them both—first the father, by the name of George Selwyn, then the baby, by the name of John Patteson. This was the special request of the parents, and as it is my dear Father's name, how could I object? He is, of course, my godson, and a dear little fellow he is. At the end of my sermon, I added a few words to "George," and besought the prayers of the Nengone people for him and his child. We have now four regular communicants among them—Wadrokala, Mark (Kainwhat), Carry and Sarah. George is baptized, and baby; and Sarah's child, Lizzy, I baptized long ago. In about two months (D. V.), we are off for a good spell of four or five months among the islands, taking back this party, though some of them will, by and by, rejoin us again, I hope.'

The plan of starting in April for a four or five months' cruise was disconcerted, as regarded Bishop Selwyn, by the delay of Bishop Harper and the Archdeacons in arriving for the intended Synod, which was thus put off till May, too wintry a month for the Melanesians to spend in New Zealand. After some doubt, it was decided that Mr. Patteson should make a short voyage, for the mere purpose of returning his scholars to their homes, come back to Auckland, and make a fresh start when the Bishop was ready.

In prospect of the parting, Patteson writes to his beloved old governess (March 19, 1857):—

'You will like a report of my pupils, especially as I can give most of them a good ticket, little mark and all, as we used to say of yours (though not as often as we ought to have done) to our dear mother. You never had such willing pupils, though you turned out some, I hope, eventually as good. In your hands these lads would be something indeed. Really they have no faults that I can detect, and when their previous state is considered, it is wonderful; for all this time they have been with us, the greatest fault has been a fit of sulkiness, lasting about half a day, with three of them. Their affection, gentleness, unselfishness, cheerfulness, willingness to oblige, in some of them a natural gentlemanly way of doing things, and sometimes indications of what we should call high principle—all these things give one great hopes, not for them only, but for all these nations, that, refined by Christianity, they may be bright examples of manly virtues and Christian graces.'

To some, no doubt, these expressions will seem exaggerated, but not to those who have had any experience of the peculiar suavity and grace that often is found in the highbred men of native races, before they are debased by the corruptions brought in by white men. Moreover, in every case, the personal influence of the teacher when in immediate contact with a sufficiently small number, is quite enough to infuse good habits and obviate evil ones to an extent quite inconceivable to those who have not watched the unconscious exertion of this power. Patteson knew that too much reliance must not be placed on present appearance.

'It is dangerous (he says), to have persons clinging to you too much. I feel that; but then these fellows, I take it, are very impulsive, and no doubt the cocoanuts in their own land will exercise a counter-influence to mine, and so I shall soon be undeceived if I learn to think too much of their personal affection; but I never knew such dear lads, I don't know how I shall get on without them.

'You must be looking forward to your spring and summer. How delicious some of those days are in England! We miss the freshness of a deciduous foliage, our evergreens look dull, and we have no deciduous trees as yet. A good scamper with Joan on the East Hill, or a drive with Fan in the pony carriage along a lane full of primroses and violets would be pleasant indeed, and so would a stroll with old Jem up the river be happy indeed, and I could almost quit the "Southern Cross" for dear Father's quarter-deck in the "Hermitage," but that I am, I believe, sailing in the right vessel, and, as I trust, on the right course to the haven where we may all meet and rest for ever.'

On Good Friday the three Nengone young men who had been baptized were confirmed, and on the Wednesday in Easter Week the 'Southern Cross' sailed, this time with a responsible sailing master. At Nengone Mr. Patteson had a friendly interview with Mr. Craig, the London Society's missionary, and explained to him the state of things with regard to these individual pupils; then, after being overwhelmed with presents by the Christian population, shaped his course for Bauro.

On the way he had the experience of a tropical thunderstorm, after having been well warned by the sinking of the barometer through the whole of the day, the 27th of April. 'At 7.30 the breeze came up, and the big drops began, when suddenly a bright forked flash so sustained that it held its place before our eyes like an immense white-hot crooked wire, seemed to fall on the deck, and be splintered there. But one moment and the tremendous crack of the thunder was alive and around us, making the masts tremble. For more than an hour the flashes were so continuous that I think every three seconds we had a perfect view of the whole horizon. I especially remember the firmament between the lurid thunder clouds looking quite blue, so intense was the light. The thunder rolled on without cessation, but the tremendous claps occurred only at intervals. We have no lightning conductor, and I felt somewhat anxious; went below and prayed God to preserve us from lightning and fire, read the magnificent chapter at the end of Job. As the storm went on, I thought that at that very hour you were praying "From lightning and tempest, good Lord, deliver us." We had no wind: furious rain, repeated again from midnight to three this morning. About eleven the thunder had ceased, but the broad flashes of lightning were still frequent. The lightning was forked and jagged, and one remarkable thing was the length of time that the line of intense light was kept up, like a gigantic firework, so that the shape of the flash could be drawn with entire accuracy by any one that could handle a pencil. It was a grand and solemn sight and sound, and I am very thankful we were preserved from danger, for the storm was right upon us, and the danger must have been great.'

A ready welcome awaited the 'Southern Cross' at Bauro, in a lovely bay hitherto unvisited, where a perfect flotilla of canoes came off to greet her, and the two chiefs, Iri and Eimaniaka, came on board, and no less than fifty-five men with them. The chiefs and about a dozen men were invited to spend the night on board. The former lay on the floor of the inner cabin, talking and listening while their host set before them some of the plain truths of Christianity. He landed next day, and returned the visit by going to Iri's hut, where he pointed to the skulls, discoursed on the hatefulness of such decorations, and recommended their burial. He also had an opportunity of showing a Christian's horror of unfilial conduct, when Rimaniaka struck his mother for being slow in handing yams; and when a man begged for a passage to Gera in direct opposition to his father's commands, he was dismissed with the words, 'I will have nothing to do with a man who does not obey his own father.'

At Gera there was also a great assembly of canoes, and as all hands were wanted on board, Patteson went ashore in a canoe with the brother of one of the scholars. He was told that he was the first white man who had ever landed there, and the people showed a good deal of surprise, but were quite peaceable, and the presence of women and children was a sign that there was no danger. When he tried to return to the ship, a heavy sea came on, and the canoes were forced to put back, and he thus found himself obliged to spend the night on the island. He was taken into a house with two rooms, in each of which numbers of men were lying on the ground, a small wood fire burning in the midst of each group of three or four.

A grass mat was brought him, and a bit of wood for a pillow, and as he was wet through, cold, and very tired, he lay down; but sleep was impossible, from tormenting vermin, as well as because it seemed to be the custom of the people to be going backwards and forwards all night, sitting over the fire talking, then dropping asleep and waking to talk again. A yam was brought him after about an hour, and long before dawn he escaped into the open air, and sat over a tire there till at high tide, at six o'clock in the morning, he was able to put off again and reach the ship, where forty-five natives had slept, and behaved well.

'The sense of cold and dirt and weariness was not pleasing,' he confesses, and certainly the contrast to the Eton and Oxford habits was great. There was a grand exchange of presents; hatchets, adzes, hooks and empty bottles on one side, and a pig and yams on the other. Immediately after follows a perilous adventure, which, as we shall find, made a deep impression. It is thus related in a letter for the benefit of Thorverton Rectory:—

'At Sea: Lat. 19° 50' S.; long. 167° 41' E.

'My dearest Uncle,—May is a month specially connected henceforward in my mind with a merciful deliverance from great peril, which God vouchsafed to us on May 2nd. We touched on a reef at the Isle of Guadalcanar, one of the Solomon

Islands, in lat. 9° 50', and but for God's mercy in blessing our exertions, we might have incurred fearful danger of losing the Mission vessel. As it was, in a couple of minutes we were off the reef and in deep safe water—to Him be the praise and the glory! I have written all particulars as usual to my father, and now that the danger has been averted, you will rejoice to hear how great a door is opened to us in that part of the world. Personal safety ensured, and, so far as can be judged of, no apparent obstacle in the way of the Mission in that quarter. Had this great peril not occurred—and it was to human eyes and in human language the mere "chance" of a minute—I might have dwelt with too much satisfaction on the bright side of the picture. As it is, it is a lesson to me "to think soberly." I can hardly trust myself to write yet with my usual freedom of the scenery, natives, &c. One great thought is before me—"Is it all real that we touched on that reef in the sight of hundreds of natives?" It was not a sense of personal danger—that could not occur at such a time; but the idea that the vessel might be lost, the missionary operations suspended, &c.; this shot through me in those two minutes! But I had no time for more than mental prayer, for I was pulling at ropes with all my strength; not till it was all over could I go below and fall on my knees in a burst of thanksgiving and praise. We suppose that there must be a very strong undercurrent near the reef at the mouth of the bay, for the vessel, instead of coming round as usual (and there was abundance of room), would not obey the helm, and we touched an outlying rock before we could alter the sails, when she rounded instantly on the other tack. Humanly speaking, she would have come off very soon, as the tide was flowing, and she received no damage, as we came very gently against the rock, which was only about the size of an ordinary table. But it is an event to be remembered by me with thankfulness all my life. I think the number of natives who had been on deck and about us in canoes that morning could not have been less than 450. They behaved very well. Of the five principal chiefs three could talk some Bauro language, so I could communicate with them, and this was one reason why I felt satisfied of their good-will. They gave me two pigs, about 500 or 600 cocoa-nuts, and upwards of a ton of yams, though I told them I had only two small hatchets, five or six adzes, a few gimlets, and empty bottles to give in exchange. If I had not been satisfied of their being quite friendly, I would not have put ourselves so entirely into their power; but it is of the greatest consequence to let the natives of a place see that you are not suspicious, and where there is no evident hazard in so doing, I think I ought to act upon it. Perhaps the Bishop, being an older hand at it, will think I was rash; but as far as the natives are concerned, the result shows I was quite right; the letting go a kedge in deepish water is another matter, that was a mistake I know now. But we could not work the vessel by reason of the crowds of natives, and what was I to do? Either not stand close in, as they all expected, or let go a kedge. If I did not go into the mouth of the bay, they would have said, "He does not trust us," and mutual suspicion would have been (possibly) the result, and I could not make them understand rightly the reason why I did not want to drop the kedge or small anchor.

'I had slept on shore about three miles up the bay among a number of natives, twenty-five or twenty-six in the same room with me, on the previous evening: at least, I lay down in my things, which, by the bye, were drenched through with salt and rain water. They said I was the first white person that had been ashore there. They treated me very well. How in the face of all this could I run the risk of letting them think I was unwilling to trust them? So I think still that I was right in all but one thing. I ought to have ascertained better the nature of the current and the bottom of the harbour, to see if there was good holding ground. But it is easier to do those things in an English port than in the sight of a number of natives, and especially when there is but one person able to communicate with the said natives. If I went off in the boat sounding, who was to look after the schooner? If I stayed on board, who was to explain to the natives what was being done in the boat? Besides, we have but five men on board, including the master and mate, and one of them was disabled by a bad hand, so that if I had manned the boat, I should have left only three able-bodied men on board—it was a puzzle, you see, dear Uncle. Now I have entered into this long defence lest any of you dear ones should think me rash. Indeed, I don't want to run any risks at all. But there was no risk here, as I supposed, and had we chosen to go round on the other tack we should have known nothing of a risk now. As it was, we did run a great hazard of grounding on the reef, and therefore, Laus Deo.

'Oh! dear little Pena, if you had only seen the village which, as yet, I alone of white people have been allowed to see—the great tall cocoa-nuts, so tall and slender at the top, that I was almost afraid when a boy was sent up to gather some nuts for me—the cottages of bamboo and cocoa-nut leaves—the great forest trees, the parrots flying about among the branches—the crowd of men and children and a few women all looking at, and some talking to the strange chief, "who had spoken the truth and brought their kinsman as he promised,"—the sea in the harbour shut off by small islets and looking like a beautiful lake with high wooded and steep banks—the pretty canoes on the beach, and the great state canoe lying at its stone anchor about fifty yards off, about fifty feet long, and inlaid throughout with mother-of-pearl, the spears leaning against the houses—men stalking about with a kind of club (the great chief Puruhanua gave me his);—I think your little head would have been almost turned crazy....

'June 4th, Auckland.—We reached harbour a week ago in a violent squall of wind and rain at 8.45 P.M. Anxious night after the anchor was dropped, lest the vessel should drag. Nine days coming from Norfolk Island, very heavy weather—no accident, but jib-boom pitched away while lying to in a south-easter....

'Your loving nephew,

'**J. C. P.**'

The Rev. Benjamin Thornton Dudley, for several years a most valuable helper in the work, both at home and abroad, gives the following account of his own share in it, and his recollections of that first year:—

'The first time I ever saw Mr. Patteson was in the beginning of 1856, when you (this is a letter to Mrs. Selwyn) all visited Lyttelton in the newly arrived "Southern Cross." That indescribable charm of manner, calculated at once to take all hearts by storm, was not perhaps as fully developed in him then as afterwards, and my experience was then comparatively limited, yet his words in the sermon he preached on behalf of the Melanesian Mission (a kind of historical review of the growth and spread of the Gospel), although coming after the wonderful sermon of the Bishop in the morning, made a deep impression on several of us, myself among the number.

'You came to Lyttelton at the end of 1856 again, this time without him, and the Bishop brought me up to St. John's College, and placed me under him there. I remember at first how puzzled I felt as to what my position was, and what I was expected to do. Not a single direction was given me by Mr. Patteson, nor did he invite me to take a class in the comparatively small Melanesian school. Gradually it dawned upon me that I was purposely left there, and that I was expected to offer myself for anything I could do. When I offered myself I was allowed to assist in this and that, until at length I fell into my regular place. Although the treatment I received in this respect puzzled me, I felt his great kindness from the first. How bright he was in those days, and how overflowing with spirits when among the Melanesians. What fun there used to be of a morning, when he would come and hunt the lazy ones out of bed, drive them down to the bath house, and there assist their ablutions with a few basins of water thrown at them; and what an amount of quiet "chaff" used to go on at breakfast time about it as we sat with them in the great hall, without any of those restraints of the "high table" which were introduced at dinner.

'During the first voyage made that year to return our Melanesian party, I think Mr. Patteson was feeling very much out of sorts. I do not remember any time during the years in which I was permitted to see so much of him when he took things so easily. He spoke of himself as lazy, and I confess I used to wonder somewhat how it was that he retired so completely into the cabin, and did apparently so little in the way of study. He read the "Heir of Redclyffe," and other books of light reading in that voyage. I understood better afterwards what, raw youth as I was at the time, puzzled me in one for whom I was already beginning to entertain a feeling different from any previously experienced. That seems to me now to have been quite a necessary pause in his life after he had with wholeheartedness and full intention given himself to his work, but before he had fully faced all its requirements and had learnt to map out his whole time with separate toil.'

So concluded what may be called the first term of Coley Patteson's tutorship of his island boys. His work is perhaps best summed up in this sentence in a letter to me from Mrs. Abraham: 'Mr. Patteson's love for them, and his facility in communicating with them in their own tongue, make his dealing with the present set much more intimate and effective than it has ever been before, and their affections towards him are drawn out in a lively manner.'

CHAPTER VIII. ST. JOHN'S COLLEGE AND LIFU. 1857-1859.

It seems to me that the years between 1856 and 1861 were the very brightest of

Coleridge Patteson's life. He had left all for Christ's sake and the Gospel's, and was reaping the blessing in its freshness. His struggles with his defects had been successful, the more so because he was so full of occupation that the old besetting trouble, self-contemplation, had been expelled for lack of opportunity; and he had become far more simple, since humility was ceasing to be a conscious effort.

There is a light-heartedness about his letters like that of the old Eton times. Something might have been owing to the impulse of health, which was due to the tropical heat. Most probably this heat was what exhausted his constitution so early, but at first it was a delightful stimulus, and gave him exemption from all those discomforts with which cold had affected him at home. This exhilaration bore him over the many trials of close contact with uncivilised human nature so completely that his friends never even guessed at his natural fastidiousness. That which might have been selfish in this fastidiousness was conquered, though the refinement remained. Even to the last, in his most solitary hours, this personal neatness never relaxed, but the victory over disgust was a real triumph over self, which no doubt was an element of happiness.

While the Bishop continued to go on the voyages with him, he had companionship, guidance, and comparatively no responsibility, while his success, that supreme joy, was wonderfully unalloyed, and he felt his own especial gifts coming constantly into play. His love for his scholars was one continual well of delight, and really seemed to be an absolute gift, enabling him to win them over, and compensating for what he had left, even while he did not cease to love his home with deep tenderness.

Another pair of New Zealand friends had to be absent for a time. Archdeacon Abraham's arm was so severely injured by an accident with a horse, that the effects were far more serious than those of a common fracture. The disaster took place in Patteson's presence. 'I shall never forget,' writes his friend, 'his gentleness and consideration as he first laid me down in a room and then went to tell my wife.'

It was found necessary to have recourse to English advice; the Archdeacon and Mrs. Abraham went home, and were never again residents at Auckland.

A letter to Mr. Justice Coleridge was written in the interval between the voyages:

'Auckland: June 12, 1857.

'My dear Uncle,—You will not give me credit for being a good correspondent, I fear; but the truth is that I seldom find time to do more than write long chatty letters to my dear father and sisters, occasionally to Thorverton, and to Miss Neill and one or two others to cheer them in their sickness and weariness. Any news from afar may be a real relaxation.

'For myself I need only say that I find these dear people most attractive and winning, that it is no effort to love them, that they display all natural gifts in a remarkable way—good temper, affection, gentleness, obedience, gratitude, &c., occasionally real self-restraint. Dear Hirika's last words to me at San Cristoval were, "Oh, I do love you so," and his conduct showed it. He is a bright handsome lad, clever but inaccurate, of most sweet disposition. In matters of personal cleanliness, healthy appearance, &c., the change in seven months was that of a lad wholly savage becoming neat, tidy in dress, and of gentlemanly appearance. In some ways he was my pet of the whole party, though I have equally bright hopes of Grariri, a sturdy, honest fellow with the best temper I almost ever found among lads of sixteen anywhere, and Kerearua is the most painstaking fellow of the lot; and a boy whose distinguishing features it would be hard to describe; but he may be summed up as a very good boy, and certainly a most loveable one. Sumaro and Kimarua older and less interesting.

'I printed short catechisms, a translation of the Lord's Prayer, Creed, General Confession, two or three other of the Common Prayer prayers, and one or two short missionary prayers in the dialect of both islands; but I can only speak at all fluently the language of San Cristoval.

'Of the Nengone people I could say much more. The two young women (married) and the two young unmarried men had been under Mr. Nihill's instruction two or three years, baptized, and were regular communicants while at the College. Simeona was baptized on the same day as his infant son, after he had been with us five months. He and the other four were confirmed at the College chapel, and he afterwards received the Holy Communion with the rest.

'Kowine, a lad of seventeen, is not baptized, though well instructed. We were not wholly satisfied about him. Of the knowledge of them all I can speak with the utmost confidence. They know more a great deal than most candidates for confirmation in a well-regulated English parish. It was delightful to work with them. We wrote Bible history, which has reached about fifty sheets in MS. in small handwriting, bringing the history to the time of Joshua; very many questions and answers, and translated ninety pages of the Prayer Book, including Services for Infant and Adult Baptism, Catechism, Burial Service, &c.

'It is most interesting work, though not easy, and much of it will no doubt be altered when we come to know the language thoroughly well. This island of Nengone (called also Maro and Britannia Island) contains about 6,500 inhabitants, of whom some profess Christianity, while the remainder are still fighting and eating one another, though accessible to white people.

'We hope to have time to see something of the heathen population, though the London Mission Society having re-occupied the island, we do not regularly visit it with the intention of establishing ourselves.... The language is confined to that island. I call it language, not dialect, for it is, I believe, really distinct from any others we have or have heard of, very soft, like Italian, and capable of expressing accurately minute shades of meaning. Causative forms, &c., remind us of the oriental structure, one peculiarity (that of the chief's dialect, or almost language, running parallel to that of common life) I think I have before mentioned.

'In about a month I suppose we shall be off again for three or four months, and we long to get hold of pupils from the Banks Archipelago, Santa Cruz, Espiritu Santo, in which no ground is broken at present. We visited them last year, but did not get any pupils; lovely islands, very populous, and the natives very bright, intelligent-looking. But how I long to see again some of my own dear boys, I do so think of them! It may be that two or three of them may come again to us, and then we may perhaps hope that they may learn enough to be really useful to their own people.... Dear uncle, I should indeed rejoice much to see my dear, dear father and sisters and Jem and all of you if it came in the way of one's business, but I think, so long as I am well, that the peculiar nature of this work must require the constant presence of one personally known to, and not only officially connected with, the natives. While I feel very strongly that in many ways intercourse occasionally resumed with the home clergy must be very useful to us, yet if you can understand that there is no one to take one's place, you see how very unlikely it must be that I can move from this hemisphere. I say "if you can understand," for it does seem sad that one should really be in such a position that one's presence should be of any consequence; but, till it please God that the Bishop shall receive other men for this Mission, there is no other teacher for these lads, and so we must rub on and do the best we can. Of course I should be most thankful, most happy if, during his lifetime, I once more found myself at home, but I don't think much nor speculate about it, and I am very happy, as I am well and hearty. You won't suspect me of any lessening of strong affection for all that savours of home. I think that I know every face in Alfington and in Feniton, and very many in Ottery as of old; I believe I think of all with increasing affection, but while I wonder at it, I must also confess that I can and do live happy day after day without enjoying the sight of those dear faces.

'Always your affectionate and grateful nephew,

'J. C. PATTESON.'

As soon as the 'Southern Cross' had carried Bishop Harper back to Lyttelton, the Melanesian voyage was recommenced, this time with a valuable assistant in Mr. Benjamin Dudley. Mrs. Selwyn was again dropped at Norfolk Island, and five young Pitcairners were taken on board to serve as a boat's crew, and also to receive instruction.

This was a more extensive voyage than the first, as more time could be spent on it, but there is less full description, as there was less time for writing; and besides, these coral islands are much alike. Futuma was the first new island visited:—

'The canoes did not venture to come off to us, so we went ashore in the boat, Bishop and I wading ankle-deep to the beach. Forty or fifty natives under a deep overhanging rock, crouching around a fire, plenty of lads and boys, no women. Some Tanna men in the group, with their faces painted red and black, hair (as you know) elaborately frizzled and dressed with coral lime. The Futuma people speak a different language from those of Anaiteum, and the Tanna people speak a third (having, moreover, four dialects of their own). These three islands are all in sight of each other. Tanna has an active volcano, now smoking away, and is like a hot-bed, wonderfully fertile. People estimate its population at 10,000, though it is not very large,—about thirty miles long. At Futuma, the process by which these coral islands have been upheaved is well seen. The volcanic rocks are lying under the coral, which has been gradually thrust upwards by them. As the coral emerged, the animal went on building under water, continually working lower and lower down upon and over the volcanic formation, as this heaved in its upward course the coral formation out of the sea.'

Erromango was occupied by the Scottish Mission, and Mr. Gordon was then living there in peace and apparent security, when a visit was paid to him, and Patteson gathered some leaves in Dillon's Bay, the spot where John Williams met his death sixteen years before, not, as now was understood, because he was personally disliked, but because he was unconsciously interfering with a solemnity that was going on upon the beach.

At Fate Isle, the people were said to be among the wildest in those seas. When the 'Royal Sovereign' was wrecked, they had killed the whole crew, nineteen in number, eaten ten at once, and sent the other nine as presents to their friends. Very few appeared, but there was a good 'opening' exchange of presents.

A great number of small islets lie around Fate, forming part of the cluster of the New Hebrides, The Bishop had been at most of them before, and with a boat's crew of three Pitcairners and one English sailor, starting early and spending all day in the boat, he and Patteson touched at eleven in three days, and established the first steps to communication by obtaining 127 names of persons present, and making gifts. These little volcanic coral isles were all much alike, and nothing remarkable occurred but the obtaining two lads from Mai, named Petere and Laure, for a ten months' visit. Poor fellows, they were very sea-sick at first, and begged to go home again, but soon became very happy, and this connection with Petere had important consequences in the end. These lads spoke a language approaching Maori, whereas the Fate tongue prevailed in the other isles.

At Mallicolo, on August 20, a horrible sight presented itself to the eyes of the two explorers when they walked inland with about eighteen most obliging and courteous natives—an open space with four hollowed trunks of trees surrounding two stones, the trees carved into the shape of grotesque human heads, and among them, a sort of temple, made of sloping bamboos and pandanus leaves meeting at the top, from whence hung a dead man, with his face painted in stripes of red and yellow, procured, it was thought, from the pollen of flowers. There was not enough comprehension of the language to make out the meaning of all this.

Ambrym, the next island, was more than usually lovely, and was destined to receive many more visits. The women made their approach crawling, some with babies on their backs. Whitsuntide, where the casks had to be filled with water, showed a great number of large, resolute-looking men, whose air demanded caution; 'but,' says the journal, 'practice makes perfect, and we get the habit of landing among strangers, the knack of managing with signs and gesticulations, and the feeling of ease and confidence which engenders confidence and good-will in the others. Quarrels usually arise from both parties being afraid and suspicious of each other.'

Leper's Isle owes its unpleasant name to its medicinal springs. It is a particularly beautiful place, containing a population of good promise. Three landings were made there, and at the fourth place Patteson jumped ashore on a rock and spent some time in calming the fears of a party of natives who had been frightened in their canoe by the boat under sail overtaking them. 'They fingered bows and arrows, but only from nervousness,' he says. However, they seem to have suspected the visitors of designs on their load of fine taro, and it was some time before the owner would come out and resume it. On all these isles the plan could as yet only be to learn names and write them down, so as to enquire for acquaintance next time, either make presents, or barter them for provisions, discover the class of language, and invite scholars for another time.

So at Star Island three or four natives said, 'In ten moons you two come back; very good, then we go with you.' 'I think,' Patteson tells his sisters, 'you would have liked to have seen me, standing on a rock, with my two supporters, two fine young men, who will I trust go with us next time, my arms round their necks, and a fine background of some thirty or forty dark figures with bows and arrows, &c., and two or three little rogues, perched on a point of rock above me, just within reach, asking for fish-hooks.' He says it in all simplicity, but the picture presupposes some strength of mind in the sisters who were to appreciate it.

Few natives appeared at Espiritu Santo, and the vessel passed on to Oanuta or Cherry Island, where the Bishop had never been, and where a race of dull, good-natured giants was found. The chief was a noble-looking man with an aquiline nose, and seemed to have them well under command, and some of the younger men, who had limbs which might have been a model for a sculptor, could have lifted an ordinary-sized Englishman as easily as a child. They were unluckily already acquainted with whalers, whom they thought the right sort of fellows, since they brought tobacco and spirits, did not interfere with native habits, nor talk of learning, for which the giants saw no need. The national complexion here was of a lighter yellow, the costume a tattooed chest, the language akin to Maori; and it was the same at Tikopia, where four chiefs, one principal one immensely fat, received their visitors seated on a mat in the centre of a wide circle formed by natives, the innermost seated, the others looking over them. These, too, were accustomed to whalers, and when they found that pigs and yams in exchange for spirits and tobacco were not the object, they were indifferent. They seemed to despise fish-hooks, and it was plain that they had even obtained muskets from the whalers, for there were six in the chiefs house, and one was fired, not maliciously but out of display. The Bishop told them his object, and they understood his language, but were uninterested. The fat chief regaled the two guests with a cocoa-nut apiece, and then seemed anxious to be rid of them.

The Banks Islands, as usual, were much more hopeful, Santa Maria coming first. Canoes came round the vessel, and the honesty of the race showed itself, for one little boy, who had had a fish-hook given him, wished to exchange it for calico, and having forgotten to restore the hook at the moment, swam back with it as soon as he remembered it. There was a landing, and the usual friendly intercourse, but just as the boat had put off, a single arrow was suddenly shot out of the bush, and fell about ten yards short. It was curious that the Spanish discoverers had precisely the same experience. It was supposed to be an act of individual mischief or fun, and the place obtained the appropriate name of Cock Sparrow Point.

It was not possible to get into the one landing-place in the wall round Mota's sugar-loaf, but there was an exchange of civilities with the Saddleites, and in

Vanua Lava, the largest member of the group, a beautiful harbour was discovered, which the Bishop named Port Patteson, after the Judge.

The Santa Cruz group was visited again on the 23rd of September. Nothing remarkable occurred; indeed, Patteson's journal does not mention these places, but that of the Bishop speaks of a first landing at Nukapu, and an exchange of names with the old chief Acenana; and the next day of going to the main island, where swarms of natives swam out, with cries of Toki, toki, and planks before them to float through the surf. About 250 assembled at the landing place, as before, chiefly eager for traffic. The Volcano Isle was also touched at, but the language of the few inhabitants was incomprehensible. The mountain was smoking, and red-hot cinders falling as before on the steep side. It was tempting to climb it and investigate what probably no white man had yet seen, but it was decided to be more prudent to abstain.

Some events of the visit to Bauro are related in the following letter to the young cousin whose Confirmation day had been notified to him in time to be thought of in his prayers:—

'Off San Cristoval: October 5, 1857.

'My dearest Pena,—It was in a heathen land, among a heathen people, that I passed the Sunday—a day most memorable in your life—on which I trust you received for the first time the blessed Sacrament of our Saviour's Body and Blood.

'My darling—, as I knelt in the chiefs house, upon the mat which was also my bed—the only Christian in that large and beautiful island—my prayers were, I hope, offered earnestly that the full blessedness of that heavenly Union with the Lord Jesus Christ, and in Him with the Father and the Holy Ghost, might rest upon you for ever. I had reckoned upon being on board that Sunday, when the Holy Eucharist was administered on board our vessel; but as we reached Mwaata, our well-known village at San Cristoval, on Saturday, we both agreed that I had better go ashore while the vessel went away, to return for me on Monday. My day was now passed strangely enough, my first Sunday in a land where no Sunday is known.

'It was about 3 P.M. on Saturday when I landed, and it was an effort to have to talk incessantly till dark. Then the chief Iri went with me to his house. It is only one oblong room, with a bamboo screen running halfway across it about half-way down the room. It is only made of bamboo at the sides, and leaves for the roof. Yams and other vegetables were placed along the sides. There is no floor, but one or two grass mats are placed on the ground to sleep on. Iri and his wife, and an orphan girl about fourteen or fifteen, I suppose, slept on the other side of the screen; and two lads, called Grariri and Parenga, slept on my side of it. I can't say I slept at all, for the rats were so very many, coming in through the bamboo on every side, and making such a noise I could not sleep, though tired. They were running all about me.

'Well, at daylight I sent Gariri to fetch some water, and shaved and washed, to the great admiration of Iri and the ladies, and of others also, who crowded together at the hole which serves for door and windows. I lay down in my clothes, all but my coat, but I took a razor and some soap ashore.

'Sunday was spent in going about to different neighbouring settlements, and climbing the coral rocks was hard work, the thermometer at sea being 85° in the cool cabin, as the Bishop told me to-day.

'Of course many people were at work in the yam grounds, several of which I saw; but I found considerable parties at the different villages, and had, on the whole, satisfactory conversations with them. They listened and asked questions, and I told them as well as I could the simplest truths of Christianity.

'I had a part of a yam and drank four cocoa-nuts during the day, besides eating some mixture of yam, taro, and cocoa-nut all pounded together.

'People offered me food and nuts everywhere. Walked back with a boy called Tahi for my guide, and stopped at several plantations, and talked with the people.

'Sat out in the cool evening on the beach at Mwaata, after much talk in a chiefs house called Tarua; people came round me on the beach, and again I talked with them (a sort of half-preaching, half-conversing these talks were), till Iri said we must go to bed. Slept a little that night.

'I can truly say that you were in my head all day. After my evening prayers, when I thought of you—for it was about 9 P.M. = 10.10 A.M. with you, and you were on your way to church—I thought of you, kneeling between your dear mamma and grandmamma, and dear grandpapa administering to his three beloved ones the Bread of Life, and I was very happy as I thought of it, for I trust, through the mercy of God, and the merits of our Lord, that we shall be by Him raised at the Last Day to dwell with Him for ever. But indeed I must not write to you how very unworthy I felt to belong to that little company.

'This morning about eleven the vessel's boat came off for me, with the Bishop. I had arranged about some lads coming on with us, and it ended in seven joining our party. Only one of our old scholars has come again: he is that dear boy Grariri, whose name you will remember.

'Now I have had a good change of shirts, etc., and feel clean and comfortable, though I think a good night's rest will do me no harm. I have written to you the first minute that I had time. What a blessed, happy day it must have been for you, and I am sure they thought of you at Feniton.

'Your loving cousin,

'J. C. P.'

This strange Sunday was spent in conversation with different sets of natives, and that some distinct ideas were conveyed was plain from what old Iri was overheard saying to a man who was asking him whether he had not a guest who spoke Bauro: 'Yes,' said Iri, adding that 'he said men were not like dogs, or pigs, or birds, or fishes, because these cannot speak or think. They all die, and no one knows anything more about them, but he says we shall not die like that, but rise up again.'

On Monday, the 7th of October, Grera was revisited, and Toto, a last year's scholar, came forth with his welcome in a canoe; but it was rather a mixed success, for the danger of the vessel on her previous visit was a warning against bringing her into the harbour, where there was no safe anchorage, and this disappointed the people. Thirteen, indeed, slept on board, and the next morning sixty canoes surrounded the vessel, and some hundred and sixty came on deck at once; but they brought only one pig and a few yams, and refused to fetch more, saying it was too far—a considerable inconvenience, considering the necessity of providing the Melanesian passengers with vegetable food. The whole nine slept in the inner cabin, Orariri on Patteson's sofa, 'feet to feet, the others on the floor like herrings in a barrel.'

The great island of New Caledonia was next visited. The Bishop had been there before, and Basset, one of the chiefs, lamented that he had been so long absent, and pleaded hard to have an English missionary placed in his part of the country. It was very sad to have no means of complying with the entreaty, and the Bishop offered him a passage to Auckland, there to speak for himself. He would have come, but that it was the season for planting his yams; but he hoped to follow, and in the meantime sent a little orphan named Kanambat to be brought up at Auckland. The little fellow was pleased enough with the ship at first, but when his countrymen who had been visiting there left her, he jumped overboard and was swimming like a duck after them, when, at a sign from the Bishop, one of the Pitcairners leapt after him, and speedily brought him back. He soon grew very happy and full of play and fun, and was well off in being away from home, for the French were occupying the island, and poor Basset shortly after was sent a prisoner to Tahiti for refusing to receive a Roman Catholic priest.

Nengone were reached on October 23, and most of the old scholars were ready with a warm welcome; but Mr. Creagh, the London missionary, had taken Wadrokala away with him on an expedition, and of the others, only Kowine was ready to return, though the two married couples were going on well, and one previous scholar of the Bishop's and four new ones presented themselves as willing to go. Urgent letters from the neighbouring isle of Lifu entreated the Bishop to come thither, and, with a splendid supply of yams, the 'Southern Cross' again set sail, and arrived on the 26th. This island had entirely abandoned heathenism, under the guidance of the Samoans. The people felt that they had come to the end of the stock of teaching of these good men, and entreated for an Englishman from the Bishop, and thus, here was the third island in this one voyage begging for a shepherd, and only one English priest had been found to offer himself to that multitude of heathen!

The only thing that could be done was to take John Cho, a former St. John's scholar, to receive instruction to fit him for a teacher, and with him came his young wife Naranadune, and their babe, whom the Bishop had just baptized in the coral-lime chapel, with three other children.

The next few days were spent in great anxiety for Wailumai, a youth from Grera, who was taken ill immediately after dinner with a most distressing difficulty of breathing. He proved to have a piece of sugar cane in his throat, which made every breath agony, and worked a small ulcer in the throat. All through the worst Patteson held him in his arms, with his hand on his chest: several times he seemed gone, and ammonia and sal volatile barely revived him. His first words after he was partially relieved were, 'I am Bishop! I am Patihana!' meaning that he exchanged names with them, the strongest possible proof of affection in Melanesian eyes. He still seemed at the point of death, and they made him say, 'God the Father, God the Son, and God the Holy Ghost! Jesus Christ, Son of God.' At last a favourable change took place, but he continued so ill for several days that his two attendants never did more than lie down in their clothes; nor was it till the third day that he at length coughed up the piece of cane that had caused the mischief. He still required so much care that Patteson did not go on shore at Norfolk Island when the five Pitcairners were exchanged for Mrs. Selwyn.

On November 15 Auckland harbour was again reached after this signally prosperous voyage. It is thus summed up in a letter written two days later:—

'November 17, 1857: St. John's College.

'My dear Miss Neill,—Thanks for your £21. 2s., and more thanks still for your prayers and constant interest in this part of the world. After nearly seventeen weeks at sea, we returned safely on Sunday morning the 15th, with thirty-three Melanesians, gathered from nine islands and speaking eight languages. Plenty of work for me: I can teach tolerably in three, and have a smattering of one or two more.

'One is the wife of a young man, John Cho, an old scholar baptized. His half-brother is chief of Lifu Isle, a man of great influence. The London Mission (Independents) are leaving all their islands unprovided with missionaries, and these people having been much more frequently visited by the Bishop than by the "John Williams," turn to him for help. By and by I will explain all this: at present no time.

'We visited sixty-six islands and landed eighty-one times, wading, swimming, &c.; all most friendly and delightful; only two arrows shot at us, and only one went near—so much for savages. I wonder what people ought to call sandal-wood traders and slave-masters if they call my Melanesians savages.

'You will hear accounts of the voyage from Fanny. I have a long journal going to my father, but I can't make time to write at length any more. I am up before five and not in bed before eleven, and you know I must be lazy sometimes. It does me good. Oh! how great a trial sickness would be to me! In my health now all seems easy. Were I circumstanced like you, how much I should no doubt repine and murmur. God has given me hitherto a most merciful share of blessings, and my dear father's cordial approbation of and consent to my proceedings is among the greatest....

'The anniversary of my dear mother's death comes round in ten days. That is my polar star (humanly speaking), and whensoever it pleases God to take my dear dear father to his rest, how blessed to think of their waiting for us, if it be His merciful will to bring me too to dwell before Him with them for ever.

'I must end, for I am very busy. The weather is cold, and my room full of lads and young men. If I was not watching like a cat they would be standing about in all sorts of places and catching cold.

'I send you in a box, a box made by Pitcairners of Pitcairn woods.

'Ever your loving old pupil,

'J. C. PATTESON.'

The little New Caledonian remained at Taurarua with the Bishop, and as there was no woman at St. John's to take the charge of Cho's wife, she was necessarily sent to Mrs. Kissling's school for Maori girls, while her husband pursued his studies at St. John's.

Patteson often gave his services at the Maori village of Orakei, where there was to be a central native school managed by Pirimona (Philemon), a well-trained man, a candidate for Holy Orders.

'However, this did not satisfy his countrymen. As if I had not enough to do, old Wi comes with a request from the folks at Orakei that I would be their "minita," and take the management of the concern. Rather rich, is it not? I said, of course, that I was minita for the islanders. "Oh, let the Bishop take another man for that, you are the minister for us." He is, you know, wonderfully tatooed, and a great object of curiosity to the boys!

Before many days had passed, there had occurred the first case of that fatal tetanus, which became only too well known to those concerned in the Mission. Of course, all weapons were taken from the scholars; but one of the San Cristoval boys, named Tohehammai, fetched one of his own arrows out of Mr. Dudley's room to exchange with an English lad for a shirt, and as he was at play, carrying the arrow in his left hand behind his back and throwing a stick like a spear with the other, he sharply pricked his right arm, within the elbow, against the point of the arrow; but thinking nothing of the hurt, and knowing that the weapons were forbidden playthings, he said nothing for twelve days, but then complained of stiffness in the arm. Two doctors happened to be at the college that day; one thought it rheumatism, the other mentioned the word tetanus, but for three days more the arm was merely stiff, it was hung in a sling, and the boy went about as usual, until, on the fifteenth day, spasmodic twitchings in the arm came on.

Liniment of chloroform was rubbed in, and the boy was kept under chloroform, but in vain; the next day his whole body was perfectly rigid, with occasional convulsions. About 4 p.m. his throat had become contracted, and the endeavour to give him nourishment brought on convulsive attacks. The Bishop came at 8. p.m., and after another attempt at giving him food, which produced a further spasm, he was lying quietly when Patteson felt his pulse stop.

"'He is dying!" the Bishop said. "'Father, into Thy hands we commend his spirit.'"

Patteson's 'Amen' came from his heart. The poor fellow made no sound as he lay with his frame rigid, his back arched so that an arm could be thrust under it. He was gone in that moment, unbaptized. Patteson writes:—

'I had much conflict with myself about it. He had talked once with me in a very hopeful way, but during his illness I could not obtain from him any distinct profession of faith, anything to make me feel pretty sure that some conviction of the truth of what he he had been taught, and not mere learning by rote, was the occasion of his saying what he did say. I did wish much that I might talk again with the Bishop about it, but his death took us by surprise. I pray God that all my omission and neglect of duty may be repaired, and that his very imperfect and unconscious yearnings after the truth may be accepted for Christ's sake.'

The arrow was reported to have been poisoned, but by the time the cause of the injury had been discovered it had been thrown away and could not be recovered for examination. Indeed, lockjaw seems to be so prevalent in the equatorial climates, and the natives so peculiarly liable to it, that poison did not seem needful to account for the catastrophe.

Altogether, these lads were exotics in New Zealand, and exceedingly fragile. In the very height of summer they had to wear corduroy trousers, blue serge shirts, red woollen comforters, and blue Scotch caps, and the more delicate a thick woollen jersey in addition; and with all these precautions they were continually catching cold, or getting disordered, and then the Bauro and Grera set could only support such treatment as young children generally need. The Loyalty Islanders were much tougher and stronger and easier to treat, but they too showed that the climate of Auckland was a hard trial to their constitutions.

On the last day of March came tidings of the sudden death of the much-beloved and honoured Dr. James Coleridge of Thorverton.

'It is a great shock,' says the letter written the same day; 'not that I feel unhappy exactly, nor low, but that many many memories are revived and keep freshening on my mind.... And since I left England his warm, loving, almost too fond letters have bound me very closely to him, and sorely I shall miss the sight of his handwriting; though he may be nearer to me now than before, and his love for me is doubtless even more pure and fervent.

'I confess I had thought sometimes that if it pleased God to take you first, the consciousness that he would be with you was a great comfort to me—not that any man is worth much then. God must be all in all. But yet he of all men was the one who would have been a real comfort to you, and even more so to others.' To his cousin he writes:—

'Wednesday in Passion Week, 1858: St. John's College.

'My dearest Sophy,—Your letter with the deep black border was the first that I opened, with trembling hand, thinking: "Is it dear dear Uncle gone to his eternal rest; or dear Aunty? not that dear child, may God grant; for that would somehow seem to all most bitter of all—less, so to speak, reasonable and natural." And he is really gone; that dear, loving, courageous, warm-hearted servant of Christ; the desire of our eyes taken away with a stroke. I read your letter wondering that I was not upset, knelt down and said the two prayers in the Burial Service, and then came the tears; for the memory of him rose up very vividly before me, and his deep love for me and the notes of comfort and encouragement he used to write were very fresh in my mind. I looked at the print of him, the one he sent out to me, with "your loving old Uncle" in pencil on it. I have all his letters: when making a regular clearance some months ago, I could not tear up his, although dangerous ones for me to read unless used as a stimulant to become what he thought me. His "Jacob" sermon in his own handwriting, I have by me. But more than all, the memory of his holy life, and his example as a minister of Christ, have been left behind for us as a sweet, undying fragrance; his manner in the sick-room —I see him now, and hear that soft, steady, clear voice repeating verses over my dear mother's death-bed; his kindly, loving ways to his poor people; his voice and look in the pulpit, never to be forgotten. I knew I should never see him again in this world. May God of His mercy take me to be with him hereafter.

'Thank you, dear Sophy, for writing to me; every word about him is precious, from his last letter to me:—

'"You will believe how sweet it is to me every month now to give the Holy Eucharist to my three dear ones."

'"All complaints of old men must be serious."

'I wish I had more time to write, but I am too busy in the midst of school, and printing Scripture histories and private prayers, and translations in Nengone, Bauro, Lifu; and as all my time out of school is spent in working in the printing office, I really have not a minute unoccupied. With one exception, I have scarcely ever taken an hour's walk for some six weeks. A large proportion of the printing is actually set up by my own fingers; but now one Nengone lad, the flower of my flock, can help me much—a young man about seventeen or eighteen, of whom I hope very much—Malo, baptized by the name of Harper, an excellent young man, and a great comfort to me. He was setting up in type a part of the little book of private prayers I am now printing for them. I had just pointed out to him the translation of what would be in English—"It is good that a man as he lies down to sleep should remember that that night he may hear the summons of the Angel of God; so then let him think of his death, and remember the words of St. Paul: 'Awake, thou that sleepest,'" etc.; when in came the man whom the Archdeacon left in charge here with my letters. "I hope, sir, there is no bad news for you;" and my eye lighted on the deep black border of your envelope.

'To-morrow, if I live, I enter upon my thirty-second year—a solemn warning I have received to-day, as another year is passing from me. May some portion of his spirit rest on me to bless my poor attempt to do what he did so devotedly for more than forty years: his duty as a soldier and servant of his Lord and Master, into whose joy he has no doubt now entered.

'Easter Day.—What an Easter for him! and doubtless we all who will by and by, as the world rolls round, receive the Holy Eucharist shall be in some way united to him as well as to all departed saints—members of His Mystical Body.

'April 12.—Bishop came out yesterday afternoon from Auckland. After baptisms at 5, and evening service at 7, sat till past 11 settling plans: thus, God willing, start this day fortnight to return the boys—this will occupy about two months; as we come back from the far north, he will drop one at Lifu, one of the Loyalty Islands, with large population; he will go on to New Zealand, stay perhaps six weeks in New Zealand, or it may be two months; so that with the time occupied by his voyage from Lifu to New Zealand, 1,000 miles and back, he will be away from Lifu about two and a half or three months. Then, picking me up (say about September 12), we go on at once to the whole number of our islands, spending three months or so among them, getting back to New Zealand about the end of November. So that I shall be in Melanesia, D.V., from the beginning of May to the end of November. I shall be able to write once more before we start —letters which you will get by the June mail from Sydney—and of course I shall send letters by the Bishop when he leaves me at Lifu. But I shall not be able to hear again from England till the Bishop comes to pick me up in September. Never mind. I shall have plenty to do; and I can think of those dear ones at home, and of you all, in God's keeping, with perfect comfort. The Lifu people are in a more critical state than any others just now, otherwise I should probably stop at San Cristoval. A few years ago they were very wild—cannibals of course; but they are now building chapels, and thirsting for the living waters. What a privilege and responsibility to go to them as Christ's minister, to a people longing for the glad tidings of the Gospel of Peace. Samoan teachers have been for a good many years among them.

'I cannot write now to dearest Aunty or Pena.

'May God bless you and abundantly comfort you.... I think I see his dear face. I see him always.

'Your loving cousin,
'J. C. PATTESON.'

Cho's wife had arrived in a cart at the College when her baby was a day old, so rapid is recovery with mothers in those climates. 'I saw the baby,' observes the journal, quite strong, not dark,—but I don't care for them till they can talk; on the contrary, I think them a great bore, especially in wooden houses, where a child with good lungs may easily succeed in keeping all the inhabitants awake.'

'April 12.—Settled that I stop at Lifu in the interval between the two voyages. I think Lifu wants me more than any other island just now. Some 15,000 or 20,000 stretching out their hands to God. The London Mission (Independent) sent Samoan teachers long ago, but no missionary, even after frequent applications. At last they applied personally to the Bishop, he being well known to them of old. I can't go for good, because I have of course to visit all these islands; but I shall try to spend all the time that I am not at sea or with boys in New Zealand, perhaps three months yearly, with them, till they can be provided with a regular clergyman.

'So I shall have no letters from you till the return of the vessel to pick me up in September. But be sure you think of me as very happy and well cared for, though, I am glad to say, not a white man on the island; lots of work, but I shall take much exercise and see most of the inhabitants. The island is large, not so large as Bauro, but still large.

'You will say all that is kind to all relations, Buckerell, etc. Thank the dear old vicar for the spurs, and tell him that I had a battle royal the other day with a colonial steed, which backed into the bush, and kicked, and played the fool amazingly, till I considerably astonished him into a gallop, in the direction I wanted to go, by a vigorous application of the said spurs.

'God bless and keep you all.

'Your loving
'J. C. PATTESON.'

A few days later he writes:—

'The "Southern Cross," returning to Lifu, will bring my letters; but unless a stray whaler comes to Lifu while I am there, on its way to Sydney, that will be the only exchange of letters. I am afraid this will be an increase of the trial of separation to you all, but it is not sent until you have learnt to do pretty well without me, and you will be comforted by knowing that this island of Lifu, with many inhabitants, is in a very critical state; that what it most wants is a missionary, and that as far as I am concerned, all the people will be very anxious to do all they can for me. I take a filter and some tea. We shall have yams, taro, cocoa-nuts, occasionally a bit of turtle, a fowl, or a bit of pork. So, you see, I shall live like an alderman; I mean, if I am to go to every part of the island, heathen and all. Perhaps 20,000 people, scattered over many miles. I say heathen and all, because only a very small number of the people now refuse to admit the new teaching. Samoans have been for some time on the island, and though, I dare say, their teaching has been very imperfect and only perhaps ten or fifteen people are baptized, they have chapels, and are far advanced beyond any of the islands except Nengone and Toke, always excepting Anaiteum. Hence it is thought the leaven may work quietly in the Solomon Islands without me, but that at Lifu they really require guidance. So now I have a parochial charge for three months of an island about twenty-five miles long and some sixteen or eighteen broad.

'I feel that my letters, after so long an absence, may contain much to make me anxious, so that I shall not look with unmixed pleasure to my return to my great packet; yet I feel much less anxiety than you might imagine; I know well that you are in God's keeping, and that is enough.'

After just touching at Nengone early in May the 'Southern Cross' went on to Lifu, and on landing, the Bishop and Mr. Patteson found a number of people ready to receive them, and to conduct them to the village, where the chief and a great number of people were drawn up in a half-circle to receive them. The young chief, Angadhohua, bowed and touched his hat, and taking Coley's hand, held it, and whispered, 'We will always live together.'

'By and by we will talk about it,' was the answer; and they were taken to a new house, belonging to one of the Samoans, built of lath plastered and thatch, with one large room and a lesser one at each of its angles. There the Bishop and Mr. Patteson sat on a chest, and seventy or eighty men squatted on mats, John Cho and the native teacher foremost. There was a five minutes' pause. Lifu was not yet familiar to Coley, who spoke it less well than he had spoken German, and John Cho said to him: 'Shall I tell them what you have said to me formerly?'

He then explained that Mr. Patteson could only offer them a visit of three or four months, and would then have the charge of lads from 'dark isles.'

Silence again; then Angadhohua asked: 'Cannot you stop always?'

'There are many difficulties which you cannot understand, which prevent me. Would you like me to shut the door which God has opened to so many dark lands?'

'No, no; but why not have the summer school here as well as the winter?'

'Because it does the lads good to see New Zealand, and because the Bishop, who knows better than I do, thinks it right.'

'And cannot we have a missionary?'

However, they were forced to content themselves with all that could be granted to them, and it was further explained that Mr. Patteson would not supersede the native teachers, nor assume the direction of the Sunday services, only keep a school which any one might join who liked. This was felt to be only right in good faith to the London Mission, in order not to make dire confusion if they should be able to fill up the gap before the Church could.

After sleeping in the house, Patteson produced the books that had been printed for them at St. John's.

'Would that you could have seen their delight! About two pages, indifferently printed, was all they had hitherto. Now they saw thirty-two clearly printed 8vo. pages of Bible History, sixteen of prayers, rubrics, &c., eight of questions and answers. "You see," said I cunningly; "that we don't forget you during these months that I can't live among you."'

They began reading at once, and crying, 'Excellent, exactly right, the very thing.'

It was thought good that some one from Lifu should join the Mission party and testify to their work, and on the invitation, the chief, Angadhohua, a bright youth of seventeen, volunteered to go. It was an unexampled thing that a chief should be permitted by his people to leave them, there was a public meeting about it, and a good deal of excitement, but it ended in Cho, as spokesman, coming forward with tears in his eyes, saying, 'Yes, it is right he should go, but bring him back soon. What shall we do?'

Patteson laid his hand on the young chief's shoulder, answering, 'God can guard him by sea as on land, and with His blessing we will bring him back safe to you. Let some of the chiefs go with him to protect him. I will watch over him, but you may choose whom you will to accompany him.'

So five chiefs were selected as a body-guard for the young Angadhohua, who was prince of all the isle, but on an insecure tenure, for the French, in New Caledonia, were showing a manifest inclination to annex the Loyalty group.

The heavily loaded boat had a perilous strife with the surf before the ship was reached, and it was a very rough passage to Anaiteum, where some goods had to be left for Mr. Inglis, and he asked that four Fate visitors might be taken home. This was done, and Mr. Grordon was visited at Erromango on the way, and found well and prosperous.

At Mai, the reception of Petere and Laure was ecstatic. There was a crowd on shore to meet them, and on the two miles' walk to the village parties met, hugged, and wept over them. At the village Mr. Patteson addressed the people for ten minutes, and Petere made an animated exposition of what he had learnt, and his speeches evidently had great effect. His younger brother and two little boys all came in his stead, and would form part of the winter school at Lifu.

The Espiritu Santo boy, the dunce of the party, was set down at home, and the Banks Islanders were again found pleasant, honest, and courteous, thinking, as it appeared afterwards, that the white men were the departed spirits of deceased friends. A walk inland at Vanua Lava disclosed pretty villages nestling under banyan trees, one of them provided with a guest-chamber for visitors from other islands. Two boys, Sarawia and another, came away to be scholars at Lifu, as well as his masters in the language, of which he as yet scarcely knew anything, but which he afterwards found the most serviceable of all these various dialects.

The 26th of May brought the vessel to Bauro, where poor old Iri was told of the death of his son, and had a long talk with Mr. Patteson, beginning with, 'Do you think I shall see him again?' It was a talk worth having, though it was purchased by spending a night in the house with the rats.

It seemed as though the time were come for calling on the Baurese to cease to be passive, and sixty or seventy men and women having come together, Mr. Patteson told them that he did not mean to go on merely taking their boys to return them with heaps of fish-hooks and knives, but that, unless they cared for good teaching, to make them good and happy here and hereafter, he should not come like a trader or a whaler. That their sons should go backwards and forwards and learn, but to teach at home; and that they ought to build a holy house, where they might meet to pray to God and learn His will.

Much of this was evidently distasteful, though they agreed to build a room.

'I think,' he writes, 'that the trial stage of the work has arrived. This has less to attract outwardly than the first beginning of all, and as here they must take a definite part, they (the great majority who are not yet disposed to decide for good) are made manifest, and the difficulty of displacing evil customs is more apparent.'

In fact, these amiable, docile Baurese seemed to have little manliness or resolution of character, and Sumaro, a scholar of 1857, was especially disappointing, for he pretended to wish to come and learn at Lifu, but only in order to get a passage to Gera, where he deserted, and was well lectured for his deceit.

The Gera people were much more warlike and turbulent, and seemed to have more substance in them, though less apt at learning. Patteson spent the night on shore at Perua, a subsidiary islet in the bay, sleeping in a kind of shed, upon two boards, more comfortably than was usual on these occasions. Showing confidence was one great point, and the want of safe anchorage in the bay was much regretted, because the people could not understand why the vessel would not come in, and thought it betokened mistrust. Many lads wished to join the scholars, but of those who were chosen, two were forced violently overboard by their friends, and only two eventually remained, making a total of twelve pupils for the winter school at Lifu, with five languages between them—seven with the addition of the Nengone and Lifu scholars.

'You see,' writes Patteson on June 10, on the voyage, 'that our difficulty is in training and organising nations, raising them from heathenism to the life, morally and socially, of a Christian. This is what I find so hard. The communication of religious truth by word of mouth is but a small part of the work. The real difficulty is to do for them what parents do for their children, assist them to—nay, almost force upon them—the practical application of Christian doctrine. This descends to the smallest matters, washing, scrubbing, sweeping, all actions of personal cleanliness, introducing method and order, habits of industry, regularity, giving just notions of exchange, barter, trade, management of criminals, division of labour. To do all this and yet not interfere with the offices of the chief, and to be the model and pattern of it, who is sufficient for it?'

On June 16, Mr. Patteson was landed at Lifu, for his residence there, with the five chiefs, his twelve boys, and was hospitably welcomed to the large new house by the Samoan. He and four boys slept in one of the corner rooms, the other eight lads in another, the Rarotongan teacher, Tutoo, and his wife in a third. The central room was parlour, school, and hall, and as it had four unglazed windows, and two doors opposite to each other, and the trade-wind always blowing, the state of affairs after daylight was much like that which prevailed in England when King Alfred invented lanterns, while in the latter end of June the days were, of course, as short as they could be on the tropic of Capricorn, so that Patteson got up in the dark at 5-30 in the morning.

At 7 the people around dropped in for prayers, which he thought it better not to conduct till his position was more defined. Then came breakfast upon yams cooked by being placed in a pit lined with heated stones, with earth heaped over the top. Mr. and Mrs. Tutoo, with their white guest, sat at the scrap of a table, 'which, with a small stool, was the only thing on four legs in the place, except an occasional visitor in the shape of a pig.' Then followed school. Two hundred Lifu people came, and it was necessary to hold it in the chapel. One o'clock, dinner on yams, and very rarely on pig or a fowl, baked or rather done by the same process; and in the afternoon some reading and slate work with the twelve Melanesians, and likewise some special instruction to a few of the more promising Lifuites. At 6.30, another meal of yams, but this time Patteson had recourse to his private store of biscuit; and the evening was spent in talk, till bedtime at 9 or 9.30. It was a thorough sharing the native life; but after a few more experiments, it was found that English strength could not be kept up on an exclusive diet of yams, and the Loyalty Isles are not fertile. They are nothing but rugged coral, in an early stage of development; great ridges, upheaved, bare and broken, and here and there with pits that have become filled with soil enough to grow yams and cocoa-nuts.

The yams—except those for five of the lads, whose maintenance some of the inhabitants had undertaken—were matter of purchase, and formed the means of instruction in the rules of lawful exchange. A fixed weight of yams were to constitute prepayment for a pair of trousers, a piece of calico, a blanket, tomahawk, or the like, and all this was agreed to, Cho being a great assistance in explaining and dealing with his people. But it proved very difficult to keep them up to bringing a sufficient supply, and as they had a full share of the universal spirit of haggling, the commissariat was a very harassing and troublesome business, and as to the boys, it was evident that the experiment was not successful. Going to New Zealand was seeing the world. Horses, cows, sheep, a town, soldiers, &c., were to be seen there, whereas Lifu offered little that they could not see at home, and schooling without novelty was tedious. Indeed, the sight of civilised life, the being taken to church, the kindness of the friends around the College, were no slight engines in their education; but the Lifu people were not advanced enough to serve as an example—except that they had renounced the more horrible of their heathen habits. They were in that unsettled state which is peculiarly trying in the conversion of nations, when the old authoritative customs have been overthrown, and the Christian rules not established.

It was a good sign that the respect for the chief was not diminished. One evening an English sailor (for there turned out to be three whites on the island) who was employed in the sandal-wood trade was in the house conversing with Tutoo, when Angadhohua interrupted him, and he—in ignorance of the youth's rank—pushed him aside out of the way. The excitement was great. A few years previously the offender would have been killed on the spot, and as it was, it was only after apology and explanation of his ignorance that he was allowed to go free; but an escort was sent with him to a place twenty miles off lest any one should endeavour to avenge the insult, not knowing it had been forgiven.

Many of the customs of these Loyalty Isles are very unhealthy, and the almost exclusive vegetable diet produced a low habit of body, that showed itself in all manner of scrofulous diseases, especially tumours, under which the sufferer wasted and died. Much of Patteson's time was taken up by applications from these poor creatures, who fancied him sure to heal them, and had hardly the power, certainly not the will, to follow his advice.

Nor had he any authority. He only felt himself there on sufferance till the promised deputation should come from Rarotonga from the London Mission, to decide whether the island should be reserved by them, or yielded to the Church. Meantime he says on Sunday:—

'Tutoo has had a pretty hard day's work of it, poor fellow, and he is anything but strong. At 9.30 we all went to the chapel, which began by a hymn sung as roughly as possible, but having rather a fine effect from the fact of some 400 or 500 voices all singing in unison. Then a long extemporary prayer, then another hymn, then a sermon nearly an hour long. It ought not to have taken more than a quarter of an hour, but it was delivered very slowly, with endless repetitions, otherwise there was some order and arrangement about it. Another hymn brought the service to an end about 11. But his work was not done; school instantly succeeded in the same building, and though seven native teachers were working their classes, the burthen of it fell on him. School was concluded with a short extemporary prayer. At three, service again—hymn, prayer, another long sermon, hymn, and at last we were out of chapel, there being no more school.'

'To be sure,' is the entry on another Sunday, 'little thought I of old that Sunday after Sunday I should frequent an Independent chapel. As for extemporary prayer not being a form, that is absurd. These poor fellows just repeat their small stock of words over and over again, and but that they are evidently in earnest, it would seem shockingly irreverent sometimes. Most extravagant expressions! Tutoo is a very simple, humble-minded man, and I like him much. He would feel the help and blessing of a Prayer-book, poor fellow, to be a guide to him; but even the Lord's Prayer is never heard among them.'

So careful was Mr. Patteson not to offend the men who had first worked on these islands, that on one Sunday when Tutoo was ill, he merely gave a skeleton of a sermon to John Cho to preach. On the 27th of July, however, the deputation arrived in the 'John Williams'—two ministers, and Mr. Creagh on his way back to Nengone, and the upshot of the conference on board, after a dinner in the house of Apollo, the native teacher, was that as they had no missionary for Lifu, they made no objection to Mr. Patteson working there at present, and that if in another year they received no reinforcement from home, they would take into consideration the making over their teachers to him. 'My position is thus far less anomalous, my responsibility much increased. God will, I pray and trust, strengthen me to help the people and build them up in the faith of Christ.'

'August 2.—Yesterday I preached my two first Lifu sermons; rather nervous, but I knew I had command of the language enough to explain my meaning, and I thought over the plan of my sermons and selected texts. Fancy your worthy son stuck up in a pulpit, without any mark of the clergyman save white tie and black coat, commencing service with a hymn, then reading the second chapter of St. Matthew, quite new to them, then a prayer, extemporary, but practically working in, I hope, the principle and much of the actual language of the Prayer-book—i.e. Confession, prayer for pardon, expression of belief and praise—then another hymn, the sermon about forty minutes. Text: "I am the Way," &c. Afternoon: "Thy Word is a lantern unto my feet."

'You can easily understand how it was simple work to point out that a man lost his way by his sin, and was sent out from dwelling with God; the recovery of the way by which we may again return to Paradise is practically the one great event which the whole Bible is concerned in teaching. The subject admitted of any amount of illustration and any amount of reference to the great facts of Scripture history, and everything converges to the Person of Christ. I wish them to see clearly the great points—first, God's infinite love, and the great facts by which He has manifested His Love from the very first, till the coming of Christ exhibited most clearly the infinite wisdom and love by which man's return to Paradise has been effected.

'Significant is that one word to the thief on the Cross "Paradise." The way open again; the guardian angel no longer standing with flaming sword in the entrance; admission to the Tree of Life.'

'The services were much shorter than usual, chiefly because I don't stammer and bungle, and take half an hour to read twenty verses of the Bible, and also because I discarded all the endless repetitions and unmeaning phrases, which took up half the time of their unmeaning harangues. About an hour sufficed for the morning-service; the evening one might have been a little longer. I feel quite at my ease while preaching, and John told me it was all very clear; but the prayers—oh! I did long for one of our Common Prayer-books.'

One effect of the Independent system began to reveal itself strongly. How could definite doctrines be instilled into the converts by teachers with hardly any books, and no formula to commit to memory? What was the faith these good Samoans knew and taught?

'No doctrinal belief exists among them,' writes Patteson, in the third month of his stay. 'A man for years has been associated with those who are called "the people that seek Baptism." He comes to me:—

'J. G. P. 'Who instituted baptism?
'A. Jesus.
'J. G. P. And He sent His Apostles to baptize in the Name of Whom?
'Dead silence.

"'Why do you wish to be baptized?'"

"'To live.'"

"'All that Jesus has done for us, and given to us, and taught us, is for that object. What is the particular benefit we receive in baptism?' 'No conception.' Such is their state.

'I would not hesitate if I thought there were any implicit recognition of the doctrine of the Trinity; but I can't baptize people morally good who don't know the Name into which they are to be baptized, who can't tell me that Jesus is God and man. There is a lad who soon must die of consumption, whom I now daily examine. He has not a notion of any truth revealed from above, and to be embraced and believed as truth upon the authority of God's Word. A kind of vague morality is the substitute for the Creed of the Apostles. What am I to do? I did speak out for three days consecutively pretty well, but I am alone, and only here for four months, and yet, I fear, I am expecting too much from them, and that I ought to be content with something much less as the (so to speak) qualifications; but surely they ought to repent and believe. To say the word, "I believe," without a notion of what they believe, surely that won't do. They must be taught, and then baptized, according to our Lord's command, suited for adults.'

Constant private teaching to individuals was going on, and the 250 copies of the Lifu primer were dispersed where some thousands were wanted, and Mr. Patteson wrote a little book of sixteen pages, containing the statement of the outlines of the faith, and of Scripture history; but this could not be dispersed till it had been printed in New Zealand.

And in the meantime a fresh element of perplexity was arising. The French had been for some time past occupying New Caledonia, and a bishop had been sent thither about the same time as Bishop Selwyn had gone to New Zealand; but though an earnest and hardworking man, he had never made much progress. He had the misfortune of being connected in the people's minds with French war ships and aggression, and, moreover, the South Sea race seem to have a peculiar distaste for the Roman Catholic branch of the Church, for which it is not easy to account.

The Loyalty Isles, as lying so near to New Caledonia, were tempting to the French Empire, and the Bishop at the same time felt it his duty to attempt their conversion.

Some priests had been placed at the north end of the island for about six months past, but the first communication was a letter on July 6, complaining, partly in French, partly in English, that since Mr. Patteson's arrival, the people had been making threatening reports. Now Mr. Patteson had from the first warned them against showing any unkindness to the French priests, and he wrote a letter of explanation, and arranged to go and hold a conference. On the way, while supping with the English sailor, at the village where he was to sleep, he heard a noise, and found the Frenchman, Pere Montrouzier, had arrived. He was apparently about forty; intelligent, very experienced in mission work, and conversant with the habits and customs of French and English in the colonies; moreover, with plenty of firmness in putting forward his cause. He seems to have been supported by the State in a manner unusual with French missions.

'I had one point only that I was determined to press (Patteson says), namely, liberty to the people to follow any form of religion they might choose to adopt. I knew that they and I were completely in his power, yet that my line was to assume that we were now about to arrange our plans for the future independently of any interference from the civil power.

'He let me see that he knew he could force upon the Lifu people whatever he pleased, the French Government having promised him any number of soldiers he may send for to take possession, if necessary, of the island. They have 1,000 men in New Caledonia, steamers and frigates of war; and he told me plainly that this island and Nengone are considered as natural appendages of New Caledonia, and practically French possessions already, so that, of course, to attempt doing more than secure for the people a religious liberty is out of the question. He promised me that if the people behaved properly to him and his people, he would not send for the soldiers, nor would he do anything to interfere with the existing state of the island.

'He will not himself remain here long, being commissioned, in consequence of his fourteen years' experience, to prepare the way for the French mission here. He told me that twenty missionaries are coming out for this group, about seven or eight of whom will be placed on Lifu, others on Nengone, &c.; that the French Government is determined to support them; that the Commandant of Nimia in New Caledonia had sent word to him that any number of men should be sent to him at an instant's notice, in a war steamer, to do what he might wish in Lifu, but that honestly he would do nothing to compel the people here to embrace Romanism; but that if necessary he would use force to establish the missionaries in houses in different parts of the island, if the chiefs refused to sell them parcels of land, for instance, one acre. The captain of the "Iris," an English frigate, called on him on Monday, and sent me a letter by him, making it quite clear that the French will meet with no opposition from the English Government. He too knew this, and of course knew his power; but he behaved, I must say, well, and if he is really sincere about the liberty of religion question, I must be satisfied with the result of our talk. I was much tired. We slept together on a kind of bed in an unfurnished house, where I was so cold that I could not sleep; besides, my head ached much; so my night was not a very pleasant one. In the morning we resumed our talk, but the business was over really. The question that we had discussed the evening before was brought to an issue, however, by his requiring from John Cho, who was with us, permission to buy about an acre of land in his territory. John was much staggered at this. It looked to him like a surrender of his rights. I told him, at great length, why I thought he must consent; but finally it was settled, that as John is not the real chief, I should act as interpreter for the Frenchmen; and send him from Mu an answer to a letter which he addresses to me, but which is, in fact, intended for the chief.

'It is, I suppose, true, that civilised nations do not acknowledge the right of a chief to prevent any one of his subjects from selling a plot of his land to a foreigner unless they may be at war with that particular nation.

'He said that France would not allow a savage chief to say "My custom in this respect is different from yours;" and again, "This is not a taking possession. It is merely requiring the right to put up a cottage for which I pay the just price." He told me plainly, if the chiefs did not allow him to do so, he would send for soldiers and put it up by force; but not use the soldiers for any other purpose. Of course I shall relate all this to Angadhohua at Mu, and make them consent.

'He told me that at New Caledonia they had reserved inalienably one-tenth of the land for the natives, that the rest would be sold to French colonists of the poor class, no one possessing more than ten acres; that 5,000 convicts would be sent there, and the ticket-of-leave system adopted, and that he thought the worst and most incorrigible characters would be sent to Lifu. Poor John! But I can't help him; he must make such terms as he can, for he and his people are wholly in their power.

'Our talk being ended, I found a great circle of men assembled on the outside with a pile of yams as usual in the centre for me. I was glad to see a small pile also for the Frenchman. I made my speech in his presence, but he knows not Lifu. "Be kind to the French, give them food and lodging. This is a duty which you are bound to pay to all men; but if they try to persuade you to change the teaching which you have received, don't listen to them. Who taught you to leave off war and evil habits, to build chapels, to pray? Remember that. Trust the teachers who have taught you the Word of God."

'This was the kind of thing I said. Then off we set—two miles of loose sand at a rattling pace, as I wanted to shake off some 200 people who were crowding about me. Then turning to the west, climbed some coral rocks very quickly, and found myself with only half my own attendants, and no strangers. Sat down, drank a cocoa-nut, and waited a long time for John, who can't walk well, and then quietly went on the remaining eight or nine miles to Zebedee's place, a Samoan teacher. They were very attentive, and gave me some supper. They had a bed, which was, of course, given up to me in spite of opposition. They regard a missionary as something superhuman almost. Sometimes I can't make them eat and drink with me; they think it would be presumptuous. Large meeting of people in the afternoon, and again the following morning, to whom I said much what I had already said at We. Then fifteen miles over to Apollo's place on the west coast, a grand bay, with perfectly calm water, delicious in the winter months. Comfortable quarters; Apollo a cleverish, free-spoken fellow.

'I went, on the same afternoon, two miles of very bad road to visit the French priest, who is living here. More talk and of a very friendly nature. He has been eighteen months at San Cristoval, but knows not the language; at Woodlark Island, New Caledonia, &c. We talked in French and English. He knows English fairly, but preferred to talk French. This day's work was nineteen miles.

Slept at Apollo's. Next morning went a little way in canoes and walked six miles to Toma's place; meeting held, speech as usual, present of yams, pig, &c. Walked back the six miles, started in double canoe for Gaicha, the other side of the bay: wind cold, some difficulty in getting ashore. Walked by the bad path to Apollo's and slept there again; Frenchman came in during the evening. Next day, Friday, meeting in the chapel. Walked twenty miles back to We, where I am now writing. Went the twenty miles with no socks; feet sore and shoes worn to pieces, cutting off leather as I came along. Nothing but broken bottles equals jagged coral. Paths went so that you never take three steps in the same direction, and every minute trip against logs, coral hidden by long leaves, arid weeds trailing over the path. Often for half a mile you jump from one bit of coral to another. No shoes can stand it, and I was tired, I assure you. Indeed, for the last two days, if I stopped for a minute to drink a nut, my legs were so stiff that they did not get into play for five minutes or so.

'July 16th.—The captain of the "Iris" frigate passing Lifu dropped me a line which satisfied me that the French will meet with no impediment from the English Government in the prosecution of their plans out here. Well, this makes one's own path just as easy, because all these things, great and small, are ordered for us; but yet I grieve to think that we might be occupying these groups with missionaries. Even ten good men would do for a few years; and is it unreasonable to think that ten men might be found willing to engage in such a happy work in such a beautiful part of the world—no yellow fever, no snakes, &c. I think of the Banks Islands, Vanua Lava, with its harbour and streams, and abundance of food, and with eight or nine small islands round it, speaking the same language, few dialectic differences of consequence, as I believe.

'Even one good man might introduce religion here as we have received it, pure and undefiled. Oh! that there were men who could believe this, and come out unconditionally, placing themselves in the Bishop's hands unreservedly. He must know the wants and circumstances of the islands far better than they can, and therefore no man ought to stipulate as to his location, &c. Did the early teachers do so? Did Titus ever think of saying to St. Paul, "Mind I must be an elder, or bishop, or whatever he was, of Crete?" Just as if that frame of mind was compatible with a real desire to do what little one can by God's help to bring the heathen to a knowledge of Christ.

'At this moment, one man for the Banks group and another for Mai and the neighbouring islands would be invaluable. If anything occurs to make me leave these Loyalty Islands as my residence during a part of the year, I am off to Banks, or Mai, or Solomon Isles. But what am I? In many respects not so well qualified for the work as many men who yet, perhaps, have had a less complete education. I know nothing of mechanics, and can't teach common things; I am not apt to teach anything, I fear, having so long deferred to learn the art of teaching, but of course exposing one's own shortcomings is easy enough. How to get the right sort of men? First qualification is common-sense, guided, of course, by religious principle. Some aptitude for languages, but that is of so little consequence that I would almost say no one was sufficient by itself as a qualification. Of course the mission work tends immensely to improve all earnest men; the eccentricities and superfluities disappear by degrees as the necessary work approves itself to the affection and intellect.'

The French question resulted in a reply in Angadhohua's name, that the people should be permitted to sell ground where the mission required it; and that in the one place specified about which there was contention, the land should be ceded as a gift from the chiefs. 'This,' observes Mr. Patteson, 'is the first negotiation which has been thrust upon me. I more than suspect I have made considerable blunders.'

By the 13th of August, he had to walk over the coral jags for another consultation with Pere Montrouzier, whose negotiation with Cho had resulted in thorough misunderstanding, each thinking the other was deceiving him, and not dealing according to promise to Mr. Patteson. The Pere had, in his fourteen years' experience, imbibed a great distrust of the natives, and thought Mr. Patteson placed too much confidence in them, while the latter thought him inclined to err the other way; however, matters were accommodated, at heavy cost to poor Coley's feet. A second pair of shoes were entirely cut to pieces, and he could not put any on the next day, his feet were so blistered.

The troubles were not ended, for when the ground was granted, there followed a stipulation that the chiefs should not hinder the men from working at the building; and when the men would not work, the chiefs were suspected of preventing it, and a note from Pere Montrouzier greatly wounded Patteson's feelings by calling John Cho faux et artificieux.

However, after another note, he retracted this, and a day or two after came the twenty miles over the coral to make a visit to the English clergyman. 'There is much to like in him: a gentleman, thoroughly well informed, anxious of course to discuss controversial points, and uncommonly well suited for that kind of work, he puts his case well and clearly, and, of course, it is easy to make their system appear most admirably adapted for carrying out all the different duties of a Church, as it is consistent in all, or nearly all, particulars, given the one or two leading points on which all depend. The Church of England here is very much in the position of any one of those other bodies, Wesleyan, Independent, or Presbyterian; and though we have a Bishop at the head—of what, however? Of one individual clergyman! Oh, that we had now a good working force—twenty or thirty men with some stuff in them; and there are plenty if they would only come. Meanwhile, France sends plenty of men; steamers bring them houses, cows for themselves and as presents for natives—supports the missionary in every way. New Caledonia is handy for the central school, everything almost that can be requisite. Never mind; work on, one small life is a mighty trifling thing considered with reference to those great schemes overruled by God to bring out of them great ultimate good, no doubt.'

There was an interchange of books between the French and English priest. Pere Montrouzier lent, and finally gave, Martinet's 'Solution de Grands Problemes,' which Patteson calls 'a very interesting book, with a great deal of dry humour about it, not unlike Newman's more recent publications. "It is," he (Montrouzier) says, "thought very highly of in France." He is a well-read man, I should imagine, in his line; and that is pretty extensive, for he is a really scientific naturalist, something of a geologist, a good botanist, besides having a good acquaintance with ecclesiastical literature.'

There was the more time for recreation with the Pere's French books, and the serious work of translating St. Mark's Grospel and part of the Litany into Lifu, as the inhabitants were all called off from school in the middle of August 'by a whale being washed ashore over a barrier reef—not far from me. All the adjacent population turned out in grass kilts, with knives and tomahawks to hack off chunks of flesh to be eaten, and of blubber to be boiled into oil; and in the meantime the neighbourhood was by no means agreeable to anyone possessing a nose.'

Meanwhile Sarawia, the best of the Banks pupils, had a swelling on the knee, and required care and treatment, but soon got better. Medical knowledge, as usual, Patteson felt one of the great needs of missionary life. Cases of consumption and scrofula were often brought to him, and terrible abscesses, under which the whole body wasted away. 'Poor people!' he writes, 'a consumptive hospital looms in the far perspective of my mind; a necessary accompaniment, I feel now, of the church and the school in early times. I wish I could contrive some remedy for the dry food, everything being placed between leaves and being baked on the ground, losing all the gravy; and when you get a chicken it is a collection of dry strings. If I could manage boiling; but there is nothing like a bit of iron for fire-place on the island, and to keep up the wood fire in the bush under the saucepan is hard work. I must commence a more practical study than hitherto of "Robinson Crusoe," and the "Swiss Family." Why does no missionary put down hints on the subject? My three months here will teach me more than anything that has happened to me, and I dare say I shall get together the things I want most when next I set forth from New Zealand.... I find it a good plan to look on from short periods to short periods, and always ask, what next? And at last it brings one to the real answer:—Work as hard as you can, and that rest which lacks no ingredient of perfect enjoyment and peace will come at last.'

Among the needs he discovered was this:—'By the bye, good cheap Bible prints would be very useful; large, so as to be seen by a large class, illustrating just the leading ideas. Schnorr's Bible prints by Rose and Bingen are something of the kind that I mean, something quite rude will do. Twenty-four subjects, comprising nothing either conventional or symbolical, would be an endless treasure for teachers; the intervening history would be filled up and illustrated by smaller pictures, but these would be pegs on which to hang the great events these lads ought to know. Each should be at least twenty-four inches by ten.

'Try to remember, in the choice of any other picture books for them, that anything that introduces European customs is no use yet. Pictures of animals are the best things. One or two of a railway, a great bridge, a view of the Thames with steamers rushing up and down, would all do; but all our habits of social life are so strange that they don't interest them yet.

'When I next reach Auckland, I suppose my eyes will rejoice at seeing your dear old likenesses. When we build our permanent central school-house at Kohimarama, I shall try to get a little snuggery, and then furnish it with a few things comfortably; I shall then invest in a chest of drawers, as I dare say my clothes are getting tired of living in boxes since March 1855.

'I can hardly tell you how much I regret not knowing something about the treatment of simple surgical cases. If when with W—— I had studied the practical—bled, drawn teeth, mixed medicines, rolled legs perpetually, it would have been worth something. Surely I might have foreseen all this! I really don't know how to find the time or the opportunity for learning. How true it is that men require to be trained for their particular work! I am now just in a position to know what to learn were I once more in England. Spend one day with old Fry (mason), another with John Venn (carpenter), and two every week at the Exeter hospital, and not look on and see others work—there's the mischief, do it oneself. Make a chair, a table, a box; fit everything; help in every part of making and furnishing a house, that is, a cottage. Do enough of every part to be able to do the whole. Begin by felling a tree; saw it into planks, mix the lime, see the right proportion of sand, &c., know how to choose a good lot of timber, fit handles for tools, &c.

'Many trades need not be attempted; but every missionary ought to be a carpenter, a mason, something of a butcher, and a good deal of a cook. Suppose yourself without a servant, and nothing for dinner to-morrow but some potatoes in the barn, and a fowl running about in the yard. That's the kind of thing for a young fellow going into a new country to imagine to himself. If a little knowledge of glazing could be added, it would be a grand thing, just enough to fit in panes to window-frames, which last, of course, he ought to make himself. Much of this cannot be done for you. I can buy window-frames in Auckland, and glass; but I can't carry a man a thousand miles in my pocket to put that glass into these frames; and if it is done in New Zealand, ten to one it gets broken on the voyage; whereas, glass by itself will pack well. Besides, a pane gets broken, and then I am in a nice fix. To know how to tinker a bit is a good thing; else your only saucepan or tea-kettle may be lying by you useless for months. In fact, if I had known all this before, I should be just ten times as useful as I am now. If anyone you know thinks of emigrating or becoming a missionary, just let him remember this.'

To these humble requisites, it appears that a missionary ought on occasion to be able to add those of a prime minister and lawgiver. Angadhohua, a bright, clever lad, only too easily led, was to be instructed in the duties of a chief; Mr. Patteson scrupulously trying in vain to make him understand that he was a person of far more consideration and responsibility than his white visitor would be in his own country. The point was to bring the Christian faith into connection with life and government. 'Much talk have I had with John in order that we may try to put before them the true grounds on which they ought to embrace Christianity,' writes Mr. Patteson, when about to visit a heathen district which had shown an inclination to abandon their old customs, 'and also the consequences to which they pledge themselves by the profession of a religion requiring purity, regularity, industry, &c., but I have little doubt that our visit now will result in the nominal profession of Christianity by many heathen. Angadhohua, John, and I go together, and Isaka, a Samoan teacher who has been a good deal among them. I shall make an arrangement for taking one of their leading men to New Zealand with me, that he may get some notion of what is meant by undertaking to become a Christian. It is in many respects a great benefit to be driven back upon the very first origin of a Christian society; one sees more than ever the necessity of what our Lord has provided, a living organised community into which the baptized convert being introduced falls into his place, as it were, naturally; sees around him everything at all times to remind him that he is a regenerate man, that all things are become new. A man in apostolic times had the lessons of the Apostles and disciples practically illustrated in the life of those with whom he associated. The church was an expression of the verbal teaching committed to its ministers. How clearly the beauty of this comes out when one is forced to feel the horrible blank occasioned by the absence of the living teacher, influencing, moulding, building up each individual professor of Christianity by a process always going on, though oftentimes unconsciously to him on whom it operates.

'But how is the social life to be fashioned here in Lifu according to the rule of Christ? There is no organised body exemplifying in daily actions the teaching of the Bible. A man goes to chapel and hears something most vague and unmeaning. He has never been taught to grasp anything distinctly—to represent any truth to his mind as a settled resting-place for his faith. Who is to teach him? What does he see around him to make him imperceptibly acquire new habits in conformity with the Bible? Is the Christian community distinguished by any habits of social order and intercourse different from non-Christians?

'True, they don't fight and eat one another now, but beyond that are they elevated as men? The same dirt, the same houses, the same idle vicious habits; in most cases no sense of decency, or but very little. Where is the expression of the Scriptural life? Is it not a most lamentable state of things? And whence has it arisen? From not connecting Christian teaching in church with the improvement in social life in the hut and village, which is the necessary corollary and complement of such teaching.

'By God's grace, I trust that some little simple books in Lifu will soon be in their houses, which may be useful. It is even a cause for thankfulness that in a few days (for the "Southern Cross" ought to be here in a week with 500 more copies) some 600 or more copies, in large type, of the Lord's Prayer, Creed, and Ten Commandments will be in circulation; but they won't use them yet. They won't be taught to learn them by heart, and be questioned upon them; yet they may follow by and by. Hope on is the rule. Give them the Bible, is the cry; but you must give them the forms of faith and prayer which Christendom has accepted, to guide them; and oh! that we were so united that we could baptize them into a real living exemplification, and expression—an embodiment of Christian truth, walking, sleeping, eating and drinking before their eyes. Christ Himself was that on earth, and His Church ought to be now. These men saw to accept His teaching was to bind themselves to a certain course of life which was exhibited before their own eyes. Hence, multitudes approved His teaching, but would not accept it—would not profess it, because they saw what was involved in that profession. But now men don't count the cost; they forget that "If any man come to Me" is followed by "Which of you intending to build a tower," &c. Hence the great and exceeding difficulty in these latter days when Christianity is popular!'

In this state of things it was impossible to baptize adults till they had come to a much clearer understanding of what a Christian ought to do and to believe; and therefore Coley's only christenings in Lifu were of a few dying children, whom he named after his brother and sisters, as he baptized them with water, brought in cocoa-nut shells, having taught himself to say by heart his own translation of the baptismal form.

He wrote the following letter towards the end of his stay:—

'September 6, 1858: Lifu, Loyalty Islands.

'My dear Miss Neill,—The delay of four or five days in the arrival of the "Southern Cross" gives me a chance of writing you a line. The Bishop dropped me here this day three months, and told me to look out for him on September 1. As New Zealand is 1,000 miles off, and he can't command winds and waves, of course I allow him a wide margin; and I begged him not to hurry over my important business in New Zealand in order to keep his appointment exactly. But his wont is to be very punctual. I have here twelve lads from the north-west islands: from seven islands, speaking six languages. The plan of bringing them to a winter school in some tropical isle is now being tried. The only difficulty here is that Lifu is so large and populous; and just now (what with French priests on it, and the most misty vague kind of teaching from Independents the only thing to oppose to the complete machinery of the Romish system) demands so much time, that it is difficult to do justice to one's lads from the distant lands that are living with one here. The Bishop had an exaggerated notion of the population here. I imagine it to be somewhere about 8,000. The language is not very hard, but has quite enough difficulty to make it more than a plaything: the people in that state when they venerate a missionary—a very dangerous state; I do my best to turn the reverence into the right channel and towards its proper object.

'You will see by the last Melanesian report of which I desired a copy to be sent to you, that our work is very rapidly increasing; that openings are being made in all directions; and that had we men of trust, we could occupy them at once. As it is, we keep up a communication with some seventy-four islands, waiting, if it may be, that men may be sent, trying to educate picked men to be teachers; but I am not very sanguine about that. At all events, the first flush of savage customs, &c., is being, I trust, removed, so that for some other body of Christians, if not the Church of England, the door may be laid open.

'Of course, the interest of the work is becoming more and more absorbing; so that, much as there is indeed going on in your world to distract and grieve one, it comes to me so weakened by time and distance that I don't sympathise as I ought with those who are suffering so dreadfully from the Indian Mutiny, or the commercial failure, or the great excitement and agitation of the country. You can understand how this can be, perhaps; for my actual present work leaves me small leisure for reflecting, and for placing myself in the position of others at a distance; and when I have a moment's time surely it is right that I should be in heart at Feniton, with those dear ones, and especially my dear dear father, of whom I have not heard for five months, so that I am very anxious as to what account of him the "Southern Cross" may bring, and try to prepare myself for news of increased illness, &c.

'You, I imagine, my dear Miss Neill, are not much changed to those who see you day by day; but I should find you much weaker in body than when I saw you last, and yet it did not seem then as if you had much strength to lose: I don't hear of any sudden changes, or any forms of illness; the gradual exhausting process is going on, but accompanied, I fear, with even greater active pain than of old; your sufferings are indeed very severe and very protracted, a great lesson to us all. Yet you have much, even speaking only of worldly comfort, which makes your position a much happier one than that of the poor suffering souls whom I see here. Their house is one round room, a log burning in the centre, no chimney, the room full of smoke, common receptacle of men, women, boys, girls, pigs, and fowls. In the corner a dying woman or child. No water in the island that is fresh, a few holes in the coral where water accumulates, more or less brackish; no cleanliness, no quiet, no cool fresh air, hot smoky atmosphere, no proper food, a dry bit of yam, and no knowledge of a life to come: such is the picture of the invalided or dying South Sea Islander. All dying children under years of discretion I baptize, and all the infants brought to the chapel by parents who themselves are seeking baptism; but I have not baptized any adults yet, they must be examined and taught for some time, for the Samoan and Rarotongan teachers sent by the Independent missionaries are very imperfectly instructed and quite incapable of conveying definite teaching to them.

'I don't see, humanly speaking, how this island is to be kept from becoming purely Roman Catholic. They have a large staff of men, and are backed up by the presence of a complete government establishment in New Caledonia, only two or three days distant, while what have we? Four months a year of the time, partially otherwise occupied by Melanesian schools, of one missionary, and while here these four months, I have my lads from many islands to teach, so that I can't lay myself out to learn this one language, &c. I am writing this on September 16. "Southern Cross" not yet come, and my lads very anxious; I confess I should like to see it, not only (as you will believe) because all my stores are gone. I have not a morsel of biscuit or grain of sugar left, and am reduced to native fare, which does not suit my English constitution for very long. Yams and taro, and a fowl now and then, will be my food until the ship comes. Hitherto I have had coffee and biscuits in addition.

'My very kind love to Mrs. S ——, and many thanks for the letters, which I much enjoy.

'Your very affectionate old pupil,

'J. C. P.'

The whole of September passed without the arrival of the 'Southern Cross.' The fact was that after Mr. Patteson had been left at Lifu, the vessel when entering Port-au-France, New Caledonia, had come upon a coral reef, and the damage done to her sheathing was so serious that though she returned to Auckland from that trip, she could not sail again without fresh coppering; and as copper had to be brought from Sydney for the purpose, there was considerable delay before she could set forth again, so that it was not till the last day of September that she gladdened Patteson's eyes, and brought the long-desired tidings from home.

This voyage was necessarily short, as there were appointments to be kept by the Bishop in New Zealand in November, and all that could be aimed at was the touching at the more familiar islands for fresh instalments of scholars. The grand comet of 1858 was one feature of this expedition—which resulted in bringing home forty-seven Melanesians, so that with the crew, there were sixty-three souls on board during the homeward voyage!

'As you may suppose, the little "Southern Cross" is cram full, but the Bishop's excellent arrangements in the construction of the vessel for securing ventilation, preserve us from harm by God's blessing. Every day a thorough cleaning and sweeping goes on, and frequent washing, and as all beds turn up like the flap of a table, and some thirty lads sleep on the floor on mats and blankets, by 7 A.M. all traces of the night arrangements have vanished. The cabin looks and feels airy; meals go on regularly; the boys living chiefly on yams, puddings, and cocoa-nuts, and plenty of excellent biscuit. We laid in so many cocoa-nuts that they have daily one apiece, a great treat to them. A vessel of this size, unless arranged with special reference to such objects, could not carry safely so large a party, but we have nothing on board to create, conceal, or accumulate dirt; no hold, no storeroom, no place where a mixed mess of spilt flour, and sugar, and treacle, and old rotten potatoes, and cocoa-nut parings and bits of candle, can all be washed together into a dark foul hold; hence the whole ship, fore and aft, is sweet and clean. Stores are kept in zinc lockers puttied down, and in cedar boxes lined with zinc. We of course distribute them ourselves; a hired steward would be fatal, because you can't get a servant to see the importance of care in such details.'

Mr. Patteson always, in the most careful manner, paid respect both to the chief's person and his dicta. He declined more than once to give directions which he said ought to issue from the chief, although on one of these occasions he was asked by the chief himself. He foresaw clearly the evils that might follow if the people's respect for recognised authority were weakened, instead of being, as it might be, turned to useful account. And so he always accorded to John Cho, and to other persons of rank when they were with us in the Mission school, just such respect as they were accustomed to receive at the hands of their own people. For instance, he would always use to a moderate extent the chief's language in addressing John Cho or any other of the Loyalty chiefs; and it being a rule of theirs that no one in the presence of the chiefs should ever presume to sit down higher than the chiefs, he would always make a point of attending to it as regarded himself; and once or twice when, on shore in the islands, the chief had chosen to squat down on the ground among the people, he would jocularly leave the seat that had been provided for him, and place himself by the chief's side on the ground. All this was keenly appreciated as significant, but alas! the Loyalty Islanders were not long to remain under his charge.

The ensuing letter was written to Sir John Taylor Coleridge, after learning the tidings of his retirement from the Bench in the packet of intelligence brought by the vessel:—

'November 10, 1858: Lat. 31° 29' S.; Long. 171° 12' E.

'My dear Uncle John,—I see by the papers that you have actually resigned, and keep your connection with the judges only as a Privy Councillor. I am of course on my own account heartily glad that you will be near my dear father for so many months of the year, and you are very little likely to miss your old occupation much, with your study at Heath's Court, so I shall often think of you in summer sitting out on the lawn, by John's Pinus excelsis, and in winter in your armchair by the fire, and no doubt you will often find your way over to Feniton. And then you have a glorious church!.... Oh! I do long for a venerable building and for the sound of ancient chants and psalms. At times, the Sunday is specially a day on which my mind will go back to the old country, but never with any wish to return. I have never experienced that desire, and think nothing but absolute inability to help on a Melanesian or a Maori will ever make a change in that respect. I feel as certain as I can be of anything that I should not be half as happy in England as I am in New Zealand, or in Lifu, in the Banks or Solomon Islands, &c. I like the life and the people, everything about it and them....

'Coppering the schooner caused delay, so that he (the Bishop) could give but two months instead of three to the Island voyage, for he starts on November 25 for a three months' Confirmation tour (1,000 miles) among the New Zealanders, which will bring him to Wellington by March 1, for the commencement of the first synod. Consequently we have only revisited some of our seventy and odd islands, but we have no less than forty-seven Melanesians from twelve islands on board, of whom three are young married women, while two are babies.

'This makes our whole number on board sixty, viz., four Pitcairners, forty-seven Melanesians, ourselves + crew = sixty-three, a number too great for so small a vessel, but for the excellent plan adopted by the Bishop in the internal arrangement of the vessel when she was built, and the scrupulous attention to cleanliness in every place fore and aft. As it is, we are not only healthy but comfortable, able to have all meals regularly, school, prayers, just as if we had but twenty on board. Nevertheless, I think, if you could drop suddenly on our lower deck at 9 P.M. and visit unbeknown to us the two cabins, you would be rather surprised at the number of the sleepers—twelve in our after-cabin, and forty-five in the larger one, which occupies two-thirds of the vessel.

'Of course we make no invasion upon the quarters forward of the four men before the mast—common seamen, and take good care that master and mate shall have proper accommodation.

'One gets so used to this sort of thing that I sleep just as well as I used to do in my own room at home, and by 6.30 or 7 A.M. all vestiges of anything connected with sleeping arrangements have vanished, and the cabins look like what they are, —large and roomy. We have, you know, no separate cabins filled with bunks, &c., abominations specially contrived to conceal dirt and prevent ventilation. Light calico curtains answer all purposes of dividing off a cabin into compartments, but we agree to live together, and no one has found it unpleasant as yet. We turn a part of our cabin into a gunaikhon at night for the three women and two babies by means of a canvas screen. Bishop looks after them, washes the babies, tends the women when sick, &c., while I, by virtue of being a bachelor, shirk all the trouble. One of these women is now coming for the second time to the college;

her name is Carry. Margaret Cho is on her second visit, and Hrarore is the young bride of Kapua, now coming for his third time, and baptized last year.

'We wish to make both husbands and wives capable of imparting better notions to their people.

'We have, I think, a very nice set on board....

'I think everything points to Vanua Lava, the principal island of the Banks group, becoming our centre of operations, i.e., that it would be the place where winter school would be carried on with natives from many islands, from Solomon Islands group to the north-west, and Santa Cruz group to north, New Hebrides to south and Loyalty Islands south-west, and also the depot among the islands, a splendid harbour, safe both from trade and hurricane winds, plenty of water, abundantly supplied with provisions, being indeed like a hot-house, with its hot springs constantly sending up clouds of vapour on the high hills, a population wholly uninjured by intercourse with traders and whalers, it being certain that our vessel was the first at all events that has ever been seen by the eyes of any member of this generation on the islands; I could prove this to you easily if I had time.

'They are most simple, gentle and docile, unwarlike, not cannibals, I verily believe as good a specimen of the natural fallen man as can be met with, wholly naked, yet with no sense of shame in consequence; timid, yet soon learning to confide in one; intelligent, and gleaming with plenty of spirit and fun. As the island, though 440 miles north of the Loyalty Isles, is not to leeward of them, it would only take us about eight days more to run down, and a week more to return to it from New Zealand, than would be the case if we had our winter school on one of the Loyalty Islands. So I hope now we may get a missionary for Lifu, and so I may be free to spend all my time, when not in New Zealand, at Vanua Lava. Temperature in winter something under 80° in the shade, being in lat. 13° 45' 5". The only thing against Vanua Lava is the fact that elephantiasis abounds among the natives, and they say that the mortality is very considerable there, so it might not be desirable to bring many lads to it from other islands; but the neighbouring islands of Mota and Valua, and Uvaparapara are in sight and are certainly healthy, and our buildings are not so substantial as to cause much difficulty in shifting our quarters if necessary. The language is very hard, but when it is one's business to learn a thing, it is done after a while as a matter of course.

'We have quite made up our mind that New Zealand itself is the right place for the head-quarters of the Mission. True, the voyage is long, and lads can only be kept there five or six months of the year, but the advantages of a tolerably settled state of society are so great, and the opportunities of showing the Melanesians the working of an English system are so many, that I think now with the Bishop that New Zealand should be the place for the summer school in preference to any other. I did not think so at one time, and was inclined to advocate the plan of never bringing the lads out of the tropics, but I think now that there are so many good reasons for bringing the lads to New Zealand that we must hope to keep them by good food and clothing safe from colds and coughs. Norfolk Island would have been in some ways a very good place, but there is no hope now of our being settled there....

'I can hardly have quite the same control over lads brought to an island itself wholly uncivilised as I can have over them in New Zealand, but as a rule, Melanesians are very tractable. Certainly I would sooner have my present school to manage, forty-five of all ages from nine to perhaps twenty-seven or eight, from twelve or thirteen islands, speaking at least eight languages, than half the number of English boys, up to all sorts of mischief....

'Thank you, dear uncle, for the Xavier; a little portable book is very nice for taking on board ship, and I dare say I may read some of his letters in sight of many a heathen island....

'Good-bye, my dear Uncle.

'Your affectionate and grateful nephew,

'J. C. PATTESON.'

'Savages are all Fridays, if you know how to treat them' is a saying of Patteson's in one of his letters, and a true one. In truth, there was no word that he so entirely repudiated as this of savage, and the courtesy and untutored dignity of many of his native friends fully justified his view, since it was sure to be called forth by his own conduct towards them.

The chiefs, having a great idea of their own importance, and being used to be treated like something sacred, and never opposed, were the most difficult people to deal with, and in the present voyage there was a time of great anxiety respecting a young chief named Aroana, from the great isle of Malanta. He fell into an agony of nervous excitement lest he should never see his island again, an attack of temporary insanity came on, and he was so strong that Mr. Patteson could not hold him down without the help of the Bishop and another, and it was necessary to tie him down, as he attempted to injure himself. He soon recovered, and the cooler latitudes had a beneficial effect on him, but there was reason to fear that in Malanta the restraint might be regarded as an outrage on the person of a chief.

The voyage safely ended on the night of the 16th of November. Here is part of a letter to Mr. Edward Coleridge, written immediately after reading the letters that had been waiting in Auckland:—

'My father writes:—"My tutor says that there must be a Melanesian Bishop soon, and that you will be the man," a sentence which amused me not a little.

'The plan is that the Bishop should gradually take more and more time for the islands, as he transfers to the General Synod all deeds, documents, everything for which he was corporation sole, and as he passes over to various other Bishops portions of New Zealand. Finally, retaining only the north part of the northern island, to take the Melanesian Bishopric.

'I urged this plan upon him very strongly one day, when somewhere about lat. 12° S. (I fancy) he pressed me to talk freely about the matter. I said: "One condition only I think should be present to your mind, viz., that you must not give up the native population in New Zealand," and to this he assented.

'If, dear tutor, you really were not in joke, just try to find some good man who would come and place himself under the Bishop's direction unreservedly, and in fact be to him much what I am + the ability and earnestness, &c. Seriously, I am not at all fitted to do anything but work under a good man. Of course, should I survive the Bishop, and no other man come out, why it is better that the ensign should assume the command than to give up the struggle altogether. But this of course is pure speculation. The Bishop is hearty, and, I pray God, may be Bishop of Melanesia for twenty years to come, and by that time there will be many more competent men than I ever shall be to succeed him, to say nothing of possible casualties, climate, &c.

'Good-bye, my dear Uncle; kind love to all.
'Your loving nephew and pupil,
'J. C. PATTESON.'

The three women and the two babies were disposed of in separate houses, but their husbands, with thirty-nine other Melanesians, four Norfolk Islanders, two printers, Mr. Dudley and Mr. Patteson, made up the dinner-party every day in the hall of St. John's College. 'Not a little happy I feel at the head of my board, with two rows of merry, happy-looking Melanesians on either side of me!'

The coughs, colds, and feverish attacks of these scholars were the only drawback; the slightest chill made them droop; and it was a subject of joy to have any day the full number in hall, instead of one or two lying ill in their tutor's own bed-chamber.

On the 29th of December came the exceeding joy of the arrival of the Judge and Mrs. Martin, almost straight from Feniton, ready to talk untiringly of everyone there. On the New Year's day of 1859 there was a joyful thanksgiving service at Taurarua for their safe return, at which all the best Church people near were present, and when John Cho made his first Communion.

On the 20th these much-loved friends came to make a long stay at the College, and the recollections they preserved of that time have thus been recorded by Lady Martin. It will be remembered that she had parted from him during the year of waiting and irregular employment:

'We were away from New Zealand nearly three years. We had heard at Feniton dear Coley's first happy letters telling of his voyages to the islands in 1856-7, letters all aglow with enthusiasm about these places and people. One phrase I well remember, his kindly regret expressed for those whose lot is not cast among the Melanesian islands. On our return we went to live for some months at St. John's College, where Mr. Patteson was then settled with a large party of scholars.

'We soon found that a great change had passed over our dear friend. His whole mind was absorbed in his work. He was always ready, indeed, to listen to anything there was to tell about his dear father; but about our foreign travels, his favourite pictures, the scenes of which we had heard so much from him, he would listen for a few minutes, but was sure in a little while to have worked round to Melanesia in general, or to his boys in particular, or to some discussion with my husband on the structure of their many languages and dialects. It was then that Bishop Abraham said that when the two came to their ninth meaning of a particle, he used to go to sleep.

'There were a very fine intelligent set of young men from the Loyalty Islands, some sleepy, lazy ones from Mai, some fierce, wild-looking lads from the Solomon Islands who had long slits in their ears and bone horns stuck in their frizzly hair. Mr. Patteson could communicate with all more or less easily, and his readily delicate hearing enabled him to distinguish accurately sounds which others could not catch—wonderful mp and piv and mbw which he was trying to get hold of for practical purposes.

'He was in comfortable quarters, in one long low room, with a sunny aspect. It looked fit for a student, with books all about, and pictures, and photos of loved friends and places on the walls, but he had no mind to enjoy it alone. There was sure to be some sick lad there, wrapped up in his best rugs, in the warmest nook by the fire. He had morning and afternoon school daily in the large schoolroom, Mr. Dudley and Mr. Lask assisting him. School-keeping, in its ordinary sense, was a drudgery to him, and very distasteful. He had none of that bright lively way and readiness in catechising which made some so successful in managing a large class of pupils at once, but every person in the place loved to come to the evening classes in his own room, where, in their own language, he opened to them the Scriptures and spoke to them of the things pertaining to the kingdom of God. It was in those private classes that he exercised such wonderful influence; his musical voice, his holy face, his gentle manner, all helping doubtless to impress and draw even the dullest. Long after this he told me once how after these evening classes, one by one, some young fellow or small boy would come back with a gentle tap at the door, "I want to talk to you," and then and there the heart would be laid open, and counsel asked of the beloved teacher.

'It was very pleasant to see him among his boys. They all used to go off for a walk on Saturday with him, sometimes to town, and he as full of fun with them as if they had been a party of Eton boys. He had none of the conventional talk, so fatal to all true influence, about degraded heathen. They were brethren, ignorant indeed, but capable of acquiring the highest wisdom. It was a joke among some of us, that when asked the meaning of a Nengone term of endearment he answered naively, "Oh, it means old fellow." He brought his fresh, happy, kindly feelings towards English lads and young men into constant play among Melanesians, and so they loved and trusted him.'

I think that exclusiveness of interest which Lady Martin describes, and which his own family felt, and which is apt to grow upon missionaries, as indeed on every one who is very earnestly engaged in any work, diminished as he became more familiar with his work, and had a mind more at liberty for thought.

Mr. Dudley thus describes the same period:—'It was during the summers of 1857-8 and 1858-9 that the Loyalty Islanders mustered in such numbers at St. John's College, as it was supposed that they, at least Lifu would be left in the hands of the Church of England. Mr. Patteson worked very hard these years at translations, and there was an immense enthusiasm about printing, the Lifuites and Nengonese striving each to get the most in their own language.

'Never shall I forget the evening service during those years held in the College chapel, consisting of one or two prayers in Bauro, Gera, and other languages, and the rest in Nengonese, occasionally changing to Lifu, when Mr. Patteson used to expound the passage of Scripture that had been translated in school during the day. Usually the Loyalty Islanders would take notes of the sermon while it went on, but now and then it was simply impossible, for although his knowledge of Nengonese at that time, as compared with what it was afterwards, was very limited, and his vocabulary a small one from which to choose his expressions, he would sometimes speak with such intense earnestness and show himself so thoroughly en rapport with the most intelligent of his hearers, that they were compelled to drop their papers and pencils, and simply to to listen. I remember one evening in particular. For some little time past the conduct of the men, especially the married men, had not been at all satisfactory. The married couples had the upper house, and John Cho, Simeona, and Kapua had obtained a draught-board, and had regularly given themselves up to draught-playing, night and day, neglecting all the household duties they were expected to perform, to the great annoyance of their wives, who had to carry the water, and do their husbands' work in other ways as well their own. This became soon known to Mr. Patteson, and without saying anything directly to the men, he took one evening as his subject in chapel those words of our Lord, "If thy hand or thy foot offend thee," &c., and spoke as you know he did sometimes speak, and evidently was entirely carried out of himself, using the Nengonese with a freedom which showed him to be thinking in it as he went on, and with a face only to be described as "the face of an angel." We all sat spellbound. John Cho, Simeona, and the other walked quietly away, without saying a word, and in a day or two afterwards I learnt from John that he had lain awake that night thinking over the matter, that fear had come upon him, lest he might be tempted again, and jumping up instantly, he had taken the draught-board from the place where he had left it and had cast it into the embers of their fire.

'Many and many a time was I the recipient of his thoughts, walking with him up and down the lawn in front of the cottage buildings of an evening, when he would try to talk himself clear. You may imagine what a willing listener I was, whatever he chose to talk upon, and he often spoke very freely to me, I being for a long time his only resident white companion. It was not long before I felt I knew his father well, and reverenced him deeply. He never was tired of talking of his home, and of former days at Eton and Oxford, and then while travelling on the Continent. Often and often during those early voyages have I stood or sat by his side on the deck of the "Southern Cross," as in the evening, after prayers, he stood there for hours, dressed in his clerical attire, all but the grey tweed cap, one hand holding the shrouds, and looking out to windward like a man who sees afar off all the scenes he was describing.'

Thinking over those times since, one understands better far than one did at the time the reality of the sacrifice he had made in devoting himself for life to a work so far away from those he loved best on earth.

The Bishop of Wellington, for to that see Archdeacon Abraham had been consecrated while in England, arrived early in March, and made a short stay at the College, during which he confirmed eleven and baptized one of Patteson's flock. Mrs. Abraham and her little boy remained at the College, while her husband went on to prepare for her at Wellington, and thus there was much to make the summer a very pleasant one, only chequered by frequent anxieties about the health of the pupils, as repeated experiments made it apparent that the climate of St. John's was too cold for them. Another anxiety was respecting Lifu for the London Missionary Society, had, after all, undertaken to supply two missionaries from England, and it was a most doubtful and delicate question whether the wishes of the natives or the established principle of noninterference with pre-occupied ground, ought to have most weight. The Primate was so occupied by New Zealand affairs that he wrote to Mr. Patteson to decide it himself and he could but wait to be guided by circumstances on the spot.

To Mr. Edward Coleridge he writes on the 18th of March:—

'I have many and delightful talks with Mr. Martin on our languages. We see already how strong an infusion of Polynesian elements exists in the Melanesian islands. With the language of four groups we are fairly acquainted now, besides some of the distinguishing dialects, which differ very much from one another; nevertheless, I think that by-and-by we shall connect them all if we live; but as some dialects may have dropped out altogether, we may want a few links in the chain to demonstrate the connection fully to people at a distance. It is a great refreshment to me to work out these matters, and the Judge kindly looked up the best books that exist in all the Polynesian languages, so that we can found our induction upon a comparison of all the dialects now from the Solomon Islands to the Marquesas, with the exception of the Santa Cruz archipelago. We have been there two or three times, but the people are so very numerous and noisy, that we never have had a chance as yet of getting into a quiet talk (by signs, &c.) with any of the people.

'Still, as we know some Polynesian inhabitants of a neighbouring isle who have large sea canoes, and go to Santa Cruz, we may soon get one of them to go with us, and so have an interpreter, get a lad or two, and learn the language.

'We are sadly in want of men; yet we cannot write to ask persons to come out for this work who may be indisposed, when they arrive in New Zealand, to carry out the particular system on which the Bishop proceeds. Any man who would come out and consent to spend a summer at the Melanesian school in New Zealand in order to learn his work, and would give up any preconceived notions of his own about the way to conduct missionary work that might militate against the Bishop's plan—such a man would be, of course, the very person we want; but we must try to make people understand that half-educated men will not do for this work. Men sent out as clergymen to the mission-field who would not have been thought fit to receive Holy Orders at home, are not at all the men we want. It is not at all probable that such men would really understand the natives, love them, and live with them; but they would be great dons, keeping the natives at a distance, assuming that they could have little in common, &c.—ideas wholly destructive of success in missionary, or in any work. That pride of race which prompts a white man to regard coloured people as inferior to himself, is strongly ingrained in most men's minds, and must be wholly eradicated before they will ever win the hearts, and thus the souls of the heathen.

'What a preachment, as usual, about Melanesia!...
'Your loving old Pupil and Nephew,
'J. C. PATTESON.'
Next follows a retrospective letter:—
'April 1, 1859: St. John's College.
'My dearest Father,—Thirty-two years old to-day! Well, it is a solemn thing to think that one has so many days and months and years to account for. Looking back, I see how fearfully I wasted opportunities which I enjoyed, of which, I fancy, I should now avail myself gladly; but I don't know that I fancy what is true, for my work now, though there is plenty of it, is desultory, and I dare say hard application, continuously kept up, would be as irksome to me as ever.

'It seems very strange to me that I never found any pleasure in classical studies formerly. Now, the study of the languages for its own sake even is so attractive to me that I should enjoy working out the exact and delicate powers of Greek particles, &c.; but I never cared for it till it was too late, and the whole thing was drudgery to me. I had no appreciation, again, of Historians, or historians; only thought Thucydides difficult and Herodotus prosy(!!), and Tacitus dull, and Livy apparently easy and really very hard. So, again, with the poets; and most of all I found no interest (fancy!) in Plato and Aristotle. They were presented to me as merely school books; not as the great effort of the cultivated heathen mind to solve the riddle of man's being; and I, in those days, never thought of comparing the heathen and Christian ethics, and the great writers had no charm for me.

'Then my French. If I had really taken any pains with old Tarver in old days— and it was your special wish that I should do so—how useful it would be to me now; whereas, though I get on after a sort, I don't speak at all as I ought to do, and might have learnt to do. It is sad to look back upon all the neglected opportunities; and it is not only that I have not got nearly (so to speak) a quantity of useful materials for one's work in the present time, but that I find it very hard to shake off desultory habits. I suppose all persons have to make reflections of this kind, more or less sad; but, somehow, I feel it very keenly now: for certainly I did waste time sadly; and it so happens that I have just had "Tom Brown's Schooldays" lent me, and that I spent some time in reading it on this particular day, and, of course, my Eton life rose up before me. What a useful book that is! A real gain for a young person to have such a book. That is very much the kind of thing that would really help a boy—manly, true, and plain.

'I hear from Sydney by last mail that the Bishop is really desirous to revive the long dormant Board of Missions. He means to propose to send a priest and a deacon to every island ready for them, and to provide for them—if they are forthcoming, and funds. Of this latter I have not much doubt....

'April 24—I have to get ready for three English full services to-morrow, besides Melanesian ditto.—So goodbye, my dearest Father,
'Your loving and dutiful Son,
'J. C. PATTESON.'
Sir John Patteson might well say, in a letter of this summer, to Bishop Selwyn:—
'As to my dear boy Coley, I am more and more thankful every day that I agreed

to his wishes; and in whatever situation he may be placed, feel confident that his heart will be in his work, and that he will do God service. He will be contented to work under any one who may be appointed Bishop of Melanesia (or any other title), or to be the Bishop himself. If I judge truly, he has no ambitious views, and only desires that he may be made as useful as his powers enable him to be, whether in a high or subordinate situation.'

Nothing could be more true than this. There was a general sense of the probability that Mr. Patteson must be the first Missionary Bishop; but he continued to work on at the immediate business, always keeping the schemes and designs which necessarily rose in his mind ready to be subjected to the control of whomsoever might be set over him. The cold had set in severely enough to make it needful to carry off his 'party of coughing, shivering Melanesians' before Easter, and the 'Southern Cross' sailed on the 18th. Patteson took with him a good store of coffee, sugar, and biscuits, being uncertain whether he should or should not again remain at Lifu.

In the outward voyage he only landed his pupils there, and then went on to the Banks Islands, where Sarawia was returned at Vanua Lava, and after Mr. Patteson had spent a pleasant day among the natives, Mota was visited next after.

'May 24.—On Monday, at 3 P.M., we sailed from Port Patteson across to Mota. Here I landed among 750 people and the boat returned to the vessel. She was to keep up to windward during the night and call for me the next morning. I walked with my large following, from the teach, up a short steep path, to the village, near to which, indeed only 200 yards off, is another considerable village. The soil is excellent; the houses good—built round the open space which answers to the green in our villages, and mighty banyan trees spreading their lofty and wide-branching arms above and around them. The side walls of these houses are not more than two feet high, made only of bamboos lashed by cocoa-nut fibre, or wattled together, and the long sloping roofs nearly touch ground but within they are tolerably clean and quite dry. The moon was in the first quarter, and the scene was striking as I sat out in the open space with some 200 people crowding round me—men, women and children; fires in front where yams were roasting; the dark brown forms glancing to and fro in the flickering light; the moon's rays quivering down through the vast trees, and the native hollow drum beating at intervals to summon the people to the monthly feast on the morrow. I slept comfortably on a mat in a cottage with many other persons in it. Much talk I had with a large concourse outside, and again in this cottage, on Christianity; and all were quiet when I knelt down as usual and said my evening prayers. Up at 5.30 A.M., and walked up a part of the Sugar Loaf peak, from which the island derives its English name, and found a small clear stream, flowing, through a rocky bed, back to the village, where were some 300 people assembled; sat some time with them, then went to the beach, where the boat soon came for me.

'After this there was a good deal of bad weather; but all the lads were restored to their islands, including Aroana, the young Malanta chief, who had begun by a fit of frenzy, but had since behaved well; and who left his English friends with a promise to do all in his power to tame his people and cure them of cannibalism.'

Then came some foul winds and hot exhausting weather.

'I have done little more than read Stanley's "Sinai and Palestine," and Helps's "Spanish America," two excellent books and most delightful to me. The characters in the Spanish conquest of Mexico and America generally; the whole question of the treatment of natives; and that nobleman, Las Casas—are more intelligible to me than to most persons probably. The circumstances of my present life enable me to realise it to a greater extent.

'Then I have been dipping into a little ethnology; yesterday a little Plato; but it is almost too hot for anything that requires a working head-piece. You know I take holiday time this voyage when we are in open water and no land near, and it is great relaxation to me.'

A pretty severe gale of wind followed, a sharp test of Patteson's seamanship.

'Then came one day of calm, when we all got our clothes dry, and the deck and rigging looked like an old clothes' shop. Then we got a fairish breeze; but we can get nothing in moderation. Very soon it blew up into a strong breeze, and here we are lying to with a very heavy sea. Landsmen would call it mountainous, I suppose. I am tired, for I have had an anxious time; and we have had but one quiet night for an age, and then I slept from 9.30 P.M. to 7.30 A.M. continuously. 'It may be that this is very good training for me. Indeed it must give me more coolness and confidence. I felt pleased as well as thankful when we made the exact point of Nengone that I had calculated upon, and at the exact time.'

On the 20th of June, Auckland harbour was safely attained; but the coming back without scholars did not make much of holiday time for their master, who was ready to give help to other clergymen whenever it might be needed, though, in fact, this desultory occupation always tried him most.

On the 25th of July he says:—

'I have had a sixty miles' walk since I wrote last; some part of it over wild country. I lost my way once or twice and got into some swamps, but I had my little pocket-compass.

'My first day was eighteen miles in pouring rain; no road, in your sense of the word; but a good warm room and tea at the end. Next day on the move all day, by land and water, seeing settlers scattered about. Third day, Sunday, services at two different places. Fourth day, walk of some twenty-seven miles through unknown regions baptizing children at different places; and reaching, after divers adventures, a very hospitable resting-place at 8 p.m. in the dark. Next day an easy walk into Auckland and Taurarua. Yesterday, Sunday, very wet day. Man-of-war gig came down for me at 9.15 A.M., took the service on board; 11 A.M. St. Paul's service; afternoon, hospital, a mile or so off; 6 P.M., St. Paul's evening service; 8.30, arrived at Taurarua dripping.'

The same letter replies to one from home:—

'I thank you, my dear father, for writing so fully about yourself, and especially, for seeing and stating so plainly your full conviction that I ought not to think of returning to England. It would, as you say, humanly speaking, interfere most seriously with the prospects of the Mission. Some dear friends write to me differently, but they don't quite understand, as you have taken pains to do, what our position is out here; and they don't see that my absence would involve great probable injury to the whole work.

'It is curious how few there are who know anything of New Zealand and Melanesia!

'Of course it is useless to speculate on the future, but I see nothing at all to make it likely that I shall ever revisit England. I can't very well conceive any such state of things as would make it a duty to gratify my constant inclination. And, my dear father, I don't scruple to say (for you will understand me) that I am happier here than I should be in England, where, even though I were absent only a few months, I should bear about with me the constant weight of knowing that Melanesia was not provided for. And, strange as it may seem, this has quite ceased to be a trial to me. The effort of subduing the longing desire to see you is no longer a great one: I feel that I am cheerful and bright, and light-hearted, and that I have really everything to make a man thankful and contented.

'And if you could see the thankful look of the Bishop, when he is again assured that there is no item of regret or desire to call me home on your part, you would feel, I know, that colonial work does require, especially, an unconditional unreserved surrender of a man to whatever he may find to do.'

But while admiring the noble spirit in which the son held fast his post, and the father forebore to unsettle him there, let not their example he used in the unkind and ignorant popular cry against the occasional return of colonial Bishops. For, be it remembered, that dire necessity was not drawing Coleridge Patteson to demand pecuniary assistance round all the platforms of English towns. The Eton, and the Australian and New Zealand Associations, supplemented by the Society for the Propagation of the Gospel and his own family, relieved him from the need of having to maintain his Mission by such means. All these letters are occupied with the arrangements for raising means for removing the Melanesian College to a less bleak situation, and it is impossible to read them without feeling what a difference it made to have a father who did not view giving to God's work as robbing his family.

On the 13th of August, Patteson was on board, preparing for the voyage; very cold, and eager for the tropics. The parting voice in his farewell letter is: 'I think I see more fully that work, by the power of God's Spirit, is the condition of us all in this world; tiny and insignificant as the greatest work of the greatest men is, in itself, yet the one talent is to be used.'

It was meant to be a farewell letter, but another followed in the leisure, while waiting for the Bishop to embark, with some strong (not to say fiery) opinions on the stern side of duty:—

'I feel anxious to try to make some of the motives intelligible, upon which we colonial folk act sometimes. First. I think that we get a stronger sense of the necessity for dispensing with that kind of courtesy and good nature which sometimes interferes with duty than people do in England.

'So a man placed as I am (for example) really cannot oftentimes avoid letting it be seen that work must come first; and, by degrees, one sympathises less than one possibly should do with drones and idlers in the hive, and feels it wrong to assent to a scheme which lets a real work suffer for the sake of acquiescing in a conventional recognition of comfort, claims of society, &c.

'Would the general of an army say to his officers, "Pray, gentlemen, don't dirty your boots or fatigue your horses to succour the inhabitants of a distant village"? Or a captain to his mates and middies: "Don't turn out, don't go aloft. It is a thing hard, and you might get wet"?

'And the difference between us and people at home sometimes is, that we don't see why a clergyman is not as much bound as an officer in the army or navy to do what he is pledged of his own act to do; and that at home the 'parsonage and pony-carriage' delusion practically makes men forget this. I forget it as much as any man, and should very likely never have seen the mistake but for my coming to New Zealand; and it is one of the great blessings we enjoy.

'There is a mighty work to be done. God employs human agents, and the Bible tells us what are the rules and conditions of their efficiency.

'"Oh! but, poor man, he has a sickly wife!" Yes, but, "it remaineth that those who have wives be as they that have none."

'True, but the case of a large family? "Whosoever loveth child more than me," &c.

'Second. The fact that we live almost without servants makes us more independent, and also makes us acquainted with the secrets of each other's housekeeping, &c. All that artificial intercourse which depends a good deal upon a well-fitted servants' hall does not find place here. More simple and more plain and homely in speech and act is our life in the colonies—e.g., you meet me carrying six or seven loaves from town to the college. "Oh, I knew that the Bishop had to meet some persons there to-day, and I felt nearly sure there would be no breakfast then." Of course an English person thinks, "Why didn't he send the bread?" To which I answer, "Who was there to send?"

'I don't mean that I particularly like turning myself into a miller one day and a butcher the next; but that doing it as a matter of course, where there is no one else to do it, one does sometimes think it unreasonable to say, as has been said to the Bishop:—"Two thousand pounds a year you want for your Mission work!" "Yes," said the Bishop, "and not too much for sailing over ten thousand miles, and for educating, clothing, and feeding some forty young men!"

'I mean that conventional notions in England are preventing people from really doing half what they might do for the good of the needy.

'I don't know how this might be said to be a theory tending to revolutionise society; but I think I do know that there is a kind of religious common sense which comes in to guide people in such matters. Only, I do not think it right to admit that plea for not doing more in the way of almsgiving which is founded upon the assumption that first of all a certain position in society must be kept up, which involves certain expenditure.

'A barrister is living comfortably on £800 a year, or a clergyman in his living of £400. The professional income of the one increases, and a fatter living is given to the other, or some money is left them. What do they do? Instantly start a carriage, another servant, put the jack-of-all-trades into a livery, turn the buttons into a flunkey, and the village girl into a ladies' maid! Is this really right? They were well enough before. Why not use the surplus for some better purpose?

'I imagine that we, the clergy, are chiefly to blame, for not only not protesting against, but most contentedly acquiescing in such a state of things. You ask now for something really demanding a sacrifice. "I can't afford it." "What, not to rescue that village from starvation? not to enable that good man to preach the Gospel to people only accessible by means of such an outlay on his vessel, &c.? Give up your carriage, your opera box; don't have so many grand balls, &c. "Oh no! it is all a corban to the genius of society.

'Now, is this Scriptural or not, my dear father? I don't mean that any individual is justified in dictating to his neighbour, still less in condemning him. But are not these the general principles of religion and morality in the Bible? There are duties to society: but a good man will take serious counsel as to what they are, and how far they may be militating against higher and holier claims.

'August 24.—Why I wrote all this, my dearest father, I hardly know, only I feel sure that unless men at home can, by taking real pains to think about it, realise the peculiar circumstances of colonial life, they will never understand any one of us.

'I have written Fan a note in which I said something about my few effects if I should die.

'One thing I should like to say to you, not as venturing to do more than let you be in full possession of my own mind on the matter. Should I die before you die, would it be wrong for me to say, "Make the Melanesian Mission my heir"?

'It may be according to the view which generally obtains that the other three should then divide my share. But now I would take what may seem the hard view of which I have been writing, and say, "They have enough to maintain them happily and comfortably." The Mission work without such a bequest will be much endangered. I feel sure that they would wish it to be so, for, of course, you know that this large sum of which you write will be, if I survive you, regarded simply as a bequest to the Mission in which I have a life interest, and the interest of which, in the main, would be spent on the Mission.

'But I only say plainly, without any reserve, what I have thought about it; not for one moment putting up my opinion against yours, of course, in case you take a contrary view.

'We sail, I hope, to-morrow, but the Bishop is more busy than ever.

'Again, my dearest Father,

'Your loving and dutiful Son,

'J. C. PATTESON.'

The history of this voyage was, as usual, given in a long letter for the Feniton fireside; but there was a parallel journal also, kept for the Bishop of Wellington, which is more condensed, and, therefore, better for quotation.

The manner in which the interest in, and connection with all English friends and relations was kept up is difficult to convey, though it was a very loveable part of the character. Little comments of condolence or congratulation, and messages of loving remembrance to persons mentioned by playful names, would only be troublesome to the reader; but it must be taken for granted that every reply to a home packet was full of these evidences that the black children on a thousand isles had by no means driven the cousins and friends of youth from a heart that was enlarged to have tenderness for all.

'Lat. 9° 29' S.; Long. 163° S.E. "Southern Cross:" October 9, 1859.

'My dear Bishop,—We are on our way from Uleawa to the Santa Cruz group, having visited the Loyalty Islands, Southern New Hebrides, Banks Island (2), and Solomon Islands.

'The Bishop so planned the voyage as to run down the wind quickly to the Solomon Islands, and do the real work coming home; not, as usual, beating up in the open water between the Santa Cruz archipelago, Banks Islands and New Hebrides to the east, and New Caledonia to the west. We are thus able to visit Vanua Lava on the way out and home also; and as we meant to make the Banks Islands the great point this voyage, that was, of course, great gain.

'We touched at Norfolk Island.... Going on to Nengone we found everybody away at the distant yam grounds, and could not wait to see them.

'At Lifu, the first thing that shocked us was John's appearance: one of those fatal glandular swellings has already produced a great change in him. He looked sallow and weak, and I fear ut sit vitalis. He spoke to me very calmly about his illness, which he thinks is unto death, and I did not contradict him.

'We had much private talk together. He is a fine fellow and, I believe, a sincere Christian man. Then came the applications to us not to desert them, and letters enumerating all the villages of Lifu almost without exception, and entreating us to suffer them to be connected with us, and we had to answer that already two missionaries from the L. M. S. are on their way from Sydney to Lifu, and that it would do harm to have two rival systems on the island. They acquiesced but not heartily, and it was a sad affair altogether, all parties unhappy and dissatisfied, and yet unable to solve the difficulty. Then came a talk with Angadhohua, John's half-brother, the real chief. The poor lad feels now what a terrible thing it will be for him and his people if they should lose John. Nothing can be nicer than his way of talking: "I know you don't think me firm enough, and that I am easily led by others. What am I to do if John dies? We all respect him. He has been taught so much, and people all listen to him." I gave him the best advice that I could and longed to be able to do something for him and his people. It was, however, a comfort to leave with them St. Mark, Scripture books, &c.

'We called at Tanna, to see poor Mr. Paton, who lost his wife last April. He is living on there quite alone, and has already lived down the first angry opposition of some of the people, and the unkind treatment that he received from men and women alike who mocked him because of his wife's death, &c. He has had much fever and looked very ill, but his heart was in his work; and the Bishop said he seemed to be one of the weak things which God hath chosen. I know he made me feel pretty well ashamed of myself.

'Next day we spent a few hours with Mr. and Mrs. Gordon at Erromango. He has a small house on the high table-land overlooking Dillon's Bay, and certainly is exposed to winds which may, for aught I know, rival those of Wellington notoriety. The situation is, however, far preferable in the summer to that on the beach, which is seldom free from malaria and ague.

'Then we sailed to the great bay of Pango, landed at Fate a fellow who had come to the Bishop in New Zealand for a passage, and in the afternoon sailed away through "the Pool" (the landlocked space between Mallicolo and Espiritu Santo to the west; Aspee, Ambrym, Whitsuntide, Aurora to the east), where for eighty miles the water is always smooth, the wind always steady, the scenery always lovely, and where, on this occasion, the volcano was bright.

'Being nearly becalmed to the south-east of Leper's Isle, the Bishop gave me the choice of a visit to Whitsuntide or Leper's Island. I voted for the latter, and delighted we were to renew an acquaintance made two years ago, and not since kept up, with these specially nice people. We were recognised at once, but we have a very small vocabulary.

'The sea was running heavily into the bay, but it is sand there and not much rock on the beach, and we had a jolly swim ashore. Then we bought a few yams, which the surf did not permit us to get to the boat, and had a very pleasant visit; for, as we sat among them, words came into one's head, or were caught from their mouth, and at the end of twenty minutes we were getting on a little. The old chief took me by the hand and led me aside to the spot where the ladies were assembled, and divining no doubt that I was a bachelor, politely offered me his daughter, and his protection, &c., if I would live among them.

'I missed seeing the Bishop knocked clean over by the breakers as he was swimming off to the boat; I was still talking to the people, with my back to the sea, and only saw him staggering to his feet again. Thinking to myself that if he was knocked over, I had better look out, I awaited a "smooth" and swam out comfortably.

'The next morning (Sunday) at ten, we dropped anchor in Port Patteson, the harbour which you know the Bishop would call after my father. The first person who came off to us was Sarawia, my old Lifu pupil, from this island! Then came a good many men. I told them there would be no going ashore and no trading till the next day. Palemana, your friend Matawathki, &c., were at church, all dressed and well-behaved. What nice orderly people they are, to be sure!

'The next day we bought lots of yams, and gave away seeds and fruit-trees, or rather planted them; and looked for a place for a station, and fixed at last on the rising-ground which forms the east side of the harbour, and the Bishop, arming himself with an axe, led a party to clear the bush, which was very thick. They made a fair path through in one afternoon to the top, and a healthy place might be found now with little trouble to return to at night from the schools, &c. in the village below, and so shirk the malaria.

'But the next day, as I had anticipated, rather changed his intentions as to the principal station being formed at Vanua Lava. We landed at Sugar Loaf Island, and with something of pride I showed off to him the beauties of the villages where I slept in May last—the dry soil, the spring of water, the wondrous fertility, the large and remarkably intelligent, well-looking population, the great banyan tree, twenty-seven paces round—and at once he said, "This is such a place as I have seen nowhere else for our purpose."

'The Bishop had seen this island before I was with him, during one of the "Border Maid's" voyages, and knew the people, of course, but had not happened to have walked in shore at all, and so the exceeding beauty and fitness of the island for a Mission station had not become so apparent to him. We know of no place where there seems to be such an unusual combination of everything that can be desired, humanly speaking, for such an institution. So that is settled (D.V.) that next winter I should be here, if alive and well; and that the Banks Islands should be regarded as the central point of the Mission.

'Such boys! Bright-eyed, merry fellows, many really handsome; of that reddish yellow tinge of colour which betokens affinity with Polynesian races, as their language also testifies. The majority of the people were pleasing in their appearance and manner. Well, all this was very hopeful, and we went off very happy, taking Eumau, the boy who first met us at Port Patteson when we found it out, and old Wompas (who was with me at Lifu), and another from Mota, to see the Northern Islands.

'I think our work is more likely now to revolve upon a fixed centre—Sugar Loaf Island in the Banks group—that we shall make the occupation of the group the first object, and do all with reference to that as the necessary part of the work to be attended to first. In the choice of scholars, e.g., we have considered whether we should not limit our selection to such as might pass the next winter with me at Sugar Loaf Island, and so that the vessel need not run down to leeward of it. Solomon Islands are the extreme verge. In the East Island, where there would be merely a question of nothing or something, we may take very young men who would perhaps not be easy to keep out of harm at Sugar Loaf, because there will be no difficulty about returning them to their homes....'

'November 11th.—We found in the Santa Cruz group that the news of Captain Front's and his two men's death in Vanikoro, and (as we suppose) the news of the "Cordelia" having been at that island to inquire into the matter, had made the people anxious, uneasy, noisy, and rather rude. That poor man went to make a station at Vanikoro in the usual way, taking three poor New Caledonian women with him. The Vanikoro people killed the three English and took away the women.

'We did not land at Sta. Cruz, but we had a more pleasant intercourse than heretofore with thirty or forty canoes' crews.

'Timelin Island we ascertained to be identical with Nukapu, an old familiar place whose latitude we had not ascertained correctly before. The small reef (Polynesian) islands did not give us so good a reception as last year, though there was no unfriendliness. The news about Vanikoro had made them suspicious of visits from white men. But they will be all right by next time....

'We saw a pleasant party at Bligh Island, brought away one young man from that island, and two lads belonging to a neighbouring small island called Eowa. The next day we watered on the north side of Vanua Lava, and in the evening went across to Santa Maria. Here we landed on the next day among two hundred or more people, shy and noisy. We bought a few yams, and I detected some young fellows stealing from our little heap I would not overlook this, but the noticing it made them more suspicious that we meant to hurt them. As the Bishop and I, after some twenty minutes, turned to rejoin the boat, the whole crowd bolted like a shot right and left into the bush. Evidently they must have had some trading crew fire a parting shot in mere wantonness at them from their boat. I expected some arrows to be shot at us; but they did not shoot any.

'The same evening (Saturday) we stood across the passage with a brisk breeze, and took up our party, consisting of five and including Sarawia and four others anciently noted as promising in appearance....

'We reached Mota (Sugar Loaf Island) in time to leave me for a night's visit to the people. I had time before the boat called next day at noon to see five or six of their villages. People quite accustomed to expect me—all most friendly, apparently pleased to be told that I would stop with them in the winter. Seven scholars joined us here....

'At Mai, I slept in the house of Petere and Laure. Things are promising. It is quite ready for a missionary. We brought away Moto, Pepeu, and the two young boys who were with me at Lifu, and very many wished to come.

'Thence we had a very long passage to Lifu. John Cho is, I am thankful to say, very much better. The two men from the London Missionary Society are on the island.... The Lifu people tell me that in the north of the island many are accepting the teaching of the two French priests. William Martin Tahia and Chakham, a principal chief and old scholar, are with us.

'At Nengone, Wadrokala, George Simeona, and Harper Malo have come away for good.... We number thirty-nine Melanesians.... This is a long letter which will try your patience.

'Always, my dear Bishop,

'Affectionately yours,

'J. C. PATTESON.'

Another long letter was written during this voyage to Mr. Edward Coleridge, a great portion of it on the expediency of the islands being taken under British protection, also much respecting the Church of New Zealand, which is scarcely relevant to the immediate subject, and only at the end is there anything more personal:—

'The last accounts of my father were unusually good, but I well know what news may be awaiting our return from a voyage whether long or short, and I try to be ready for any news; yet I suppose that I cannot at all realize what it would be. It makes some difference when the idea of meeting again in this world has been relinquished for now four and a half years, yet it is all very well to wait or think about it! I was not so upset by dear Uncle James's death as I should no doubt have been had I enjoyed the prospect of frequently seeing him. Somehow, when all ideas of time and space are annihilated by death, one must think about such separations in a religious way: for separations in any other sense to us here, from people in England, have already taken place. I must except, however, the loving wise letters, and the power of realising more clearly perhaps the occupations of those still in the body—their accustomed places and duties; though I suppose we can tell quite enough about all this in the case of those who have died in the true faith of Christ to know, at all events, that we are brought and united to them whenever we think or do anything religiously. I often think that this is well brought out in the "Heir of Redclyffe"—the loss of "the bright outside," the life and energy and vigour, and all the companionable and sociable qualities, contrasted with the power of thinking oneself into the inner spiritual relations that exist between the worlds visible and invisible.

'All this effort is much diminished in our case. There is no very great present loss; at least, it is not so sensibly felt by a great deal as it would be if we missed some one with whom we lived up to the time of his death. It is much easier to think of them as they are than it could be in the case of persons who remember so vividly what they so lately were; and this is why, I suppose, the news of Uncle James's death seemed to affect me so much less than I should have expected, and it may be so again: certain it is that I loved him dearly, and that I miss his letters very much indeed; but I think that the point I felt most about him was the sad affliction to his family, and the great loss to my dear father, who had of late seen more than ever of him.'

From the home letter I only quote from the reflections so regularly inspired by the anniversary of the 28th of November.

After lamenting that it was difficult to realise those scenes in his mother's illness which he and his brother only knew from narration, Patteson adds:—

'The memory of those days would perhaps have been more precious to me if I had witnessed more with my own eyes. And yet of course it really mattered nothing at all, because the lesson of her life does not depend on an acquaintance with a few days of it; and what I saw when I was there I never have forgotten, and hope that I never may forget.

'And indeed I feel now with regard to you, my dear Father, that I have not learned to know you better while I was with you than I do now. I think that in some ways I enter more almost into your mind and thought, or that I fancy I do so: just as the present possession of anything so often prevents our really taking pains to learn all about it. We rest content with the superficial knowledge of that which is most easily perceived and recognised in it....

'I think I know from your letters, and from the fact of my absence from you making me think more about you, as much about you as those present. I very much enjoy a letter from Joan, which gives me a kind of tableau vivant of you all. That helps me to realize the home life; so do the photographs, they help in the same way. But your letters, and the fact that I think so much about them, and about you, are my real helps.'

The voyage ended on the 7th of December. It was the last made under the guidance of the Bishop of New Zealand, and, alas! the last return of the first 'Southern Cross.'

CHAPTER IX. MOTA AND ST. ANDREW'S COLLEGE, KOHIMARAMA. 1859-1862.

With the year 1860 a new period, and one far more responsible and eventful, began. After working for four years under Bishop Selwyn's superintendence, Coleridge Patteson was gradually passing into a sphere of more independent action; and, though his loyal allegiance to his Primate was even more of the heart than of the letter, his time of training was over; he was left to act more on his own judgment; and things were ripening for his becoming himself a Bishop. He had nearly completed his thirty-third year, and was in his fullest strength, mental and bodily; and, as has been seen, the idea had already through Bishop Selwyn's letters become familiar to his family, though he himself had shrunk from entertaining it.

The first great change regarded the locality of the Melanesian school in New Zealand. Repeated experience had shown that St. John's College was too bleak for creatures used to basking under a vertical sun, and it had been decided to remove to the sheltered landing-place at Kohimarama, where buildings for the purpose had been commenced so as to be habitable in time for the freight of 1859.

It should be explained, that the current expenses of the Mission had been defrayed by the Eton and Sydney associations, with chance help from persons privately interested, together with a grant of £200, and afterwards £300 per annum from the Society for the Propagation of the Gospel. The extra expense of this foundation was opportunely met by a discovery on the part of Sir John Patteson, that his eldest son, living upon the Merton Fellowship, had cost him £200 a year less than his younger son, and therefore that, in his opinion, £800 was due to Coleridge. Moreover, the earlier voyages, and, in especial the characters of Siapo and Umao, had been so suggestive of incidents fabricated in the 'Daisy Chain,' that the proceeds of the book were felt to be the due of the Mission and at this time these had grown to such an amount as to make up the sum needful for erecting such buildings as were immediately requisite for the intended College.

These are described in the ensuing letter, which I give entire, because the form of acknowledgment is the only style suitable to what, however lightly acquired, was meant as an offering, even though it cost the giver all too little:

'Kohimarama: Dec. 21, 1859.

'My dear Cousin,—I have received at length from my father a distinct statement of what you have given to the Melanesian Mission. I had heard rumours before, and the Bishop of Wellington had spoken to me of your intentions, but the fact had not been regularly notified to us.

'I think I know you too well to say more than this. May God bless you for what you have lent to Him, and give us, who are specially connected with the Mission, grace to use your gift as you intend it to be used, to His glory in the salvation of souls.

'But you will like to hear how your gift will be appropriated. For three summers the Melanesian scholars lived at St. John's College, which is situated on a low hill, from which the ground falls away on every side, leaving it exposed to every wind that blows across and around the narrow isthmus.

'Thank God, we had no death traceable to the effect of the climate, but we had constant anxiety and a considerable amount of illness. When arrangements were completed for the arrival of a new principal to succeed the Bishop of Wellington, the college was no longer likely to be available for the Mission school. Consequently, we determined to build on the site long ago agreed upon; to put up some substantial buildings, and to remove some of the wooden buildings at the College which would not be required there, and set them up again at Kohimarama.

'Just opposite the entrance into the Auckland harbour, between the island of Eangitoto with its double peak and the easternmost point of the northern shore of the harbour, lies a very sheltered bay, with its sea-frontage of rather more than a quarter of a mile, bounded to the east, south, and west by low hills, which where they meet the sea become sandy cliffs, fringed with the red-flower-bearing pohutakawa. The whole of this bay, the seventy acres of flat rich soil included within the rising ground mentioned, and some seventy acres more as yet lying uncleared, adjoining the same block of seventy acres, and likely to be very valuable, as the land is capital—the whole of this was bought by the Bishop many years ago as the property of the Mission, and is the only piece of Church land over which he retains the control, every other bequest or gift to the amount of 14,000 acres, having been handed over by him to the General Synod. This he retains till the state of the Melanesian Mission is more definitely settled.

'On the west corner of this bay we determined to build. A small tide creek runs for a short way about S.S.E. from the extreme end of the western part of the beach, then turns early eastward, and meets a small stream coming down from the southern hill at its western extremity. This creek encloses a space extending along the whole width of the bay of about eighteen or twenty acres.

'At the east end stand three wooden cottages, occupied by the master, mate, and a married seaman of the "Southern Cross." At the west end stands the Melanesian school. Fences divide the whole space into three portions, whereof the western one forms our garden and orchard; and the others pasture for cows and working bullocks; small gardens being also fenced off for the three cottages. The fifty acres of flat land south of the creek we are now clearing and ploughing.

'The situation here is admirably adapted for our school. Now that we have a solid wall of the scoria from the volcanic island opposite, we have a complete shelter from the cold south wind. The cliff and hill to the west entirely shut off the wind from that quarter, and the north and east winds are always warm. The soil is very dry, and the beach composed exclusively of small "pipi" shells—small bivalves. So that by putting many cart-loads of these under our wooden floors, and around our buildings, we have so perfect a drainage that after heavy rain the soil is quite dry again in a few hours. It causes me no anxiety now, when I am for an hour away from my flock, to be thinking whether they are lying on the ground, forgetting that the hot sun overhead does not destroy the bad effect of a damp clay soil such as that at St. John's College.

'The buildings at present form three sides of a quadrangle, but the south side is only partly filled up. The large schoolroom, eighty feet long, with three sets of transepts, has been removed from the College, and put up again so as to form the east side of the quadrangle. This is of wood; so is the small wooden quadrangle which serves now for dormitories, and a part of which I occupy; my house consisting of three little rooms, together measuring seventeen feet by seven. These dormitories are the southern side of the quadrangle, but do not reach more than half-way from the east to the west side, room being left for another set of dormitories of equal size, when we want them and can afford them. The west side consists of a very nice set of stone buildings, including a large kitchen, store room, and room for putting things in daily and immediate use; and the hall, which is the northern part of the side of the quadrangle, is a really handsome room, with simple open roof and windows of a familiar collegiate appearance. These buildings are of the dark grey scoria, almost imperishable I suppose, and look very well. The hall is just long enough to take seven of us at the high table (so to speak), and thirty-four at the long table, stretching from the high table to the end of the room.

'At present this is used for school also, as the carpenters who are making all our fittings, shelves, &c., are still in the large schoolroom. We take off the north end of the schoolroom, including one set of transepts for our temporary chapel. This part will be lined, i.e. boarded, neatly inside. The rest of the building is very rough, but it answers its purpose.

'In all the stone buildings, the rough stone is left inside just as it is outside. It does not look bad at all to my eye, and I doubt if I would have it lined if we had funds to pay for it.

'I hope eventually that stone buildings will take the place of the present wooden schoolroom and dormitories; but this ought to last many years. Here we live most happily and comfortably. The climate almost tropical in summer. The beautiful scenery of the harbour before our eyes, the smooth sea and clean dry beach within a stone's throw of my window. The lads and young men have their fishing, bathing, boating, and basking in the sun, which all day from sunrise to sunset beats right upon us; for the west cliff does not project more than a few yards to the north of us, and the eastern boundary is low and some way off. I see the little schooner at her moorings whenever I look off my book or my paper, and with an opera-glass can see the captain caulking the decks. All is under my eye; and the lads daily say, "College too cold; Kohimarama very good; all the same Bauro, Mota," as the speaker belongs to one or other of our fourteen islands represented.... The moment we heard of your gift, we said simultaneously, "Let it be given to this or to some specific and definite object." I think you will like to feel not only that the money came most opportunely, but that within the walls built with that money, many many hundreds, I trust, of these Melanesian islanders will be fed and taught, and trained up in the knowledge and fear of God....

'Your affectionate Cousin,
'J. C. PATTESON.'

Before the old year was out came the tidings of the death of good Miss Neill, the governess whom Patteson had so faithfully loved from early childhood, and whose years of suffering he had done his best to cheer. 'At rest at last.' In the same letter, in answer to some complaint from his sister of want of detail in the reports, he says: 'Am I trying to make my life commonplace? Well, really so it is more or less to me. Things go on in a kind of routine. Two voyages a year, five months in New Zealand, though certainly two-thirds of my flock fresh every year. I suppose it still sounds strange to you sometimes, and to others always, but they should try to think for themselves about our circumstances.

'And you know, Fan, I can't write for the world at large anecdotes of missionary life, and swell the number of the "Gems" and other trashy books. If people who care to know, would think of what their own intuition tells them of human nature, and history tells them of heathenism, they can make out some notion of real missionary work.

'The school is the real work. Teaching adults to read a strange tongue is hard work; I have little doubt but that the Bishop is right in saying they must be taught English; but it is so very difficult a language, not spelt a bit as pronounced; and their language is all vocalic and so easy to put into writing.

'But if you like I will scatter anecdotes about—of how the Bishop and his chaplain took headers hand in hand off the schooner and roundhouse; and how the Bishop got knocked over at Leper's Island by a big wave; and how I borrowed a canoe at Tariko and paddled out yams as fast as the Bishop brought them to our boat, &c.—but this is rubbish.'

This letter is an instance of the reserve and reticence which Mr. Patteson felt so strongly with regard to his adventures and pupils. He could not endure stories of them to become, as it were, stock for exciting interest at home. There was something in his nature that shrank from publishing accounts of individual pupils as a breach of confidence, as much, or perhaps even more, than if they had been English people, likely to know what had been done. Moreover, instances had come to his knowledge in which harm had been done to both teachers and taught by their becoming aware that they were shown off to the public in print. Such things had happened even where they would have seemed not only unlikely, but impossible; and this rendered him particularly cautious in writing of his work, so that his reports were often dry, while he insisted strongly on his letters to his family being kept private.

The actual undertakings of the Mission did not exceed its resources, so that there was no need for those urgent appeals which call for sensation and incident to back them; and thus there sometimes seemed to the exterior world to be a lack of information about the Mission.

The letters of January 1860 show how the lads were fortified against weather: 'They wear a long flannel waistcoat, then a kind of jersey-shaped thing, with short trousers, reaching a little below the knee, for they dabble about like ducks here, the sea being not a hundred yards from the building. All the washing, of course, and most of the clothes-making they can do themselves; I can cut out after a fashion, and they take quickly to needle and thread; but now the Auckland ladies have provided divers very nice garments, their Sunday dresses are very nice indeed.'

The question of the Bishopric began to come forward. On the 18th of January a letter to Sir John Patteson, after speaking of a playful allusion which introduced the subject, details how Mrs. Selwyn had disclosed that a letter had actually been despatched to the Duke of Newcastle, then Colonial Secretary, asking permission to appoint and consecrate John Coleridge Patteson as Missionary Bishop of the Western Pacific Isles.

J.C.P.—'Well, then, I must say what I feel about it. I have known for some time that this was not unlikely to come some day; but I never spoke seriously to you or to the Martins when you insinuated these things, because I thought if I took it up gravely it would come to be considered a settled thing.'

Mrs. S.—'Well, so it has been, and is——'

J.C.P.—'But has the Bishop seriously thought of this, that he has had no trial of any other man; that I could give any other man who may come, perhaps, the full benefit of my knowledge of languages, and of my acquaintance with the islands and the people, while we may reasonably expect some one to come out before long far better fitted to organise and lead men than I am? Has he fairly looked at all the per contra?

Mrs. S.—'I feel sure he has.'

J.C. P.—'I don't deny that my father tells me I must not shrink from it; that some things seem to point to it as natural; that I must not venture to think that I can be as complete a judge as the Bishop of what is good for Melanesia—but what necessity for acting now?'

Here came an interruption, but the conversation was renewed later in the day with the Bishop himself, when Patteson pleaded for delay on the score that the isles were as yet in a state in which a missionary chaplain could do all that was requisite, and that the real management ought not to be withdrawn from the Bishop; to which the reply was that at the present time the Bishop could do much to secure such an appointment as he wished; but, in case of his death, even wishes expressed in writing might be disregarded. After this, the outpouring to the father continues:—

'I don't mean to shrink from this. You tell me that I ought not to do so, and I quite believe it. I know that no one can judge better than you can as to the general question, and the Bishop is as competent to decide on the special requirements of the case.

'But, my dear father, you can hardly tell how difficult I find it to be, amidst all the multiplicity of works, a man of devotional prayerful habits; how I find from time to time that I wake up to the fact that while I am doing more than I did in old times, yet that I pray less. How often I think that "God gives" habitually to the Bishop "all that sail with him;" that the work is prospering in his hands; but will it prosper in mine? I know He can use any instrument to His glory: I know that, and that He will not let my sins and shortcomings hinder His projects of love and blessing to these Melanesian islanders; but as far as purity of motive, and a spirit of prayer and self-denial do go for anything in making up the qualification on the human side for such an office—in so far, do they exist in me? You will say I am over sensitive and expect too much. That, I think, very likely may be true. It is useless to wait till one becomes really fit, for that of course I never shall be. But while I believe most entirely that grace does now supply all our deficiencies when we seek it fully, I do feel frightened when I see that I do not become more prayerful, more real in communion with God. This is what I must pray for earnestly: to become more prayerful, more constantly impressed with the necessity of seeking for everything from Him.

'You all think that absence from relations, living upon yams, want of the same kind of meat and drink that I had at home, that these things are proofs of sincerity, &c. I believe that they all mean just nothing when the practical result does not come to this—that a man is walking more closely with his God. I dare not say that I can feel humbly and reverently that my inner life is progressing. I don't think that I am as earnest in prayer as I was. Whether it be the effect of the amount of work distracting me; or, sometimes, of physical weariness, or of the self-indulgence (laugh as you may) which results from my never being contradicted or interfered with, or much worried, still I do feel this; and may He strengthen me to pray more for a spirit of prayer.

'I don't know that the actual time for my being consecrated, if I live, is nearer by reason of this letter: I think it most probable that it may take place when the General Synod meets, and, consequently, five bishops will be present, in 1862, at Nelson. But I suppose it is more fixed than it has been hitherto, and if the Bishop writes to you, as he may do, even more plainly than he speaks to me, you will know what especially to ask for me from God, and all you dear ones will recollect daily how I do inwardly tremble at the thoughts of what is to come. Do you remember how strangely I was upset before leaving home for my ordination as a deacon; and now it is coming to this—a church to be planted, organised, edified among the wild heathen inhabitants of Melanesia; and what hope can there be for me if there is to be no growth of a fervent, thankful, humble spirit of prayer and love and adoration? Not that, as I feel to my great comfort, God's work is dependent upon the individual growth in grace even of those who are entrusted with any given work; but it is in some way connected with it.

'And yet, the upshot of it all is that I shall do (D.V.) what the Bishop tells me is right. I hope he won't press on the matter, but I am content now to leave it with him, knowing what you have said, and being so thankful to leave it with you and him.'

There is a letter to his sister Fanny of the same date, beginning merrily about the family expostulation on receiving a box of reports where curiosities had been expected:—

'Fancy not thinking your worthy brother's important publications the most satisfactory treasures that any box could contain! The author's feelings are seriously injured! What are Melanesian shells to Melanesian statistics, and Lifu spears to a dissertation on the treatment of Lifu diseases? Great is the ingratitude of the houses of Feniton and Dawlish!

'Well, it must have been rather a "sell," as at Eton it is called, to have seen the long-desired and highly-paid-for box disgorge nought but Melanesian reports! all thanks to Mrs. Martin, who packed it after I was off to the Islands.

'I cannot send you anything yet, but I will bear in mind the fact that reports by themselves are not considered satisfactory. Does anybody read them, after all? for they really cost me some days' trouble, which I can't find time for again. This year's report (for I suppose there must be one) is not begun, and I don't know what to put in it. I have but little news beyond what I have written once for all to Father.

'The decisive letter from the Bishop of New Zealand to the Duke of Newcastle is in the Governor's hands, and all discussion of the question is at an end. May God bring out of it all that may conduce to His glory; but how I dread what is to come, you, who remember my leaving home first for my deacon's ordination, can well imagine.

'It is true I have seen this coming for a year or two, and have seen no way of preventing its coming upon me—no one else has come out; the Bishop feels he cannot work his present diocese and Melanesia: he is satisfied that he ought to take New Zealand rather than the islands; that the time is come for settling the matter while he is able to settle it; and I had nothing to say, for all personal objections he overruled. So then, if I live, it is settled; and that, at all events, is a comfort.... Many of my Melanesians have heavy coughs—some twelve, but I don't think any of them seriously ill, only needing to be watched. I am very well, only I want some more exercise (which, by the bye, it is always in my power to take), and am quite as much disposed as ever to wish for a good game at tennis or fives to take it out of me.

'Your loving Brother,
'J. C. PATTESON.'

The birthday letter of February 11 is a happy one, though chiefly taken up with the business matters respecting the money required for the Mission, of which Sir John was one trustee. Life was pleasant then, for Patteson says:—

'I do feel sometimes that the living alone has its temptations, and those great ones; I mean that I can arrange everything—my work, my hours, my whole life—after my own pleasure a great deal more than probably is good for me; and it is very easy to become, in a manner, very self-indulgent. I think that most likely, as our work (D.V.) progresses, one or two men may be living with me, and that will supply a check upon me of some kind. At present I am too much without it. Here I am in my cosy little room, after my delicious breakfast of perfect coffee, made in Jem's contrivance, hot milk and plenty of it, dry toast and potato. Missionary hardships! On the grass between me and the beach—a distance of some seventy yards—lie the boys' canvas beds and blankets and rugs, having a good airing. The schooner lies at anchor beyond; and, three or four miles beyond the schooner, lies Eangitoto, the great natural breakwater to the harbour. With my Dollond's opera-glass that you gave me, I can see the master and mate at their work refitting. Everything is under my eye. Our long boat and whale boat (so-called from their shapes) lie on the beach, covered with old sails to protect them from the sun. The lads are washing clothes, or scrubbing their rooms, and all the rooms—kitchen, hall, store-room, and school-room. There is a good south-western breeze stirring —our cold wind; but it is shut off here, and scarcely reaches us, and the sun has great power.

'I have the jolliest little fellows this time—about seven of them—fellows scarcely too big to take on my knee, and talk to about God, and Heaven, and Jesus Christ; and I feel almost as if I had a kind of instinct of love towards them, as they look up wonderingly with their deep deep eyes, and smooth and glossy skins, and warm soft cheeks, and ask their simple questions. I wish you could have seen the twenty Banks Islanders as I told them that most excellent of all tales—the story of Joseph. How their eyes glistened! and they pushed out their heads to hear the sequel of his making himself known to his brethren, and asking once more about "the old man of whom ye spake, is he yet alive?"

'I can never read it with a steady voice, nor tell it either.'

Sir John had thus replied to the tirade against English conventional luxury:—

'The conventional notions in this old country are not always suited to your country, and I quite agree that even here they are carried too far. Yet there are other people than the needy whose souls are entrusted to the clergy here, and in order to fulfil that trust they must mix on some degree of equality with the gentry, and with the middle classes who are well-to-do. Then again, consider both as to clergy and laity here. If they were all to lower themselves a peg or two, and give up many not only luxuries, but comforts, numbers of tradesmen, and others working under them, aye, even merchants, manufacturers, and commercial men of all sorts, would be to some extent thrown out of employ. The artificial and even luxurious state of society here does really prevent many persons from falling into the class of the needy. All this should be regulated in its due proportion. Every man ought so to limit his expenses as to have a good margin for charitable purposes of all sorts, but I cannot think that he is doing good by living himself like a pauper in order to assist paupers. If all men did so, labour of all kinds would be overstocked with hands, and more paupers created. True it is, that we all are too apt as means increase, some to set our hearts upon them, which is wickedness; some to indulge in over much luxury, which is wicked also; there should be moderation in all things. I believe that more money is given in private charities of various kinds in helping those who are struggling with small means, and yet not apparently in the class of the needy, than the world is aware of; and those who do the most are precisely those who are never heard of. But do not mistake me. I am no advocate for luxury and idle expenditure. Yet I think you carry your argument a little farther than is just. The impositions that are practised, or attempted to be practised, upon charitable people are beyond all conception.'

The following is the answer:—

'April 23, 1860.

'My dearest Father,—Thank you for writing your views about luxuries, extravagant expenditure, and the like. I see at once the truth of what you say.

'What I really mean is something of this kind. A high degree of civilisation seems to generate (perhaps necessarily) a state of society wherein the natural desires of people to gratify their inclinations in all directions, conjoined with the power of paying highly for the gratification of such inclinations, tends to call forth the ingenuity of the working class in meeting such inclinations in all agreeable ways. So springs up a complicated mechanism, by which a habit of life altogether unnecessary for health and security of life and property is introduced and becomes naturalised among a people.

If this is the necessary consequence of the distinction between rich and poor, and the course of civilisation must result in luxury and poverty among the two classes respectively (and this seems to be so), it is, of course, still more evident that the state of society being once established gradually, through a long course of years, no change can subsequently be introduced excepting in one way. It is still in the power of individuals to act upon the community by their example—e.g., the early Christians, though only for a short time, showed the result of the practical acceptance of the Lord's teaching in its effect upon society. Rich and poor, comparatively speaking, met each other half way. The rich man sold his possessions, and equal distribution was made to the poor.

'All that I contend for is that, seeing the fearful deterioration, and no less fearful extravagance, of a civilised country, the evil is one which calls loudly for careful investigation. Thousands of artisans and labourers who contribute nothing to the substantial wealth of the country, and nothing towards the production of its means of subsistence, would be thrown out of employment, and therefore that plan would be wrong. Jewellers, &c., &c., all kinds of fellows who simply manufacture vanities, are just as honest and good men as others, and it is not their fault, but the fault (if it be one at all) of civilisation that they exist. But I don't see why, the evil being recognised, some comprehensive scheme of colonisation might not be adopted by the rulers of a Christian land, to empty our poor-houses, and draft off the surplus population, giving to the utterly destitute the prospect of health, and renewed hopes of success in another thinly-inhabited country, and securing for those who remain behind a more liberal remuneration for their work by the comparative absence of competition.

'I hardly know what to write to you, my dear Father, about this new symptom of illness. I suppose, from what you say, that at your time of life the disease being so mild in its form now, will hardly prove dangerous to you, especially as you submit at once to a strictness of diet which must be pretty hard to follow out—just the habit of a whole life to be given up; and I know that to forego anything that I like, in matters of eating and drinking, wants an effort that I feel ashamed of being obliged to make. I don't, therefore, make myself unnecessarily anxious, though I can't help feeling that such a discipline must be hard. You say that in other respects you are much the same; but that means that you are in almost constant pain, and that you cannot obtain entire relief from it, except in bed.

'Still, my dear Father, as you do bear it all, how can we wish that God should spare you one trial or infirmity, which, we know, are, in His providence, making you daily riper and riper for Heaven? I ought not to write to you like this, but somehow the idea of our ever meeting anywhere else has so entirely passed from my mind, that I try to view things with reference to His ultimate purpose and work.

'Your loving and dutiful Son,
'J. C. PATTESON.'

The most present trouble of this summer was the sickness of Simeona. The account of him on Ash Wednesday is: 'He is dying of consumption slowly, and may go back with us two months hence, but I doubt it. Poor fellow, he makes the worst of his case, and is often discontented and thinks himself aggrieved because we cannot derange the whole plan of the school economy for him. I have everything which is good for him, every little dainty, and everyone is most kind; but when it comes to a complaint because one pupil-teacher is not set apart to sit with him all day, and another to catch him fish, of course I tell him that it would be wrong to grant what is so unreasonable. Some one or other of the most stupid of the boys catches his fish just as well as a pupil-teacher, and he is quite able to sit up and read for two or three hours a day, and would only be injured by having another lad in the room on purpose to be the receptacle of all his moans and complaints, yet I know, poor fellow! it is much owing to the disease upon him.'

In spite of his fretfulness and exactions, the young man, meeting not with spoiling, but with true kindness, responded to the touch. Lady Martin tells us: 'I shall never forget dear Mr. Patteson's thankfulness when, after a long season of reserve, he opened his heart to him, and told him how, step by step, this sinfulness of sin had been brought home to him. He knew he had done wrong in his heathen boyhood, but had put away such deeds when he was baptized, and had almost forgotten the past, or looked on it as part of heathenism. But in his illness, tended daily and hourly by our dear friend, his conscience had become very tender. He died in great peace.'

His death is mentioned in the following letter to Sir John Coleridge:—

'March 26, 1860. '(This day 5 years I left home. It was a Black Monday indeed.)

'My dear Uncle,—At three this morning died one of my old scholars, by name George Selwyn Simeona, from Nengone. He was here for his third time; for two years a regular communicant, having received a good deal of teaching before I knew him. He was baptized three years ago. I did not wish to bring him this time, for it was evident that he could not live long when we met last at Nengone, and I told him that he had better not come with us; but he said, "Heaven was no farther from New Zealand than from Nengone;" and when we had pulled some little way from shore, he ran down the beach, and made us return to take him in. Gradual decline and chronic bronchitis wore him to a skeleton. On Thursday the Bishop and I administered the Holy Eucharist to him; and he died at 3 A.M. to-day, with his hand in mine, as I was in the act of commending his soul to God. His wife, a sweet good girl, one of Mrs. Selwyn's pupils from Nengone in old times, died last year. They leave one boy of three years, whom I hope to get hold of entirely, and as it were adopt him.

'The clear bright moon was right over my head as after a while, and after prayer with his friends, I left his room; the quiet splash of the tiny waves on our sheltered shore, and the little schooner at her anchorage: and I thanked God that one more spirit from among the Melanesian islanders was gone to dwell, we trust, with JESUS CHRIST in Paradise.

'He will not be much missed in the Melanesian school work, for, for months, he could not make one of us....

'I find Trench's Notes on the Authorised Version of the New Testament very useful, chiefly as helping one to acquire a habit of accurate criticism for oneself, and when we come (D.V.) to translate any portion of the Scriptures, of course such books are very valuable.'

'Last mail brought me but a very few letters. The account of my dear Father's being obliged to submit to discipline did not alarm me, though I know the nature of the disease, and that his father died of it. It seems in his case likely to be kept under, but (as I have said before) I cannot feel uneasy and anxious about him, be the accounts what they may. It is partly selfish, for I am spared the sight of his suffering, but then I do long for a look at his dear face and for the sound of his voice. Five years of absence has of course made so much change in my mind in this respect, that I do not now find myself dreaming of home, constantly thinking of it; the first freshness of my loss is not felt now. But I think I love them all and you all better than ever; and I trust that I am looking inward on the whole to the blessedness of our meeting hereafter.

'But this work has its peculiar dangers. A man may become so familiarised with the habits of the heathen that insensibly his conscience becomes less sensitive.

'There is a danger in living in the midst of utter lawlessness and violence; and though the blessings and privileges far excel the disadvantages, yet it is not in every way calculated to help one forward, as I think I have in some ways found by experience.

'Well, this is all dull and dry. But our life is somewhat monotonous on shore, varied only by the details of incidents occurring in school, and witnessing to the growth of the minds of my flock. They are a very intelligent set this year, and there are many hopeful ones among them. We have worked them hard at English, and all can read a little; and some eight or ten really read nicely, but then they do not understand nearly all they read without an explanation, just like an English boy beginning his knowledge of letters with Latin (or French, a still spoken language).

'In about a month we shall (D.V.) start to take them back; but the vessel will be absent but a short time, as I shall keep the Solomon Islanders with me in the Banks Archipelago for the winter, and so avoid the necessity of the schooner running 200 or 300 miles to leeward and having to make it up again. I have slept ashore twice in the Banks Islands, but no other white man has done so, and that makes our course very clear, as they have none of the injuries usually committed by traders, &c., to revenge.

'Good-bye once more, my dearest Uncle,

'Your affectionate and grateful Nephew,

'J. C. PATTESON.'

The calmness of mind respecting his father which is here spoken of was not perpetual, and his grief broke out at times in talks with his young friend and companion, Mr. Dudley, as appears by this extract:—

'I remember his talking to me more than once on the subject of his father, and especially his remarking on one occasion that his friends were pressing him to come out there oftener, and suggesting, when he seemed out of health and spirits, that he was not taking care of himself; but that it was the anguish he endured, as night after night he lay awake thinking of his father gradually sinking and craving for him, and cheerfully resigning him, that really told upon him. I know that I obtained then a glimpse of an affection and a depth of sorrow such as perfectly awed me, and I do not think I have witnessed anything like it at all, either before or since. It was then that he seemed to enter into the full meaning of those words of our Lord, in St. Mark x. 29-30, i.e., into all that the "leaving" there spoken of involved.'

Yet in spite of this anxiety there was no flinching from the three months' residence at Mota, entirely out of reach of letters. A frame house, with planks for the floor, was prepared at Auckland to be taken out, and a stock of wine, provisions, and medicines laid in. The Rev. B. Y. Ashwell, a New Zealand clergyman, joined the Mission party as a guest, with two Maori youths, one the son of a deacon; and, besides Mr. Dudley, another pupil, Mr. Thomas Kerr, was beginning his training for service in the Mission. Sailing on one of the last days of April, there was a long passage to Nengone, where the party went ashore, and found everything in trouble, the French constantly expected, and the chiefs entreating for a missionary from the Bishop, and no possibility of supplying them. Lifu was rendered inaccessible by foul winds.

'Much to my sorrow,' writes Mr. Patteson, 'I could not land my two pupil-teachers, who, of course, wished to see their friends, and who made me more desirous to give them a run on shore, by saying at once: "Don't think of us, it is not safe to go." But I thought of what my feelings would be if it were the Devonshire coast, somewhere about Sidmouth, and no landing!' However, they, as well as the three Nengonese, Wadrokala, Harper Malo, and Martin Tahia, went on contentedly.

'Off Mai, May 19th.—Mr. Kerr has been busy taking bearings, &c., for the purpose of improving our MS. chart, and constructing a new one. Commodore Loring wanted me to tell him all about Port Patteson, and asked me if I wished a man-of-war to be sent down this winter to see me, supposing the New Zealand troubles to be all over. I gave him all the information he wanted, told him that I did not want a vessel to come with the idea of any protection being required, but that a man-of-war coming with the intention of supporting the Mission, and giving help, and not coming to treat the natives in an off-hand manner, might do good. I did not speak coldly; but really I fear what mischief even a few wildish fellows might do on shore among such people as those of the Banks Islands!

'A fore-and-aft schooner in sight! Probably some trader. May be a schooner which I heard the French had brought for missionary purposes. What if we find a priest or two at Port Patteson! However, my course is clear any way: work straight on.

'May 21st.—Schooner a false alarm. We had a very interesting visit on Saturday afternoon at Mai. We could not land till 4 P.M.; walked at once to the village, a mile and a half inland. After some excitement caused by our appearance, the people rushing to welcome us, we got them to be quiet, and to sit down. I stood up, and gave them a sermonette, then made Dudley, who speaks good Mai, say something. Then we knelt down, and I said the second Good Friday Collect, inserted a few petitions which you can imagine anyone would do at such a time, then a simple prayer in their language, the Lord's Prayer in English, and the Grace.'

On Friday Mota was reached, and the people showed great delight when the frame of the house was landed at the site purchased for a number of hatchets and other goods, so that it is the absolute property of the Mission. Saturday was spent in a visit to Port Patteson, where the people thronged, while the water-casks were being filled, and bamboos cut down, with entreaties that the station might be there; and the mosquitoes thronged too—Mr. Patteson had fifty-eight bites on one foot.

On Whit Sunday, after Holy Communion on board, the party went on shore, and prayed for, 'I cannot say with the people of Vanua Lava.'

And on Whit Monday the house was set up 'in a most lovely spot,' says Mr. Dudley, 'beneath the shade of a gigantic banyan tree, the trunk and one long horizontal branch of which formed two sides of as beautiful a picture as you would wish to look upon; the sloping bank, with its cocoa-nut, bread-fruit, and other trees, forming the base of the picture; and the coral beach, the deep, clear, blue tropical ocean, with others of the Banks Islands, Valua, Matlavo, and Uvaparapara, in the distance, forming the picture itself.'

At least a hundred natives came to help, pulling down materials from their own houses to make the roof, and delighted to obtain a bit of iron, or still better of broken glass, to shave with. In the afternoon, the master of the said house, using a box for a desk, wrote: 'Our little house will, I think, be finished to-night; anyhow we can sleep in it, if the walls are but half ready; they are merely bamboo canes tied together. We sleep on the floor boarded and well raised on poles, two feet and more from the ground—beds are superfluous here.'

Here then was the first stake of the Church's tabernacle planted in all Melanesia!

The boards of the floor had been brought from New Zealand, the heavy posts on which the plates were laid were cut in Vanua Lava, and the thatch was of cocoa-nut leaves, the leaflets ingeniously bound together, native fashion, and quite waterproof; but a mat or piece of canvas had to be nailed within the bamboo walls to keep out the rain.

On Wednesday a short service was held, the first ever known in Mota; and then Mr. Ashwell and Mr. Kerr embarked, leaving Mr. Patteson and Mr. Dudley with their twelve pupils in possession. Mr. Dudley had skill to turn their resources to advantage. Space was gained below by making a frame, to which knapsacks, bags, &c., could be hung up, and the floor was only occupied by the four boxes, which did the further part of tables, desks, and chairs in turn. As to beds, was not the whole floor before them? and, observes the Journal: 'Now I see the advantage of having brought planks from New Zealand to make a floor. We all had something level to lie on at night, and when you are tired enough, a good smooth plank or a box does just as well as a mattress.'

Fresh water was half a mile off, and had to be fetched in bamboos; but this was a great improvement upon Lifu, where there was none at all; and a store of it was always kept in four twenty-gallon casks, three on the beach, and one close to the house.

The place was regularly purchased:—

'June 8th.—I have just bought for the Mission this small clearing of half an acre, and the two acres (say) leading to the sea, with twenty or more bread-fruits on it. There was a long talk with the people, and some difficulty in finding out the real proprietors, but I think we arranged matters really well at last. You would have been amused at the solemnity with which I conducted the proceeding: making a great show of writing down their names, and bringing each one of the owners up in their turn to see his name put down, and making him touch my pen as I put a cross against his name. Having spent about an hour in enquiring whether any other person had any claim on the land or trees, I then said, "Now this all belongs to me," and they assented. I entered it in my books—"On behalf of the Melanesian Mission," but they could only understand that the land belonged to the Bishop and me, because we wanted a place where some people might live, who should be placed by the Bishop to teach them. Of course the proceeding has no real validity, but I think they will observe the contract: not quite the same thing as the transfer of land in the old country! Here about 120 men, quite naked, represented the interests of the late owners, and Dudley and I represented the Mission.'

The days were thus laid out—Morning school in the village, first with the regular scholars, then with any one who liked to come in; and then, when the weather permitted, a visit to some village, sometimes walking all round, a circuit of ten miles, but generally each of the two taking a separate village, talking to the people, teaching them from cards, and encouraging interrogatories. Mr. Patteson always had such an attraction for them that they would throng round him eagerly wherever he went.

The Mota people had a certain faith of their own; they believed in a supreme god called Ikpat, who had many brothers, one of whom was something like Loki, in the Northern mythology, always tricking him. Ikpat had disappeared in a ship, taking the best of everything with him. It was also believed that the spirits of the dead survived and ranged about at night, maddening all who chanced to meet them; and, like many other darkly coloured people, the Motans had begun by supposing their white visitors to be the ghosts of their deceased friends come to revisit them.

There were a good many other superstitions besides; and a ceremony connected with one of them was going on the second week of the residence at Mota—apparently a sort of freemasonry, into which all boys of a certain age were to be initiated.

The Journal says:—

'There is some strange superstitious ceremony going on at this village. A space had been enclosed by a high hedge, and some eighteen or nineteen youths are spending a month or more inside the fence, in a house where they lie wrapped up in mats, abundantly supplied with food by the people, who, from time to time, assemble to sing or perform divers rites. I had a good deal of trouble with the father of our second year's pupil Tagalana, who insisted upon sending his son thither. I warned him against the consequences of hindering his son, who wished to follow Christ. He yielded, because he was evidently afraid of me, but not convinced, as I have no right to expect he should be.

'The next morning comes an old fellow, and plants a red-flowering branch in our small clearing, whereupon our Mota boys go away, not wishing to go, but not daring to stay. No people came near us, but by-and-by comes the man who had planted it, with whom I had much talk, which ended in his pulling up and throwing away the branch, and in the return of our boys.

'In the evening many people came, to whom I spoke very plainly about the necessity of abandoning these customs if they were in earnest in saying they wished to embrace the Word of God. On Sunday they gave up their singing at the enclosure, or only attempted it in a very small way.

'June 6th.—I am just returned from a village a mile and a half off, called Tasmate, where one of their religious ceremonies took place this morning. The village contains upwards of twenty houses, built at the edge of the bush, which consists here almost exclusively of fruit-bearing trees—cocoa-nut trees, bananas, bread-fruit, and large almond trefts are everywhere the most conspicuous. The sea view looking south is very beautiful.

'I walked thither alone, having heard that a feast was to be held there. As I came close to the spot, I heard the hum of many voices, and the dull, booming sound of the native drum, which is nothing but a large hollow tree, of circular shape, struck by wooden mallets. Some few people ran off as I appeared, but many of them had seen me before. The women, about thirty in number, were sitting on the ground together, in front of one of the houses, which enclosed an open air circular space; in front of another house were many children and young people. In the long narrow house which forms the general cooking and lounging room of the men of each village, and the sleeping room of the bachelors, were many people preparing large messes of grated yam and cocoa-nut in flat wooden dishes. At the long oblong-shaped drum sat the performers, two young men, each with two short sticks to perform the kettledrum part of the business, and an older man in the centre, whose art consisted in bringing out deep, hollow tones from his wooden instrument. Around them stood some thirty men, two of whom I noticed especially, decked out with red leaves, and feathers in their hair. Near this party, and close to the long, narrow house in the end of which I stood, was a newly raised platform of earth, supported on stones. On the corner stone were laid six or eight pigs' jaws, with the large curling tusks left in them. This was a sacred stone. In front of the platform were three poles, covered with flowers, red leaves, &c.

'For about an hour and a half the men at or around the drum kept up an almost incessant shouting, screaming and whistling, moving their legs and arms in time, not with any wild gesticulations, but occasionally with some little violence, the drum all the time being struck incessantly. About the middle of the ceremony, an old, tall, thin man, with a red handkerchief, our gift at some time, round his waist, began ambling round the space in the middle of the houses, carrying a boar's skull in his hand. This performance he repeated three times. Then a man jumped up upon the platform, and, moving quickly about on it and gesticulating wildly, delivered a short speech, after which the drum was beat louder than ever; then came another speech from the same man; and then the rain evidently hastening matters to a conclusion to the whole thing, without any ceremony of consecrating the stone, as I had expected.

'In the long room afterwards I had the opportunity of saying quietly what I had said to those about me during the ceremony: the same story of the love of God, especially manifested in JESUS CHRIST, to turn men from darkness to light, and from the power of Satan unto God. With what power that verse speaks to one while witnessing such an exhibition of ignorance, or fear, or superstition as I have seen to-day! And through it all I was constantly thinking upon the earnestness with which these poor souls follow out a mistaken notion of religion. Such rain as fell this morning would have kept a whole English congregation from going to church, but they never sought shelter nor desisted from their work in hand; and the physical effect was really great, the perspiration streamed down their bodies, and the learning by heart all the songs and the complicated parts of the ceremony implied a good deal of pains. Christians do not always take so much pains to fulfil scrupulously their duties as sometimes these heathens do. And, indeed, their bondage is a hard one, constant suspicion and fear whenever they think at all. Everything that is not connected with the animal part of our nature seems to be the prey of dark and gloomy superstitions; the spiritual part is altogether inactive as an instrument of comfort, joy, peace and hope. You can imagine that I prayed earnestly for these poor souls, actually performing before me their strange mysteries, and that I spoke earnestly and strongly afterwards.

'The argument with those who would listen was: What good comes of all this? What has the spirit you call Ikpat ever done for you? Has he taught you to clothe yourselves, build houses, &c.? Does he offer to make you happy? Can you tell me what single good thing has come from these customs? But if you ask me what good thing has come to us from the Word of God, first you had better let me tell you what has happened in England of old, in New Zealand, Nengone, or Lifu, then I will tell you what the Word of God teaches;—and these with the great outline of the Faith.'

Every village in the island had the platforms, poles, and flowers; and the next day, at a turn in the path near a village, the Mission party suddenly came upon four sticks planted in a row, two of them bearing things like one-eyed masks; two others, like mitres, painted red, black, and white. As far as could be made out, they were placed there as a sort of defiance to the inhabitants; but Mr. Patteson took down one, and declared his intention of buying them for fish-hooks, to take to New Zealand, that the people might see their dark and foolish customs!

Some effect had already been produced, the people declared that there had been much less of fighting since the missionaries had spoken to them eighteen months back, and they had given up some of the charms by which they used to destroy each other; but there was still much carrying of bows; and on the way home from this expedition, Mr. Patteson suddenly came on six men with bows bent and arrows pointed in his direction. He at once recognised a man from Veverao, the next village to the station, and called out 'All right!' It proved that a report had come of his being attacked or killed on the other side of the island, and that they had set out to defend or avenge him.

He received his champions with reproof:—'This is the very thing I told you not to do. It is all your foolish jealousy and suspicion of them. There is not a man on the island who is not friendly to me! And if they were not friendly, what business have you with your bows and arrows? I tell you once more, if I see you take your bows again, though you may do it as you think with a good intention towards me, I will not stay at your village. If you want to help me, receive the Word of God, abandon your senseless ceremonies. That will be helping me indeed!'

'Cannot you live at peace in this little bit of an island?' was the constant theme of these lectures; and when Wompas, his old scholar, appeared with bow and arrows, saying, I am sent to defend you,' the answer was, 'Don't talk such nonsense! Give me the bow!' This was done, and Patteson was putting it across his knee to break it, when the youth declared it was not his. 'If I see these things again, you know what will become of them!'

The mitres and masks were gone; but the Veverao people were desperately jealous of the next village, Auta, alleging that the inhabitants were unfriendly, and by every means trying to keep the guest entirely to themselves; while he resolutely forced on their reluctant ears, 'If you are sincere in saying that you wish to know God, you must love your brother. God will not dwell in a divided heart, nor teach you His truth while you wilfully continue to hate your brother!'

The St. Barnabas Day on which most of this was written was a notable one, for it was marked by the first administration of both the Sacraments in Mota. In the morning one English and four Nengonese communicants knelt round their pastor; and, in the evening, after a walk to Auta, and much of this preaching of peace and goodwill, then a dinner, which was made festive with preserved meat and wine, there came a message from one Ivepapeu, a leading man, whose child was sick. It was evidently dying, and Mr. Patteson, in the midst of the people, told them that—

'The Son of God had commanded us to teach and baptize all nations; that they did not understand the meaning of what he was about to do, but that the word of JESUS the Son of God was plain, and that he must obey it; that this was not a mere form, but a real gift from heaven, not for the body but the soul; that the child would be as likely to die as before, but that its spirit would be taken to God, and if it should recover, it must be set apart for God, not taken to any heathen rites, but given to himself to be trained up as a child of God.' The parents consented: 'Then,' he continues, 'we knelt, and in the middle of the village, the naked group around me, the dying child in its mother's lap, I prayed to God and Christ in their language to bless the child according to His own promise, to receive it for His own child, and to convey to it the fulness of the blessing of His holy Sacrament. Then while all were silent, I poured the water on its head, pronouncing the form of words in English, and calling the child John, the first Christian child in the Banks Islands. Then I knelt down again and praised God for His goodness, and prayed that the child might live, if it were His good pleasure, and be educated to His glory; and then I prayed for those around me and for the people of the island, that God would reveal to them His Holy Name and Word and Will; and so, with a few words to the parents and people, left them, as darkness settled down on the village and the bright stars came out overhead.'

The innocent first-fruits of Mota died three days later, and Mr. Patteson found a great howling and wailing going on over its little grave under a long low house. This was hushed when he came up, and spoke of the Resurrection, and described the babe's soul dwelling in peace in the Kingdom of the Father, where those would join it who would believe and repent, cast away their evil practices, and be baptized to live as children of God. Kneeling down, he prayed over it, thanking God for having taken it to Himself, and interceding for all around. They listened and seemed touched; no opposition was ever offered to him, but he found that there was much fighting and quarrelling, many of the villages at war with each other, and a great deal too much use of the bow and arrow, though the whole race was free from cannibalism. They seemed to want to halt between two opinions: to keep up their orgies on the one hand, and to make much of the white teacher on the other; and when we recollect that two unarmed Englishmen, and twelve blacks from other islands, were perfectly isolated in the midst of a heathen population, having refused protection from a British man-of-war, it gives a grandeur to the following narrative:—

'June 7th.—One of their chief men has just been with two bread-fruit as a present. I detected him as a leader of one of their chief ceremonies yesterday, and I have just told him plainly that I cannot accept anything from him, neither can I suffer him to be coming to my place while it is notorious that he is teaching the children the very things they ought not to learn, and that he is strongly supporting the old false system, while he professes to be listening attentively to the Word of God. I made him take up his two bread-fruit and carry them away; and I suppose it will be the story all over the village that I have driven him away.

'"By-and-by we will listen to the Word of God, when we have finished these ceremonies."

'"Yes, you hearken first to the voice of the evil spirit; you choose him firsthand then you will care to hear about God."'

The ceremony was to last twenty days, and only affected the lads, who were blackened all over with soot, and apparently presented pigs to the old priest, and were afterwards admitted to the privileges of eating and sleeping in the separate building, which formed a kind of club-house for the men of each village, and on which Mr. Patteson could always reckon as both a lecture room and sleeping place.

The people kept on saying that 'by-and-by' they would make an end of their wild ritual, and throw down their enclosures, and at the same time they thronged to talk to him at the Mission station, and built a shed to serve for a school at Auta.

Meantime the little estate was brought into order. A pleasant day of landscape-gardening was devoted to clearing gaps to let in the lovely views from the station; and a piece of ground was dug and planted with pine-apples, vines, oranges, and cotton, also a choicer species of banana than the indigenous one. Bread-fruit was so plentiful that breakfast was provided by sending a boy up a tree to bring down four or five fruits, which were laid in the ashes, and cooked at once; and as to banana leaves 'we think nothing of cutting one down, four feet long and twenty inches wide, of a bright pale green, just to wrap up a cooked yam or two.'

The first week in July, with Wadrokala, Mark, and two Malanta men, Mr. Patteson set forth in the boat that had been left with him, for an expedition among the other islands, beginning with Saddle Island, or Valua, which was the proper name.

The day after leaving Eowa, the weather changed; and as on these perilous coasts there was no possibility of landing, two days and the intervening night had to be spent in the open four-oared boat, riding to a grapnel!

Very glad they were to get into Port Patteson, and to land in the wet, 'as it can rain in the tropics.' The nearest village, however, was empty, everybody being gone to the burial wake of the wife of a chief, and there was no fire to cook the yams, everything dreary and deserted, but a short walk brought the wet and tired party to the next village, where they were made welcome to the common house; and after, supping on yams and chocolate, spent a good night, and found the sea smooth the next day for a return to head-quarters.

These first weeks at Mota were very happy, but after that the strain began to tell. Mr. Patteson had been worn with anxiety for his father, and no doubt with awe in the contemplation of his coming Episcopate, and was not in a strong state of health when he left Kohimarama, and the lack of animal food, the too sparing supply of wine, and the bare board bed told upon him. On the 24th of July he wrote in a letter to his Uncle Edward:—

'I have lost six days: a small tumour formed inside the ear about two inches from the outer ear, and the pain has been very considerable, and the annoyance great. Last night I slept for the first time for five nights, and I have been so weary with sleeplessness that I have been quite idle. The mischief is passing away now. That ear is quite deaf; it made me think so of dear Father and Joan with their constant trial. I don't see any results from our residence here; and why should I look for them? It is enough that the people are hearing, some of them talking, and a few thinking about what they hear. All in God's own time!'

Mr. Dudley adds: 'His chief trouble at this time was with one of his ears. The swelling far in not only made him deaf while it lasted, but gave him intense and protracted agony. More than once he had to spend the whole night in walking up and down the room. But only on one occasion during the whole time do I remember his losing his patience, and that was when we had been subjected to an unusually protracted visitation from the "loafers" of the village, who would stretch themselves at full length on the floor and table, if we would let them, and altogether conduct themselves in such a manner as to call for summary treatment, very different from the more promising section. The half jocular but very decided manner in which he cleared the house on this occasion, and made them understand that they were to respect our privacy sometimes, and not make the Mission station an idling place, was very satisfactory. It was no small aggravation of the pain to feel that this might be the beginning of permanent deafness, such as would be fatal to his usefulness in a work in which accuracy of ear was essential.'

However, this gradually improved; and another boat voyage was made, but again was frustrated by the torrents of rain. In fact, it was an unusually wet and unwholesome season, which told upon everyone. Mark Chakham, the Nengonese, was brought very near the grave by a severe attack of dysentery. All the stores of coffee, chocolate, wine and biscuit were used up. The 'Southern Cross' had been due full a month, and nothing was heard of her through the whole of September.

Teaching and conversation went on all this time, trying as it was; and the people still came to hear, though no one actually undertook to forsake his idols.

'I am still hopeful about these people,' is the entry on September 18, 'though all their old customs and superstitions go on just as before. But (1) they know that a better teaching has been presented to them. (2) They do not pursue their old habits with the same unthinking-security. (3) There are signs of a certain uneasiness of mind, as if a struggle was beginning in them. (4) They have a vague consciousness, some of them, that the power is passing away from their witchcrafts, sorceries, &c., by which unquestionably they did and still do work strange effects on the credulous people, like 'Pharaoh's magicians of old.'

This was ground gained; and one or two voyages to Vanua Lava and the other isles were preparatory steps, and much experience had been acquired, and resulted in this:—

'The feasibility of the Bishop's old scheme is more and more apparent to me. Only I think that in taking away natives to the summer school, it must be understood that some (and they few) are taken from new islands merely to teach us some of their languages and to frank us, so that we may have access in safety to their islands. Should any of them turn out well, so much the better; but it will not be well to take them with the expectation of their becoming teachers to their people. But the other section of the school will consist of young men whose behaviour we have watched during the winter in their own homes, whose professions we have had an opportunity of testing—they may be treated as young men on the way to become teachers eventually to their countrymen. One learns much from living among a heathen people, and only by living in our pupils' homes shall we ever know their real characters. Poor fellows! they are adepts in all kinds of deceitfulness at a very early age, and so completely in our power on board the schooner and at Kohimarama, that we know nothing of them as they are.'

The very paper this is copied from shows how the stores were failing, for the full quarto sheets have all failed, and the journal is continued on note paper.

Not till October 1 was Mr. Patteson's watch by a poor dying woman interrupted by tidings that a ship was in sight. And soon it was too plain that she was not the 'Southern Cross,' though, happily, neither trader nor French Mission ship. In a short time there came ashore satisfactory letters from home, but with them the tidings that the little 'Southern Cross' lay in many fathoms water on the New Zealand coast!

On her return, on the night of the 17th of June, just as New Zealand itself was reached, there was a heavy gale from the north-east. A dangerous shoal of rocks, called the Hen and Chickens, stands out from the head of Ngunguru Bay; and, in the darkness and mist, it was supposed that these were safely passed, when the ship struck on the eastern Chicken, happily on a spot somewhat sheltered from the violence of the breakers. The two passengers and the crew took refuge in the rigging all night; and in the morning contrived to get a line to land, on which all were safely drawn through the surf, and were kindly received by the nearest English settlers.

So, after five years' good service, ended the career of the good 'Southern Cross' the first. She had gone down upon sand, and much of the wreck might have been recovered and made useful again had labour not been scarce at that time in New Zealand that the Bishop could find no one to undertake the work, and all he could do was to charter another vessel to be despatched to bring home the party from Mota. Nor were vessels fit for the purpose easy to find, and the schooner 'Zillah'—welcome as was the sight of her—proved a miserable substitute even in mere nautical capabilities, and her internal arrangements were of course entirely inappropriate to the peculiar wants of the Mission.

This was the more unfortunate because the very day after her arrival Mr. Dudley was prostrated by something of a sunstroke. Martin Tehele was ill already, and rapidly became worse; and Wadrokala and Harper Malo sickened immediately, nor was the former patient recovered. Mr. Dudley, Wadrokala and Harper were for many days in imminent danger, and were scarcely dragged through by the help of six bottles of wine, providentially sent by the Bishop. Mr. Dudley says:—

'During the voyage Mr. Patteson's powers of nursing were severely tried. Poor Martin passed away before we arrived at Nengone, and was committed to the deep. Before he died he was completely softened by Mr. Patteson's loving care, and asked pardon for all the trouble he had given and the fretfulness he had shown. Poor fellow! I well remember how he gasped out the Lord's Prayer after Mr. Patteson a few minutes before he died. We all who had crawled up round his bed joining in with them.

'Oh, what a long dreary time that was! Light baffling winds continually, and we in a vessel as different from the "Southern Cross" as possible, absolutely guiltless, I should think, of having ever made two miles an hour to windward "in a wind." The one thing that stands out as having relieved its dreariness is the presence of Mr. Patteson, the visits he used to pay to us, and the exquisite pathos of his voice as, from the corner of the hold where we lay, we could hear him reading the Morning and Evening Prayers of the Church and leading the hymn. These prevented these long weary wakeful days and nights from being absolutely insupportable.'

At last Nengone was reached, and Wadrokala and Harper were there set ashore, better, but very weak. Here the tidings were known that in Lifu John Cho had lost his wife Margaret, and had married the widow of a Karotongan teacher, a very suitable match, but too speedy to be according to European ideas; and on November 26 the 'Zillah' was off the Three Kings, New Zealand.

'Monday: Nov. 26, 1860. '"Zillah" Schooner, off the Three Kings, N. of New

Zealand.

'You know pretty well that Kohimarama is a small bay, about one-third of a mile along the sea frontage, two-and-a-half miles due east of Auckland, and just opposite the entrance into the harbour, between the North Head and Eangitoto. The beach is composed entirely of the shells of "pipi" (small cockles); always, therefore, dry and pleasant to walk upon. A fence runs along the whole length of it. At the eastern end of it, a short distance inside this N. (= sea) fence, are the three cottages of the master and mate and Fletcher. Sam Fletcher is a man-of-war's man, age about thirty-eight, who has been with us some four years and a half. He has all the habits of order and cleanliness that his life as coxswain of the captain's gig taught him; he is a very valuable fellow. He is our extra man at sea.

'Each of these cottages has its garden, and all three men are married, but only the master (Grange) has any family, one married daughter.

'Then going westward comes a nine-acre paddock, and then a dividing fence, inside (i.e. to W.) of which stand our buildings.

'Now our life here is hard to represent. It is not like the life of an ordinary schoolmaster, still less like that of an ordinary clergyman. Much of the domestic and cooking department I may manage, of course, to superintend. I would much rather do this than have the nuisance of a paid servant.

'So at 5 A.M., say, I turn out; I at once go to the kitchen, and set the two cooks of the week to work, light fire, put on yams or potatoes, then back to dress, read, &c.; in and out all the time, of the kitchen till breakfast time: say 8 or 8.30. You would be surprised to see how very soon the lads will do it all by themselves, and leave me or Mr. Kerr to give all our attention to school and other matters.

'So you can fancy, Joan, now, the manner of life. My little room with my books is my snuggery during the middle of the day, and at night I have also a large working table at one end of the big school-room, covered with books, papers, &c., and here I sit a good deal, my room being too small to hold the number of books that I require to have open for comparison of languages, and for working out grammatical puzzles. Then I am in and out of the kitchen and store-room, and boys' rooms, seeing that all things, clothes, blankets, floors, &c., are washed and kept clean, and doing much what is done in every house.'

Snuggery no doubt it looked compared with the 'Zillah;' but what would the 'Eton fellow' of fifteen years back have thought of the bare, scantily furnished room, with nothing but the books, prints, and photographs around to recall the tastes of old, and generally a sick Melanesian on the floor? However, he was glad enough to return thither, though with only sixteen scholars from ten places. Among them was Taroniara from Bauro, who was to be his follower, faithful to death. The following addition was made to the letter to Mr. Edward Coleridge, begun in Banks Islands:—

'Kohimarama: Dec. 1, 1860.

'One line, my dear tutor, before I finish off my pile of hastily written letters for this mail.

'Alas! alas! for the little schooner, that dear little vessel, our home for so many months of each year, so admirably qualified for her work. Whether she may be got off her sandy bed, no one can say. Great expense would certainly be incurred, and the risk of success great also.

'I have not yet had time to talk to the Bishop, I only reached New Zealand on November 28. We cannot, however, well do our work in chartered vessels [then follows a full detail of the imperfections of the 'Zillah' and all other Australian merchant craft; then—But, dear old tutor, even the "Southern Cross" (though what would I give to see her now at her usual anchorage from the window at which I am now sitting!) for a time retires into the distance, as I think of what is to take place (D.V.) in January next.

'I hoped that I had persuaded the Bishop that the meeting of the General Synod in February 1862 would be a fit time. I do not see that the Duke's despatch makes any difference in the choice of the time. But all was settled in my absence; and now at the Feast of the Epiphany or of the Conversion of St. Paul (as suits the convenience of the Southern Bishops) the Consecration is to take place. I am heartily glad that the principle of consecrating Missionary Bishops will be thus affirmed and acted upon; but oh! if some one else was to be the Bishop!

'And yet I must not distrust God's grace, and the gift of the Holy Spirit to enable me for this work. I try and pray to be calm and resigned, and I am happy and cheerful.

'And it is a blessed thing that now three of your old dear friends, once called Selwyn, Abraham, Hobhouse should be consecrating your own nephew and pupil, gathered by God's providence into the same part of God's field at the ends of the earth.'

Still with his heart full of the never-forgotten influence of his mother, he thus begins his home letter of the same date:—

'Kohimarama: Dec. 1.

'My dearest Father,—I could not write on November 28, but the memory of that day in 1842 was with me from morning to night. We anchored on that day at 1 A.M., and I was very busy till late at night. I had no idea till I came back from the Islands that there was any change in the arrangements for the consecration in February 1862. But now the Bishops of Wellington and Nelson have been summoned for the Feast of the Epiphany, or of the conversion of St. Paul, and all was done in my absence. I see, too, that you in England have assumed that the consecration will take place soon after the reception of the Duke's despatch.

'I must not now shrink from it, I know. I have full confidence in your judgment, and in that of the Bishop; and I suppose that if I was speaking of another, I should say that I saw reasons for it. But depend upon it, my dear Father, that a man cannot communicate to another the whole of the grounds upon which he feels reluctant to accept an office. I believe that I ought to accept this in deference to you all, and I do so cheerfully, but I don't, say that my judgment agrees wholly with you all.

'And yet there is no one else; and if the separation of New Zealand and Melanesia is necessary, I see that this must be the consequence. So I regard it now as a certainty. I pray God to strengthen and enable me: I look forward, thanks to Him, hopefully and cheerfully. I have the love and the prayers of many, many friends, and soon the whole Church of England will recognise me as one who stands in special need of grace and strength from above.

'Oh! the awful power of heathenism! the antagonism, not of evil only, but of the Evil One, rather, I mean the reality felt of all evil emanating from a person, as St. Paul writes, and as our Lord spoke of him. I do indeed at times feel overwhelmed, as if I was in a dream. Then comes some blessed word or thought of comfort, and promised strength and grace.

'But enough of this.

'The "Southern Cross" cannot, I think, be got off without great certain expense and probable risk. I think we shall have to buy another vessel, and I dare say she may be built at home, but I don't know what is the Bishop's mind about it....

'I shall write to Merton, I don't know why I should needs vacate my fellowship. I have no change of outward circumstances brought upon me by my change presently from the name of Presbyter to Bishop, and we want all the money.

'What you say about a Missionary Bishop being for five months of the year within the diocese of another Bishop, I will talk over with the Bishop of New Zealand. I think our Synodical system will make that all right; and as for my work, it will be precisely the same in all respects, my external life altered only to the extent of my wearing a broader brimmed and lower crowned hat. Dear Joan is investing moneys in cutaway coats, buckles without end, and no doubt knee-breeches and what she calls "gambroons" (whereof I have no cognizance), none of which will be worn more than (say) four or five times in the year. Gambroons and aprons and lawn sleeves won't go a-voyaging, depend upon it. Just when I preach in some Auckland church I shall appear in full costume; but the buckles will grow very rusty indeed!

'How kind and good of her to take all the trouble, I don't laugh at that, and at her dear love for me and anxiety that I should have everything; but I could not help having a joke about gambroons, whatever they are....

'Good-bye once more, my dearest Father. You will, I trust, receive this budget about the time of your birthday. How I think of you day and night, and how I thank you for all your love, and perhaps most of all, not only letting me come to Melanesia, but for your great love in never calling me away from my work even to see your face once more on earth.

'Your loving and dutiful son,

'J. C. PATTESON.'

Remark upon a high-minded letter is generally an impertinence both to the writer and the reader, but I cannot help pausing upon the foregoing, to note the force of the expression that thanks the father for the love that did not recall the son. What a different notion these two men had of love from that which merely seeks self-gratification! Observe, too, how the old self-contemplative, self-tormenting spirit, that was unhappiness in those days of growth and heart-searching at the first entrance into the ministry, had passed into humble obedience and trust. Looking back to the correspondence of ten years ago, volumes of progress are implied in the quiet 'Enough of this.'

There were, however, some delays in bringing the three together, and on the

New Year's Day of 1861, the designate writes to Bishop Abraham: 'I dare say the want of any positive certainty as to the time of the Consecration is a good discipline for me. I think I feel calm now; but I know I must not trust feelings, and when I think of those islands and the practical difficulty of getting at them, and the need of so many of those qualities which are so wonderfully united in our dear Primate, I need strength from above indeed to keep my heart from sinking. But I think that I do long and desire to work on by God's grace, and not to look to results at all.'

A 'supplementary mail' made possible a birthday letter (the last) written at 6 A.M. on the 11th of February: 'I wanted of course to write to you to-day. Many happy returns of it I wish you indeed, for it may yet please God to prolong your life; but in any case you know well how I am thinking and praying for you that every blessing and comfort may be given you. Oh I how I do think of you night and day. When Mrs. Selwyn said "Good-bye," and spoke of you, I could not stand it. I feel that anything else (as I fancy) I can speak of with composure; but the verses in the Bible, such as the passage which I read yesterday in St. Mark x., almost unnerve me, and I can't wish it to be otherwise. But I feel that my place is here, and that I must look to the blessed hope of meeting again hereafter....

'Of course no treat is so great to me as the occasional talks with the Bishop. Oh! the memory of those days and evenings on board the "Southern Cross." Well, it was so happy a life that it was not good for me, I suppose, that it should last. But I feel it now that the sense of responsibility is deepening on me, and I must go out to work without him; and very, very anxious I am sometimes, and almost oppressed by it.

'But strength will come; and it is not one's own work, which is the comfort, and if I fail (which is very likely) God will place some other man in my position, and the work will go on, whether in my hands or not, and that is the real point.

'Some talk I find there has been about my going home. I did not hear of it until after Mrs. Selwyn had sailed. It was thought of, but it was felt, as I certainly feel, that it ought not to be.... My work lies out here clearly; and it is true that any intermission of voyages or residences in the islands is to be avoided.'

Mrs. Selwyn had gone home for a year, and had so arranged as to see the Patteson family almost immediately on her return. Meantime the day drew on. The Consecration was not by Royal mandate, as in the case of Bishops of sees under British jurisdiction; but the Duke of Newcastle, then Colonial Secretary, wrote:—'That the Bishops of New Zealand are at liberty, without invasion of the Royal prerogative or infringement of the law of England, to exercise what Bishop Selwyn describes as their inherent power of consecrating Mr. Patteson or any other person to take charge of the Melanesian Islands, provided that the consecration should take place beyond British territory.'

In consequence it was proposed that the three consecrating Bishops should take ship and perform the holy rite in one of the isles beneath the open sky; but as Bishop Mackenzie had been legally consecrated in Cape Town Cathedral, the Attorney-General of New Zealand gave it as his opinion that there was no reason that the consecration should not take place in Auckland.

'Kohimarama: Feb. 15, 1861.

'My dearest Father,—Mr. Kerr, who has just returned from Auckland, where he spent yesterday, brings me the news that the question of the Consecration has been settled, and that it will take place (D.V.) on Sunday week, St. Matthias Day, February 24.

'I ought not to shrink back now. The thought has become familiar to me, and I have the greatest confidence in the judgment of the Bishop of New Zealand; and I need not say how your words and letters and prayers too are helping me now.

'Indeed, though at any great crisis of our lives no doubt we are intended to use more than ordinary strictness in examining our motives and in seeking for greater grace, deeper repentance, more earnest and entire devotion to God, and amendment of life, yet I know that any strong-emotion, if it existed now, would pass away soon, and that I must be the same man as Bishop as I am now, in this sense, viz., that I shall have just the same faults, unless I pray for strength to destroy them, which I can do equally well now, and that all my characteristic and peculiar habits of mind will remain unchanged by what will only change my office and not myself. So that where I am indolent now I shall be indolent henceforth, unless I seek to get rid of indolence; and I shall not be at all better, wiser, or more consistent as Bishop than I am now by reason simply of being a Bishop.

'You know my meaning. Now I apply what I write to prove that any strong excitement now would be no evidence of a healthy state of mind. I feel now like myself, and that is not at all like what I wish to be. And so I thank God that as before any solemn season special inducements to earnest repentance are put into our minds, so I now feel a special call upon me to seek by His grace to make a more faithful use of the means of usefulness which He gives me, that I may be wholly and entirely turned to Him, and so be enabled to do His will in Melanesia. You know, my dearest Father, that I do not indeed undervalue the grace of Ordination; only I mean that the right use of any great event in one's life, as I take it, is not to concentrate feeling so much on it as earnestness of purpose, prayer for grace, and for increase of simplicity and honesty and purity of heart. Perhaps other matters affect me more than my supposed state of feeling, so that my present calmness may be attributed to circumstances of which I am partially ignorant; and, indeed, I do wonder that I am calm when one moment's look at the map, or thought of the countless islands, almost overwhelms me. How to get at them? Where to begin? How to find men and means? How to decide upon the best method of teaching, &c.? But I must try to be patient, and to be content with very small beginnings—and endings, too, perhaps.

'Sunday, Feb. 24, St. Matthias, 10 A.M.—The day is come, my dearest Father, and finds me, I thank God, very calm. Yesterday, at 6 P.M., in the little chapel at Taurama, the three Bishops, the dear Judge, Lady Martin, Mrs. Abraham, Mr. Lloyd and I met together for special prayer. How we missed Mrs. Selwyn, dear dear Mrs. Selwyn, from among us, and how my thoughts passed on to you! Evening hymn, Exhortation in Consecration Service, Litany from the St. Augustine's Missionary Manual, with the questions in Consecration Service turned into petitions, Psalm cxxxii., cxxxi., li.; Lesson i Tim. iii.; special prayer for the

Elect Bishop among the heathen, for the conversion of the heathen; and the Gloria in Excelsis.

'Then the dear Bishop walked across to me, and taking my hand in both of his, looking at me with that smile of love and deep deep thought, so seldom seen, and so deeply prized. "I can't tell you what I feel," he said, with a low and broken voice. "You know it—my heart is too full! "

'Ah! the memory of six years with that great and noble servant of God was in my heart too, and so we stood, tears in our eyes, and I unable to speak.

'At night again, when, after arranging finally the service, I was left with him alone, he spoke calmly and hopefully. Much he said of you, and we are all thinking much of you. Then he said: "I feel no misgiving in my heart; I think all has been done as it should be. Many days we three have discussed the matter. By prayer and Holy Communion we have sought light from above, and it is, I believe, God's will." Then once more taking both hands, he kissed my forehead: "God bless you, my dear Coley. I can't say more words, and you don't desiderate them."

'"No," said I; "my heart, as yours, is too full for words. I have lived six years with you to little purpose, if I do not know you full well now!"

'And then I walked, in the perfect peace of a still cloudless night—the moon within two days of full—the quarter of a mile to St. Stephen's schools, where I slept last night. On the way I met the Bishop of Wellington and Mrs. Abraham, coming up from St. Stephen's to the Bishop's house.

J. C. P.—What a night of peace! the harbour like a silver mirror!

'B. of W.—Dominus tecum.

'Mrs. A.—I trust you will sleep.

'J. C. P.—I thank you; I think so. I feel calm.

'Sunday Night, 10 P.M. (Feniton, Sunday, 10.40 A.M.)—It is over—a most solemn blessed service. Glorious day. Church crowded—many not able to find admittance; but orderly. More than two hundred communicants. More to-morrow (D.V.). All day you have been in our minds. The Bishop spoke of you in his sermon with faltering voice, and I broke down; yet at the moment of the Veni Creator being sung over me, and the Imposition of Hands, I was very calm. The Bible presented is the same that you gave me on my fifth birthday with your love and blessing. Oh! my dear dear Father, God will bless you for all your love to me, and your love to Him in giving me to His service. May His heavenly blessing be with you—all your dear ones for ever!

'Your most loving and dutiful Son,

'J. C. PATTESON, Missionary Bishop.

'February 25th.—I am spending to-day and to-morrow here—i.e., sleeping at the Judge's, dining and living half at his house, and half at the Bishop's—quiet and calm it is, and I prize it. The music yesterday was very good; organ well played. The choirs of the three town churches, and many of the choral society people, filled the gallery—some eighty voices perhaps. The Veni Creator the only part that was not good, well sung, but too much like an anthem.

'Tagalana, half-sitting, half-kneeling behind me, held the book for the Primate to read from at the Imposition of Hands—a striking group, I am told.'

Here ends the letter, to which a little must be added from other pens; and, first, from Mrs. Abraham's letter for the benefit of Eton friends:—

'The Consecration was at St. Paul's Church, in default of a Cathedral. Built before the Bishop arrived, St. Paul's has no chancel: and the Clergy, including a Maori Deacon, were rather crowded within the rail. Mr. Patteson was seated in a chair in front, ten of his island boys close to him, and several working men of the rougher sort were brought into the benches near. We were rather glad of the teaching that none were excluded. The service was all in harmony with the occasion; and the sermon gave expression to all the individual and concentrated feeling of the moment, as well as pointing the Lesson and its teaching.

'The sermon was on the thought of the Festival: "And they prayed, and said, Thou, Lord, which knowest the hearts of all men, show whether of these two Thou hast chosen." (Acts i. 24.) After speaking of the special import and need of the prayers of those gathered to offer up their prayers at the Holy Communion, for those who were to exercise the office of apostles in their choice, he spoke in words that visibly almost overpowered their subject:—

'"In this work of God, belonging to all eternity, and to the Holy Catholic Church, are we influenced by any private feelings, any personal regard? The charge which St. Paul gives to Timothy, in words of awful solemnity, 'to lay hands suddenly on no man,' may well cause much searching of heart. 'I charge thee before God, and the Lord Jesus Christ, and the elect angels, that thou observe these things, without preferring one before another, doing nothing by partiality.' Does our own partial love deceive us in this choice? We were all trained in the same place of education, united in the same circle of friends; in boyhood, youth, manhood, we have shared the same services, and joys, and hopes, and fears. I received this, my son in the ministry of Christ Jesus, from the hands of a father, of whose old age he was the comfort. He sent him forth without a murmur, nay, rather with joy and thankfulness, to these distant parts of the earth. He never asked even to see him again, but gave him up without reserve to the Lord's work. Pray, dear brethren, for your Bishops, that our partial love may not deceive us in this choice, for we cannot so strive against natural affection as to be quite impartial."

'And again, as the Primate, addressing more especially his beloved son in the ministry, exclaimed, "May Christ be with you when you go forth in His name, and for His sake, to those poor and needy people," and his eye went along the dusky countenances of his ten boys, Coleridge Patteson could hardly restrain his intensity of feeling.'

Another letter from the same lady to the sisters adds further details to the scene, after describing the figures in the church:—

'Lady Martin, who had never seen the dress (the cassock and rochet) before, said that Coley reminded her of the figures of some young knight watching his armour, as he stood in his calm stedfastness, and answered the questions put to him by the Primate.

'The whole service was very nicely ordered, and the special Psalm well chanted. With one exception (which was, alas! the Veni Creator), the music was good, and

Coley says was a special help to him; the pleasure of it, and the external hold that it gave, helping him out of himself, as it were, and sustaining him.'

Lady Martin adds her touch to the picture; and it may perhaps be recorded for those who may in after times read the history of the first Bishop of the Melanesian Church, that whatever might be wanting in the beauty of St. Paul's, Auckland, never were there three Bishops who outwardly as well as inwardly more answered to the dignity of their office than the three who stood over the kneeling Coleridge Patteson.

'I shall never forget the expression of his face as he knelt in the quaint rochet. It was meek and holy and calm, as though all conflict was over and he was resting in the Divine strength. It was altogether a wonderful scene: the three consecrating Bishops, all such noble-looking men, the goodly company of clergy and Hohua's fine intelligent brown face among them, and then the long line of island boys, and of St. Stephen's native teachers and their wives, were living testimonies of Mission work. Coley had told us in the morning of a consecration he had seen at Rome, where a young Greek deacon had held a large illuminated book for the Pope to read the words of Consecration. We had no such gorgeous dresses as they, but nothing could have been more simply beautiful and touching than the sight of Tagalana's young face as he did the same good office. There was nothing artistic about it; the boy came forward with a wondering yet bright look on his pleasant face, just dressed in his simple grey blouse.

'You will read the sermon, so there is no need to talk about it. Your brother was overcome for a minute at the reference to his father, but the comfort and favour of His Heavenly Master kept him singularly calm, though the week before he had undoubtedly had much struggle, and his bodily health was affected.'

All the friends who were thus brought together were like one family, and still called the new Bishop by the never disused abbreviation that recalled his home. He was the guest of the now retired Chief Justice and Lady Martin, who were occupying themselves in a manner probably unique in the history of law and lawyers, by taking charge of the native school at St. Stephen's.

The next two were great days of letter writing. Another long full letter was written to the father, telling of the additional record which each of the three consecrating Bishops had written in the Bible of his childhood, and then going into business matters, especially hoping that the Warden and Fellows of Merton would not suppose that as a Bishop he necessarily had £5,000 a year and a palace, whereas in fact the see had no more than the capital of £5,000 required by Government! He had already agreed with his father that his own share of the inheritance should go to the Mission; and, as he says, on hearing the amount:—

'Hard enough you worked, my dear Father, to leave your children so well off. Dear old Jem will have enough; and my children now dwell in 200 islands, and will need all that I can give them. God grant that the day may come when many of them may understand these things, and rise up and call your memory blessed!

'Your words of comfort and blessing come to me with fresh strength just now, two days only after the time when you too, had you been here, would in private have laid your hand on my head and called down God's blessing upon me. I shall never know in this world what I owe to your prayers.'

There is much, too, of his brother's marriage; and in a separate letter to the sisters there are individual acknowledgments of each article of the equipment, gratifying the donor by informing her that the 'cutaway' coat was actually to be worn that very evening at a dinner party at the Chief Justice's, and admiring the 'gambroon,' which turned out to be the material of the cassock, so much as to wish for a coat made of it for the islands. Apropos of the hat:— 'You know my forehead is square, so that an oval hat does not fit; it would hang on by the temples, which form a kind of right angle with the forehead.'

Another letter of that 26th was from the Bishop of Wellington to Dr. Goodford respecting this much-loved old pupil:—

'Anything more conscientious and painstaking cannot be conceived than the way he has steadily directed every talent, every hour or minute of his life, to the one work he had set before him. However small or uncongenial or drumdrudgery-like his occupation, however hard, or dangerous, or difficult, it seemed to be always met in the same calm, gentle, self-possessed spirit of love and duty, which I should fancy that those who well knew his good and large-minded, large-hearted father, and his mother, whom I have always heard spoken of as saintly, could best understand. Perhaps the most marked feature in his character is his genuine simplicity and humility. I never saw it equalled in one so gifted and so honoured and beloved.

'It is really creditable to the community to see how universal is the admiration for his character, for he is so very good, so exceedingly unworldly, and therefore such a living rebuke to the selfishness of the world; and though so gentle, yet so firm and uncompromising that you would have supposed he would hardly be popular outside the circle of friends who know him and understand him. Certainly he is the most perfect character I ever met.'

The last day of February was that of the Installation.

Again Mrs. Abraham must speak:—

'On Thursday last we had another happy day at Kohimarama, where Bishop Patteson was duly installed in the temporary chapel of St. Andrew's College, as we hope to call it, after the church at Cocksmoor, in "The Daisy Chain." The morning was grey, and we feared rain would keep our ladies away, but we made the venture with our willing squire, Mr. M——, in the "Iris" boat to help us. The pity was, that after all Lady Martin could not go, as she had an invalid among her Maori flock, whom she could not trust all day by herself. The day lightened, and our sail was pleasant.

'The Primate and Missionary Bishop planted a Norfolk pine in the centre of the quadrangle—"the tree planted by the water side," &c. The Bishop then robed and proceeded to chapel, and the Primate led the little service in which he spoke the words of installation, and the mew Bishop took the oath of allegiance to him. The Veni Creator was sung, and the Primate's blessing-given. The island boys looked on from one transept, the "Iris" sailors from another, and Charlie stood beside me. I am afraid his chief remembrance of the day is fixed upon Kanambat's tiny boat and outrigger, which he sat in on the beach, and went on voyages, in which the owner waded by his side, and saw him (Kanambat) skim along the waves like a white butterfly. We all dined in hall, after the boys, on roast beef and plum pudding, melons and water melons, and strolled about the place and beach at leisure, till it was time to sail back again.'

On the Sunday the new Bishop preached at St. Mary's one of the sermons that broke from him when he was too much excited (if the word may be used) for his usual metaphysical style. The subject was the promise of the Comforter, His eternal presence and anointing, and the need of intercessory prayer, for which the preacher besought earnestly, as one too young for his office, and needing to increase in the Holy Spirit more and more. Very far were these from being unrealised words. God's grace had gone along with him, and had led him through every step and stage of his life, and so mastered his natural defects, that friends who only knew him in these years hear with incredulous indignation of those flaws he had conquered in his younger days. 'Fearless as a man, tender as a woman, showing both the best sides of human nature,' says one of the New Zealand friends who knew him best; 'always drawing out the good in all about him by force of sympathy, and not only taking care that nothing should be done by others that he would not do himself, but doing himself what he did not like to ask of them, and thinking that they excelled him.' Humility, the effort of his life, was achieved at last the more truly because not consciously.

The letter to his father was again almost wholly on money matters; but at the end come two notable sentences:—

'How can I thank you for giving me up to this work, and for all the wise and loving words with which you constantly cheer me and encourage me? Your blessing comes now to strengthen me, as work and responsibilities are fast accumulating upon me. I thank God that He enables us at the two ends of the world to see this matter in the same way, so that no conflict of duties arises in my mind.

'This book, "Essays and Reviews," I have, but pray send your copy also; also any good books that may be produced bearing on that great question of the Atonement, and on Inspiration, Authority of Scripture, &c. How sad it is to see that spirit of intellectualism thinking to deal with religion in forgetfulness of the necessary conditions of humility and faith! How different from the true gnosis!'

'Kohimarama: April 29, 1861.

'My dearest Father,—As I read your letters of Feb. 21-25, you are, I trust, reading mine which tell you of what took place on Feb. 24. That point is settled. I almost fear to write that I am a Bishop in the Church of Christ. May God strengthen me for the duties of the office to which I trust He has indeed called me!

'As I read of what you say so wisely and truly, and dear Joan and Fan and Aunt James and all, of my having expected results too rapidly at Mota, I had sitting with me that dear boy Tagalana, who for two months last winter was in the great sacred enclosure, though, dear lad, not by his own will, yet his faith was weak, and no wonder.

'Now, God's holy name be praised for it, he is, I verily believe, in his very soul, taught by the Spirit to see and desire to do his duty. I feel more confidence about him than I have done about anyone who has come into my hands originally in a state of complete heathenism. It is not that his knowledge only is accurate and clearly grasped, but the humility, the loving spirit, the (apparent) personal appropriation of the blessing of having been brought to know the love of God and the redemption wrought for him by the death of Christ; this is what, as I look upon his clear truthful eyes, makes me feel so full of thankfulness and praise.

"'But Tagalana, if I should die, you used to say that without my help you should perhaps fall back again: is that true?"

"'No, no; I did not feel it then as I do now in my heart. I can't tell how it came there, only I know He can never die, and will always be with me. You know you said you were only like a sign-post, to point out the way that leads to Him, and I see that we ought to follow you, but to go altogether to Him."

'I can't tell you, my dearest Father, what makes up the sum of my reasons for thinking that God is in His mercy bringing this dear boy to be the first-fruits of Mota unto the Christ, but I think that there is an inward teaching going on now in his heart, which gives me sure hope, for I know it is not my doing.

'All you all say about Mota is most true: I never thought otherwise really, but I wrote down my emotions and impulses rather than my deliberate thoughts, that my letter written under such strange circumstances might become as a record of the effect produced day by day upon us by outward circumstances.

'What some of you say about self-possession on one's going about among the people being marvellous, is just what of course appears to me commonplace. Of course it is wrong to risk one's life, but to carry one's life in one's hand is what other soldiers besides those of the Cross do habitually; and no one, as I think, would willingly hurt a hair of my head in Melanesia, or that part of it where I am at all known.

'How I think of those islands! How I see those bright coral and sandy beaches, strips of burning sunshine fringing the masses of forest rising into ridges of hills, covered with a dense mat of vegetation. Hundreds of people are crowding upon them, naked, armed, with wild uncouth cries and gestures; I cannot talk to them but by signs. But they are my children now! May God enable me to do my duty to them!

'I have now as I write a deepening sense of what the change must be that has passed upon me. Again I go by God's blessing for seven months to Melanesia. All that our experience has taught us we try to remember: food, medicine, articles of trade and barter.

'But what may be the result? Who can tell? You know it is not of myself that I am thinking. If God of His great mercy lead me in His way, to me there is little worth living for but the going onward with His blessed work, though I like my talks with the dear Bishop and the Judge. But others are committed to me—Mr. Pritt and Mr. Kerr go with me. Shall I find dear old Wadrokala and Harper alive, and if alive, well?

'And yet, thank God, we go on day by day, so happy, so hopeful!

'I see two sermons by the Bishop of Oxford, "God's Revelation Man's Trial," please send them. They bear, I conclude, on the controversy of the day. I need not tell you that I find a very great interest in reading these books, or rather at present in talking now and then, when we meet, with the Judge on the subject of which those books treat. The books I have not read. But I know no refreshment so great as the reading any books which deal with these questions thoughtfully. I hope you don't think it wrong and dangerous for me to do so; pray tell me. I don't believe that I am wrong in doing it, yet it may be that I read them as an intellectual treat, and prefer them to thoughtful books on other subjects, because they deal with a study which I am a little more conversant with than with history, science, &c.

'Besides, I do see that we have, many of us, very vague notions of the meaning of terms which we use, and I see that I must be prepared (I speak for myself) to expect that a clergyman may not with impunity use a language wanting in definiteness and precision. It is possible that men do too passively receive hereditary and conventional opinions which never have a living reality to them. But this, you know, I do not confound with the humble submission to authoritative teaching, given upon authority, to supersede the necessity of every person investigating for himself the primary grounds of his religious convictions.'

It is worth noting how the Bishop submits his reading to his father's approval, as when he was a young boy. Alas! no more such letters of comfort and counsel would be exchanged. This one could hardly have been received by that much-loved father.

Preparations for the voyage were going on; but the 'Dunedin,' the only vessel to be procured, at best a carthorse to a racer compared with the 'Southern Cross,' was far from being in a satisfactory state, as appears in a note of 3rd of May to the Bishop of Wellington:—

'Here we are still. The only vessel that I could make any arrangement about not yet returned, and known to be in such a state that the pumps were going every two hours. I have not chartered her, but only agreed with the owner a month ago nearly that I would take her at a certain sum per day, subject to divers conditions about being caulked (which is all she wants, I have ascertained), being provided with spare sails, spars, chronometer, boat, &c., and all agreement to be off unless by a certain day (already past) she was in a state satisfactory to Mr. Kerr. But there is, I fear, none other, and I am in a difficulty.'

Of the same day is a letter to the Rev. Stephen Hawtrey:—

'Taurarua, Auckland: May 6, 1861.

'My dear Mr. Hawtrey,—I was highly pleased to receive a note from you. Though I never doubt of the hearty sympathy and co-operation of all Eton friends (how could you do so with such an annual subscription list?), yet it is very pleasant and more than pleasant to be reminded by word or by letter that prayers and wishes are being offered up for Melanesia by many good men throughout the world.

'I should like to send a special appeal for a Mission Vessel by the next mail. We cannot get on without one. Vessels built for freight are to the "Southern Cross" as a cart-horse to a thoroughbred steed, and we must have some vessel which can do the work quickly among the multitude of the isles, and many other reasons there are which we seamen only perhaps can judge fully, which make it quite essential to the carrying on this peculiar Mission that we should have a vessel of a peculiar kind.

'Tagalana, from Mota (Sugar Loaf Island), in the Banks Archipelago, is, I think, likely by God's great mercy to become the first-fruits of that cluster of islands unto Christ. He is here for the third time; and I have infinite comfort in seeing the earnestness of his character, and the deep sense of what he was, and what he is going to be, so truly realised.

'He is now so unlike what still his people are, so bright and open in manner, and all who see him say, "What is come to the lad, his manner and very appearance so changed!" "Clothed," thank God, he is, "and in his right mind," soon to sit, if not already seated, at the feet of Christ. You may, if you think fit, let your thoughts centre more especially in him. He, of all who have come into my hands absolutely stark naked and savage, gives now the greatest ground for hope and thanksgiving. I shall (D.V.) think of all your dear friends assembled in your church and house on St. Barnabas Day. May God bless and reward you all for your work of charity to Melanesia!

'Very sincerely yours,

'J. C. PATTESON, Missionary Bishop.

'P.S.—I hope to baptize that dear boy Tagalana on his own island in the course of the winter. I should wish to make the service as impressive as possible, in the presence of as many islanders as I can bring to the spot, under the shadow of a mighty banyan tree, and above the sparkling waves of the great Pacific.'

The 'Dunedin' was patched up into sailing with the new Bishop for his cathedral —the banyan tree of Mota.

It carried him away to his work, away from all knowledge of the blow that was preparing for him at home, and thinking of the delight that was in store for his family in a visit from Mrs. Selwyn, who, immediately after his Consecration, had returned home to spend a year in England on business.

Sir John Patteson's happiness in his son's work and worth were far greater than those of the actual worker, having none of the drawbacks that consciousness of weakness must necessarily excite. The joy this gave his heart may, without exaggeration, he deliberately said to have been full compensation for the loss of the presence so nobly sacrificed. On January 22 he had written to the Bishop of New Zealand:—

'You write most kindly touching him, dear fellow, and truly I am to be envied, qui natum haberem tali ingenio praeditum. Not for a moment have I repented of giving my sanction to his going out to New Zealand; and I fully believe that God will prosper his work. I did not contemplate his becoming a Bishop, nor is that the circumstance which gives me the great satisfaction I feel. It is his devotion to so good a work, and that he should have been found adequate to its performance; whether as a Bishop or as a Priest is not of itself of so much importance.

'Perhaps he may have been consecrated before I am writing this, though I am puzzled as to the time....

'May God bless with the fullest success the labours of both of you in your high and Christian works!'

There had for more than a year been cause of anxiety for Sir John's health, but it was not the disease that had then threatened which occasioned the following calm-hearted letter to be written to his son:—

'Feniton Court: March 22, 1861.

'My own dearest Coley,—I promised always to tell you the truth respecting myself, and will do so. About a month ago, on my rising from reading prayers, the girls and the Dawlish party who were here exclaimed that my voice was broken, at which I laughed. Whitby was in London, but his partner happened to call, and looking at my throat found it relaxed, and recommended a mustard poultice on the front. When we came to put it on, we discovered that the glands of the throat were much swelled and in hard knots. Whitby returned in two days, and was much alarmed. He declared that it was serious, and nothing but iodine could check it. I had been unable to take iodine under Watson some years ago, as it affected my head tremendously, so he applied it outwardly by painting; this painting did not reduce them, and he strongly pressed my having London advice, for he said that if not reduced and the swellings increased internally, they would press on the windpipe and choke me: it was somewhat a surgical matter. So on Tuesday the 12th inst. we went to London, and I consulted Paget. He entirely agreed with Whitby, and thought it very serious, and ordered iodine internally at all hazards. I took it, and by God's mercy it agreed with me. Paget wished to talk over the case with Watson, and they met on the 16th, Saturday. They quite agreed, and did not conceal from me that if iodine did not reduce the swellings, and they should increase internally, the result must be fatal. How soon, or in what particular manner, they could not tell; it might even become cancerous. They did not wish me to stay in town, but thought I was better here, and Paget, knowing Whitby, has perfect confidence in his watching, and will correspond with him, if necessary. At present there is no reduction of the swellings. The iodine has certainly lessened the pains in my limbs, but does not seem, so to speak, to determine to the throat, but it may be there has been hardly time to say that it will not. My own impression is, that it will not, and that it is highly improbable that I shall last very long. I mean that I shall not see 1862, nor perhaps the summer or autumn of this year. I cannot tell why, but this near prospect of death has not given me any severe shock, as perhaps it ought to have done. It brings more than ever to my mind serious recollection of the sins of my youth, and the shortcomings of my after life in thousands of instances. I have never been a hardened sinner, but years ago, if I did what was sin, it smote me, and I tried to repent; yet there has always been in me a want of fervid love to God, and to my blessed Redeemer for His unspeakable love in suffering for my sins; but it has been cold—that may have been the natural constitution of the man, I cannot tell—but I never have placed my hopes of forgiveness and of blessedness hereafter in anything but in His merits, and most undeserved goodness in offering me salvation, if I have not thrown it away. But what shall I say? As the time approaches, it may please Him in His mercy to give me a warmer heart, and a more vivid perception of all that He has done for me. If I were to say that I am not a sinner, the truth would not be in me; and if I am washed in His blood and cleansed, it is not by any efforts or merits of my own, but by His unlimited mercy and goodness. Pray for me, that when the time comes I may not for any fears of death fall from Him. You know that as far as regards this world and its enjoyments, save the love of my dear good children, they have sate but lightly upon me for some time; but it is not because we have nothing that we are unwilling to leave, therefore we are prepared for that which is to come. Perhaps it may please God to give me still a short time that I may try more strenuously to prepare myself. We shall never meet again in this world. Oh! may Almighty God in His infinite mercy grant us to meet again in His kingdom, through the merits of our blessed Redeemer....

'Oh! my dearest Coley, what comfort I have had in you—what delightful conversations we have had together, and how thankful we ought to be to our gracious God for allowing it to be so: and still not less thankful for the blessings of being watched and comforted and soothed by the dear girls, and by that dear and good Jem. All so good in their various ways, and I so little worthy of them...of Francis. That will indeed, humanly speaking, be a terrible loss to his family, for they want his fatherly care, and will do so for years. Not so with me; and as I am in my seventy-second year, it cannot be said that I am cut off prematurely: but on the contrary, fall like a fruit or a sheaf at its proper ripeness. Oh! that it may be so spiritually indeed.'

Another letter followed the next month:—

'Feniton Court: April 24, 1861.

'My own dearest Coley,—How many more letters you may receive from me, God only knows, but, as I think, not many. The iodine fails altogether, and has produced no effect on the swellings in my throat; on the contrary, they steadily increase, though not rapidly. Doubtless they will have their own course, and in some way or other deliver my soul from the burden of the flesh. Oh! may it by God's mercy be the soul of a faithful man! Faith and love I think I have, and have long had: but I am not so sure that I have really repented for my past sins, or only abandoned them when circumstances had removed almost the temptation to commit them. Yet I do trust that my repentance has generally been sincere, and though I may have fallen again, that I may by God's grace have risen again. I have no assurance that I have fought the good fight like St. Paul, and that henceforth there is laid up a crown of gold; yet I have a full and firm hope that I am not beyond the pale of God's mercy, and that I may have hold of the righteousness of Christ, and may be partaker of that happiness which he has purchased for His own, by His atoning blood. No other hope have I; and in all humility I from my heart feel that any apparent good that I may have done has been His work in me and not my own. May it please Him that you and I, my dear son, may meet hereafter, together with all those blessed ones, who have already departed this life in His faith and fear, in His kingdom above.

'My head aches occasionally, and is not so clear as it used to be.... The next mail will bring us more definite news, if indeed I am not myself removed before then.... I am afraid that you discern by what I have written that I am become stupid, and though I could never write decently, yet you will see that continued dull pain in the head, and other pains in various parts, have made me altogether heavy and stupid. I have had the kindest letters and messages from various quarters when it became known, as it is always very soon, that my health was in a precarious state: one particularly from the Bishop of Lichfield (all companions in Old Court, King's, you know) which is very consoling. He says, If not for such as you, for whom did Christ die? I will not go on in such strains, for it is of no use. Only do not despair of me, my beloved Son, and believe me always,

'Your loving Father,
'J. PATTESON.'

'Feniton Court: May 25, 1861.

'O my own dearest Coley,—Almighty God be thanked that He has preserved my life to hear from you and others of your actual consecration as a Missionary Bishop of the Holy Catholic Church: and may He enable you by His grace and the powerful assistance of His Spirit to bring to His faith and fear very many who have not known Him, and to keep and preserve in it many others who already profess and call themselves Christians.

'I was too ill to be present at the whole service on Sunday, but I attended the Holy Sacrament, and hope to do so to-morrow. We have with us our dear Sarah Selwyn, who came on Thursday: she came in the most kind and affectionate spirit, the first visit that she could make, that she might if possible see me: "I will go and see him before he dies." What delight this has been to me you may easily imagine, and what talk, and what anecdotes we have had about you and all your circle; for though your letters have all along let us in wonderfully into your daily life, yet there were many things to be filled up, which we have now seen more clearly and more perfectly recollect as long as our lives are spared.

'What at present intensely fills our hearts and minds is all that took place on St. Matthias Day, and the day or two before and after. Passages and circumstances there were, which it is almost wonderful that you all could respectively bear, some affecting one the more and some the other; but the absorbing feeling that a great work was then done, and the ardent trust and prayer that it might turn out to the glory of God, and the good of mankind, supported every one, I have no doubt. It was about one of those days that I was first informed of the nature of the complaint which had just been discovered, and which is bringing me gradually to the grave.

'Trinity Sunday.—I am just returned from receiving the Holy Sacrament. You will do so the same in a few hours, and they may well be joined together, and probably the last that you and I shall receive together in this world. My time is probably very short. Dear Sarah will hereafter tell you more particulars of these few days. Dear Joan and Fanny are watching me continually; it is hard work for them continually and most uncertain, but in my mind it cannot be very long. Jem is here helping them continually, but his wife's mother is grievously ill at a relation's in Gloucestershire, and I will not have him withdrawn from her. I hope that next week she may be removed to Jem's new cottage, next Hyde Park, and then they, Joan and Fanny will watch me, and Jem on a telegraph notice may come to me. If I dare express a hope, it is that this state of things may not last long. But I have no desire to express any hope at all; the matter is in the hands of a good God, who will order all things as is best.... I would write more, but I am under the serious impression that I shall be dead before this letter reaches you.

'May our Almighty God, three Persons, blessed for evermore, grant that we may meet hereafter in a blessed eternity!'

One more letter was written:—

'Feniton Court, Honiton: June 12, 1861.

'Oh! my dearest Right Reverend well-beloved Son, how I thank God that it has pleased Him to save my life until I heard of the actual fact of your being ordained and consecrated, as I have said more than once since I heard of it. May it please Him to prolong your life very many years, and to enable you to fulfil all those purposes for which you have been now consecrated, and that you may see the fruit of your labour of love before He calls you to His rest in Heaven. But if not, may you have laid such foundations for the spread of God's Word throughout the countries committed to your charge, that when it pleases God to summon you hence, you may have a perfect consciousness of having devoted all your time and labour, and so far as you are concerned have advanced all the works as fastly and as securely as it seemed fit to your great Assister, the Holy Spirit, that they should be advanced. Only conceive that an old Judge of seventy-two, cast out of his own work by infirmity, should yet live to have a son in the Holy Office of Bishop, all men rejoicing around him; and so indeed they do rejoice around me, mingling their loving expressions at my illness and approaching death....

'I shall endeavour to write at intervals between this and July mail. It tries me to write much at a time.

'Your loving Father,

'J. PATTESON.'

The calm of these letters was the pervading spirit of Feniton. With perfect cheerfulness did the aged Judge await the summons, aware that he carried the 'sentence of death within himself,' and that the manner of his summons would probably be in itself sudden—namely, one of the choking fits that increased in frequency. He lived on with his children and relations round him, spending his time in his usual manner, so far as his strength permitted—bright, kind, sunny as ever, and not withdrawing his interest from the cares and pleasures of others, but glad to talk more deeply, though still peacefully, of his condition and his hopes. One thing only troubled him. Once he said, and with tears in his eyes, to his beloved brother-in-law, Sir John Coleridge: 'Woe unto you when all men shall speak well of you,' adding to this effect, 'Alas! That this has been my lot without my deserts. It pains me now!'

But as this popularity had come of no self-seeking nor attempt to win applause, it was a grief that was soon dispelled. Perhaps if there was one strong wish, it was to hear of his son's actually having been received into the order of Bishops, and that gratification was granted to him. The letters with the record of consecration arrived in time to be his Whitsuntide joy—joy that he still participated in the congregation, for though not able to be at church for the whole service, he still was always present at the celebration of the Holy Communion.

On the day the letters came there was great peace, and a kind of awful joy on all the household. For many weeks past, Sir John had not attempted to read family prayers, but on this evening he desired his daughters to let him do so. Where in the prayer for missionaries he had always mentioned, 'the absent member of this family,' he added in a clear tone, 'especially for John Coleridge Patteson, Missionary Bishop.' That was the father's one note of triumph, the last time he ever led the household prayers. In a day or two Mrs. Selwyn came to him, and he wrote the following to the Bishop of New Zealand:—

'Feniton Court: May 24, 1861.

'My very dear Friend,—Here I am, and I have with me your dear and good wife, who arrived yesterday. She looks well, and I trust is so. She has arranged her visits so as to come to me as soon as possible. "I will go and see him before he die," and I feel sensibly the kindness of it. What a mercy is it that my life should have been preserved to receive from my dear son Coley and from you by letter the account of his having been consecrated by you as Bishop of the true Catholic Church. There were [accounts?] of that most impressive service, which, had I been present, would have, I fear, sent me to the floor; and you and Coley must have had difficulty in holding up at those feeling statements of your having received him at my old hands. When you so received him, it was known I was satisfied that his heart was really fixed on this missionary work—that he felt a call to it. I believe, you know, and I am sure God knows, that I had not the most distant notion in my mind that it would lead to his becoming a Bishop, nor do I now rejoice in the result, simply on account of the honour of the office; but because my confidence in the honesty and sincerity of his then feelings has been justified, and that it has pleased God to endow him with such abundant graces. May it please God that you should continue together in your respective governments in His Church many years, and that we may all meet together in his kingdom above!

'When I parted with him I did not expect to see his face on earth, yet perhaps I hardly expected that our separation would be so soon, though I am in my seventy-second year. But in February I discovered these swellings in my throat; which, humanly speaking, could only be cured by iodine. Iodine has failed, and other attempts at a cure fail also; and it is only a question of time when the soul will be delivered from the burthen of the flesh. So indeed it is with all human beings; but it is one thing to know this as a general proposition, and another to know that the particular minister of death has hold of you, and that you are really only living from day to day.

'For all your many kindnesses to all of us and to my son, I thank you from the very bottom of my soul, and pray that we may meet hereafter, through the merits, and for the sake of our blessed Mediator and Redeemer Jesus Christ our Lord, that as we have striven on earth to be followers of Him and His glory, so we may be partakers of it in Heaven.

'Your loving Friend,

'J. PATTESON.'

The July mail was without a letter from the father. The end had come in the early morning of June 28, 1861, with a briefer, less painful struggle than had been thought probable, and the great, sound, wise, tender heart had ceased to beat.

There is no need to dwell on the spontaneous honours that all of those who had ever been connected with him paid to the good old Judge, when he was laid beside his much-loved wife in Feniton churchyard. Bishop Sumner of Winchester, the friend of his boyhood, read the funeral service.

'His works do follow him:' and we turn to that work of his son's in which assuredly he had his part, since one word of his would have turned aside the course that had brought such blessing on both, had he not accepted the summons, even as Zebedee, when he was left by the lake side, while his sons became fishers of men.

Unknowing of the tidings in reserve for him, the Bishop was on his voyage, following the usual course; hearing at Anaiteum that a frightful mortality had prevailed in many of these southern islands. Measles had been imported by a trader, and had, in many cases, brought on dysentery, and had swept away a third of Mr. Geddie's Anaiteum flock. Mr. Gordon's letters had spoken of it as equally fatal in Erromango, and there were reports of the same, as well as of famine and war, in Nengone.

'God will give me men in His time; for could I be cut up into five pieces already I would be living at Nengone, Lifu, Mai, Mota, and Bauro!' was the comment on this visit; and this need of men inspired a letter to his uncle Edward, on a day dear to the Etonian heart:—

'Schooner "Dunedin," 60 tons.

'In sight of Erromango, New Hebrides: June 4, 1861.

'My dear Tutor,—Naturally I think of Eton and of you especially to-day. I hope you have as fine a day coming on for the cricket-match and for Surley as I have here. Thermometer 81°; Tanna and Erromango, with their rugged hilly outlines, breaking the line of the bright sparkling horizon.

'I managed to charter the vessel for the voyage just in time to escape cold weather in New Zealand. She is slow, but sound; the captain a teetotaller, and crew respectable in all ways. So the voyage, though lengthy, is pleasant.

'I have some six or seven classes to take, for they speak as many more languages; and I get a little time for reading and writing, but not much.

'I need not tell you how heavily this new responsibility presses on me, as I see the islands opening, and at present feel how very difficult it must be to obtain men to occupy this opening—

'True, we have not to contend with subtle and highly-elaborated systems of false religion. It is the ignorantia purae negationis, comparatively speaking, in some of the islands; yet, generally, there is a settled system of some kind observed among them, and in the Banks Islands, an extraordinarily developed religion, which enters into every detail of social and domestic life, and is mixed up with the daily life of every person in the archipelago.

'I think, therefore, that men are needed who have what I may call strong religious common sense to adapt Christianity to the wants of the various nations that live in Melanesia, without compromising any truth of doctrine or principle of conduct—men who can see, in the midst of the errors and superstitions of a people, whatever fragment of truth or symptom of a yearning after something better may exist among them, and make that the point d'appui, upon which they may build up the structure of Christian teaching. Men, moreover, of industry they must be, for it is useless to talk of "picking up languages." Of course, in a few days a man may learn to talk superficially and inaccurately on a few subjects; but to teach Christianity, a man must know the language well, and this is learnt only by hard work.

'Then, again, unless a man can dispense with what we ordinarily call comfort or luxuries to a great extent, and knock about anywhere in Melanesian huts, he can hardly do much work in this Mission. The climate is so warm that, to my mind, it quite supplies the place of the houses, clothing, and food of old days, yet a man cannot accommodate himself to it all at once. I don't say that it came naturally to me five years ago, as it does now, when I feel at home anywhere, and cease to think it odd to do things which, I suppose, you would think very extraordinary indeed.

'But most of all—for this makes all easy—men are wanted who really do desire in their hearts to live for God and the world to come, and who have really sought to sit very loosely to this world. The enjoyment, and the happiness, and the peace all come, and that abundantly; but there is a condition, and the first rub is a hard one, and lasts a good while.

'Naturally buoyant spirits, the gift of a merry heart, are a great help; for oftentimes a man may have to spend months without any white man within hundreds of miles, and it is very depressing to live alone in the midst of heathenism. But there must be many many fellows pulling up to Surley to-night who may be well able to pull together with one on the Pacific—young fellows whose enthusiasm is not mere excitement of animal spirits, and whose pluck and courage are given them to stand the roughnesses (such as they are) of a missionary life. For, dear Uncle, if you ever talk to any old pupil of yours about the work, don't let him suppose that it is consistent with ease and absence of anxiety and work. When on shore at Kohimarama, we live very cosily, as I think. Some might say we have no society, very simple fare, &c.; I don't think any man would really find it so. But in the islands, I don't wish to conceal from anyone that, measured by the rule of the English gentleman's household, there is a great difference. Why should it, however, be measured by this standard? I can truly say that we have hitherto always had what is necessary for health, and what does one need more? though I like more as much as anyone.

'How you will wonder at the news of my consecration, and, indeed, well you may! I would, indeed, that there were a dozen men out here under whom I was working, if only they were such men as the Primate would have chosen to the work.

'But it is done now, and I know I must not shrink from it. Never did I need the love and prayers of my dear relations and friends as I do now. Already difficulties are rising up around me, and I am so little fit to be a leader of work like this. Don't forget, dear Tutor, your old pupil, who used to copy the dear Bishop's letters in your study from Anaiteum, Erromango, &c.; and little thought that he would write from these islands to you, himself the Missionary Bishop.

'With kind love to all,

'Your loving old Pupil and Nephew,

'J. C. PATTESON, Missionary Bishop.'

This thoughtful and beautiful letter was written in sight of Erromango, a sandal-wood station, whence a trader might be found to take charge of it. The ink was scarcely dry before the full cost of carrying the Gospel among the heathen was brought before the writer. Not only houses and brethren must be given up, but the 'yea and his own life also' was now to be exemplified almost before his eyes.

The Erromaugo Mission, like that of Anaiteum, came from the Scottish Kirk. Mr. and Mrs. Gordon, as has been seen, had been visited on every voyage of the 'Southern Cross' during their three years' residence there, and there was a warm regard between them and the Bishop. It was then a great shock to hear a Nengone man call out from a sandal-wood vessel, lying in Dillon's Bay, that they had both been killed!

It was but too true. The Erromango people had been little inclined to listen to Mr. Gordon's warnings, and he, a young and eager man, had told them that to persevere in their murders and idolatries would bring a judgment upon them. When therefore the scourge of sickness came, as at Anaiteum, they connected him with it; and it was plain from his diary that he had for some months known his life to be in danger, but he had gone about them fearlessly, like a brave man, doing his best for the sick.

On May 20 he was in a little wood, putting up a house instead of one that had been blown down by a hurricane, and he had sent his few faithful pupils to get grass for the thatch. Nine natives from a village about three hours' walk distant came to the house where his wife was, and asked for him. She said he was in the little wood. They went thither, and while eight hid themselves in the bush, one went forward and asked for some calico. Mr. Gordon took a bit of charcoal and wrote on a bit of wood directions to his wife to give the bearer some cotton, but the man insisted that he must come himself to give out some medicine for a sick man. Mr. Gordon complied, walking in front as far as the place where lay the ambush, when the man struck him with a tomahawk on the spine, and he fell, with a loud scream, while the others leaping out fell upon him with blows that must have destroyed life at once, yelling and screaming over him. Another went up to the house. Mrs. Gordon had come out, asking what the shouts meant. 'Look there!' he said, and as she turned her head, he struck her between the shoulders, and killed her as soon as she had fallen.

Another native had in the meantime rushed down the hill to the sandal-wood station half a mile off on the beach, and the trader, arming his natives, came up too late to do more than prevent the murderers from carrying off the bodies or destroying the house. The husband and wife were buried in the same grave; the natives fenced it round; and now, on June 7, eighteen days after, Bishop Patteson read the Burial Service over it, with many solemn and anxious thoughts respecting the population, now reduced to 2,500, and in a very wild condition.

At Mai the Bishop spent two hours the next day, and brought away one old scholar and one new one.

At Tariko, where he had been three years before with the Primate, the Episcopal hat brought the greeting 'Bishop,' as the people no doubt thought the wearer identical. Of Ambrym there is a characteristic sentence: 'As we left the little rock pool where I had jumped ashore, leaving, for prudence sake, the rest behind me in the boat, one man raised his bow and drew it, then unbent it, then bent it again, but apparently others were dissuading him from letting fly the arrow. The boat was not ten yards off, I don't know why he did so; but we must try to effect more frequent landings.'

On June 12 Mota was reached, and the next morning the Mission party landed, warmly welcomed by the inhabitants. The house was found safely standing and nearly weather-proof.

'June 13th.—This morning I put up the framework for another small house, where I shall put Wadrokala, his child-wife, and many of our boxes. We had to carry up the timber first from the beach, and it was rather hot work, as also the carpentering, as I chose a place for the house where no falling bread-fruit or branches of trees would hurt it, and the sun was so hot that it almost burnt my hand when I took up a handful of nails that had been lying for ten minutes in the sun. So our picnic life begins again, and that favourably. I feel the enjoyment of the glorious view and climate, and my dear lads, Tagalana and Parenga, from Bauro, are with me, the rest in Port Patteson, &c., coming over in the vessel to-morrow, which I shall then discharge. I see that the people are very friendly; they all speak of your bread-fruit tree, your property. The house had not been entered, a keg of nails inside it not touched.

'Tagalana's father is dead. His first words to me were, "Oh that the Word of God had come in old times to Mota, I should not then cry so much about him. Yes, it is true, I know, I must be thankful it is come now, and I must remember that, and try to help others who may die too before they believe it."

'"Yes, I am quite your child now! Yes, one Father for us all in Heaven. You my father here! Yes, I stop always with you, unless you send me away. They ask me with whom I shall live now; I say with the Bishop."

'How I was praising and rejoicing in my heart as the dear boy was speaking: "Yes, I am feeling calm again now. When people die at Mota, you know they make a great shouting, but soon forget the dead person. But I am able to be quiet and calm now, as you talk to me about God and Jesus Christ. Yes, He rose again. Death is not the end. I know you said it is for those who repent and believe in Christ the Door to enter into life eternal. How different it all seems then!"

'When you read this you will say, "Thank God that I sent him out to Melanesia with my blessing on his head. I too may see Tagalana one day with Him who is the Father of us all."

'One soul won to Christ, as I hope and believe, by His love and power, and if in any degree by my ministry, to God be the praise!'

The comfort sent home to the sisters with the letter respecting this voyage is:—
'Mota: June 14, 1861.

'Now, dear Joan, don't any of you think too much about the murder of Mr. and Mrs. Gordon, as if my life was exposed to the same kind of risk.

'Certainly it is not endangered here. It may be true that at places where I am not known some sudden outbreak may occur; but humanly speaking, there are not many places that as yet I am able to visit where I realise the fact of any danger being run.

'Yet it may happen that some poor fellow, who has a good cause to think ill of white men, or some mischievous badly disposed man, may let fly a random arrow or spear some day.

'If so, you will not so very much wonder, nor be so very greatly grieved. Every clergyman runs at least as great a risk among the small-pox and fevers of town parishes. Think of Uncle James in the cholera at Thorverton.'

So with the 'Dunedin' dismissed, Bishop Patteson, Mr. Pritt, Mr. Kerr, and their pupils recommenced their residence at Mota. The Banks Islanders returned to their homes; and when the Bishop came to Aroa, Tagalana's native place, three weeks lately the little fellow received him affectionately, cooked yams, fetched mats, and was not ashamed before his own people to kneel down, and join audibly in hymn and prayer. The people begged for Wadrokala or some other teacher to be placed among them. The Journal continues:—

'On Friday, at 8.30, I started, not quite knowing whither I should go, but soon saw that I could fetch round the south end of Vanua Lava, which was well. The sea, when it comes through the passage between Mota and Valua, is heavy, but the boat had great way on her, sailing very fast, so that I could steer her well, and we did not take very long crossing to the small reef islands. I passed between Pakea and Vanua Lava (Dudley Passage), and then we had unexpectedly a very heavy sea, a strong tide up. I did not like it, but, thank God, all went well. One very heavy sea in particular I noticed, which broke some twenty yards ahead, and about the same distance astern of us, while the exact part of it which came down upon us was only a black wall of water, over which we rode lightly and dry. I think that it might have swamped us had it broken upon the boat. My boat is an open four-oared one, 26 feet long, and about five wide, strong but light. She sails admirably with a common lug sail. I had one made last summer, very large, with two reefs, so that I can reduce it to as small a sail as I please. By 4 or 5 P.M. I neared Aruas, in the bay on the west side of Vanua Lava; the same crowd as usual on the beach, but I did not haul the boat up. I had a grapnel, and dropped it some fifty yards from the beach.

'Somehow I did not much like the manner of some of the people; they did not at night come into the Ogamal, or men's common eating and sleeping house, as before, and I overheard some few remarks which I did not quite like—something about the unusual sickness being connected with this new teaching—I could not be quite sure, as I do not know the dialect of Aruas. There were, however, several who were very friendly, and the great majority were at least quiet, and left us to ourselves. The next morning I started at about eight, buying two small pigs for two hatchets, and yams and taro and dried bread-fruit for fish-hooks. I gave one young man a piece of iron for his attention to us. As we pulled away, one elderly man drew his bow, and the women and children ran off into the bush, here, as everywhere almost in these islands, growing quite thickly some twenty yards above high-water mark. The man did not let fly his arrow: I cannot tell why this small demonstration took place.'

When an arrow was pointed at him, it was Bishop Patteson's custom to look the archer full in the face with his bright smile, and in many more cases than are here hinted at, that look of cheery confidence and good-will made the weapon drop.

After a few more visits to the coasts of this archipelago the boat returned to Mota, where Mr. Pritt and Mr. Kerr had kept school every day, besides getting the station into excellent order and beauty. Their presence at the head-quarters left the Bishop free to circulate in the villages, sleeping in the Ogamals, where he could collect the men. They always seemed pleased and interested, and their pugnacious habits were decidedly diminishing, though their superstitious practices and observances were by no means dropped.

The Diary, on July 24, thus speaks of the way of life; which, however, was again telling on the health of the party:—

'I am so accustomed to sleeping about anywhere that I take little or no account of thirty, forty, fifty naked fellows, lying, sitting, sleeping round me. Someone brings me a native mat, someone else a bit of yam; a third brings a cocoa-nut; so I get my supper, put down the mat (like a very thin door-mat) on the earth, roll up my coat for a pillow, and make a very good night of it. I have had deafness in my right ear again for some days; no pain with it, but it is inconvenient.

'Several of our lads have had attacks of fever and ague; Wadrokala and his child of a wife, Bum, a Bauro boy, &c. The island is not at all unhealthy, but natives cannot be taught caution. I, thank God, am in robust health, very weather-beaten. I think my Bishop's dress would look quite out of keeping with such a face and pair of hands!

'There is much as usual in such cases to encourage and to humble us. Some few people seem to be in earnest. The great majority do their best to make me think they are listening. Meanwhile, much goes on in the island as of old.

'Sunday, July 28th, 11.45 A.M.—I have much anxiety just now. At this moment Wadrokala is in an ague fit, five or six others of my party kept going by quinine and port wine, and one or other sickening almost daily. Henry Hrahuena, of Lifu, I think dying, from what I know not—I think inflammation of the brain, induced possibly by exposure to the sun, though I have not seen him so exposed, and it is a thing I am very careful about with them. I do what I can in following the directions of medical books, but it is so hard to get a word from a native to explain symptoms, &c.; besides, my ear is now, like last year, really painful; and for two nights I have had little sleep, and feel stupid, and getting a worn-out feeling. With all this, I am conscious that it is but a temporary depression, a day or two may bring out the bright colours again. Henry may recover by God's mercy, the boys become hearty again; my ear get right. At present I feel that I must rub on as

I can, from hour to hour.

'If I find from experience that natives of Melanesia, taken to a different island, however fertile, dry, and apparently healthy, do seem to be affected by it, I must modify my plans, try as soon as possible to have more winter schools, and, what is of more consequence, I must reconsider the whole question of native teachers. If a great amount of sickness is to be the result of gathering scholars around me at an island, I could do, perhaps, more single-handed, in health, and with no one to look after, than with twenty fellows of whom half are causing continual anxiety on the score of health. Now were I alone, I should be as brisk as a bee, but I feel weighed down somewhat with the anxiety about all these fellows about me.

'I must balance considerations, and think it out. It requires great attention. It is at times like these that I experience some trials. Usually my life is, as you know, singularly free from them.

'July 31st.—Henry died on Sunday about 4 A.M. Wadrokala is better. The boys are all better. I have had much real pain and weariness from sleepless nights, owing to the small tumour in my ear. What a sheet of paper for you to read! And yet it is not so sad either. The boys were patient and good; Wadrokala takes his ague attacks like a man; and about Henry I had great comfort.

'He was about eighteen or nineteen, as I suppose, the son of the great enchanter in Lifu in old times—the hereditary high priest of Lifu indeed. He was a simple-minded, gentle, good fellow, not one probably who would have been able to take a distinct line as a teacher, yet he might have done good service with a good teacher. We found that afternoon a slate on which he had written down some thoughts when first taken ill, showing that he felt that he was sick unto death. Very full of comfort were his written as well as his spoken words.'

On August 1, while the Bauro scholars were writing answers to questions on the Lord's Prayer, a party of men and women arrived, headed by a man with a native scarf over his shoulders. They had come to be taught, bringing provisions with them, and eating them, men and women together, a memorable infringement of one of the most unvarying customs of the Banks inhabitants; and from the conversation with them and with others, Bishop Patteson found that the work of breaking down had been attained, that of building up had to be begun. They must learn that leaving off heathen practices was not the same thing as adopting the religion of Christ, and the kind of work which external influences had cut short in Lifu had to be begun with them.

'Soon, I think, the great difficulty must be met in Mota of teaching the Christian's social and domestic life to people disposed to give up much of their old practices. This is the point at which I suppose most Missions have broken down. It is a great blessing indeed to reach it, but the building up of converts is the harder work. Here, for example, a population of 1,500 people; at present they know all that is necessary for the cultivation of yams, &c., they build houses sufficient for the purpose of their present life, they are giving up fighting, losing-faith in their old charms and contrivances for compassing the death of their enemies; they will very likely soon be at peace throughout the whole island. Well, then, they will be very idle, talk infinite scandal, indulge in any amount of gluttony; professing to believe our religion, their whole life will contradict that profession, unless their whole social and domestic life be changed, and a new character infused into them. It would be a great mistake to suppose that the English aspect of the Christian's social life is necessarily adapted to such races as these. The Oriental tendencies of their minds, the wholly different circumstances of their lives, climate, absence of all poverty or dependence upon others, &c., will prevent them from ever becoming a little English community; but not, I trust, their becoming a Christian community. But how shall I try to teach them to become industrious, persevering, honest, tidy, clean, careful with children, and all the rest of it? What a different thing from just going about and teaching them the first principles of Christianity! The second stage of a Mission is the really difficult one.'

A few days after the foregoing observations were written, H.M.S. 'Cordelia,' a war steamer, entered Port Patteson, and Captain Hume himself came across by boat to Mota, to communicate to Bishop Patteson his instructions to offer him a cruise in the vessel, render him any assistance in his power in the Solomon Islands, and return him to any island he might desire. Letters from the Primate assumed that the proposal should be accepted; it was an opportunity of taking home the Bauro and Grera boys; moreover there was a quarrel between English and natives to be enquired into at Ysabel Island, where the Bishop could be useful as interpreter; and, as he could leave his two friends to carry on the school at Mota, he went on board, and very good it was for him, in the depressed state of health brought on by rude bed and board, to be the guest on board a Queen's ship and under good medical care.

For the 'Cordelia' had brought out the letters which gave the first intimation of his father's state; and without the privacy, and freedom from toil and responsibility, he could hardly have borne up under the blow. The first day was bad enough: 'a long busy day on shore with just one letter read, and the dull heavy sensation of an agony that was to come, as soon as I could be alone to think.' Arrangements had to be made; and there was not one solitary moment till 9 P.M. in the cabin when this loving and beloved son could shut himself in, kneel down, and recover composure to open the two letters in his father's hand.

He wrote it all—his whole heart—as of old to the father who had ever shared his inmost thoughts:—

'It may be that as I write, your blessed spirit, at rest in Paradise, may know me more truly than ever you did on earth; and yet the sorrow of knowing how bitter it is within may never be permitted to ruffle your everlasting peace.

'I may never see you on earth. All thought of such a joy is gone. I did really cling to it (I see it now) when most I thought I was quite content to wait for the hope of the great meeting. I will try to remember and to do what you say about all business matters.

'I will pray God to make me more desirous and more able to follow the holy example you leave behind. Oh that the peace of God may be given to me also when I come to die; though how may I dare to hope for such an end, so full of faith and love and the patient waiting for Christ!

'I must go on with my work. This very morning I was anxious, passing shoal water with the captain and master beside me, and appealing to me as pilot. I must try to be of some use in the ship. I must try to turn to good account among the islands this great opportunity. Probably elasticity of mind will come again now for very pain of body. Oh! how much more sorrow and heavy weight on my heart! I am quite worn out and weary. It seems as if the light were taken from me, as if it was no longer possible to work away so cheerily when I no longer have you to write to about it all, no longer your approval to seek, your notice to obtain.

'I must go on writing to you, my own dearest Father, even as I go on praying for you. It is a great comfort to me, though I feel that in all human probability you are to be thought of now as one of the blessed drawn wholly within the veil. Oh! that we may all dwell together hereafter for His blessed sake who died for us. Now more than ever your loving and dutiful Son,' &c.

Such another letter was written to his sister Fanny; but it is dated four days later, when he was better in health, and was somewhat recovered from the first shock; besides which, he felt his office of comforter when writing to her. So the letter is more cheerful, and is a good deal taken up with the endeavour to assure the sisters of his acquiescence in whatever scheme of life they might adopt, and willingness that, if it were thought advisable, Feniton Court should be sold. 'This is all cold and heartless,' he says, 'but I must try and make my view pretty clear.' Towards the end occurs the following:—

'Last night, my slight feverish attack over, my ears comfortable, with the feeling of health and ease returning, I lay awake, thought of dear Uncle Frank, and then for a long time of dear Mamma. How plainly I saw her face, and dear dear Uncle James, and I wondered whether dear dear Father was already among them in Paradise. It is not often that I can fasten down my mind to think continuously upon those blessed ones; I am too tired, or too busy; and this climate, you know, is enervating. But last night I was very happy, and seemed to be very near them. The Evening Lesson set me off, 1 John iii. How wonderful it is! But all the evening I had been reading my book of Prayers and Meditations. Do you know, Fan, at times the thought comes upon me with a force almost overpowering, that I am a Bishop; and that I must not shrink from believing that I am called to a special work. I don't think that I dwell morbidly on this, but it is an awful thought. And then I feel just the same as of old, and don't reach out more, or aim more earnestly at amendment of life and strive after fresh degrees of enlightenment and holiness. But probably I have to learn the lesson, which it may be only sickness will teach me, of patient waiting, that God will accomplish His own work in His own time.'

Some of this is almost too sacred for publication, and yet it is well that it should be seen how realising the Communion of Saints blessed the solitary man who had given up home. The next letter is to Sir J. T. Coleridge:—

'H.M.S. "Cordelia," September 11, 1861.

'My dearest Uncle,—It is now nearly five weeks since I learnt from my letters of March and April, brought to me by this ship, the very precarious state of my dear Father.

'He has never missed a mail since we have been parted, never once; and he wrote as he always did both in March and April. I had read a letter from the good Primate first; because I had to make up my mind whether I could, as I was desired, take a cruise in this vessel; and in his letter I heard of my dear Father's state. With what reverence I opened his letters! With what short earnest prayers to God that I might have strength supplied and resignation I had kept them till the last. All day at Mota I had been too busy to read any but the Primate's letters. I had many matters to arrange...and it was not until night that I could quietly read my letters in the captain's cabin. My dear Father's words seem to come to me like a voice from another world. I think from what he says, and what they all say, that already he has departed to be with Christ.

'I think of him and my dear mother, and those dear uncles James and Frank, so specially dear to me, and others gone before. I think of all that he has been to me, and yet how can I be unhappy? The great shock to me was long overpast: it is easy for me to dwell on his gain rather than my loss; yet how I shall miss his wise loving letters and all the unrestrained delights of our correspondence.

'It is not with me as with those dear sisters, or with old Jem. Theirs is the privilege of witnessing the beauty and holiness of his life to the end; and theirs the sorrow of learning to live without him. Yet I feel that the greatest perhaps of all the pleasures of this life is gone. How I did delight in writing to him and seeking his approval of what I was about! How I read and re-read his letters, entering so entirely into my feelings, understanding me so well in my life, so strangely different from what it used to be.

'Well, it should make me feel more than ever that I have but one thing to live for —the good, if so it may please God, of these Melanesian islands.

'I cannot say, for you will like to know my feelings, that I felt so overwhelmed with this news as not to be able to go about my usual business. Yet the rest on board the vessel has been very grateful to me. The quiet cheerfulness and briskness will all come again, as I think; and yet I think too that I shall be an older and more thoughtful man by reason of this.

'There has been reported a row at Ysabel Island, one of the Solomon group, eighteen months ago. This vessel, a screw steamer, ten guns and a large pivot gun, came to enquire, with orders from the Commodore of the station to call at Mota and see me, and request me to go with the vessel if I could find time to do so; adding that the vessel was to take me to any island which I might wish to be returned to. Now I have long wished to indoctrinate captains of men-of-war with our notions of the right way to settle disputes between natives and traders. Secondly, I had a passage free with my Solomon Islanders, and consequently all October and half November I may devote to working up carefully (D.V.) the Banks and New Hebrides group without being under the necessity of going down to the Solomon Islands. Thirdly, I had an opportunity of going further to the westward than I had ever been before, and of seeing new ground. Fourthly, the Primate, I found, assumed that I should go. So here I am, in great clover, of course: the change from Mota to man-of-war life being amusing enough. Barring some illness, slight attacks of fever, I have enjoyed myself very much. The seeing

Ysabel Island is a real gain. I had time to acquire some 200 words and phrases of the language, which signify to me a great deal more. The language is a very remarkable one, very Polynesian; yet in some respects distinguished from the Polynesian, and most closely related to Melanesian dialects.

'I need not enter into all this. It is my business, you know, to work at such things, and a word or two often tells me now a good deal of the secrets of a language—the prominent forms, affixes, &c., &c.; the way in which it is linked on to other dialects by peculiar terminations, the law by which the transposition of vowels and consonants is governed in general. All these things soon come out, so I am very sanguine about soon, if I live, seeing my way in preparing the way for future missionaries in the far West.

'But I must not forget that I have some islands to visit in the next month or two where the people are very wild, so that I of all people have least reason to speculate about what I may hope to do a year hence.

'The real anxiety is in the making up my own mind whether or not I ought to lower the boat in such a sea way; whether or not I ought to swim ashore among these fellows crowded there on the narrow beach, &c.

'When my mind is made up, it is not so difficult then. But, humanly speaking, there are but few islands now where I realise the fact of there being any risk; at very many I land with confidence. Yet I could enumerate, I dare say, five-and-twenty which we have not visited at all, or not regularly; and where I must be careful, as also in visiting different parts of islands already known to us in part. Poor poor people, who can see them and not desire to make known to them the words of life? I may never forget the Bishop's words in the Consecration Service: —"Your office is in the highest sense to preach the Gospel to the poor;" and then his eye glanced over the row of Melanesians sitting near me.

'How strange that I can write all this, when one heavy sense of trouble is hanging vaguely over me. And yet you will be thankful that I can think, as I trust, heartily of my work, and that my interest is in no way lessened. It ought to be increased. Yet I scarce realise the fact of being a Bishop, though again it does not seem unnatural. I can't explain what I mean. I suppose the fact that I knew for so long before that it must come some day if I lived, makes the difference now.

'I don't think, however, that your words will come true of my appearing in shovel hat, &c., at Heath's Court some fine day. It is very improbable that I shall ever see the northern hemisphere, unless I see it in the longitude of New Guinea.

'I must try to send a few island shells to M——, B——, and Co.; those little ones must not grow up, and I am sure that you all do not suffer them to grow up, without knowing something about "old cousin Coley" tumbling about in a little ship (albeit at present in a war steamer) at the other end of the world. Seriously, dear Uncle, as they grow older, it may be some help for them to hear of these poor Melanesians, and of our personal intercourse with them, so to speak.

'I have but little hope of hearing, if I return safe to New Zealand at the end of November, that this disastrous war is over. I fear that the original error has been overlaid by more recent events, forgotten amongst them. The Maori must suffer, the country must suffer. Confession of a fault in an individual is wrong in a State;

indeed, the rights of the case are, and perhaps must be, unknown to people at a distance. We have no difficulty here in exposing the fallacies and duplicities of the authors of the war, but we can't expect (and I see that it must be so) people in England to understand the many details. To begin with, a man must know, and that well, Maori customs, their national feeling, &c. It is all known to One above, and that is our only hope now. May He grant us peace and wisdom for the time to come!

'I have been reading Helps again this voyage, a worthy book, and specially interesting to me. How much there is I shall be glad to read about. What an age it is! America, how is that to end? India, China, Japan, Africa! I have Jowett's books and "Essays and Reviews." How much I should like to talk with you and John, in an evening at Heath's Court, about all that such books reveal of Intellectualism at home. One does feel that there is conventionalism and unreality in the hereditary passive acceptance of much that people think they believe. But how on Jowett's system can we have positive teaching at all? Can the thing denoted by "entering into the mind of Christ or St. Paul" be substituted for teaching the Catechism?

'Not so, writes my dear Father in the depth of his humility and simplicity, writing to me what a father could scarcely say to a son! But our peculiar circumstances have brought this blessing to me, that I think he has often so "reamed out" his heart to me in the warmth of his love to a son he was never again to see in the body, that I know him better even than I should have done had I remained at home.

'So wonderful was my dearest Father's calmness when he wrote on the 24th of April, that if he was alive to write again in May, I think it not impossible that he may allude to these matters. If so, what golden words to be treasured up by me! I have all his letters. You will see, or have seen him laid by my dear Mother's side. They dwell together now with Him in Paradise.

'Good-bye, my dearest Uncle. Should God spare your life, my letters will be more frequent to you now.

'My kindest love to Aunt.

'Your affectionate and grateful Nephew,

'J. C. PATTESON, Missionary Bishop.'

There is little more record of this voyage. There was less heart and spirit than usual for the regular journalizing letter; but the five weeks' voyage had been most beneficial in restoring health and energy, and it had one very important effect upon the Mission, for it was here that Lieutenant Capel Tilly, R.N., became so interested in the Mission and its head, as to undertake the charge of the future 'Southern Cross.' The 'Cordelia' was about to return to England, where, after she was paid off, Mr. Tilly would watch over the building of the new vessel on a slightly larger scale than the first, would bring her out to Kohimarama, and act as her captain.

So great a boon as his assistance did much to cheer and encourage the Bishop, who was quite well again when he landed at Mota on September 17, and found Mr. Pritt convalescent after a touch of ague, and Mr. Kerr so ill as to be glad to avail himself of Captain Hume's kind offer to take him back to Auckland in the

'Cordelia.'

Probably all were acclimatised by this time, for we hear of no more illness before the 'Sea Breeze,' with Mr. Dudley, came, on the 10th of October, to take the party off.

He says:—'The Bishop and Mr. Pritt both looked pale and worn. There were, however, signs in the island of a great advance in the state of things of the previous year. An admirable schoolroom had been built; and in the open space cleared in front of it, every evening some hundred people would gather, the older ones chatting, the younger ones being initiated in the mysteries of leap-frog, wrestling, and other English games, until prayer time, when all stood in a circle, singing a Mota hymn, and the Bishop prayed with and for them.

'That voyage was not a long one. We did not go to the Solomon Islands and the groups to the north, but we worked back through the New Hebrides, carefully visiting them.'

Mr. Dudley had brought letters that filled the Bishop's heart to overflowing, and still it was to his father that he wrote: 'It seems as if you had lived to see us all, as it were, fixed in our several positions, and could now "depart in peace, according to His word."'

The agony and bitterness seem to have been met and struggled through, as it were, in those first days on board the 'Cordelia.' In this second letter there is infinite peace and thankfulness; and so there still was, when, at Norfolk Island, the tidings of the good old man's death met him, as described in the ensuing letter:—

'"Sea Breeze," one hundred miles south-east of Norfolk Island: 8 A.M.

'My dearest Sisters,—Joy and grief were strangely mingled together while I was on shore in Norfolk Island, from 6 P.M. Saturday to 8 P.M. Sunday (yesterday).

'I was sitting with Mr. Nobbs (Benjamin Dudley the only other person present) when he said, "We have seen in our papers from Sydney the news of the death of your revered Father." He concluded that I must have known of it.

'How wonderful it seems to me that it did not come as a great shock. I showed by my face (naturally) that I had not known before that God had taken him unto Himself, but I could answer quite calmly, "I thank God. Do not be distressed at telling me suddenly, as you see you have done inadvertently. I knew he could not live long. We all knew that he was only waiting for Christ."

'And, dear dear John and Fan, how merciful God has been! The last part of his letter to me, of date June 25, only three days before his call came, so that I know (and praise God for it) that he was spared protracted suffering. Shall I desire or wish to be more sorry than I am? Shall I try to make myself grieve, and feel unhappy? Oh, no; it is of God's great mercy that I still feel happy and thankful, for I cannot doubt the depth of my love to him who has indeed been, and that more than ever of late, the one to whom I clung in the world.

'I could be quiet at night, sleeping in Mr. Nobbs's house, and yet I could not at once compose myself to think it all over, as I desired to do. And then I had much to do, and here was the joy mingling with the sorrow.

'For the Norfolk Island people have come to see how wise was the Primate's original plan, and now they much desire to connect themselves more closely with the Mission.

'Mr. and Mrs. Nobbs desire their son Edwin, who was two years at the Governor's at Sydney, and is now eighteen and a half years old, to be given wholly to us.... So said Simon Young of his boy Fisher, and so did three others. All spoke simply, and without excitement, but with deep feeling. I thought it right to say that they should remain at Norfolk Island at present, that we all might prove them whether they were indeed bent upon this work, that we might be able to trust that God had indeed called them. To the lads I said, "This is a disappointment, I know, but it is good for you to have to bear trials. You must take time to count the cost. It is no light thing to be called to the work of a teacher among the heathen. In giving up your present wish to go immediately, you are obeying your parents and others older than yourselves, and your cheerful obedience to them is the best evidence that you wish to act upon a sense of duty, and not only from impulse; but don't think I wish to discourage you. I thank Him who has put the good desire into your hearts. Prove yourselves now by special prayer and meditation."

'Then came the happy, blessed service, the whole population present, every confirmed person communicating, my voice trembling at the Fifth Commandment and the end of the Prayer for the Church Militant, my heart very full and thankful. I preached to them extempore, as one can preach to no other congregation, from the lesson, "JESUS gone to be the guest of a man that is a sinner," the consequences that would result in us from His vouchsafing to tabernacle among us, and, as displayed in the Parable of the Pounds, the use of God's gifts of health, influence, means; then, specifying the use of God's highest gifts of children to be trained to His glory, quoting 1 Samuel i. 27, 28, "lent to the Lord," I spoke with an earnestness that felt strange to me at the time.

'Simon Young said afterwards: "My wife could not consent months ago to Fisher's going away, but she has told me now that she consents. She can't withhold him with the thought of holy Hannah in her mind." And I felt as if I might apply (though not in the first sense) the prophecy "Instead of thy fathers, thou shalt have children."

'To add to all, Mr. Nobbs said: "I have quite altered my mind about the Melanesian school, I quite see that I was mistaken;" and the people are considering how to connect themselves closely with us.

'You may imagine, dear Joan, that joy and grief made a strange, yet not unhappy tumult in my mind. I came away at 3 P.M. (the wind being very fair) hoping to revisit them, and, by the Bishop of Tasmania's desire, hold a confirmation in six months' time. How I am longing to hear the last record of the three days intervening between June 25 and 28, you may well imagine.... Already, thank God, four months have passed, and you are recovering from the great shock. Yours is a far harder trial than mine. May God comfort and bless us all, and bring us to dwell with our dear parents in heaven, for our blessed Lord's sake.

'Your very loving Brother,
'J. C. PATTESON.'

And this most touching account from within is supplemented by the following, by Mr. Dudley, from without:—

'He took it [the tidings of his father's death] quite calmly. Evidently it had been long expected and prepared for. He was even cheerful in his quiet grave way. In the evening there was singing got up for him by some of the Norfolk Islanders, in one of the large rooms of the old barracks. He enjoyed it; and after it had gone on some time, he thanked them in a few touching words that went home, I am sure, to the hearts of many of them, and then we all knelt down, and he prayed extempore. I wish I had kept the words of that prayer! Everyone was affected, knowing what was then occupying his mind, but we were still more so next morning, at the service in church. His voice had that peculiarly low and sweet tone which always came into it when he was in great anxiety or sorrow, but his appeal to the congregation was inspiring to the last degree. It was the Twenty-third Sunday after Trinity, and the subject he took was from the second lesson, the Parable of the Pounds, in St. Luke xix., and so pointed out the difficulties between the reception of a talent and the use of it. He showed that the fact of people's children growing up as wild and careless as heathen was no proof that no grace had been bestowed upon them; on the contrary, in the baptized it was there, but it had never been developed; and then came the emphatic assertion, "The best way of employing our gifts of whatever kind—children, means, position—is by lending them to the Lord for His service, and then a double blessing will be returned for that we give. Hannah giving her child to the Lord, did she repent of it afterwards, think you, when she saw him serving the Lord, the one upright man of the house of Israel?"'

No doubt these words were founded on those heartfelt assurances which stirred his very soul within him that his own father had never for a moment regretted or mourned over the gift unto the Lord, which had indeed been costly, but had been returned, 'good measure, pressed together, and flowing over,' in blessing! can I grieve and sorrow about my dear dear Father's blessed end?' are the words in a letter to myself written on the 19th. It further contained thanks for a photograph of Hursley Church spire and Vicarage, which had been taken one summer afternoon, at the desire of Dr. Moberly (the present Bishop of Salisbury), and of which I had begged a copy for him. 'I shall like the photograph of Hursley Vicarage and Church, the lawn and group upon it. But most shall I like to think that Mr. Keble, and I dare say Dr. Moberly too, pray for me and this Mission. I need the prayers of all good people indeed.' I quote this sentence because it led to a correspondence with both Mr. Keble and Dr. Moberly, which was equally prized by the holy and humble men of heart who wrote and received the letters:—

'St. Andrew's, Kohimarama: November 20, 1861.

"Thank you, my dearest Sophy, for your loving letters, and all your love and devotion to him.

'I fear I do not write to those two dear sisters of mine as they and you all expect and wish. I long to pour it all out; I get great relief in talking, as at Taurarua I can talk to the dear Judge and Lady Martin. She met me with a warm loving kiss that was intended to be as home-like as possible, and for a minute I could not speak, and then said falteringly, "It has been all one great mercy to the end. I have heard at Norfolk Island." But I feel it still pent up to a great extent, and yet I have a great sense of relief. I fancy I almost hear sometimes the laboured breathing, the sudden stop—the "thanks be to God, he has entered into his rest."

'What his letters are, I cannot even fully say to another, perhaps never fully realise myself.

'As I write, the tears come, for it needs but a little to bring them now, though I suppose the world without thinks that I "bear up," and go on bravely.

'But when any little word or thought touches the feelings, the sensitive rather than the intellectual part of me, then I break down.

'And yet it seems to bring thoughts and hopes into more definite shape. How I read that magnificent last chapter of Isaiah last Sunday. I seemed to feel my whole heart glowing with wonder, and exultation, and praise. The world invisible may well be a reality to us, whose dear ones there outnumber now those still in the flesh. Jem's most beautiful, most intensely affecting letter, with all his thoughtfulness about the grave, &c., fairly upset me. I let the Judge and Lady Martin read some parts of it, and they returned it, saying it had quite overcome them. Now all day I feel really as much as at those moments, only the special circumstances give more expression at one time than at another to the inward state of mind.

'How I treasure up many many of his words and actions!

'What a history in these words: "All times of the day are alike to me now; getting near, I trust, the time when it will be all day."

'Those are the things that break me down. I see his dear face, and hear him slowly and calmly saying such words of patient trust and faith, and it is too much. Oh! that I might live as the son of such parents ought to live!

'And then I turn to the practical duties again, and get lost in the unceasing languages and all the rest of it.

'Now enough—but I write what comes uppermost.

'Your loving Cousin,

'**J. C. PATTESON.**'

Very soon after the return, on the 6th December, 1861, an Ordination was held at St. Paul's, Auckland, when the Primate ordained two Maori deacons, and Bishop Patteson, the Rev. Benjamin Dudley.

Sir William and Lady Martin spent part of this summer in the little cottage at Kohimarama where the sailing master of the late 'Southern Cross' had lived: and again we have to thank her for a picture of life at St. Andrew's. She says:—

'The new settlement was then thought to be healthy, and he and his boys alike rejoiced in the warmth of the sheltered bay, after the keenness of the air at St. John's on higher ground. The place looked very pretty. The green fields and hawthorn hedges and the sleek cattle reminded one of England. As a strong contrast, there was the white shelly beach and yellow sands. Here the boys sunned themselves in play hours, or fished on the rocks, or cooked their fish at drift-wood fires. On calm days one or two would skim across the blue water in their tiny canoes. One great charm of the place was the freedom and naturalness of the whole party. There was no attempt to force an overstrained piety on these wild fellows, who showed their sincerity by coming with the Bishop. By five in the morning all were astir, and jokes and laughter and shrill unaccountable cries would rouse us up, and go on all day, save when school and chapel came to sober them.

'The Bishop had not lost his Eton tastes, and only liked to see them play games, and the little fat merry-faced lads were always on the look-out for a bit of fun with him. One evening a tea-drinking was given in the hall in honour of us. The Mota boys sung in twilight the story of the first arrival of the Mission vessel and of their wonder at it. The air, with a monotonous, not unpleasing refrain, reminded us of some old French Canadian ditties. I remember well the excitement when the Bishop sent up a fire balloon. It sailed slowly towards the sea, and down rushed the whole Melanesian party, shrieking with delight after it. Our dear friend's own quarters were very tiny, and a great contrast to his large airy room at St. John's. He occupied a corner house in the quadrangle, to be close to the boys. Neither bedroom nor sitting-room was more than ten feet square. Everything was orderly, as was his wont. Photographs of the faces and places he loved best hung on the walls. Just by the door was his standing desk, with folios and lexicons. A table, covered with books and papers in divers languages, and a chair or two, completed his stock of furniture. The door stood open all day long in fine weather, and the Bishop was seldom alone. One or other of the boys would steal quietly in and sit down. They did not need to be amused, nor did they interrupt his work. They were quite content to be near him, and to get now and then a kind word or a pleasant smile. It was the habitual gentle sympathy and friendliness on his part that won the confidence of the wild timid people who had been brought up in an element of mistrust, and which enabled them after a while to come and open their hearts to him.

'How vividly the whole scene comes back to me as I write! The Bishop's calm thoughtful face, the dusky lads, the white-shelled square in front, relieved by a mass of bright geraniums or gay creepers, the little bed-room with its camp bed, and medicine bottles and good books, and, too often, in spite of our loving remonstrances, an invalid shivering with ague, or influenza, in possession. We knew that this involved broken nights for him, and a soft board and a rug for a couch. He was overtasking his powers during those years. He was at work generally from five A.M. to eleven P.M., and this in a close atmosphere; for both the schoolroom and his own house were ill-ventilated. He would not spare time enough either for regular exercise. He had a horse and enjoyed riding, but he grudged the time except when he had to come up to town on business or to take Sunday services for the English in the country. It was very natural, as he had all a student's taste for quiet study, yet could only indulge it by cutting off his own hours for relaxation. He was constantly called off during the day to attend to practical work, teaching in school, prescribing for and waiting on the sick, weighing out medicines, keeping the farm accounts, besides the night classes in several languages.

'He was really never so happy as among his boys or his books. He had no liking for general society, though his natural courteousness made him shrink from seeming ungracious. He did thoroughly enjoy a real talk with one or two friends at a time, but even this he denied himself.'

Fanny Patteson had spent several days at Hursley in the course of the winter, and the Vicar and Mrs. Keble had greatly delighted in hearing her brother's letters. The following letter from Mr. Keble was written, as will be perceived, immediately after hearing the account of the baptism of the dying child at Mota:—

'Hursley, February 19, 1862.

'My dear Bishop Patteson,—I seat myself down on a low chair between the pictures of your uncle and your Metropolitan, and that by command of your sister, who is on a footstool in the corner opposite, I to send two words, she 200, or, for aught I know, 2,000, to greet you on the other side of the world. We have the more right, as your kind sisters have kept us well up to your Missionary doings from time to time, and we seem to be very often with you on board or in your islands (I say we, for my dear wife is more than half of me, as you may well suppose, in such sympathies), and it seems to me that, perhaps, in the present state of your island or sea-work you may have more time than by-and-by for thinking of one and another; anyhow we trust that that may happen which we ask for every evening—that we may be vouchsafed a part in the holy prayers which have been that day offered to the Throne of Grace, in Melanesia or elsewhere. I don't know whether I am right, but I fancy you at times something between a Hermit and a Missionary. God grant you a double blessing! and as you are a Bishop besides, you will breathe us a blessing in return for this, such as it is. Fanny's visit has been, as you know it would be, most charming and genial to us old folks (not that my wife ought to be so spoken of), and I shall always think it so kind of her to have spared us the time when she had so much to do and so short a time to do it in; but she seems like one going about with a bag of what Bishop Selwyn calls "hope-seed," and sowing it in everyplace; yet when one comes to look close at it, it all consists of memories, chiefly you know of whom. I only wish I could rightly and truly treasure up all she has kindly told us of your dear Father; but it must be a special grace to remember and really understand such things. It will be a most peculiar satisfaction, now that we have had her with us in this way, to think of you all three together, should God's Providence allow the meeting of which we understand there is a hope. The last thing she has told us of is the baptism on St. Barnabas' Day—"the first fruits of Mota unto Christ." What a thought—what a subject for prayer and thanksgiving! God grant it may prove to you more than we can ask or think.

'Ever yours, my dear Bishop,

'**J. K.**

'Don't trouble yourself to write, but think of us.'

Of course there was no obeying this postscript, and the immediate reply was:—

'My dear dear Mr. Keble,—Few things have ever given me more real pleasure than the receipt of your letter by this mail. I never doubted your interest in New Zealand and Melanesia, and your affection for me for my dear Father's sake. I felt quite sure that prayers were being offered up for us in many places, and where more frequently than at Hursley? Even as on this day, five years ago, when I touched the reef at Guadalcanar, in the presence of three hundred armed and naked men, (I heard afterwards) prayers were being uttered in the dead of your night by my dear old governess, Miss Neill, that God would have me in His safe keeping. But it is most pleasant, most helpful to me, to read your letter, and to feel that I have a kind of right now to write to you, as I hope I may do while I live fully and freely.

'I do not say a word concerning the idea some of you in England seem to take of my life here. It is very humbling to me, as it ought to be, to read such a letter from you. How different it is really!

'If my dear sisters do come out to me for a while, which, after their letters by this February mail, seems less impossible than before, they will soon see what I mean: a missionary's life does not procure him any immunity from temptations, nor from falling into them; though, thanks be to God, it has indeed its rich and abundant blessings. It is a blessed thing to draw a little fellow, only six months ago a wild little savage, down upon one's knee, and hear his first confession of his past life, and his shy hesitating account of the words he uses when he prays to his newly-found God and Saviour. These are rare moments, but they do occur; and, if they don't, why the duty is to work all the same.

'The intelligence of some of these lads and young men really surprises me. Some with me now, last October were utterly wild, never had worn a stitch of clothing, were familiar with every kind of vice. They now write an account of a Scripture print, or answer my MS. questions without copy, of course, fairly and legibly in their books, and read their own language—only quite lately reduced to writing—with ease. What an encouragement! And this applies to, I think, the great majority of these islanders.

'One child, I suppose some thirteen or fourteen years of age, I baptized on Christmas Day. Three days afterwards I married her to a young man who had been for some years with us. They are both natives of Nengone, one of the Loyalty Isles. I administered the Holy Eucharist to her last Saturday, and she is dying peacefully of consumption. What a blessed thing! This little one, fresh from Baptism, with all Church ministrations round her, passing gently away to her eternal rest. She looks at me with her soft dark eyes, and fondles my hand, and says she is not unhappy. She has, I verily believe, the secret of real happiness in her heart.

'I must write more when at sea. I have very little time here.

'I hope by God's blessing to make a long round among my many islands this winter; some, I know, must be approached with great caution. Your prayers will be offered for me and those with me, I know, and am greatly comforted by the knowledge of it.

'Fanny tells me what you have said to her about supplying any deficit in the money required for our vessel. I feel as if this ought not in one sense to come upon you, but how can I venture to speak to you on such matters? You know all that I think and feel about it. Send me more your blessing. I feel cares and anxieties now. My kind love to Mrs. Keble.

'J. C. PATTESON, Missionary Bishop.'

Two more notes followed in quick succession to Hursley Vicarage, almost entirely upon the matter of the new 'Southern Cross,' which was being built under Mr. Tilly's eye. The two Bishops were scrupulous about letting Mr. Keble give more than a fair proportion towards the vessel, which was not to cost more than £3,000, though more roomy than her lamented predecessor. Meantime the 'Sea Breeze' was 'again to serve for the winter voyage:—

'St. Barnabas Day, Auckland: 1862.

'My dear Sisters,—Think of my being ashore, and in a Christian land on this day. So it is. We sail (D.V.) in six days, as it may be this day week. The Melanesians are very good and pretty well in health, but we are all anxious to be in warm climates. I think that most matters are settled. Primate and I have finished our accounts. Think of his wise stewardship! The endowment in land and money, and no debts contracted! I hope that I leave nothing behind me to cause difficulty, should anything happen. The Primate and Sir William Martin are my executors; Melanesia, as you would expect, my heir. I may have forgotten many items, personal reminiscences. Ask for anything, should anything happen. I see no reason to anticipate it, humanly speaking, but it is always well to think of such things. I am just going to the little Taurarua chapel to our Melanesian Commemoration service with Holy Communion.

'Oh! if it should please God to grant us a meeting here!

'Great blessings have been given me this summer in seeing the progress made by the scholars, so great as to make me feel sober-minded and almost fearful, but that is wrong and faithless perhaps, and yet surely the trials must come some day.

'God bless you all, and keep you all safe from all harm.

'Your loving Brother,

'J. C. PATTESON, Bishop.'

'Friday, June 27th, 2 P.M.—How you are thinking of all that took place that last night on earth. He was taking his departure for a long voyage, rather he was entering into the haven where he would be! May God give us grace to follow his holy example, his patient endurance of his many trials, the greatest his constant trial of deafness.

'I think if the weather be fair, that we shall go off to-morrow. Oh! if we do meet, and spend, it may be, Christmas together.

28th, 3 P.M.—The first anniversary of our dear Father's death. How you are all recalling what took place then! How full of thankfulness for his gain, far outweighing the sorrow for our loss! And yet how you must feel it, more than I do, and yet I feel it deeply: but the little fond memories of the last months, and above all the looks and spoken words of love, I can't altogether enter into them. His letters are all that letters can be, more than any other letters can be, but they are not the same thing in all ways. The Primate has left us to hurry down the sailing master of the "Sea Breeze." It was a very rough morning, but is calm now, boats passing and repassing between the shore and the schooner at anchor off Kohimarama.'

The habit of writing journals was not at once resumed by Bishop Patteson when his father was not there to read them; and the chance of seeing his sisters, no doubt, made him write less fully to them, since they might be on the voyage when the letters arrived in England. Thus the fullest record of the early part of the voyage is in a report which he drew up and printed in the form of a letter to the Rev. J. Keble:—

'We chartered the "Sea Breeze" schooner in June last for four months: she is a vessel of seventy tons register, a little larger than the old "Southern Cross," and as well suited for our purpose as a vessel can be which is built to carry passengers in the ordinary way. No voyage can of course equal in importance those early expeditions of the Primate, when he sailed in his little schooner among seas unknown, to islands never before visited, or visited only by the sandal-wood traders. But I never recollect myself so remarkable a voyage as this last. I do not mean that any new method was adopted in visiting islands, or communicating with the natives. God gave to the Bishop of New Zealand wisdom to see and carry out from the first the plan, which more and more approves itself as the best and only feasible plan, for our peculiar work. But all through this voyage, both in revisiting islands well known to us, and in recommencing the work in other islands, where, amidst the multitude of the Primate's engagements, it had been impossible to keep up our acquaintance with the people, and in opening the way in islands now visited for the first time, from the beginning to the end, it pleased God to prosper us beyond all our utmost hopes. I was not only able to land on many places where, as far as I know, no white man had set foot before, but to go inland, to inspect the houses, canoes, &c., in crowded villages (as at Santa Cruz), or to sit for two hours alone amidst a throng of people (as at Pentecost Island), or to walk two and a half miles inland (as at Tariko or Aspee). From no less than eight islands have we for the first time received, young people for our school here, and fifty-one Melanesian men, women, and young lads are now with us, gathered from twenty-four islands, exclusive of the islands so long-known to us of the Loyalty Group. When you remember that at Santa Cruz, e.g., we had never landed before, and that this voyage I was permitted to go ashore at seven different places in one day, during which I saw about 1,200 men: that in all these islands the inhabitants are, to look at, wild, naked, armed with spears and clubs, or bows and poisoned arrows; that every man's hand (as, alas! we find only too soon when we live among them) is against his neighbour, and scenes of violence and bloodshed amongst themselves of frequent occurrence; and that throughout this voyage (during which I landed between seventy and eighty times) not one hand was lifted up against me, not one sign of ill-will exhibited; you will see why I speak and think with real amazement and thankfulness of a voyage accompanied with results so wholly unexpected. I say results, for the effecting a safe landing on an island, and much more the receiving a native lad from it, is, in this sense, a result, that the great step has been made of commencing an acquaintance with the people. If I live to make another voyage, I shall no longer go ashore there as a stranger. I know the names of some of the men; I can by signs remind them of some little present made, some little occurrence which took place; we have already something in common, and as far as they know me at all, they know me as a friend. Then some lad is given up to us, the language learned, and a real hold on the island obtained.

'The most distant point we reached was the large island Ysabel, in the Solomon Archipelago. From this island a lad has come away with us, and we have also a native boy from an island not many miles distant from Ysabel, called Anudha, but marked in the charts (though not correctly) as Florida.

'It would weary you if I wrote of all the numerous adventures and strange scenes which in such a voyage we of course experience. I will give you, if I can, an idea of what took place at some few islands, to illustrate the general character of the voyage.

'One of the New Hebrides Islands, near the middle of the group, was discovered by Cook, and by him called "Three Hills." The central part of it, where we have long-had an acquaintance with the natives, is called by them "Mai." Some six years ago we landed there, and two young men came away with us, and spent the summer in New Zealand. Their names were Petere and Laure; the former was a local chief of some consequence. We took a peculiar interest in this island, finding that a portion of the population consists of a tribe speaking a dialect of the great Polynesian language of which another dialect is spoken in New Zealand. Every year we have had scholars from Mai, several of whom can read and write. We have landed there times without number, slept ashore three or four times, and are well known of course to the inhabitants.

'The other day I landed as usual among a crowd of old acquaintances, painted and armed, but of that I thought nothing. Knowing them to be so friendly to us, instead of landing alone, I took two or three of our party to walk inland with me; and off we started, Mr. Dudley and Wadrokala being left sitting in the boat, which was, as usual, a short distance from the beach. We had walked about half a mile before I noticed something unusual in the manner of the people, and I overheard them talking in a way that made me suspect that something had happened which they did not want me to know. Petere had not made his appearance, though in general the first to greet us, and on my making enquiries for him, I was told that he was not well. Not long afterwards I overheard a man say that Petere was dead, and taking again some opportunity that offered itself for asking about him, was told that he was dead, that he had died of dysentery. I was grieved to hear this, because I liked him personally and had expected help from him when the time came for commencing a Mission station on the island. The distance from the beach to the village where Petere lived is about one and a half mile, and a large party had assembled before we reached it. There was a great lamentation and crying on our arrival, during which I sat down on a large log of a tree. Then came a pause, and I spoke to the people, telling them how sorry I was to hear of Petere's death. There was something strange still about their manner, which I could not quite make out; and one of our party, who was not used to the kind of thing, did not like the looks of the people and the clubs and spears. At last one of them, an old scholar of ours, came forward and said, "The men here do not wish to deceive you; they know that you loved Petere, and they will not hide the truth; Petere was killed by a man in a ship, a white man, who shot him in the forehead." Of course I made minute enquiries as to the ship, the number of masts, how many people they saw, whether there was anything remarkable about the appearance of any person on board, &c. The men standing round us were a good deal excited, but the same story was told by them all.

'After a while I walked back to the beach, no indication having been made of unfriendliness, but I had not gone more than a quarter of a mile when three men rushed past me from behind, and ran on to the beach. Meanwhile Mr. Dudley and Wadrokala in the boat were rather uneasy at the manner of the people standing near them on the reef; and they too suspected that something unusual had occurred. Presently they saw these three men rush out of the bush on to the beach and distribute "kava" (leaves of the pepper plant) among the people, who at once changed their manner, became quite friendly and soon dispersed. It was quite evident that a discussion had taken place on shore as to the treatment we were to receive; and these men on the beach were awaiting the result of the discussion, prepared to act accordingly. There was scarcely any danger in our case of their deciding to injure us, because they knew us well; but had we been strangers we should have been killed of course; their practice being, naturally enough, to revenge the death of a countryman on the arrival of the next man who comes from what they suppose to be their enemies' country.

'This story may show you that caution is necessary long after the time that a real friendship has commenced and been carried on. We never can tell what may have taken place during the intervals of our visits. I returned to the village, with Mr. Kerr and Mr. Dudley and slept ashore, thinking it right to restore mutual confidence at once; and there was not the slightest risk in doing so.

'Now let me tell you about an island called Ambrym, lying to the south of Aurora and Pentecost, the two northernmost islands of the New Hebrides group.

'Ambrym is a grand island, with a fine active volcano, so active on this last occasion of our visiting it, that we were covered and half-blinded by the ashes; the deck was thickly covered with them, and the sea for miles strewed with floating cinders. We have repeatedly landed in different parts of the island, but this time we visited an entirely new place. There was a considerable surf on the beach, and I did not like the boat to go near the shore, partly on that account, but chiefly because our rule is not to let the boat approach too near the beach lest it should be hauled up on shore by the people and our retreat to the schooner cut off. So I beckoned to some men in a canoe (for I could not speak a word of the language), who paddled up to us, and took me ashore.

'As I was wading to the beach, an elderly man came forward from the crowd to the water's edge, where he stood holding both his arms uplifted over his head. Directly that I reached him, he took my hand, and put it round his neck, and turned to walk up the beach. As I walked along with him through the throng of men, more than three hundred in number, my arm all the while round his neck, I overheard a few words which gave me some slight clue as to the character of their language, and a very few words go a long way on such occasions. We went inland some short distance, passing through part of a large village, till we came to a house with figures, idols or not, I hardly know, placed at some height above the door.

'They pointed to these figures and repeated a name frequently, not unlike the name of one of the gods of some of the islands further to the north; then they struck the hollow tree, which is their native drum, and thronged close round me, while I gave away a few fish-hooks, pieces of red braid, &c. I asked the names of some of the people, and of objects about me, trees, birds, &c. I was particularly struck with two boys who kept close to me. After some time I made signs that I would return to the beach, and we began to move away from the village; but I was soon stopped by some men, who brought me two small trees, making signs that I should plant them.

'When I returned to the beach, the two boys were still with me, and I took their hands and walked on amidst the crowd. I did not imagine that they would come away with me, and yet a faint hope of their doing so sprang up in my mind, as I still found them holding my hands, and even when I began to wade towards the boat still close by my side in the water. All this took place in the presence of several hundred natives, who allowed these boys to place themselves in the boat and be taken on board the schooner.

'I was somewhat anxious about revisiting an island called Tikopia. Once we were there, five or six years ago. The island is small, and the inhabitants probably not more than three hundred or four hundred. They are Polynesians, men of very large stature, rough in manner, and not very easily managed. I landed there and waded across the reef among forty or fifty men. On the beach a large party assembled. I told them in a sort of Polynesian patois, that I wished to take away two lads from their island, that I might learn their language, and come back and teach them many things for their good. This they did not agree to. They said that some of the full-grown men wished to go away with me; but to this I in my turn could not agree. These great giants would be wholly unmanageable in our school at present. I went back to the edge of the reef—about three hundred yards—and got into the boat with two men; we rowed off a little way, and I attempted, more quietly than the noisy crowd on shore would allow, to explain to them my object in coming to them. After a while we pulled back to the reef, and I waded ashore again; but I could not induce them to let me take any one away who was at all eligible for the school. Still I was very thankful to have been able twice to land and remain half an hour or more on shore among the people. Next year (D.V.) I may be able to see more of them, and perhaps may obtain a scholar, and so open the island. It is a place visited by whalers, but they never land here, and indeed the inhabitants are generally regarded as dangerous fellows to deal with, so I was all the more glad to have made a successful visit.

'Nothing could have been more delightful than the day I spent in making frequent landings on the north side of Santa Cruz. This island was visited by Spaniards, under the command of Mendana, nearly three hundred years ago. They attempted to found a colony there, but after a short time were compelled, by illness and the death of Mendana and his successor, to abandon their endeavour. It is apparently a very fertile island, certainly a very populous one. The inhabitants are very ingenious, wearing beautiful ornaments, making good bags woven of grass stained with turmeric, and fine mats. Their arrows are elaborately carved, and not less elaborately poisoned: their canoes well made and kept in good order.

We never before landed on this island; but the Primate, long before I was in this part of the world, and two or three times since, had sailed and rowed into the bay at the north-west end, called Graciosa Bay, the fine harbour in which the Spaniards anchored. I went ashore this last voyage in seven different places, large crowds of men thronging down to the water's edge as I waded to the beach. They were exceedingly friendly, allowed me to enter the houses, sit down and inspect their mode of building them. They brought me food to eat; and when I went out of the houses again, let me examine the large sea-going canoes drawn up in line on the beach. I wrote down very many names, and tried hard to induce some young people to come away with me, but after we had pulled off some way, their courage failed them, and they swam back to the shore.

'Two or three of the men took off little ornaments and gave them to me; one bright pretty boy especially I remember, who took off his shell necklace and put it round my neck, making me understand, partly by words, but more by signs, that he was afraid to come now, but would do so if I returned, as I said, in eight or ten moons.

'Large baskets of almonds were given me, and other food also thrown into the boat. I made a poor return by giving some fish-hooks and a tomahawk to the man whom I took to be the person of most consequence. On shore the women came freely up to me among the crowd, but they were afraid to venture down to the beach. Now this is the island about which we have long felt a great difficulty as to the right way of obtaining any communication with the natives. This year, why and how I cannot tell, the way was opened beyond all expectation. I tried hard to get back from the Solomon Islands so as to revisit it again during the voyage, but we could not get to the eastward, as the trade-wind blew constantly from that quarter.

'At Leper's Island I had just such another day—or rather two days were spent in making an almost complete visitation of the northern part of the island—the people were everywhere most friendly, and I am hoping to see them all again join us soon, when some may be induced to.

'It would be the work of days to tell you all our adventures. How at Malanta I picked two lads out of a party of thirty-six in a grand war canoe going on a fighting expedition—and very good fellows they are; how we filled up our water-casks at Aurora, standing up to our necks in the clear cool stream rushing down from a cataract above, with the natives assisting us in the most friendly manner; how at Santa Maria, which till this year we never visited without being shot at, I walked for four or five hours far inland wherever I pleased, meeting great crowds of men all armed and suspicious of each other—indeed actually fighting with each other—but all friendly to me; how at Espiritu Santo, when I had just thrown off my coat and tightened my belt to swim ashore through something of a surf, a canoe was launched, and without more ado a nice lad got into our boat and came away with us, without giving me the trouble of taking a swim at all; how at Florida Island, never before reached by us, one out of some eighty men, young and old, standing all round me on the reef, to my astonishment returned with me to the boat, and without any opposition from the people quietly seated himself by my side and came away to the schooner; how at Pentecost Island, Taroniara (a lad whom the Primate in old days had picked up in his canoe paddling against a strong head wind, and kept him on board all night, and sent him home with presents in the morning) now came away with me, but not without his bow and poisoned arrows, of which I have taken safe possession; how Misial felt sea-sick and home-sick for a day or two, but upon being specially patronised by the cook, soon declared "that no place could compare with the galley of a Mission vessel," to the truth of which declaration the necessity of enlarging his scanty garments soon bore satisfactory testimony; how at Ysabel the young chief came on board with a white cockatoo instead of a hawk on his wrist, which he presented to me with all the grace in the world, and with an enquiry after his good friend Captain Hume, of H.M.S. "Cordelia," who had kindly taken me to this island in the winter of 1861.'

To this may be added some touches from the home letter of August 27, off Vanikoro:—

'I don't deny that I am thankful that the Tikopia visit is well over. The people are so very powerful and so independent and unmanageable, that I always have felt anxious about visiting them. Once we were there in 1856, and now again. I hope to keep on visiting them annually. Sydney traders have been there, but have never landed; they trade at arm's length from their boat and are well armed. It is a strange sensation, sitting alone (say) 300 yards from the boat, which of course can't be trusted in their hands, among 200 or more of people really gigantic. No men have I ever seen so large—huge Patagonian limbs, and great heavy hands clutching up my little weak arms and shoulders. Yet it is not a sensation of fear, but simply of powerlessness; and it makes one think, as I do when among them, of another Power present to protect and defend.

'They perfectly understood my wish to bring away lads. Full-grown Brobdignag men wished to come, and some got into the boat who were not easily got out of it again. Boys swam off, wishing to come, but the elder people prevented it, swimming after them and dragging them back. It was a very rough, blustering day; but even on such a day the lee side of the island is a beautiful sight, one mass of cocoa-nut trees, and the villages so snugly situated among the trees.

'Just been up the rigging to get a good look at this great encircling reef at Vanikoro. Green water as smooth as glass, inside the reef for a mile, and then pretty villages; but there is no passage through the reef, it is a continuous breakwater. We are working up towards a part of the reef where I think there may be a passage. Anyhow I am gaining a good local knowledge of this place, and that saves time another year.

'The ten lads on board talk six languages, not one of which do I know; but as I get words and sentences from them, I see how they will "work in" with the general character of the language of which I have several dialects. It is therefore not very difficult to get on some little way into all at once; but I must not be disappointed if I find that other occupations take me away too much for my own pleasure from this particular branch of my work.'

A long letter to Sir John T. Coleridge gives another aspect of the voyage:—

'"Sea Breeze" Schooner: off Rennell Island. 'Therm. 89° in shade; lat. 11° 40', long. 160° 18' 5". 'September 7, 1862.

'My dear Uncle,—I can hardly keep awake for the unusually great heat. The wind is northerly, and it is very light, indeed we are almost becalmed, so you will have a sleepy letter, indeed over my book I was already nodding. I think it better to write to you (though on a Sunday) than to sleep. What a compliment! But I shall grow more wakeful as I write. Perhaps my real excuse for writing is that I feel to-day much oppressed with the thought of these great islands that I have been visiting, and I am sadly disappointed in some of my scholars from San Cristoval.

'Leaving New Zealand on June 20th, I sailed to Norfolk Island, where I held my first Confirmation. By desire of the Bishop of Tasmania, I act as Bishop for the Norfolk Islanders. This was, as you know, a very solemn time for me; sixteen dear children were confirmed. Since that time I have visited very many islands with almost unequalled success, as far as effecting landings, opening communication, and receiving native lads are concerned. I have on board natives from many places from which we have never received them before. Many I have left with Mr. Dudley and Mr. Pritt on Mota Island at school, but I have now twenty-one, speaking eleven languages. At many places where we had never landed, I was received well.

'The state of things, too, in the Banks Islands is very encouraging. What do you think of my having two married (after their fashion) couples on board from the Solomon Islands (San Cristoval and Contrariete)? This was effected with some difficulty. Both the men are old scholars, of course. I ought therefore to be most thankful; and yet my heart is sad because, after promises given by Grariri and his wife, Parenga and Kerearua (all old scholars, save Mrs. Garm), not one came away with me yesterday, and I feel grieved at the loss of my dear boys, who can read and write, and might be taught so much now! It is all very faithless; but I must tell it all to you, for indeed I do not feel as if I had any right to expect it otherwise, but in the moment of perceiving and confessing that it is very good for me, I find out for the first time how much my heart was set upon having them.

'And then San Cristoval, sixty miles long, with its villages and languages, and Malanta over eighty miles long, and Guadalcanar, seventy! It is a silly thought or a vain, human wish, but I feel as if I longed to be in fifty or a hundred places at once. But God will send qualified men in good time. In the meanwhile (for the work must be carried on mainly by native teachers gathered from each island), as some fall off I must seek to gain others. Even where lads are only two, or even one year with mer and then apparently fall back to what they were before, some good may be done, the old teaching may return upon them some day, and they may form a little nucleus for good, though not now.

'As for openings for men of the right sort, they abound. Really if I were free to locate myself on an island instead of going about to all, I hardly know to which of some four or five I ought to go. But it is of no use to have men who are not precisely the kind of men wanted. Somehow one can't as yet learn to ask men to do things that one does oneself as a matter of course. It needs a course of training to get rid of conventional notions. I think that Norfolk Island may supply a few, a very few fellows able to be of use, and perhaps New Zealand will do so, and I have the advantage of seeing and knowing them. I don't think that I must expect men from England, I can't pay them well; and it is so very difficult to give a man on paper any idea of what his life will be in Melanesia or Kohimarama. So very much that would be most hazardous to others has ceased to be so to me, because I catch up some scrap of the language talked on the beach, and habit has given an air of coolness and assurance. But this does not come all at once, and you cannot talk about all this to others. I feel ashamed as I write it even to you. They bother me to put anecdotes of adventures into our Report, but I cannot. You know no one lands on these places but myself, and it would be no good to tell stories merely to catch somebody's ear. It was easier to do so when the Bishop and I went together, but I am not training up anyone to be the visitor, and so I don't wish anybody else to go with me. Besides Mr. Pritt and Mr. Dudley are bad swimmers, and Mr. Kerr not first-rate. My constant thought is "By what means will God provide for the introduction of Christianity into these islands," and my constant prayer that He will reveal such means to me, and give me grace to use them.

'What reality there is in such a work as this! What continual need of guidance and direction! I here see before me now an island stretching away twenty-five miles in length! Last night I left one sixty miles long. I know that hundreds are living there ignorant of God, wild men, cannibals, addicted to every vice. I know that Christ died for them, and that the message is for them, too. How am I to deliver it? How find an entrance among them? How, when I have learnt their language, speak to them of religion, so as not to introduce unnecessary obstacles to the reception of it, nor compromise any of its commands?

'Thank God I can fall back upon many solid points of comfort—chiefest of all, He sees and knows it all perfectly. He sees the islanders too, and loves them, how infinitely more than I can! He desires to save them. He is, I trust, sending me to them. He will bless honest endeavours to do His will among them. And then I think how it must all appear to angels and saints, how differently they see these things. Already, to their eyes, the light is breaking forth in Melanesia; and I take great comfort from this thought, and remember that it does not matter whether it is in my time, only I must work on. And then I think of the prayers of the Church, ascending continually for the conversion of the heathen; and I know that many of you are praying specially for the heathen of Melanesia. And so one's thoughts float out to India, and China, and Japan, and Africa, and the islands of the sea, and the very vastness of the work raises one's thoughts to God, as the only One by whom it must be done.

'Now, dear Uncle, I have written all this commonplace talk, not regarding its dulness in your eyes, but because I felt weary and also somewhat overwrought and sad; and it has done me much good, and given me a happy hour.

'We had our service on board this morning, and the Holy Eucharist afterwards; Mr. Kerr, two Norfolk Islanders, a Maori, and a Nengone man present. I ought not to be faint-hearted. My kind love to Aunt and Mary.

'Your affectionate and dutiful Nephew,

'J. C. PATTESON, Missionary Bishop.'

The climate of Mota had again disagreed with Mr. Dudley, who was laid up with chronic rheumatism nearly all the time he was there; and the Bishop returned from his voyage very unwell; but Mr. Pritt happily was strong and active, and the elder Banks Island scholars were very helpful, both in working and teaching, so that the schools went on prosperously, and the custom of carrying weapons in Mota was dropped.

On November 7 the 'Sea Breeze' was again in harbour; and on the 15th, after mature consideration, was written this self-sacrificing letter:—

'St. Andrew's: November 15, 1862.

'My dearest Sisters,—I returned from a voyage unusually interesting and prosperous on the 7th of this month; absent just nineteen weeks. We were in all on board seventy-one.

'I found all your letters from April to August 25. How thankful I am to see and know what I never doubted, the loving manner in which my first and later letters about New Zealand were taken. How wise of you to perceive that in truth my judgment remained all through unaltered, though my feelings were strongly moved, indeed the good folk here begged me to reconsider my resolution, thinking no doubt kindly for me that it would be so great a joy to me to see you. Of course it would; were there no other considerations that we already know and agree upon, what joy so great on earth! But I feel sure that we are right. Thank God that we can so speak, think, and act with increasing affection and trust in each other!

'The more I think of it, the more I feel "No, it would not do! It would not be either what Joan expects or what Fan expects. They look at it in some ways alike —i.e., in the matter of seeing me, which both equally long to do. In some ways they regard it differently. But it would not to one or the other be the thing they hope and wish for. They would both feel (what yet they would not like to acknowledge) disappointment." Though, therefore, I could not help feeling often during the voyage, "What if I hear that they may be with me by Christmas!" yet it was not exactly unwelcome to hear that you do not come. I recognised at once your reading of my letters as the right one; and my feelings, strong as they are, give way to other considerations, especially when, from my many occupations, I have very little time to indulge them.

'But for the thought of coming, and your great love to me, I thank you, dear ones, with all my heart. May God bless you for it!...

'Good-bye, my dear Sisters; we are together in heart at all events.

'Your loving Brother, 'J. C. P.'

The judgment had decided that the elder sister especially would suffer more from the rough life at Kohimarama than her brother could bear that she should undergo, when he could give her so little of his society as compensation, without compromising his own decided principle that all must yield to the work. Perhaps he hardly knew how much he betrayed of the longing, even while deciding against its gratification; but his sisters were wise enough to act on his judgment, and not on their own impulse; and the events of the next season proved that he had been right. To Sir John Coleridge he wrote:—

'Kohimarama: November 15, 1862.

'My dear Uncle,—I should indeed, as you say, delight to have a ramble in the old scenes, and a good unburthening of thoughts conceived during the past seven or eight years.

'And yet you see I could not try the experiment of those dear good sisters of mine coming out. It would not have been what they expected and meant to come out to. I am little seen by any but Melanesians, and quite content that it should be so. I can't do what I want with them, nor a tenth part of it as it is. I cannot write to you of this last voyage—in many respects a most remarkable one—indicating, if I am not over hopeful, a new stage in our Mission work. Many islands yielding scholars for the first time; old scholars, with but few exceptions, steadfast and rapidly improving; no less than fifty-seven Melanesians here now from twenty-four islands, exclusive of the Loyalty Islands, and five bright Pitcairners, from twenty-four to sixteen, helpful, good, conscientious lads. There are eight languages that I do not know, besides all the rest; yet I can see that they are all links in the great chain of dialects of the great "Pacific language,"—yet dialects very far removed sometimes from one another.

'I find it not very easy to comply with reasonable demands from men in Europe, who want to know about these things. If I had time and ability, I think I should enjoy really going into philology. I get books sent me from people such as Max Muller, Grabalentz, &c.; and if I write to them at all, it is useless to write anything but an attempt at classification of the dialects; and that is difficult, for there are so many, and it takes so long to explain to another the grounds upon which I feel justified in connecting dialects and calling them cognate. It becomes an instinct almost, I suppose, with people in the trade.

'But I hardly know how far I ought to spend any time in such things. Elementary grammars for our own missionaries and teachers are useful, and the time is well spent in writing them. Hence it is that I do not write longer letters. Oh! how I enjoy writing un-business letters; but I can't help it—it's part of my business now to write dull Reports—i.e. reports that I can't help making dull, and all the rest of it....

'I cannot write about Bishop Mackenzie. Mr. Pritt (at 9.30 P.M. the night we landed) put his head into my room and said, "Bishop Mackenzie is dead," and I sat and sat on and knelt and could not take it all in! I cannot understand what the papers say of his modus operandi, yet I know that it was an error of judgment, if an error at all, and there may be much which we do not know. So I suspend my opinion.'

In a letter to myself, written by the same mail, in reply to one in which I had begged him to consider what was the sight, to a Christian man, of slaves driven off with heavy yokes on their necks, and whether it did not justify armed interposition, he replies with arguments that it is needless now to repeat, but upholding the principle that the shepherd is shepherd to the cruel and erring as well as to the oppressed, and ought not to use force. The opinion is given most humbly and tenderly, for he had a great veneration for his brother Missionary

Bishop. Commenting on the fact that Bishop Selwyn's speech at Cambridge had made Charles Mackenzie a missionary, and that he would gladly have hailed an invitation to the Australasian field of labour, the letter proceeds:—

'How wonderful it is to reflect upon the events of the last few years! Had he come out when I did to New Zealand, I might be now his Missionary Chaplain; and yet it is well that there should be two missionary dioceses, and without the right man for the African Mission, there might have been a difficulty in carrying out the plan.

'The chapel is not built yet, for I have sixty mouths to feed, and other buildings must be thought of for health's sake. But I have settled all that in my will.'

'In a postscript is mentioned the arrival of some exquisite altar plate for the College chapel, which had been offered by a lady, who had also bountifully supplied with chronometers and nautical instruments the 'Southern Cross,' which was fast being built at Southampton.

The above letter was accompanied by one to Dr. Moberly:—

'St. Andrew's College, Kohimarama: Nov. 18, 1862.

'My dear Dr. Moberly,—Thank you heartily for writing to me. It is a real help to me and to others also, I think, of my party to be in communication with those whom we have long respected, and whose prayers we now more than ever earnestly ask. We returned on November 7 from a very remarkable voyage.

'I was nineteen weeks absent all but a day: sailed far beyond our most distant island in my previous voyage, landed nearly eighty times amidst (often) 300 and more natives, naked, armed, &c., and on no less than thirty or forty places never trodden before (as far as I know) by the foot of a white man. Not one arm was lifted up against me, not one bow drawn or spear shaken. I think of it all quietly now with a sort of wondering thankfulness.

'From not less than eight islands we have now for the first time received native lads; and not only are openings being thus made for us in many directions, but the permanent training of our old scholars is going on most favourably; so that by the blessing of God we hope, at all events in the Banks Islands, to carry on continuously the Mission Schools during the winter and summer also. We have spent the three last winters here, but it would not be wise to run the risk of the damp hot climate in the summer. Natives of the island must do this, and thank God there are natives being raised up now to do it. The enclosed translation of a note. It is but three or four years since the language was reduced to writing, and here is a young man writing down his thoughts to me after a long talk about the question of his being baptized.

'Four others there are soon, by God's blessing, to be baptized also—Sarawia from Vanua Lava, Tagalana from Aroa, Pasvorang from Eowa, Woleg from Mota, and others are pressing on; Taroniara from San Cristoval, Kanambat from New Caledonia, &c. I tell you their names, for you will I know, remember them in your prayers.

'Will you kindly let Mr. Keble see the enclosed note? It does not, of course, give much idea of the lad's state of mind; but he is thoroughly in earnest, and as for his knowledge of his duty there can be no question there. He really knows his

Catechism. I have scarcely a minute to write by this mail. Soon you will have, I hope, a sketch of our last voyage. We remember you all, benefactors and benefactresses, daily. Thank you again for writing to me: it humbles me, as it ought to do, to receive such a letter from you.

'Very faithfully yours,

'J. C. PATTESON, Missionary Bishop.'

These names deserve note: Sarawia the first to be ordained of the Melanesian Church; and Taroniara, who was to share his Bishop's death. B———, as will be seen, has had a far more chequered course. Tagalana is described in another letter as having the thoughtfulness of one who knows that he has the seeds of early death in him; but he, the living lectern at the consecration, has lived to be the first deacon of his island of Aroa.

The ensuing is to the Rev. Derwent Coleridge, at that time Principal of St. Mark's Training College, Chelsea, upon the question whether that institution would afford assistants:—

'Auckland, New Zealand: Nov. 15, 1862.

'My dear Cousin,—You will not be surprised, I hope, to hear from me; I only wish I had written to you long ago. But until quite recently we could not speak with so much confidence concerning the Melanesian Mission, and it is of little use to write vaguely on matters which I am anxious now to make known to you.

'The general plan of the Mission you may get some notion of from the last year's Report (which I send), and possibly you may have heard or seen something about it in former years. This last voyage of nineteen weeks, just concluded, has determined me to write to you; for the time is come when we want helpers indeed, and I think that you will expect me naturally to turn to you.

'It is not only that very many islands throughout the South Pacific, from the Loyalty Islands on to the northwest as far as Ysabel Island in the Solomon group, are now yielding up scholars and affording openings for Mission stations, though this indeed is great matter for thankfulness; but there is, thank God, a really working staff gathered round us from the Banks Archipelago, which affords a definite field, already partially occupied with a regular system at work in it; and here young persons may receive the training most needed for them, actually on a heathen island, though soon not to be without some few Christians amongst its population. Now I can say to anyone willing and qualified to help me:—

'In the six summer months there is the central school work in New Zealand, where now there are with me fifty-one Melanesians from twenty-four islands, speaking twenty-three languages; and in the six winter months there is a station regularly occupied on Mota Island, where all the necessary experience of life in the islands can be acquired.

'I am not in any hurry for men. Norfolk Island has given me five young fellows from twenty-one to sixteen years of age, who already are very useful. One has been with me a year, another four months. They are given unreservedly into my hands, and already are working well into our school, taking the superintendence of our cooking, e.g., off our hands; with some help from us, they will be very useful at once as helpers on Mota, doing much in the way of gardening, putting up huts, &c., which will free us for more teaching work, &c., and they are being educated by us with an eye to their future employment (D.V.) as missionaries. I would not wish for better fellows; their moral and religious conduct is really singularly good—you know their circumstances and the character of the whole community. But I should be thankful by-and-by to have men equally willing to do anything, yet better educated in respect of book knowledge. No one is ever asked to do what we are not willing to do, and generally in the habit of doing ourselves —cooking, working, &c., &c. But the Melanesian lads really do all this kind of work now. I have sixty mouths to fill here now; and Melanesian boys, told out week by week, do the whole of the cooking (simple enough, of course) for us all with perfect punctuality. I don't think any particular taste for languages necessary at all. Anyone who will work hard at it can learn the language of the particular class assigned to him. Earnest, bright, cheerful fellows, without that notion of "making sacrifices," &c., perpetually occurring to their minds, would be invaluable. You know the kind of men, who have got rid of the conventional notion that more self-denial is needed for a missionary than for a sailor or soldier, who are sent anywhere, and leave home and country for years, and think nothing of it, because they go "on duty." Alas! we don't so read our ordination vows. A fellow with a healthy, active tone of mind, plenty of enterprise and some enthusiasm, who makes the best of everything, and above all does not think himself better than other people because he is engaged in Mission work—that is the fellow we want. I assume, of course, the existence of sound religious principle as the greatest qualification of all. Now, if there be any young persons whom you could wish to see engaged in this Mission now at St. Mark's, or if you know of any such and feel justified in speaking to them, you will be doing a great kindness to me, and, I believe, aiding materially in this work.

'I should not wish at all any young man to be pledged to anything; as on my part I will not pledge myself to accept, much less ordain, any man of whom I have no personal knowledge. But let anyone really in earnest, with a desire and intention (as far as he is concerned) to join the Mission, come to me about December or January in any year. Then he will live at the Mission College till the end of April, and can see for himself the mode of life at the Central Summer School in New Zealand. Then let him take a voyage with me, see Melanesians in their own homes, stop for a while at Mota—e.g. make trial of the climate, &c., &c., and then let me have my decisive talk with him.

'If he will not do for the work, I must try and find other employment for him in some New Zealand diocese, or help to pay his passage home. I don't think such a person as you would recommend would fail to make himself useful; but I must say plainly that I would rather not have a man from England at all, than be bound to accept a man who might not thoroughly and cordially work into the general system that we have adopted. We live together entirely, all meals in common, same cabin, same hut, and the general life and energy of us all would be damaged by the introduction of any one discordant element. You will probably say, "Men won't go out on these terms," and this is indeed probable, yet if they are the right fellows for this work—a work wholly anomalous, unlike all other work that they have thought of in many respects—they will think that what I say is reasonable, and like the prospect all the better (I think) because they see that it means downright work in a cheery, happy, hopeful, friendly spirit.

'A man who takes the sentimental view of coral islands and cocoa-nuts, of course, is worse than useless; a man possessed with the idea that he is making a sacrifice will never do; and a man who thinks any kind of work "beneath a gentleman" will simply be in the way, and be rather uncomfortable at seeing the Bishop do what he thinks degrading to do himself. I write all this quite freely, wishing to convey, if possible, some idea to you of the kind of men we need. And if the right fellow is moved by God's grace to come out, what a welcome we will give him, and how happy he will soon be in a work the abundant blessings of which none can know as we know them. There are three clergymen with me. Mr. Pritt, who came out with the Bishop of Nelson as his chaplain, but who, I am thankful to say, is regularly part and parcel of the Mission staff; Mr. Dudley, ordained last year, who for six years has been in the Mission, and has had the special advantage of being trained under the Primate's eye; and Mr. Kerr who was also ordained about ten months ago.

'I give 100 pounds to a clergyman when ordained, increasing it 101 annually to a maximum of 150 pounds. But this depends upon subscriptions, &c. I could not pledge myself even to this, except in the case of a man very highly recommended. But of this I will write more.

'Again let me say that I do not want anyone yet, not this year. I shall be off again (D.V.) in the beginning of May 1863, for six months; and if then I find on my return (D.V.) in November, letters from you, either asking me to write with reference to any young man, or informing me that one is on the way out, that will be quite soon enough.

'I need not say I don't expect any such help so soon, if at all.

'Finally, pray don't think that I underrate the great advantage of having such persons as St. Mark's produces; but I write guardedly. My kind love to Mrs. Derwent.

'Affectionately yours,

'J. C. PATTESON, Missionary Bishop.'

On the 29th of December, after two pages of affectionate remarks on various family incidents, the letter proceeds:—

'We are having an extra scrubbing in preparation for our visitors on Thursday, who may wish to be with us on the occasion of the baptism of our six Banks Islanders; and I am writing in the midst of it, preferring to sit in the schoolroom to my own room, which is very tiny and very hot.

'We have some eight only out of the fifty-one whom I am obliged to treat rather as an awkward squad, not that they are too stupid to learn, but that we cannot give them the individual attention that is necessary. They teach me their language; but I cannot put them into any class where they could be regularly taught—indeed, they are not young fellows whom I should bring again. They do the work of introducing us to their islands, and of teaching us something of their language. So I continue to give them what little time I can—the real strength of our force being given to those whom we hope to have here again.

'We are all on the qui vive about our beautiful vessel, hoping to see it in about six or eight weeks. It will, please God, be for years the great means by which we may carry on the Mission if we live; and all the care that has been spent upon it has been well spent, you may be sure.

'I don't want to appear as if I expected this to be done in one sense, but it is only when I think of the personal interest shown in it that I suppose it right to thank people much. I don't want it to be thought of any more than you do as a gift to us particular missionaries. It is the Church carrying on its own work. Yet, as you truly say, private feelings and interests are not to be treated rudely; and I do think it a very remarkable thing that some 2,000 pounds should be raised by subscriptions, especially when one knows that so very few people have an idea of the work that is being done.'

'What a blessed New Year's rejoicing in hope here follows:—

'Kohimarama: Jan. 1, 1863.

'My dearest Sisters,—The first letter of the year to you! Thank God for bringing us to see it! It is 1 P.M., and at 4.30 P.M. six dear children (from twenty-two to fourteen) are to be baptized. Everything in one sense is done; how very little in the other and higher sense! May Almighty God pour the fulness of His blessing upon them! I sit and look at them, and my heart is too full for words. They sit with me, and bring their little notes with questions that they scarcely dare trust themselves to speak about. You will thank God for giving me such comfort, such blessings, and such dear children. How great a mercy it is! How unexpected! May God make me humble and patient through it all!

'What a sight it would be for you four hours hence! Our party of sixty-one, visitors from Auckland, the glorious day, and the holy service, for which all meet.

'I use Proper Psalms, 89, 96, 126, 145, and for lessons a few verses, 2 Kings v. 9-15, and Acts viii. 35-9. After the third Collect, the Primate may say a few words, or I may do so; and then I shall use our usual Melanesian Collect for many islands, very briefly named; and so conclude with the Blessing.

'What this is to me you must try and realise, that you may be partakers of my joy and thankfulness. To have Christians about me, to whom I can speak with a certainty of being understood, to feel that we are all bound together in the blessed Communion of the Body of Christ, to know that angels on high are rejoicing and evil spirits being chased away, that all the Banks Islands and all Melanesia are experiencing, as it were, the first shock of a mighty earthquake, that God who foresees the end may, in his merciful Providence, be calling even these very children to bear His message to thousands of heathens, is not it too much? One's heart is not large enough for it, and confession of one's own unworthiness breaks off involuntarily into praise and glory!

'I know, my dear Sisters, that this is most likely one of the great blessings that precede great trials. I can't expect or wish (perhaps) always to sail with a fair wind, yet I try to remember that trial must come, without on that account restraining myself from a deep taste of the present joy. I can't describe it!

'Then we have now much that we ever can talk about—deep talk about Mota and the other islands, and the special temptations to which they must be exposed; that now is the time when the devil will seek with all his might to "have" them, and so hinder God's work in the land; that they have been specially blest by God to be the first to desire to know His will, and that they have heavy responsibilities.

'"Yes," they say, "we see man does not know that his room is dirty and full of cobwebs while it is all dark; and another man, whose room is not half so dirty, because the sun shines into it and shows the dirt, thinks his room much worse than the other. That is like our hearts. It is worse now to be angry than it was to shoot a man a long time ago. But the more the sun shines in, the more we shall find cobwebs and dirt, long after we thought the room was clean. Yes, we know what that means. We asked you what would help us to go on straight in the path, now that we are entering at the gate. We said prayer, love, helping our countrymen. Now we see besides watchfulness, self-examination; and then you say we must at once look forward to being confirmed, as the people you confirmed at Norfolk Island. Then there is the very great thing, the holy and the great, the Supper of the Lord." So, evening by evening and day by day, we talk, this being of course not called school, being, indeed, my great relaxation, for this is the time when they are like children with a father.

'I know I feel it so. Don't take the above as a fair sample of our talk, for the more solemn words we say about God's Love, Christ's Intercession, and the Indwelling of the Spirit, I can hardly write down now.

'Your loving Brother,

'**J. C. P.**

'P.S.—Feast of the Epiphany. Those dear children were baptized on Thursday. A most solemn interesting scene it was!'

Thoroughly happy indeed was the Bishop at this time. In a note of February 3 to the Bishop of Wellington, he speaks of the orderly state of the College:—

'Mr. Pritt has made a complete change in the Melanesian school, very properly through me; not putting himself forward, but talking with me, suggesting, accepting suggestions, giving the benefit of his great knowledge of boys and the ways to educate them. All the punctuality, order, method, &c., are owing to him; and he is so bright and hearty, thoroughly at ease with the boys, and they with him.'

The same note announces two more recruits—Mr. John Palmer, a theological student at St. John's, and Joseph Atkin, the only son of a settler in the neighbourhood, who had also held a scholarship there. He had gained it in 1860, after being educated at the Taranaki Scotch School and the Church of England Grammar School at Parnell, and his abilities were highly thought of. The Bishop says:—

'Joe Atkin, you will be glad to hear, has joined us on probation till next Christmas, but he is very unlikely to change his mind. He and his father have behaved in a very straightforward manner. I am not at all anxious to get fellows here in a hurry. The Norfolk Islanders, e.g., are in need of training much more than our best Melanesians, less useful as teachers, cooks, even as examples. This will surprise you, but it is so.

'I have long suspected that Joe thought about joining us. He tells me, "You never would give me a chance to speak to you, Sir."

"Quite true, Joe; I wished the thought to work itself out in your own mind, and then I thought it right to speak first to your father."

'I told him that I could offer but "a small and that an uncertain salary" should he be ordained five years hence; and that he ought to think of that, that there was nothing worldly in his wishing to secure a maintenance by-and-by for wife and child, and that I much doubted my power to provide it. But this did not at all shake either his father or him. I have a great regard for the lad, and I know you have.'

From that time forward reading with and talking with 'Joe Atkin' was one of the chief solaces of the Bishop's life, though at present the young man was only on trial, and could not as yet fill the place of Mr. Benjamin Dudley, who, soon after the voyage, married, and returned to Canterbury settlement. The loss was felt, as appears in the following:—

'Kohimarama; Saturday, 1 P.M., Feb. 7, 1863.

'My dearest Sisters,—I have a heavy cold, so you must expect a stupid letter. I am off in an hour or two for a forty-mile ride, to take to-morrow's services (four) among soldiers and settlers. The worst of it is that I have no chance of sleep at the end, for the mosquitos near the river are intolerable. How jolly it would be, nevertheless, if you were here, and strong enough to make a sort of picnic ride of it. I do it this way: strap in front of the saddle a waterproof sheet, with my silk gown, Prayer-book, brush and comb, razor and soap, a clean tie, and a couple of sea biscuits. Then at about 3 P.M. off I go. About twenty miles or so bring me to Papakura, an ugly but good road most of the way. Here there is an inn. I stop for an hour and a half, give the horse a good feed, and have my tea. At about 7.30 or 8 I start again, and ride slowly along a good road this dry weather. The moon rises at 9.30, and by that time I shall be reaching the forest, through which a good military road runs. This is the part of the road I should like to show you. Such a night as this promises to be! It will be beautiful. About 11 I reach a hut made of reeds on the very brink of the river, tether the horse, give him a feed, which I carry with me from Papakura, light a fire (taking matches) inside the hut, and try to smoke away mosquitos, lie down in your plaid, Joan—do you remember giving it to me?—and get what sleep I can. To-morrow I work my way home again, the fourth service being at Papakura at 4 P.M., so I ought to be at Kohimarama by 9 P.M., dead tired I expect. I think these long days tire me more than they did; and I really do see not a few white hairs, a dozen or so, this is quite right and respectable.

'I am writing now because I am tired with this cold, but chiefly because when I write only for the mail I send you such wretched scrawls, just business letters, or growls about something or other which I magnify into a grievance. But really, dear Joan and Fan, I do like much writing to you; only it is so very seldom I can do so, without leaving undone some regular part of the day's work. I am quite aware that you want to know more details about my daily life, and I really wish to supply them; but then I am so weary when I get a chance of writing, that I let my mind drift away with my pen, instead of making some effort to write thoughtfully. How many things I should like to talk about, and which I ought to write about: Bishops Mackenzie and Colenso, the true view of what heathenism is, Church government, the real way to hope to get at the mass of heathens at home, the need of a different education in some respects for the clergy, &c. But I have already by the time I begin to write taken too much out of myself in other ways to grapple with such subjects, and so I merely spin out a yarn about my own special difficulties and anxieties.

'Don't mind my grumbling. I think that it is very ungrateful of me to do so, when, this year especially, I am receiving such blessings; it is partly because I am very much occupied, working at high pressure, partly because I do not check my foolish notions, and let matters worry me. I don't justify it a bit; nor must you suppose that because I am very busy just now, I am really the worse for it. The change to sea life will set me all to rights again; and I feel that much work must be done in a little time, and a wise man would take much more pains than I do to keep himself in a state fit to do it.

'I have told you about our manner of life here. Up at 5, when I go round and pull the blankets, not without many a joke, off the sleeping boys, many of the party are already up and washing. Then, just before prayers, I go into the kitchen and see that all is ready for breakfast. Prayers at 5.45 in English, Mota, Baura, &c., beginning with a Mota Hymn, and ending with the Lord's Prayer in English. Breakfast immediately after: at our table Mr. Pritt, Mr. Kerr, and young Atkin who has just joined us. At the teachers' table, five Norfolk Islanders, Edward (a Maori), five girls and two of their husbands, and the three girls being placed at this table because they are girls; Melanesians at the other three tables indiscriminately. There are four windows, one at the north, three at the east side. The school and chapel, in one long modern building, form the corresponding wing on the eastern side of my little room, and the boys dormitories between.

'We are daily expecting the vessel, though it will be a quick passage for her if she comes in the next ten days, and then what a bustle!

'We send Dudley and his wife away to Canterbury for eight or nine months; he is so weak as to make the change, which I had urged him to try for some time past, quite necessary.

'Next Sunday a Confirmation at Orehunga, eight miles off; back to Auckland for catechising and Baptism at 3 p.m. and evening service at 6.30, and never a word of either sermon written, and all the school work! Never mind, a good growl to you is a fine restorative, and really I get on very well somehow.

'Well, good-bye, you dear Sisters,

'Your affectionate Brother,

'J. C. P.'

On the last day of February came the new 'Southern Cross,' and two delightful notes announced it to the Vicar of Hursley and to myself in one envelope.

'St. Andrew's: Feb. 28, 1863.

'My dear Cousin,—The "Southern Cross" arrived safely this morning. Thanks to God!

'What it is to us even you can hardly tell; I know not how to pour out my thankfulness. She seems admirably adapted for the work. Mr. Tilly's report of her performance is most satisfactory: safe, fast, steers well, and very manageable. Internal arrangements very good; after cabin too luxurious, but then that may be wanted for sick folk, and as it is luxurious, why I shall get a soft bed, and take to it very kindly.

'Pray let dear Mr. Keble and Dr. Moberly know at once how very happy and thankful I am for this blessing. I know all you good friends at home will try to picture to yourselves my delight as I jumped on board!

'The boys are, of course, wild with excitement. It is blowing very hard. Last night (when we were thinking of them) it was an anxious night for them close on the coast.

'I have no time to write more. I thought of Lady... as I looked at the chronometers and instruments, and of you all as I looked at the beautiful vessel slipping along through the water with scarce a stitch of canvas. I pray that she may be spared many years to the Mission, and that we may have grace to use her, as she ought to be used, to His glory.

'Your affectionate Cousin,

'J. C. PATTESON, Bishop.

'You know that you are daily remembered in our prayers. God bless you.'

'10.30 P.M., March 1, 1863.

'My dear Mr. Keble,—One line, though on Sunday night, to tell you of the safe arrival of the "Southern Cross." You have a large share in her, and she has a large share in your good wishes and prayers, I am sure.

'Solemn thoughts on this day, an Ordination Sunday, mingle with the joy at the coming of this messenger (I trust of mercy and peace). I need not ask you to pray continually for us, for I know you do so. But indeed, now is the time when we seem especially to need your prayers.

'The lads have no lack of intellectual capacity, they not unfrequently surprise me. Now is the time when they are in the receptive state, and now especially any error on our part may give a wrong direction to the early faith of thousands! What an awful thought! We are their only teachers, the only representatives of Christianity among them. How inexpressibly solemn and fearful! This is the thought so perpetually present to me. The training of the future missionaries of Melanesia is, by God's Providence, placed in our hands. No wonder that I feel sometimes overwhelmed at the thought!

'But I know that if God gives me grace to become more simple-minded and humble, He will order even this aright. You I know will pray more than ever for me. My kindest regards to Mrs. Keble; I hope she is better.

'Your affectionate and grateful young Friend,

'J. C. PATTESON, Missionary Bishop.'

Before the first joy of the arrival was over, ere the 'Southern Cross' could make her first voyage among the multitude of isles, a great calamity had fallen upon St. Andrew's. Whether it was from the large numbers, or the effect of the colder climate, or from what cause could not be told, but a frightful attack of dysentery fell upon the Melanesians, and for several weeks suffering and death prevailed among them. How Bishop Patteson tended them during this time can be better guessed than described.

Archdeacon Lloyd, who came to assist in the cares of the small party of clergy, can find no words to express the devotion with which the Bishop nursed them, comforting and supporting them, never shrinking from the most repulsive offices, even bearing out the dead silently at night, lest the others should see and be alarmed.

Still no mail, except during the voyages, had ever left New Zealand without a despatch for home; and time was snatched in the midst of all this distress for a greeting, in the same beautiful, clear minute hand as usual:—

'Hospital, St. Andrew's: Saturday night, 9 P.M., March 22, 1863.

'My dearest Brother and Sister,—I write from the dining hall (now our hospital), with eleven Melanesians lying round me in extremity of peril. I buried two to-day in one grave, and I baptized another now dying by my side.

'God has been pleased in His wisdom and mercy to send upon us a terrible visitation, a most virulent form of dysentery. Since this day fortnight I have scarce slept night or day, but by snatching an hour here and there; others are working quite as hard, and all the good points of our Melanesian staff are brought out, as you may suppose.

'The best medical men cannot suggest any remedy. All remedies have been tried and failed. Every conceivable kind of treatment has been tried in vain. There are in the hall (the hospital now) at this moment eleven—eleven more in the little quadrangle, better, but in as anxious a state as can be; and two more not at all well.

'I have sent all the rest on board to be out of the way of contagion. How we go on I scarce know.... My good friend, Mr. Lloyd, is here, giving great help; he is well acquainted with sickness and a capital nurse.

'I have felt all along that it would be good for us to be in trouble; we could not always sail with a fair wind, I have often said so, and God has sent the trial in the most merciful way. What is this to the falling away of our baptized scholars!

'But it is a pitiful sight! How wonderfully they bear the agony of it. No groaning.

'When I buried those two children to-day, my heart was full, I durst not think, but could only pray and believe and trust in Him. God bless you.

'Your loving Brother,

'**J. C. P.**

'O Lord, correct me, but with judgment!'

On the 25th, two more were dead, and buried without time to make coffins, for thirteen still hung between life and death, while fresh cases were sent from on board ship. Mr. Pritt and Mr. Palmer cooked nourishing food and prepared rice-water unceasingly; while the others tended the sick, and the Primate returned from a journey to give his effective aid. On the night of the 30th, a fifth died unexpectedly, having only been ill a week, the only scholar from Pentecost Island. One of these lads, when all hope was over, was wrapped in his white winding sheet, carried into the chapel, and there baptized by the Bishop, with choked voice and weeping eyes.

Over those who had not faith enough to justify him in baptizing them, he said the following prayers as he laid them in their graves:—

'Sentences. Psalms from the Burial Service.

'Forasmuch as it hath pleased Thee, O Almighty God, to take from amongst us the souls of these two children committed to our charge, we therefore commit their bodies to the ground; earth to earth, ashes to ashes, dust to dust; humbly commending to Thy Fatherly mercy these and all other Thy children who know not Thee, whom Thou knowest, who art the Father and Lord of all things in heaven and earth, to whom be all praise and glory, with Thy Son, Jesus Christ, and the Holy Spirit, for ever and ever. Amen.

'We humbly beseech Thee, most merciful God, to remember for good the inhabitants of the islands of Melanesia, and specially we pray God by the grave of these children, for the dwellers in Vanua Lava and Ambrym that Thou wouldest cause the light of the Gospel to shine in their hearts. Give unto Thy servants grace in their sight, that we may go forth in peace, and return if it be Thy will in safety, to the honour and glory of Thy Name, through Jesus Christ our Lord.

'O Almighty God, Father of Mercy, we cry unto Thee in our sorrow and distress, most humbly confessing that we have most justly provoked Thy wrath and heavy indignation.

'We know, O Lord, that this is a dispensation of mercy, a gift from Thee, to be used, as all things may be used to Thy glory. Yet, O Lord, suffer not our unworthiness to hinder Thy work of mercy!

'O Lord, look down from heaven, visit with Thy tender compassion Thy children lying under Thy hand in grievous sufferings of body. Restore them if it be Thy good pleasure to health and strength, or if it be Thy good will to take them out of this world, receive them to Thy tender mercies for His blessed sake who died for all men, Thy Son our Lord.

'Lord's Prayer. Grace.'

This was written down for use, in great haste, in the same spirit that breathes through the account of the next death: the entry dated on Coleridge Patteson's thirty-sixth birthday, April 1, 1863, which must be transcribed, though much of the detail of this time of trial has been omitted.

'Sosaman died at 9 A.M. this day—a dear lad, one of the Banks Islanders, about ten or twelve years old. As usual I was kneeling by him, closing his eyes in death. I can see his poor mother's face now! What will she say to me? she who knows not the Christian's life in death! Yet to him, the poor unbaptized child, what is it to him? What a revelation! Yes, the names he heard at our lips were names of real things and real persons! There is another world! There is a God, a Father, a Lord Jesus Christ, a Spirit of holiness, a Love and Glory. So let us leave him, O Father, in Thy hands, who knowest him who knew not Thee on earth. Thy mercies never fail. Thou hast created all things, and for Thy pleasure they are and were created.

'I washed him, and laid him out as usual in a linen sheet. How white it looked! So much more simple and touching than the coffin—the form just discernible as it lay where five had lain before; and then I knelt down in our little chapel; and, I thank God, I could still bless and praise Him in my heart!

'How is it that I don't pray more? I pray in one sense less than usual—am not so long on my knees. I hope it is that I am so worn out, and so very, very much occupied in tending the sick and dying, but I am not sure.

'Anyhow I am sure that I am learning at terrible cost lessons which, it may be, God would have taught me more gently if I had ears to hear. I have not in all things depended upon Him, and perpetually sought help from Him.

'Oh that my unworthiness may not hinder His work of mercy!

'If I live, the retrospect of this most solemn time will, I hope, be very useful. I wonder if I ever went through such acute mental suffering, and yet, mind! I feel perfectly hardened at times—quite devoid of sensibility.'

He said in another letter that he felt that if he relaxed his self-command for one moment he should entirely break down. To him writing to his beloved home was what speaking, nay, almost thinking, would be in another man; it gave an outlet to his feeling, and security of sympathy. There was something in his spiritual nature that gave him the faculty of realising the Communion of Saints in its fullest sense, both with those on earth and in Paradise; and, above all, with his Heavenly Father, so that he seems as complete an example as ever lived of the reality of that privilege, in which too often we only express our belief.

Sosaman's was the last death. On a fragment of pink paper, bearing the date of the next day, it is declared that an alleviation in the worst symptoms had taken place, and that the faces and eyes were less haggard. 'Oh! if it be God's will to grant us now a great deliverance, all glory be to Him!'

The deliverance was granted. The next mail brought tidings of gladness:—

'St. Andrew's: April 17, 1863.

'My dearest Sisters,—You know the calm yet weary feeling that succeeds to the period of intense anxiety and constant watchfulness. Six dear children are taken from us, as you know already. Some twenty-one others have been very ill, nigh unto death. Two or three are still weak, but doing well.

'All the rest are convalescent. Oh! I look at them, to see the loving bright smile again on their poor wan faces. I don't mind breaking down now; yet I have experienced no decided reaction; only I am very indolent, like one who, for six weeks, has not had his usual allowance of sleep. What abundant cause we have for thankfulness! All the many hours that I spent in that atmosphere, and yet not a whit the worse for it. What a sight it was! What scenes of suffering! There seemed to be no end to it; and yet there was always strength for the immediate work in hand. Tending twenty-four sick, after hurrying back from burying two dear lads in one grave, or with a body lying in its white sheet in the chapel; and once, after a breathless watch of two hours, while they all slept the sleep of opium, for we dared almost anything to obtain some rest, stealing at dead of night across the room to the figure wrapped so strangely in its blanket, and finding it cold and stiff, while one dying lay close by. It has been a solemn time indeed. And now the brightness seems to be coming back.

'I have not yet ceased to think of the probable consequences; but, speaking somewhat hastily, I do not think that this will much retard the work. I may have to use some extra caution in some places—e.g., one of the two first lads brought from Ambrym is dead: one lad, the only one ever brought from the middle of Whitsuntide Island, is dead; I must be careful there. The other four came from Mota, Matlavo, Vanua Lava (W. side), and Guadalcanar; for the six who died came from six islands.

'One dear lad, Edmund Quintal, sixteen or seventeen years old, was for a while in a critical state. Fisher Young, a little older, was very unwell for three or four days. They came from Norfolk Island.

'The last six weeks have been very unhealthy. We had an unusually hot dry summer—quite a drought; the wells, for example, were never so tried. There was also an unusual continuance of north-east winds—our sultry close wind. And when the dry weather broke up, the rain and damp weather continued for many days. Great sickness prevailed in Auckland and the country generally.

'The Norfolk Islanders, now four in number—Edwin Nobbs, Gilbert Christian, Fisher Young, and Edmund Quintal—have behaved excellently. Oh, how different I was at their age! It is pleasant, indeed, to see them so very much improved; they are so industrious, so punctual, so conscientious. The fact seems to be that they wanted just what I do hope the routine of our life has supplied—careful supervision, advice, and, when needed, reproof. They had never had any training at all.

'But there was something better—religious feeling—to work on! and the life here has, by God's blessing, developed the good in them. I am very hopeful about then now. Not, mind! that any one of them has a notion of teaching, but they are acquiring habits which will enable them to be good examples in all points of moral conduct to those of the Melanesians who are not already like B——, &c. The head work will come by-and-by, I dare say.

'April 22.—The storm seems to have passed, though one or two are still very weak. But there are no active symptoms of disease. How mercifully God has dealt with us! I have been very seedy for a few days, and am so still. In spite of two teeth taken out a fortnight ago, my whole jaw has been paining me much, heavy cold, and I can't get good sleep by reason of the pain, and I want sleep much. I think I must go to the dentist again. You see we hope to sail in ten days or so, and I want to be well.

'We have just washed and scrubbed the hall thoroughly, and once again it ceases to be our hospital. That looks bright, does not it? You must let all friends know about us, for I shall not be able to write to many, and perhaps I shall not have time to write at all. In the midst of all this, I have so much work about the management of the Mission farm and property, and the St. John's College estate, and educational prospects.'

The 'Southern Cross' was at sea again on May 2, and approved herself entirely to her owners' satisfaction.

Moreover, another clergyman had come on board for a trial trip, the Rev. Robert Codrington, a Fellow of Wadham, Oxford, who brought the University culture which was no small personal pleasure to Bishop Patteson in the companion of his labours. So that the staff consisted of Mr. Pritt, Mr. Kerr, Mr. Codrington, Mr.

Palmer and Mr. Atkin, besides Mr. Tilly, whose management of the vessel left the Bishop free from cares whenever his knowledge of the coast was not needed. Some of the results of his leisure on the outward voyage here appear:—

'I am glad I have read the accounts which Bishop Mackenzie's sister sent me. I know more about it now. Work and anxiety and necessity for action all came upon them so rapidly, that there was but little time for forming deliberate plans. I can well realise the finding oneself surrounded with a hundred poor creatures, diseased and hungered, the multitude of questions how to feed, lodge, and clothe them. How far it is right to sanction their mode of life, &c. One thing I am glad to notice, that the Bishop abstained from all attempts to convey religious instruction, because he was not sufficiently acquainted with the language to know what ideas he might or might not be suggesting. That was wise, and yet how unlike many hot-headed men, who rush with unintentional irreverence into very dangerous experiments.

'I confess, as you know, that there seems to me far too cumbrous and expensive and talkative a method employed in England, for raising supplies for that Mission and Columbia, Honolulu, &c. I never think of all that fuss of the four Universities, and all the meetings and speeches, without some shame. But united action will come in the train of real synodical action; and if I understand aright, the last Convocation of Canterbury accepted all that we are trying for, taking the right view in the question of Provinces, Metropolitans, position of Colonial Churches, joint action of the Church at large, &c. Extension of Episcopate in England. Oh, thanks be to God for it all. What a work for this branch of the Catholic Church! How can people sit quiet, not give their all!

'I like very much Vaughan's work on the Epistle to the Romans. That is the book to teach young students how to read their Greek Testament. Accurate scholarship, no private notions imported into the Greek text. I should like to hear Mr. Keble speak about the law underlying the superstitions of heathenism, the way to deal with the perversions of truth, &c. Somehow I get to marvel at and love that first book of Hooker more and more. It is wonderful. It goes to the bottom of the matter; and then at times it gives one to see something of the Divine wisdom of the Bible as one never saw it before.

'But I fear that I seek too much after a knowledge and understanding of principles of action which are attainable by a scholar and man of real reasoning power, but which I am not able to make of practical use, having neither the brains nor the goodness. This is what I really mean.

'May 20th.—Any really good book on the New Testament, especially dealing critically with the Greek text, I certainly wish to have. I feel that the great neglect of us clergy is the neglect of the continual study most critically and closely of the grammatical meaning of the Hebrew and Greek texts. Oh! that in old days I had made myself a good scholar! Oh! that I did really know Hebrew and Greek well! What a blessing and delight it would be now! I fear that I shall never be a good Hebrew scholar, I can't make time for it; but a decent Greek scholar I hope to be. I work away, but alas I for want of time, only by fits and starts, at grammars, and such a book as Vaughan's "Epistle to the Romans," an excellent specimen of the way to give legitimate help to the student. Trench's books I delight in. The Revision by Five Clergymen is an assistance. There was a review in the Quarterly the other day on the Greek Testament, very nearly an excellent one. The ordinary use of folio commentaries I don't wish to depreciate, but I think it far less valuable than the diligent study for oneself with the best grammatical aids of the original text. I always assume an acquaintance with the true mind and spirit of the Church of England as a substratum of interpretation. I like Westcott's book on the "Introduction to the Study of the Gospels."

'Oh! why, when I sat evening after evening with our dear Father, did I not ask him on all these points much more than I did? He did talk of such things! But I suppose it is partly the impulse given to such studies by the tendency of present religious thought. Yet ought it not to have been always put forward at Eton and Oxford that the close study of the text of the Bible is the first duty of a Christian scholar. I never really thought of it till I came out here, and then other occupations crowded upon me, and so it was too late to make myself a scholar. Alas!

'Now I really think nothing is so great a relaxation tome as a good book by Trench, or Vaughan, or Ellicott, or Dr. Pusey, and I do enjoy it. Not that I can keep up my attention for very long so as to make it profitable, but even then it is delightful, only I must go over it again, and so it is perhaps time wasted.

'But I greatly miss the intimate friend with whom to fix what I read by conversation and communication of mutual difficulties in understanding passages. I don't often forget points on which the Judge and I have had a talk, but what I read by myself I read too quickly, and forget. I want to fix it by subsequent discussion and enquiry with a competent friend. If I have intelligent young men to read with, that will almost do, it will easily help me to remember what I have read. It won't be suggestive, like the Judge's conversation; yet if one tries to teach conscientiously one does learn a great deal. I am puzzled as to books for my Norfolk Islanders. I should like much the "Conversations on the Catechism." Are they published separately? Shall I ask Miss Yonge to give me a copy? And the "Plain Commentary" would be useful too, if (which I doubt) it is plain enough.'

'"Southern Cross:" May 9, 1863.

'My dear Joan,—You ask me about qualifications which a man had better possess for this Mission, so perhaps I had better ask you to enquire of cousin Derwent Coleridge and of Ernest Hawkins for letters written to them some six months ago in which (if I remember rightly) I succeeded as well as I am likely to do now in describing the class of men I should like some day to have. I dare say they have not kept the letters, I forgot that, because although they took me some little time to write, they may have chucked them away naturally enough. Still if they have them and can find them, it may be worth while for you to keep a copy by you to show to any person who wishes for information.

'It is not necessary at all that a man should have a taste for languages or a faculty of acquiring them. What I want now is not a linguist, but a well-trained schoolmaster of black boys and men, who will also put his hand to any kind of work—a kindly, gentle, cheerful, earnest fellow, who will make light of all little inconveniences, such as necessarily attend sea life, &c., who is so much of a gentleman that he can afford to do any kind of work without being haunted by the silly thought that it "is beneath him," "not his business." That is the fellow for me. He would have to learn one language, the language of the particular class given over to him, and I think that a person of any moderate ability might soon do this with our teaching. If I could get him to take an interest in the general science of language and to go into philological points, of course his work would be lighter, and he would have soon the advantage of knowing dialects cognate to that which he must know. But that is not necessary.

'The real thing is to train a certain number of lads in habits of attention, punctuality, tidiness, &c., to teach them also upon a plan, which I should show him, to read and write. The religious instruction I should take, and the closer investigation of the language too, unless he showed a capacity for going into the nicer points of structure, &c.

'But somehow a cut and dried teaching machine of a man, however methodical, and good, and conscientious, won't do. There must be a vivacity, an activity of mind, a brightness about the man, so that a lesson shall never be mere drudgery; in short, there must be a real love in the heart for the scholars, that is the qualification.

'One man and one only I hope to have some day who ought to be able to learn scraps at least of many languages, but he will have a different work to do. No work can be considered to be satisfactorily carried on while it depends on the life of any one man. Someone to take my place will come, I hope, some day. He would have to go round the islands with me, and acquire a knowledge of the whole field of work—the wading and swimming, the mode of dealing with fellows on a first meeting, &c.; he will not only have one class to look after, but he must learn the same kind of lesson that I learnt under the Primate. Where to get such a man, I'm sure I don't know. He must be of standing and ability to be acceptable to the others should I die, &c., &c.

'So we need not speculate about him, and the truth is, I am not in any hurry to get men from home. We are educating ourselves lads here who will very likely learn to do this kind of work fairly well. Mr. Palmer will, I hope, be ordained at Christmas. Young Atkin will be useful some day. By-and-by if I can get one or two really first-rate men, it will indeed be a great thing. But who knows anything of me in England? I don't expect a really able man to come out to work with me. They will go to other parts of the world kept more before the notice of the public by committees and meetings and speeches, &c.; and indeed I am very thankful for it. I am not old nor wise enough to be at the head of a party of really able men. I must be more fit to lead before I can ask men to follow.

'Of course I know that the work, if I chose to speak out, is second to none in interest and importance, and that very little comparatively is known about it in England. But it is evidently far better that it should go quietly on without attracting much notice, and that we all should remain unknown at all events at present. By-and-by, when by God's blessing things are more ripe for definite departments of work, and men can have distinct duties at once assigned to them, and our mode of carrying on the Mission has been fairly tested, then it will be high time to think about first-rate men.

'And, presumptuous and strange as it may seem for me to say it, a man confessedly second-rate, unfit to hold a position with the best stamp of English clergymen, I had rather not have. I can get the material cheaper and made to my own hand out here.

'Some men are dull though good, others can't get away from their book life and the proprieties, others are donnish, others are fine gentlemen, others are weak in health, most have preconceived and, many, mistaken views about heathenism, and the way to deal with it; some would come out with the notion that England and English clergymen were born to set the colonies right.

'How few would say, "There's a young man for the Bishop, only a second-class man, no scholar, not remarkable in any way, but he has learnt his work in a good school, and will go out to him with the purpose of seeing how he carries on the work, and learning from him." I don't expect men worth anything to say this. Of course I don't; and yet you know, Joan, I can't take them on any other terms. No, I prefer taking promising lads here, and training them up, not with any pledge that I will employ them in the Mission, but with the promise of giving them every chance of becoming qualified for it.'

The voyage was much shorter than had been intended, and its history is best summed up here:—

'"Southern Cross," Kohimarama: Aug. 6, 1863.

'My dear Cousin,—This date, from this place, will surprise you. We returned yesterday, after a short voyage of only three months. I had arranged my plans for a long voyage, hoping to revisit all our known islands, and that more than once. We sailed to Norfolk Island, thence at once to Mota. I spent two days there, and left the Rev. L. Pritt in charge of the station; Mr. Palmer being with him and the four Norfolk Islanders, and several old scholars.

'I spent a fortnight in the Banks Archipelago, returning some scholars, and taking away others from divers islands; and then went back to Mota, bringing some sixteen or seventeen lads to the central school. I found them all pretty well; the whole island at peace, people moving about everywhere unarmed, and a large school being gathered together.

'I went off again to the south (the New Hebrides group), returning scholars who had been in New Zealand, purchasing yams for axes and iron, &c., to supply the large number of scholars at Mota. The season had been unfavourable, and the crop of yams in some islands had almost failed. However, in another fortnight I was again at Mota with some six or seven tons of yams. I found things lamentably changed. A great mortality was going on, dysentery and great prostration of strength from severe influenza.

'But of those not actually boarding at the station, the state was very sad indeed. About twenty-five adults were dead already, several of them regular attendants at school, of whom we were very hopeful.

'I spent two days and a half in going about the island, the wet incessant, the ground steaming and reeking with vegetable exhalations. During those days twenty-seven adults died, fifty-two in all, and many, many more were dying, emaciated, coughing, fainting; no constitutional vigour of body, nor any mutton broth, or beef tea, or jellies, or chickens, or wine, &c. Mr. Pritt did what he could, and more than I thought could have been done; but what could be done? How could nourishing food be supplied to dozens of invalids living miles off, refusing to obey directions in a country which supplies no food to rally the strength of persons in illness?

'I decided to remove the whole party at once, explaining to the people that we were not afraid to share with them the risk of dying, but that if Mr. Pritt and the others died, there were no teachers left. I felt that our Banks Island scholars must be removed, and that at once lest they should die. I could not send the vessel to the Solomon Islands without me, for Mr. Tilly was completely laid up and unable to move from rheumatic gout, and no one else on board knows those languages.

'I could not leave the party at Mota in the sickness, and I could not well send the vessel to Port Patteson for a time, for the danger was imminent. So I took them all away, in all thirty-nine.

'But now the vessel was full, more than sixty on board, and I had reckoned upon an empty vessel in the hot Santa Cruz and Solomon Island latitudes. Moreover, the weather was extraordinarily unfavourable—damp, foul winds, squalls, calms, unhealthy weather. Mr. Tilly was being greatly pulled down, and everything seemed to point out that the voyage ought not to be long. I made my mind up, took back the Solomon Island scholars; and, with heavy sea and baffling winds and one short gale, sailed back to New Zealand.

'How mysteriously our plans are overruled for good! I came back to hear of the war; and to learn to be thankful for my small, very young and very manageable party. Thirty-three Banks Islanders, the baptized party and select lads from their islands, one New Caledonian, four Ysabel lads, constitute this summer's Melanesian school.

'Don't be disappointed; I was at first, but I had the comfort of having really no alternative. I had, indeed, a great desire to make a thorough visitation of Leper's Island, and Santa Cruz especially; but the wind, usually so fair, was dead against me, we had, so to speak, no trade winds, and I had to give it up. It was certainly my duty to get to the south with my invalids as soon as I could, and alter my plans, which, you know, always are made with a view to divers modifications being rendered necessary.

'Training the baptized scholars, and putting into shape such knowledge as I have of Melanesian tongues, that made a good summer programme, as I was obliged to content myself with a small party gathered from but few islands. Concentration v. diffusion I soon began to think a very good thing.

'Well, so it is, and now I see great reason to be thankful. Why do we not always give thanks whether we see the reason or not?

'The vessel behaves admirably. I have written to Jem at length, and he must be applied to for my account of her. Pray tell Mr. Keble all this. I have a most valuable letter from Dr. Moberly, a great delight and honour to me. It is very kind of him to write; and his view of Church matters is really invaluable, no papers can give that which his letter gives, and only he and a very few others could give an opinion which I so greatly value. He speaks hopefully of Church matters in general, and there are great reasons surely for thankfulness and hope.

'Yet men such as he see far and wide, and to their great hearts no very violent storms are caused by such things as sorely trouble others. He sees the presumption and weakness, the vain transitory character of that phase of modern thought which Bishop Colenso represents, and confidently expects its speedy disappearance. But it does try the earnest, while it makes shipwreck of the frivolous, and exercises the faith and humility of all. Even a very poor scholar can see that his reasoning is most inconclusive, and his reading superficial and inferences illogical.

'God bless you, my dear Cousin.

'Your affectionate Cousin,

'J. C. PATTESON, Missionary Bishop.'

Perhaps this is the fittest place to give Mr. Tilly's description of the Bishop in his voyages:—

'My acquaintance with the late Bishop Patteson began at Port Patteson, in the Banks Islands, in 1861. He went with us in H.M.S. "Cordelia" to the Solomon Islands, and after being together some two months we again left him at Port Patteson on our way back to Auckland. During the time he was on board the "Cordelia" it was arranged that I was to sail the new vessel (the present "Southern Cross"), then about to be built by the Messrs. Wigram, and the size, internal arrangements, &c. were told me by him. He did not trouble me with much detail, referring me almost altogether to Bishop Selwyn—and gave no written directions; the little he said I carefully noted, observing that he spoke as with a thorough knowledge of the subject (so far as I could be a judge) as to sea-going qualities, capacity, &c., and to the best of my recollection, I found that while the vessel was building these few directions were the main ones to be kept in view. We entered Auckland harbour (from England) early on the morning of February 28, 1863, and hove to off the North Head, to wait for the Bishop coming off from Kohimarama before going up the harbour. It had been blowing hard outside the night before from the N.E., and there was still much wind, and some sea, even in the harbour. I was much struck by his appearance and manner. Having to launch his boat through a surf at Kohimarama beach, he had only on a shirt and trousers, and was of course drenched. He stepped on board more like a sailor than a clergyman, and almost immediately made one or two sailor-like remarks about the vessel, as if he understood her qualities as soon as he felt her in motion; and he was quite right in what he said.

'Before the building of the present vessel he had (I am told) navigated at different times to and from the islands; of his capacity in this respect, therefore, others who knew him there can speak. During the time I remained in the "Southern Cross," he never in any way, to the best of my recollection, interfered in the navigation or management of the vessel; but I came to know—almost at once—that his general planning of a voyage, knowledge of local courses and distances, the method by which it could be done most quickly and advantageously, and the time required to do it in, were thorough; and, in fact, I suppose, that almost without knowing it, in all this I was his pupil, and to the last felt the comfort of his advice or assistance, as, e.g., when looking out together from aloft he has seen shoal water more quickly than myself, or has decided whether certain doubtful appearances ahead were or were not sufficient to make us alter our course, &c.; and always speaking as no one who was what sailors call a landsman could have done. There was, of course, always a great deal of boat work, much of it to be done with a loaded boat in a seaway, requiring practical knowledge of such matters, and I do not remember any accidents, such as staving a boat on a reef, swamping, &c. in all those years; and he invariably brought the boat out when it was easy for the vessel to pick her up, a matter not sufficiently understood by many people. This was where Mr. Atkin's usefulness was conspicuous. Mr. Atkin was a fearless boatman, and the knowledge of boating he gained with us at sea was well supplemented when in Auckland, where he had a boat of his own, which he managed in the most thorough manner, Auckland being at times a rough place for boating. He (Mr. Atkin) pulled a good and strong oar, and understood well how to manage a boat under sail, much better in fact than many sailors (who are not always distinguished in that respect). His energy, and the amount of work he did himself were remarkable; his manner was quiet and undemonstrative. He took all charge—it may in a manner be said—of the boys on board the vessel, regulated everything concerning meals, sleeping arrangements, &c., how much food had to be bought for them at the different islands, what "trade" (i.e. hatchets, beads, &c.) it was necessary to get before starting on a voyage, calculated how long our supply of water would last, and in fact did so much on board as left the master of the vessel little to do but navigate. With regard to the loss the Mission has sustained in Mr. Atkin, speaking from my personal knowledge of his invaluable services on a voyage, I can safely say there is no one here now fitted to take his place. He had always capital health at sea, and was rarely sea-sick, almost the only one of the party who did not suffer in that way. And his loss will be the more felt now, as those who used to help in the boat are now otherwise employed as teachers, &c.; and as Norfolk Island is a bad place to learn boating, there is great need of some one to take his place, for a good boat's crew is a necessity in this work as may be readily understood when the boat is away sometimes for the greater part of the day, pulling and sailing from place to place. At those places where the Bishop landed alone, Mr. Atkin gradually acquired the experience which made him so fit to look after the safety of the boat and crew. In this manner he, next to the Bishop, became best known to the natives throughout the islands, and was always looked for; in fact, at many places they two were perhaps only recognised or remembered.

'Bishop Patteson was hardly what could be called a good sailor in one sense of the word; rough weather did not suit him, and although I believe seldom if ever actually sea-sick, he was now and then obliged to lie down the greater part of the day, or during bad weather. He used to read and write a great deal on board, and liked to take brisk walks up and down the deck, talking to whoever happened to be there. He was orderly and methodical on board, liked to see things in their places, and was most simple in all his habits. He always brought a good stock of books on board (which we all made use of), but very few clothes.

'The living on board was most simple, much the same as the crew, those in the cabin waiting on themselves (carrying no steward), until gradually boys used to volunteer to do the washing up, &c. School with all the boys was kept up when practicable; but the Bishop was always sitting about among them on the deck, talking to one and another, and having classes with him in the cabin. There were regular morning and evening native and English prayers. The sermons on Sundays were specially adapted for the sailors, and listened to with marked attention, as indeed they well might be, being so earnest, simple, and suitable.

'Speaking for myself, I used to look forward to the voyage as the time when I should have the privilege of being much with him for some months. While on shore at Kohimarama I saw but comparatively little of him, except at meals; but during the voyage I saw of course a great deal of him, and learned much from him—learned to admire his unselfishness and simplicity of mode of life, and to respect his earnestness and abilities. His conversation on any subject was free and full; and those on the few nights when quietly at anchor they could be enjoyed more, will be long remembered. Of his manner to Melanesians, others will, no doubt, say enough, but I may be excused for mentioning one scene that very much struck me, and of which I am now the only (white) one left who was present at it. We were paying a visit for the first time to an island, and—the vessel being safe in the offing—the Bishop asked me if I would go with them as he sometimes did on similar occasions. We pulled in to a small inner islet among a group, where a number of (say 200) natives were collected on the beach. Seeing they looked as if friendly, he waded on shore without hesitation and joined them; the reception was friendly, and after a time he walked with them along the beach, we in the boat keeping near. After a while we took him into the boat again, and lay off the beach a few yards to be clear of the throng, and be able to get at the things he wanted to give them, they coming about the boat in canoes; and this is the fact I wished to notice—viz., the look on his face while the intercourse with them lasted. I was so struck with it, quite involuntarily, for I had no idea of watching for anything of the sort; but it was one of such extreme gentleness, and of yearning towards them. I never saw that look on his face again, I suppose because no similar scene ever occurred again when I happened to be with him. It was enough in itself to evoke sympathy; and as we pulled away, though the channel was narrow and winding, yet, as the water was deep, we discussed the possibility of the schooner being brought in there at some future time. I am quite aware of my inability to do justice to that side of the Bishop's character, of which, owing to the position in which I stood to him as master of the Mission vessel, I have been asked to say a few words. There are others who know far better than myself what his peculiar qualifications were. His conduct to me throughout the time was marked by an unvarying confidence of manner and kindliness in our everyday intercourse, until, gradually, I came to think I understood the way in which he wished things done, and acted in his absence with an assurance of doing his wishes, so far as I could, which I never had attained to before with anyone else, and never shall again. And, speaking still of my own experience, I can safely say the love we grew to feel for him would draw such services from us (if such were needed) as no fear of anyone's reproof or displeasure ever could do. And perhaps this was the greatest privilege, or lesson, derived from our intercourse with him, that "Love casteth out fear!"

'Tiros. CAPEL TILLY.

'Auckland: October 28, 1872.'

This letter to Mr. Derwent Coleridge follows up the subject of the requisites for missionary work:—

'"Southern Cross," Kohimarama: August 8, 1863.

'My dear Cousin,—Thank you for a very kind letter which I found here on my return from a short three months' voyage in Melanesia. You will, I am sure, give me any help that you can, and a young man trained under your eye would be surely of great use in this work. I must confess that I distrust greatly the method adopted still in some places of sending out men as catechists and missionaries, simply because they appear to be zealous and anxious to engage in missionary work. A very few men, well educated, who will really try to understand what heathenism is, and will seek, by God's blessing, to work honestly without prejudice and without an indiscriminating admiration for all their own national tastes and modes of thought—a few such men, agreeing well together and co-operating heartily, will probably be enabled to lay foundations for an enduring work. I do not at all wish to apply hastily for men—for any kind of men—to fill up posts that I shall indeed be thankful to occupy with the right sort of men. I much prefer waiting till it may please God to put it into the head of some two or three more men to join the Mission—years hence it may be. We need only a few; I don't suppose that ten years hence I should (if alive) ever wish to have more than six or eight clergy; because their work will be the training of young natives to be themselves teachers, and, I pray God, missionaries in due time. I am so glad that you quite feel my wants, and sympathise with me. It is difficult to give reasons—intelligible to you all at a distance—for everything that I may say and do, because the circumstances of this Mission are so very peculiar. But you know that I have always the Primate to consult with as to principles; and I must, for want of a better course, judge for myself as to the mode of working them out in detail.

'Two plans are open for obtaining a supply of young men. First, I may receive some few ready-trained men, who nevertheless will have to learn the particular lessons that only can be taught here on the spot. Secondly, I may have youths of (say) sixteen to eighteen years of age, sent out from such a school as Stephen Hawtrey's for example, who will come with a good general knowledge of ordinary things, and receive a special training from myself. I think, too, that New Zealand will now and then supply an earnest, active-minded young fellow—who will be a Greek or Latin scholar, yet may find a useful niche in which he may be placed. At present I have means only to maintain one or two such persons, and this because I am able to use the money my dear Father left me for this purpose. Indeed, I have no other use for it. The money received on public account would not keep the Mission in its present state, and the expenditure ought to be increased by maintaining more scholars and teachers. I don't forget what you say about the philological part of my business. My difficulty is this, mainly: that it is next to impossible to secure a few hours of continuous leisure. You can have no idea of the amount of detail that I must attend to: seeing everything almost, and having moreover not a few New Zealand matters to employ my time, besides my Melanesian work. I have, I suppose, a considerable amount of knowledge of Melanesian tongues, unknown by name to anyone else perhaps; I quite feel that this ought not to die with me, if anything should suddenly happen to me. I hoped this summer to put together something; but now there is this Maori war, and an utterly unsettled state of things. I may have to leave New Zealand with my Melanesians almost any day. But I will do what I can, and as soon as I can. Again: I find it so hard to put on paper what I know. I could talk to a philologist, and I fancy that I could tell him much that would interest him; but I never wrote anything beyond a report in my life, and it is labour and grief to me to write them —I can't get on as a scribe at all. Then, for two or three years I have not been able to visit some islands whose language I know just enough of to see that they supply a valuable link in the great Polynesian chain. One might almost get together all the disjecta membra and reconstruct the original Polynesian tongue. But chiefly, of course, my information about Melanesia may be interesting. I have begun by getting together numerals in forty quite unknown dialects. I will give, at all events, short skeleton grammars too of some. But we have no time. Why, I have from five hundred to two thousand or more carefully ascertained words in each of several dialects, and of course these ought to be in the hands of you all at home. I know that, and have known it for years; but how to do it, without neglecting the daily necessary work?

'Again: the real genius of the language, whatever it may be, is learned when I can write down what I overhear boys saying when they are talking with perfect freedom, and therefore idiomatically, about sharks, cocoa-nuts, yams, &c. All translations must fail to represent a language adequately, and most of all the translation into a heathen language of religious expressions. They have not the ideas, and the language cannot be fairly seen in the early attempts to make it do an unaccustomed work.

'I remember more of you and my Aunt than you suppose. Even without the photograph (which I am very glad to have—thank you for it), I could have found you and Aunt out in a crowd. I can't say that I remember my own generation so well.

'Thank you again for writing so kindly.

'Always, my dear Cousin,

'Affectionately yours,

'J. C. PATTESON, Missionary Bishop.'

The next mail carried the reply to Johanna's sympathy with the troubles of the time of sickness in the early part of the year.

'August 28, 1863.

'My dear Joan,—Very full of comfort to have all your kind loving thoughts and words about our sickness. I know you thought and talked much about it, and indeed it was a very heavy visitation viewed in one way, though in another (and I really can't analyze the reason why) there was not only peace and calmness, but even happiness. I suppose one may be quite sure one is receiving mercies, and be thankful for them, although one is all the time like a man in a dream. I can hardly think of it all as real. But I am sure that God was very, very merciful to us. There was no difficulty anywhere about the making known the death of the lads to their relatives. I did not quite like the manner of the people at Guadalcanar, from which island poor Porasi came; and I could not get at the exact place from which Taman came, though I landed on the same island north and south of the beach from which I brought him.

'I do not at all think that any interruption of the work has been occasioned by it. It was very unfortunate that I could not, last voyage, make visits (and long ones too, as I had hoped) to many islands where in the voyage before I had met with such remarkable tokens of good-will, especially Leper's Island and Santa Cruz, but I think that if I can make a regular good round next time, it may be all as well. I imagine that in a great many islands it would now take a good deal to shake their confidence in us. At the same time it was and is a matter of great regret that I did not at once follow up the openings of the former year, and by returning again to the New Hebrides and Solomon Islands (as in the contemplated six months' voyage I intended to do), strengthen the good feeling now existing. Moreover, many scholars who were here last year would have come again had I revisited them and picked them up again. But the Mota sickness, the weather, and Mr. Tilly's illness made it more prudent to return by what is on the whole the shorter route, i.e., to the west of New Caledonia.

'You should have been with me when, as I jumped on shore at Mota, I took Paraskloi's father by the hand. That dear lad I baptized as he lay in his shroud in the chapel, when the whole weight of the trial seemed, as it were, by a sudden revelation to manifest itself, and thoroughly overwhelmed and unnerved me. I got through the service with the tears streaming down my cheeks, and my voice half choked. He was his father's pride, some seventeen years old. A girl ready chosen for him as his wife. "It is all well, Bishop, he died well. I know you did all you could, it is all well." He trembled all over, and his face was wet with tears; but he seemed strangely drawn to us, and if he survives this present epidemic, his son's death may be to him the means in God's hands of an eternal life. Most touching, is it not, this entire confidence?

'At Aruas, the small island close to Valua, from which dear Sosaman came, it was just the same; rather different at the west side of Vanua Lava, where they did not behave so well, and where (as I heard afterwards) there had been some talk of shooting me; but nothing occurred while I was on shore with them to alarm me.

'At Ambrym I landed with Talsil (Joval, from the same place, had died), a great crowd, all friendly, walked into the village and sat down, speechifying by the principal man, a presentation to me of a small pig; but such confidence that this man came back with me on board, where I gave him presents. I much wished to land at Taman's place, but could not do so, though I tried twice, without causing great delay.

'I could have brought away any number of scholars from almost any of these islands, probably from all. I have great reason to regret not having revisited Ambrym and other islands, but I think that a year hence, if alive, I may feel that it is better as it is.

'These Norfolk Islanders, four of them, I take as my children, for I can't fairly charge them (except Edwin Nobbs) to the Mission, and I wish to give Norfolk Island some help, as it is really, though not by letters patent, part of my charge. Edwin Nobbs is a thoroughly good fellow, and Fisher Young is coming on very well.

'Now, my dearest Joan, good-bye. My hats will come no doubt in good time, my present chapeau is very seedy, very limp and crooked and battered; as near green as black almost—a very good advertisement of the poverty of the Mission. But if I go about picking up gold in Australia, I shall come out in silk cassock and all the paraphernalia—very episcopal indeed!

'Your loving Brother,
'**J. C. PATTESON.**'

Herewith was a letter for Dr. Moberly:—

'St. Andrew's College, Kohimarama: August 29, 1863. 'My dear Dr. Moberly,—Thank you for a very kind and most interesting letter written in May. I know that you can with difficulty find time to write at all, and thank you all the more. If you knew the real value to us of such letters as you have now sent, containing your impressions and opinions of things in general, men, books, &c., you would be well rewarded for your trouble, I assure you. To myself, I must say to you, such letters are invaluable; they are a real help to me, not only in that they supply information from a very good authority on many questions which I much desire to understand, but even more because I rise up or kneel down after reading them, and think to myself, "how little such men who so think of me really know me; how different I ought to be," and then it is another help to me to try and become by God's grace less unlike what you take me to be. Indeed, you must forgive me for writing thus freely. I live very much alone as far as persons of the same language, modes of thought, &c., are concerned. I see but little (strange as it may seem to you) even of my dear Primate. We are by land four or five miles apart, and meet perhaps once or twice a month for a few minutes to transact some necessary business. His time is, of course, fully occupied; and I never leave this place, very seldom even this little quadrangle, and when other work does not need immediate attention (a state of things at which I have not arrived as yet), there are always a dozen new languages to be taken up, translations to be made, &c. So that when I read a letter which is full of just such matters as I think much of, I naturally long to talk on paper freely with the writer. Were I in England, I know scarcely any place to which I would go sooner than Winchester, Hursley, Otterbourne, and then I should doubtless talk as now I write freely. All that you write of the state of mind generally in England on religious questions is most deeply interesting. What a matter of thankfulness that you can say, "With all the sins and shortcomings that are amongst us, there is an unmistakeable spreading of devotion and the wish to serve God rightly on the part of very many."

'Then, the Church preferments have lately been good; Bishop Ellicott, one of your four coadjutors in the revision of the A. V., especially. I know some part of his Commentary, and am very glad to find that you speak so very highly of it. What a contrast to be sure between such work as his and Jowett's and Stanley's! Jowett actually avows a return to the old exploded theory of the inaccurate use of language in the Greek Testament. This must make men distrust him sooner or later as an interpreter of Scripture. I thank you heartily for your offer of sending me Bishop Ellicott's Commentary, but I hardly like you to send me so valuable a gift. What if you substitute for it a copy of what you have written yourself, not less valuable to me, and less expensive to you? I hardly like to write to ask favours of such people as Bishop Ellicott; I mean I have no right to do so; yet I almost thought of asking him to send a copy of his Commentaries to us for our library. I have ventured to write to Dean Trench: and I am pretty sure that Mr. Keble will send me his "Life of Bishop Wilson." But pray act as you wish. I am very grateful to you for thinking of it at all; and all such books whether yours or his will be used and valued, I can undertake to say. My good friend Kidding knows that I was, alas! no scholar at Eton or Oxford. I have sought to remedy this in some measure as far as the Greek Testament is concerned, and there are some excellent books which help one much; yet I can never make myself a good scholar, I fear; one among many penalties I pay for want of real industry in old days.

'Miss Yonge will hear from my sisters, and you from her, I have no doubt, my very scanty account of a very uninteresting voyage. I see everywhere signs of a change really extraordinary in the last few years. I can tell no stories of sudden conversions, striking effects, &c. But I know that in twenty, thirty, perhaps forty places, where a year or two ago no white man could land without some little uncertainty as to his reception, I can feel confident now of meeting with friends; I can walk inland—a thing never dreamt of in old days, sleep ashore, put myself entirely into their hands, and meet with a return of the confidence on their part. We have, too, more dialects, talk or find interpreters in more places; our object in coming to them is more generally known—and in Mota, and two or three other small islands of the Banks group, there is almost a system of instruction at work. The last voyage was a failure in that I could not visit many islands, nor revisit some that I longed to land at for the second or third time. But I don't anticipate any difficulty in reestablishing (D. V.) all the old familiarity before long. No doubt it is all, humanly speaking, hazardous where so much seems to depend upon the personal acquaintance with the people.

'By-and-by I hope to have some young man of character and ability enough to allow of his being regarded as my probable successor, who may always go with me—not stop on any one island—but learn the kind of work I have to do; then, when I no longer can do the work, it will be taken up by a man already known to the various islanders.

'I have not touched on many points in your letter. Again, thank you for it: it is very kind of you to write. I must send a line to Dr. Eidding.

'I am, my dear Dr. Moberly,

'Yours very truly,

'J. C. PATTESON, Bishop.'

The next of the closely written sheets that every mail carried was chiefly occupied with the Maori war and apostasy, on which this is not the place to enter, until the point where more personal reflections begin.

'How all this makes me ponder about my own special work I need not say. There is not the complication of an English colony, it is true; that makes a great difference.

'My own feeling is that one should teach positive truth, the plain message of Christianity, not attacking prejudices. Conviction as it finds its way into the heart by the truth recommending itself will do the work of casting out the old habits. I do not mean to say that the devil is not in a special way at work to deceive people to follow lying delusions. But all error is a perversion of truth; it has its existence negatively only, as being a negation of truth. But God is truth, and therefore Truth is ———. Now this is practically to be put, it seems to me, in this way. Error exists in the mind of man, whom God has created, as a perversion of truth; his faculties are constructed to apprehend and rest satisfied with truth. But his faculties are corrupted, and the devil supplies a false caricature of truth, and deceives him to apprehend and rest satisfied with a lie. But inasmuch as his nature, though damaged, is not wholly ruined by the Fall, therefore it is still not only possible for him to recognise positive truth when presented to him, but he will never rest satisfied with anything else—he will be restless and uneasy till he has found it.

'It is because I feel that it is more natural to man to follow truth than error ("natural" being understood to mean correspondent to the true nature) that I believe the right thing is to address oneself to the principle in a man which can and will recognise truth. Truth when recognised expels error. But why attack error without positively inculcating truth? I hope it does not bore you for me to write all this. But I wish you to learn all that may explain my way of dealing with these questions.'

The next day, October 25, a headache gives the Bishop a reason for indulging himself, while waiting for his pupils, in calling up and setting down a realisation of his sisters' new home at St. Mary Church, where for the time he seems to go and live with them, so vividly does he represent the place to himself. His first return to his own affairs is a vision that once more shows his unappeased craving for all appliances 'for glory and for beauty' in the worship of God.

'I may some day have a connection with Mary Church marbles. Sometimes I have a vision—but I must live twenty years to see more than a vision—of a small but exceedingly beautiful Gothic chapel, rich inside with marbles and stained glass and carved stalls and encaustic tiles and brass screen work. I have a feeling that a certain use of really good ornaments may be desirable, and being on a very small scale it might be possible to make a very perfect thing some day. There is no notion of my indulging such a thought. It may come some day, and most probably long after I am dead and gone. It would be very foolish to spend money upon more necessary things than a beautiful chapel at present, when in fact I barely pay my way at all. And yet a really noble church is a wonderful instrument of education, if we think only of the lower way of regarding it. Well, you have a grand church, and it is pleasant to think of dear dear Father having laid the stone, and of Cousin George. What would he say now to Convocation and Synods, and the rapid progress of the organisation of the Church?

'I think that what you say, Fan, about my overvaluing the world's opinion is very true. Self-consciousness and a very foolish sinful vanity always have been and are great sources of trial to me. How often I have longed for that simplicity and truthfulness of character that we saw so beautifully exemplified in our dear Father! How often I think that it is very good for me that I am so wanting in all personal gifts! I should be intolerable! I tell you this, not to foster such feelings by talking of them, but because we wish to know and be known to each other as we are. It is a very easy thing to be a popular preacher here, perhaps anywhere. You know that I never write a really good sermon, but I carry off platitudes with a sort of earnest delivery, tolerably clear voice, and with all the prestige of being a self-devoted Missionary Bishop. Bless their hearts! if they could see me sipping a delicious cup of coffee, with some delightful book by my side, and some of my lads sitting with me, all of them really loving one, and glad to do anything for one!

'A less self-conscious person could do what I can hardly do without danger. I see my name in a book or paper, and then comes at once a struggle against some craving after praise. I think I know the fault, but I don't say I struggle against it as I ought to do. It is very hard, therefore, for me to write naturally about work in which I am myself engaged. But I feel that a truthful account of what we see and hear ought to be given, and yet I never speak about the Mission without feeling that I have somehow conveyed a false impression.'

Again there was a time of sickness. The weather alternated between keen cutting winds and stifling heat; and there was much illness among the colonists, as well as a recurrence of the dreadful disease of the former year among the scholars of St. Andrew's, though less severe, and one boy died after fourteen days' sickness, while two pulled through with difficulty. In the midst came the Ember Week, when Mr. Palmer was ordained Deacon; and then the Bishop collapsed under ague, and spent the morning of Christmas Day in bed, but was able to get up and move into chapel for the celebration, and afterwards to go into hall and see the scholars eat their Christmas dinner.

In the letter he wrote in the latter part of the day, he confessed that 'he felt older and less springy;' though, as he added, there was good reason for it in the heavy strain that there had been upon him throughout the year, though his native, scholars were all that he could desire.

A few days' holiday and change at the Primate's brought back spirits and strength; but the question whether under any circumstances New Zealand would be a safe residence for the great body of Melanesian scholars was becoming doubtful, and it seemed well to consider of some other locality. Besides, it was felt to be due to the supporters of the Mission in Australia to tell them personally how great had been the progress made since 1855; and, accordingly, on one of the first days of February, Bishop Patteson embarked in a mail steamer for Sydney, but he was obliged to leave six of his lads in a very anxious state with a recurrence of dysentery. However, the Governor, Sir George Grey, had lent his place on the island of Kawau, thirty miles north of Auckland, to the party, so that there was good hope that change would restore the sick.

'Fancy me,' says the Journal of February 6, 'on board a screw steamer, 252 feet long, with the best double cabin on board for my own single use, the manager of the company being anxious to show me every attention, eating away at all sorts of made dishes, puddings, &c., and lounging about just as I please on soft red velvet sofas and cushions.'

The rest and good living were the restorative he needed; and, in spite of anxiety about the patients at home, he enjoyed and profited by it.

On February 6, Sydney was reached, but the Bishop sailed on at once for his farthest point. At Melbourne, on the 11th, he quaintly declares, after describing his kind reception: 'I feel at present a stranger among strangers; no new thing to me, especially if they are black, and begin by offering me cocoa-nut instead of bread and butter. This place looks too large for comfort—like a section of London, busy, bustling, money-making. There are warm hearts somewhere amid the great stores and banks and shops, I dare say. But you know it feels a little strange, and especially as I think it not unlikely that a regular hearty Church feeling may not be the rule of the place. Still I am less shy than I was, and with real gentlemen feel no difficulty in discussing points on which we differ.

It is the vulgar uneducated fellow that beats me. The Melanesians, laugh as you may at it, are naturally gentlemanly and courteous and well-bred. I never saw a "gent" in Melanesia, though not a few downright savages. I vastly prefer the savage.'

Melbourne was, however, to be taken on the return; and he went on to Adelaide, where Bishop Short and the clergy met him at the port, and he was welcomed most heartily. The Diocesan Synod assembled to greet him, and presented an address; and there were daily services and meetings, when great interest was excited, and tangibly proved by the raising of about £250. He was perfectly astonished at the beauty and fertility of the place, and the exceeding luxuriance of the fruit. One bunch of grapes had been known to weigh fourteen pounds. As to the style of living with all ordinary English comforts and attendance, he says:—'I feel almost like a fish out of water, and yet I can't help enjoying it. One very easily resumes old luxurious habits, and yet the thought of my dear boys, sick as I fear some must be, helps to keep me in a sober state of mind.'

On St. Matthew's Day he assisted at an Ordination: and on the 27th returned to Melbourne for three weeks, and thence to Sydney. His time was so taken up that his letters are far more scanty and hurried than usual.

'I have been running no little risk of being spoilt, and I don't say that I have come off uninjured. In Melbourne I was told by the Dean (the Bishop is in England) and by Judge Pohlman (an excellent good man) that they remembered no occasion during the twenty-two years of sojourn (before Melbourne was more than a village) when so much interest had been shown in Christian work, especially Mission work. This is a thing to be very thankful for. I felt it my duty to speak strongly to them on their own duties, first to Aborigines, secondly to

Chinese (of whom some 40,000 live in Victoria), thirdly to Melanesians. I did not aim only at getting money for Melanesia; I took much higher ground than that. But the absence of the ordinary nonsense about startling conversions, rapid results, &c., and the matter-of-fact unsentimental way of stating the facts of heathenism, and the way to act upon it, did, no doubt, produce a very remarkable effect.

'I need not tell you that I did pray for strength to make good use of such unexpected and very unusual opportunities. Crowded meetings, nothing before like it in Melbourne or the provinces. I did not feel nervous, much to my surprise; I really wonder at it, I had dreaded it much.

'It was a sight to see St. George's Hall crowded, children sitting on the floor, platform, anywhere, and very many adults (about 500) besides. Now you know my old vanity. Thank God, I don't think it followed me very much here. There was a strong sense of a grand opportunity, and the need of grace to use it.'

The enthusiasm at Victoria resulted in 350 pounds, and pledges of future assistance; and at Sydney there was the like grand meeting, the like address, and hearty response; and the Churches of Australia pledged themselves to bear the annual expenses of the voyages of the 'Southern Cross.' A number of young clerks and officials, too, united in an arrangement by which she could be insured, high as was the needful rate.

The preaching and speeches produced an immense feeling, and the after review of the expedition is thus recorded:—

'As for my sermons in Australia, I found to my surprise that every minute was so occupied that I could not make time to write; and as for doing so in New Zealand before I started, why, I systematized and put into the printer's hands, in about four months, grammars, &c., more or less complete, of seventeen languages, working up eight or ten more in MS.!

'I had to preach extempore for the most part: I did not at all like it, but what could I do? Sermons and speeches followed like hail—at least one, sometimes two on week-days, and three on Sundays. I preached on such points as I had often talked out with the Primate and Sir William, and illustrated principles by an occasional statement of facts drawn from missionary experience.

'Now, old Fan, as you know, the misery of self-consciousness and conceit clings to me. I can't, as dear old father could, tell you what actually occurred without doing myself harm in the telling of it.

'It pleased God to make me able to say all through what I think it was good for people to hear. All meetings and services (with a few, very few exceptions, from heavy rains, &c.) were crowded. I could not in a few minutes speak with any degree of completeness on subjects which for years had occupied my thoughts: I was generally about an hour and a half, occasionally longer—I tried to be shorter. But people were attentive and interested all through. At Melbourne, it was said that 1,500 children (at a meeting for them) were present, and 500 adults, including many of the most educated people. All, children included, were as still as mice for an hour and a half, except occasional cheers.

'But generally there was little excitement. I did not, as you can suppose, take the sensation line; spoke very rapidly, for I had no time to spare—but clearly and quietly, sometimes gravely, sometimes with exceeding earnestness, and exposed sophistries and fallacies and errors about the incapacity of the black races, &c. There were times when I lost all sense of nervousness and self, and only wished that 10,000 people had been present, for I felt that I was speaking out, face to face, plain simple words of truth.

'The effect at the time was no doubt very remarkable. The Dean of Melbourne, e.g., said publicly that no such earnestness in religious, matters had ever been exhibited there. The plan of Mission work was simple, practicable, commended itself to hard-headed men of business. Many came to hear who had been disgusted with the usual sentimentalism and twaddle, the absence of knowledge of human nature, the amount of conventional prejudice, &c. They were induced to come by friends who represented that this was something quite different, and these men went away convinced in many cases, seconding resolutions and paying subscriptions.

'I said what was true, that I was the mouthpiece of the Bishop of New Zealand; that I could speak freely of the plan of the Mission, for it was not my plan, &c. How I was carried through it all, I can't say. I was unusually well, looked and felt bright, and really after a while enjoyed it, though I was always glad when my share in the speechifying was over. Yet I did feel it a blessing, and a privilege, to stand up there and speak out; and I did speak out, and told them their plain duties, not appealing to feelings, but aiming at convincing the judgment. I told 1,500 people in church at Sydney, "I speak as to wise men, judge ye what I say." Do you know, Fan, I almost feel that if I live a few years I ought to write a book, unless I can get the Primate to do it? So much that is self-evident to us, I now see to be quite unknown to many good educated men. I don't mean a silly book, but a very simple statement of general principles of Christian work, showing the mode that must be adopted in dealing with men as partakers of a common nature, coupled with the many modifications and adaptations to circumstances which equally require special gifts of discernment and wisdom from on high. Then occasional narratives, by way of illustration, to clench the statement of principles, might be introduced; but I can't write, what I might write if I chose, folios of mere events without deducing from them some maxims for Christian practice.'

The impression produced was deep and lasting at all the Australian capitals, including Brisbane.

A plan was even set on foot for transferring a part of the Melanesian school to a little island not far from the coast of Queensland, in a much warmer climate than Kohimarama, where it was thought Australian natives might be gathered in.

Here is the description of the place, written a day or two after the return to New Zealand:—

'St. Andrew's: April 27, 1864.

'My dear Cousin,—I returned on the 24th from Australia. I visited the dioceses of Adelaide, Melbourne, Sydney, and Brisbane. Everywhere I met with great encouragement; and indeed, I thank God that (as I had hoped) the special work of the Mission became the means of exciting unusual interest in the work of the

Church generally. It was a great opportunity, a great privilege in the crowded meetings to tell people face to face their duties, to stand up as the apologist of the despised Australian black, and the Chinese gold-digger, and the Melanesian islander.

'All the Primate had taught me—what heathenism is, how to deal with it, the simple truisms about the "common sin, common redemption," the capacity latent in every man, because he is a man, and not a fallen angel nor a brute beast, the many conventional errors on Mission (rather) ministerial work—many, many things I spoke of very fully and frequently. I felt it was a great responsibility. How strange that I forgot all my nervous dread, and only wished there could be thousands more present, for I knew that I was speaking words of truth, of hope, and love; and God did mercifully bless much that He enabled, me to say, and men's hearts were struck within them, though, indeed, I made no effort to excite them.

'Much may result from it. We may have a branch school on the S.W. of Curtis Island, on the east coast of Queensland, healthy, watered, wooded, with anchorage, about 25° S. latitude, a fair wind to and from some of the islands; to which place I could rapidly carry away sick persons.

'There I could convey two hundred or more scholars, in the same time required to bring sixty to New Zealand; there yams can be grown; there it may be God's will that a work may be commenced at length among the remnant that is left of the Australian blacks. The latter consideration is very strongly urged upon me by the united voice of the Australian Churches, by none more strongly than by the Bishop of Sydney. I dare to hope that the communion of the Australian and New Zealand Churches will be much strengthened by the Mission as a link. What blessings, what mercies!

'This will not involve an abandonment of St Andrew's, but the work must expand. I think Australia will supply near 1,000 pounds a year, perhaps more before long.

'To teach me that all is in His hands, we have again had a visitation from dysentery. It has been very prevalent everywhere, no medical men remember such a season. We have lost from consumption two, and from dysentery six this year; in fourteen months not less than fourteen: more than in all the other years put together. Marvellous to relate, all our old baptized and confirmed scholars are spared to us. Good-bye, and God ever bless and keep you.

'Your affectionate cousin,

'J. C. PATTESON, Bishop.'

One of these deaths was that of Kareambat, the little New Caledonian confided to the Bishop of New Zealand by poor Basset. He had been christened on the previous Epiphany.

No doubt this grief on coming home increased the effect of this year of trial. Indeed even on the voyage there had been this admission, 'Somehow I don't feel right with all this holiday; I have worked really very hard, but "change of work is the best holiday." I don't feel springy. I am not so young as I was, that's the truth of it, and this life is not likely to be a long one. Yet when used up for this work, absence of continual anxiety and more opportunity of relaxation may carry a man on without his being wholly useless!'

The Maori war was a constant grief and anxiety to all the friends on shore, and there was thus evidently much less elasticity left to meet the great shock that was preparing for the voyagers in the expedition of 1864. Mr. Codrington was not of the party, having been obliged to go to England to decide whether it was possible to give himself wholly to the Mission; and the staff therefore consisted of Mr. Pritt, Mr. Kerr, and Mr. Palmer, with Mr. Joseph Atkin, whose journal his family have kindly put at my disposal.

The endeavour was to start after the Ascension Day Communion, but things were not forward enough. May was not, however, very far advanced before the 'Southern Cross' was at sea.

On May 17, Norfolk Island was visited, and Edwin Nobbs and Fisher Young had what proved to be their last sight, of their home and friends. The plan was to go on to Nengone and Erromango, take up the stores sent to the latter place from Sydney, drop the two clergymen at Mota, and after a stay there, go to the New Hebrides, and then take up the party, and if possible leave them to make experiment of Curtis Island, while going to those Santa Cruz islands for which he always seems to have had such a yearning.

'I feel as usual,' he finishes the letter sent from Norfolk Island, 'that no one can tell what may be the issue of such voyages. I pray and trust that God will mercifully reveal to me "what I ought to do, and give me grace and power to fulfil the same."

'I have now been for some time out of the way of this kind of work, but I hope that all may be safely ordered for us. It is all in His hands; and you all feel, as I try to do, that there should be no cause for anxiety or trouble.

'Yet there are moments when one has such an overwhelming sense of one's sins and negligences provoking God to chastise one. I know that His merciful intention towards men must be accomplished, and on the whole I rest thankfully in that, and feel that He will not suffer my utter unworthiness to hinder His work of love and goodness.'

At Mota, Mr. Atkin's journal shows to what work a real helper needed to be trained:—

'The Mission-house had lost its roof in a gale of wind. The epidemic that was raging last year did not seem to have continued long after with such violence; some more of the people were dead, but not very many. We took off all the Mota boys, and things that were wanted in three boat-loads, the last time leaving the Bishop. There was, fortunately, very little surf, and we got nothing wet, but as the tide was high, we had to carry the things over the coral reefs with the water a little above our knees.

'About an hour later we dropped anchor at Vanua Lava. On Saturday morning I went ashore with the boat, and got water for washing and sand for scrubbing decks, and several tons of taro and yams discharged on board the vessel. Then made another trip, left all the boys on shore for a holiday, and took off twelve or fourteen cwt. of yams, taro, and cocoa-nuts. After dinner and washing up, went to fetch boys back. Where we bought the yams there was such a surf breaking that we could not haul the boat on the beach, and we had to wade and carry them out. After we got on board, we had a bathe. Two of the Solomon Islanders distinguished themselves by jumping off the fore-yard, and diving under the ship. Mr. Tilly and the mates had been stowing, and the rest of us had been getting yams all day, and if our friends could have seen us then, haggard-looking and dirty, singing choruses to nigger melodies, how shocked they would have been!

'Next Thursday went across to Mota, took the Bishop on board, and sailed south as fast as possible.

'Sunday morning we were at the entrance of the passage between Ambrym and Mallicolo, without a breath of wind. We had service at 10 A.M.; and in the afternoon, psalms and hymns and chants in the cabin, the Bishop doing most of the singing.

'June 6th.—On Monday morning we landed at the old place at Tariko. We began to buy some yams. The Bishop and William Pasvorang went ashore, and the rest of us stayed in the boat, keeping her afloat and off the reefs. Unfortunately the place where we landed was neutral ground between two tribes, who both brought yams to the place to sell. One party said another was getting too many hatchets, and two or three drew off and began shooting at the others. One man stood behind the Bishop, a few feet from him, and fired away in the crowd with a will. The consternation and alarm of both parties were very ludicrous. Some of each set were standing round the boat, armed with bows and arrows, but they were so frightened that they never seemed to think of using them, but ran off as hard as they could scamper to the shallow water, looking over their shoulders to see if the enemies' arrows were after them. One arrow was fired at the Bishop from the shore, and one hit the boat just as we pushed off.

'The Bishop himself says of this fray:—"I was in the middle, one man only remained by me, crouching under the lee of the branch of the tree, and shooting away from thence within a yard of me. I did not like to leave the steel-yard, and I had to detach it from the rope with which it was tied to the tree, and the basket too was half full of yams and heavy, so that it was some time before I got away, and walked down the beach, and waded to the boat, shooting going on all round at the time; no one shooting at me, yet as they shot on both sides of me at each other, I was thankful to get well out of it. I thought of him who preserves from 'the arrow that flieth by day,' as He has so mercifully preserved so many of us from 'the sickness.'" Now don't go and let this little affair be printed.'

At Parama there was a friendly landing. At Sopevi Mr. Atkin says: 'We could not find the landing place where the Bishop two years ago found several people. We saw three or four on the shore. They were just the same colour as the dust from the volcano. What a wretched state they must be in! If they go to the neighbouring-isles they will be killed as enemies, and if they stay at home they are constantly suffocated by the ashes, which seemed to have fallen lately to the depth of more than afoot.'

At Mallicolo a landing place was found, and an acquaintance begun by means of gifts of calico. At Leper's Island St. Barnabas Day was celebrated by bringing off two boys, but here again was peril. The Bishop writes:—

'The people, though constantly fighting, and cannibals and the rest of it, are to me very attractive, light-coloured, and some very handsome. As I sat on the beach with a crowd about me, most of them suddenly jumped up and ran off. Turning my head I saw a man (from the boat they saw two men) a few yards from me, corning to me with club uplifted. I remained sitting, and held out a few fish-hooks to him, but one or two men jumped up and seizing him by the waist forced him off. After a few minutes (lest they should think I was suspicious of them), I went back to the boat. I found out from the two young men who went away with me from another place, just what I expected to hear, viz. that a poor fellow called Moliteum was shot dead two months ago by a trader for stealing a bit of calico. The wonder was, not that they wanted to avenge the death of their kinsman, but that the others should have prevented it. How could they possibly know that I was not one of the wicked set? Yet they did discriminate; and here again, always by the merciful Providence of God, the plan of going among the people unarmed and unsuspiciously has been seen to disarm their mistrust and to make them regard me as a friend.'

Curtis Island was inspected, but there was no possibility of leaving a party to make experiment on it; and then the 'Southern Cross' sailed for the Santa Cruz cluster, that group whose Spanish name was so remarkable a foreboding of what they were destined to become to that small party of Christian explorers. Young Atkin made no entry in his diary of those days, and could never bear to speak of them; and yet, from that time forward, his mind was fully made up to cast in his lot with the Mission.

It was on August 15 that the first disaster at these islands took place. Not till the 27th could the Bishop—on his sister Fanny's birthday—begin a letter to her, cheering himself most touchingly with the thought of the peace at home, and then he broke off half way, and could not continue for some days:—

'My dearest Fan,—You remember the old happy anniversaries of your birthday —the Feniton party—the assembly of relations—the regular year's festivity.

'No doubt this anniversary brings as much true happiness, the assurance of a more abiding joy, the consciousness of deeper and truer sympathy. You are, I hope, to pass the day cheerfully and brightly with perhaps —— and —— about you.... Anyhow, I shall think of you as possibly all together, the remnant of the old family gathering, on a calm autumn day, with lovely South Devon scenery around you.

'The day comes to me in the midst of one of the deepest sorrows I have ever known—perhaps I have never felt such sorrow...perhaps I have never been so mercifully supported under it. It is a good and profitable sorrow I trust for me: it has made so much in me reveal itself as hollow, worldly, selfish, vainglorious. It has, I hope, helped to strip away the veil, and may be by God's blessing the beginning of more earnest life-long repentance and preparation for death.

'On August 15 I was at Santa Cruz. You know that I had a very remarkable day there three years ago. I felt very anxious to renew acquaintance with the people, who are very numerous and strong.

'I went off in the boat with Atkin (twenty), Pearce (twenty-three or twenty-four years old), Edwin Nobbs, Fisher Young, and Hunt Christian, the last three Norfolk Islanders. Atkin, Edwin and Fisher have been with me for two or three years—all young fellows of great promise, Fisher perhaps the dearest of all to me, about eighteen, and oh! so good, so thoroughly truthful, conscientious, and unselfish!

'I landed at two places among many people, and after a while came back as usual to the boat. All seemed pleasant and hopeful. At the third place I landed amidst a great crowd, waded over the broad reef (partially uncovered at low water), went into a house, sat down for some time, then returned among a great crowd to the boat and got into it. I had some difficulty in detaching the hands of some men swimming in the water.

'Well, when the boat was about fifteen yards from the reef, on which crowds were standing, they began (why I know not) to shoot at us.—(Another letter adds) 300 or 400 people on the reef, and five or six canoes being round us, they began to shoot at us.—I had not shipped the rudder, so I held it up, hoping it might shield off any arrows that came straight, the boat being end on, and the stern, having been backed into the reef, was nearest to them.

'When I looked round after a minute, providentially indeed, for the boat was being pulled right into a small bay on the reef, and would have grounded, I saw Pearce lying between the thwarts, with the long shaft of an arrow in his chest, Edwin Nobbs with an arrow as it seemed in his left eye, many arrows flying close to us from many quarters. Suddenly Fisher Young, pulling the stroke oar, gave a faint scream; he was shot through the left wrist. Not a word was spoken, only my "Pull! port oars, pull on steadily." Once dear Edwin, with the fragment of the arrow sticking in his cheek, and the blood streaming down, called out, thinking even then more of me than of himself, "Look out, sir! close to you!" But indeed, on all sides they were close to us!

'How we any of us escaped I can't tell; Fisher and Edward pulled on, Atkin had taken Pearce's oar, Hunt pulled the fourth oar. By God's mercy no one else was hit, but the canoes chased us to the schooner. In about twenty minutes we were on board, the people in the canoes round the vessel seeing the wounded paddled off as hard as they could, expecting of course that we should take vengeance on them. But I don't at all think that they were cognisant of the attack on shore.'

Several letters were written about this adventure; but I have thought it better to put them together, every word being Bishop Patteson's own, because such a scene is better realised thus than by reading several descriptions for the most part identical. What a scene it is! The palm-clad island, the reef and sea full of the blacks, the storm of long arrows through the air, the four youths pulling bravely and steadily, and their Bishop standing over them, trying to ward off the blows with the rudder, and gazing with the deep eyes and steadfast smile that had caused many a weapon to fall harmless!

Pearce, it should be observed, was a volunteer for the Mission then on a trial-trip.

There was an even more trying time to come on board. The Bishop continues:

'I drew out the arrow from Pearce's chest: a slanting wound not going in very deep, running under the skin, yet of apparently almost fatal character to an ignorant person like myself; Five inches were actually inside him. The arrow struck him almost in the centre of the chest and in the direction of the right breast. There was no effusion of blood, he breathed with great difficulty, groaning and making a kind of hollow sound, was perfectly composed, gave me directions and messages in case of his death. I put on a poultice and bandage, and leaving him in charge of some one, went to Fisher. The wrist was shot through, but the upper part of the arrow broken off and deep down; bleeding profuse, of which I was glad; I cut deeply, though fearing much to cut an artery, but I could not extract the wooden arrow-head. At length getting a firm hold of the projecting point of the arrow on the lower side of his wrist, I pulled it through: it came out clean. The pain was very great, he trembled and shivered: we gave him brandy, and he recovered. I poulticed the wound and went to Edwin. Atkin had got out the splinter from his wound; the arrow went in near the eye and came out by the cheek-bone: it was well syringed, and the flow of blood had been copious from the first. The arrows were not bone-headed, and not poisoned, but I well knew that lock-jaw was to be dreaded. Edwin's was not much more than a flesh wound. Fisher's being in the wrist, frightened me more: their patience and quiet composure and calm resignation were indeed a strength and comfort to us all.

'This was on Monday, August 15. All seemed doing well for a day or two, I kept on poultices, gave light nourishing food, &c. But on Saturday morning Fisher said to me, "I can't make out what makes my jaws feel so stiff."

'Then my heart sank down within me, and I prayed earnestly, earnestly to God. I talked to the dear dear lad of his danger, night and day we prayed and read. A dear guileless spirit indeed. I never saw in so young a person such a thorough conscientiousness as for two years I witnessed in his daily life, and I had long not only loved but respected him.

'We had calm weather and could not get on. By Saturday the jaws were tight-locked. Then more intense grew the pain, the agony, the whole body rigid like a bar of iron! Oh! how I blessed God who carried me through that day and night. How good he was in his very agonies, in his fearful spasms, thanking God, praying, pressing my hand when I prayed and comforted him with holy words of Scripture. None but a well-disciplined, humble, simple Christian could so have borne his sufferings: the habit of obedience and faith and patience; the childlike unhesitating trust in God's love and fatherly care, supported him now. He never for a moment lost his hold upon God. What a lesson it was! it calmed us all. It almost awed me to see in so young a lad so great an instance of God's infinite power, so great a work of good perfected in one young enough to have been confirmed by me.

'At 1 A.M. (Monday) I moved from his side to my couch, only three yards off. Of course we were all (I need not say) in the after cabin. He said faintly, "Kiss me. I am very glad that I was doing my duty. Tell my father that I was in the path of duty, and he will be so glad. Poor Santa Cruz people!" Ah! my dear boy, you will do more for their conversion by your death than ever we shall by our lives. And as I lay down almost convulsed with sobs, though not audible, he said (so Mr. Tilly afterwards told me), "Poor Bishop!" How full his heart was of love and peace, and thoughts of heaven. "Oh! what love," he said. The last night when I left him for an hour or two at 1 A.M. only to lie down in my clothes by his side, he said faintly (his body being then rigid as a bar of iron), "Kiss me, Bishop." At 4 A.M. he started as if from a trance; he had been wandering a good deal, but all his words even then were of things pure and holy. His eyes met mine, and I saw the consciousness gradually coming back into them. "They never stop singing there, sir, do they?"—for his thoughts were with the angels in heaven. Then, after a short time, the last terrible struggle, and then he fell asleep. And remember, all this in the midst of that most agonizing, it may be, of all forms of death. At 4 A.M. he was hardly conscious, not fully conscious: there were same fearful spasms: we fanned him and bathed his head and occasionally got a drop or two of weak brandy or wine and water down. Then came the last struggle. Oh! how I thanked God when his head at length fell back, or rather his whole body, for it was without joint, on my arm: long drawn sighs with still sadder contraction of feature succeeded, and while I said the Commendatory Prayer, he passed away.

'The same day we anchored in Port Patteson, and buried him in a quiet spot near the place where the Primate and I first landed years ago. It seems a consecration of the place that the body of that dear child should be resting there.

'Some six years ago, when Mrs. Selwyn stopped at Norfolk Island she singled him out as the boy of special promise. For two or three years he had been with me, and my affection flowed out naturally to him. God had tried him by the two sicknesses at Kohimarama and at Mota, and by his whole family returning to Pitcairn. I saw that he had left all for this work. He had become most useful, and oh! how we shall miss him!

'But about five days after this (August 22) Edwin's jaws began to stiffen. For nine or ten days there was suspense, so hard to bear. Some symptoms were not so bad, it did not assume so acute a form. I thought he ought to be carried through it. He was older, about twenty-one, six feet high, a strong handsome young man, the pride of Norfolk Island, the destined helper and successor (had God so willed) of his father, the present Clergyman. The same faith, the same patience, the same endurance of suffering.

'On Friday, September 2, I administered the Holy Communion to him and Pearce. He could scarce swallow the tiniest crumb. He was often delirious, yet not one word but spoke of things holy and pure, almost continually in prayer. He was in the place where Fisher had died, the best part of the cabin for an invalid. Sunday came: he could take no nourishment, stomach and back in much pain: a succession of violent spasms at about 10.30 A.M., but his body never became quite rigid. The death struggle at 1 A.M. September 5, was very terrible. Three of us could scarcely hold him. Then he sank back on my arm, and his spirit passed away as I commended his soul to God. Then all motionless. After some minutes, I said the first prayer in the Burial Service, then performed the last offices, then had a solemn talk with Pearce, and knelt down, I know not how long.

'We buried him at sea. All this time we were making very slow progress; indeed the voyage has been very remarkable in all respects. Pearce seems to be doing very well, so that I am very hopeful about him. The temperature now is only 72 degrees, and I imagine that his constitution is less liable to that particular disease. Yet punctured wounds are always dangerous on this account.

'Patience and trust in God, the same belief in His goodness and love, that He orders all things for our good, that this is but a proof of His merciful dealing with us: such comforts God has graciously not withheld. I never felt so utterly broken down, when I thought, and think, of the earthly side of it all; never perhaps so much realised the comfort and power of His Presence, when I have had grace to dwell upon the heavenly and abiding side of it. I do with my better part heartily and humbly thank Him, that He has so early taken these dear ones by a straight and short path to their everlasting home. I think of them with blessed saints, our own dear ones, in Paradise, and in the midst of my tears I bless and praise God.

'But, dear Fan, Fisher most of all supplied to me the absence of earthly relations and friends. He was my boy: I loved him as I think I never loved any one else. I don't mean more than you all, but in a different way: not as one loves another of equal age, but as a parent loves a child.

'I can hardly think of my little room at Kohimarama without him. I long for the sight of his dear face, the sound of his voice. It was my delight to teach him, and he was clever and so thoughtful and industrious. I know it is good that my affections should be weaned from all things earthly. I try to be thankful, I think I am thankful really; time too will do much, God's grace much more. I only wonder how I have borne it all. "In the multitude of the sorrows that I had in my heart, Thy comforts have refreshed my soul." Mr. Tilly has been and is full of sympathy, and is indeed a great aid. He too has a heavy loss in these two dear ones. And now I must land at Norfolk Island in the face of the population crowding the little pier. Mr. Nobbs will be there, and the brothers and sisters of Edwin, and the uncles and aunts of Fisher.

'Yet God will comfort them; they have been called to the high privilege of being counted worthy to suffer for their Savior's sake. However much I may reproach myself with want of caution and of prayer for guidance (and this is a bitter thought), they were in the simple discharge of their duty. Their intention and wish were to aid in bringing to those poor people the Gospel of Christ. It has pleased God that in the execution of this great purpose they should have met with their deaths. Surely there is matter for comfort here!

'I can't write all this over again.... I have written at some length to Jem also; put the two letters together, and you will be able to realise it somewhat.

'This is a joint letter to you and Joan. It was begun on your birthday, and it has been written with a heavy, dull weight of sorrow on my heart, yet not unrelieved by the blessed consciousness of being drawn, as I humbly trust, nearer to our most merciful Father in heaven, if only by the very impossibility of finding help elsewhere. It has not been a time without its own peculiar happiness. How much of the Bible seemed endued with new powers of comfort.... How true it is, that they who seek, find. "I sought the Lord, and He heard me." The closing chapters of the Gospels, 2 Corinthians, and how many other parts of the New Testament were blessings indeed! Jeremy Taylor's "Life of Christ," and "Holy Living and Dying," Thomas a Kempis, most of all of course the Prayer-book, and such solemn holy memories of our dear parents and uncles, such blessed hopes of reunion, death brought so near, the longing (if only not unprepared) for the life to come: I could not be unhappy. Yet I could not sustain such a frame of mind long; and then when I sank to the level of earthly thoughts, then came the weary heartache, and the daily routine of work was so distasteful, and I felt sorely tempted to indulge the "luxury of grief." But, thanks be to God, it is not altogether an unhealthy sorrow, and I can rest in the full assurance that all this is working out God's purposes of love and mercy to us all—Melanesians, Pitcairners, and all; and that I needed the discipline I know full well....

'Your loving Brother,

'**J. C. P.**'

It was not possible to touch at Norfolk Island, each attempt was baffled by the winds; and on September 16 the 'Southern Cross' anchored at Kohimarama, and a sad little note was sent up to the Primate with the announcement of the deaths and losses.

In spite of the comfort which, as this note said, Patteson felt 'in the innocence of their lives, and the constancy of their faith' unto the death, the fate of these two youths, coming at the close of a year of unusual trial, which, as he had already said, had diminished his elasticity, had a lasting effect. It seemed to take away his youthful buoyancy, and marked lines of care on his face that never were effaced. The first letter after his return begins by showing how full his heart was of these his children:—

'Kohimarama: Sunday, September 18, 1864.

'My dearest Fan,—I must try to write without again making my whole letter full of dear Edwin and Fisher. That my heart is full of them you can well believe.

'These last five weeks have taught me that my reading of the Bible was perhaps more intellectual and perhaps more theological than devotional, to a dangerous extent probably; anyhow I craved for it as a revelation not only of truth, but of comfort and support in heavy sorrow. It may be that when the sorrow does not press so heavily, the Bible cannot speak so wonderfully in that particular way of which I am writing, and it is right to read it theologically also.

'But yet it should always be read with a view to some practical result; and so often there is not a special, though many general points which may make our reading at once practical. Then comes the real trial, and then comes the wondrous power of God's Word to help and strengthen.

'Now it helps me to know where I am, to learn how others manage to see where they are.

'All that you say about self-consciousness, &c., can't I understand it! Ah! when I saw the guileless pure spirit of those two dear fellows ever brightening more and more for now two years. I had respected them as much as I loved them. I used to think, "Yes, we must become such as they; we too must seek and pray for the mind of a little child."

'And surely the contemplation of God is the best cure. How admirable Jeremy Taylor is on those points! Oh that he had not overlaid it all with such superabundant ornamentation of style and rhetoric. But it is the manner of the age. Many persons I suppose get over it, perhaps like it; but I long for the same thoughts, the same tenderness and truthfulness, and faithful searching words with a clear, simple, not unimaginative diction. Yet his book is a great heritage.

'Newman has a sermon on Contemplation or Meditation, I forget which; and my copy is on board. But I do hope that by praying for humility, with contemplation of God's majesty and love and our Savior's humility and meekness, some improvement may be mercifully vouchsafed to me.

'To dwell on His humiliation, His patience, that He should seek for heavenly aids, accept the ministration of an angel strengthening Him, how full of mystery and awe! and yet written for us! And yet we are proud and self-justified and vainglorious!

'The Archbishop of York, in "Aids to Faith," on the Death of Christ, has some most solemn and deep remarks on the Lord's Agony. I don't know that it could ever be quite consistent with reverence to speak on what is there suggested. Yet if I could hear Mr. Keble and Dr. Pusey (say) prayerfully talking together on that great mystery, I should feel that it might be very profitable. But he must be a very humble man who should dare to speak on it. Yet read it, Fan, it cannot harm you; it is very awful, it is fully meant that He was sinless, without spot, undefiled through all. It makes the mystery of sin, and of what it cost to redeem our souls, more awful than ever.

'And then, surely to the contemplation of God and the necessary contrast of our own weakness and misery, we add the thought of our approaching death, we anticipate the hours, the days, it may be the weeks and months, even the years of weariness, pain, sleeplessness, thirst, distaste for food, murmuring thoughts, evil spirits haunting us, impatient longings after rest for which we are not yet prepared, the thousand trials, discomforts, sadnesses of sickness—yes, it must come in some shape; and is it to come as a friend or an enemy to snatch us from what we love and enjoy, or to open the gates of Paradise?

'I humbly thank God that, while I dare not be sure that I am not mistaken, and suppose that if ready to go I should be taken, the thought of death at a distance is the thought of rest and peace, of more blessed communion with God's saints, holy angels and the Lord. Yet I dare not feel that if death was close at hand, it might not be far otherwise. How often the "Christian Year," and all true divinity helps up here! Why indulge in such speculations? Seek to prepare for death by dying daily. Oh! that blessed text: Be not distracted, worry not yourselves about the morrow, for the morrow shall, &c. How it does carry one through the day! Bear everything as sent from God for your good, by way of chastisement or of proving you. Pusey's sermon on Patience, Newman's on a Particular Providence, guarding so wisely against abuse as against neglect of the doctrine. How much to comfort and guide one! and then, most of all, the continual use of the Prayer-book. Do you often use the Prayer at the end of the Evening Service for Charles the Martyr? Leave out from "great deep...teach us to number"—and substitute "pride" for "splendour." Leave out "according to... blessed martyr." In the Primate's case, it is a prayer full of meaning, and it may have a meaning for us all.

'Once more, the love of approbation is right and good, but then it must be the love of the approbation of God and of good men. Here, as everywhere, we abuse His gift; and it is a false teaching which bids us suppress the human instinct which God implanted in us, but a true leading, which bids us direct and use it to its appointed and legitimate use. On this general subject, read if you have not read them, and you can't read them too often, Butler's Sermons; you know, the great Butler. I think you will easily get an analysis of them, such as Mill's "Analysis of Pearson on the Creed," which will help you, if you want it. Analyse them for yourself, if you like, and send me out your analysis to look at. There is any amount of fundamental teaching there and the imprimatur of thousands of good men to assure us of it.

'I think, as I have written to Joan, that if I were with you, after the first few days my chiefest delight would be in reading and talking over our reading of good books. Edwin and Fisher were beginning to understand thoughtful books; and how I did delight in reading with them, interspersing a little Pitcairn remark here and there! Ah! never more! never more! But they don't want books now. All is clear now: they live where there is no night, in the Glory of God and of the Lamb, resting in Paradise, anticipating the full consummation of the Life of the Resurrection. Thanks be to God, and it may not be long—but I must not indulge such thoughts.

'I feel better, but at times this sad affliction weighs me down much, and business of all kinds seems almost to multiply. Yet there are many many comforts, and kindest sympathy.

'Your loving Brother,

'J. C. P.'

Just at this time heavy sorrow fell upon Bishop Hobhouse of Nelson; and the little council of friends at Auckland decided that Bishop Patteson should go at once to do his best to assist and comfort him, and bring him back to Auckland. There was a quiet time of wholesome rest at Nelson; and the effects appeared in numerous letters, and in the thinking out of many matters on paper to his sisters.

'Oh! how I think with such ever-increasing love of dear Fisher and Edwin! How I praised God for them on All Saints' Day. But I don't expect to recover spring and elasticity yet awhile. I don't think I shall ever feel so young again. Really it is curious that the number of white hairs is notably increased in these few weeks (though it is silly to talk about it. Don't mention it!), and I feel very tired and indolent. No wonder I seem to "go softly." But I am unusually happy down in the depths, only the surface troubled. I hope that it is not fancy only that makes the shortness and uncertainty of this life a ground of comfort and joy. Perhaps it is, indeed I think it is, very much a mere cowardly indolent shirking of work.

'Did I say I thought I might some day write a book? It will be some day indeed. It seems funny enough to think of such a thing. The fact is, it is much easier to me to speak than to write. I think I could learn with a good deal of leisure and trouble to write intelligibly, but not without it. I am so diffusive and wanting in close condensed habits of thought. How often I go off in a multitude of words, and really say nothing worthy to be remembered.

'How I should enjoy, indeed, a day or two at Hursley with Mr. and Mrs. Keble. A line from him now and then, if he can find time, would be a great delight to me; but I know that he thinks and prays, and that is indeed a great happiness.

'Oh, the blessing of such thoughts as All Saints' Day brings!—and now more dear than ever, every day brings!—"Patriarchs, prophets, apostles, martyrs, and every spirit made perfect in the faith of Christ," as an old Liturgy says. And the Collects in the Burial Service! How full, how simple and soothing, how full of calm, holy, tender, blessed hopes and anticipations!

'So you think the large Adelaide photograph very sad. I really don't remember it; I fancy I thought it a very fair likeness. But you know that I have a heavy lumpy dull look, except when talking—indeed, then too for aught I know—and this may be mistaken for a sad look when it is only a dull stupid one. You can't get a nice picture out of an ugly face, so it's no use trying, but you are not looking for that kind of thing. You want to see how far the face is any index of the character and life and work.

I don't think it odd that I should look careworn. I have enough to make me so! And yet if I were with you now, brightened up by being with you, you would say, "How well he looks!" And you would think I had any amount of work in me, as you saw me riding or walking or holding services. And then I had to a very considerable extent got over that silly shyness, which was a great trial and drawback to me of old, and sadly prevented me from enjoying the society of people (at Oxford especially) which would have done me much good. But without all these bodily defects, I should have been even more vain, and so I can see the blessing and mercy now, though how many times I have indulged murmuring rebellious thoughts!

'Perhaps I shall live ten or twenty years, and look back and say, "I recollect how in '64 I really almost thought I should not last long." But don't fancy that I am morbidly cherishing such fancies. Only I like you all to know me as I am changing in feeling from time to time. There is quite enough to account for it all.'

A few days later he returned to Auckland, and thence wrote to me a letter on the pros and cons of a move from New Zealand. The sight of ships and the town he had ceased to think of great importance, and older scholars had ceased to care for it, and there was much at that time to recommend Curtis Island to his mind. The want of bread-fruit was the chief disadvantage he then saw in it, but he still looked to keeping up Kohimarama for a good many years to come. I cannot describe how tender and considerate he was of feelings he thought I might possibly have of disappointment that St. Andrew's was not a successful experiment as far as health was concerned, evidently fearing that I had set my hopes on that individual venture, and that my feelings might be hurt if it had to be deserted.

The next letters are a good deal occupied with the troubles incident to the judgment upon 'Essays and Reviews.' He took a view, as has been seen, such as might be expected of the delicate refining metaphysical mind, thinking out points for itself, and weighing the possible value of every word, and differed from those who were in the midst of the contest, and felt some form of resistance and protest needful. He was strongly averse to agitation on the subject, and at the same time grieved to find himself for the first time, to his own knowledge, not accepting the policy of those whom he so much respected; though the only difference in his mind from theirs was as to the manner of the maintenance of the truth, and the immediate danger of error going uncondemned—a point on which his remote life perhaps hardly enabled him to judge.

All these long letters and more, which were either in the same tone, or too domestic to be published, prove the leisure caused by having an unusually small collection of pupils, and happily all in fair health; but with Christmas came a new idea, or rather an old one renewed. Instead of only going to Norfolk Island, on sufferance from the Pitcairn Committee, and by commission from the Bishop of Tasmania, a regular request was made, by Sir John Young, the Governor of Australia, that the Pitcairners might be taken under his supervision, so that, as far as Government was concerned, the opposition was withdrawn which had hindered his original establishment there, though still Curtis Island remained in the ascendency in the schemes of this summer. The ensuing is a reply to Sir John Coleridge's letter, written after hearing of the attack at Santa Cruz:—

'Kohimarama: March 3, 1865.

'My dearest Uncle,—Many many thanks for your letter, so full of comfort and advice. I need not tell you that the last budget of letters revived again most vividly not only the actual scene at Santa Cruz, but all the searchings of heart that followed it. I believe that we are all agreed on the main point. Enough ground has been opened for the present. Codrington was right in saying that the object of late has been to fill up gaps. But some of the most hazardous places to visit lie nearest to the south, e.g. some of the New Hebrides, &c., south of the Banks Islands. My notion is, that I ought to be content even to pass by (alas!) some places where I had some hold when I had reason to feel great distrust of the generally kind intentions of the people (that is a dark sentence, but you know my meaning). In short, there are very few places where I can feel, humanly speaking, secure against this kind of thing. It is always in the power of even one mischievous fellow to do mischief. And if the feeling of the majority might be in my favour, yet there being no way of expressing public opinion, no one cares to take an active part in preventing mischief. It is not worth his while to get into a squabble and risk his own life.

'But I shall be (D.V.) very cautious. I dare say I was becoming presumptuous: one among the many faults that are so discernible. It is, dear Uncle, hard to see a wild heathen party on the beach, and not try to get at them. It seems so sad to leave them. But I know that I ought to be prudent, even for my own sake (for I quite suppose that, humanly speaking, my life is of consequence for a few years more), and I can hardly bear the thought of bringing the boat's crew, dear good volunteers, into danger. Young Atkin, the only son of my neighbour, behaved admirably at Santa Cruz, and is very staunch. But his parents have but him and one daughter, and I am bound to be careful indeed. But don't think me careless, if we get into another scrape. There is scarcely one island where I can fully depend upon immunity from all risk. There was no need to talk so much about it all before.

'As to Curtis Island, I need not say that I have no wish indeed to take Australian work in hand. I made it most clear, as I thought, that the object of a site on Curtis Island was the Melanesian and not the Australian Mission. I offered only to incorporate Australian blacks, if proper specimens could be obtained, into our school, regarding in fact East Australia as another Melanesian island. This would only have involved the learning a language or two, and might have been of some use. I did not make any pledge. But I confess that I think some such plan as this one only feasible one. I don't see that the attempts at mission work are made on the most hopeful plan. But I have written to the Brisbane authorities, urging them to appropriate large reserves for the natives. I tell them that it is useless for them to give me a few acres and think they are doing a mission work, if they civilize the native races off their own lands. In short, I almost despair of doing anything for blacks living on the same land with whites. Even here in New Zealand, the distrust now shown to us all, to our religion even, is the result in very great measure of the insolent, covetous behaviour exhibited by the great majority of the white people to the Maori. Who stops in Australia to think whether the land which he wants for his sheep is the hunting ground of native people or not?

'I confess that while I can't bear to despair and leave these poor souls uncared for, I can't propose any scheme but one, and who will work that? If, indeed, one or two men could be found to go and live with a tribe, moving as they move and really identifying himself with their interests! But where are such men, and where is a tribe not already exasperated by injurious treatment?

'It was the statement for our mode of action which commended itself so much to people in Australia, that they urged me to try and do something. But I answered as I have now written; and when at one meeting in Sydney I was asked whether I would take Australians into my school, I said, "Yes, if I can get the genuine wild man, uncontaminated by contact with the white man." I can't, in justice to our Melanesian scholars, take the poor wretched black whose intercourse with white men has rendered him a far more hopeless subject to deal with than the downright ferocious yet not ungenerous savage. "If," was the answer, "you can get them, I will pay for them."

'Indeed, dear Uncle, I don't want more but less work on my hands: yet as I look around, I see (as far as I can judge) so great a want of that prudence and knowledge and calm foresight that the Primate has shown so remarkably, that I declare I do think his plan is almost the only reasonable one for dealing with black races. Alas! you can't put hearty love for strangers into men's hearts by paying them salaries.

'I think that in two or three years I may, if I live, have some preparatory branch school at Curtis Island. If it should clearly succeed, then I think in time the migration from New Zealand might take place. I do not think two schools in two different countries would answer. We want the old scholars to help us in working the school; we can't do without them, and the old scholars can't be trained without the younger ones, the material on whom their teaching, and training faculties must be exercised.

'You all know how deeply I feel about dear Mr. Keble!

'Thank God, we have as yet no dysentery. I baptized last week a lad dying of consumption. There are many blessings, as all clergymen know, in having death scenes so constantly about one; and the having to do everything for these dear fellows makes one love them so....

'Your affectionate and dutiful Nephew,

'J. C. P.'

The above sentence refers to the paralytic attack Mr. Keble had on November 30, 1864. Nevertheless, almost at that very time, he was writing thus:—

'Penzance: March 7, 1865.

'My dear and more than dear Bishop,—It would be vain for me to write to you, if I pretended to do more than just express my heart's wish that I could say something of the doings and sufferings which now for years past we of course associate with your name, so as to encourage and support you in your present manifold distress. But (especially for reasons known only to myself) I must leave that altogether to Him who helps His own to do and suffer. One thing only I would say, that to us at our great distance it looks as if the sanguis martyrum were being to you as the semen Ecclesiae, and you know how such things were hailed in the time of St. Cyprian. May it please God before long to give you some visible earnest of this sure blessing! but I suppose that if it tarry, it may be the greater when it comes. Our troubles as a Church, though of a different kind, are not small. The great point with me is, lest, if in our anxiety to keep things together, we should be sinfully conniving at what is done against the faith, and so bringing a judgment upon ourselves. I do not for a moment think that by anything which has yet been done or permitted our being as a Church is compromised (though things look alarmingly as if it might be before long), but I fear that her well-being is more and more being damaged by our entire and conscious surrender of the disciplinary part of our trust, and that if we are apathetic in such things we may forfeit our charter. There is no doubt, I fear, that personal unbelief is spreading; but I trust that a deeper faith is spreading also; it is (at Oxford, e.g.) Pusey and Moberly, &c., against the Rationalists and other tempters. As to the question of the Bible being (not only containing) the Word, I had no scruples in signing that Declaration. One thought which helped me was, the use made in the New Testament of the Old, which is such as to show that we are not competent judges as to what passages convey deep moral or religious meanings or no. Another, that in every instance where one had the means of ascertaining, so far as I have known, the Bible difficulty has come right: therefore, it is reasonable to conclude that so it would be in all the rest, if we knew the right reading and the right interpretation of the words. And as to what are called the Divine and Human Elements, I have seemed to help myself with the thought that the Divine adoption (if so be) of the human words warrants their truthfulness, as a man's signature makes a letter his own; but whether this is relevant, I doubt. My wife and I are both on the sick list, and I must now only add that we never forget you.

'Ever yours,
'J. K.

Nothing has hitherto been said of this term at St. Andrew's: so here is an extract from a letter to one of the cousinhood, who had proposed a plan which has since been carried out extensively and with good effect:—

'The difficulty about scholars appropriated to certain places or parishes is this: I cannot be sure of the same persons remaining with me. Some sickness in an island, some panic, some death of a relative, some war, or some inability on my part from bad weather or accident to visit an island, may at any time lose me a scholar. Perhaps he may be the very one that has been appropriated to some one, and what am I to say then?

'This year we have but thirty-eight Melanesians, we ought to have sixty. But after dear Edwin and Fisher's wounds, I could not delay, but hurried southwards, passing by islands with old scholars ready to come away. This was sad work, but what could I do?

'I will gladly assign, to the best of my power, scholars whom I think likely to remain with me to various places or persons; but pray make them understand that their scholar may not always be forthcoming. Anyhow, their alms would go to the support of some Melanesian, who would be their scholar as it were for the time being.

'You would perhaps feel interested in knowing that the Gospel of St. Luke has been printed in the Mota language, to a great extent by our scholars, and that George Sarawia is printing now the Acts, composing it, and doing press-work and all. Young Wogale (about thirteen) prints very fairly, and sent off 250 copies of a prayer, which the Bishop of Nelson wanted for distribution, of which everything was done by him entirely. They both began to learn about last November.

'When morning school is over at 10 A.M., all hands, "dons" and all, are expected to give their time to the Mission till 12.45. Mr. Pritt is general overlooker (which does not mean doing nothing himself) of domestic work: kitchen, garden, farm, dairy, &c. You know that we have no servants. Mr. Palmer prints and teaches printing. Atkin works at whatever may be going on, and has a large share of work to get ready for me, and to read with me: Greek Testament, 12 to 12.45, Greek and Latin from 2 to 3. So all the lads are busy at out-door work from 10 to 12.45; and I assure you, under Mr. Pritt's management, we begin to achieve considerable results in our farm and garden work. We are already economising our expenditure greatly by keeping our own cows, for which we grow food (a good deal artificial), and baking our own bread. We sell some of our butter, and have a grand supply of milk for our scholars, perhaps the very best kind of food for them.

'If we can manage to carry on a winter's school here with some ten or twelve of the lads left under Mr. Pritt's charge, while I go off with the rest, I really think that the industrial department may become something considerable. It is an essential part of the system, for we must begin with teaching habits of order, punctuality, &c:, in respect of those things with which they have already some acquaintance. No Melanesian can understand why he is to sit spelling away at a black board; and he is not like a child of four or five years old, he must be taught through his power of reasoning, and perceiving the meaning of things. Secondly, we can gradually invest the more advanced scholars with responsible duties. There are the head cooks in the various weeks, the heads of departments in garden work, &c., &c. As these lads and men are being trained (we hope) to teach others, and as we want them to teach industry, decency, cleanliness, punctuality, to be, and to teach others to be honest, and careful, and thoughtful, so we find all these lessons are learnt more in the industrial work than in the mere book work, though that is not neglected. Indeed school, in the restricted sense of the word, is going on for four or four and a half hours a day.

'The main difficulty remains, of retaining our hold upon boys. Oh that I could live permanently in twenty islands at once! But I can't do so even in one; and all the letter-writing and accounts, and, worst of all, the necessity for being trustee for matters not a bit connected with Melanesia, because there is no one else, interferes sadly with my time. I think I could work away with the languages, &c., and really do something with these fellows, but I never get a chance. I never have two days together which I can spend exclusively at Melanesian work. And I ought to have nothing whatever to distract me. Twenty languages calling for arrangement and comparison causes confusion enough!'

These interruptions made the Kohimarama life trying. 'As for correspondence,' says the birthday despatch to Fanny, 'why this mail my letters to Victoria alone are twelve, let alone Sydney, Brisbane, Adelaide, Tasmania, New Zealand, and England. Then three sermons a week, occasional services, reading up for a most difficult session of General Synod, with really innumerable interruptions from persons of all kinds. Sometimes I do feel tempted to long for Curtis Island merely to get away from New Zealand! I feel as if I should never do anything here. Everything is in arrears. I turn out of a morning and really don't know what to take up first. Then, just as I am in the middle of a letter (as yesterday) down comes some donkey to take up a quarter of an hour (lucky if not an hour) with idle nonsense; then in the afternoon an invasion of visitors, which is worst of all. That fatal invention of "calling"! However, I never call on anyone, and it is understood now, and people don't expect it. I have not even been to Government House for more than a year!

'There, a good explosion does one good! But why must idle people interfere with busy men? I used to make it up by sitting up and getting up very early indeed; but somehow I feel fit for nothing but sleeping and eating now.'

After an absence of three weeks at the General Synod at Christchurch, the Bishop took up such of his party as were to return, and sailed home, leaving those whom he thought able to brave the winter with Mr. and Mrs. Pritt, on one of the first days of June. The first visit was one to the bereaved family at Norfolk Island, whence a brief note to his brother on the 9th begins:—

'Nothing can be more comforting to me than the loving patient spirit of these dear people. Poor Mr. and Mrs. Nobbs and all the brothers and sisters so good and so full of kindness to me. It was very trying when I first met them yesterday. They came and kissed me, and then, poor things, fairly gave way, and then I began to talk quietly about Edwin and Fisher, and they became calm, and we knelt and prayed together.'

After landing the Bishop at Mota, the others crossed to Port Patteson where they found Fisher Young's grave carefully tended, kept clear of weeds, and with a fence round it. After establishing Mr. Palmer at the station at Mota, the Bishop re-embarked for Santa Maria, where, at the north-east—Cock Sparrow Point, as some one had appropriately called it—the boat was always shot at; but at a village called Lakona, the people were friendly, and five scholars had come from thence, so the Bishop ventured on landing for the night, and a very unpleasant night it, was—the barrack hut was thronged with natives, and when the heat was insufferable and he tried to leave it, two of his former scholars advised him strongly to remain within.

It was bad weather too, and there was some difficulty in fetching him off, and he was thankful that the wet had hindered more than 300 or 400 natives from collecting; there was no possibility of speaking to them quietly, for the sight of the boat suggested trading, and they flocked round as he was fetched off, half a dozen swimming out and begging to go to New Zealand. He took three old scholars and one new one, and sent the others off with fish-hooks, telling them that if they would not behave at Lakona as he liked, he would not do as they liked. However, no arrows were shot.

Then while the 'Southern Cross,' with Mr. Tilly and Mr. Atkin, went on to land the Solomon Island scholars, the work at Mota was resumed in full force. It seems well worth while to dwell on the successive steps in the conversion of this place, and the following letter shows the state of things in the season of 1865:—

'Mota: July 4, 1865.

'My dearest Sisters and Brother,—I must write a joint letter for all, with little notes if I have anything more special for anyone of you. I wish you could see this place. The old hut is queer enough certainly, quite open on one side, and nearly so on another, but it is weather-tight in the middle, with forms to sit on and a table or two like a kitchen table, on which I read and write by day, and sleep by night. Last night we killed five lizards; they get on the roof and drop down and bite pretty severely, so seeing these running all about, we made a raid upon them, poor things. The great banyan tree is as grand as ever, a magnificent tree, a forest in itself, and the view of the sea under its great branches, and of the islands of Matlavo and Valua, is beautiful.

'At daylight I turn off my table and dress, not elaborately—a flannel shirt, old trousers and shoes; then a yam or two is roasted on the embers, and the coffee made, and (fancy the luxury here in Mota!) delicious goat's milk with it. Then the morning passes in reading, writing, and somewhat desultory talking with people, but you can't expect punctuality and great attention. Then at one, a bit of biscuit and cheese (as long as the latter lasts). Mr. Palmer made some bread yesterday. Then generally a walk to meet people at different villages, and talk to them, trying to get them to ask me questions, and I try to question them. Then at 6 P.M., a tea-ation, viz., yam and coffee, and perhaps a crab or two, or a bit of bacon, or some good thing or other. But I forgot! this morning we ate a bit of our first full-grown and fully ripe Mota pine-apple (I brought some two years ago) as large and fine as any specimens I remember in hot-houses. If you mention all these luxuries, we shall have no more subscriptions, but you may add that there is as yet no other pineapple, though our oranges, lemons, citrons, guavas, &c., are coming on. Anyone living here permanently might make a beautiful place indeed, but it becomes sadly overgrown in our absence, and many things we plant are destroyed by pigs, &c.

'Then after tea—a large party always witnessing that ceremony—there is an hour or so spent in speaking again to the people, and then I read a little with Wadrokala and Carry. Then Mr. Palmer and I read a chapter of Vaughan on the Revelation, then prayers, and so to bed. It seems as if little was done—certain talks with people, sometimes many, sometimes few; yet, on the whole, I hope an increased acquaintance with our teaching. You can well understand that the consciousness of sin and the need of a Redeemer may be talked about, but cannot be stated so as to make one feel that one has stated it in the most judicious and attractive manner. Of course it is the work of God's Spirit to work this conviction in the heart. But it is very hard so to speak of it as to give (if you can understand me) the heathen man a fair chance of accepting what you say. Forgetfulness of God; ingratitude to the Giver of life, health, food; ignorance of the Creator and the world to come, of the Resurrection and Life Everlasting, are all so many proofs to us of a fallen and depraved state. But the heathen man recognises some outward acts as more or less wrong; there he stops. "Yes, we don't fight now, nor quarrel, nor steal so much as we used to do. We are all right now."

'"Are you? I never taught you to think so. You tell me that you believe that the Son of God came down from heaven. What did He come for? What is the meaning of what you say that He died for us?"

'It is the continual prayer and effort of the Christian minister everywhere, that God would deepen in his own heart the sense of sin, and create it in the mind of the heathen. And then the imperfect medium of a language very far from thoroughly known! It is by continual prayer, the intercession of Christ, the power of the Spirit (we well know) that the work must be carried on. How one does understand it! The darkness seems so thick, the present visible world so wholly engrosses the thoughts, and yet, you see, there are many signs of progress even here, in changed habits to some extent, in the case of our scholars, real grounds of hope for the future. One seems to be doing nothing, yet surely if no change be wrought, what right have we to expect it. It is not that I looked for results, but that I seek to be taught how to teach better. The Collect for the first Sunday after Epiphany is wonderful.

'It requires a considerable effort to continually try to present to oneself the state of the heathen mind, to select illustrations, &c., suitable to his case. And then his language has never been used by him to set forth these new ideas; there are no words which convey the ideas of repentance, sin, heartfelt confession, faith, &c. How can there be, when these ideas don't exist? Yet somehow the language by degrees is made the exponent of such ideas, just as all religious ideas are expressed in English by words now used in their second intention, which once meant very different and less elevated ideas.

'I find everywhere the greatest willingness to listen. Everywhere I take my pick of boys, and now for any length of time. That is the result of eleven scholars remaining now in New Zealand. Everyone seems to wish to come. I think I shall take away five or six young girls to be taught at Kohimarama, to become by and by wives for scholars. Else the Christian lad will have to live with a heathen girl. But all this, if carried out properly, would need a large number of scholars from only one island. At Curtis Island, indeed (should it answer and supply plenty of food), we might hope to have a school some day of 300 or 400, and then thirty or forty from each island could be educated at once; but it can't be so in New Zealand. And a good school on an island before a certain number are trained to teach could not, I think, be managed successfully. I feel that I must concentrate more than hitherto. I must ascertain—I have to some extent ascertained—the central spots upon which I must chiefly work. This is not an easy thing, nevertheless, to find out, and it has taken years. Then using them as centres, I must also find out how far already the dialect of that spot may extend, how far the people of the place have connections, visiting acquaintances, &c. elsewhere, and to use the influence of that place to its fullest extent. Many islands would thus fall under one centre, and thus I think we may work. My mind is so continually, day and night, I may say, working on these points, that I dare say I fill up my letters with nothing else. But writing on these points helps me to see my way.'

On July 7, an expedition to Aroa seems to have overtired Bishop Patteson, and a slight attack of fever and ague came on. One of his aunts had provided him with a cork bed, where, after he had exerted himself to talk to his many visitors, he lay 'not uncomfortably.' He was not equal to going to a feast where he hoped to have met a large concourse, and after a day of illness, was taken back to Mota in the bottom of the boat; but in another week more revived, and went on with his journal, moralising on the books he had been reading while laid up.

'I looked quite through Bishop Mackenzie's life. What a beautiful story it is! what a truthful, simple, earnest character, and that persuasiveness that only real humility and self-forgetfulness and thoughtfulness can give. Then his early desire to be useful, his Cambridge life, the clear way in which he was being led on all through. It is very beautiful as an illustration of the best kind of help that God bestows on His children. Here was one so evidently moulded and fashioned by Him, and that willingly, for so it must be, and his life was just as it should be, almost as perfect perhaps as a life can be. What if his work failed on the Shire? First, his work has not failed to begin with, for aught we know; and secondly his example is stimulating work everywhere. I shall indeed value his Thomas a Kempis. [A copy sent home from the Zambesi stained with the water of the Shire, and sent to the Bishop by Miss Mackenzie].

The ship returned with tidings that the more important scholars would be ready to come back after a short holiday with their friends, and the Bishop embarked again on the 29th. At Mai he landed, and slept ashore, when little Petere, the son of the young man whose death had so nearly been revenged on the Bishop, a boy of eight years old, did the honours as became a young chief, and announced, 'I am going to New Zealand with you.' No one made any attempt to prevent him; but the old scholars did not show themselves helpful, and only one of them, besides three more new ones, came away. The natives were personally friendly, but there was no sign of fighting being lessened among them.

At Whitsuntide there was a brisk trade in yams, but no scholars were brought away; the parents would not part with any young enough to be likely to be satisfactory pupils, nor would the one last year's scholar come. Here intelligence was received that a two-masted ship had been at Leper's Island, a quarrel had taken place and some natives had been shot. It was therefore decided that it would not be safe to land, but as the vessel sailed along the coast, numerous canoes came out, bringing boars' tusks for sale. Three boys who had been taken on a cruise of six weeks the year before, eagerly came on board, and thirty or forty more. All the parents were averse to letting them go, and only two ended by being brought away: Itole, a young gentleman of fourteen or so, slim and slight, with a waist like a wasp, owing to a cincture worn night and day, and his hair in ringlets, white with coral-lime; his friend a little older, a tall, neat-limbed fellow, not dark and with little of the negro in his features.

A letter to me was written during this cruise, from which I give an extract:—

'It was a great delight to me to receive a letter from Mr. Keble, by the February mail from England. How kind of him to write to me; and his words are such a help and encouragement.

'I dare say I shall see Merivale's Lectures soon. Nothing can well be so wonderful, as a proof of God's hand controlling and arranging all the course of history to those who need it, as a subject for adoration and praise, to those who need not such proof, than the vast preparation made for the coming of Christ and the spreading of the Gospel. To popularise this the right way, and bring it home to the thought of many who have not time nor inclination for much reading, must be a good work. I suppose that all good Church histories deal with that part of the subject; it is natural for the mere philosopher to do so.

'And think how the early Alexandrian teachers used the religious yearnings of the East to draw men to the recognition of their wants, supplied and satisfied only in Christianity. Often it is the point d'appui that the Missionary must seek for. There is an element of faith in superstition; we must fasten on that, and not rudely destroy the superstition, lest with it we destroy the principle of faith in things and beings unseen. I often think, that to shake a man's faith in his old belief, however wrong it may be, before one can substitute something true and right, is, to say the least, a dangerous experiment. But positive truth wins its way without controversy, while error has no positive existence, and there is a craving for truth deep down in the heathen heart.

'Do you remember that grand passage of Hooker, where he says that he cannot stand to oppose all the sophisms of Romanism, only that he will place against it a structure of truth, before which, as Dagon before the Ark, error will be dashed in fragments?

'In our work (and so I suppose in a Sunday school) one must think out each step, anticipate each probable result, before one states anything. It is of course full of the highest interest. Can't you fancy a party of twenty or thirty dark naked fellows, when (having learnt to talk freely to them) I question them about their breakfast and cocoa-nut trees, their yams and taro and bananas, &c., "Who gave them to you? Can you make them grow? Why, you like me and thank me because I give you a few hatchets, and you have never thought of thanking Him all these long years."

'"It is true, but we didn't think."

'"But will you think if I tell you about Him?"

'"He gave them rain from heaven and fruitful seasons."

'How it takes one back to the old thoughts, the true philosophy of religion. Sometimes I lie awake and think "if Jowett and others could see these things!"

'And yet, if it is not presumptuous in me to say so, I do think that this work needs men who can think out principle and supply any thoughtful scholar or enquirer with some good reason for urging this or that change in the manners and observances of the people. Often as I think of it, I feel how greatly the Church needs schools for missionaries, to be prepared not only in Greek and Latin and manual work, but in the mode of regarding heathenism. It is not a moment's work to habitually ask oneself, "Why feel indignant? How can he or she know better?" It is not always easy to be patient and to remember the position which the heathen man occupies and the point of view from which he must needs regard everything brought before him.

'Thank you for Maclear's book. It is a clear statement of the leading facts that one wishes to know, a valuable addition to our library. You know, no doubt, a book which I like much, Neander's "Light in Dark Places."

'I shall remember about Miss Mackenzie's memoir of that good Mrs. Robertson. I wonder that men are not found to help Mr. Robertson. Here, as you know, the climate (as in Central Africa) is our difficulty. I think sometimes I make too much of it, but really I don't see how a man is to stand many months of it. But I can't help thinking and hoping that if that difficulty did not exist I could see my way to saying, "Now, a missionary is wanted for these four or five or six islands, one for each, and a younger man as fellow-helper to that missionary," and they would be forthcoming.

'Yet doubtless I don't estimate fairly the difficulties and hardships as they appear to the man who has never left England, and is not used to knocking about. I should have felt the same years ago but for the thought of being with the Primate, at least I suppose so.

'Well, I have written a very dull letter, but the place from which it comes will give it some interest. I really think that not Mota only, but the Banks Islands are in a hopeful state.

'Next year (D.V.) Mr. Palmer will try the experiment of stopping here for eight or ten months. I almost dare to hope that a few years may make great changes. Yet it seems as if nothing were done in comparison with what remains to be done.

'Sarah, Sarawia's wife, pronounced that as she was always ill at home, she would risk the New Zealand winter; two more married pairs came, and four little maidens to be bred up under Mrs. Pritt, girls from twelve to eight years old, of whom Sarah was quite able to take charge.'

There was the usual proportion of lads from various islands; but the most troublesome member of the community seems to have been Wadrokala's three years old daughter. 'I have daily to get Wadrokala and Carry to prevent their child from being a nuisance to everybody.' But this might have been a difficulty had she been white.

This large party had to be taken to the Solomon Isles to complete the party, sailing in company with the 'Curacoa,' the Commodore's ship, when the local knowledge and accurate surveying done by Mr. Tilly and Mr. Kerr proved very valuable, and Sir William Wiseman gave most kind and willing assistance.

Since his short interview with the Bishop off Norfolk Island, he had been cruising in the New Hebrides. There some of the frequent outrages of the traders had made the people savage and suspicious, and one of the Missionaries of the London Missionary Society living at Tanna had been threatened, driven away across the island, and his property destroyed. He had appealed for protection as a British subject, and Sir William Wiseman had no choice but to comply; so after warning had been sent to the tribe chiefly concerned to quit their village, it was shelled and burnt. No one seems to have been hurt, and it was hoped that this would teach the natives to respect their minister—whether to love his instruction was another question.

This would not have been worth mentioning had not a letter from on board the 'Curacoa' spoken of chastising a village for attacking a Missionary. It went the round of the English papers, and some at once concluded that the Missionary could be no other than the Bishop. Articles were published with the usual disgusting allusions to the temptation presented by a plump missionary; and also observing with more justice that British subjects had no right to run into extraordinary peril and appeal to their flag for protection.

Every friend or relative of Bishop Patteson knew how preposterous the supposition was, and his brother took pains to contradict the rumour. As a matter of fact, as his letters soon proved, he was not only not in company with the 'Curacoa' at the time, but had no knowledge either of the outrage or the chastisement, till Sir William Wiseman mentioned it to him when they were together at Sydney.

At Ysabel or Mahya, the party was made up to sixty, seven married couples and seven unmarried girls among them. The female population was stowed away at night in the after cabins, with 'arrangements quite satisfactory to them, as they were quite consistent with propriety, but which would somewhat startle unaccustomed folk.'

The 'Curapoa' stood in the offing while Sta. Cruz was visited, or rather while the 'Southern Cross' approached, for the Bishop thought it better not to risk landing; but numerous canoes came off, and all the curiosities were bought which were offered in hopes of reestablishing a friendly relation. There was reason to think the people of this group more than usually attached to the soil, and very shy and distrustful, owing perhaps to the memories left by the Spaniards.

Thence the 'Southern Cross' sailed across for an inspection of Curtis Island, and again with a favourable impression; but the Brisbane Parliament had just been prorogued, everyone was taking holiday, and the Bishop therefore gave up his visit to that place, and sent the vessel straight home to Auckland with her cargo of souls, while he returned to Sydney to carry on the same work as in the former year. Here one great delight and refreshment to him was a visit to Mr. and Mrs. Mort at their beautiful home at Greenoaks. What a delight it must have been to find himself in a church built by his host himself! 'one of the most beautiful things I have seen, holds about 500 people; stained glass, carved stalls, stone work, &c.,—perfect.' And the house, 'full of first-rate works of art, bronzes, carvings, &c.,' was pleasant to the eyes that had been so enthusiastic in Italy and Germany, and had so long fasted from all beauty but that of Nature, in one special type. The friends there were such as to give life and spirit to all these external charms, and this was a very pleasant resting place in his life. To Sir John Coleridge he writes:—

'I am having a real holiday. This place, Greenoaks, the really magnificent place of my good friends Mr. and Mrs. Mort, is lovely. The view of the harbour, with its land-locked bays, multitude of vessels, wooded heights, &c., is not to be surpassed; and somehow I don't disrelish handsome rooms and furniture and pictures and statues and endless real works of art in really good taste.

'One slips into these ways very readily. I must take care I am not spoilt. Everyone, from the governor downwards, lays himself out to make my visit pleasant. They work me hard on Sundays and week days, but it is a continual round of, I don't deny, to me, pleasurable occupation. Kindly people asked to meet me, and the conversation always turned to pleasant and useful subjects: Church government, principles of Mission work, &c. These colonies, unfortunate in many ways, are fortunate in having governors and others in high position who are good men, and the class of people among whom my time is spent might (me judice) hold its position among the best English society.

'I am very intimate with some few families, drop in and set the young ladies down to play Beethoven and Mendelssohn, and it is a nice change, and refreshes me.'

From Sydney the Bishop went to Adelaide and Melbourne, and these five weeks in Australia obtained about 800 pounds for the Mission; the Bishop of Sydney had hoped to raise more, but there had been two years of terrible drought and destruction of cattle, and money was not abundant. The plan of sending Australian blacks to be educated with the Melanesians was still entertained; but he had not much hope of this being useful to the tribes, though it might be to the individuals, and none of them ever were sent to him.

But what had a more important effect on the Mission was a conference between Sir William Wiseman and Sir John Young, the Governor of New South Wales, resulting in an offer from the latter of a grant of land on Norfolk Island for the Mission, for the sake of the benefit to the Pitcairners; at the same time the Commodore offered him a passage in the 'Curacoa' back to Auckland, touching at Norfolk Island by the way. The plan was carried out, and brought him home in time for Christmas, to find all and prosperous under Mr. Pritt at St. Andrew's. His mind was nearly made up on the expedience of a change to a place which was likely to suit both English and tropical constitutions alike, and he hoped to make the experiment the ensuing winter with Mr. Palmer and a small body of scholars.

CHAPTER X. THE EPISCOPATE AT KOHIMARAMA. 1866.

The removal of his much-loved correspondent did not long withhold the outpouring of Bishop Patteson's heart to his family; while his work was going on at the College, according to his own definition of education which was given about this time in a speech at St. John's: 'Education consists in teaching people to bear responsibilities, and laying the responsibilities on them as they are able to bear them.'

Meanwhile, he wrote as follows to Miss Mackenzie, on receiving the book she had promised to send him as a relic of her brother:—

'January 1, 1866.

'My dear Miss Mackenzie,—I have this evening received your brother's Thomas a Kempis, and your letter. I valued the letter much, as a true faithful record of one whom may God grant that I may know hereafter, if, indeed, I may be enabled to follow him as he followed Christ. And as for the former, what can I say but I hope that the thought of your dear brother may help me to read that holy book in something of the spirit in which he read and meditated on it.

'It seems to bring me very near to him in thought. Send me one of his autographs to paste into it. I don't like to cut out the one I have in the long letter to the Scottish Episcopal Church, which you kindly sent me.

'I found, too, in one of Mr. Codrington's boxes, a small sextant for me, which, being packed with the Thomas a Kempis, I think may have been your brother's. Do you really mean this for me too? If so, I shall value it scarcely less than the book. Indeed, I think that, divided as I am from all relations and home influences and affections, I cling all the more to such means as I may still enjoy of keeping up associations. I like to have my father's watch-chain in use, and to write on his old desk. I remember my inkstand in our drawing-room in London. So I value much these memorials of the first Missionary Bishop of the Church of England, in modern days at all events, and night by night as I read a few lines in his book, and think of him, it brings me, I hope, nearer in spirit to him and to others, who, like him, have done their duty well and now rest in Christ.

'We are pretty well now (Jan. 20), but one very promising lad sank last week in low fever; a good truthful lad he was, and as I baptized him at midnight shortly before he died, I felt the great blessing of being able with a very clear conscience to minister to him that holy sacrament; and so he passed away, to dwell, I trust, with his Lord.

'What a revelation to that spirit in its escape from the body! But I must not write on. With many thanks once again for these highly-valued memorials of your brother,

'I remain, my dear Miss Mackenzie,
'Very truly yours,
'J. C. PATTESON.'

The sandal-wood referred to in the following letter was the brother's gift to a church, All Saints, Babbicombe, in which his sisters were deeply interested, and of which their little nephew laid the first stone:—

'St. Matthias' Day.

'My dearest Sisters,—You are thinking of me to-day, I know, but you hardly know that in an hour or two I hope the Primate will ride down and baptize nine of our Melanesian scholars.

'The last few weeks have been a happy, though of course an anxious time, and now to-day the great event of their lives is to take place. May God grant that the rest of their lives may be like this beginning!

'We avoid all fuss. I don't like anyone being here but the Primate and Mrs. Selwyn, yet I think some dozen more may come, though I don't like it. I need not say that making a scene on such occasions is to my mind very objectionable. I could much prefer being quite alone. I have translated some appropriate Psalms, but the 2nd and 57th they hardly know as yet quite well; so our service will be Psalms 96, 97, 114; 1st lesson 2 Kings, v. 9—15, Magnificat; 2nd lesson Acts viii. 5-12, and the Baptismal Service. Henry Tagalana reads the first, and George Sarawia the second lesson. Then will come my quiet evening, as, I trust, a close of an eventful day. I have your English letters of December, with the news of Johnny laying the stone. I am thankful that that good work is begun. Sir John Young writes to me that I can have a gift of 100 acres at Norfolk Island, with permission to buy more. I think that, all being well, I shall certainly try it with a small party next summer, the main body of scholars being still brought to Kohimarama.

'The sandal-wood is not yet gone! But, my dear Joan, the altar of sandal-wood! If it is to be solid and not veneered, why, £50 would not buy it at Erromango. It sells in Sydney for about £70 a ton, and it is very heavy wood. However, I will send some of the largest planks I ever saw of the wood, and it is now well seasoned. It cost me £14 merely to work it into a very simple lectern, so hard is the grain.

'What has become of the old Eton stamp of men? Have you any in England? I must not run the risk of the Mission being swamped, by well-intentioned, but untaught men. We must have gentlemen of white colour, or else I must rely wholly, as I always meant to do chiefly, on my black gentlemen; and many of them are thorough gentlemen in feeling and conduct, albeit they don't wear shoes.

'It was a most impressive service. The dear Primate looking worn and somewhat aged, very full of feeling; the two most advanced, George and Henry, in their surplices, reading the Lessons; the nine candidates looking so reverent and grave, yet not without self-possession.

'As he signed each one with the sign of the Cross, his left hand resting on the head of each, the history of the Mission rushed into my mind, the fruit of the little seed be sowed when, eight years ago, he thought it wisest not to go ashore at

Mota, and now more than twenty Christians of the Banks Islands serve God with prayers night and day.

'What would you have thought, if you could have been there? Our little chapel looked nice with the red hangings and sandal-wood lectern.

'Then we had a quiet cup of tea, and the old and new baptized party had a quiet talk with me till 8.30, when I sent them away.

'And then after an hour I was alone. That I should have been already five years a Bishop, and how much to think of and grieve over, something too to be thankful for. Perhaps after all, dear Edwin and Fisher stand out most clearly from all the many scenes and circumstances.

'And now what is to come? This move to Norfolk Island? Or what? "Something," you say; "perhaps in time showing the Governor that the Melanesians are not so very wild." But it is another Governor; and so far from the Melanesians being wild, it is expressly on the ground that the example of the school will be beneficial that I am asked to go!

'Tell all who may care to know it about our St. Matthias' Day, I must give myself the pleasure of writing one line to Mr. Keble. I won't write many lest I weary him, dear good man. I like to look at his picture, and have stuck the photograph of Mr. and Mrs. Keble which Charlotte Yonge sent me into the side of it. How I value his prayers and thoughts for us all!

'Your loving brother,

'J. C. P.

'P.S.—No terms of full communion between the Home and the Colonial Church can be matter of Parliamentary legislation. It is the "One Faith, One Lord," that binds us together; and as for regulating the question of colonially ordained clergy ministering in English dioceses, you had better equalise your own Church law first for dealing with an Incumbent and a Curate.'

'Auckland: Tuesday in Holy Week.

'My dear Uncle,—I have long owed you a letter, but I have not written because I have had an unusual time of distraction. Now, all my things being on board the "Southern Cross," I am detained by a foul wind. We can do nothing till it changes; and I am not sorry to have a few quiet hours, though the thought of a more than usually serious separation from the dear Primate and Mrs. Selwyn, Sir William and Lady Martin, hangs over my head rather gloomily. Still I am convinced, as far as I can be of such matters, that this move to Norfolk Island is good for the Mission on the whole. It has its drawbacks, as all plans have, but the balance is decidedly in favour of Norfolk Island as against New Zealand. I have given reasons at length for this opinion in letters to Joan and Fan, and also, I think, to Charlotte Yonge, who certainly deserves to know all my thoughts about it.

'But I may shortly state some of them, in case you may not have heard them, because I should like this step to approve itself to your mind:—

'1. Norfolk Island is 600 miles nearer to Melanesian islands than Auckland, and not only nearer in actual distance, but the 600 miles from Norfolk Island to Auckland are the cold and boisterous miles that must be passed at the extremities of the voyages with no intervening lands to call at and obtain a change for our large party on board.

'2. The difficulty usually is to get westward when sailing from New Zealand, by the North Cape of New Zealand, because the prevalent winds are from the west. So that usually the passage to Norfolk Island is a long-one.

'3. New Zealand is much to the east of Norfolk Island, and to go from the Loyalty, New Hebrides, Banks, and Santa Cruz groups to New Zealand, it is necessary to make a long stretch out to the N.E. (the trades blowing from about S.E. by E.), standing down to S. on the other tack. But Norfolk Island is almost due S. of other those groups.

'4. I cannot come back from the islands during my winter voyage to New Zealand, it is too distant; the coast is dangerous in the winter season and the cold too great for a party of scholars first coming from the tropics. But I can go backwards and forwards through the islands and Norfolk Island during the five winter months. It is not wise to sail about in the summer, hurricanes being prevalent then.

'5. As I can only make one return from the islands to New Zealand in the year, I can only have a school consisting of (say) sixty Melanesians brought in the very crowded vessel + (say) thirty left in New Zealand for the winter; and I dare not attempt to leave many, for so much care is needed in the cold season. But in Norfolk Island I can have a school of any number, because I can make separate voyages thither from the Banks and Solomon Islands, &c., each time bringing a party of sixty, if I think fit.

'6. The productions of Norfolk Island include the yam, taro (Caladium esculentum), sweet potato, sugar-cane, banana, almond, orange, pine-apple, coffee, maize. Only cocoa-nut and bread-fruit are wanting, that natives of Melanesia care much about.

'7. There is no necessity for so violent a contrast as there must be in New Zealand between the life with us and in their homes in respect of dress, food, and houses.

'Light clothing and an improved style of native house and more cleanly way of eating their food—not of cooking it, for they are cleanly already in that—may be adopted, and more easily perpetuated in their own homes than the heavy clothing necessary here, and the different style of houses and more English food.

'This is very important, because with any abrupt change of the outer man, there is sometimes a more, very more natural abandonment of the inner thoughts and disposition and character. Just as men so often lose self-respect when they take to the bush life; or children who pray by their own little bedside alone, leave off praying in "long chamber," the outward circumstances being altered.

'I have for years thought that we seek in our Missions a great deal too much to make English Christians of our converts. We consciously and unanimously assume English Christianity (as something distinct I mean from the doctrines of the Church of England), to be necessary; much as so many people assume the relation of Church and State in England to be the typical and normal condition of the Church, which should be everywhere reproduced. Evidently the heathen man is not treated fairly if we encumber our message with unnecessary requirements.

'The ancient Church had its "selection of fundamentals"—a kind of simple and limited expansion of the Apostles' Creed for doctrine and Apostolic practice for discipline.

'Notoriously the Eastern and Western mind misunderstood one another. The speculative East and the practical West could not be made to think after the same fashion. The Church of Christ has room for both.

'Now any one can see what mistakes we have made in India. Few men think themselves into the state of the Eastern mind, feel the difficulties of the Asiatic, and divine the way in which Christianity should be presented to him.

'We seek to denationalise these races, as far as I can see; whereas we ought surely to change as little as possible—only what is clearly incompatible with the simplest form of Christian teaching and practice.

'I don't mean that we are to compromise truth, but to study the native character, and not present the truth in an unnecessarily unattractive form.

'Don't we overlay it a good deal with human traditions, and still more often take it for granted that what suits us must be necessary for them, and vice versa.

'So many of our missionaries are not accustomed, not taught to think of these things. They grow up with certain modes of thought, hereditary notions, and they seek to reproduce these, no respect being had to the utterly dissimilar character and circumstances of the heathen.

'I think much about all this. Sir William Martin and I have much talk about it; and the strong practical mind of the Primate, I hope, would keep me straight if I was disposed to theorise, which I don't think is the case.

'But Christianity is the religion for humanity at large. It takes in all shades and diversities of character, race, &c.

'The substratum of it is, so to say, inordinate and coextensive with the substratum of humanity—all men must receive that. Each set of men must also receive many thing of secondary, yet of very great importance for them; but in this class there will be differences according to the characteristic differences of men throughout the world.

'I can't explain myself fully; but, dear Uncle, I think there is something in what I am trying to say.

'I want to see more discrimination, more sense of the due proportion, the relative importance of the various parts which make up the sum of extra teaching.

'There is so great want of order in the methods so often adopted, want of arrangement, and proper sequence, and subordination of one to another.

'The heathen man will assume some arbitrary dictate of a missionary to be of equal authority and importance with a moral command of God, unless you take care. Of course the missionary ought not to attempt to impose any arbitrary rule at all; but many missionaries do, and usually justify such conduct on the ground of their "exceptional position."

'But one must go much further. If I tell a man just beginning to listen, two or three points of Christian faith, or two or three rules of Christian life, without any orderly connection, I shall but puzzle him.

'Take, e.g., our English Sunday, I am far from wishing to change the greater part of the method of observing it in England.

'I hope the Melanesian Christians may learn to keep holy the Lord's Day. But am I to begin my teaching of a wild Solomon Islander at that end; when he has not learned the evil of breaking habitually the sixth, seventh, and eighth Commandments?

'I notice continually the tendency of the teaching of the very men who denounce "forms" to produce formation.

'It is nearest to the native mind; it generates hypocrisy and mere outward observance of certain rules, which, during the few years that the people remain docile on their first acceptance of the new teaching, they are content to submit to.

'I see the great difficulty of making out all this. It necessitates the leaving so very much to the discretion of the pioneer. Ergo the missionary must not be the man who is not good enough for ordinary work in England, but the men whom England even does not produce in large numbers with some power of dealing with these questions.

'It is much better and safer to have a regular well-known rule to act by; but I don't see how you can give me, e.g., precise directions. It seems to me that you must use great care in selecting your man, and then trust him fully.

'I hope it is not an excess of self-conceit and self-reliance which makes me pass by, rather lightly, I confess, some of the advice that very well-intentioned people occasionally volunteer to missionaries. I have had (D. Gr.) the Primate and Sir William Martin's men, who know what heathenism is, and the latter of whom has deeply studied the character of the various races of the world.

'I mean that when some one said, "Do you really mean to place those savage Melanesians among the immaculate Pitcairners?" the natural answer seemed to me to be, "I am not aware that you ever saw either a Pitcairner or a Melanesian." I thought it rather impertinent. The truth is, that the great proportion of our Melanesian scholars in our school, i.e., not standing alone, but helped by the discipline of the school, are quite competent to set an example to the average Pitcairners. But this I mark only as an illustration of my meaning. Occasionally I hear of some book or sermon or speech in which sound views (as I venture to call them) are propounded on these points.

'Always your loving and grateful Nephew,

'**J. C. PATTESON.**'

The next letter was called forth by my sorrowful communication of the shattered state of both my dear friends; of whom, one, at the very time that my Cousin wrote, was already gone to his rest, having been mercifully spared the loneliness and grief we had feared for him.

'St. Andrew's: April 24, 1866.

'My dear Cousin,—I write a line at once in reply to a letter of January 29, for I see that a great sorrow is hanging over you, is perhaps already fallen on you, and I would fain say my word of sympathy, possibly of comfort.

'One, perhaps, of the great blessings that a person in my position enjoys is that he must perforce see through the present gloom occasioned by loss of present companionship on to the joy beyond. I hear of the death of dear Uncle, and friends, and even of that loving and holy Father of mine, and somehow it seems all peace, and calmness, and joy. It would not be so were I in England, to actually experience the sense of loss, to see the vacant seat, and miss the well-known voice; but it is (as I see) a great and most blessed alleviation to the loss of their society here below. You feel that when those loving hearts at Hursley can no longer be a stay and comfort to you here, you will have a sense almost of desolation pressing on you. You must, we all have, many trials and some sorrows, and I suppose Hursley has always been to you a city of refuge and house of rest.

'But I think the anticipation is harder than the reality. For him, but how can I speak of such as he is? Why should we feel anxiety? Surely he is just the man upon whom we should expect some special suffering, which is but some special mark of love and (may we not say in such a case?) of approbation. Some special aid to a very close conformity to the mind and character of Christ, to be sent in special love and mercy.

'I always seem to think that in the case of good men the suffering is the sure earnest of special nearness to God. It surely—if one may dare so to speak, and the case of Job warrants it, and the great passage "Simon, Simon, Satan hath desired to have you" (all)—is true that God is glorified in the endurance of sufferings which He lays upon the saints. And if dear Mr. Keble must suffer this last blow, as all through his life he has felt the care of the Churches pressing sorely on him, and has even had to comfort the weary, and guide the wayward, and to endure disappointment, and to restrain the over zealotish, and reprove the thoughtless, and bear in his bosom the infirmities of many people—why must we be unhappy about him, and why mourn for ourselves? God forbid! It is only one mark of the cross stamped upon him, only one more draught of the cup of the lacking measures of the afflictions of Christ. But you must, more than I, know and feel all this; and it is only in attempting to put before your eyes your own thoughts, that I have written this. For, indeed, I do sympathise with you, and I think how to me, who knew him so little yet yield to no one in deep reverence and love for him, his departure would be almost what the passing away of one of those who had seen the Lord must have been to those of old time; yet our time is not so very long now, and may be short, and we have had this blessed example for a long time, and there is on all accounts far more cause for joy than for sorrow.

'You must not think me unkind to Miss Mackenzie, because I have written to Fan to say that my letters and anecdotes are not to be fishes to swim in her "Net." It may be unwise in me to write all that kind of thing, but it does such an infinity of harm by its reflex action upon us who are engaged in this work. And I can write brotherly letters, if they are to be treated as public property. I could not trust my own brother to make extracts from my letters. No one in England can be a judge of the mischief that the letters occasion printed contrary to my wish by friends. We in the Mission think them so infinitely absurd, one-sided, exaggerated, &c., though we don't mean to make them so when we write them.

'We are all well, thank God, except a good fellow called Walter Hotaswol, from Matlavo (Saddle Island), who is in a decline. He has had two bad haemorrhages;

but he is patient, simple-minded, quite content to die, and not doubting at all his Father's love, and his Saviour's merits, so I cannot grieve for him, though he was the one, humanly speaking, to have led the way in his home.

'You know that I sympathise with all your anxieties about Church matters. Parliamentary legislation would be the greatest evil of all. All your troubles only show that synodical action, and I believe with the laity in the Synod, is the only cure for these troubles.

'God bless you, my dear Cousin,
'Your affectionate Cousin,
'J. C. PATTESON.'

To the sisters he wrote at the same time:—

'I hear from Miss Yonge that Mrs. Keble is very ill—dying. But, as I wrote to her, why should such things grieve us? He will soon rejoin her, and so it is all peace and comfort. He was seventy-five, I think, last St. Mark's Day, and I began a letter to him, but it was not fair to him to give him the trouble of reading it, and I tore it up. He knows without it how I do love and revere him, and I cannot pluck up courage to ask for some little book which he has used, that there may be a sort of odour of sanctity about it, just as Bishop Mackenzie's Thomas a Kempis, with him on the Zambesi, is on my table now.'

Before going forth with this 'lonely watcher' upon his voyage, the description of this season's work with his scholars must be given from a Report which he brought himself to write for the Eton Association. After saying how his efforts were directed to the forming a number of native clergy in time to work among their own people, he continues:—'When uncivilised races come into contact with civilised men, they must either be condemned to a hopeless position of inferiority, or they must be raised out of their state of ignorance and vice by appealing to those powers within them which God intended them to use, and the use of which will place them by His blessing in the possession of whatever good things may be denoted by the words Religion and Civilisation.

'Either we may say to our Melanesian scholars, "You can't expect to be like us: you must not suppose that you can ever cease to be dependent on us, you must be content always to do as you are told by us, to be like children, as in malice so in knowledge; you can never be missionaries, you may become assistant teachers to English missionaries whom you must implicitly obey, you must do work which it would not be our place to do, you must occupy all the lower and meaner offices of our society;"—or, if we do not say this (and, indeed, no one would be likely to say it), yet we may show by our treatment of our scholars that we think and mean it.

'Or we may say what was, e.g., said to a class of nineteen scholars who were reading Acts ix.

'"Did our Lord tell Saul all that he was to do?"

'"No."

'"What! not even when He appeared to him in that wonderful way from Heaven?"

'"No."

"'What did the Lord say to him?"

"'That he was to go into Damascus, and there it would be told him what he was to do."

"'What means did the Lord use to tell Saul what he was to do?"

"'He sent a man to tell him."

"'Who was he?"

"'Ananias.'"

"'Do we know much about him?"

"'No, only that he was sent with a message to Saul to tell him the Lord's will concerning him and to baptize him."

"'What means did the Lord employ to make His will known to Saul?"

"'He sent a disciple to tell him.' 'Did He tell him Himself immediately?'"

"'No, He sent a man to tell him."

"'Mention another instance of God's working in the same way, recorded in the Acts."

"'The case of Cornelius, who was told by the angel to send for Peter."

"'The angel then was not sent to tell Cornelius the way of salvation?"

"'No, God sent Peter to do that."

"'Jesus Christ began to do the same thing when He was on earth, did He not, even while He was Himself teaching and working miracles?"

"'Yes; He sent the twelve Apostles and the seventy disciples."

"'But what is the greatest instance of all, the greatest proof to us that God chooses to declare His will through man to man?"

"'God sent His own Son to become man."

"'Could He not have converted the whole world in a moment to the obedience of faith by some other way?"

"'Yes."

"'But what did He in His wisdom choose to do?"

"'He sent His Son to be born of the Virgin Mary, to become man, and to walk on this earth as a real man, and to teach men, and to die for men."

"'What does Jesus Christ call us men?"

"'His brethren.' 'Who is our Mediator?'"

"'The Man Christ Jesus."

"'What means does God employ to make His will known to us?"

"'He uses men to teach men."

"'Can they do this by themselves?"

"'No, but God makes them able."

"'How have you heard the Gospel?"

"'Because God sent you to us."

"'And now, listen. How are all your people still in ignorance to hear it? What have I often told you about that?"

'Whereupon the scholars looked shy, and some said softly, "We must teach them."

"'Yes, indeed you must!"

'And so the lesson ended with questioning them on the great duty and privilege of prayer for God's Holy Spirit to give them both the will and the power to do the work to which God is calling them.

'So we constantly tell them "God has already been very merciful to you, in that He has called you out of darkness into His marvellous light. He has enabled you to receive the knowledge of His will, and to understand your relations to Him. He has taught you to believe in Him, to pray to Him, to hope for salvation through the merits of His Son's death and resurrection. He has made you feel something of the power of His love, and has taught you the duty of loving Him and serving your brother. He calls upon you now to rouse yourself to a sense of your true position, to use the gifts which He has given you to His glory and the good of your brethren. Don't suppose that you are unable to do this. You are unable to do it, as you were unable to believe and love Him by yourselves, but He gives you strength for this very purpose that you may be able to do it. You can do it through Christ, who strengtheneth you. Our fathers were not more able to teach their people once than you to teach your people now!"

'We make no distinction whatever between English and Melanesian members of the Mission as such. No Melanesian is excluded from any office of trust. No classification is made of higher and lower kinds of work, of work befitting a white man and work befitting a black man. English and Melanesian scholars or teachers work together in the school, printing-office, dairy, kitchen, farm. The senior clergyman of the Mission labours most of all with his own hands at the work which is sometimes described as menial work; and it is contrary to the fundamental principle of the Mission that anyone should connect with the idea of white man the right to fag a black boy.

'Young men and lads come to us and say, "Let me do that. I can't write the languages, or do many things you or Mr. Pritt or Mr. Palmer do, so let me scrub your floor, or brush your shoes, or fetch some water." And of course we let them do so, for the doing it is accompanied by no feeling of degradation in their minds; they have seen us always doing these things, and not requiring them to do them as if it were the natural work for them, because they are black, and not proper for us, because we are white.

'Last night, a young man, sitting by the fire, said to the Bishop, "They want you to stop with them in my land."

'"I wish with all my heart I could."

'"Yes, I know, you must go to so many places."

'"But they are different in your land now."

'"Oh! yes, they don't fight now as they used to do; they don't go about armed now."

'"Well, that is a thing to be thankful for. What is the reason of it, do you think?"

"Why they know about you, and see you now and then, and Henry Tagalana talked to them, and I talked a little to them, and they asked me about our ways here, and they want to learn."

'"Well, there are now five of you from your island, and you must try hard to learn, that you may teach them, for remember you must do it, if God spares your life."'

'During the year 1865 a great advance was made in the industrial department of our work. About seventeen acres of land were taken in hand and worked by Mr. Pritt, with the Melanesian lads. We have our own dairy of thirteen cows, and, besides supplying the whole Mission party, numbering in all seventy-seven persons, with abundance of milk, we sell considerable quantities of butter. We grow, of course, our own potatoes and vegetables, and maize, &c., for our cows. The farm and dairy work affords another opportunity for teaching our young people to acquire habits of industry.'

Cooking, farm, gardening, dairy-work, setting out the table, &c., were all honourable occupations, and of great importance in teaching punctuality and regularity, and the various arts and decencies of life to the youths, who were in time to implant good habits in their native homes. Their natural docility made them peculiarly easy to manage and train while in hand; the real difficulty was that their life was so entirely different from their home, that there was no guessing how deep the training went, and, on every voyage, some fishes slipped through the meshes of the net, though some returned again, and others never dropped from their Bishop's hands. But he was becoming anxious to spare some of his scholars the trial of a return to native life; and, as the season had been healthy, he ventured on leaving twenty-seven pupils at St. Andrew's with Mr. and Mrs. Pritt, among them George and Sarah Sarawia.

After Trinity Sunday, May 27, the 'Southern Cross' sailed, and the outward voyage gave leisure for the following letter to Prof. Max Muller, explaining why he could not make his knowledge of languages of more benefit to philology while thus absorbed in practical work:—

'"Southern Cross," off Norfolk Ireland: June 6, 1866.

'My dear Friend,—I am about to tire your patience heavily. For I must find you some reasons for doing so little in making known these Melanesian dialects, and that will be wearisome for you to read; and, secondly, I cannot put down clearly and consecutively what I want to say. I have so very little time for thinking out, and working at any one subject continuously, that my whole habit of mind becomes, I fear, inaccurate and desultory. I have so very many and so very different occupations, and so much anxiety and so many interruptions, as the "friction" that attends the working, of a new and somewhat untried machine.'

'You know that we are few in number; indeed (Codrington being absent) I have but two clergymen with me, and two young men who may be ordained by-and-by. Besides, had I the twenty troublesome men, whom you wish to banish into these regions, what use would they or any men be until they had learnt their work? And it must fall to me to teach them, and that takes again much of my time; so that, as a matter of fact, there are many things that I must do, even when all is going on smoothly; and should sickness come, then, of course, my days and nights are spent in nursing poor lads, to whom no one else can talk, cheering up poor fellows seized with sudden nervous terror, giving food to those who will take it from no one else, &c.

'Then the whole management of the Mission must fall upon me; though I am most thankful to say that for some time Mr. Pritt has relieved me from the charge of all domestic and industrial works. He does everything of that kind, and does it admirably, so that our institution really is a well-ordered industrial school, in which kitchen work, dairy work, farm work, printing, clothes making and mending, &c., are all carried on, without the necessity of having any foreign importation of servants, who would be sure to do harm, both by their ideas as to perquisites (= stealing in the minds of our Melanesians), and by introducing the idea of paid labour; whereas now we all work together, and no one counts any work degrading, and still less does any one qua white consider himself entitled to fag a Melanesian.

'Mr. Tilly, R.N., has also quite relieved me from my duties as skipper, and I have no trouble about marine stores, shipping seamen, navigating the vessel now. I cannot be too thankful for this; it, saves me time, anxiety, and worry; yet much remains that I must do, which is not connected with peculiar work directly.

'I can't refuse the Bishop of New Zealand when he presses me (for want of a better man) to be trustee of properties, and to engage in managing the few educational institutions we have. I can't refuse to take some share in English clerical work while on shore; indeed, in 1865, my good friend Archdeacon Lloyd being ill, I took his parish (one and a half hour distant from Kohimarama), the most important parish in Auckland, for some three months; not slacking my Melanesian work, though I could only avoid going back by hard application, and could make no progress. Then I must attend our General Synod; and all these questions concerning the colonial churches take some time to master, and yet I must know what is going on.

'Then I must carry on all the correspondence of the Mission. I am always writing letters. Every £5 from any part of New Zealand or Australia I must acknowledge; and everyone wants information, anecdotes, &c., which it vexes my soul to have to supply, but who else can do it? Then I keep all the accounts, very complicated, as you would say if you saw my big ledger. And I don't like to be altogether behindhand in the knowledge of theological questions, and people sometimes write to me, and their letters need to be answered carefully. Besides, take my actual time spent in teaching. Shall I give you a day at Kohimarama?

'I get in the full summer months an hour for reading by being dressed at 5.30 A.M. At 5.30 I see the lads washing, &c., 7 A.M. breakfast all together, in hall, 7.30 chapel, 8-9.30 school, 9.30-12.30 industrial work. During this time I have generally half an hour with Mr. Pritt about business matters, and proof sheets are brought me, yet I get a little time for preparing lessons. 12.45 short service in chapel, 1 dinner, 2-3 Greek Testament with English young men, 3-4 classics with ditto, 5 tea, 6.30 evening chapel, 7-8.30 evening school with divers classes in rotation or with candidates for Baptism or Confirmation, 8.30-9 special instruction to more advanced scholars, only a few. 9-10 school with two other English lay assistants. Add to all this, visitors interrupting me from 4-5, correspondence, accounts, trustee business, sermons, nursing sick boys, and all the many daily unexpected little troubles that must be smoothed down, and questions inquired into, and boys' conduct investigated, and what becomes of linguistics? So much for my excuse for my small progress in languages! Don't think all this egotistical; it is necessary to make you understand my position.

'If I had spare time, leisure for working at any special work, perhaps eleven years of this kind of life have unfitted me for steady sustained thought. And you know well I bring but slender natural qualifications to the task. A tolerably true ear and good memory for words, and now something of the instinctive insight into new tongues, but that is chiefly from continual practice.

'But when I attempt to systematise, I find endless ramifications of cognate dialects rushing through my brain, by their very multitude overwhelming me, and though I see the affinities and can make practical use of them, I don't know how to state them on paper, where to begin, how to put another person in my position.

'Again, for observation of the rapid changes in these dialects, I have not much opportunity. For no one in Melanesia can be my informant. It is not easy where so many dialects must be known for practical purposes, for the introductory part of Mission work, to talk to some wild naked old fellow, and to make him understand what I am anxious to ascertain. It is a matter that has no interest for him, he never thought of it, he doesn't know my meaning, what have we in common? How can I rouse him from his utter indifference, even if I know his language so well as to talk easily, not to a scholar of my own, but to an elderly man, with none but native ideas in his head?

'All that I can do is to learn many dialects of a given archipelago, present their existing varieties, and so work back to the original language. This, to some extent, has been done in the Banks group, and in the eastern part of the Solomon Isles. But directly I get so far as this, I am recalled to the practical necessity of using the knowledge of the several dialects rather to make known God's truth to the heathen than to inform literati of the process of dialectic variation. Don't mistake me, my dear friend, or suspect me of silly sentimentalism. But you can easily understand what it is to feel "God has given to me only of all Christian men the power of speaking to this or that nation, and, moreover, that is the work He has sent me to do." Often, I don't deny, I should like the other better. It is very pleasant to shirk my evening class, e.g. and spend the time with Sir William Martin, discussing some point of Melanesian philosophy. But then my dear lads have lost two hours of Christian instruction, and that won't do.

'I don't need to be urged to do more in working out their languages. I am quite aware of the duty of doing all that I can in that way, and I wish to do it; but there are only twenty-four hours in the day and night together! I feel that it is a part of my special work, for each grammar and dictionary that I can write opens out the language to some other than myself. But I am now apologising rather for my fragmentary way of writing what I do write by saying that what I find enough, with my help given in school to enable one of my party to learn a dialect, I am almost obliged to regard as a measure of the time that I ought to spend on it.

'Another thing, I have no outline provided for me, which I can fill up. My own clear impression is that to attempt to follow the analogy of our complicated Greek and Latin grammars would not only involve certain failure, but would mislead people altogether. I don't want to be hunting after a Melanesian paulo-post-futurum. I had rather say, "All men qua men think, and have a power of expressing their thoughts. They have wants and express them. They use many different forms of speech in making that statement, if we look superficially at the matter, not so if we look into it," and so on. Then, discarding the ordinary arrangement of grammars, explain the mode of thought, the peculiar method of thinking upon matters of common interest, in the mind of the Melanesian, as exhibited in his language. An Englishman says, "When I get there, it will be night." But a Pacific Islander says, "I am there, it is night." The one says, "Go on, it will soon be dark." The other, "Go on, it has become already night." Anyone sees that the one possesses the power of realising the future as present, or past; the other now whatever it may have been once, does not exercise such power. A companion calls me at 5.30 A.M., with the words, "Eke! me gong veto," (Hullo! it is night already). He means, "Why, we ought to be off, we shall never reach the end of our journey before dark." But how neatly and prettily he expresses his thought! I assure you, civilised languages, for common conversational purposes needed by travellers, &c., are clumsy contrivances! Of course you know all this a hundred times better than I do. I only illustrate my idea of a grammar as a means of teaching others the form of the mould in which the Melanesian's mind is cast. I think I ought to go farther, and seek for certain categories, under which thought may be classified (so to say), and beginning with the very simplest work on to the more complicated powers.

'But I haven't the head to do this; and suppose that I did make such a framework, how am I to fill it in so as to be intelligible to outsiders? For practical purposes, I give numerals, personal, possessive, and demonstrative pronouns, the mode of qualifying nouns, e.g., some languages interpose a monosyllable between the substantive and adjective, others do not. The words used (as it is called) as prepositions and adverbs, the mode of changing a neuter verb into a transitive or causative verb, usually by a word prefixed, which means do or make, e.g., die, do-die, do-to-the-death, him.

'Then I teach orally how the intonation, accentuation, pause in the utterance, gesticulation, supply the place of stops, marks of interrogation, &c.

'Then giving certain nouns, verbs, &c., make my English pupils construct sentences; then give them a vocabulary and genuine native stories, not translations at all, least of all of religious books, which contain very few native ideas, but stories of sharks, cocoa-nuts, canoes, fights, &c. This is the apparatus. This gives but little idea of a Melanesian dialect to you. I know it, and am anxious to do more.

'This last season I have had some three or four months, during which I determined that I must refuse to take so much English work, &c. I sat and growled in my den, and of course rather vexed people, and perhaps, for which I should be most heartily grieved, my dear friend and leader, the Bishop of New Zealand. But I stuck to my work. I wrote about a dozen papers of phrases in as many dialects, to show the mode of expressing in those dialects what we express by adverbs and prepositions, &c. This is, of course, the difficult part of a language for a stranger to find out. I also printed three, and have three more nearly finished in MS., vocabularies of about 600 words with a true native sehdia on each word. The mere writing (for much was written twice over) took a long time. And there is this gained by these vocabularies for practical purposes: these are (with more exceptions, it is true, than I intended) the words which crop up most readily in a Melanesian mind. Much time I have wasted, and would fain save others from wasting, in trying to form a Melanesian mind into a given direction into which it ought, as I supposed, to have travelled, but which nevertheless it refused to follow. Just ten years' experience has, of course, taught me a good deal of the minds of these races; and when I catch a new fellow, as wild as a hawk, and set to work at a new language, it is a great gain to have even partially worked out the problem, "What words shall I try to get from this fellow?" Now I go straight to my mark, or rather I am enabling, I hope, my young friends with me to do so, for of course, I have learnt to do so myself, more or less, for some time past. Many words may surprise you, and many alterations I should make in any revision. I know a vast number of words not used in these vocabularies, in some languages I daresay five times the number, but I had a special reason for writing only these. The rest must come, if I live, by-and-by.

'Of course these languages are very poor in respect of words belonging to civilised and literary and religious life, but exceedingly rich in all that pertains to the needs and habits of men circumstanced as they are. I draw naturally this inference, "Don't be in any hurry to translate, and don't attempt to use words as (assumed) equivalents of abstract ideas. Don't devise modes of expression unknown to the language as at present in use. They can't understand, and therefore don't use words to express definitions."

But, as everywhere, our Lord gives us the model. A certain lawyer asked Him for a definition of his neighbour, but He gave no definition, only He spoke a simple and touching parable. So teach, not a technical word, but an actual thing.

'Why do I write all this to you? It is wasting your time. But I prose on.—(A sheet follows on the structure of the languages.)

'Well, I have inflicted a volume on you. We are almost becalmed after a weary fortnight of heavy weather, in which we have been knocked about in every direction in our tight little 90-ton schooner. And my head is hardly steady yet, so excuse a long letter, or rather long chatty set of desultory remarks, from

'Your old affectionate Friend,

'J. C. PATTESON.'

A little scene from Mr. Atkin's journal shows how he had learnt to talk to natives. He went ashore with the Bishop and some others at Sesaki for yams:—

'It has been by far the pleasantest day of the kind that I have seen here. The people are beginning to understand that they can do no better than trade fairly with us, and to-day they on the whole behaved very well. A very big fellow had been ringing all the changes between commanding and entreating me to give him a hatchet (I was holding the trade bag). When he found it was no use, he said, "I was a bad man, and never gave anything." I said "Yes, I was." He said the Bishops were very good men, they gave liberally. He had better go and ask the Bishop for something, for he was a good man, though I was not.'

After landing Mr. Palmer at Mota, the vessel went onto the Solomon Isles, reaching Bauro on the 27th:—

'About 8.30 in the evening the boat was lowered, and the party pulled towards the village, which was the home of Taroniara, in a fine clear moonlit night, by the fires which people had lit for the people on shore, and directed by Taroniara himself to the opening in the reef. They landed in the midst of a group of dark figures, some standing in a brook, some by the side under a large spreading tree, round a fire fed by dry cocoa-nut leaves; and in the background were tall cocoa-nuts with their gracefully drooping plumes, and the moon behind shining through them made the shade seem darker and deeper as the flashing crests of the surf, breaking on the reef, made the heaving sea beyond look murkier. It was a sight worth going a long way to see,' so says Mr. Atkin's journal.

The next sight was, however, still more curious. The Bishop relented so far towards 'the Net,' as to write an account of it on purpose for it. Ysabel Island is, like almost all the rest, divided among many small communities of warlike habits. And some years previously the people of Mahaga, the place with which he was best acquainted, had laid an ambush for those of Hogirano, killed a good many, and, cutting off their heads, had placed them in a row upon stones, and danced round them in a victorious suit of white-coral lime. However, a more powerful tribe, not long after, came down upon Mahaga and fearfully avenged the massacre of Hogirano. All were slain who could not escape into the bush; and when the few survivors, after days and nights of hunger, ventured back, they found the dwellings burnt, the fruit trees cut down, the yam and taro grounds devastated, and more than a hundred headless bodies of their kindred lying scattered about.

This outrage had led to the erection of places of refuge in the tops of trees; and Bishop Patteson, who had three Mahagan scholars, went ashore, with the hope of passing the night in one of these wonderful places, where the people always slept, though by day they lived in the ordinary open bamboo huts.

After landing in a mangrove swamp, and wading through deep mud, he found that the Mahaga people had removed from their old site, and had built a strong fortification near the sea; and close above, so as to be reached by ladders resting on the wall, were six large tree-houses.

It had been raining heavily for a day or two, and the paths were so deep in mud that the bed of a water-course was found preferable to them. The bush had been cleared for some distance before the steep rocky mound where the village stood, surrounded by a high wall of stones, in which one narrow entrance was left, approached by a fallen trunk of a tree lying over a hollow. The huts were made of bamboo canes, and the floors, raised above the ground, were nearly covered with mats and a kind of basket work.

The tree-houses, six in number, were upon the tops of trees of great height, 50 feet round at the base, and all branches cleared off till near the summit, where two or three grew out at right angles, something after the manner of an Italian stone pine:—

'From the top of the wall the ladder that led to one of these houses was 60 feet long, but it was not quite upright, and the tree was growing at some little distance from the bottom of the rock, and the distance by a plumb line from the floor of the verandah to the ground on the lower side of the tree was 94 feet. The floor of the house, which is made first, was 23 feet long and about 11 broad; a narrow verandah is left at each end, and the inside length of the house is 18 feet, the breadth 10 feet, the height to the ridge pole 6 feet. The floor was of bamboo matted, the roof and sides of palm-leaf thatch. The ladders were remarkable contrivances: a pole in the centre, from 4 to 6 inches in diameter, to which were lashed by vines cross pieces of wood, about two feet long. To steady these and hold on by were double shrouds of supple-jacks. The rungs of the ladder were at unequal distances, 42 upon the 50 feet ladder.'

The Bishop and Pasvorang, who had gone ashore together, beheld men, women, and children running up and down these ladders, and walking about the bare branches, trusting entirely to their feet and not touching with their hands. The Bishop, in his wet slippery shoes, did not think it right to run the risk of an accident: and though Pasvorang, who was as much at home as a sailor among the ropes of the 'Southern Cross,' made the ascent, he came down saying, 'I was so afraid, my legs shook. Don't you go, going aloft is nothing to it;' but the people could not understand any dread; and when the Bishop said, 'I can't go up there. I am neither bird nor bat, and I have no wings if I fall,' they thought him joking. At the same time he saw a woman with a load on her back, quietly walking up a ladder to another tree, not indeed so lofty as that Pasvorang had tried, but as if it were the most natural thing in the world, and without attempting to catch hold with her hands.

'At night,' says the Bishop, 'as I lay ignominiously on the ground in a hut, I heard the songs of the women aloft as voices from the clouds, while the loud croaking of the frogs, the shrill noise of countless cicadas, the scream of cockatoos and parrots, the cries of birds of many kinds, and the not unreasonable fear of scorpions, all combined to keep me awake. Solemn thoughts pass through the mind at such times, and from time to time I spoke to the people who were sleeping in the hut with me. It rained heavily in the night, and I was not sorry to find myself at 7 A.M. on board the schooner.'

The next day was spent in doing the honours of the ship, a crowd on board all day; and on July 2 the Bishop landed again with Mr. Atkin, and mounted up to this wonderful nest, where all these measurements were made. It proved much more agreeable to look at from below than to inhabit 'the low steaming bamboo huts—the crowds, the dirt, the squalling of babies—you can't sit or stand, or touch anything that is not grimy and sooty and muddy. It is silly to let these things really affect one, only that it now seems rather to knock me up. After such a day and night I am very tired, come back to our little ship as to a palace, wash, and sit down on a clean, if not a soft stool, and am free for a little while from continual noise and the necessity of making talk in an imperfectly known language.

'It is really curious to see how in some way our civilised mode of life unfits one for living among these races. It is not to be denied that the want of such occupations as we are employed in is a large cause of their troubles. What are they to do during the long hours of night, and on wet, pouring days? They can't read, they can't see in their huts to do any work, making baskets, &c. They must lie about, talking scandal and acquiring listless indolent habits. Then comes a wild reaction. The younger people like excitement as much as our young men like hunting, fishing, shooting, &c. How can they get this? Why, they must quarrel and fight, and so they pass their time. It does seem almost impossible to do much for people so circumstanced; yet it was much the same in Mota and elsewhere, where things are altered for the better.'

It was bad and trying weather, and it was well to have only two old Banks Islanders on board, besides three Ysabel lads. The Bishop had plenty of time for writing; and for the first time in his life 'pronounced himself forward with that Report which was always on his mind.' He goes on: 'I read a good deal, but I don't say that my mind is very active all the time, and I have some schooling. Yet it is not easy to do very much mental work. I think that I feel the heat more than I used to do, but that may be only my fancy.

'You meantime are, I hope, enjoying fine summer weather. Certainly it must be a charming place that you have, close to that grand Church and grand scenery. I think my idea of a cosy home is rather that of a cottage in the Isle of Wight, or, better still, a house near such a Cathedral as Wells, in one of the cottages close to the clear streams that wind through and about the Cathedral precincts. But I can form no real notions about such things. Only I am pretty sure that there is little happiness without real hard work. I do long sometimes for a glorious Cathedral service, for the old chants, anthems, not for "functions" and "processions," &c. I have read Freeman's pamphlet on "Ritual" with interest; he really knows what he writes about, and has one great object and a worthy one, the restoration of the universal practice of weekly communion as the special Sunday service. That all our preachifying is a wide departure from the very idea of worship is self-evident, when it is made more than a necessary part of the religious observance of the Lord's Day, and catechising is worth far more than preaching (in the technical sense of the word).'

A first visit was paid to Savo; where numerous canoes came out to meet them, one a kind of state galley, with the stem and stern twelve feet high, inlaid with mother-of-pearl, and ornamented with white shells (most likely the ovum or poached egg), and containing the chief men of the island. The people spoke the Ysabel language, and the place seemed promising.

Some little time was spent in beating up to Bauro; where the Bishop again landed at Taroniara's village, and slept in his hut, which was as disagreeable as all such places were:—'Such a night always disturbs me for a time, throws everything out of regular working order; but it always pays, the people like it, and it shows a confidence in them which helps us on.

'I was disappointed though in the morning, when Taroniara declined to come with me to this place.

'My people say, "Why do you go away?"—the old stupid way of getting out of an engagement.' However, two others came to 'this place,' which was a hut in the village of Wango, which the Bishop had hired for ten days for the rent of a hatchet.

'A very sufficient rent too, you would say, if you could see the place. I can only stand upright under the ridge pole, the whole of the oblong is made of bamboo, with a good roof that kept out a heavy shower last night. There is a fresh stream of water within fifteen yards, where I bathed at 9 P.M. yesterday; and as I managed to get rid of strangers by 8.30, it was not so difficult to manage a shift into a clean and dry sleeping shirt, and then, lying down on Aunt William's cork-bed (my old travelling companion), I slept very fairly.

'People about the hut at earliest dawn; and the day seems long, the sustained effort of talking, the heat, the crowd, and the many little things that should not but do operate as an annoyance, all tire one very much. But I hope that by degrees I may get opportunities of talking about the matter that I come to talk about. Just now the trading with the vessel, which is detained here by the weather, and surprise at my half-dozen books, &c., prevent any attention being paid to anything else.

'7 P.M.—The vessel went off at 10.30 A.M. I felt for a little while rather forlorn, and a little sinking at the heart. You see I confess it all, how silly! Can't I after so many years bear to be left in one sense alone? I read a little of you know what Book, and then found the feeling pass entirely away.

'But, more than that, the extreme friendliness of the people, the real kindness was pleasant to me. One man brought his child, "The child of us two, Bishop." Another man, "These cocoa-nut trees are the property of us two, remember." A third, "When you want yams, don't you buy them, tell me."

'But far better still. Many times already to-day have I spoken to the people; they have so far listened that they say, "Take this boy, and this boy, and this boy. We see now why you don't want big men, we see now that you can't stop here long, what for you wish for lads whom you may teach, we see that you want them for a long time. Keep these lads two years."

'"Yes, two or three or four. By-and-by you will understand more and more my reason."

'Then came the talks that you too may experience when dealing with some neglected child in London, or it may be in the country; but which, under the cocoa-nut tree, with dark naked men, have a special impressiveness. It was the old lesson, of the Eternal and Universal Father, who has not left Himself without witness in that He gives us all rain from Heaven, &c., and of our ingratitude, and His love; of His coming down to point out the way of life, and of His Death and Rising again; of another world, Resurrection, and Judgment. All interrupted, now and then, by exclamations of surprise, laughter, or by some one beginning to talk about something that jarred sadly on one's ear, and yet was but natural. But I do hope that a week may pass not unprofitably. In one sense, I shall no doubt be glad when it is over; but I think that it may, by God's great goodness, be a preparation for something more to come.

'Last night, my little hired hut being crowded as usual, they all cried out at once "Numu" (earthquake). I should not the least have known that anything had occurred. I said I thought it was a pig pushing against the bamboo wall of the hut. They say that they have no serious shocks, but very many slight ones. Crocodiles they have too, but, they say, none in this stream.

'July 22nd.—It is 9 P.M., the pleasantest time, in one sense, of my twenty-four hours, for there are only two people with me in the hut.

'My arrangements are somewhat simple; but I am very comfortable. Delicious bathes I have in the stream: yams and fish are no bad fare; and I have some biscuit and essence of coffee, and a few books, and am perfectly well. The mode of life has become almost natural to me. I am on capital terms with the people, and even the babies are no longer afraid of me. Old and young, men and women, boys and girls about me of course all day; and small presents of yams, fish, bananas, almonds, show the friendliness of the people when properly treated. But the bunches of skulls remain slung up in the large canoe houses, and they can be wild enough when they are excited.'

[The home diary continues, on the 26th]:—'I am expecting the schooner, and shall be glad to get off if it arrives to-day, for it is very fine. I don't think I could do any good by staying a few days more, so I might as well be on my way to Santa Cruz. If I were here for good, of course I should be busy about many things that it would be useless to attempt now, e.g., what good would it be to induce half-a-dozen boys to learn "a," when I should be gone before they could learn "b"? So I content myself with making friends with the people, observing their ways, and talking to them as I can. It is hot, now at 8.30 A.M. What will it be at 2 P.M.? But I may perhaps be able to say something to cheer me up. One of the trials of this kind of thing is that one seems to be doing nothing. Simply I am here! Hardly in one hour out of the twenty-four am I sure to be speaking of religion. Yet the being here is something, the gaining the confidence and goodwill of the people. Then comes the thought, who is to carry this on? And yet I dare not ask men to come, for I am certain they would after all my pains find something different from what they expect.

My death would very likely bring out some better men for the work, with energy and constructive power and executive genius, all of which, guided by Divine Wisdom, seem to be so much wanted! But just now, I don't see what would become of a large part of the work if I died. I am leaving books somewhat more in order; but it is one thing to have a book to help one in acquiring a language, quite another to speak it freely, and to be personally known to the people who speak it.

'11th Sunday after Trinity.—Off Anudha Island, 4 P.M. Thermometer 88° in the empty cabin, everyone being on deck. Well, dear old Joan and Fan, refreshed by—what do you think? O feast of Guildhall and Bristol mayors! Who would dream of turtle soup on board the "Southern Cross" in these unknown seas? Tell it not to Missionary Societies! Let no platform orator divulge the great secret of the luxurious self-indulgent life of the Missionary Bishop! What nuts for the "Pall Mall Gazette"! How would all subscriptions cease, and denunciations be launched upon my devoted head, because good Mr. Tilly bought, at San Cristoval, for the price of one tenpenny hatchet, a little turtle, a veritable turtle, with green fat and all the rest of it, upon which we have made to-day a most regal feast indeed.

'But seriously. There has been much to make me hopeful, and something to disappoint me, since I last wrote.'

The two days at Santa Cruz were hopeful—[Mr. Atkin says that the natives came on board with readiness and stole with equal readiness; but this was all in a friendly way]—and a small island, named Piteni, was visited, and judged likely to prove a means of reaching the larger isle.

The disappointment is not here mentioned, unless it was the missing some of the Ysabel scholars, and bringing away only three; but this mattered the less, as the Banks Island party, which, as forming a nucleus, was far more important, was now considerable. Sixty-two scholars were the present freight, including nine little girls, between eight and twelve, mostly betrothed to old pupils.

At Malanta, a new village called Saa was visited. The 'harbour' was a wall of coral, with the surf breaking upon it, but a large canoe showed the only accessible place, and this was exposed to the whole swell of the Pacific.

'The natives,' writes Mr. Atkin, 'held the boat in water up to their knees, but the seas that broke thirty yards outside washed over their shoulders and sometimes their heads. We might have taken away half the people of the village, and had no trouble in getting two nice-looking little boys. About 320 miles from Norfolk Island, one of these little boys, Wate, playing, fell overboard: we were going ten knots at the time, right before the wind; it was a quarter of an hour before we picked him up, as it took five minutes to stop the vessel and ten to get to him. Wate seemed all the better for his ducking.' This little Wate became Mr. Atkin's especial child, his godson and devoted follower.

On October 2, Norfolk Island was reached, and there, a wooden house having been conveyed thither by H.M.S. 'Falcon,' Mr. Palmer and fifteen scholars were placed to spend the winter. The Pitcairners welcomed the Mission, but were displeased at the Government assuming a right to dispose of the land which they had fancied entirely their own.

One of the letters written separate from the journal during this voyage gives a commission for photographs from the best devotional prints, for the benefit chiefly of his young colonial staff:—'I have not the heart to send for my Lionardo da Vinci,' (he says), that much valued engraving, purchased at Florence, and he wishes for no modern ones, save Ary Scheffer's 'Christis Consolator,' mentioning a few of his special favourites to be procured if possible. For the Melanesians, pictures of ships, fishes, and if possible tropical vegetation, was all the art yet needed, and beads, red and blue, but dull ones; none not exactly like the samples would be of any use. 'It is no good sending out any "fancy" articles such as you would give English children. "Toys for savages" are all the fancies of those who manufacture such toys for sale. Of course, any manufacturer who wishes to give presents of knives, tools, hatchets, &c., would do a great benefit, but then the knives must be really strong and sharp.'

I have concluded the letters of the island voyage, before giving those written on the homeward transit from Norfolk Island, whither the 'Falcon' had conveyed the letters telling of the departure of both Mr. and Mrs. Keble. The first written under this impulse was of course to Sir John Coleridge, the oldest friend:—

'At Sea, near Norfolk Island: October 3, 1866.

'My dear, dear Uncle,—How can I thank you enough for telling me so much of dear saintly Mr. Keble and his wife? He has been, for my dear father and mother's sakes, very loving to me, and actually wrote me two short letters, one after his seizure, which I treasure. How I had grown to reverence and love him more and more you can easily believe; and yesterday at Norfolk Island, whither some letters had been sent, I read with a very full heart of the peaceful close of such a holy life. And I do love to think too of you and him, if I may speak freely of such as you; and the weight attached to all you say and do (you two I mean) in your several occupations seems at all events one hopeful sign among not a few gloomy ones. I suppose you and Mr. Keble little estimated the influence which even a casual word or sentence of yours exercises upon a man of my age, predisposed (it is true) to hearken with attention and reverence....

'Is it possible that fifty years hence any similar event, should there be such, which should so "stir the heart of the country" (as you say about Mr. Keble's death), might stimulate people to raise large sums for the endowment of a Church about to be, or already separated from the State? I can't avoid feeling as if God may be permitting the extension of the Colonial Churches, partly and in a secondary sense that so the ground may be travelled over on a small scale before the Church at home may be thrown in like manner upon its own resources. The alliance is a very precarious one surely, and depends upon the solemn adherence to a fiction. It is extraordinary that some Colonial Bishops should seek to reproduce the state of things which is of course peculiar to England, the produce of certain historical events, and which can have no resemblance whatever to the circumstances of our Colonies.

'The mail closes just after our arrival; and I am very busy at first coming on shore with such a party. Goodbye for the present, my dear dear Uncle,

'Your loving and grateful Nephew, 'J. C. P.'

To me the condolence was:—

'October 6, 1866.

'And so, my dear Cousin, the blow has fallen upon you, and dear Mr. and Mrs. Keble have passed away to their eternal rest. I found letters at Norfolk Island on October 2, not my April letters, which will tell me most about him, but my May budget.

'How very touching the account is which my Uncle John sends me of dear Mrs. Keble, so thankful that he was taken first, so desirous to go, yet so content to stay! And how merciful it has all been. Such a calm holy close to the saintly life. May God bless and support all you who feel the bereavement! Even I feel that I would fain look for one more letter from him, but we have his "Christian Year," and other books. Is it not wonderful that all the wisdom and love and beauty of the "Christian Year," to say nothing of the exquisite and matured poetry, should have been given to him so early in life? Why, as I gather, the book was finished in the year 1825, though not published till 1827. He wrote it when he was only 33 years old, and for 45 years he lived after he was capable of such a work. Surely such a union of extreme learning, wisdom, and scholarship, with humility and purity of heart and life has very seldom been found. Everyone wishes to say something to everyone else of one so dear to all, and no one can say what each and all feel. We ought indeed to be thankful, who not only have in common with all men his books, but the memory of what he was personally to us.

'The change must needs be a great one to you. I do feel much for you indeed. But you will bear it bravely; and many duties and the will and power to discharge them occupy the mind, and the elasticity comes back again after a time. I know nothing of the Keble family, not even how they were related to him, so that my interest in Hursley is connected with him only. Yet it will always be a hallowed spot in the memory of English Churchmen. You will hear the various rumours as to who is to write his life, &c. Let me know what is worth knowing about it.

'Kohimarama. Anchored on October 8, after an absence of exactly six weeks; all well on board and ashore.

'Thanks be to God for so many mercies. The mail is gone, and alas! all my letters and newspapers were sent off a few days since in the "Brisk" to Norfolk Island. We passed each other. They did not expect me back so soon, so I have no late news, and have no time to read newspapers.

'May God bless you, my dear Cousin,

'Your affectionate Cousin, 'J. C. PATTESON.'

In spite of this deep veneration for Mr. Keble and for his teachings, Bishop Patteson did not embrace to the full the doctrine which had been maintained in 'Eucharistic Adoration,' and which he rightly perceived to lie at the root of the whole Ritualistic question. His conclusions had been formed upon the teachings of the elder Anglican divines, and his predilections for the externals of worship upon the most reverent and beautiful forms to which he had been accustomed before he left home.

After an All Saints' Communion, the following letter was written:—

'All Saints' Day, 1866.

'My dear Cousin,—You know why I write to you on this day. The Communion of Saints becomes ever a more and more real thing to us as holy and saintly servants of God pass beyond the veil, as also we learn to know and love more and more our dear fellow-labourers and fellow-pilgrims still among us in the flesh.

'Such a day as this brings, thanks be to God, many calm, peaceful memories with it. Of how many we may both think humbly and thankfully whose trials and sorrows are over for ever, whose earthly work is done, who dwell now in Paradise and see His Face, and calmly wait for the great consummation. To you the sense of personal loss must be now—it will always be—mixed up with the true spirit of thankfulness and joy; but remember that as they greatly helped you, so you in no slight measure have received from God power to help others, a trust which I verily believe you are faithfully discharging, and that the brightness of the Christian life must be not lost sight of in our dealings with others, would we really seek to set forth the attractiveness of religion.

'I don't mean that I miss this element in any of your writings; rather I am thankful to you because you teach so well how happiness and joy are the portion of the Christian in the midst of so much that the world counts sorrow and loss. But I think that depression of mind rapidly communicates itself, and you must be aware that you are through your books stamping your mind on many people.

'Do you mind my saying all this to you? only I would fain say anything that at such a time may, if only for a minute, help to keep the bright side before you. The spirit of patience did seem so to rest upon him and his dear saintly wife. The motto of the Christian Year seemed to be inwoven into his life and character. I suppose he so well knew the insignificance of what to us mortals in our own generation seems so great, that he had learned to view eternal truths in the light of Him who is eternal. He fought manfully for the true eternal issues, and everything else fell into its subordinate place. Is not one continually struck with his keen sense of the proportion of things? He wastes no time nor strength in the accidents of religion; much that he liked and valued he never taught as essential, or even mentioned, lest it might interfere with essentials.

'Oh! that his calm wise judgment, his spiritual discernment, may be poured out on many earnest men who I can't help thinking lack that instinct which divinely guided the early Church in the "selection of fundamentals." We must all grieve to see earnest, zealous men almost injuring the good cause, and placing its best and wisest champions in an unnecessarily difficult position, because they do not see what I suppose Mr. Keble did see so very clearly.

'I know that these questions present themselves somewhat differently to those situated severally as you and we are. But it is, I suppose, by freely interchanging amongst ourselves thoughts that the general balance is best preserved. Pray, when you have time, write freely to me on such matters if you think it may be of use to do so. The Church everywhere ought to guard, and teach, and practise what is essential. In non-essentials I suppose the rule is clear. I will eat no meat, &c.

'And now good-bye, my dear Cousin; and may God ever bless and comfort you.
'Your affectionate Cousin,
'J. C. PATTESON.'

Sir William and Lady Martin had just paid their last visit to Kohimarama, and here is the final record by Lady Martin's hand of the pleasant days there spent:—

'One more visit we paid to our dear friend in November 1866, a few months before he left Kohimarama for Norfolk Island. He invited my dear husband specially for the purpose of working together at Hebrew, with the aid of the lights they thought our languages throw on its grammatical structure.

'The Bishop was very happy and bright. He was in his new house, a great improvement upon the stuffy quarters in the quad. His sitting-room was large and lofty, and had French windows which opened on a little verandah facing the sea.

'The Mission party were most co-operative, and would not let the Bishop come into school during the three weeks of our stay, so he had a working holiday which he thoroughly enjoyed. The weather was lovely, the boys were all well, and there was no drawback to the happiness of that time. At seven the chapel bell rang and we walked across with him to the pretty little chapel. The prayers and hymn were in Mota, the latter a translation by the Bishop of the hymn "Now that the daylight fills the sky." The boys all responded heartily and were reverent in demeanour. After breakfast the two wise men worked steadily till nearly one. We were not allowed to dine in Hall as the weather was very warm, and we inveigled the Bishop to stay out and be our host.

'A quaint little procession of demure-looking little maidens brought our dinner over. They were grave and full of responsibility till some word from 'Bisop' would light up their faces with shy smiles.

'What pleasant walks we had together before evening chapel under the wooded cliffs or through the green fields. Mr. Pritt had by this time brought the Mission farm into excellent working order by the aid of the elder lads alone. Abundance of good milk and butter (the latter getting ready sale in town) and of vegetables. His gifts too in school-keeping were invaluable.

'I wish I could recall some of the conversations with our dear friend. A favourite topic was concerning the best modes of bringing the doctrines of the Christian religion clearly and fully within the comprehension of the converts. Some of their papers written after being taught by him showed that they did apprehend them in a thoughtful intelligent way.

'At half-past six we had a short service, again in Mota, in chapel, and then we rarely saw our dear friend till nine. He would not neglect any of his night classes. At half-past nine the English workers gathered together in the Bishop's room for prayers and for a little friendly chat. Curiously enough, the conversation I most distinctly remember was one with him as we rode up one Saturday from Kohimarama to St. John's College. I got him to describe the game of tennis, and he warmed up and told me of games he had played at.

'How that cheery talk came to mind as I drove down the same road last year just after fine weather had come! It was the same season, and the hedges on each side of the narrow lane were fragrant as then with may and sweet briar.'

CHAPTER XI. ST. BARNABAS COLLEGE, NORFOLK ISLAND. 1867 —1869.

A new phase of Coleridge Patteson's life was beginning with the year 1867, when he was in full preparation for the last of his many changes of home, namely, that to Norfolk Island, isolating him finally from those who had become almost as near kindred to him, and devoting him even more exclusively to his one great work. No doubt the separation from ordinary society was a relief, and the freedom from calls to irregular clerical duty at Auckland was an immense gain; but the lack of the close intercourse with the inner circle of his friends was often felt, and was enhanced by the lack of postal communication with Norfolk Island, so that, instead of security of home tidings by every mail, letters and parcels could only be transmitted by chance vessels touching at that inaccessible island, where there was no harbour for even the 'Southern Cross' to lie.

But the welfare of the Mission, and the possible benefit to the Pitcairners, outweighed everything. It is with some difficulty that the subject of this latter people is approached. They have long been the romance of all interested in Missionary effort, and precious has been the belief that so innocent and pious a community existed on the face of the earth. And it is quite true that when they are viewed as the offspring of English mutineers and heathen Tahitians, trained by a repentant old sailor, they are wonderful in many respects; and their attractive manners and manifest piety are sure to strike their occasional visitors, who have seldom stayed long enough to penetrate below the surface.

But it has been their great disadvantage never to have had a much higher standard of religion, morals, civilisation, or industry set before them, than they had been able to evolve for themselves; and it is a law of nature that what is not progressive must be retrograde. The gentle Tahitian nature has entirely mastered the English turbulence, so that there is genuine absence of violence, there is no dishonesty; and drunkenness was then impossible; there is also a general habit of religious observance, but not including self-restraint as a duty, while the reaction of all the enthusiastic admiration expressed for this interesting people has gendered a self-complacency that makes them the harder to deal with. Parental authority seems to be entirely wanting among them, the young people grow up unrestrained; and the standard of morality and purity seems to be pretty much what it is in a neglected English parish, but, as before said, without the drunkenness and lawlessness, and with a universal custom of church-going, and a great desire not to expose their fault to the eyes of strangers. The fertile soil, to people of so few wants, and with no trade, prevents the necessity of exertion, and the dolce far niente prevails universally. The Government buildings have fallen into entire ruin, and the breed of cattle has been allowed to become worthless for want of care. The dwellings are uncleanly, and the people so undisciplined that only their native gentleness would make their present self-government possible; and it is a great problem how to deal with them.

The English party who were to take up their abode on Norfolk Island consisted of the Bishop, the Rev. Mr. Palmer, who was there already, Mr. Atkin, and Mr. Brooke. The Rev. R. Codrington was on his way from England with Mr. Bice, a young student from St. Augustine's, Canterbury; but Mr. and Mrs. Pritt had received an appointment at the Waikato, and left the Mission. The next letter to myself tells something of the plans:—

'January 29, 1867.

'My dear Cousin,—I enclose a note to Miss Mackenzie, thanking her for her book about Mrs. Robertson. It does one good to read about such a couple. I almost feel as if I should like to write a line to the good man. There was the real genuine love for the people, the secret of course of all missionary success, the consideration for them, the power of sympathy, of seeing with the eyes of others, and putting oneself into their position. Many a time have I thought: "Yes, that's all right, that's the true spirit, that's the real thing."

'Oh that men could be trained to act in that way. It seems as if mere common sense would enable societies and men to see that it must be so. And yet how sadly we mismanage men, and misuse opportunities.

'Men should be made to understand that they cannot receive training for this special Mission work except on the spot; at the institution the aim should be to give them a thorough grounding in Greek and Latin, the elements of Divinity, leaving out all talk about experiences, and all that can minister to spiritual pride, and delude men into the idea that the desire (as they suppose) to be missionaries implies that they are one whit better than the baker and shoemaker next door.

'The German system is very different. The Moravians don't handle their young candidates after this fashion.

'Now Mr. Robertson and his good wife refresh one by the reality and simplicity of their life, the simple-mindedness, the absence of all cant and formalism. I mean the formal observance of a certain set of views about the Sabbath, about going to parties, about reading books, &c., the formal utterance of an accepted phraseology.

'Would that there were hundreds such! Would that his and her example might stir the hearts of many young people, women as well as men! Well, I like all that helps me to know him and her in the book, and am much obliged to Miss Mackenzie for it.

'We have had a trying month, unusually damp close weather, and influenza has been prevalent. Many boys had it, one little fellow died. He was very delirious at last, and as he lay day and night on my bed we had often to hold him. But one night he was calm and sensible, and with Henry Tagalana's help I obtained from him such a simple answer or two to our questions that I felt justified in baptizing him. He was about ten years old, I suppose one of our youngest.

'Last Saturday, at 12.45 A.M., he passed away into what light, and peace, and knowledge, and calm rest in his Saviour's bosom! we humbly trust. God be praised for all His mercies! It was touching, indeed, to hear Henry speaking to his little friend. He spoke so as to make me feel very hopeful about his work as a teacher being blessed, his whole heart on his lips and in his voice and manner and expression of face.

'But, my dear Cousin, often I think that I need more than ever your prayers that I may have the blessing for which we pray in our Collect for the First Sunday after Epiphany: grace to use the present opportunities aright. My time may be short; we are very few in number: now the young English and Melanesian teachers ought to be completely trained, that so, by God's blessing, the work may not come to nought. Codrington's coming ought to be a great gain in this way. A right-minded man of age and experience may well be regarded as invaluable indeed. I so often feel that I am distracted by multitudinous occupations, and can't think and act out my method of dealing with the elder ones, so as to use them aright. So many things distract—social, domestic, industrial matters and general superintendence, and my time is of course always given to anyone who wants it.

'The change to Norfolk Island, too, brings many anxious thoughts and cares, and the state of the people there will be an additional cause of anxiety. I think that we shall move en masse in April or May, making two or three trips in the schooner. Palmer has sixteen now with him there. I shall perhaps leave ten more for the winter school and then go on to the islands, and return (D.V.) in October, not to New Zealand, but to Norfolk Island; though, as it is the year of the meeting of the General Synod, i.e., February 1868, I shall have to be in New Zealand during that summer. You shall have full information of all my and our movements, as soon as I know myself precisely the plan.

'And now good-bye, my dear Cousin; and may God ever bless and keep you. I think much of you, and of how you must miss dear Mr. Keble.

'Your affectionate Cousin,

'**J. C. P.**'

'Sunday, February 10, 1867.

'My dear old Fan,—No time to write at length. We are pretty well, but coughs and colds abound, and I am a little anxious about one nice lad, Lelenga, but he is not very seriously ill.

'I have of course occasional difficulties, as who has not? Irregularities, not (D. Gr.) of very serious nature, yet calling for reproof; a certain proportion of the boys, and a large proportion of the girls careless, and of course, like boys and girls such as you know of in Devonshire, not free from mischief.

'Indeed, it is a matter for great thankfulness that, as far as we know, no immorality has taken place with fifteen young girls in the school. We take of course all precautions, rooms are carefully locked at night. Still really evil-minded young persons could doubtless get into mischief, if they were determined to do so. Only to-day I spoke severely, not on this point, but on account of some proof of want of real modesty and purity of feeling. But how can I be surprised at that?

'All schoolmaster's work is anxious work. It is even more so than the ordinary clergyman's work, because you are parent and schoolmaster at once.

'You may suppose that as time approaches for Codrington and Bice to arrive, and for our move to Norfolk Island, I am somewhat anxious, and have very much to do. Indeed, the Norfolk Island people do sadly want help.

'Your affectionate Brother,

'**J. C. P.**

'P. S.—You may tell your boys at night school, if you think it well, that no Melanesian I ever had here would be so ungentlemanly as to throw stones or make a row when a lady was present.'

'St. Matthias Day, 1867.

'My dearest Joan and Fan,—The beginning of the seventh year of my Bishop's life! How quickly the time has gone, and a good deal seems to have taken place, and yet (though some experience has been gained) but little sense have I of real improvement in my own self, of "pressing onwards," and daily struggles against faults. But for some persons it is dangerous to talk of such things, and I am such a person. It would tend to make me unreal, and my words would be unreal, and soon my thoughts and life would become unreal too. I am conscious of very, very much that is very wrong, and would astonish many of even those who know me best, but I must use this consciousness, and not talk about it any more.

'I am in harness again for English work. How can I refuse? I am writing now between two English services.

'Indeed, no adequate provision is made here for married clergymen with families; £300 a year is starvation at present prices. Men can't live on it; and who can work vigorously with the thought ever present to him, "When I die, what of my wife and family?" What is to be done?

'I solve the difficulty in Melanesian work by saying, "Use Melanesians." I tell people plainly, "I don't want white men."

'I sum it all up thus: They cost about ten times as much as the Melanesian (literally), and but a very small proportion do the work as well.

'I was amused at some things in your December letters. How things do unintentionally get exaggerated! I went up into the tree-house by a very good ladder of bamboos and supple-jacks, quite as easily as one goes up the rigging of a ship, and my ten days at Bauro were spent among a people whose language I know, and where my life was as safe and everybody was as disposed to be friendly as if I had been in your house at Weston. But, of course, it is all "missionary hardships and trials." I don't mean that you talk in this way.

'Our first instalment of scholars with Messrs. Atkin and Brooke will go off (D.V.) about March 21. Then my house is taken down; the boys who now live in it having been sent off: and on the schooner's return about April 15, another set of things, books, houses, &c. Probably a third trip will be necessary, and then about May 5 or 6 I hope to go. It will be somewhat trying at the end. But I bargain for all this, which of course constitutes my hardest and most trying business. The special Mission work, as most people would regard it, is as nothing in comparison. Good-bye, and God bless you.

'Your loving Brother,

'J. C. P.'

On March 5 Mr. Codrington safely arrived, bringing with him Mr. Bice. The boon to the Bishop was immense, both in relief from care and in the companionship, for which he had henceforth to depend entirely on his own staff. The machinery of the routine had been so well set in order by Mr. Pritt that it could be continued without him; and though there was no English woman to superintend the girls, it was hoped that Sarah Sarawia had been prepared by Mrs. Pritt to be an efficient matron.

'Kohimarama: March 23, 1867.

'My dear Cousin,—Our last New Zealand season, for it may be our last, draws near its close. On Monday, only two days hence, the "Southern Cross" sails (weather permitting) with our first instalment. Mr. Palmer has got his house up, and they must stow themselves away in it, three whites and forty-five blacks, the best way they can. The vessel takes besides 14,000 feet of timber, 6,000 shingles for roofing, and boxes of books, &c., &c., without end.

'I hope she may be here again to take me and the remaining goods, live and inanimate, in about eighteen or twenty days. I can't tell whether I am more likely to spend my Easter in New Zealand or Norfolk Island.

'I see that in many ways the place is good for us. The first expense is heavy. I have spent about £1,000 already, sinking some of my private money in the fencing, building, &c., but very soon the cost of all the commissariat, exclusive of the stores for the voyage, and a little English food for the whites, will be provided. Palmer has abundance of sweet potatoes which have been planted in ground prepared by our lads since last October. The yam crop is coming on well: fish are always abundant.

'I think that in twelve months' time we ought to provide ourselves with almost everything in the island. The ship and the clergymen's stipends and certain extras will always need subscriptions, but we ought at once to feed ourselves, and soon to export wool, potatoes, corn (maize I mean), &c.

'I never forget about the idea of a chapel. At present the Norfolk Island Chapel will be only a wing of my house: which will consist of two rooms for myself, a spare room for a sick lad or two, and a large dormitory which, if need be, can be turned into a hospital, and the other end a wing in the chapel, 42 x 18 feet, quite large enough for eighty or more people. The entrance from without, and again a private door from my sitting room. All is very simple in the plan. It seem almost selfish having it thus as a part of my dwelling house; but it will be such a comfort, so convenient for Confirmation and Baptism and Holy Communion classes, and so nice for me. Some ladies in Melbourne give a velvet altar cloth, Lady S. in Sydney gives all the white linen: our Communion plate, you know, is very handsome. Some day Joan must send me a solid block of Devonshire serpentine for my Font, such a one as there is at Alfington, or Butterfield might now devise even a better.

'But I think, though I have not thought enough yet, that in the diocese of Norfolk Island, and in the islands, the running stream of living water and the Catechumens "going down" into it is the right mode of administering the holy sacrament. The Lectern and the small Prayer-desk are of sandal-wood from Erromango.

'It will be far more like a Church than anything the Pitcairners have ever seen. Perhaps next Christmas—but much may take place before then—I may ordain Palmer Priest, Atkin and Brooke Deacons, and there may be a goodly attendance of Melanesian communicants and candidates for baptism. If so, what a day of hope to look forward to! And then I think I see the day of dear George Sarawia's Ordination drawing nigh, if God grant him health and perseverance. He is, indeed, and so are others, younger than he, all that I could desire.

'So, my dear Cousin, see what blessings I have, how small our trials are. They may yet come, but it is now just twelve years, exactly twelve years on Monday, since I saw my Father's and Sisters' faces, and how little have those years been marked with sorrows. My lot is cast in a good land indeed. I read and hear of others, such as that noble Central African band, and I wonder how men can go through it all. It comes to me as from a distance, not as to one who has experienced such things. We know nothing of war, or famine, or deadly fever; and we seem now to have a settled plan of work, one of the greatest comforts of all; but while I write thus brightly I don't forget that a little thing (humanly speaking) may cause great reverses, delays, and failures.

'I am very glad you understand my unwillingness to write, and still more to print over much about our proceedings. I do speak pretty freely in New Zealand and Australia, from whence I profess and mean to draw our supplies.

'Accurate information is all very well, but to convey an idea of our life and work is quite beyond my powers. Still, everything that helps the ordinary men and women of England to look out into the world a bit, and see that the Gospel is a power of God, is good.

'And now, good-bye, my dear Cousin. May God bless and keep you.

'Your affectionate Cousin,
'J. C. PATTESON.'
On Lady Day the Bishop wrote to his sisters:—

'This day, twelve years ago, I saw your faces for the last time; and so I told Mary Atkin, my good young friend's only sister, as we stood on the beach just now, watching the 'Southern Cross' carrying away her only brother and some forty other people to Norfolk Island.

The first detachment is therefore gone; I hope that we, the rest, will follow in about sixteen or eighteen days. I think back over these twelve years. On the whole, how smoothly and easily they have passed with me! Less of sorrow and anxiety than was crowded into one short year of Bishop Mackenzie's life. I have been reading Mr. Rowley's book on the University Mission to Central Africa, and am glad to have read it. They were indeed fine gallant fellows, full of faith and courage and endurance.

'As I write, some dozen boys are on the roof, knocking away the shingles, i.e., the wooden tiles of roofing, a carpenter is taking down all that needs some more skilled handiwork. In a week the house will all be tied up in bundles of boarding, battens, about 14,000 or 15,000 feet of timber in all. Yesterday I was with the Primate; I went up indeed on Monday afternoon, as the "Southern Cross" sailed with thirty-one Melanesians at 11 A.M., and I could get away. It was rather a sad day. I was resigning trusts, and it made the departure from New Zealand appear very real.

'April 1st.—My fortieth birthday. It brings solemn thoughts. Last night I had to take the service at St. Paul's, and as I came back I thought of many things, and principally of how very different I ought to be from what I am.

'All are well here at Kohimarama. My house knocked down and arrangements going on, the place leased to Mr. Atkin, Joe Atkin's father, my trusts resigned, accounts almost made up, many letters written, business matters arranged.'

In a few days more the last remnant of St. Andrew's was broken up; and the first letter to the Bishop of New Zealand was written from Norfolk Island before the close of the month:—

'St. Barnabas' Mission School: April 29, 1867.

My dear Primate,—We had a fair wind all the way, and having shortened sail during all Friday so as not to reach Norfolk Island in the night, made the lead at 5 A.M. on Saturday morning. But a sad casualty occurred; we lost a poor fellow overboard, one of the seamen. He ought not to have been lost, and I blame myself. He was under the davits of the boat doing something, and the rope by which he was holding parted; the life-buoy almost knocked him as he passed the quarter of the vessel, and I, instead of jumping overboard, and shouting to the Melanesians to do the same, rushed to the falls. The boat was on the spot where his cap was floating within two and a half minutes of the time he fell into the sea, but he was gone.

'Fisher in the hurry tore his nail by letting the falls run through his hand too fast. I was binding it up, the boat making for the poor fellow faster than any swimmer could have done. How it was that he did not lay hold of the buoy, or sank so soon, I can't say; the great mistake was not jumping overboard at once. This is a gloomy beginning, and made us all feel very sad. He was not married and was a well-behaved man.

'It was blowing fresh on Saturday, but we anchored under Nepean Island, and by hard work cleared the vessel by 5 P.M.; all worked hard, and all the things were landed safely. Palmer, with the cart and boys, was on the pier, and the things were carted and carried into the store as they arrived. I came on shore about 5, found all well and hearty, the people very friendly, nothing in their manner to indicate any change of feeling.

'I walked up to our place. It is, indeed, a beautiful spot. Palmer has worked with a will. I was surprised to see what was done. Some three and a half acres of fine kumaras, maize, yams, growing well; a yam of ten pounds weight, smooth and altogether Melanesian, just taken up, not quite ripe, so the boys say they will grow much bigger. Abundant supply of water, though the summer has been dry.

'Much of the timber has been carted up, more has been stacked at the top of the hill. This was carried by the boys, and will be carted along the pine avenue; a good deal is still near the pines, but properly stacked. I see nothing anywhere thrown about, even here not a chip to be seen, all buried or burnt, and the place quite neat though unfinished.

'1. House, on the plan of my old house just taken down by Gray, but much larger.

'2. Kitchen of good size.

'3. Two raupo outhouses.

'4. Cow-shed.

'I find it quite assumed here that the question is settled about our property here; but I have not thought it desirable to talk expressly about it. They talk about school, doctor, and other public arrangements as usual.

'It seems that it was on St. Barnabas Day that, after Holy Communion, we walked up here last year and chose the site of the house. The people have of their own accord taken to call the place St. Barnabas; and as this suits the Eton feeling also, and you and others never liked St. Andrew's, don't you think we may adopt the new name? Miss Yonge won't mind, I am sure.

'I could not resist telling the people that you and Mrs. Selwyn might come for a short time in September next to see them, and they are really delighted; and so shall we be, I can tell you indeed....

'Your affectionate

'**J. C. PATTESON.**'

The time for the island voyage was fully come; and, after a very brief stay in the new abode, the Bishop sailed again for Mota, where the old house was found (May 8) in a very dilapidated condition; and vigorous mending with branches was needed before a corner could be patched up for him to sleep on his table during a pouring wet night, having first supped on a cup of tea and a hot yam, the latter brought from the club-house by one of his faithful adherents; after which an hour and a half's reading of Lightfoot on the Epistle to the Galatians made him forget every discomfort.

There had, however, been a renewal of fighting of late; and at a village called Tasmate, a man named Natungoe had ten days previously been shot in the breast with a poisoned arrow, and was beginning to show those first deadly symptoms of tetanus. He had been a well-conducted fellow, though he had hitherto shown indifference to the new teaching; and it had not been in a private quarrel that he was wounded, but in a sudden attack on his village by some enemies, when a feast was going on.

On that first evening when the Bishop went to see him it was plain that far more of the recent instruction had taken root in him than had been supposed. 'He showed himself thoroughly ready to listen, and manifested a good deal of simple faith. He said he had no resentment against the person who had shot him, and that he did wish to know and think about the world to come. He accepted at once the story of God's love, shown in sending Jesus to die for us, and he seemed to have some apprehension of what God must be, and of what we are—how unlike Him, how unable to make ourselves fit to be with Him. He certainly spoke of Jesus as of a living Person close by him, willing and able to help him. He of his own accord made a little prayer to Him, "Help me, wake me, make my heart light, take away the darkness. I wish for you, I want to go to you, I don't want to think about this world."'

Early the next morning the Bishop went again, taking George Sarawia with him. The man said, 'I have been thinking of what you said. I have been calling on the Saviour (i Vaesu) all night.' The Bishop spoke long to him, and left Sarawia with him, speaking and praying quietly and earnestly.

Meanwhile continues the diary:—

'I went to the men in the village, and spoke at length to them: "Yes, God will not cast out those who turn to Him when they are called, but you must not suppose that it is told us anywhere that He will save those who care nothing about Him through their years of health, and only think about Him and the world to come when this world is already passing away."

'How utterly unable one feels to say or do the right thing, and the words fall so flat and dull upon careless ears!'

Every day for ten days the poor sufferer Natungoe was visited, and he listened with evident faith and comprehension. On May 15 the entry is:—

'I was so satisfied with his expressions of faith in the Saviour, of his hope of living with Him; he spoke so clearly of his belief in Jesus having been sent from the Great Creator and Father of all to lead us back to Him, and to cleanse us from sin, which had kept us from our Father, by His Death for us; he was so evidently convinced of the truth of our Lord's Resurrection and of the resurrection of us all at the last day—that I felt that I ought to baptize him. I had already spoken to him of Baptism, and he seemed to understand that, first, he must believe that the water is the sign of an inward cleansing, and that it has no magical efficacy, but that all depended on his having faith in the promise and power of God; and second, that Jesus had commanded those who wished to believe and love Him to be baptized.

"The expression Nan ive Maroo i Vaesu, "I wish for the Saviour," had been frequently used by him; and I baptized him by the name of Maroovaesu, a name instantly substituted for his old name Natungoe by those present.

'I have seen him again to-day; he cannot recover, and at times the tetanus spasms are severe, but it is nothing like dear Fisher's case. He can still eat and speak; women sit around holding him, and a few people sit or lie about in the hut. It looks all misery and degradation of the lowest kind, but there is a blessed change, as I trust, for him.'

On Sunday the 19th the last agony had come. He lay on a mat on the ground, in the middle of the village, terribly racked by convulsions, but still able in the intervals to speak intelligibly, and to express his full hope that he was going to his Saviour, and that his pain would soon be over, and he would be at rest with Him, listening earnestly to the Bishop's prayers. He died that night.

In the meantime, the Bishop had not neglected the attacking party. Of them, one had been killed outright, and two more were recovering from their wounds, and it was necessary to act as pacificator.

'Meanwhile, I think how very little religion has to do directly with keeping things quiet; in England (for example) men would avenge themselves, and steal and kill, were it not for the law, which is, indeed, an indirect result of religion; but religion simply does not produce the effect, i.e. men are not generally religious in England or Mota. I have Maine's Book of "Ancient Law" among the half-dozen books I have brought on shore, and it is extremely interesting to read here.'

How he read, wrote, or did anything is the marvel, with the hut constantly crowded by men who had nothing to do but gather round, in suffocating numbers, to stare at his pen travelling over the paper. 'They have done so a hundred times before,' he writes, actually under the oppression, 'but anything to pass an hour lazily. It is useless to talk about it, and one must humour them, or they will think I am vexed with them.'

The scholars, neatly clothed, with orderly and industrious habits, were no small contrast: 'But I miss as yet the link between them and the resident heathen people. I trust and pray that George and others may, ere long, supply it.

'But it is very difficult to know how to help them to change their mode of life. Very much, even if they did accept Christianity, must go on as before. Their daily occupations include work in the small gardens, cooking, &c., and this need not be changed.

'Then as to clothing. I must be very careful lest they should think that wearing clothes is Christianity. Yet certain domestic changes are necessary, for a Christian life seems to need certain material arrangements for decency and propriety. There ought to be partition screens in the hut, for example, and some clothing is desirable no doubt. A resident missionary now could do a good deal towards showing the people why certain customs, &c., are incompatible with a Christian life. His daily teaching would show how Christ acted and taught, and how inconsistent such and such practices must be with the profession of faith in Him. But regulations imposed from without I rather dread, they produce so often an unreasoning obedience for a little while only.

The rules for the new life should be very few and very simple, and carefully explained. "Love to God and man," explained and illustrated as the consequence of some elementary knowledge of God's love to us, shown of course prominently in the giving His own Son to us. There is no lack of power to understand simple teaching, a fair proportion of adults take it in very fairly. I was rather surprised on Friday evening (some sixty or seventy being present) to find that a few men answered really rather well questions which brought out the meaning of some of our Saviour's names.

'"The Saviour?"

'"The saving His people."

'"Not all men? And why not all men? And from what poverty, sickness, &c., here below?"

'"From their sins."

'"What is sin?"

'"All that God has forbidden."

'"What has He forbidden? Why? Because He grudges us anything? Why do you forbid a child to taste vangarpal ('poison'), &c. &c.?"

'"The Way," "the Mediator," "the Redeemer," "the Resurrection," "the Atoner," "the Word." Some eight days' teaching had preceded this; but I dare say there are ten or fifteen people here now, not our scholars, who can really answer on these points so as to make it clear that they understand something about the teaching involved in these names. Of course, I had carefully worked out the best way to accept these names and ideas in Mota; and the illustrations, &c., from their customs made me think that to some extent they understood this teaching.

'Of course the personal feeling is as pleasant as can be, and I think there is something more: a real belief that our religion and our habits are good, and that some day they will be accepted here. A considerable number of people are leading very respectable lives on the whole. But I see that we must try to spend more time here. George Sarawia is being accepted to some extent as one whom they are to regard as a teacher. He has a fair amount of influence. But in this little spot, among about 1,500 people, local jealousies and old animosities are so rife, that the stranger unconnected with any one of them has so far a better chance of being accepted by all; but then comes, on the other hand, his perfect knowledge and our comparative ignorance of the language and customs of the people. We want to combine both for a while, till the native teacher and clergyman is fully established in his true position.

'It is a curious thing that the Solomon Islanders from the south-east part of that group should have dropped so much behind the Banks Islanders. I knew their language before I knew the language of Mota, they were (so to say) my favourites. But we can't as yet make any impression upon them. The Loyalty Islanders have been suffered to drop out; and so it is that all our leading scholars, all who set good examples, and are made responsible for various duties, are (with the sole exception of Soro, from Mai Island, New Hebrides) from the Banks group. Consequently, their language is the lingua franca of the school—not that we made it so, or wished it rather than any other to be so; indeed Bauro is easier, and so are some others: but so it is. It is an excellent thing, for any Melanesian soon acquires another Melanesian language, however different the vocabulary may be. Their ideas and thoughts and many of their customs are similar, the mode of life is similar, and their mode of expressing themselves similar. They think in the same way, and therefore speak in the same way. Their mode of life is natural; ours is highly artificial. We are the creatures of a troublesome civilisation to an extent that one realises here. When I go ashore for five weeks, though I could carry all my luggage, yet it must comprise a coffee-pot, sugar, biscuits, a cork bed, some tins of preserved meat, candles, books, and my hut has a table and a stool, and I have a cup, saucer, plate, knife, fork, and spoon. My good friend George, who I think is on the whole better dressed than I am, and who has adopted several of our signs of civilisation, finds the food, cooking, and many of the ways of the island natural and congenial, and would find them so throughout the Pacific.

'May 21st.—The morning and evening school here is very nice. I doubt if I am simple enough in my teaching. I think I teach too much at a time; there is so much to be taught, and I am so impatient, I don't go slowly enough, though I do travel over the same ground very often. Some few certainly do take in a good deal.

'A very hot day, after much rain. This morning we took down our old wooden hut, that was put up here by us six years ago. Parts of it are useless, for in our absence the rain damaged it a good deal. I mean to take it across to Arau, Henry Tagalana's little island, for there, even in very wet weather, there is little fear of ague, the soil being light and sandy. It would be a great thing to escape from the rich soil and luxuriant vegetation in the wet months, if any one of us spent a long time here. It was hot work, but soon over. It only took about two and a half hours to take down, and stack all the planks, rafters, &c. Two fellows worked well, and some others looked on and helped now and then.

'I have had some pleasant occupation for an hour or so each day in clearing away the bush, which in one year grows up surprisingly here. Many lemon, citron, and orange trees that we planted some years ago. cocoa-nut trees also, were almost, some quite overgrown, quite hidden, and our place looked and was quite small and close; but one or two hours for a few days, spent in clearing, have made a great difference. I have planted out about twenty-five lemon suckers, and as many pine-apples, for our old ones were growing everywhere in thick clumps, and I have to thin them out.

'Yesterday was a great day; we cut down two large trees, round one of which I had carelessly planted orange, lemon, and cocoa-nut trees, so that we did not know how to fell it so as to avoid crushing some fine young trees; but the tree took the matter into its own hands, for it was hollow in the centre, and fell suddenly, so that the fellows holding the rope could not guide it, and it fell at right angles to the direction we had chosen, but right between all the trees, without seriously hurting one. It quite reminds me of old tree-cutting days at Feniton; only here I see no oaks, nor elms, nor beeches, nor firs, only bread-fruit trees and almond trees, and many fruit-bearing trees—oranges, &c., and guavas and custard-apples—growing up (all being introduced by us), and the two gigantic banyan trees, north and south of my little place. It is so very pretty!

'I don't trouble myself much about cooking. My little canteen is capital; and I can make myself all sorts of good things, if I choose to take the trouble, and some days I do so. I bake a little bread now and then, and natter myself it is uncommonly good; and one four-pound tin of Bloxland's preserved meat from Queensland has already lasted me twelve days, and there is about half of it remaining. He reckons each pound well soaked and cooked to be equal to three pounds, and I think he is right. A very little of this, with a bit of yam deliciously cooked, and brought to me each day as a present by some one from their cooking ovens, makes a capital dinner. Then I have some rice and sugar for breakfast, a biscuit and coffee, and a bit of bread-fruit perhaps; and all the little delicacies are here—salt, pepper, mustard, even to a bottle of pickles—so I am pretty well off, I think.

'I find that the white ant, or an insect like it, is here. The plates of our old hut are quite rotten, the outside still untouched, all within like tinder. They call the insect vanoa; it is not found in New Zealand, but it is a sad nuisance in Australia.

'I do not read much here this time, so much of every day is taken up with talking to the people about me. That is all right, and I generally can turn the talk to something that I wish them to hear, so it is all in the way of business here. And I am glad to say that my school, and conversations and lessons, need some careful preparation. I have spent some time in drawing up for myself a little scheme of teaching for people in the state of my friends here. I ought of course to have done it long ago, and it is a poor thing now. I cannot take a real pleasure in teaching, and so I do it badly. I am always, almost always, glad when school is over, though sometimes I get much interested myself, though not often able to interest others.

'I am reading some Hebrew nearly every day, and Lightfoot on the Galatians, Tyler's "Researches into the Early History of Mankind," Dollinger's "First Ages of the Church," and "Ecce Homo." I tried Maine's "Ancient Law," but it is too tough for the tropics, unless I chance to feel very fresh. I generally get an hour in the evening, if I am sleeping at home.

'May 23rd.—I suppose anyone who has lived in a dirty Irish village—pigs, fowls, and children equally noisy and filthy, and the parents wild, ignorant, and impulsive—may have some notion of this kind of thing. You never get a true account, much less a true illustration of the real thing. Did you happen to see a ridiculous engraving on one of the S. P. Gr. sheets some years ago, supposed to be me taking two Ambrym boys to the boat? (Footnote: No such engraving can be found by the S. P. Gr. It was probably put forth in some other publication.) Now it is much better not to draw at all than to draw something which can only mislead people. If Ambrym boys really looked like those two little fellows, and if the boat with bland-looking white men could quietly be pulled to the beach, and if I, in a respectable dress, could go to and from the boat and the shore, why the third stage of Mission work has been reached already! I don't suppose you can picture to yourselves the real state of things in this, and in many of these islands, and therefore the great difficulty there is in getting them out of their present social, or unsocial, state!

'To follow Christian teaching out in detail, to carry it out from the school into the hut, into the actual daily life of the dirty naked women, and still dirtier though not more naked children; to get the men really to abandon old ways from a sense of responsibility and duty and love to God, this of course comes very slowly. I am writing very lazily, being indeed tired with heat and mosquitos. The sun is very hot again to-day. I have no thermometer here, but it feels as if it ought to be 90° in the shade.

'May 25th.—George Sarawia spent yesterday here, and has just gone to his village. He and I had a good deal of conversation. I copied out for him the plan of teaching drawn up from books already printed in their language. He speaks encouragingly, and is certainly recognised as one who is intended to be the teacher here. No one is surprised that he should be treated by me in a very different way from anyone else, with a complete confidence and a mutual understanding of each other. He is a thoroughly good, simple-minded fellow, and I hope, by God's blessing, he may do much good. He told me that B—— wants to come with me again; but I cannot take him. As we have been living properly, and for the sake of the head school and our character in the eyes of the people here, I cannot take him until he shows proof of a real desire to do his duty. I am very sorry for it. I have all the old feeling about him; and he is so quick and intelligent, but he allows himself again and again to be overcome by temptation, hard I dare say to withstand; but this conduct does disqualify him for being chosen to go with us. I am leaving behind some good but dull boys, for I can't make room as yet for them, and I must not take an ill-conducted fellow because he is quick and clever. He has some sort of influence in the place from his quickness, and from his having acquired a good deal of riches while with us. He says nothing, according to Sarawia, for or against our teaching. Meanwhile, he lives much like a somewhat civilised native. Poor fellow! I sent a message to him by George that if he wished to see me, I should be very willing to have a talk with him.

'Yesterday we made some sago. A tree is cut down in its proper stage of growth, just when it begins to flower. The pith is pulled and torn into shreds and fibres, then the juice is squeezed out so as to allow it to run or drip into some vessel, while water is poured on the pith by some one assisting the performer. The grounds (as say of coffee) remain at the bottom when the water is poured off, and an hour of such a sun as we had yesterday dries and hardens the sago. It is then fit for use. I suppose that it took an hour and a half to prepare about a slop-basin full of the dried hard sago. I have not used it yet. We brought tapioca here some years ago, and they used it in the same way, and they had abundance of arrow-root. On Monday I will make some, if all is well. Any fellow is willing to help for a few beads or fish-hooks, and they do all the heavy work, the fetching water, &c.

'I never saw anything like the pigeons in the great banyan tree close by. They eat its berries, and I really think there are at times more than a hundred at once in it. Had I a gun here I think I might have brought down three or four at a shot yesterday, sitting shot of course, but then I should shoot "for the pot." Palmer had his gun here last year, and shot as many as he wanted at any time. The bats at night are innumerable; they too eat the banyan berries, but chiefly the ripening bread-fruit. The cats we brought here have nearly cleared the place of the small rats which used to abound here; but lizards abound in this hut, because it is not continually smoke-dried.

'Last night I think some of the people here heard some rather new notions, to them, about the true relation of man and woman, parent and child, &c. They said, as they do often say, "Every word is true! how foolish we are!" But how to get any of them to start on a new course is the question.

'Ascension Day, May 30th.—There is a good deal of discussion going on now among the people. I hear of it not only from our old scholars, but from some of the men. I have been speaking day by day more earnestly to the people; always reading here and there verses of the Gospels or the Acts, or paraphrasing some passage so that they may have the actual words in which the message is recorded. They say, "This is a heavy, a weighty word," and they are talking, as they say, night after night about it. Some few, and they elderly men, say, "Let us talk only about our customs here." Others say, "No, no; let us try to think out the meaning of what he said." A few come and ask me questions, only a few, not many are in earnest, and all are shy. Many every night meet in Robert Pantatun's house, twenty-five or thirty, and ask him all manner of questions, and he reads a little. They end with prayer.

'They have many strange customs and superstitious observances peculiar to this group. They have curious clubs, confraternities with secret rites of initiation. The candidate for admission pays pigs and native money, and after many days' seclusion in a secret place is, with great ceremony, recognised as a member. No woman and none of the uninitiated may know anything of these things.

'In every village there is a Sala Goro, a place for cooking, which only those who have "gazed at the sacred symbol" may frequent. Food cooked there may not be eaten by one uninitiated, or by women or children. The path to the Sala Goro is never trodden by any woman or matanomorous ("eye closed"). When any ceremony is going on the whole of the precincts of the Sala Goro are sacred. At no time dare any woman eat with any man, no husband with his wife, no father with his daughter as soon as she is no longer a child.

'Of course such a system can be used by us in two ways. I say, "You have your method of assembling together, and you observe certain customs in so doing; so do we, but yours is an exclusive and selfish system: your secret societies are like our clubs, with their entrance fees, &c. But Christ's society has its sacred rite of admission, and other mysteries too, and it is for all who wish to belong to it. He recognises no distinction of male or female, bond or free."

'Some of the elder men are becoming suspicious of me. I tell them plainly that whatever there may be in their customs incompatible with the great law of Love to God and man must come to nought. "You beat and terrify matanomorous in order to make them give, that you may get pigs and native money from them. Such conduct is all wrong, for if you beat or frighten a youth or man, you certainly can't love him."

'At the same time I can't tell how far this goes. If there were a real ceremony of an idol or prayer to it, of course it would be comparatively easy to act in the matter; but the ceremony consists in sticking a curious sort of mitre, pointed and worked with hair, on the head of the candidate, and covering his body with a sort of Jack-in-the green wicker work of leaves, &c., and they joke and laugh about it, and attach, apparently, no religious significance to it whatever.

'I think it has the evil which attends all secret societies, that it tends to produce invidious distinctions and castes. An instinct impels men to form themselves into associations; but then Christ has satisfied that instinct legitimately in the Church.

'Christianity does meet a human instinct; as, e.g., the Lord's Supper, whatever higher and deeper feelings it may have, has this simple, but most significant meaning to the primitive convert, of feasting as a child with his brethren and sisters at the Father's Board.

'The significance of this to people living as more than half the human beings in the world are living still, is such as we have lost the power of conceiving; the Lord's Supper has so long had, so to say, other meanings for many of us. Yet to be admitted a member of God's family, and then solemnly at stated times to use this privilege of membership, strengthening the tie, and familiarising oneself more and more with the customs of that heavenly family, this surely is a very great deal of what human instinct, as exhibited in almost universal customs, requires.

'There are depths for those who can dive into them; but I really think that in some of these theological questions we view the matter solely from our state of civilisation and thought, and forget the multitudes of uneducated, rude, unrefined people to whom all below the simple meaning is unmeaning. May I not say to Robert Pantatun, "Christ, you know, gave His Body and Blood for us on the Cross, He gives them to you now, for all purposes of saving you and strengthening your spiritual life, while you eat and drink as an adopted child at your Father's Table"?

'It is the keeping alive the consciousness of the relation of all children to God through Christ that is needed so much. And with these actual sights before me, and you have them among you in the hundreds of thousands of poor ignorant creatures, I almost wonder that men should spend so much time in refining upon points which never can have a practical meaning for any persons not trained to habits of accurate thought and unusual devotion. But here I am very likely wrong, and committing the very fault of generalizing from my own particular position.

'June 4th.—I was greatly pleased, on Friday evening last which George Sarawia spent here with me, to hear from him that he had been talking with the Banks Islanders at Norfolk Island, and on board ship, about a plan which he now proposed to me. I had indeed thought of it, but scarcely saw my way. It is a new proof of his real earnestness, and of his seeking the good of his people here. The plan is this:—

'G. S. "Bishop, we have been talking together about your buying some land here, near your present place, where we all can live together, where we can let the people see what our mode of life is, what our customs are, which we have learnt from you."

'J. C. P. "Capital, George, but are you all willing to give up your living in villages among your own particular relations?"

'G. S. "Yes, we all agreed about it. You see, sir, if we live scattered about we are not strong enough to hold our ground, and some of the younger ones fall back into their old ways. The temptations are great, and what can be expected of one or two boys among eighty or ninety heathen people?"

'J. C. P. "Of course you know what I think about it. It is the very thing I have always longed for. I did have a general school here, as you know."

'G. S. "Yes, but things are different now. People are making enquiries. Many young fellows want to understand our teaching, and follow it. If we have a good large place of our own there, we can carry on our own mode of living without interfering with other people."

'J. G. P. "Yes, and so we can, actually in the midst of them, let them see a Christian village, where none of the strange practices which are inconsistent with Christianity will be allowed, and where the comforts and advantages of our customs may be actually seen."

'G. S. "By-and-by it will be a large village, and many will wish to live there, and not from many parts of Mota only."

'Well, I have told you, I suppose, of the fertility of this island, and how it is far more than sufficient to supply the wants of the people. Food is wasted on all sides. This very day I have plucked ten large bread-fruits, and might have plucked forty now nearly ripe, simply that the bats may not get them. I gave them away, as I can't eat more than a third part of one at a meal.

'So I went with George on Saturday, and we chose such a beautiful property, between Veverao and Maligo, I dare say about ten acres. Then I spoke to the people here, explaining my wishes and motives. To-day we have been over it with a large party, that all might be done publicly and everybody might hear and know. The land belongs to sixteen different owners; the cocoa-nut trees, breadfruit, almond, and other fruit-trees are bought separately.

'They all agree; indeed, as they have abundance of space of spare land just as good all about, and they will get a good stock of hatchets, pigs, &c., from me, for this land, there is not much doubt about that. But it is pleasant to hear some of them say, "No, no, that is mine and my son's, and he is your boy. You can have that for nothing."

'I shan't take it; it is safer to buy, but it is pleasant to see the kind feeling.

'If it be God's will to prosper this undertaking, we should begin next year with about fifteen of our own scholars, and a goodly number of half-scholars, viz., those who are now our regular scholars here, but have not been taken to New Zealand.

'Fencing, clearing, &c., could go on rapidly. Many would help, and small payments of beads and fish-hooks can always secure a man's services.

'I should build the houses with the material of the island, save only windows, but adopt of course a different shape and style for them. The idea would be to have everything native fashion, but improved, so as to be clearly suitable for the wants of people sufficiently civilised. All that a Christian finds helpful and expedient we ought to have, but to adopt English notions and habits would defeat my object. The people could not adopt them, there would be no teaching for them. I want to be able to say: "Well, you see, there is nothing to prevent you from having this and that, and your doing this and that."

'We must have some simple rules about cleanliness, working hours, &c., but all that is already familiar to those who have been with us at Kohimarama and Norfolk Island. Above all, I rejoice in the thought that the people understand that very soon this plan is to be worked by George Sarawia. He is to be the, so to say, head of the Christian village. I shall be a kind of Visitor. Palmer will, of course, be wanted at first, but must avoid the fault of letting the people, our own pupils as well as others, become dependent upon us. The Paraguay Mission produced docile good-natured fags for the missionaries, but the natives had learnt no self-respect, manliness, nor positive strength of character. They fought well, and showed pluck when the missionaries armed them, but they seem to have had no power of perpetuating their newly-learnt customs, without the continual guidance of the missionaries. It may be that such supervision is necessary; but I do not think it is so, and I should be sorry to think it is so.'

As usual, the Mota climate told on the health of the party, there was general influenza, and the Bishop had a swelling under his left arm; but on Whitsunday the 'Southern Cross,' which had been to set down the Solomon Islanders, returned, and carried him off. Vanua Lava was touched at, and a stone, carved by John Adams, put up at Fisher Young's grave, which was found, as before, well kept in order. Then the round of the New Hebrides was made; but new volunteers were refused, or told to wait ten moons, as it was an object to spend the first season in the new locality with tried scholars.

At 'the grand island, miscalled Leper's,' the Bishop slept ashore for the first time, and so also at Whitsuntide.

At Espiritu Santo much friendliness was shown, and a man would not take a present Mr. Atkin offered, because he had nothing, to pay for it. Santa Cruz, as usual, was disappointing, as, Mr. Atkin says, the only word in their mouths, the only thought in their heads, was 'iron;' they clamoured for this, and would not listen; moreover, their own pronunciation of their language was very indistinct, owing to their teeth being destroyed by the use of the betel-nut, so that they all spoke like a man with a hot potato in his mouth.

'So again we leave this fine island without any advance, as far as we can see, having been made. I may live to think these islanders very wild, and their speech very difficult, yet I know no more of them now than I did years ago. Yet I hope that some unforeseen means for "entering in among" them may be given some day. Their time is to come, sooner or later, when He knows it to be the right time.'

Savo was then touched at; and the Bishop slept ashore at Florida, and left Mr. Brooke there to the hospitality of three old scholars for a few days, by way of making a beginning. The observations on the plan show a strange sense of ageing at only forty:—

'He speaks the language fairly; and his visit will, I hope, do good. Of course he will be tired, and will enjoy the quiet of the schooner after it. I know what that is pretty well, and it takes something to make one prefer the little vessel at sea to any kind of shore life. However, he has youth and cheery spirits at command, and that makes life on an island. A man whose tastes naturally are for books, &c., rather than for small talk, and who can't take much interest in the very trifling matters that engage the attention of these poor fellows, such a man finds it very tiring indeed sometimes, when a merry bright good-natured fellow would amuse himself and the natives too.

'In these introductory visits, scarcely anything is done or said that resembles Mission work as invented in stories, and described by the very vivid imagination, of sensational writers. The crowd is great, the noise greater, the heat, the dirt, the inquisitiveness, the endless repetition of the same questions and remarks, the continual requests for a fish-hook, for beads, &c.—this is somewhat unlike the interesting pictures, in a Missionary Magazine, of an amiable individual very correctly got up in a white tie and black tailed coat, and a group of very attentive, decently-clothed and nicely-washed natives. They are wild with excitement, not to hear "the good news," but to hear how the trading went on: "How many axes did they sell? How many bits of iron?"

'You say, "Why do you trade at all?" Answer: In the first visits that we make we should at once alienate all the goodwill of the people from us unless we so far complied with their desire to get iron tools, or to trade more or less with them. As soon as I can I give presents to three or four leading men, and then let the buying curiosities be carried on by the crew and others; but not to trade at all would be equivalent to giving up hope of establishing any intercourse with the people.

'But in new islands, and upon our first visits, if we do get a chance of saying something amid the uproar, what can we say about religion that will be intelligible to men whose language has never been used to express any thought of ours that we long to communicate, and whose minds are pre-occupied by the visit of the vessel, and the longing for our articles of trade? Sometimes we do try to say a few words; sometimes we do a little better, we get a hearing, some persons listen with some interest; but usually, if we can merely explain that we don't come to trade, though we trade to please them, that we wish to take lads and teach them, we are obliged to be satisfied. "Teach them! teach them what?" think the natives. Why, one old hatchet would outweigh in their minds all that boy or man can gain from any teaching. What appreciable value can reading, writing, wearing clothes, &c., have in their eyes? So we must in first visits (of which I am now thinking) be thankful that we can in safety sleep on shore at all, and regard the merely making friends with the people as a small beginning of Mission work.

'Poor fellows! they think it very strange! As you lie down in the dark and try to sleep, you presently feel hands stroking your arms and legs, and feeling you about to make sure that the stranger has the same allowance of arms and legs that they have; and you overhear such quaint remarks as you lie still, afraid to let them know that you are awake, lest they should oblige you to begin talking over again the same things that you have already said twenty times.'

Mr. Brooke stayed four days at Florida; and came away with three former pupils, and four new ones, one of them grown up, a relative of the leading man of the island. Taroniara was the only Bauro scholar brought away this time; but so many were taken from Mota that the whole party numbered thirty-seven, seven of them girls, all betrothed to one or other of the lads. The entire colony at St. Barnabas, including English, was thus raised to seventy, when the 'Southern Cross' returned thither in August. On the 23rd, Bishop Patteson writes:—

'I wish you could see this place and the view from this room. I have only got into it within this hour. The carpenters are just out of it. You know that I left Palmer here about eleven months ago, on the return from that island voyage. He had sixteen lads with him, of whom eleven were good stout fellows.

'He did work wonderfully. The place I chose for the site of the station is about three miles from the settlement—the town, as the people call it. If you have a map of the island, you will see Longridge on the western part of it. Follow on the principal road, which goes on beyond Longridge in a N. and NW. direction, and about a mile beyond Longridge is our station. The top of Mount Pitt is nearly opposite our houses, of which two are now habitable, though not finished. The third, which is the house at Kohimarama which I had for one year, and in which Sir W. and Lady Martin spent ten days, will be begun on Monday next, I hope. The labour of getting all these things from New Zealand and then landing them (for there is no harbour), and then carting them up here (for there are no really good horses here, but the two I bought and sent down), was very considerable. Palmer and his boys worked admirably. He was industrious indeed. He and they lived at first in a little cottage, about three-quarters of a mile from our place, i.e., about a quarter of a mile from Longridge. During the first month, while they had no cart or horses as yet (for I had to send them down from Auckland), they fenced in some lands (the wire for which I had bought at Sydney, and a man-of-war brought it hither), planted yams (which grow excellently, such a crop never was seen here) and sweet potatoes, melons, vegetables, &c. Meanwhile, the timber for the houses was being sent as I had opportunity, a large quantity having been already taken to Norfolk Island in a man-of-war. Luckily, timber was selling very cheap at Auckland.

'After this first month, Palmer set to work at house building. He built entirely by himself, save the chimney and some part of the shingling (wooden roofing). As yet, no rooms have any ceiling or lining; they might by innocent people be thought to resemble barns, but they are weather-proof, strong, and answer all present purposes. The verandah, about 8 feet broad, is another great room really.

'I am still buying and sending down bricks, timber, &c. Two Auckland carpenters, thoroughly steady men, left Norfolk Island, about three weeks after we left it, for the Melanesian islands. They have been putting up my special building. We have no doors like hall doors, as all the rooms open with glass doors on to the verandah, and they are the doors for going in and out. Comprenez-vous? The ground slopes away from these two houses for some 200 yards or more to a little stream; and this slope is all covered with sweet potatoes and vegetables, and Codrington and Palmer have planted any number of trees, bushes, flowers, &c. Everything grows, and grows luxuriantly. Such soil, such a climate!

'By-and-by I shall have, I hope, such myrtles and azaleas, kalmias and crotons, and pine-apples and almond trees, bananas and tree-ferns, and magnolias and camellias, &c., all in the open air.

'The ground slopes up beyond the little stream, a beautiful wooded bank, wooded with many kinds of trees and bushes, large Norfolk Island pines; cattle and sheep stray about. Oh! how very pretty it is! And then beyond and above this first slope, the eye travels along the slopes of the Pitt to its summit, about 1,000 feet, a pretty little hill. It is, indeed, a calm peaceful scene, away from noise and bustle, plenty of pleasant sounds of merry boys working in the gardens, and employing themselves in divers ways. The prospect is (D. Gr.) a very happy one. It is some pleasure to work here, where the land gives "her increase" indeed.

'All seem very happy and well pleased with the place. I don't see how it can be otherwise, and yet to the young people there may be something attractive in society. But the young ones must occasionally go to Auckland or Sydney, or whithersoever they please, for a two or three months' holiday. For me, what can I desire more than this place affords? More than half of each year spent here if I live, and quietly, with any amount of work, uninterrupted work, time for quiet reading and thought. This room of mine in which I now am sitting is magnifique, my dear Joan; seriously, a very good room. You see it will be full of boys and girls; and I must have in it many things, not books only, for the general use of all here, so that I determined to make it a nice place at once.

'This room then, nicely lined, looking rather like a wooden box, it is true, but clean and airy, is 22 feet x 14 feet 6 in., and the wall plates 9 feet 6 in. high, the ceiling coved a little, so as to be nearly 14 feet high in the centre. What do you think of that for a room? It has a fire-place, and wide verandah, which is nearly 6 feet above the ground, so that I am high and dry, and have all the better view too, quite a grand flight of steps—a broad ladder—up into my house. The Mahaga lads and I call it my tree-house.

'Then I have one great luxury. I thought I would have it, and it is so nice. My room opens into the Chapel by red baize swinging doors; my private entrance, for there is a regular porch where the rest go in.

'Service at 7 A.M. and 8 P.M. But it is always open, boys come in of a morning to say their private prayers, for sleeping together in one room they have little privacy there. And I can go in at all hours. Soon it will become a sacred spot to us. It is really like a Chapel.

'August 27th.—Your birthday, my dear old Fan! God bless you, and grant you all true happiness, and the sense of being led onwards to the eternal peace and joy above. The parting here is a long one; and likely to be a parting for good, as far as this world is concerned.

'Last night was the coldest night that they have had during the whole winter; the thermometer touched 43°—Codrington has regular registering thermometers, so you see what a charming climate this is for us. Palmer was here all the summer, and he says that the heat, though great as marked by thermometer, was never trying, relaxing, and unfitting for work, as at Kohimarama.'

Thus began the first period of the residence in Norfolk Island; where Mr. Codrington's account of the way of life shall supplement the above:—

'When the Bishop returned in August 1867, our party consisted of himself, Mr. Palmer in Deacon's orders, and myself, Mr. Atkin and Mr. Brooke already experienced in the work, and Mr. Bice, who had with myself lately arrived from

England. The whole number of Melanesians was about sixty; among the eldest of these the most intelligent and advanced of the few then baptized, George, Henry, B———, Robert and Edward. There were then, I think, thirteen baptized, and two Communicants. To this elder class, the Bishop, as far as I can recollect, devoted the greater part of his time. He said that now for the first time he was able without interruption to set to work to teach them, and he certainly made great progress in those months. I remember that every evening they used to sit in Chapel after prayers, and consider what difficulty or question they should propound to him; and he would come in after a time, and, after hearing the question, discuss the subject, discourse upon it, and end with prayer. They were at the time, I remember, much impressed by this; and those who were the most advanced took in a great deal of an elevated strain of doctrine which, no doubt, passed over the heads of the greater number, but not without stirring up their hearts.

'It became a regular custom on the evening before the Communion Sunday, i.e., every other Sunday, to give the Communicants instruction and preparation after the Chapel service. At this time there was no Sunday sermon in Chapel. The Bishop used to say that the preaching was done in the school; but much of his school was of a hortatory kind in the Chapel, and often without taking off the surplice.

'At this time I should add that he used from time to time to have other boys with him to school, and particularly Solomon Islanders, whose languages he alone could generally speak. He had also a good deal with him the second set of eight Banks Islanders, who were by this time recognised Catechumens.

'There were other occupations of the Bishop's time, besides his school with Melanesians. The hour from 12 to 1 was devoted to instruction given to the two young men, one from New Zealand and one a son of Mr. Nobbs, who were working with the Mission; and on alternate days to the younger members of the Mission, who were being prepared for Ordination.

'The reading with the younger clergy continued to be to the last one of the most regular and most fruitful of the Bishop's engagements. The education which Mr. Atkin had for many years received from the Bishop had set him considerably above the average of young English clergy, not only in scholarship and information, but also in habits of literary industry. The Bishop, with his own great interest in Hebrew, enjoyed very much his Hebrew reading with Mr. Atkin and Mr. Bice.

'The Bishop also began as soon as he could to pay attention to the teaching of the young Norfolk Islanders. He preached very often in their Church, and went down on Wednesdays to take a class of candidates for Confirmation. He said, and I believe with truth, that he wasted a great deal of time in preparing his lessons with the candidates for Ordination or younger clergy; that is, he looked up the subject in some book, and read on and on till he had gone far beyond the point in search of which he started, and had no time left to take up the other points which belonged to the subject he had in view. I should say he was always a desultory scholar, reading very much and to very great purpose, but being led continually from one subject or one book to another long before coming to an end of the first. He was always so dissatisfied with what he did, that whereas there are remaining several beginnings of one or two pages on one subject or another, there is no paper of his which is more than a fragment—that is, in English. There is one series of Notes on the Catechism in Mota complete. In those days I was not myself able to converse sufficiently in Mota to learn much from the elder boys about the teaching they were receiving; but it was evident that they were much impressed and stirred up, they spent much time with their books by themselves, and one could not fail to form a high estimate of the work that was going on. Now they say they never had school like that before or since. The Bishop was, in fact, luxuriating in the unbroken opportunity of pouring out instruction to intelligent and interested scholars. I think it was altogether a happy time to him; he enjoyed the solitude, the advantages of the move to the island were apparent in the school work, and were anticipated in the farm, and the hope of doing something for the Pitcairn people, which I believe had much to do with fixing the Mission here, was fresh.'

This judgment is thoroughly borne out by the Bishop's own letter to his sisters of October 27, wherein it appears how considerable an element of his enjoyment and comfort was Mr. Codrington's own companionship, partly as a link with the younger members of the little community:—

'Do I feel doubtful about an early Communion Service, Codrington, when I broach the matter, takes it up more eagerly almost than I do; and then I leave him to talk with the others, who could hardly differ from me on such a point if they wished to do so, but will speak freely to him. Not that, mind, I am aware of there being anything like a feeling of distance between me and them, but necessarily they must just feel that I am forty and their Bishop, and so I might perhaps influence them too much, which would be undesirable.

'Then I can talk with him on matters which of course have special interest for me, for somehow I find that I scarcely ever read or think on any points which do not concern directly my work as clergyman or language-monger. It is very seldom that I touch a book which is not a commentary on the Bible or a theological treatise, scarcely ever, and of course one likes to talk about those things of which one's mind is full. That made the talks with the Judge so delightful. Now young people, of course, have their heads full (as I used to have mine) of other things, and so my talk would be dull and heavy to them.

'No doubt, if you had me at home you would find that I am pretty full of thoughts on some points, but not very well able to express myself, and to put my thoughts into shape. It is partly want of habit, because, except as one speaks somewhat dictatorially to pupils, I do not arrange my ideas by conversing with others—to a great extent, from want of inclination, i.e., indolence, and also I have not the brains to think out a really difficult subject. I am amused occasionally to see what a false estimate others form of me in that way. You see it has pleased God to give me one faculty in rather an unusual degree, that of learning languages, but in every other respect my abilities are very moderate indeed. Distance exaggerates of course, and I get credit with some folks for what if I had it would simply be a gift and no virtue in me; but I attain anything I work at with very considerable labour, and my mind moves very sluggishly, and I am often very dull and stupid. You may judge, therefore, of the great advantage of having a bright, cheery, intelligent, well-informed man among us, without whom every meal would be heavy and silent, and we should (by my fault) get into a mechanical grind....

'As for your own worthy Brother, I don't think I knew what rest meant till I got here. I work, in one sense, as hard as before, i.e., from early morn till 10 P.M., with perhaps the intermission of a hour and a half for exercise, besides the twenty minutes for each of the three meals; and did my eyes allow it, I could go on devouring books much later. But then I am not interrupted and distracted by the endless occupation of the New Zealand life. Oh! how utterly distasteful to me were all those trustee meetings, those English duties of all kinds, and most of all, those invasions of Kohimarama by persons for whom I could get up no interest. I am not defending these idiosyncrasies as if they were all right, but stating what I felt and what I feel. I am indeed very happy here; I trust not less useful in my way. School of course flourishes. You would be surprised at the subjects that I and my first class work at. No lack of brains! Perhaps I can express it briefly by saying that I have felt for a year or more the need of giving them the Gospel of St. John. Because they were ready, thank God, for those marvellous discourses and arguments in that blessed Gospel, following upon the record of miracles wrought or events that happened.

'Of course the knowledge of the facts must come first, but there was always in school with me—either they have it as a natural gift, or my teaching takes naturally that line—a tendency to go deeper than the mere apprehension of a fact, a miracle wrought, or a statement made. The moral meaning of the miracle, the principle involved in the less important expression of it, or particular manifestation of it, these points always of late I am able to talk about as to intelligent and interested listeners. I have these last six weeks been translating St. John; it is nearly done. Think, Fan, of reading, as I did last night, to a class of fifteen Melanesian Christians, the very words of St. John vi. for the first time in their ears! They had heard me paraphrase much of it at different times. I don't notice these things, unless (as now) I chance to write about them. After 6 P.M. Chapel, I remain with some of the lads, the first class of boys, men, and women, every night, and in addition, the second class every other night (not on the nights when I have had them from 7 to 8). I used to catechise them at first, starting the subject myself. Now, I rejoice to say, half goes very quickly in answering questions, of which they bring me plenty.

Then, at about 8.50 or 9, I leave them alone in the Chapel (which opens, as you know, into my sitting-room), and there they stay till past 10, talking over points among themselves, often two or three coming in to me, "Bishop, we can't quite make out this." What do they know and ask? Well, take such a subject as the second Psalm, and they will answer you, if you ask them, about prophecy and the prophetic state. Test them as to the idea they form of a spiritual vision of something seen, but not with the fleshly eye, and they will say, "Yes, our minds have that power of seeing things. I speak of Mota, it is far off, but as I speak of it, I see my father and my mother and the whole place. My mind has travelled to it in an instant. I am there. Yes, I see. So David, so Moses, so St. Peter on the housetop, so St. Paul, caught up into the third heaven, so with his mind."

"'But was it like one of our dreams?"

"'Yes and No—Yes, because they were hardly like waking-men. No, because it was a real true vision which God made them see."

'Ask them about the object of prophecy, and they will say, in quaint expression, it is true, what is tantamount to this—it was not only a prediction of things to come, but a chief means of keeping before the minds of the Jews the knowledge of God's true character as the moral Governor of their nation, and gradually the knowledge was given of His being the Lord and Ruler of all men. The Prophet was the teacher of the present generation as well as the utterer of truths that, when fulfilled in after ages, would teach future ages.

'I mention these fragmentary sentiments, merely to show you how I can carry these fellows into a region where something more than memory must be exercised. The recurrence of the same principles upon which God deals with us is an illustration of what I mean; e.g., the Redemption out of Egypt from the Captivity and the Redemption involve the same principle. So the principle of Mediation runs through the Bible, the Prophet, Priest, King, &c. Then go into the particular Psalm, ask the meaning of the words, Anointed, Prophet, Priest, King —how our Lord discharged and discharges these offices. What was the decree? The Anointed is His Son. "This day have I begotten Thee"—the Eternal Generation—the Birth from the grave. His continual Intercession. Take up Psalm cx., the Priest, the Priest for ever, not after the order of Aaron. Go into the Aaronical Priesthood. Sacrifices, the idea of sacrifice, the Mosaic ritual, its fulfilment; the principle of obedience, as a consequence of Faith, common to Old and New Testaments, as, indeed, God's Moral Law is unchangeable, but the object of faith clearly revealed in the New Testament for the first time, &c., &c.

'Christ's Mediatorial reign, His annihilation of all opposition in the appointed time, the practical Lesson the Wrath of the Lamb.

'Often you would find that pupils who can be taught these things seem and are very ignorant of much simpler things; but they have no knowledge of books, as you are aware, and my object is to teach them pretty fully those matters which are really of the greatest importance, while I may fill up the intervening spaces some day, if I live. To spend such energy as they and I have upon the details of Jewish history, e.g., would be unwise. The great lessons must be taught, as, e.g., St. Paul in 1 Cor. x. uses Jewish history.

'October 15, I finished my last chapter of St. John's Gospel in the Mota language; we have also a good many of the Collects and Gospels translated, and some printed. What is better than to follow the Church's selection of passages of Scripture, and then to teach them devotionally in connection with the Collects?

'Brooke works away hard at his singing class in the afternoon. We sing the Venite, Magnificat, Nunc dimittis, &c., in parts, to single and double chants, my old favourite "Jacob's" for the Venite, also a fine chant of G. Elvey's. They don't sing at all well, but nevertheless, though apt to get flat, and without good voices, there is a certain body of sound, and I like it. Brooke plays the harmonium nicely.

'The Norfolk Island people, two or three only, have been here at evening service, and are extremely struck with the reverence of the Melanesians.

'I work away with my Confirmation class, liking them personally, but finding no indication of their having been taught to think in the least. It is a relief to get back to the Melanesians.'

The visit of the Bishop of New Zealand which had been hoped for, had been prevented by the invitation to attend the Synod of the Church held at Lambeth, in the autumn of 1867, and instead of himself welcoming his friends, Bishop Patteson was picturing them to himself staying with his sisters at Torquay, and joining in the Consecration Services of the Church of All Saints, at Babbicombe, where the altar stood, fragrant with the sandal wood of the Pacific isles. The letters sent off by an opportunity in November were to family and friends, both in England. The one to his sister Joanna narrates one of those incidents that touched the Bishop most deeply:—

'On Friday last we had such a very, very solemn service in our little Chapel. Walter Hotaswol, from Matlavo Island, is dying—he has long been dying, I may say—of consumption. For two winters past he has remained with us rather than in his own island, as he well knew that without good food and care he would sink at once. Years ago he was baptized, and after much time spent in preparation, Tuesday, at 7.30 A.M., was the day when we met in Chapel. Walter leant back in a chair. The whole service was in the Mota language, and I administered the Holy Communion to eleven of our Melanesian scholars, and last of all to him. Three others I trust I may receive to Holy Communion Sunday next. Is not this a blessed thing? I think of it with thankfulness and fear. My old text comes into my mind—"Your heart shall fear and be enlarged." I think there is good hope that I may baptize soon seven or eight catechumens.'

The letter to Bishop Selwyn despatched by the same vessel on November 16, gives the first hint of that 'labour traffic' which soon became the chief obstacle to the Mission.

After describing an interview with an American captain, he continues: —'Reports are rife of a semi-legalised slave-trading between the South Sea Islands and New Caledonia and the white settlers in Fiji. I have made a little move in the matter. I wrote to a Wesleyan Missionary in Fiji (Ovalau) who sent me some books. I am told that Government sanctions natives being brought upon agreement to work for pay, &c., and passage home in two years. We know the impossibility of making contracts with New Hebrides or Solomon natives. It is a mere sham, an evasion of some law, passed, I dare say, without any dishonourable intention, to procure colonial labour. If necessary I will go to Fiji or anywhere to obtain information. But I saw a letter in a Sydney paper which spoke strongly and properly of the necessity of the most stringent rules to prevent the white settlers from injuring the coloured men.'

So first loomed the cloud that was to become so fatal a darkening of the hopes of the Mission, all the more sad because it was caused by Christian men, or men who ought to have been Christian. It will be seen, however, that Bishop Patteson did not indiscriminately set his face against all employment of natives. Occupation and training in civilised customs were the very things he desired for them, but the whole question lay in the manner of the thing. However, to him as yet it was but a report, and this Advent and Christmas of 1867 were a very happy time. A letter to me describes the crowning joy.

'Norfolk Island: Christmas Day, 1867.

'My dear Cousin,—One line to you to-day of Christmas feelings and blessings. Indeed, you are daily in my thoughts and prayers. You would have rejoiced could you have seen us last Sunday or this morning at 7 A.M. Our fourteen Melanesian Communicants so reverent, and (apparently) earnest. On Sunday I ordained Mr. Palmer Priest, Mr. Atkin and Mr. Brooke Deacons.

'The service was a solemn one, in the Norfolk Island Church, the people joining heartily in the first ordination they had seen; Codrington's sermon excellent, the singing good and thoroughly congregational, and the whole body of confirmed persons remaining to receive the Holy Communion. Our own little Chapel is very well decorated (Codrington again the leader) with fronds of tree-ferns, arums, and lilies; "Emmanuel, God amemina" (with us), in large letters over the altar.

'And now (9.30P.M.) they are practising Christmas hymns in Mota for our 11 A.M. service. Then we have a regular feast, and make the day a really memorable one for them. The change from the old to the new state of things, as far as our Banks Islanders are concerned, is indeed most thankworthy. I feel that there is great probability of George Sarawia's ordination before long. This next year he will be left alone (as far as we whites are concerned) at Mota, and I shall be able to judge, I hope, of his fitness for carrying on the work there. If it be God's will to give him health of body and the will and power to serve Him, then he ought to be ordained. He is an excellent fellow, thoughtful, sensible, and my right hand among the Melanesians for years. His wife, Sara Irotaviro, a nice gentle creature, with now a fine little boy some seven months old. She is not at all equal to George in intelligence, and is more native in habits, &c. But I think that she will do her best.

'You know I have long felt that there is almost harm done by trying to make these islanders like English people. All that is needful for decency and propriety in the arrangement of houses, in dress, &c., we must get them to adopt, but they are to be Melanesian, not English Christians. We are so far removed from them in matters not at all necessarily connected with Christianity, that unless we can denationalise ourselves and eliminate all that belongs to us as English, and not as Christians, we cannot be to them what a well-instructed fellow-countryman may be. He is nearer to them. They understand him. He brings the teaching to them in a practical and intelligible form.

'I hope and pray that dear old George may be the first of such a band of fellow-workers. Others—Henry Tagalana, who is, I suppose, about eighteen, Fisher Pantatun, about twenty-one, Edward Wogale (George's own brother), about sixteen, Robert Pantatun, about eighteen—are excellent, all that I could wish; and many younger ones are coming up. They stay with us voluntarily two or three years now without any going home, and the little ones read and write surprisingly well. They come to me very often and say, "Bishop, I wish to stop here again this winter."

'They come for help of the best kind. They have their little printed private prayers, but some are not content with this. Marosgagalo came last week with a slip of paper—

'"Well, Maros, what is it?"

'He is a shy little fellow who has been crippled with rheumatism.

'"Please write me my prayer."

'And as my room opens into the Chapel, and they are told to use that at all times (their sleeping-rooms not allowing much privacy), I know how they habitually come into it early (at 5 A.M.) and late at night for their private prayers. You cannot go into the Chapel between 5 and 6.30 A.M. without seeing two or three kneeling about in different corners. As for their intelligence, I ought to find time to send you a full account of them, translations of their answers, papers, &c., but you must be content to know that I am sure they can reason well upon facts and statements, that they are (the first class) quite able to understand all the simpler theological teaching which you would expect Communicants and (I pray) future clergymen to understand. Of some six or seven I can thus speak with great confidence, but I think that the little fellows may be better educated still, for they are with us before they have so much lee-way to make up—jolly little fellows, bright and sharp. The whole of the third Banks Island class (eight of them) have been with me for eighteen months, and they have all volunteered to stay for eighteen months more. They ought to know a great deal at the end of that time, then they will go home almost to a certainty only for two or three months, and come back again for another long spell.

'All this is hopeful, and we have much to be thankful for indeed; but I see no immediate prospect of anything like this in the other islands at present. We know very many of the islanders and more or less of their languages; we have scholars who read and write, and stop here with us, and who are learning a good deal individually, but I have as yet no sense of any hold gained upon the people generally. We are good friends, they like us, trust young people with us, but they don't understand our object in coming among them properly. The trade and the excitement of our visit has a good deal to do with their willingness to receive us and to give us children and young men. They behave very well when here, and their people treat us well when we are with them. But as yet I see no religious feeling, no apprehension of the reality of the teaching: they know in one sense, and they answer questions about the meaning of the Creed, &c., but they would soon fall again into heathen ways, and their people show no disposition to abandon heathen ways. In all this there is nothing to surprise or discourage us. It must be slow work, carried on without observation amidst many failures and losses and disappointments. If I wished to attribute to secondary causes any of the results we notice, I might say that our having lived at Mota two or three months each year has had a great deal to do with the difference between the Banks and the other islanders.

'It may be that, could we manage to live in Bauro, or Anudha, or Mahaga, or

Whitsuntide, or Lepers' Island, or Espiritu Santo, we might see soon some such change take place as we notice in Mota; but all that is uncertain, and such thoughts are useless. We must indeed live in those other islands as soon as we can, but it is hard to find men able to do so, and only a few of the islands are ripe for the attempt.

'I feel often like a horse going his regular rounds, almost mechanically. Every part of the day is occupied, and I am too tired at night to think freshly. So that I am often like one in a dream, and scarcely realise what I am about. Then comes a time when I wish to write, e.g. (as to you now) about the Mission, and it seems so hard to myself to see my way, and so impossible to make others see what is in my mind about it. Sometimes I think these Banks Islanders may be evangelists beyond the limits of their own islands. So many of the natives of other islands live here with them, and speak the language of Mota, and then they have so much more in common with them than with us, and the climate and food and mode of life generally are familiar to them alike. I think this may come to pass some day; I feel almost sure that I had better work on with promising islanders than attempt to train up English boys, of which I once thought. I am more and more confirmed in my belief that what one wants is a few right-minded, well-educated English clergymen, and then for all the rest trust to native agency.

'When I think of Mr. Robertson and such men, and think how they work on, it encourages me. And so, where do I hear of men who have so many comforts, so great immunity from hardship and danger as we enjoy? This is nothing to the case of a London parish.

'Fanny has sent me out my old engravings, which I like to look at once more, although there is only one really good one among them, and yet I don't like to think of her no longer having them. I have also a nice selection of photographs just sent out, among which the cartoons from Hampton Court are especially good. That grand figure of St. Paul at Athens, which Raphael copied from Masaccio's fresco, always was a favourite of mine.

'I feel at home here, more so than in any place since I left England; but I hope that I may be able to spend longer intervals in the islands than the mere sixteen or eighteen weeks of the voyage, if I have still my health and strength. But I think sometimes that I can't last always; I unconsciously leave off doing things, and wake up to find that I am shirking work.

'Holy Innocents' Day.—I don't think I have sufficiently considered your feelings in suffering the change of name in the Mission School that took place, and I am rather troubled about it. I came back from the last voyage to find that as I had selected a site for the buildings on St. Barnabas Day, which was, by a coincidence, the day I spent here on my outward voyage in 1866, the people had all named the place St. Barnabas. Then came the thought of the meetings on St. Barnabas, and the appropriateness of the Missionary Apostle's name, and I, without thinking enough about it, acquiesced in the change of name. I should have consulted you, —not that you will feel yourself injured, I well know; but for all that, I ought to have done it. It was the more due to you, because you won't claim any right to be consulted. I am really sorry for it, and somewhat troubled in mind. (Footnote: 'He need not have been sorry. I give this to show his kind, scrupulous consideration; but I, like everyone else, could not help feeling that it was more fitting that the germ of a missionary theological college should not bear a name even in allusion to a work of fiction.)

'The occasional notices of Mr. and Mrs. Keble in your letters, and the full account of him and her as their end drew nigh, is very touching. How much, how very much there is that I should like to ask him now! How I could sit at his feet and listen to him! These are great subjects that I have neither time nor brains to deal with, and there is no one here who can give me all the help I want. I think a good deal about Ritualism, more about Union, most about the Eucharistic question; but I need some one with whom to talk out these matters. When I have worked out the mind of Hooker, Bull, Waterland, &c., and read Freeman's "Principles," and Pusey's books, and Mr. Keble's, &c., then I want to think it out with the aid of a really well-read man. It is clearly better not to view such holy subjects in connection with controversy; but then comes the thought—"How is Christendom to be united when this diversity exists on so great a point?" And then one must know what the diversity really amounts to, and then the study becomes a very laborious and intricate enquiry into the ecclesiastical literature of centuries. Curiously enough, I am still waiting for the book I so much want, Mr. Keble's book on "Eucharistic Adoration." I had a copy, of course, but I lent it to some one. I lose a good many books in that way.

'The extraordinary change in the last thirty years will of course mark this time hereafter as one of the most noticeable periods in the history of the Church, indeed one can't fail to see it, which is not always the case with persons living in the time of great events. The bold, outspoken conduct of earnest men, the searching deeply into principles, the comparative rejection of conventionalities, local prejudices, exclusive forms of thought and practice, must strike everyone. But one misses the guiding, restraining hand...the man in the Church corresponding to "the Duke" at one time in the State, the authority.

'One thing I do think, that the being conversant only with thoughtful educated Christians may result in a person ignoring the simpler idea of the Eucharist which does not in the least divest it of its mysterious character, but rather, recognising the mystery, seeks for no solution of it. How can I teach my fifteen Melanesian Communicants the points which I suppose an advanced Ritualist would regard as most essential? But I can give them the actual words of some of the ancient, really ancient, Liturgies, and teach them what Christ said, and St. Paul said, and the Church of England says, and bid them acquiesce in the mystery.

'Yet I would fain know more. I quite long for a talk with Mr. Keble. Predisposed on every account to think that he must be right, I am not sure that I know what he held to be the truth, nor am I quite sure that I would see it without much explanation; but to these holy men so much is revealed that one has no right to expect to know. What he held was in him at all events combined with all that a man may have of humility, and learning, and eagerness for union with God.'

This letter was sent with these:—
'Norfolk Island: December 16, 1867.

'My dear Mr. Atkin,—The "Pacific" arrived on Friday after a quick passage. All our things came safely. She leaves to-morrow for Sydney, and we are in a great hurry. For (1) we have three mails all at once, and I have my full share of letters, public and private; and (2) we have had last week our first fall of rain for some three and a half months, and we are doing our best to plant kumaras, &c., which grow here wonderfully, if only they get anything like a fair chance.

'Joe as usual is foremost at all work; fencing, well-sinking, &c. And he proves the truth of the old saying, that "the head does not suffer by the work of the hand." His knowledge of Scripture truth, of what I may fairly call the beginning of theological studies, gives me great comfort. I am quite sure that in all essentials, in all which by God's blessing tends to qualify a man for teaching faithfully, and with sufficient learning and knowledge of the Word of God, he is above the average of candidates for ordination in England.

'I don't say that he would pass the kind of examination before an English Bishop so well as a great many—they insist a good deal on technical points of historical knowledge, &c.—but in all things really essential—in his clear perception of the unity of the teaching of the Bible; in his knowledge of the Greek Testament, in his reading with me the Articles, Prayer Book, &c., I am convinced that he is well fitted to do his work well and truly. We have had more than one talk on deeper matters still, on inward feelings and thoughts, on prayer and the devotional study of God's Word, and divinity in general. I feel the greatest possible thankfulness and happiness as I think of his ordination, and of what, by the grace of God, he may become to very many both heathens and Christians, if his life be spared.

'Once again, my dear friends, I thank you for giving him to this work. He is the greatest conceivable comfort and help to me. I always feel when he is walking or working with others, that there is one on whose steadiness and strong sense of duty I can always rely. May God bless him with His richest blessings....

'On Sunday next (D.V.) we shall not forget you, as I well know your thoughts and prayers will be with us; and we sing "Before JEHOVAH'S awful Throne" to the Old Hundredth; 2nd, No. 144 of the Hymnal, after third Collect; and before sermon, 3rd, No. 143; after sermon, 4th, No. 19; after Litany, 5th, Veni Creator to All Saints.

The ordination will be in the Norfolk Island Church.—My kind regards to Mrs. Atkin and Mary.

'Always, my dear friend, very truly yours,

'J. C. PATTESON.'

'December 16, 1867.

'My dear Miss Mackenzie,—Your brother's pedometer reached me safely three days ago. I feel most truly unworthy to receive such gifts. I have now his sextant, his pedometer, and, most precious of all, his "Thomas a Kempis"; they ought to help me to think more of him, and his holy example. Your letter commenting on the published life makes me know him pretty well. He was one to love and honour; indeed, the thorough humility and truthfulness, the single-mindedness of the man, the simple sense of duty and unwearied patience, energy, and gentleness

—indeed you must love to dwell on the memory of such a brother, and look forward with hope and joy to the reunion.

'We are fast settling ourselves into our headquarters here. Our buildings already sufficient to house eighty or one hundred Melanesians. We are fencing, planting, &c., &c., vigorously, and the soil here repays our labours well. The yam and sweet potatoes grow excellently, and the banana, orange, lemon, and nearly all semi-tropical fruits and vegetables. I think that our commissariat expenditure will soon be very small, and we ought to have an export before long.

'Two things seem to be pretty clear: that there is no lack of capacity in the Melanesian, and no probability of any large supply of English teachers and clergymen, even if it were desirable to work the Mission with foreign rather than native clergymen. My own mind is, and has long been in favour of the native pastorate; but it needs much time to work up to such a result.

'All our party are well in health, save one good fellow, Walter Hotaswol, who is dying of consumption, in faith and hope. "Better," he says, "to die here with a bright heart than to live in my own land with a dark one." It is a solemn Ember week for us.

'I remain, dear Miss Mackenzie, very truly yours,

'J. C. PATTESON.

'I quite agree with you that you cannot educate tropical and semi-tropical people in England; and you don't want to make them English Christians, you know.'

Walter's history is here completed:—

'January 22, 1868.

'My dear Cousin,—I write you a line: I have not time for more in addition to my other epistle, to tell you that I purpose to baptize, on Sunday next, eight Melanesian youths and one girl. You will, I know, thank God for this. Indeed I hope (though I say it with a kind of trembling and wonder) that a succession of scholars is now regularly established from the Banks Islands.

'These nine are being closely followed by some ten or twelve more, younger than they, averaging from seven to eleven years, who all read and write and know the elements of Christian teaching, but you should see them, bright merry little fellows, and the girls too, full of play and fun. Yet so docile, and obedient, and good-tempered. They all volunteer to stay here again this winter, though they have not been at home since they first left it, in July and August 1866. They have a generation of Christians—I mean one of our generations—some two dozen or more, to help them; they have not the brunt of the battle to bear, like dear George and Henry and others; and because, either here or there, they will be living with Christians; I need not, I think, subject them to a probation. Next year (D.V.) they may be baptized, and so the ranks are being filled up.

'I would call the girl Charlotte were she a favourite of mine, but I wait in hopes that a nicer girl (though this one is good and nice too) may be baptized by your and Mrs. Keble's name. You may well believe that my heart and mind are very full of this. May God grant that they may continue His for ever!

'I confirm on the same day fourteen Norfolk Islanders.

'Walter Hotaswol, from Matlavo, the southern part of Saddle Island, died on the evening of the Epiphany: a true Epiphany to him, I trust. He was remarkably gentle and innocent for one born in a heathen land. His confession, very fully made to me before his first Communion, was very touching, simply given, and, thank God, he had been wonderfully kept from the sins of heathenism. With us, his life for years was blameless. He died almost without pain, after many weeks of lingering in consumption, I verily believe in full faith in his Saviour and his God.

'During his last illness, and for a short time before he actually took to his bed, he frequently received the Holy Communion. And very remarkable were his words to me the day after his first Communion. I was sitting by him, when he said, apropos of nothing, "Very good!"

'"What is very good, Walter?"

'"The Lord's Supper."

'"Why do you think so?"

'"I can't talk about it. I feel it here (touching his heart), I don't feel as I did!"

'"But you have long believed in Him."

'"Yes, but I feel different from that; I don't feel afraid for death. My heart is calm (me masur kal, of a calm following a gale)." His look was very earnest as he added: "I do believe that I am going to Him." Presently, "Bishop!"

'"Well."

'"Last night—no, the night before I received the Lord's Supper, I saw a man standing there, a tanum liana (a man of rank, or authority). He said Your breath is bad, I will give you a new breath."'

'"Yes."

'"I thought it meant, I will give you a new life. I thought it must be JESUS."

'He was weak, but not wandering. "Yes, better to die here with a bright heart than to live in my old home with a dark one."

'January 28th.—The nine young Christians were baptized on Sunday evening; a very touching and solemn service it was, very full of comfort. It may be that now, in full swing of work, I am too sanguine, but I try to be sober-minded, thankful, and hopeful. I try, I say—it is not easy.

'God bless you, my dear Cousin, and as I pray for you, so I know you pray for us.

'Your affectionate Cousin,

'J. C. PATTESON.'

A long letter to James Patteson, which was begun a few days later, goes into the man's retrospect of the boy's career:—

'March 3rd.—I think often of your boys. Jack, in two or three years, will be old enough for school, and I suppose it must make you anxious sometimes. I look back on my early days, and see so much, so very much to regret and grieve over, such loss of opportunities, idleness, &c., that I think much of the way to make lessons attractive to boys and girls. I think a good deal may be done simply by the lessons being given by the persons the children love most, and hence (where it can be done) the mother first, and the father too (if he can) are the best people. They know the ways of the child, they can take it at the right times. Of course, at first it is the memory, not the reasoning power, that must be brought into exercise.

Young children must learn by heart, learn miles which they can't understand, or understand but very imperfectly. I think I forget this sometimes, and talk to my young Melanesians as I should to older persons. But I feel almost sure that children can follow a simple, lively account of the meaning and reasons of things much more than one is apt to fancy. And I don't know how anything can be really learnt that is not understood. A great secret of success here is an easy and accurate use of illustration—parabolic teaching.

'Every day of my life I groan over the sad loss I daily experience in not having been grounded properly in Latin and Greek. I have gone on with my education in these things more than many persons, but I can never be a good scholar; I don't know what I would not give to have been well taught as a boy. And then at Eton, any little taste one might have had for languages, &c., was never called out.

My fault again, but I can't help thinking that it was partly because the reason of a rule was never explained. Who ever taught in school the difference between an aorist and a perfect, e.g.? And at college I was never taught it, because it was assumed that I knew it. I know that at ten, fifteen, or twenty, I should not in any case have gone into languages as I do now. But I might have learnt a good deal, I think. A thoroughly good preparatory school is, I dare say, very difficult to find. I would make a great point, I think, to send a boy to a good one; not to cram him or make a prig of him, but simply to give him the advantage which will make his whole career in life different from what it will be if his opening days pass by unimproved. Cool of me, Jem, to write all this; but I think of this boy, and my boyish days, and what I might have been, and am not.

'I was always shallow, learned things imperfectly, thought I knew a thing when I knew scarce any part of it, scrawling off common-place verses at Eton, and, unfortunately, getting sent up for them. I had a character which passed at school and at home for that of a fair scholar. Thence came my disgrace at being turned out of the select, my bad examination for the Balliol scholarship, my taking only a second, &c. Nothing was really known! Pretty quick in seizing upon a superficial view of a matter, I had little patience or determination to thoroughly master it. The fault follows me through life. I shall never, I fear, be really accurate and able to think out a matter fully. The same fault I see in my inner life. But it is not right to talk perhaps too much of that, only I know that I get credit for much that I don't do, and for qualities which I don't possess. This is simple truth, not false humility. Some gifts I have, which, I thank God, I have been now taught to employ with more or less of poverty in the service.'

The vessel that took away the above despatches brought the tidings of New Zealand's beloved Primate being appointed to the See of Lichfield. It was another great wrench to the affectionate heart, as will be seen in this filial reply to the intelligence:—

'2nd Sunday in Lent, 10 P.M.

'My dear, dear Bishop,—I don't think I ever quite felt till now what you have been to me for many a long year. Indeed, I do thank God that I have been taught to know and dearly love you; and much I reproach myself (not now for the first time) that I have been wilful, and pained you much sometimes by choosing for myself when I ought to have followed your choice. I could say much, but I can't say it now, and you don't desire it. You know what I think and feel. Your letter of the 3rd reached me last night. I don't yet realise what it is to me, but I think much more still of those dear people at Taurarua. It is perfectly clear to my mind that you could not have acted otherwise. I don't grudge you to the Mother Church one atom!

'I write at this time because I think you may possibly be soon beginning your first Ordination Service in your Cathedral. It was almost my first thought when I began to think quietly after our 8 P.M. prayers. And I pray for those whom you may be leading to their work, as so often you have laid your hands on me. I understand Bishop Andrewes' [Greek text] now.

'What it must have been to you and still is!...

'This move to Norfolk Island does make a great difference, no doubt. And full well I know that your prayers will be around us; and that you will do all that mortal man can do for us and for the islands. Indeed, you must not trouble yourself about me too much. I shall often need you, often sadly miss you, a just return for having undervalued the blessing of your presence. But I do feel that it is right. I humbly pray and trust that God's blessing may be on us all, and that a portion of your spirit may be with us.

'More than ever affectionately yours,

'J. C. PATTESON.'

The tidings had come simultaneously with the history of the Consecration of All Saints, Babbicombe, for indeed the Bishop and Mrs. Selwyn were staying with Joanna and Fanny Patteson for the Octave Services when the first offer arrived. So that the two mails whose contents were transported together to Norfolk Island contained matter almost overwhelming for the brother and friend, and he had only one day in which to write his answers. To the sisters the assurance is, 'Only be quite comforted about me!' and then again, 'No, I don't grudge him one bit. There is no room for small personal considerations when these great issues are at stake.'

'I don't think I quite know yet what it is to me. I can't look at his photograph with quite dry eyes yet. But I don't feel at all sad or unhappy. You know the separation, if God, in His mercy, spare me at last, can't be long; and his prayers are always around us, and he is with us in spirit continually, and then it will be such joy and delight to me to watch his work.

'I think with such thankfulness of the last Holy Week; the last Easter Sunday spent wholly with him. I think too, and that sadly enough, of having pained him sometimes by being self-willed, and doing just what he has not done, viz., chosen for myself when I ought to have followed him.

'Do you remember when, on the morning of Mamma's death, we came into the study where Uncle and Aunt Frank were, and our dear Father in his great faith and resignation said, with broken voice, "I thank God, who spared her to me so long"? Surely I may with far greater ease say, "I thank God for the blessing for now thirteen, years of his example and loving care of me." Had he been taken away by death we must have borne it, and we can bear this now by His grace.'

The thought engrossed him most completely. It is plain in all his letters that it was quite an effort to turn his mind to anything but the approaching change. His Primate had truly been a 'Father in God' to him. His affections had wound themselves about him and Mrs. Selwyn, and the society that they formed together with Sir William and Lady Martin had become the next thing to his home and family. Above all, the loneliness of sole responsibility was not complete while the Primate was near to be consulted. There had been an almost visible loss of youth and playfulness ever since the voyages had been made without the leader often literally at the helm; and though Bishop Patteson had followed his own judgment in two decided points—the removal to Norfolk Island, and the use of Mota language instead of English, and did not repent having done so, yet still the being left with none to whom to look up as an authority was a heavy trial and strain on mind and body, and brought on another stage in that premature age that the climate and constant toil were bringing upon him when most men are still in the fulness of their strength.

The next letter spoke the trouble that was to mark the early part of the year 1868 as one of sickness and sorrow.

'Our two Ambrym boys are coming out; and I am hopeful as to some more decided connection with the north face of the Island. Mahaga lads very promising, but at present Banks Islanders much ahead of the rest. Indeed, of some of them, I may say that while they have no knowledge of many things that an English lad ought to know, yet they have a very fair share of intelligence concentrated on the most important subject, and know a good deal about it. They think.'

Then follows a working out of one of the difficult questions that always beset missionaries respecting the heathen notions—or no notions—about wedlock. Speaking of the persons concerned, the journal continues:—

'They were not able to understand—and how can a man and woman, or rather a girl and boy, understand—what we understand by marriage. They always saw men and women exchanging husbands and wives when they pleased, and grew up in the midst of such ideas and practices, so that there never was a regular contract, nor a regularly well-conceived and clearly-understood notion of living together till "death us do part" in their minds. You will say, "And yet they were baptized." Yes, but I did not know so much about heathen ways then, and, besides, read St. Paul to the Corinthians, and see how the idea of sanctity of marriage, and of chastity in general is about the last idea that the heathen mind comprehends. Long after the heathen know that to break the sixth, eighth, even the ninth and tenth Commandments is wrong, and can understand and practically recognise it to be so, the seventh is a puzzle to them. At the best they only believe it because we say that it is a Commandment of God. Look at the Canons of the early Church on the question; look how Luther sanctioned the polygamy, the double marriage, of the Landgrave of Hesse! So that although now, thank God, our scholars understand more of what is meant by living with a woman, and the relation of husband and wife is not altogether strange to them, yet it was not so at first, and is not likely to be so with any but our well-trained scholars for a long time.'

'Norfolk Island: March 26, 1868. 'My dearest Sisters,—How you are thinking of me this anniversary? Thirteen years since I saw your dear faces and his face. Oh! how thankful I am that it is so long ago. It was very hard to bear for a long long time. Last night as I lay awake I thought of that last Sunday, the words I said in church (how absurdly consequential they seem to me now), the walk home, calling to see C. L., parting with the Vicar and M., the last evening—hearts too full to say what was in them, the sitting up at night and writing notes. And then black Monday! Well, I look back now and see that it was very hard at first, and I don't deny that I found the mere bodily roughnesses very trying at first, but that has long past. My present mode of life is agreeable to me altogether now. Servants and company would be a very great bore indeed. So even in smaller ways, you see, I have all that I can desire. I always try to remember that I may miss these things, and specially miss you if it should please God to send any heavy sickness upon me. I dare say I should be very impatient, and need kind soothing nurses. But I must hope for the best.

'Just now we have some anxiety. There has been and is a bad typhoid fever among the Pitcairners: want of cleanliness, no sewerage, or very bad draining, crowded rooms, no ventilation, the large drain choked up, a dry season, so that the swampy ground near the settlement has been dry, these are secondary causes. For two months it has been going on. I never anticipated such a disease here.

'But the fever is bad. Last night two died, both young women of about twenty. Two, one a married man of thirty, with five children, the other a girl of twelve, had died before. I have been backwards and forwards, but no one else of the party. The poor people like to see me. For three weeks I have felt some anxiety about four or five of our lads, and they have been with me in my room. I don't like the symptoms of one or two of them. But it is not yet a clear case of the fever.'

'Easter Eve.—Dear Sisters, once more I write out of a sick hospital. This typhoid fever, strongly marked, as described in Dr. Watson's books, Graye's edition of Hooper's "Vade Mecum," and, as a very solemn lesson of Lent and Holy Week, seven Pitcairners have died. For many weeks the disease did not touch us; we established a regular quarantine, and used all precautions. We had, I think, none of the predisposing causes of fever at our place. It is high, well-drained, clean, no dirt near, excellent water, and an abundant supply of it; but I suppose the whole air is impregnated with it. Anyhow, the fever is here.

'April 23rd.—My house consists, you know, of Chapel, my rooms, and hospital. This is the abode of the sick and suspected. The hospital is a large, lofty, well-ventilated room; a partition, 6 feet high, only divides it into two; on one side are the sick, on the other side sleep those who are sickening.

'As yet twenty have been in my quarters. Of these seven are now in Codrington's house, half-way between hospital and ordinary school life. They are convalescents, real convalescents. You know how much so-called convalescents need care in recovering from fever, but these seven have had the fever very slightly indeed, thank God; the type of the disease is much less severe than it was at first. One lad of about sixteen, Hofe from Ysabel Island, died last Friday morning. The fever came on him with power from the first. He was very delirious for some days, restless, sleepless, then comatose. The symptoms are so very clearly marked, and my books are so clear in detail of treatment, that we don't feel much difficulty now about the treatment, and the nursery and hospital work we are pretty well used to.

'Barasu, from Ysabel Island, who was near dying on Thursday week, a fortnight ago to-day, has hovered between life and death. I baptized him at 9 P.M. on Holy Thursday (the anniversary of Mr. Keble's death). John Keble: rather presumptuous to give such a name, but I thought he would not have been named here by it for many hours. He is now sitting by the hospital fire. I have just fed him with some rice and milk; and he is well enough to ask for a bit of sweet potato, which he cannot yet hold, nor guide his hand to his mouth. He has had the regular fever, and is now, thank God, becoming convalescent. No other patient is at present in a dangerous state; all have the fever signs more or less doubtful. No one is at present in a precarious state. It has been very severe in the town, and there are many cases yet. Partly it is owing to the utter ignorance or neglect of the most ordinary rules of caution and nursing. Children and men and women all lie on the ground together in the fever or out of it. The contagion fastens upon one after another. In Isaac Christian's house, the mother and five children were all at one time in a dangerous state, wandering, delirious, comatose. Yet the mortality has been small. Only seven have died; some few are still very ill, yet the character of the fever is less severe now. We had some sharp hospital work for a few days and nights, all the accompaniments of the decay of our frail bodies. Now we have a respite. Codrington, Palmer, and I take the nursing; better that the younger ones, always more liable to take fever, should be kept out of contagion; to no one but I have gone among the sick in town, or to town at all. We are all quite well.

'Beef tea, chicken broth, mutton broth, wine, brandy, milk to any extent, rice, &c.—Palmer manufactures all. The Pitcairners, most improvident people, are short of all necessary stores. I give what I can, but I must be stingy, as I tell them, for I never anticipated an attack of typhus here. They will, I trust, learn a lesson from it, and not provoke a recurrence of it by going on in their old ways.

'I don't deny that at times I have been a good deal depressed: about Holy Week and Easter Week was the worst time. Things are much brighter now; though I fully expect that several others, perhaps many others, will yet have the attack, but I trust and fancy it may be only in a modified form. We have regular Chapel and school, but the school is a mild affair now; I who am only in bed from 12.30 or 1 to 5, and in the hospital all day, cannot be very bright in school. I just open a little bit of my red baize door into Chapel, so that the sick in my room join in the service. Nice, is it not?

'This will greatly unsettle plans for the voyage. The "Southern Cross" is expected here about May 10; but I can't leave any sick that may want my care then, and I can't take back to the islands any that are only just convalescent, or indeed any of the apparently healthy who may yet have the seeds of the fever in them. It would be fearful if it broke out on the islands. I must run no risk of that;

so I think that very likely I may keep the whole party here another year, and make myself a short visitation. I suppose that the Bishop will come to New Zealand, and I must try to meet him; I should like to see his face once more; but if he doesn't come, or if I can't (by reason of this sickness) go to meet him—well, I shall be spared the parting if I don't have the joy of the meeting, and these things are not now what they once were.

'April 28th.—Barasu (John Keble) died this morning as I read the Commendatory Prayer by his side. He had a relapse some five days ago, how we cannot say, he was always watched day and night. I had much comfort in him, he was a dear lad, and our most hopeful Ysabel scholar. His peaceful death, for it was very peaceful at the last, may work more than his life would have done; some twenty others convalescent, or ailing, or sick. At this moment another comes to say that he feels out of sorts; you know that sensation, and how one's heart seems to stop for a minute, and then one tries to look and speak cheerfully.

'April 29th.—I read the Service over another child to-day, son of James and Priscilla Quintall, the second child they have lost within a few days, and Priscilla herself is lying ill of the fever. Poor people, I did what little I could to comfort them; the poor fellow is laid up too with a bad foot; a great many others are very ill, some young ones especially.

'May 5th.—Jemima Young sent for me yesterday morning. I was with her the day before, and she was very ill. I reached the room at 11.45, and she died at noon. [Jemima Young had been particularly bright, pleasant, and helpful when Mrs. Selwyn was on the island].

'May 7th.—The sick ones doing pretty well. You must not think it is all gloom, far from it, there is much to cheer and comfort us. The hearty co-operation of these excellent fellow-workers is such a support, and is brought out at such times.

'We are going on with divers works, but not very vigorously just now. We are sawing the timber for our large hall: the building still to be put up, and then our arrangements will be complete for the present.

'Then our fencing goes on. We have one large field of some ninety or one hundred acres enclosed, the sea and a stream bounding two sides, and two other fields of about forty and twenty acres. I have good cart mares and one cart horse, a riding mare which I bought of Mr. Pritt, and Atkin has one also, eleven cows, and as many calves, poultry (sadly destroyed by wild cats) and pigs, and two breeding sows, and a flock of fifty well-bred sheep imported. These cost me £4. 10s. a head; I hope they are the progenitors of a fine flock. The ram cost £12. We have plenty of work, and must go on fencing and subdividing our fields. Most of the land is wooded; but a considerable quantity can easily be cleared. Indeed 200 or 300 acres are clear now of all but some smaller stuff that can easily be removed. A thick couch-grass covers all. It is not so nutritious as the ordinary English grasses; but cattle, sheep, and horses like it, only a larger quantity is needed by each animal. It gives trouble when one wants to break it up, it is such a network of roots; but once out of the ground and the soil clear, and it will grow anything. Our crops of sweet potatoes are excellent. The ordinary potato does very well too; and maize, vegetables of all sorts, many fruit trees, all the semi-tropical things, capitally; guavas by the thousand, and very soon I hope oranges; lemons now by thousands, melons almost a weed, bananas abundant; by-and-by coffee, sugar-cane, pineapples (these last but small), arrowroot of excellent quality. Violets from my bed, and mignonette from Palmer's, scent my room at this minute. The gardeners, Codrington, Palmer, and Atkin, are so kind in making me tidy, devising little arrangements for my little plot of ground, and my comfort and pleasure generally. Well, that is a nice little chat with you. Now it is past 8 P.M., and the mutton broth for Clement and Mary is come. I must feed my chicks. Excellent patients they are, as good as can be. They don't make the fuss that I did in my low fever when I was so savage with your doves that would go on cooing at my window, don't you remember?

'My dear Bishop will be touched by the confidence in him shown by his late Diocesan Synod in entrusting to him the nomination of his successor. It was clearly the right thing to do. As for me, no one who knows anything about it or me would dream of removing me from Melanesia, as long as I have health and strength, and still less of putting me into another diocese. When I break down, or give up, it will not be to hold any other office, as I think.

'May 8th.—All going on pretty well, thank God. Mary is weak, but I think better; did not wander last night. Clement, with strong typhoid symptoms, yet, at all events, not worse. But he is a very powerful, thickset fellow, not a good subject for fever. I feel that I am beginning to recover my interest in things in general, books, &c. For two months I was entirely occupied with hospital work, and with visiting daily the sick Pitcairners, and I was weary and somewhat worn out. Now I am better in mind and body; some spring in me again. This may be to fit me for more trials in store; but I think that the sunshine has come again.'

There were, however, two more deaths—the twins of Mwerlau. Clement died on the 24th of May; the other brother, Richard, followed him a fortnight later. They were about seventeen, strong and thick-set; Clement had made considerable progress during his two years of training, and had been a Communicant since Christmas. Before passing to the other topics with which, as the Bishop said, he could again be occupied, here is Mr. Codrington's account of this period of trouble:—

'A great break in the first year was caused by the visitation of typhus fever in the earlier part of 1868. This disease, brought as I always believed by infection from a vessel that touched here, first attacked a Norfolk Islander who did not live in the town. He was ill in the middle of February, others of the Pitcairn people soon after. The Bishop began at once to visit the sick very diligently, and continued to visit them throughout, though after a time our own hospital was full. Our first case was on the 11th of March, and our last convalescents did not go out until near the end of June. For some time there was hard work to be done with nursing the sick. The Bishop had the anxiety and the charge of medically treating the sick. Mr. Nobbs, as always, was most kind in giving the benefit of his experience, but he was too fully occupied with the care of his own flock to be able to help us much. It was agreed, as soon as we saw the disease was among us, that the three elder members of the Mission should alone come into communication with the sick.

We kept watch in turns, but the Bishop insisted on taking a double share, i.e., he allowed us only to take regular watches in the night, undertaking the whole of the day's work, except during the afternoon when he was away with the Pitcairn people. He seemed quite at home in the hospital, almost always cheerful, always very tender, and generally very decided as to what was to be done. He was fond of doctoring, read a good deal of medical books, and knew a good deal of medical practice; but the weight of such a responsibility as belonged to the charge of many patients in a fever of this kind was certainly heavy upon him. The daily visit to the Pitcairn people on foot or on horseback was no doubt a relief, though hard work in itself. Of the four lads we lost, two, twins, had been some time christened, one was baptized before his death, the first who died had not been long with the Mission. It is characteristic of Bishop Patteson that I never heard him say a word that I remember of religion to one of the sick. On such things he would not, unless he was obliged, speak except with the patient alone.

'Before the sickness was quite over, the "Southern Cross" arrived for the winter voyage. The danger of carrying infection to the islands could not be incurred, and the vessel was sent back to Auckland for a time.'

The letters she carried back refer again to the growing anxiety about the 'labour traffic.'

'May 6th.—I am corresponding with a Wesleyan Missionary in Ovalau (Fiji) on a matter that you may see mentioned some day in the papers, a very questionable practice of importing from the Southern New Hebrides (principally Tanna) natives to work on the cotton plantations of white settlers in Fiji. It is all, as I am assured, under the regulation of the Consul at Ovalau, and "managed" properly. But I feel almost sure that there is, or will be, injuries done to the natives, who (I am sure) are taken away under false pretences. The traders don't know the Tannese language, and have no means of making the people understand any terms, and to talk of any contract is absurd. Yet, a large number of Tanna men, living on really well-conducted plantations, owned by good men, might lead to a nucleus of Christian Tannese. So says Mr. M. True, say I, if (!) you can find the good planters and well-conducted plantations. Mr. M. assures me that they (the Wesleyan Missionaries) are watching the whole thing carefully. He writes well and sensibly on the whole, and kindly asks me to visit his place, and judge for myself.

'Tanna is in the hands of the Nova Scotia Presbyterians—Mr. Greddie, Inglis, and others; but the adjacent islands we have always visited and considered ours, and of course a plague of this kind soon spreads. My letter to Mr. Attwood on the matter was read by Sir John Young and Commodore Lambert, and they expressed a warm interest in the matter. Mr. M. says that they think it would be well to accept some rule of conduct in the matter from the Commodore, which is, I think, likely to do good.'

By the 15th of June the glad intelligence was received that the hospital had been empty for a fortnight; and the house that was to have been carried to Mota was put up for the married couples, for whom it afforded separate sleeping rooms, though the large room was in common. Two weddings were preparing, and B —— and his wife had become reconciled.

'We may hope that this time it is not a case of two children, then unbaptized, living together, heathen fashion, obeying mere passion, ignorant of true love, but a sober, somewhat sad reunion of two clever and fairly-educated grown-up people, knowing much of life and its sad experience, understanding what they are about, and trying to begin again with prayer to God and purposes of a good life.'

This time of convalescence was a time of great progress. A deep impression had been made on many, and there was a strong spirit of enquiry among them. The Bishop then began a custom of preaching to his black scholars alone after the midday service, dismissing his five or six white companions after prayers, because he felt he could speak more freely and go more straight to the hearts of his converts and catechumens if he had no other audience.

The other inhabitants of the island suffered long after the St. Barnabas scholars were free, and deaths continued. It was impossible to enforce on such an undisciplined race the needful attention to cleanliness, or even care of the sick; the healthy were not kept apart, nor was the food properly prepared for the sick. It was impossible to stir or convince the easy-going tropical nature, and there was no authority to enforce sanitary measures, so the fever smouldered on, taking first one, then another victim, and causing entire separation from St. Barnabas, except as far as the Bishop was concerned.

Meantime, a house was being put up to receive Mr. Palmer's intended wife, the daughter of that Mr. Ashwell who had shared in the disastrous voyage when the 'Southern Cross' had been wrecked. She had been brought up to Mission work, and was likely to be valuable among the young girls. After this announcement, the Bishop continues:—

'My mind is now made up to take the great step of ordaining dear George Sarawia, for nine years my pupil, and for the last three or four my friend and helper. Codrington is only surprised that he is not ordained already. Humanly speaking, there can be no doubt of his steadfastness. He is, indeed, a thoroughly good conscientious man, humble without servility, friendly and at his ease without any forwardness, and he has a large share of good sense and clear judgment. Moreover, he has long held a recognised position with all here and in New Zealand, and for the last two years the Mota people and the neighbouring islanders have quite regarded him as one whom they recognise as their leader and teacher, one of our own race, yet not like us—different; he knows and does what we can't do and don't know.

'They quite look upon him as free from all the difficulties which attend a man's position as inheriting feuds, animosities, &c. He goes anywhere; when the island may be in a disturbed state, no one would hurt him; he is no partisan in their eyes, a man of other habits and thoughts and character, a teacher of all.

'I think, oh! with such feelings of thankfulness and hope too, of the first Melanesian clergyman! I should almost like to take him to Auckland, that the Bishop might ordain him; but he ought to be ordained here, in the presence of the Melanesians; and in the hasty confusion of the few weeks in New Zealand, George would be at a sad loss what to do, and the month of October is cold and raw. But you may get this just in time to think of his Ordination, and how you will pray for him! His wife Sara is a weakly body, but good, and she and I are, and always have been, great friends. She has plenty of good sense. Their one child, Simon, born in Norfolk Island some fourteen months ago, is a very nice-looking child, and healthy enough.

Meantime the spirit of enquiry and faith was making-marked progress. Mr. Codrington says: 'The stir in the hearts and minds of those already christened might be called a revival, and the enquiring and earnest spirit of many more seemed to be working towards conversions. During this time, there might be seen on the cliff or under the trees in the afternoon, or on Sundays, little groups gathered round some of the elder Christians, enquiring and getting help. It was the work that George evidently was enabled to do in this way that convinced everyone that the time had quite come for his Ordination. It is worth mentioning that the boys from one island, and one individual in particular, were much influenced by the last conversations of the first Christian who died here (Walter Hotaswol), who had told his friends to be "sure that all the Bishop had told them was true."'

This quickening and its results are further described in the ensuing letter, wherein is mention of the Bauro man Taroniara, the most remarkable of the present conversions, and destined three years after to die with the Bishop and Mr. Atkin.

'June 20, 9 P.M., 1868.

'My dear Sisters,—You know how I am thinking of him to-day. Seven years ago! I think that he seems more and more present to my mind than ever. How grateful it is to me to find the dear Bishop ever recurring to him in his sermons, &c.; but indeed we all have the great blessing and responsibility of being his children. The thought of meeting him again, if God be so merciful, comes over me sometimes in an almost overpowering way: I quite seem to see and feel as if kneeling by his side before the Great Glory, and even then thinking almost most of him. And then, so many others too—Mamma, Uncle James, Frank, &c., and you, dear Joan, think of your dear Mother. It seems almost too much. And then the mind goes on to think of the Saints of God in every generation, from one of the last gathered in (dear Mr. Keble) to the very first; and as we realise the fact that we may, by God's wonderful mercy, be companions, though far beneath the feet, of Patriarchs, and Apostles, and Martyrs, and even see Him as He is—it is too great for thought! and yet, thank God, it is truth.

'My heart is full too of other blessed thoughts. There seems to be a stirring of heart among our present set of scholars, the younger ones I mean; they come into my room after evening Chapel and school, one or two at a time, but very shy, sit silent, and at last say very softly, "Bishop, I wish to stop here for good."

'"Why?"

'"I do wish to be good, to learn, to be like George and Henry and the rest."

'This morning I baptized Charlotte and Joanna. Charlotte will be married to Fisher on Wednesday, when Benjamin and Marion will also be married. Oh, what blessings are these! I spoke earnestly of the service in my preachment.

'Taroniara, from San Cristoval, said to me the other night, "Bishop, why is it that now I think as I never thought before? I can't tell quite what I think. You know I used to be willing to learn, but I was easily led away on my own island; but I think that I shall never wish again to listen to anything but the Word of God. I know I may be wrong, but I think I shall never be inclined to listen to anything said to me by my people to keep me from you and from this teaching. I feel quite different: I like and wish for things I never really used to care for; I don't care for what I used to like and live for. What is it?"

"'What do you think it is?"

"'I think—but it is so (mava) great—I think it is the Spirit of God in my heart."

'As for the Mota and Matlavo fellows, and the girls too, they have now good examples before them, and one and all wish to stop here as long as I please. And that being so, the return to their homes not being a return to purely heathen islands, I trust that they may soon be baptized. So my heart is full of thankfulness and wonder and awe.

'All this time I write with a full sense of the uncertainty of this and every human work. I know the Bishop is preaching on failures, and I try to think he is preaching to me.

'July 2nd, 8 A.M.—My dear Sisters, what a day we had yesterday! so full of happiness and thankfulness. It was the wedding-day of Fisher and Charlotte, Benjamin and Marion.

'The chapel was so prettily dressed up by Mr. Codrington and Mr. Bice, under whose instructions some of the lads made evergreen ornaments, &c., large white arums and red flowers also.

'At 7 A.M. Morning-Prayers, as usual. At 9.30 the wedding. All the Melanesians in their places in Chapel; and as we came into the Chapel from my room, the 100th Psalm was chanted capitally. Mr. Codrington said he never was present at so thoroughly devotional a wedding. It was a really solemn religious service.

'Then I gave good presents to everyone in the school, even the smallest boys came in for a knife, beads, &c. Then cricket, for the day was beautifully fine, though it is midwinter. And all sorts of fun we had. Then a capital dinner, puddings, &c. Then cricket, running races, running in sacks (all for prizes), then a great tea, 7 P.M. Chapel, then native dances by a great bonfire. Then at 10 P.M. hot coffee and biscuits, then my little speech, presenting all our good wishes to the married couples, and such cheering, I hope it may be well remembered. The deeper feeling of it all is bearing fruit. Already lads and young men from the Solomon Islands say, "We begin to see what is meant by a man and woman living together." The solemnity of the service struck them much.

'The bridegrooms wore their Sunday dresses, nice tidy trousers of dark tweed, Crimean shirt, collar and tie, and blue serge coat. The brides, white jackets trimmed with a bit of red, white collar and blue skirts. All the answers quietly and reverently made; the whole congregation answering "Amen" to the word of blessing in an unmistakeable way. The 67th Psalm was chanted, of course.

'My plan is to have Psalms, with reading and singing to suit each day, regarded as commemorative of the great facts and doctrines, so that every week we read in chapel about forty Psalms, and sing about twelve hymns. These are pretty well known by heart, and form already a very considerable stock of Scriptural reference. The Resurrection and the Gift of the Spirit, the Nativity, Manifestation, Betrayal, Ascension, Crucifixion, Burial, with the doctrines connected with them, come in this way every week before their minds. I translated Psalms chosen with reference to this plan, and wrote hymns, &c. in the same way.

'I wish you could have been with us yesterday. It was really a strikingly solemn service. Then our fortnightly 7 A.M. Communions, our daily 7 A.M. and 7 P.M. Services, our Baptisms, yes and our burials too, all are so quiet, and there is so much reverence. You see that they have never learnt bad habits. A Melanesian scholar wouldn't understand how one could pray in any other posture than kneeling.

'The evening Catechumen classes, so happy. And then the dear fellows at their private prayers. The Chapel is always open, you know, and in the early morning and late evening little knots of three and four, or eight and ten, are kneeling about, quietly saying their prayers. The sick lads—dear Clement and Richard who died—as long as they could move, knelt up in hospital to say their prayers, and all but quite the new comers did the same. It was touching to see them, weak and in much pain, yet I did not of course tell them that they might as well pray as they lay on their rugs. Better for them even if it did a little exhaust them. It is no mere formal observance of a rule, for there never has been any rule about it. I have given them short simple prayers, and they first learn to kneel down with me here in my room, or with Codrington in his room, &c. But I merely said (long ago at Kohimarama), "You know you can always go into the Chapel whenever you like."

'Sometimes I do wish you could see them; but then unless you could talk with them, and indeed unless you knew the Melanesian mind and nature, you couldn't estimate these things rightly.

'But never did I feel so hopeful, though my old text is ever in my mind, Isaiah lx. 5: "Thine heart shall fear, and be enlarged." That's exactly it.

'July 18th.—To-morrow I baptize Taroniara, of San Cristoval, a young man full of promise. He has a wife and little girl of about four years old. He may become, by God's blessing, the teacher of the people of his island.'

(From a letter of the same date to myself, I add the further particulars about one who was to teach by his death instead of his life, and for whom the name of the first martyr was chosen):—

'He has been with me for some years, always good and amiable; but too good-natured, too weak, so that he did not take a distinct line with his people. He is a person of some consequence in his neighbourhood. Now he gives all the proofs that can well be given of real sincerity. He wonders himself, as he contrasts his present with his former thoughts. I feel, humanly speaking, quite convinced that he is thoroughly in earnest. His wife and little child are in the islands. "How foolish of me not to have listened to you, and brought them here at once. Then we could stop here for good." But he will return with them, all being well, or without them, if anything has happened to them, and I see in him, as I hope and pray, the pioneer for San Cristoval at last.

'(Resuming the home letter.) The language of Mota now is beginning to be a very fair channel for communicating accurate theological teaching. We have, of course, to a large extent made it so by assigning deeper meanings to existing words (we have introduced very few words). This is the case in every language. On Sunday night, if you had been here, and been able to understand my teaching on St. John vi. to the Communicants, you would have been surprised, I think. Something of Hooker's fifth book was being readily taken in by several of those present. An Old Testament history they don't learn merely as certain events. They quickly take up the meaning, the real connection. I use the "Sunday Teaching," or work them at all events on that plan. Well, you mustn't say too much of the bright side of the picture. It is so easy to misunderstand.

'The time has been bad for our "lambing." We have thirty-five lambs, looking well, and have lost, I think, nine. Yesterday a great event occurred. One of the cart-mares foaled; great was the satisfaction of the Melanesians at the little filly. Calves are becoming too common, as we have now fourteen or fifteen cows, and five more are owing to us for goods which the people take in exchange—not money, which would not suit them as well. We have fenced in plenty of grass, and I don't wan't to pay any more for keep. Of course, we use a good deal of salt beef on shore here, as well as seek to supply the "Southern Cross" on her voyages.

'It is pleasant to walk about and see the farm and gardens thriving. All being well, we shall have some 300 bananas next year, lots of sugar-canes; many fruit trees are being planted, pine-apples, coffee, &c. Guavas grow here like weeds. I don't care for these things; but the others do, and of course the scholars rejoice in them.

'I think of the islands, and see them in my waking dreams, and it seems as if nothing was done. But I think again of what it was only a very short time ago, and oh! I do feel thankful indeed, and amazed, and almost fearful. I should like much, if I am alive and well, to see my way to spending more of my time on the islands. But the careful training of picked scholars for future missionaries is, I am sure, the most important part of our work (though it must be combined as much as possible with residence in the islands). If I could feel that the school was well able to get on without me, I would be off to the islands for a good spell. On the other hand, I feel most strongly that my chief business is to make such provision as I may for the multiplication of native missionaries, and the future permanent development and extension of the Mission; and to do this, our best scholars must be carefully trained, and then we may hope to secure a competent staff of native clergymen for the islands.

'Mind, I am not disposed to act in a hasty way. Only I don't mean to let conventional notions about an English clergyman hinder my providing Melanesian islands with a Melanesian ministry. These scholars of ours know very much more, and I imagine possess qualifications of all kinds for their work in Melanesia, greater than the majority of the missionaries in the old missionary times.

'How many men did good work who could hardly read, only repeat a few portions of the Service-book, &c.!

'I need not say that we wish to educate them up to the maximum point of usefulness for their practical work. But, given earnestness and steadfastness of character, a fair amount of teaching power, and a sound knowledge of fundamental truths, of the Church Services, and the meaning and spirit of the Prayer-book, and we may surely trust that, by God's grace, they may execute the office of the Ministry to the glory of God, and the edification of the Church.

'They have now in Mota, in print, St. Luke, the Acts; soon will have St. John, which is all ready; the Prayer-book, save some of the Psalms, and a few other small portions. And in MS. they have a kind of manual of the Catechism, abstract of the Books of the Old Testament, papers on Prophecy, &c., &c. All this work, once done in Mota, is, without very much labour, to be transferred into Bauro, Mahaga, Mara, &c., &c. as I hope; but that is in the future.'

In the birthday letter to his sister Fanny, his chilly nature confesses that August cold was making itself felt; and it was becoming time for him to make a journey to the settled world, both on account of a small tumour under his eyelid, and of the state of his teeth. Moreover, no letters from home had reached him since the 2nd of March. But he writes on the 7th of September to his brother:—

'This does not a bit distress me. I like the freedom from all external excitement. It gives me uninterrupted time from my own work; and the world does not suffer from my ignorance of its proceedings. How you exist with all the abominations of daily papers, I can't imagine. Your life in England seems to be one whirl and bustle, with no real time for quiet thought and patient meditation, &c. And yet men do think and do great things, and it doesn't wear them out soon either. Witness Bishops and Judges, &c., living to eighty and even ninety in our own days.

'I like quiet and rest, and no railroads and no daily posts; and, above all, no visitors, mere consumers of time, mere idlers and producers of idleness. So, without any post, and nothing but a cart on wheels, save a wheelbarrow, and no visitors, and no shops, I get on very happily and contentedly. The life here is to me, I must confess, luxurious, because I have what I like, great punctuality, early hours, regular school work, regular reading, very simple living; the three daily meals in hall take about seventy minutes all put together, and so little time is lost; and then the climate is delightful. Too cold now, but then I ought to be in the islands. The thermometer has been as low as 56° in my room; and I am standing in my room and writing now with my great coat on, the thermometer being 67°.

'You know that I am not cut out for society, never was at my ease in it, and am glad to be out of it. I am seldom at my ease except among Melanesians: they and my books are my best companions. I never feel the very slightest desire for the old life. You know how I should like to see you dear ones, and...[others by name] but I couldn't stand more than a week in England, if I could transplant myself there in five minutes! I don't think this augurs any want of affection; but I have grown into this life; I couldn't change it without a most unpleasant wrench.'

The letter was at this point, when the 'Southern Cross' arrived, on September 10, to carry off the Bishop and Mr. Palmer: the one to the General Synod, and to take leave of his most loved and venerated friend; the other, to fetch his bride.

He arrived on the 18th of the month, looking ill, and much worn and even depressed, more so than Lady Martin had ever seen him, for the coming parting pressed heavily upon him. The eye and teeth were operated upon without loss of time, and successfully; but this, with the cold of the voyage, made him, in his own word, 'shaky,' and it was well that he was a guest at Taurarua, with Lady Martin to take care of him, feed him on food not solid, and prevent him on the ensuing Sunday from taking more than one of the three services which had been at once proffered to him.

It was no small plunge from the calm of St. Barnabas. 'We agree,' said Lady Martin, in a note within his envelope, 'that we cannot attempt to write letters just now. We are in a whirl, mental and bodily; one bit of blue sky has just shown itself, viz. that Coley may possibly stay on with us for a week or two after the Selwyns have left us. This really is proeter spem, and I mean to think that it will come to pass.'

But in all this bustle, he found time to enclose a kind little note to me; showing his sympathy with the sorrow of that summer, in my mother's illness:—

'Auckland. October 3, 1868.

'I add one line, my dear Cousin, to assure you of my prayers being offered for you, now more especially when a heavy trial is upon you and a deep sorrow awaiting you. May God comfort and bless you! Perhaps the full experience of such anxiety and the pressure of a constant weight may, in His good Providence, qualify you more than ever to help others by words put into your mouth out of your own heart-felt troubles.

'Yet in whatever form the sorrow comes, there is the blessing of knowing that she is only being mysteriously prepared for the life of the world to come. There is no real sorrow where there is no remorse, nor misery for the falling away of those we love. You have, I dare say, known (as I have) some who have the bitterness of seeing children turn out badly, and this is the sorrow that breaks one down.'

It was during these spring days of October, that last Sunday before the final parting, that being hindered by pouring rain from going with the Primate, who was holding a farewell service with the sick at the hospital, Bishop Patteson said the prayers in the private chapel. After these were ended (Lady Martin says), 'he spoke a few words to us. He spoke of our Lord standing on the shore of the Lake after His Resurrection; and he carried us, and I think himself too, out of the heaviness of sorrow into a region of peace and joy, where all conflict and partings and sin shall cease for ever. It was not only what he said, but the tones of his musical voice, and expression of peace on his own face, that hushed us into a great calm. One clergyman, who was present, told Sir William Martin that he had never known anything so wonderful. The words were like those of an inspired man.

'Three days after, our dear friends sailed. I will not dwell on the last service at St. Paul's Church, when more than four hundred persons received the Holy Communion, where were four Bishops administering in the body of the church and the transepts; but in the chancel, the Primate and his beloved son in the faith were partaking together for the last time of the Bread of Life.

'From the Church we accompanied our beloved friends to the ship, and drove back on a cold, dry evening, a forlorn party, to the desolate house. But from that time dear Bishop Patteson roused himself from his natural depression (for to whom could the loss be greater than to him?) and set himself to cheer and comfort us all. How gentle and sympathising he was! He let me give him nourishing things, even wine—which he had long refused to take—because I told him Mrs. Selwyn wished him to have it. Many hearts were drooping, and he no longer shrank from society, but went about from one to another in the kindest manner. I do not know how we could have got on without him. He loved to talk of the Bishop. In his humility he seemed to feel as if any power of usefulness in himself had been gained from him. It was like him to think of our Auckland poor at this time. They would so miss the Bishop and Mrs. Selwyn. He prayed me to draw £50 a year for the next year or two, to be spent in any way I should think best. And he put it as a gift from his dear Father, who would have wished that money of his invested here should be used in part for the good of the townspeople. This did not include his subscriptions to the Orphan Home and other charities.'

To make his very liberal gifts in time of need in the name of his Father, was his favourite custom; as his former fellow-labourer, the Rev. B. T. Dudley, found when a case of distress in his own parish in the Canterbury Settlement called forth this ready assistance.

Perhaps the young Church of New Zealand has never known so memorable or so sorrowful a day as that which took from her her first Bishop: a day truly to be likened to that when the Ephesians parted with their Apostle at Miletus. The history of this parting Bishop Patteson had himself to read on Saturday, October 17, the twenty-seventh anniversary of Bishop Selwyn's Consecration. It was at the Celebration preceding the last meeting of the Synod, when Collect, Epistle, and Gospel were taken from the Order for the Consecration of Bishops; and as the latter says,—'He has always told me to officiate with him, and I had, by his desire, to read Acts xx. for the Epistle. I did read it without a break-down, but it was hard work.' Then followed the Sunday, before described by Lady Martin; and on Tuesday the 20th, that service in St. Mary's—the parting feast:—

'Then,' writes the younger Bishop, 'the crowded streets and wharf, for all business was suspended, public offices and shops shut, no power of moving about the wharf, horses taken from the carriage provided for the occasion, as a mixed crowd of English and Maoris drew them to the wharf. Then choking words and stifled efforts to say, "God bless you," and so we parted!

'It is the end of a long chapter. I feel as if "my master was taken from my head."

'Ah! well, they are gone, and we will try to do what we can.

'I feel rather no-how, and can't yet settle down to anything!'

But to the other sister on the same day comes an exhortation not to be alarmed if friends report him as 'not up to the mark.' How could it be otherwise at such a time? For truly it was the last great shock his affections sustained. In itself, it might not be all that the quitting home and family had been; but not only was there the difference between going and being left behind, but youth, with its spirit of enterprise and compensation, was past, and he was in a state to feel the pain of the separation almost more intensely than when he had walked from the door at

Feniton, and gathered his last primrose at his mother's grave. Before leaving Auckland, the Bishop married the Rev. John Palmer to Miss Ashwell; and while they remained for a short time in New Zealand, he returned for the Ember Week.

'St. Thomas, Norfolk Island: December 21, 1868.

'My dear Cousin,—I must write you a few lines, not as yet in answer to your very interesting letter about Mr. Keble and about Ritualism, &c., but about our great event of yesterday.

'George Sarawia was ordained Deacon in our little chapel, in the presence of fifty-five Melanesians and a few Norfolk Islanders. With him Charles Bice, a very excellent man from St. Augustine's, was ordained Deacon also. He has uncommon gifts of making himself thoroughly at home with the Melanesians. It comes natural to him, there is no effort, nothing to overcome apparently, and they of course like him greatly. He speaks the language of Mota, the lingua franca here, you know.

'But what am I to say of George that you cannot imagine for yourself? It was in the year 1857 that the Bishop and I first saw him at Vanua Lava Island. He has been with us now ten years; I can truly say, that he has never given me any uneasiness. He is not the cleverest of our scholars; but no one possesses the confidence of us all in the same degree. True, he is the oldest of the party, he can hardly be less than twenty-six years old, for he had been married a year when first we saw him; but it is his character rather than his age which gives him his position. For a long time he has been our link with the Melanesians themselves whenever there was something to be done by one of themselves rather than by us strangers. Somehow the other scholars get into a way of recognising him as the A 1 of the place, and so also in Mota and the neighbouring islands his character and reputation are well known. The people expect him to be a teacher among them, they all know that he is a person of weight.

'The day was warm and fine.

'At 7.20 A.M. we had the Morning Service, chanting the 2nd Psalm. I read Isa. xlii. 5-12 for the First Lesson, and 1 Tim. iii. 8-13 for the Second, and the Collect in the Ordination Service before the Prayer of St. Chrysostom. Mr. Codrington, as usual, read the prayers to the end of the third Collect, after which we sang our Sunday hymn.

'At 11 A.M. we began the Ordination Service. One Epiphany hymn, my short sermon, then Mr. Codrington presented the candidates, speaking Mota for one and English for the other. The whole service was in Mota, except that I questioned Bice, and he answered in English, and I used the English words of Ordination in his case. George was questioned and answered in Mota, and then Bice in English, question by question. Mr. Nobbs was here and a few of the people, Mr. Atkin, Mr. Brooke, so we made a goodly little party of seven in our clerical supper.

'What our thoughts were you can guess as we ordained the first Melanesian clergyman. How full of thankfulness, of awe, of wonderment, the fulfilment of so much, the pledge of it, if it be God's will, of so much more! And not a little of anxiety, too—yet the words of comfort are many; and it does not need much faith, with so evident a proof of God's Love and Power and Faithfulness before our very eyes, to trust George in His Hands.

'The closing stanzas of the Ordination Hymn in the "Christian Year" comforted me as I read them at night; but I had peace and comfort, thank God, all through.

'Others, too, are pressing on. I could say, with truth, to them in the evening in the Chapel, "This is the beginning, only the beginning, the first fruit. Many blossoms there are already. I know that God's Spirit is working in the hearts of some of you. Follow that holy guidance, I pray always that you may be kept in the right way, and that you may be enabled to point it out to others, and to guide them in it."

'And yet no words can express what the recoil of the wave heathenism is, but "when the enemy shall come in like a flood," and it has indeed its own glorious word of Promise. It is like one who was once a drunkard and has left off drinking, and then once more tastes the old deadly poison, and becomes mad for drink; or like the wild furious struggles (as I suppose) of poor penitents in penitentiaries, when it seems as if the devil must whirl them back into sin. You know we see things which look like "possession," a black cloud settling down upon the soul, overwhelming all the hopeful signs for a time. And then, when I have my quiet talk with such an one (and only very few, and they not the best among us), he will say, "I can't tell, I didn't mean it. It was not I. What was it?" And I say, "It was the devil, seeking to devour you, to drag you back into the old evil dark ways." "It is awful, fearful." "Then you must gird your loins and pray the more, and remember that you are Christ's, that you belong to Him, that you are God's child, that Satan has no right to claim you now. Resist him in this name, in the strength of the Spirit whom Christ has sent to us from the Father, and he will flee from you."

'It is of course the same more or less with us all, but it comes out in, a shape which gives it terrible reality and earnestness. Only think, then, more than ever, of them and of me, and pray that "the Spirit of the Lord may lift up a standard against the enemy." At times we do seem to realise that it is a downright personal struggle for life or death.'

There the writer paused, and the next date is

'Christmas Day, 1868.

'My dearest Sisters,—What a happy happy day! At 12.5 A.M. I was awoke by a party of some twenty Melanesians, headed by Mr. Bice, singing Christmas carols at my bedroom door. It is a glass window, opening on to the verandah. How delightful it was! I had gone to bed with the Book of Praise by my side, and Mr. Keble's hymn in my mind; and now the Mota versions, already familiar to us, of the Angels' Song and of the "Light to lighten the Gentiles," sung too by some of our heathen scholars, took up as it were the strain. Their voices sounded so fresh and clear in the still midnight, the perfectly clear sky, the calm moon, the warm genial climate.

'I lay awake afterwards, thinking on the blessed change wrought in their minds, thinking of my happy happy lot, of how utterly undeserved it was and is, and (as is natural) losing myself in thoughts of God's wonderful goodness and mercy and love.

'Then at 4.45 A.M. I got up, a little later perhaps than usual. Codrington and Brooke were very soon at work finishing the decorations in the Chapel; branches of Norfolk Island pines, divers evergreens, pomegranates and oleanders and lilies (in handfuls) and large snow-white arums; on the altar-table arums above, and below lilies and evergreens. Oleanders and pomegranates marked the chancel arch. The rugs looked very handsome, the whole floor at the east end is covered with a red baize or drugget to match the curtains.

'7 A.M., Holy Communion. Six clergymen in surplices and fifteen other communicants. At 10 A.M., a short, very bright, joyful service, the regular Morning Prayers, Psalms xcv. xix. cx. all chanted. Proper Lessons, two Christmas hymns.

'Then games, cricket, prisoner's base, running races. Beef, pork, plum-puddings.

'Now we shall soon have evening Chapel, a great deal of singing, a few short words from me; then a happy, merry, innocent evening, native dances, coffee, biscuit, and snapdragons to finish with.

'If you had been here to-day, you would indeed have been filled with surprise and thankfulness and hope. There is, I do think, a great deal to show that these scholars of ours so connect religion with all that is cheerful and happy. There is nothing, as I think, sanctimonious about them. They say, "We are so happy here! How different from our lands!"

'And I think I can truly say that this is not from want of seriousness in those of an age to be serious.

'I pour this out to you in my happy day—words of hope and joy and thankfulness! But remember that I feel that all this should make me thoughtful as well as hopeful. How can I say but what sorrow and trial may even now be on their way hither? But I thank God, oh! I do thank Him for his great love and mercy, and I do not think it wrong to give my feelings of joy some utterance.'

With this year the Eucharist was administered weekly, the Melanesians still attending fortnightly; but it proved to have been a true foreboding that a sorrow was on its way:—

'January 8th.—A very joyful Christmas, but a sad Epiphany!

'U——, dearer to me than ever, has (I now hear from him) been putting himself in the way of temptation. I had noticed that he was not like himself, and spoke to him and warned him. I told him that if he wished to be married at once, I was quite willing to marry him; but he said they were too young, and yet he was always thinking of the young fiancée. Alas! he had too often (as he says) put himself in the way of temptation with his eyes open, and he fell. He was frightened, terrified, bewildered.

'Alas! it is our first great sorrow of the kind, for he was a Communicant of nearly three years' standing. Yet I have much comfort.

'I can have no doubt, 1st, that a fall was necessary, I believe fully. His own words (not suggested by me) were, "I tempted God often, and He let me fall; I don't mean He was the cause of it, it is of course only my fault; but I think I see that I might have gone on getting more and more careless and wandering further and further from Him unless I had been startled and frightened." And then he burst out, "Oh! don't send me away for ever. I know I have made the young ones stumble, and destroyed the happiness of our settlement here. I know I must not be with you all in Chapel and school and hall. I know I can't teach any more, I know that, and I am miserable, miserable. But don't tell me I must go away for ever. I can't bear it!"

'I did manage to answer almost coldly, for I felt that if I once let loose my longing desire to let him see my real feeling, I could not restrain myself at all. "Who wishes to send you away, U—? It is not me whom you have displeased and injured."

'"I know. It is terrible! But I think of the Prodigal Son. Oh! I do long to go back! Oh! do tell me that He loves me still."

'Poor dear fellow! I thought I must leave him to bear his burthen for a time. We prayed together, and I left him, or rather sent him away from my room, but he could neither eat nor sleep.

'The next day his whole manner, look, everything made one sure (humanly speaking) that he was indeed truly penitent; and then when I began to speak words of comfort, of God's tender love and compassion, and told him how to think of the Lord's gentle pity when He appeared first to the Magdalene and Peter, and when I took his hand in the old loving way, poor fellow, he broke down more than ever, and cried like a child.

'Ah! it is very sad; but I do think he will be a better, more steadfast man: he has learnt his weakness, and where to find strength, as he never had before. And the effect on the school is remarkable. That there should be so much tenderness of conscience and apprehension of the guilt of impurity among the children of the heathen in among many brought up in familiarity with sin, is a matter for much thankfulness.'

To this may well be added an extract from Joseph Atkin's journal, showing his likemindedness both in thoughtfulness and charity:—

'I feel quite sure that we must be prepared for many such cases. The whole associations and training of the early lives of these people must influence them as long as they live. The thought of what my mother and sister would think, never occur to them as any influence for good; and although this may be said to be a low motive for doing right, it is a very powerful one, and it is more tangible because it is lower.

'The Bishop, in speaking of it to-day, told the boys that they ought not to do right to please him, but because it was right to please God; but I can't help thinking that pleasing the Bishop may and can help the other very much. Is it not right for a child to do right to please its parents, and for older children too to be helped by the thought that they are pleasing those they love and honour?

'We had a council to-day of all the Church members to talk about how U—— was to be treated. For himself, poor fellow, I should think kindness would be harder to bear than neglect.

'Mr. Codrington says, "On this occasion all the male Communicants went together to some little distance, where a group of boulders under the pines gave a convenient seat. The Bishop set out the case, and asked what was the opinion of the elder boys as to the treatment of the offender. They were left alone to consider; and when we came back, they gave their judgment, that he should not eat in the hall at what may be called the high table, that he should not teach in school, and should not come into Chapel."

'This was of course what was intended, but the weight of the sentence so given was greater with the school, and a wholesome lesson given to the judges. How soon the Bishop's severity, which never covered his pity, gave way to his affection for one of his oldest and dearest pupils, and his tenderness for the penitent, and how he took a large share of blame upon himself, just where it was not due, can well be understood by all who knew him.'

There was soon a brighter day. On January 25, writes Mr. Atkin:—

'We had a great day. In the morning some who were baptized last summer were confirmed, and at night there were baptized three girls and thirteen boys. Most of them were quite little fellows. I don't think any of us will easily forget their grave and sober but not shy looks, as one by one they stepped up to the Bishop. I think that all understood and meant what they said, that Baptism was no mere form with them, but a real solemn compact. All who were in my class (nine), or the Sunday morning school, were baptized in the evening. While we were standing round the font, I thought of you at home, and half wished that you could have seen us there. I was witness for my son (Wate); he was called Joseph, so that I shall lose my name that I have kept so long.'

Joseph Wate, the little Malanta boy, was always viewed by the Atkin family as a kind of child, and kept up a correspondence with his godfather's sister, Mother Mary as he called her.

On the same day the Bishop wrote to Judge Pohlman:—

'My very dear Friend,—I must not let our correspondence drop, and the less likely it seems to be that we may meet, the more I must seek to retain your friendship, by letting you know not only the facts that occur here, but my thoughts and hopes and fears about them.'

(Then, after mentioning the recent transgression, the letter continues respecting the youth.)

'His fright and terror, his misery and deep sorrow, and (I do believe) godly repentance, make me say that he is still, as I trust, one of our best scholars. But it is very sad. For three weeks he did not come even into chapel with us. He not only acquiesced, but wished that it should be so.

'Last Saturday evening he was readmitted, without any using of fine names. I did as a matter of fact do what was the practice of the early Christians, and is recognised in our Ash Wednesday service now. It was very desirable that great notice should be taken of the commission of an act which it is hard for a heathen to understand to be an act of sin, and the effect upon the whole school of the sad and serious way in which this offence was regarded has been very good.

'In the circumstances it is so easy to see how the discipline of the early Church was not an artificial, but a necessary system, though by degrees elaborated in a more complicated manner. But I find, not seldom, that common sense dictates some course which afterwards I come across in Bingham, or some such writer, described as a usage of the early Christians.

'In our English nineteenth century life such practices could hardly be reintroduced with benefit. Yet something which might mark open offences with the censure of the Christian Body is clearly desirable when you can have it; and of course with us there is no difficulty whatever.

'I cannot be surprised, however deeply grieved at this sad occurrence; and though it is no comfort to think how many English persons would think nothing of this, and certainly not show the deep compunction and sorrow which this poor fellow shows, yet, as a matter of fact, how few young Englishmen are there who would think such an act, as this young Melanesian thinks it to be, a grievous sin against God, and matter for continual sorrow and humiliation. So I do rejoice that he is sorrowing after a godly sort.

'In other respects there is a very hopeful promising appearance just now. We number seven clergymen, including myself. We have a very efficient band of Melanesian teachers, and could at this moment work a school of 150 scholars.

'George Sarawia will (D.V.) start with a little company of Christian friends at his own island. The scholars from all the different islands fraternise excellently well, and in many cases the older and more advanced have their regular chums, by private arrangement among themselves, whom they help, and to whose islands they are quite prepared to be sent, if I think fit so to arrange; and I really do believe that from the Banks Islands we may send out missionaries to many of the Melanesian islands, as from Samoa and Karotonga they have gone out to the islands of the Eastern Pacific. Humanly speaking, I see no difficulty in our drawing into our central school here any number of natives that we can support, from the New Hebrides, Banks and Solomon Islands, and I trust soon from the Santa Cruz Islands also.

'Here must be the principal work, the training up missionaries and steadfast Christian men and women, not of ability sufficient to become themselves missionaries, but necessary to strengthen the hands of their more gifted countrymen. This training must be carried on here, but with it must be combined a frequent visitation and as lengthened sojourns in the islands as possible. The next winter we hope that the Rev. J. Atkin will be some time at San Cristoval, the Rev. C. H. Brooke at Florida, the Rev. J. Palmer at Mota. But I am more than ever convinced that the chiefest part of our work is to consist in training up Melanesian clergymen, and educating them up to the point of faithfully reproducing our simple teaching. We must hope to see native self-supporting Melanesian Churches, not weak indolent Melanesians dependent always on an English missionary, but steadfast, thoughtful men and women, retaining the characteristics of their race so far as they can be sanctified by the Word of God in prayer, and not force useless imitations of English modes of thought and nineteenth century civilisation.

'It is sometimes a consequence of our national self-conceit, sometimes of want of thought, that no consideration is shown to the characteristic native way of regarding things. But Christianity is a universal religion, and assimilates and interpolates into its system all that is capable of regeneration and sanctification anywhere.

'Before long I hope to get something more respectable in the way of a report printed and circulated. It seems unreasonable to say so, but really I have very little time that I can spare from directly Melanesian work, what with school, translations, working out languages, and (thank God) the many, many hours spent in quiet interviews with Melanesians of all ages and islands, who come to have private talks with me, and to tell me of their thoughts and feelings. These are happy hours indeed. I must end. Always, my dear friend, affectionately and sincerely yours,

'J. C. PATTESON.'

The readmission thus mentioned was by the imposition of hands, when the penitent was again received, and his conduct ever since has proved his repentance true.

February brought Mr. and Mrs. Palmer to their new home, and carried away Mr. Codrington for a holiday. The budget of letters sent by this opportunity contained a remarkable one from young Atkin. Like master, like scholar:—

'February 24, 1869.

'My dear Mother,—You must not think about my coming back; I may have to do it, but if I do, it will seem like giving up the object of my life. I did not enter upon this work with any enthusiasm, and it is perhaps partly from that cause that I am now so attached to it that little short of necessity would take me away; my own choice, I think, never. I know it is much harder for you than for me. I wish I could lighten it to you, but it cannot be. It is a great deal more self-denial for you to spare me to come away than for me to come away. You must think, like David, "I will not offer unto the Lord my God of that which doth cost me nothing." If you willingly give Him what you prize most, however worthless the gift may be, He will prize it for the willingness with which it is given. If it had been of my own choosing that I came away, I should often blame myself for having made a selfish choice in not taking harder and more irksome work nearer home, but it came to me without choosing. I can only be thankful that God has been so good to me.'

Well might the Bishop write to the father, 'I thank you in my heart for Joe's promise.'

How exactly his own spirit, in simple, unconscious self-abnegation and thorough devotion to the work. How it chimes in with this, written on the self-same morning to the Bishop of Lichfield:—

'St. Matthias Day, 6.45 A.M., 1869.

My dear Bishop,—You do not doubt that I think continually of you, yet I like you to have a line from me to-day. We are just going into Chapel, altering our usual service to-day that we may receive the Holy Communion with special remembrance of my Consecration and special prayer for a blessing on the Mission. There is much to be thankful for indeed, much also that may well make the retrospect of the last eight years a somewhat sad and painful one as far as I am myself concerned. It does seem wonderful that good on the whole is done. But everything is wonderful and full of mystery....

'It is rather mean of me, I fear, to get out of nearly all troubles by being here. Yet it seems to me very clear that the special work of the Mission is carried on more conveniently (one doesn't like to say more successfully) here, and my presence or absence is of no consequence when general questions are under discussion....

'Your very affectionate
'J. C. PATTESON.'

The same mail brought a letter to Miss Mackenzie, with much valuable matter on Mission work:—

'February 26, 1869.

'Dear Miss Mackenzie,—I have just read your letter to me of April 1867, which I acknowledged, rather than answered, long ago.

'I can't answer it as it deserves to be answered now. I think I have already written about thirty-five letters to go by this mail, and my usual work seldom leaves me a spare hour.

'But I am truly thankful for the hopes that seem to show themselves through the mists, in places where all Christian men must feel so strong an interest. I do hope to hear that the new Bishopric may soon be founded, on which Mr. Robertson and you and others have so set your hearts. That good man! I often think of him, and hope soon to send him, through you, £10 from our Melanesian offertory.

'You know we have, thank God, thirty-nine baptized Melanesians here, of whom fifteen are communicants, and one, George Sarawia, a clergyman. He was ordained on December 20.

'There are many little works usually going ons which I don't consider it fair to reckon among the regular industrial work of the Mission. I pay the young men and lads and boys small sums for such things, and I think it right to teach the elder ones the use of money by giving them allowances, out of which they buy their clothing, &c., when necessary, all under certain regulations. I say this that you may know that our weekly offertory is not a sham. No one knows what they give, or whether they give or not. A Melanesian takes the offertory bason, and they give or not as they please. I take care that such moneys as are due to them shall be given in 3d., 4d., and 6d. pieces.

'Last year our offertory rather exceeded £40, and it is out of this that my brother will now pay you £10 for the Mackenzie fund. I write all this because you will like to think that some of this little offertory comes bond fide from Melanesians.

'...You take me to mean, I hope, that Christianity is the religion for mankind at large, capable of dealing with the spiritual and bodily needs of man everywhere.

'It is easy for us now to say that some of the early English Missions, without thinking at all about it, in all probability, sought to impose an English line of thought and religion on Indians and Africans. Even English dress was thought to be almost essential, and English habits, &c., were regarded as part of the education of persons converted through the agency of English Missions. All this seems to be burdening the message of the Gospel with unnecessary difficulties.

The teacher everywhere, in England or out of it, must learn to discriminate between essentials and non-essentials. It seems to me self-evident that the native scholar must be educated up to the highest point that is possible, and that unless one is (humanly speaking) quite sure that he can and will reproduce faithfully the simple teaching he has received, he ought not to teach, much less to be ordained.

'All our elder lads and girls here teach the younger ones, and we know what they teach. Their notes of our lessons are brought to me, books full of them, and there I see what they know; for if they can write down a plain account of facts and doctrines, that is a good test of their having taken in the teaching. George Sarawia's little essay on the doctrine of the Communion is to me perfectly satisfactory. It was written without my knowledge. I found it in one of his many note-books accidentally.

'As for civilisation, they all live entirely with us, and every Melanesian in the place, men and women, boys and girls, three times a day take their places with all of us in hall, and use their knives and forks, plates, cups and saucers (or, for the passage, one's pannikins) just as we do. George and two others, speaking for themselves and their wives, have just written out, among other things, in a list which I told them to make out: plates, cups, saucers, knives, forks, spoons, tubs, saucepans, kettles, soap, towels, domestic things for washing, ironing, &c.

'The common presents that our elder scholars take or send to their friends include large iron pots for cooking, clothing, &c. They build improved houses, and ask for small windows, &c., to put in them, boxes, carpet bags for their clothes, small writing desks, note-books, ink, pens. They keep their best clothes very carefully, and on Sundays and great days look highly respectable. And for years we know no instance of a baptized Melanesian throwing aside his clothing when taking his holiday at home.

'As far as I can see my way to any rule in the matter, it is this: all that is necessary to secure decency, propriety, cleanliness, health, &c., must be provided for them. This at once involves alteration of the houses, divisions, partitions. People who can read and write, and cut out and sew clothes, must have light in their houses. This involves a change of the shape and structure of the hut. They can't sit in clean clothes on a dirty floor, and they can't write, or eat out of plates and use cups, &c., without tables or benches, and as they don't want to spend ten hours in sleep or idle talk, they must have lamps for cocoa-nut and almond oil.

'These people are not taught to adopt these habits by word of mouth. They live with us and do as we do. Two young married women are sitting in my room now. I didn't call them in, nor tell them what to do. "We didn't quite understand what you said last night." "Well, I have written it out,—there it is." They took, as usual, the MS., sat down, just as you or anyone would do, at the table to read it, and are now making their short notes of it. Anyone comes in and out at any time, when not at school, chapel, or work, just as they please. We each have our own sitting-room, which is in this sense public property, and of course they fall into our ways.

'There is perhaps no such thing as teaching civilisation by word of command, nor religion either. The sine qua non for the missionary—religious and moral character assumed to exist—is the living with his scholars as children of his own.

And the aim is to lift them up, not by words, but by the daily life, to the sense of their capacity for becoming by God's grace all that we are, and I pray God a great deal more; not as literary men or scholars, but as Christian men and women, better suited than we are for work among their own people. "They shall be saved even as we." They have a strong sense of and acquiescence in, their own inferiority. If we treat them as inferiors, they will always remain in that position of inferiority.

'But Christ humbled Himself and became the servant and minister that He might make us children of God and exalt us.

'It is surely very simple, but if we do thus live among them, they must necessarily accept and adopt some of our habits. Our Lord led the life of a poor man, but He raised His disciples to the highest pitch of excellence by His Life, His Words, and His Spirit, the highest that man could receive and follow. The analogy is surely a true one. And exclusiveness, all the pride of race must disappear before such considerations.

'But it is not the less true that He did not make very small demands upon His disciples, and teach them and us that it needs but little care and toil and preparation to be a Christian and a teacher of Christianity. The direct contrary to this is the truth.

'The teacher's duty is to be always leading on his pupils to higher conceptions of their work in life, and to a more diligent performance of it. How can he do this if he himself acquiesces in a very imperfect knowledge and practice of his duty?

'"And yet the mass of mediaeval missionaries could perhaps scarce read." That may be true, but that was not an excellence but a defect, and the mass of the gentry and nobility could not do so much. They did a great work then. It does not follow that we are to imitate their ignorance when we can have knowledge.

'But I am wasting your time and mine.

'Yours very truly,

'**J. C. PATTESON.**

'P.S.—George and his wife and child, Charles and his wife, Benjamin and his wife, will live together at Mota on some land I have bought. A good wooden house is to be put up by us this winter (D.V.) with one large room for common use, school, &c., and three small bed-rooms opening on to a verandah. One small bed-room at the other end which any one, two or three of us English folks can occupy when at Mota. I dare say, first and last, this house will cost seventy or eighty pounds.

'Then we hope to have everything that can be sown and planted with profit in a tropical climate, first-class breed of pigs, poultry, &c., so that all the people may see that such things are not neglected. These things will be given away freely- settings of eggs, young sows, seeds, plants, young trees, &c. All this involves expense, quite rightly too, and after all, I dare say that dear old George will cost about a sixth or an eighth of what we English clergymen think necessary. I dare say £25 per annum will cover his expenses.'

On Easter Sunday the penitent was readmitted to the Lord's Table. A happy letter followed:—

'Easter Tuesday, 1869.

'My dearest Sisters,—Another opportunity of writing. I will only say a word about two things. First, our Easter and the Holy Week preceding it; secondly, how full my mind has been of Mr. Keble, on his two anniversaries, Holy Thursday and March 29. And I have read much of the "Christian Year," and the two letters I had from him I have read again, and looked at the picture of him, and felt helped by the memory of his holy saintly life, and I dared to think that it might be that by God's great mercy in Christ, I might yet know him and other blessed Saints in the Life to come.

'Our Holy Week was a calm solemn season. All the services have long been in print. Day by day in school and chapel we followed the holy services and acts of each day, taking Ellicott's "Historical Lectures" as a guide.

'Each evening I had my short sermonet, and we sought to deepen the impressions made evidently upon our scholars by whatever could make it a real matter of life and death to them and us. Then came Good Friday and Easter Eve, during which the Melanesians with Mr. Brooke were busily engaged in decorating the Chapel with fronds of tree-ferns, bamboo, arums, and oleander blossoms.

'Then, at 7 A.M. on Easter Morning, thirty of us—twenty-one, thank God, being Melanesians—met in Chapel for the true Easter Feast.

'Then, at 11 A.M., how we chanted Psalms ii, cxiii, cxiv, and Hymn, and the old Easter Hallelujah hymn to the old tune with Mota words. Then at 7 P.M. Psalms cxviii, cxlviii, to joyful chants, and singing Easter and other hymns.

'So yesterday and so to-day. The short Communion Service in the morning with hymn, and in the evening we chant Psalm cxviii, and sing out our Easter hymn. Ah well! it makes my heart very full. It is the season of refreshing, perhaps before more trails.

'Dear U—— was with us again on Easter morn, a truly repentant young man, I verily believe, feeling deeply what in our country districts is often not counted a sin at all to be a foul offence against his Father and Saviour and Sanctifier.

'Six were there for their first Communion, among them honest old Stephen Taroniara, the first and only communicant of all the Solomon Isles—of all the world west of Mota, or east of any of the Bishop of Labuan's communicants. Think of that! What a blessing! What a thought for praise and hope and meditation!

'I sit in my verandah in the moonlight and I do feel happy in spite of many thoughts of early days which may well make me feel unhappy.

'But I do feel an almost overpowering sensation of thankfulness and peace and calm tranquil happiness, which I know cannot last long. It would not, I suppose, be good: anyhow it will soon be broken by some trial which may show much of my present state to be a delusion. Yet I like to tell you what I think, and I know you will keep it to yourselves.

'Good-bye, and all Easter blessings be with you.

'Your loving brother,

'J. C. PATTESON '

The island voyage was coming near, and was to be conducted, on a larger scale, after the intermission of a whole year. Mr. Brooke was to make some stay at Florida, Mr. Atkin at Wango in Bauro, and the Bishop himself was to take the party who were to commence the Christian village at Mota, while Mr. Codrington and Mr. Bice remained in charge of twenty-seven Melanesians. The reports of the effects of the labour traffic were becoming a great anxiety, and not only the Fiji settlers, but those in Queensland were becoming concerned in it.

The 'Southern Cross' arrived in June, but the weather was so bad that, knocking about outside the rocks, she sustained some damage, and could not put her freight ashore for a week. However, on the 24th she sailed, and put down Mr. Atkin at Wango, the village in Bauro where the Bishop had stayed two years previously.

Mr. Atkin gives a touching description of Taroniara's arrival:—

'Stephen was not long in finding his little girl, Paraiteka. She was soon in his arms. The old fellow just held her up for the Bishop to see, and then turned away with her, and I saw a handkerchief come out privately and brush quickly across his eyes, and in a few minutes he came back to us.'

The little girl's mother, for whose sake Taroniara had once refused to return to school, had been carried off by a Maran man; and as the heathen connection had been so slight, and a proper marriage so entirely beyond the ideas of the native state, it was thought advisable to leave this as a thing of heathen darkness, and let him select a girl to be educated into becoming fit for his true wife.

Besides Stephen, Joseph Wate and two other Christian lads were with Mr. Atkin, and he made an expedition of two days' visit to Wate's father. At Ulava he found that dysentery had swept off nearly all the natives, and he thought these races, even while left to themselves, were dying out. 'But,' adds the brave man in his journal, 'I will never, I hope, allow that because these people are dying out, it is of no use or a waste of time carrying the Gospel to them. It is, I should rather say, a case where we ought to be the more anxious to gather up the fragments.'

So he worked on bravely, making it an object, if he could do no more, to teach enough to give new scholars a start in the school, and to see who were most worth choosing there. He suffered a little loss of popularity when it was found that he was not a perpetual fountain of beads, hatchets, and tobacco, but he did the good work of effecting a reconciliation between Wango and another village named Hane, where he made a visit, and heard a song in honour of Taroniara. He was invited to a great reconciliation feast; which he thus describes, beginning with his walk to Hane by short marches:—

'We waited where we overtook Taki, until the main body from Wango came up. They charged past in fine style, looking very well in their holiday dress, each with his left hand full of spears, and one brandished in the right. It looked much more like a fighting party than a peace party; but it is the custom to make peace with the whole army, to convince the enemy that it is only for his accommodation that they are making peace, and not because they are afraid to fight him. It was about 12 o'clock when we reached the rendezvous. There was a fine charge of all, except a dozen of the more sedate of the party; they rattled their spears, and ran, and shouted, and jumped, even crossing the stream which was the neutral ground. We halted by the stream for some time; at last some Hane people came to their side; there was a charge again almost up to them, but they took it coolly. At about 10 o'clock the whole body of the Hane men came, and two or three from Wango went across to them. I was tired of waiting, and asked Taki if I should go. "Yes, and tell them to bring the money," he said.

'While I was wading through the stream, the Hane men gathered up and advanced; I turned back with them. They rushed, brandishing their spears, to within ten or twelve paces of the Wango party, who had joined into a compact body, and so seated themselves as soon as they saw the movement.

'Kara, a Hane man, made his speech, first running forwards and backwards, shaking his spear all the time; and at the end, he took out four strings of Makira money, and gave it to Taki. Hane went back across the stream; and Wango went through the same performance, Taki making the speech. He seemed a great orator, and went on until one standing by him said, "That's enough," when he laughed, and gave over. He gave four strings of money, two shorter than the others, and the shortest was returned to him, I don't know why; but in this way the peace was signed.'

After nineteen days, during which the Bishop had been cruising about, Mr. Atkin and his scholars were picked up again, and likewise Mr. Brooke, who had been spending ten days at Florida with his scholars, in all thirty-five; and then ensued a very tedious passage to the Banks Islands, for the vessel had been crippled by the gale off Norfolk Island, and could not be pressed; little canvas was carried, and the weather was unfavourable.

However, on September 6, Mota was safely reached; and great was the joy, warm the welcome of the natives, who eagerly assisted in unloading the vessel, through storms of rain and surf.

The old station house was in entire decay; but the orange and lemon trees were thirty feet high, though only the latter in bearing.

The new village, it was agreed, should bear the name of Kohimarama, after the old home in New Zealand, meaning, in Maori, 'Focus of Light.' After landing the goats, the Bishop, Mr. Atkin, and five more crossed to Valua. They were warmly welcomed at Ara, where their long absence had made the natives fancy they must all be dead. The parents of Henry, Lydia, and Edwin were the first to approach the boat, eager to hear of their children left in Norfolk Island; and the mother walked up the beach with her arm round Mr. Atkin's neck. But here it appeared that the vessels of the labour traffic had come to obtain people to work in the cotton plantations in Queensland, and that they had already begun to invite them in the name of the Bishop, whose absence they accounted for by saying his ship had been wrecked, he had broken his leg, he had gone to England, and sent them to fetch natives to him. No force had been used as yet, but there was evident dread of them; and one vessel had a Mota man on board, who persuaded the people to go to Sydney. About a hundred natives had been taken from the islands of Valua, Ara, and Matlavo, and from Bligh Island twenty-three were just gone, but Mota's inaccessibility had apparently protected it. It will be remembered that it has a high fortification of coral all round the beach, with but one inconvenient entrance, and that the people are little apt to resort to canoes. This really has hitherto seemed a special Providence for this nucleus of Christianity.

They spent the night at Ara, making a fire on the sandy beach, where they boiled their chocolate, and made gravy of some extract of meat to season their yam, and supped in public by firelight, reclining upon mats. Afterwards they went up to the Ogamal, or barrack tent: it was not an inviting bed-chamber, being so low that they could only kneel upright in it, and so smoky that Stephen remarked, 'We shall be cooked ourselves if we stay here,' proving an advance in civilisation. One of the private houses was equally unattractive, and the party slept on the beach.

The next morning they started to walk round the island: taking two cork beds, a portmanteau and a basket of provisions; stopping wherever a few people were found, but it was a thinly peopled place, and the loss of the men carried off was sensibly felt.

One village had had a fight with a boat's crew from Sydney. They made no secret of it, saying that they would not have their men taken away; and they had been sharp enough to pour water into the guns before provoking the quarrel.

Further on there was a closer population, where the Bishop was enthusiastically welcomed, and an Ogamal was found, making a good shelter for the night. Then they returned to Ara, where Mr. Atkin notes, in the very centre of the island, a curious rock, about 200 feet high, and on the top, 20 or 30 feet from the nearest visible soil, a she-oak stump, and two more green and flourishing a little below. The rock was of black scoriae, too hot in the middle of the day to sit upon, and near it was a pool of water. 'Such water, so rotten.' The water used by the visitors had been brought from Auckland. The natives do not trouble water much, I don't think they ever drink it, and they certainly don't look as if they ever washed.

On the following day they recrossed to Vanua Lava, where they spent a quiet calm Sunday in the vessel, landing in the afternoon to see Fisher Young's grave, which they found well kept and covered with a pretty blue creeper.

The next Sunday they spent at Kohimarama: beginning with Celebration at 7.30 A.M., and in the afternoon making the circuit of the island, about ten miles. In one place Mr. Atkin bent over the edge of the natural sea wall, and saw the sea breaking 150 or 200 feet below!

After a fortnight spent in this manner, he and the other two clergymen carried off their Melanesians to Norfolk Island, leaving the Bishop to be fetched away in a month's time. Here is the letter written during his solitude:—

'Kohimarama, Mota Island: September 23, 1869.

'My dearest Joan and Fan,—Here I am sitting in a most comfortable house in our new Kohimarama, for so the Melanesians determine to call our station in Mota. The house is 48 feet by 18, with a 9-foot verandah on two sides. It has one large room, a partition at each end, one of which is subdivided into two small sleeping rooms for George and his wife, and Charles and his wife. There is no ceiling, so that we have the full advantage of the height of the house, and plenty of ventilation, as the space beyond where the roof comes down upon the wall plates is left open.

'The verandah is a grand lounging place; very commodious for school also, when other classes fill the large room, and a delightful place to sit or lie about on in this genial warm climate. These bright moonlight nights are indeed delicious. The mosquito gives no trouble here to speak of. The cocoa-nut trees, the bread-fruit trees, yam gardens, and many kinds of native trees and shrubs, are all around us; the fine wooded hill of Mota shows well over the house. The breeze always plays round it; and though it is very hot, it is only when the wind comes from the north and north-west, as in the midsummer, that the heat is of an oppressive and sickly nature.

'About twenty lads and young men live here, and about forty attend daily school; but I think there is every indication of all Mota sending its young people here as soon as we have our crops of yams, &c., &c., to provide sufficient food. Improved native huts will, I think, soon be built over our little estate here.

'Many girls I hope to take to Norfolk Island. They could hardly be brought together with safety to this place yet. The parents see and admit this, and consent to my taking them. I tell them that their sons will not marry ignorant heathen girls (their sons I mean who have been and are still with us); that all the young fellows growing up at Kohimarama must have educated wives provided for them, and that I must therefore take away many young girls with me to Norfolk Island. The fashion here is to buy at an early age young girls for their sons, though occasionally a girl may be found not already betrothed, but almost grown up. I now say, "I want to train up wives for my sons," and the fashion of the place allows of my buying or appropriating them. You would be amused to see me engaged in this match-making. It is all the same a very important matter, for clearly it is the best way to secure, as I trust, the introduction of Christian family life among these people.

'George and I are satisfied that things are really very promising here. Of course, much old heathen ignorance, and much that is very wrong, will long survive. So you recollect perhaps old Joe (great-Uncle Edward's coachman) declaring that C. S. as a witch, and there is little proof of practical Christianity in the morals of our peasants of the west, and of Wales especially.

'It is not that one should acquiesce in what is wrong here, but one ought not to be surprised at it. Public opinion, the constraint of law, hereditary notions, are more effective in preventing the outbreak of evil passions into criminal acts in very many cases and districts in England.

'Now these restraints are, indeed, indirect consequences of Christianity, but do not imply any religion in the individuals who are influenced by them. These restraints don't exist here. If they did, I think these Mota people now would live just as orderly decent lives as average English folk. Christianity would not be a vigorous power in the one case or in the other. Exceptional cases would occur here and there.

'If I am asked for proofs of the "conversion" of this people, I should say, "Conversion from what to what?" and then I should say, "Ask any close observer in England about the commercial and social morality existing in not only the most ignorant ranks of society: how much is merely formal, and therefore, perhaps, actually detrimental to a true spirit of religion!" Here you don't find much that you associate with religion in England, in the external observances of it; but there are not a few ignorant people (I am not speaking of our trained scholars) who are giving up their old habits, adopting new ways, accepting a stricter mode of life, foregoing advantages of one kind and another, because they believe that this "Good news," this Gospel, is true, and because the simple truths of Christianity are, thank God, finding some entrance into their hearts.

'I dread the imposition from without of some formal compliances with the externals of religion while I know that the meaning and spirit of them cannot as yet be understood. Can there be conceived anything more formal, more mischievous, than inculcating a rigid Sabbatarian view of the Lord's Day upon a people who don't know anything about the Cross and the Resurrection? Time enough to talk about the observance when the people have some knowledge of the vital living truth of a spiritual religion.

'So about clothing. If I tried to do it, I think I could make the people here buy, certainly accept, and wear, clothing. With what result at present? That they would think that wearing a yard of unbleached calico was a real evidence of the reception of the new teaching.

'Such things are, in this stage of Mission work, actually hurtful. The mind naturally takes in and accepts the easy outward form, and by such treatment you actually encourage it to do so, and to save itself the trouble of thinking out the real meaning and teaching which must of course be addressed to the spirit.

'These outward things all follow as a matter of course after a time, as consequences of the new power and light felt in the soul; but they may be so spoken of as to become substitutes for the true spiritual life, and train up a people in hypocrisy.

'I beg your pardon really for parading all these truisms. Throw it in the fire.

'I don't for a moment mean or think that religion is to be taught by mere prudence and common sense. But a spiritual religion is imperilled the moment that you insist upon an unspiritual people observing outward forms which are to them the essence of the new teaching. Anything better than turning heathens into Pharisees! What did our Lord call the proselytes of the Pharisee and the Scribe?

'And while I see and love the beauty of the outward form when it is known and felt to be no more than the shrine of the inward spiritual power; while I know that for highly advanced Christians, or for persons trained in accurate habits of thought, all that beauty of holiness is needful; yet I think I see that the Divine wisdom of the Gospel would guard the teacher against presenting the formal side of religion to the untaught and ignorant convert. "God is a Spirit, and they that worship Him must worship Him in spirit and in truth," is the great lesson for the heathen mind chained down as it is to things of sense.

'"He that hateth his brother is a murderer:" not the outward act, but the inward motive justifies or condemns the man. Every day convinces me more and more of the need of a different mode of teaching than that usually adopted for imperfectly taught people. How many of your (ordinary) parishioners even understand the simple meaning of the Prayer-book, nay, of their well-known (as they think) Gospel miracles and parables? Who teaches in ordinary parishes the Christian use of the Psalms? Who puts simply before peasant and stone-cutter the Jew and his religion, and what he and it were intended to be, and the real error and sin and failure?—the true nature of prophecy, the progressive teaching of the Bible, never in any age compromising truth, but never ignoring the state, so often the unreceptive state, of those to whom the truth must therefore be presented partially, and in a manner adapted to rude and unspiritual natures? What an amount of preparatory teaching is needed! What labour must be spent in struggling to bring forth things new and old, and present things simply before the indolent, unthinking, vacant mind! How much need there is of a more special training of the Clergy even now! Many men are striving nobly to do all this. But think of the rubbish that most of us chuck lazily out of our minds twice a week without method or order. It is such downright hard work to teach well. Oh! how weary it makes me to try. I feel as if I were at once aware of what should be attempted, and yet quite unable to do it!

'St. Michael's Day.—[After an affectionate review of most of his relations at home.]—When the Bishop and Mrs. Selwyn pressed me a good deal to go with them to England, it obliged me a little to analyse my feelings. You won't suspect me of any want of longing to see you, when I say that it never was a doubtful matter to me for five minutes. I saw nothing to make me wish to go to England in comparison with the crowd of reasons for not doing so. They, good people, thought it would be rest and refreshment to me. Little they know how a man so unlike them takes his rest! I am getting it here, hundreds of miles out of reach of any white man or woman, free from what is to me the bother of society. I am not defending myself; but it is true that to me it is a bore, the very opposite of rest, to be in society. I like a good talk with Sir William Martin above anything, but I declare that even that is dearly purchased by the other accompaniments of society.

'And I could not spend a quiet month with you at Weston. I should have people calling, the greatest of all nuisances, except that of having to go out to dinner. I should have to preach, and perhaps to go to meetings, all in the way of my business, but not tending to promote rest.

'Seriously, I am very well now; looking, I am sure, and feeling stronger and stouter than I was in New Zealand in the winter. So don't fret yourself about me, and don't think that I shouldn't dearly love to chat awhile with you. What an idle, lazy letter. You see I am taking my rest with you, writing without effort.'

He was looking well. Kohimarama must be more healthily situated than the first station, for all his three visits there were beneficial to him; and there seems to have been none of the tendency to ague and low fever which had been the trouble of the first abode.

Mr. Codrington and Mr. Bice came back in the schooner early in October, and were landed at Mota, while the Bishop went for a cruise in the New Hebrides; but the lateness of the season and the state of the vessel made it a short one, and he soon came back with thirty-five boys. Meanwhile, a small harmonium, which was to be left with the Christian settlement, had caused such an excitement that Mr.

Bice was nearly squeezed to death by the crowds that came to hear it. He played nearly all day to successive throngs of men, but when the women arrived, they made such a clatter that he was fain to close the instrument. Unbleached calico clothing had been made for such of the young ladies as were to be taken on board for Norfolk Island, cut out by the Bishop and made up by Robert, William, and Benjamin, his scholars; and Mr. Codrington says, 'It was an odd sight to see the Bishop on the beach with the group of girls round him, and a number of garments over his arm. As each bride was brought by her friends, she was clothed and added to the group.

'Esthetically, clothes were no improvement. "A Melanesian clothed," the Bishop observes, "never looks well; there is almost always a stiff, shabby-genteel look. A good specimen, not disfigured by sores and ulcers, the well-shaped form, the rich warm colour of the skin, and the easy, graceful play of every limb, unhurt by shoe or tight-fitting dress, the flower stuck naturally into the hair, &c., make them look pleasant enough to my eye. You see in Picture Bibles figures draped as I could wish the Melanesians to be clothed."'

To continue Mr. Codrington's recollections of this stay in Mota:—

'I remember noticing how different his manner was from what was common at home. His eyes were cast all about him, keeping a sharp look-out, and all his movements and tones were quick and decisive. In that steaming climate, and those narrow paths, he walked faster than was at all agreeable to his companions, and was dressed moreover in a woollen coat and waistcoat all the time. In fact, he thoroughly enjoyed the heat, though no doubt it was weakening him; he liked the food, which gave him no trouble at all to eat, and he liked the natives.

'He felt, of course, that he was doing his work all the while; but the expression of his countenance was very different while sitting with a party of men over their food at Mota, and when sitting with a party in Norfolk Island.

'The contrast struck me very much between his recluse studious life there, and his very active one at Mota, with almost no leisure to read, and very little to write, and with an abundance of society which was a pleasure instead of a burthen.

'I think that the alert and decisive tone and habit which was so conspicuous in the islands, and came out whenever he was roused, was not natural to his disposition, but had been acquired in early years in a public school, and faded down in the quiet routine of St. Barnabas, and was recalled as occasion required with more effort as time went on. No doubt, his habitual gentleness made his occasional severity more felt, but at Mota his capacity for scolding was held in respect. I was told when I was last there, that I was no good, for I did not know how to scold, but that the Bishop perfectly well understood how to do it. Words certainly would never fail him in twenty languages to express his indignation, but how seldom among his own scholars had he to do it in one!'

This voyage is best summed up in the ensuing letter to one of the Norfolk relations:—

'"Southern Cross" Schooner, 20 miles East of Star Island.

'My dear Cousin,—We are drawing near the end of a rather long cruise, as I trust, in safety. We left Norfolk Island on the 24th June, and we hope to reach it in about ten days. We should have moved about in less time, but for the crippled state of the schooner. She fell in with a heavy gale off Norfolk Island about June 20th-23rd; and we have been obliged to be very careful of our spars, which were much strained. Indeed, we still need a new mainmast, main boom, and gaff, a main topmast, foretopmast, and probably new wire rigging, besides repairs of other kinds, and possibly new coppering. Thank God, the voyage has been so far safe, and, on the whole, prosperous. We sailed first of all to the Banks Islands, only dropping two lads at Ambrym Island on our way. We spent a week or more at Mota, while the vessel was being overhauled at the harbour in Vanua Lava Island, seven miles from Mota. It was a great relief to us to get the house for the station at Mota out of the vessel, the weight of timber, &c., was too much for a vessel not built for carrying freight. After a few days we left Mr. Palmer, George Sarawia, and others at Mota, busily engaged in putting up the house, a very serious matter for us, as you may suppose.

'Our party was made up of Mr. Atkin, Mr. Brooke, and two Mota volunteers for boat work, and divers Solomon Islanders. We were absent from Mota about seven years, during which time we visited Santa Cruz, and many of the Solomon Isles. Mr. Atkin spent three weeks in one of the isles, and Mr. Brooke in another, and we had more than thirty natives of the Solomon Islands on board, including old scholars, when we left Ulava, the last island of the Solomon group at which we called.

'Mr. Palmer, Mr. Atkin, and Mr. Brooke went on to Norfolk Island, the whole number of Melanesians on board being sixty-two. I had spent a very happy month at Mota when the vessel returned from Norfolk Island both with Mr. Codrington and Mr. Bice on board, bringing those of the Melanesians (nearly thirty in all) who chose to stay on Norfolk Island. Then followed a fortnight's cruise in the New Hebrides, and now with exactly fifty Melanesians on board from divers islands, we are on our way to Norfolk Island. We have fourteen girls, two married, on board, and there are ten already at Norfolk Island. This is an unusual number; but the people understand that the young men and lads who have been with us for some time, who are baptized and accustomed to decent orderly ways, are not going to marry heathen wild girls, so they give up these young ones to be taught and qualify to become fit wives for our rapidly increasing party of young men.

'It is quite clear that we must aim at exhibiting, by God's blessing, Christian family life in the islands, and this can only be done by training up young men and women.

'Three married couples, all Communicants, live now at Kohimarama, the station at Mota. George has two children, Benjamin one. It is already a small specimen of a little Christian community, and it must be reinforced, year by year, by accessions of new couples of Christian men and women.

'About twenty lads live at the station, and about forty more come daily to school. It may grow soon into a real working school, from which the most intelligent and best conducted boys may be taken to Norfolk Island for a more complete education. I am hopeful about a real improvement in Mota and elsewhere.

'But a new difficulty has lately been caused by the traders from Sydney and elsewhere, who have taken many people to work in the plantations at Brisbane, Mimea, (New Caledonia), and the Fiji Islands, actual kidnapping, and this is a sad hindrance to us. I know of no case of actual violence in the Banks Islands; but in every case, they took people away under false pretences, asserting that "the Bishop is ill and can't come; he has sent us to bring you to him." "The Bishop is in Sydney, he broke his leg getting into his boat, and has sent us to take you to him," &c., &c. In many of these places some of our old scholars are found who speak a little English, and the traders communicated with them.

'In most places where any of our young people happened to be on shore, they warned their companions against these men, but not always with success. Hindrances there must be always in the way of all attempts to do some good. But this is a sad business, and very discreditable to the persons employed in it and the Government which sanctions it, for they must know that they cannot control the masters of the vessels engaged in the trade; they may pass laws as to the treatment the natives are to receive on the plantations, as to food, pay, &c., the time of service, the date of their being taken home, but they know that the whole thing is dishonest. The natives don't intend or know anything about any service or labour; they don't know that they will have to work hard, and any regular steady work is hard work to South Sea Islanders. They are brought away under false pretences, else why tell lies to induce them to go on board?

'I dare say that many young fellows go on board without much persuasion. Many causes may be at work to induce them to do so, e.g., sickness in the island, quarrels, love of excitement, spirit of enterprise, &c., but if they knew what they were taken for, I don't think they would go.

'November 2nd.—In sight of Norfolk Island. All well on board.

'November 6th.—Yesterday we all landed safely, and found our whole party quite well. Our new hall is finished, and in good time to receive 134 Melanesians.'

Before the full accumulation of letters arrived from Auckland, a report by a passing ship from Sydney stirred the hermit Bishop deeply, and elicited the following warm congratulation:—

'Norfolk Island: November 17, 1869.

'My dear Dr. Moberly,—Since my return—a fortnight since—from the islands a rumour has reached us, brought hither in a small trader, that the Bishop of Winchester has resigned his see, and that you are his successor. It is almost too good to be true. I am waiting with great anxiety for a vessel expected soon; I have had no English news since letters of April. But in all seriousness, private news is of small moment compared with the news of what is to become of that great Diocese. And especially now, when almost all the south of England is so sadly in want of officers to command the Church's army. Exeter, Bath and Wells, Salisbury, Chichester (very old), and till now (if this rumour be true) Winchester, from old age or sickness almost, if not quite, unfit for work. If indeed I hear that God's Providence has placed you in charge of that great see, it will give a different hue to the prospect, dreary enough, I confess, to me; though I hope I am mistaken in my gloomy forebodings of the results of all those many Dioceses being so long without active Bishops. Salisbury of course I except, and Chichester is a small Diocese comparatively, and the good Bishop, I know, works up to the maximum of his age and strength. But if this be a true rumour, and I do sincerely trust and pray that it may be so, indeed it will give hope and courage and fresh life and power to many and many a fainting soul. If I may presume to say so, it is (as Mrs. Selwyn wrote to me when he was appointed to Lichfield) "a solemn and anxious thing to undertake a great charge on the top of such great expectations." But already there is one out here anyhow who feels cheered and strengthened by the mere hope that this story is true; and everywhere many anxious men and women will lift up their hearts to God in thankfulness, and in earnest prayers that you may indeed do a great work to His glory and to the good of His Church in a new and even greater sphere of usefulness. No doubt much of my thoughts and apprehensions about the religious and social state of England is very erroneous. I have but little time for reading about what is going on, and though I have the blessing of Codrington's good sense and ability, yet I should like to have more persons to learn from on such matters. I am willing and anxious to believe that I am not cheerful and faithful enough to see the bright side as clearly as I ought. Your letters have always been a very great help to me; not only a great pleasure, much more than a pleasure. I felt that I accepted, occasionally even that I had anticipated, your remarks on the questions of the day, the conduct of parties and public men, books, &c. It has been a great thing for me to have my thoughts guided or corrected in this way.

'Your last present to me was your volume of "Bampton Lectures," of which I need not say how both the subject and the mode of treating it make them especially valuable just now. And there is a strong personal feeling about the work and writings of one where the public man is also the private friend, which gives a special zest to the enjoyment of reading a work of this kind.

'Certainly it is one of the many blessings of my life that I should somehow have been allowed to grow into this degree of intimacy with you, whom I have always known by name, though I don't remember ever to have seen you. I think I first as a child became familiar with your name through good Miss Rennell, whom I dare say you remember: the old Dean's daughter. What a joy this would have been to dear Mr. and Mrs. Keble; what a joy it is to Charlotte Yonge; and there may be others close to Winchester whose lives have been closely bound up with yours.

'But, humanly speaking, the thing is to have Bishops who can command the respect and love and dutiful obedience of their clergy and laity alike.

'One wants men who, by solid learning, and by acquaintance too with modern modes of criticism and speculation, by scholarship, force of character, largeness of mind, as well as by their goodness, can secure respect and exercise authority. It is the lawlessness of men that one deplores; the presumption of individual priests striking out for themselves unauthorised ways of managing their parishes and officiating in their churches. And, if I may dare to touch on such a subject, is there not a mode of speaking and writing on the Holy Eucharist prevalent among some men now, which has no parallel in the Church of England, except, it may be, in some of the non-jurors, and which does not express the Church of England's mind; which is not the language of Pearson, and Jackson, and Waterland, and Hooker, no, nor of Bull, and Andrewes, and Taylor, &c.? I know very little of such things—very little indeed. But it is oftentimes a sad grief to me that I cannot accept some of the reasonings and opinions of dear Mr. Keble in his book on "Eucharistic Adoration." I know that I have no right to expect to see things as such a man saw them: that most probably the instinctive power of discerning truth—the reward of a holy life from early childhood—guided him where men without such power feel all astray. But yet, there is something about the book which may be quite right and true, but does not to me quite savour of the healthy sound theology of the Church of England; the fragrance is rather that of an exotic plant; here and there I mean—though I feel angry with myself for daring to think this, and to say it to you, who can understand him.

'November 27th.—I leave this as I wrote it, though now I know from our mails, which have come to us, that you are Bishop of Salisbury, not of Winchester. I hardly stop to think whether it is Winchester or Salisbury, so great is my thankfulness and joy at the report being substantially true. Though it did seem that Winchester was a natural sphere for you, I can't help feeling that at Salisbury you can do (D.V.) what perhaps scarcely any one else could do. And now I rejoice that you have had the opportunity of speaking with no uncertain sound in your "Bampton Lectures." Anyone can tell what the Bishop of Salisbury holds on the great questions of Church Doctrine and Church Government. The diocese knows already its Bishop, not only by many former but by his latest book. Surely you will have the confidence of all Churchmen, and be blessed to do a great work for the glory of God and the edification of the Church.

'And now, my dear Bishop of Salisbury, you will excuse my writing on so freely, too freely I fear. I do like to think of you in that most perfect of Cathedrals. I hope and trust that you will have ere long, right good fellow-workers in Exeter, Winton, and Bath and Wells.

'But in the colonies you have a congeries of men from all countries, and with every variety of creed, jumbled up together, with nothing whatever to hold them together—no reverence—no thoughts of the old parish church, &c. They are restless, worldly people to a great extent, thinking of getting on, making money. To such men the very idea of the Church as a Divine Institution, the mystical Body of the Lord, on which all graces are bestowed, and through whose ministrations men are trained in holiness and truth, is wholly unknown. The personal religion of many a man is sincere; his position and duty as a Churchman he has never thought about. I wish the clergy would master that part, at all events, of your Lectures which deals with this great fundamental point, and then, as they have opportunity, teach it to their people. And by-and-by, through the collective life of the Church in its synods, &c., many will come to see it, we may hope.

'I think that I may give you a cheering account of ourselves. I was nineteen weeks in the islands—met with no adventures worth mentioning, only one little affair which was rather critical for a few minutes, but ended very well—and in some of the Solomon Islands made more way than heretofore with the people.

We have 134 Melanesians here and a baby. George Sarawia and his wife and two children, and two other married couples—all Communicants—are at Mota, in a nice place, with some twenty-two lads "boarding" with them, and about thirty more coming to daily school.

'The vessel was much knocked about in a violent gale in June off Norfolk Island, and we had to handle her very carefully. The whole voyage was made with a mainmast badly sprung, and fore topmast very shaky. Mr. Tilly was very watchful over the spars, and though we had a large share of squally weather, and for some days, at different times, were becalmed in a heavy swell, the most trying of all situations to the gear of a vessel, yet, thank God, all went well, and I have heard of the schooner safe in Auckland harbour. About forty of our Melanesians here are Solomon Islanders, from seven different islands; a few came from the New Hebrides, the rest from the Banks Islands. We are already pretty well settled down to our work. Indeed, it took only a day or two to get to work; our old scholars are such great helpers to us. We number six clergymen here (G. Sarawia being at Mota). Ten or twelve of the sixth form are teachers. If you care to hear more; I must refer you to a letter just written to Miss Yonge. But it is not easy to write details about 134 young people. Their temptations are very great when they return to their islands; every inducement to profligacy, &c., is held out to them. One of our young baptized lads fell into sinful ways, and is not now with us. He was not one of whom we had great expectations, though we trusted that he would go on steadily. Many others, thank God, were kept pure and truthful in the midst of it all, refusing even to sleep one night away from our little hut, and in some cases refusing even to leave the schooner. "No, I will wait till I am married," said two lads to me, who were married here to Christian girls on November 24th, "and then go ashore for a time with my young wife. I don't think I should yield, but I don't want to put myself in the way of such temptations." And so, when I had naturally expected that they would take their six weeks' holiday on shore, while the "Southern Cross" went from Mota to Norfolk Island and back (during my stay at Mota), they remained on board, rejoining me, as they were two of my boating crew, for the New Hebrides trip! This was very comforting. And when I married three couples on November 24th, and knew that they were pure, youths and girls alike, from the great sin of heathenism, you can well think that my heart was very full of thankfulness and hope.

'I must end my long letter. How will you find time to read it? Send me some day a photograph of your beautiful Cathedral.

'Yours very faithfully,

'J. C. PATTESON.'

Before the letter to which Bishop Moberly is referred, Mr. Codrington's bit about the weddings seems appropriate:—

'These wedding days were great festivals, especially before many had been seen. The Chapel was dressed with flowers, the wedding party in as new and cheerful attire as could be procured, the English Marriage Service translated into Mota. We make rings out of sixpences or threepenny bits. The place before is full of the sound of the hammer tapping the silver on the marlingspike. The wedding ceremony is performed with as much solemnity as possible, all the school present in their new clothes and with flowers in their hair. There is even a kind of processional Psalm as the wedding party enters the Chapel. There is of course a holiday, and after the service they all go off, taking with them the pig that has been killed for the feast. An enormous quantity of plum pudding awaits them when, in the evening, they come back to prayers and supper. Rounds of hearty cheers, led off by the Bishop, used to complete the day. Weddings of this kind between old scholars, christened, confirmed, and trustworthy, represented much anxiety and much teaching and expense, but they promise so much, and that so near of what has been worked for, that they have brought with them extraordinary pleasure and satisfaction.'

'Norfolk Island: November 24, 1869.

'My dear Cousin,—To-day we married three young couples: the bridegrooms. Robert Pantatun, William Pasvorang, and Marsden Sawa, who have been many years with us, and are all Communicants; the brides, Emily Milerauwe, Lydia Lastitia, and Rhoda Titrakrauwe, who were baptized a year ago.

'The Chapel was very prettily dressed up with lilies and many other flowers. The bridegrooms wore white trousers, shirts, &c., the brides wore pretty simple dresses and flowers in their hair. We crowded as many persons as possible into our little Chapel. Mr. Nobbs and some ten or twelve of our Pitcairn friends were all the visitors that we could manage to make room for.

'Great festivities followed, a large pig was killed yesterday and eaten to-day, and Mr. Palmer had manufactured puddings without end, a new kind of food to many of the present set of scholars, but highly appreciated by most of them. Then followed in the evening native dances and songs, and a supper to end with, with cheers for the brides and bridegrooms.

'There are now six married couples here, three more at Mota, and one or two more weddings will take place soon. Very fortunately, a vessel came from Auckland only three or four days ago, the first since the "Southern Cross," in June, It brought not only five mails for us English folk, but endless packages and boxes for the Mission, ordered by us long ago, stores, clothing, &c. We had all ordered more or less in the way of presents for scholars, and though we keep most of these treasures for Christmas gifts, yet some are distributed now.

'These presents are for the most part really good things. It is quite useless for kind friends to send presents to Melanesians as they would do to an English lad or girl. To begin with, most of our scholars are grown up, and are more like English young people of twenty or eighteen years old than like boys and girls, and not a few are older still; and secondly, no Melanesian, old or young, cares a rush about a toy. They, boys and girls, men and women, take a practical view of a present, and are the very reverse of sentimental about it, though they really do like a photograph of a friend. But a mere Brummagem article that won't stand wear is quite valueless in their eyes.

'Whatever is given them, cheap or dear, is estimated according to its usefulness; and whatever is given, though it may cost but a shilling, must be good of its kind. For example, a rough-handled, single-bladed knife, bought for a shilling, they fully appreciate; but a knife with half-a-dozen blades, bought for eighteen-pence, they would almost throw away. And so about everything else. I mention this as a hint to kind friends. They do like to hear that people think of them and are kind to them, but they don't understand why useless things should be sent from the other end of the world when they could buy much better things with their own money out of the mission store here.

'They are very fond of anything in the way of notebooks, 8vo and 12mo sizes (good paper), writing-cases (which must be good if given at all), patent safety inkstands—these things are useful on board ship, and can be carried to the islands and brought back again safely. Work-baskets or boxes for the girls, with good serviceable needles, pins, thread, scissors, thimbles, tapes, &c. &c., not a plaything. Here we can buy for them, or keep in the store for them to buy, many things that are much too bulky to send from a distance, the freight would be ruinous. The "Southern Cross" brings them usually to us. Such things I mean as good carpet-bags, from 5s. to 10s., stout tin boxes with locks and keys, axes, tools, straw hats, saucepans, good strong stuff (tweed or moleskin) for trousers and shirts, which they cut out and make up for themselves, quite understanding the inferior character of "slop" work, good flannel for under-shirts, or for making up into Crimean shirts, Nottingham drill, good towelling, huckaback, &c., ought to be worth while to send out, and if bought in large quantities at the manufacturer's, it would pay us to get it in England, especially if the said manufacturer reduced the price a little in consequence of the use to be made of his goods.

'Dull small blue beads are always useful, ditto red. Bright glittering ones are no use, few Melanesians would take them as a gift. Some islanders like large beads, as big or bigger than boys' marbles. These are some hints to any kind people who may wish to contribute in kind rather than in money.

'Mr. Codrington has given these fellows a great taste for gardening. Much of their spare hours (which are not many) are spent in digging up, fencing in and preparing little pieces of land close about the station, two or three lads generally making up a party, and frequently the party consists of lads and young men from different islands. Then they have presents of seeds, cuttings, bulbs, &c., from Mr. Codrington chiefly, and Mrs. Palmer and others contribute. Some of these little gardens are really very nicely laid out in good taste and well looked after. They have an eye to the practically useful here too, as every garden has its stock of bananas, and here and there we see the sugar-cane too.

'From 3.30 P.M. to 6 P.M. is the play time, although they do not all have this time to themselves. For three lads must milk from 5 to 6, one or two must drive in the cows, seven or eight are in the kitchen, three or four must wash the horses, one must drive the sheep into the fold, all but the milkers have only their one week of these diverse occupations. There are about twelve head cooks, who choose their helpers (the whole school, minus the milkers and two or three overlookers, being included), and so the cooking work comes only once in twelve weeks. The cooks of the one week drive up the cows and water the horses the next week, and then there is no extra work, that is, nothing but the regular daily work from 9.30 A.M. after school to 1 P.M. Wednesday is a half-holiday, Saturday a whole holiday. There are six milkers, one of whom is responsible for the whole. One receives 2s. 0d. per week, his chief mate 1s. 6d., and the other four 1s. each. They take it in turns, three each week. This is the hardest work in one sense; it brings them in from their play and fishing, or gardening, &c., and so they are paid for it. We do not approve of the white man being paid for everything, and the Melanesian being expected to work habitually extra hours for nothing. There are many other little extra occupations for which we take care that those engaged in them shall have some reward, and as a matter of fact a good deal of money finds its way into the hands of the storekeeper, and a very fair amount of 3d., 4d. and 6d. pieces may be seen every Sunday in the offertory bason.

'Perhaps I should say that we have seldom seen here any indications of these Melanesians expecting money or presents; but we want to destroy the idea in their minds of their being fags by nature, and to help them to have some proper self-respect and independence of character. We see very little in them to make us apprehensive of their being covetous or stingy, and indisposed to give service freely.

'School hours 8-9.20, 2-3.30, singing 7-8 P.M., chapel 6.45 A.M., 6.30 P.M.

'Of the 134 Melanesians, besides the baby, ten are teachers, and with their help we get on very fairly. There are sixteen of us teachers in all, so that the classes are not too large.

'Mr. Codrington takes at present the elder Banks Islanders, Mr. Palmer the next class, and Mr. Bice the youngest set of boys from the same group.

'Mr. Atkin takes the Southern Solomon Islanders, and Mr. Brooke those from the northern parts of the same group. I have been taking some Leper's Islanders and Maiwo or Aurora Islanders as new comers, and other classes occasionally.

'Out of so many we shall weed out a good number no doubt. At present we don't condemn any as hopelessly dull, but it will not be worth while to spend much time upon lads who in five months must go home for good, and some such there must be; we cannot attempt to teach all, dull and clever alike. We must make selections, and in so doing often, I dare say, make mistakes. But what can we do?

'Our new hall is a great success. We had all the framework sawn out here; it is solid, almost massive work, very unlike the flimsy wooden buildings that are run up in a week or two in most colonial villages. It is so large that our party of 145, plus 9 English, sit in the aisles without occupying any part of the middle of the room. This gives us ample accommodation for the present. Indeed we might increase our numbers to 200 without any more buildings being necessary. The married people give the most trouble in this respect, as they have their separate rooms, and four or five married couples take up more room than three times the number of single folk. However we have here room for all, I am thankful to say, though we must build again if more of our young people take it into their heads to be married. They pass on quickly, however, when married, into the next stage, the life in their own islands, and so they leave their quarters here for some successors.

'I hope you can understand this attempt at a description, but I never could write properly about such things, and never shall do so, I suppose. I like the life, I know, a great deal better than I can write about it. Indeed, it is a quiet restful life here, comparatively. Some anxieties always, of course, but, as compared with the distractions of New Zealand life, it is pleasant indeed. We have very few interruptions here to the regular employment of our time, and need not waste any of it in visits or small talk, which seems to be a necessary, though most wearisome part of civilised life.

'Your namesake goes on well; not a clever girl, but very steady and good; her sister and brother are here; the sisters are much alike in character and ability, the brother is sharper. You will, I know, specially think of George Sarawia and his wife Sarah at Mota, with Charles and Ellen, Benjamin and Marion. They are all Communicants, but the temptations which surround them are very great, and early familiarity with heathen practices and modes of thought may yet deaden the conscience to the quick apprehension of the first approaches of sin. They do indeed need the earnest prayers of all.

'Your affectionate Cousin,

'**J. C. PATTESON.**'

How many sons who have lost a mother at fifteen or sixteen dwell on the thought like this affectionate spirit, twenty-seven years later?

'Advent Sunday, November 20, 1869.

'It is a solemn thing to begin a new year on the anniversary of our dear Mother's death. I often think whether she would approve of this or that opinion, action, &c. Wright's painting is pleasant to look upon. I stand in a corner of my room, at father's old mahogany desk. Her picture and his, the large framed photographs from Richmond's drawing, and a good photograph of the Bishop are just above. I wish you could see my room. I write now on December 3, a bright summer day, but my room with its deep verandah is cool and shady. It is true that I refuse carpet and curtains. They only hold dust and make the room fusty. But the whole room is filled with books, and those pictures, and the Lionardo da Vinci over the fireplace, and Mr. Boxall's photograph over it, and his drawing vis-a-vis to it at the other end of the room, and by my window a splendid gloxinia with fine full flowers out in a very pretty porcelain pot, both Mr. Codrington's gift. On another glass stand (also his present) a Mota flower imported here, a brilliant scarlet hibiscus, and blossoms of my creepers and bignonia, most beautiful. So fresh and pretty. The steps of the verandah are a mass of honeysuckle. The stephanotis, with the beautiful scented white flowers and glossy leaves, covers one of the posts. How pleasant it is. Everyone is kind, all are well, all are going on well just now. Such are missionary comforts. Where the hardships are I have not yet discovered. Your chain, dear Joan, is round my neck, and the locket (Mamma's) in which you, Fan, put the hair of you five, hangs on it.

'I am dipping my pen into the old silver inkstand which used to be in the front drawing-room. Every morning at about 5 A.M. I have a cup of tea or coffee, and use Grandmamma Coleridge's old-fashioned silver cream-jug, and the cup and saucer which Augusta sent out years ago, my old christening spoon, and the old silver tea-pot and salver. Very grand, but I like the old things.

'This day fortnight (D.V.) I ordain J. Atkin and C. H. Brooke Priests.

'I have no time to answer your April and September letters. I rejoice with all my heart to hear of Dr. Moberly's appointment. What a joyful event for Charlotte Yonge. That child Pena sent me Shairp's (dear old Shairp) book, which I wanted. I must write to Sophy as soon as I can. You will forgive if I have seemed to be, or really have been, unmindful of your sorrows and anxieties. Sometimes I think I am in too great a whirl to think long enough to realise and enter into all your doings.

'Your loving Brother,

'J. C. P.'

The intended letter to Mrs. Martyn was soon written. The death there referred to was that of Mrs. William Coleridge, widow of the Bishop of Barbadoes:—

'Norfolk Island: December 14, 1869.

'My dear Sophy,—I should be specially thinking of you as Christmas draws nigh with its blessed thoughts, and hopes, and the St. Stephen's memories in any case I should be thinking of you. But now I have lately received your long loving letter of last Eastertide, partly written in bed.

Then your dear child's illness makes me think greatly (and how lovingly!) of you three of the three generations. Lastly, I hear of dear Aunt William's death. You know that I had a very great affection for her, and I feel that this is a great blow probably to you all, though dear Aunty (as I have noticed in all old persons, especially when good as well as old) takes this quietly, I dare say. The feeling must be, "Well, I shall soon meet her again; a few short days only remain."

'I suppose that you, with your quarter of a century's widowhood, still feel as if the waiting time was all sanctified by the thought of the reunion. Oh! what a thought it is: too much almost to think that by His wonderful mercy, one may hope to be with them all, and for ever; to behold the faces of Apostles, and Apostolic men, and Prophets, and Saints, holy men and women; and, as if this were not enough, to see Him as He is, in His essential perfections, and to know Him. One can't sustain the effort of such a thought, which shows how great a change must pass on one before the great Consummation. Well, the more one can think of dear Father and Mother, and dear dear Uncle James and Uncle Frank, and Cousin George, and Uncle and Aunt William, others too, uncles and aunts, and your dear Fanny, and your husband, though it would be untrue to say I knew him, taken so early—the more one thinks of them all the better. And I have, Sophy, so many very different ones to think of Edwin and Fisher, and so many Melanesians taken away in the very first earnestness and simplicity of a new convert's faith. How many have died in my arms—God be thanked—in good hope!

'If by His great mercy there be a place for me there, I feel persuaded that I shall there find many of those dear lads, whom indeed I think of with a full heart, full of affection and thankfulness.

'I have been reading the "Memoir of Mr. Keble," of course with extreme interest. It is all about events and chiefly about persons that one has heard about or even known. I think we get a little autobiography of our dear Uncle John in it too, for which I don't like it the less.

There are passages, as against going to Rome, which I am glad to see in print; they are wanted now again, I fear. I am glad you like Moberly's "Bampton Lectures." His book on "The Great Forty Days," his best book (?) after all, has the germ of it all. I am so thankful for his appointment to Salisbury. I dare say you know that he is kind enough to write to me occasionally; and he sends me his books, one of the greatest of the indirect blessings of being known to Mr. Keble. I do very little in the way of reading, save that I get a quiet hour for Hebrew, 5-6 A.M., and I do read some theology. In one sense it is easier reading to me than other books, history, poetry, because, though I don't know much about it, I know nothing about them.

'My pleasure would be, if with you, in talking over such little insight as I may have received into the wondrous harmony and symmetry of the whole Bible, by tolerably close examination of the text of the Greek, and to some extent of the Hebrew. The way in which a peculiar word brings a whole passage or argument en rapport with a train of historical associations or previous statements is wonderful; e.g., the verb of which Moses is formed occurs only in Exodus ii. 10, 2 Samuel xxii. 17, Psalm xviii. 16. See how the magnificent description of the Passage of the Red Sea in Psalm xviii. is connected with Moses by this one word. These undesigned coincidences, and (surely) proofs of inspiration are innumerable.

'I do delight in it: only I want more help, far more. We have great advantages in this generation. Dear Uncle James had no Commentary, one might almost say, on Old Testament or New Testament. Ellicott, Wordsworth, and Alford on the New Testament were not in existence; and the Germans, used with discrimination, are great helps. An orthodox Lutheran, one Delitzsch (of whom Liddon wrote that Dr. Pusey thinks highly of his Hebrew scholarship), helps me much in Isaiah. He has sucked all the best part out of Vitringa's enormous book, and added much minute, and I am told correct criticism. And how grand it is! This morning—it is now 6.15 A.M.—I have been reading part of that wonderful chapter xxvi.

'It strikes me that the way to teach a class or a congregation is to bring out the doctrine from the very words of Scripture carefully, critically examined and explained. Only think, Sophy, of the vague desultory way in which we all, more or less, read; and we have accepted a phraseology without enquiring to a great extent, and use words to which we attach no definite meaning. Few in the congregation could draw out in clear words what they mean when they talk of faith, justification, regeneration, conversion, &c. &c. All language denoting ideas and thoughts is transferred to the region of the mind from denoting at first only external objects and sensations. This is in accordance with the mystery of all, the union of mind and matter—which no pagan philosopher could comprehend— the extreme difficulty of solving which caused Dualism and Asceticism on the one hand, and neglect of all bodily discipline on the other. Mind and matter must be antagonistic, the work of different beings: man must get rid of his material part to arrive at his true end and perfection.

'So some said, "Mortify, worry the body, which is essentially and inherently evil." "No," said others, "the sins of the body don't hurt the mind; the two things are distinct, don't react on one another." (St. Paul deals with all this in the Colossians.)

The Incarnation is the solution or the culmination of the mystery.

'What a prose! but I meant, that people so often use words as if the use of a word was equivalent to the knowledge of the thought which, in the mind of an accurate thinker, accompanies the utterance of the word.

'I should think that three-fourths of what we clergymen say is unintelligible to the mass of the congregation. We assume an acquaintance with the Bible and Prayer-book, thought, and a knowledge of the meaning of words which few, alas! possess. We must begin, then, with the little ones; as far as I see, all children are apt to fail at the point when they ought to be passing from merely employing the memory (in learning by heart, e.g., the Catechism) by exercising the reasoning and thinking faculty.

'"Well now, you have said that very well, now let us think what it means."

'How well Dr. Pusey says, in his Sermons, "Not altogether intentional deliberate vice, but thoughtlessness is destroying souls."

'I run on at random, dear Sophy, hoping to give you one and a half hour's occupation on a sick bed or couch, and because, as you say, this is the only converse we are likely to have on earth.

'I think I am too exclusively fond of this reading, very little else interests me. I take up a theological book as a recreation, which is, perhaps, hardly reverent, and may narrow the mind; but even Church history is not very attractive to me. I like Jackson and Hooker, and some of the moderns, of whom I read a good many; and I lose a good deal of time in diving into things too deep by half for me, while I forget or don't learn simple things.

'All this modern rage for reviews, serials, magazines, I can't abide. My mind is far too much distracted already, and that fragmentary mode of reading is very bad for many people, I am sure.

'Naturally enough at forty-two years of age ninety-nine hundredths of the "lighter" books seem to me mere rubbish. They come to me occasionally. However, there are younger ones here, so it isn't sheer waste to receive such donations: they soon get out of my room. Not, mind you, that I think this the least evidence of my being wiser, or employing my time more carefully than other folk. Only I want you to know what I am, and what I think.

'Pena has sent me a nice book which I wanted: 1st. Because I have a great personal liking for Shairp, a simple-minded, affectionate man, with much poetical feeling and good taste-a kindly-natured man. 2nd. Because he writes in an appreciative kind of way, and is the very opposite of .... whom I can't stand with his insufferable self-sufficiency, and incapacity for appreciating the nobler, simpler, more generous natures who are unlike him. Well! that is fierce. But there is a school of men whom I can't stand. Their nature repels me, and I hardly wish to like them; which is an evil feeling.

'I shall add a line in a few days.

'My very dearest love to Aunty—dear Aunty; and if I can't write to Pena, give her my best love and thanks for her book.

'Dear Sophy, your loving Cousin,

'J. C. P.'

Two other letters, one to each of the sisters, were in progress at this time. To Joanna, who had been grieved for the poor girl whose transgression had occurred in the beginning of the year, he says:—

'About Semtingvat, you must be comforted about her. For a poor child who, two short years before, had assumed as a matter of course that a woman simply existed to be a man's slave in every kind of way, her fault could not, I think, be regarded as very great. Indeed, there was much comfort from the first; and since that time they not only have gone on well, but I do believe that their religious character has been much strengthened by the kind of revelation they then obtained of what Christianity really does mean. Anyhow, all notice the fact that U —— has improved very much, and they all sing Semtingvat's praises. I had no difficulty about marrying them after a little while. I spoke openly in chapel to everyone about it. Their wedding was not as other weddings—no festivity, no dressing of the chapel, no feast, no supper and fun and holiday. It was perfectly understood to be in all respects different from a bright, happy wedding. But it was quite as much for the sake of all, for the sake of enforcing the new teaching about the sanctity of marriage, that we made so very much of what (as men speak) was under the circumstances a comparatively light fault, less than an impure thought on the part of such as have been taught their duty from their childhood.

'I am almost confused with the accounts from England. All seems in a state of turmoil and confusion; all the old landmarks being swept away by a deluge of new opinions as to all matters civil and ecclesiastical. I don't think that we ought to refuse to see these signs of a change in men's mode of regarding great political and religious questions. A man left high and dry on the sand-bank of his antiquated notions will do little good to the poor folk struggling in the sea way, though he is safer as far as he is himself concerned by staying where he is than by plunging in to help them.

'It is a critical time in every sense. Men and women can hardly be indifferent; they must be at the pains of making up their minds. As for us clergy, everywhere but in Norfolk Island, we must know that people are thinking of matters which all were content a few years ago to keep back in silence, and that they expect us to speak about them. How thankful I am that we fortunate ones are exempt from this. Yet in my way I, too, try to think a bit about what is going on; and I don't want to be too gloomy, or to ignore some good in all this ferment in men's minds. It is better than stagnation and indolent respectability. There is everywhere a consciousness of a vast work to be done, and sincere efforts are made to do it. I suppose that is a fact; many, many poor souls are being taught and trained for heaven through all these various agencies which seem to a distant and idle critic to be so questionable in some ways.

'Of old one thought that the sober standard of Church of England divinity was the rule to which all speculations should be reduced; and one thought that Pearson, Hooker, Waterland, Jeremy Taylor also, and Andrewes, and Bull, and Jackson, and Barrow, &c., stood for the idea of English divinity. Now we are launched upon a wider sea. Catholic usage and doctrine take the place of Church of England teaching and practice; rightly, I dare say, only it may be well to remember that men who can perhaps understand a good deal of the English divines, can hardly be supposed to be equally capable of understanding the far wider and more difficult range of ecclesiastical literature of all ages and all writers.

'Everyone knows and is struck by the fact that passages of old writers are continually quoted by men of quite different schools of thought in favour of their own (different) views. Clearly they can't both understand the mind and spirit of these writers; and the truth is, isn't it, that only they who by very long study, and from a large share of the true historical imagination, sympathise with and really enter into the hearts and minds of these writers, are competent to deal with and decide upon such wide and weighty matters?

'It seems to me as if men who are in no sense divines, theologians, or well read, speak strongly and use expressions and teach doctrines which, indeed, only very few men should think of uttering or teaching.

'And yet, don't think I wish to be only an exclusive Anglican, without sympathy for East or West; still less that I wish to ignore the Catholic Church of the truly primitive times; but I take the real, so to say, representative teaching of the Church of England to be the divinity of the truly primitive Church, to which our formularies and reformers appeal. I know, moreover, that our dear Father accepted Jackson and Waterland; and I don't feel disposed to disparage them, as it is the fashion to do nowadays. Few men, in spite of occasional scholastic subtlety, go so deep in their search right down into principles as Jackson. Few men so analyse, dissect, search out the precise, exact meaning of words and phrases, so carry you away from vague generalities to accurate defined meanings and doctrines. He had an honest and clear brain of his own, though he was a tremendous book-worm; and I think he is a great authority, though I know about him and his antagonism to Rome. I don't fear to weary you by this kind of talk; but don't I wish I could hear three or four of our very best men discuss these points thoroughly. In all sincerity I believe that I should be continually convinced of error, shallow judgments, and ignorance. But then I should most likely get real light on some points where I would fain have it.'

To this unconscious token of humility, another must be added, from the same letter, speaking of two New Zealand friends:—'To me she has always been kindness itself, with her husband overrating me to such an amusing extent that I don't think it hurt even my vanity.'

Full preparation was going on for the ordination, of the two priests.

No special account of the actual service seems to have been written; and the first letter of January was nearly absorbed by the tidings of the three Episcopal appointments of the close of 1869, the Oxford choice coming near to Bishop Patteson by his family affections, and the appointment to Exeter as dealing with his beloved county at home.

And now, before turning the page, and leaving the period that had, on the whole, been full of brightness, will be the best time to give Mr. Codrington's account of the manner of life at St. Barnabas, while the Bishop was still in his strength:—

'Certainly one of the most striking points to a stranger would have been the familiar intercourse between the Bishop and his boys, not only the advanced scholars, but the last and newest comers. The kindly and friendly disposition of the Melanesians leads to a great deal of free and equal familiarity even where there are chiefs, and the obsequious familiarity of which one hears in India is here quite unknown. Nevertheless, I doubt very much whether other Melanesians live in the same familiarity with their missionaries—e.g., Carry, wife of Wadrokala, writes thus:—"I tremble very much to write to you, I am not fit to write to you, because, does an ant know how to speak to a cow? We at Nengone would not speak to a great man like you; no, our language is different to a chief and a missionary."

'Making every allowance, and, looking at the matter from within, that perfect freedom and affectionateness of intercourse that existed with him seems very remarkable.

'The secret of it is not far to seek. It did not lie in any singular attractiveness of his manner only, but in the experience that everyone attracted gained that he sought nothing for himself; he was entirely free from any desire to be admired, or love of being thought much of, as he was from love of commanding for the sake of being obeyed. The great temptations to missionaries among savage people, as it seems, are to self-esteem, from a comparison of themselves with their European advantages and the natives among whom they live; and to a domineering temper, because they find an obedience ready, and it is delightful to be obeyed. Bishop Patteson's natural disposition was averse to either, and the principles of missionary work which he took up suited at once his natural temper and his religious character. He was able naturally, without effort, to live as a brother among his black brothers, to be the servant of those he lived to teach. The natural consequence of this was, the unquestioned authority which he possessed over those with whom he lived on equal terms. No one could entertain the idea that anything was ordered from a selfish motive, for any advantage to himself, or that anything was forbidden without some very good reason. This familiarity with a superior, which is natural with Melanesians, is accompanied, especially in Banks Islanders, with a very great reserve about anything that touches the feelings or concerns character. Thus a boy, who would use the Bishop's room as if it were his own, coming in unasked, to read or write, or sit by the fire there, would with very great difficulty get over the physical trembling, which their language implies, that would come upon him, if he wished to speak about his own feelings on religious matters, or to tell him something which he well knew it was his duty to make known. When one knows how difficult it is to them to speak openly, their openness with the Bishop is more appreciated, though he indeed often enough complained of their closeness with him. The real affection between the boys and the Bishop required no acquaintance with the character of either to discern, and could surprise no one who knew anything of the history of their relation one to another. It is well known that he wished his elder boys to stand in the place of the sixth form of a public school; and to some extent they did so, but being mostly Banks Islanders, and Banks Islanders being peculiarly afraid of interfering with one another, his idea was never reached. Still no doubt a good deal is attained when they arrive rather at the position of pupil-teacher in a National School; and this at least they occupy very satisfactorily, as is shown by the success with which so large a school has been carried on since the Bishop's death. No doubt the Ordination of more from among their number would go far to raise them in their own estimation.

'In truth, the carrying out of the principle of the equality of black and white in a missionary work, which is the principle of this mission, is very difficult, and cannot be done in all particulars in practice by anyone, and by most people, unless brought up to it, probably not at all. Nevertheless, it is practicable, and, as we think, essential, and was in all main points carried out by Bishop Patteson. But the effect of this must not be exaggerated. It is true that we have no servants, yet a boy regularly brought water, &c., for the Bishop, and a woman regularly swept and cleaned his rooms, and received regular wages for it. The Bishop never cooked his dinner or did any such work except upon occasions on which a bachelor curate in England does much of the kind, as a matter of course. The extraordinary thing is that it is, as he at any rate supposed, the custom in other missions to make scholars and converts servants as a matter of course; and the difference lies not in the work which is done or not done by the one party or the other, but in the social relation of equality which subsists between them, and the spirit in which the work is asked for and rendered.

'The main thing to notice about the Bishop is that there was nothing forced or unnatural in his manner of taking a position of equality, and equality as real in any way as his superiority in another. Consequently, there was never the least loss of dignity or authority on his part.

'There never was visible the smallest diminution of freedom and affection in the intercourse that went on. It required some knowledge in one respect to appreciate the extraordinary facility with which he conversed with boys from various islands. A stranger would be struck with his bright smiles and sweet tones as he would address some little stranger who came into his room; but one who knew a little of the languages alone could know with what extraordinary quickness he passed from one language to another, talking to many boys in their own language, but accommodating his tongue with wonderful readiness to each in succession. It would be hard to say how many languages he could speak; those which he spoke quite freely, to my knowledge, were not so many: Mota, Bauro, Mahaga, and Nengone, certainly; some others no doubt quite readily when among the people who spoke them; and very many only with a small vocabulary which was every instant being enlarged. It does not appear to me that his scientific philological acquirements were extraordinary; but that his memory for words giving him such a command of vocabulary, and so wide a scope for comparison, and his accurate and delicate ear to catch the sounds, and power of reproducing them, were altogether wonderful and very rarely equalled. A man of his faculty of expression and powers of mind could not speak like a native; he spoke better than a native, than a native of Mota at least. That is that, although no doubt he never was quite master of the little delicate points of Mota scholarship, which no one not a native can keep quite right, and no native can account for, yet his vocabulary was so large and accurate, and his feeling of the native ways of looking at things and representing them in words so true, that he spoke to them more clearly and forcibly than even any native spoke, and with the power of an educated mind controlling while following the native taste. He was an enthusiast, no doubt, about these languages, and jealous of their claim to be considered true language, and not what people suppose them to be, the uncouth jargon of savages. I will only say that his translations of some of the Psalms into Mota are as lofty in their diction and as harmonious in their rhythm, in my estimation, as anything almost I read in any language. This no doubt sounds exaggerated, and must be taken only for what it is worth.

'It was probably in a great measure because his natural power of acquiring languages was so extraordinary, and needed so very little labour in him, that he did so very little to put on paper what he knew of all those many tongues. All there is in print I have put together. Besides this, he carried the same unfortunate way of leaving off what he had begun into these notes on language also. In the year '63-'64 he got printed a number of small grammatical papers in almost all the languages he knew, because he felt he ought not to subject them to the risk of being lost. Another reason why he did not go into any laborious manuscript or printing work with the various languages was, that he saw as time went on, first, that it was so very uncertain what language would come in practice into request; and, secondly, that one language would suffice for the use, in practice, of all natives of a neighbourhood. For example, the language of part of Mae (Three Hills), in the New Hebrides, was once studied and well known. Nothing whatever came of the intercourse with that island, once so constant, I don't know why, and now the people themselves are destroyed almost, and hopes of doing them good destroyed by the slave trade. And, secondly, the use of the Mota language in our ordinary intercourse here has very much diminished the need for any one's knowing a particular language beyond the missionary who has charge of the boys who speak it. Thus the Bishop rather handed over the language of Bauro to Mr. Atkin, of Florida to Mr. Brooke, of Leper's Island to Mr. Price; and as the common teaching of all boys who belonged to either of the principal groups into which the school fell went on in Mota, there was no practical use in the other tongues the Bishop knew, except in his voyages, and in giving him more effectual powers of influencing those to whom he could speak in their own tongue. Besides, he saw so clearly the great advantage, on the one hand, of throwing together in every possible way the boys from all the islands, which was much helped by the use of one language, and, on the other hand, the natural tendency in a group of boys from one island or neighbourhood to keep separate, and of the teacher of a particular set to keep them separate with himself, that, without saying much about it, he discouraged the printing of other languages besides Mota, and in other ways kept them rather in the background. How things would have arranged themselves if Mota had not by circumstances come into such prominence I cannot say, but the predominance of Mota came in with the internal organisation of the Mission by Mr. Pritt. It is impossible for one who knew

Bishop Patteson intimately, and the later condition of the Mission intimately, to lose sight for long of Mr. Pritt's influence and his useful work.'

Perhaps this chapter can best be completed by the external testimony of a visitor to Norfolk Island, given in a letter to the Editor of the 'Australian Churchman':—

'Daily at 7 A.M. the bell rings for chapel about one minute, and all hands promptly repair thither. In spite of the vast varieties of language and dialect spoken by fifty or sixty human beings, collected from twenty or thirty islets of the Pacific main, no practical difficulty has been found in using the Mota as the general language in Chapel and school, so that in a short time a congregation of twenty languages are able to join in worship in the one Mota tongue, more or less akin to all the rest, and a class of, say, nine boys, speaking by nature five different languages, easily join in using the one Mota language, just as a Frenchman, a German, a Russian, a Pole, an Italian, and an Englishman, all meeting in the same cafe or railway carriage, on the same glacier or mountain top, might harmoniously agree to use the French language as their medium of communication. So the service is conducted in Mota with one exception only. The collect for the day is read in English, as a brief allowable concession to the ears and hearts of the English members of the Mission. The service consists of the greater part of the Church of England Service translated. Some modifications have been made to suit the course of religious instruction. The Psalms are chanted and hymns sung in parts, and always in admirable tune, by the congregation. Noteworthy are the perfect attention, the reverent attitude, the hearty swing and unison of the little congregation, a lesson, I felt with shame, to many of our white congregations.

'Immediately after service clinks out the breakfast bell, and, with marvellous promptitude and punctuality, whites and blacks, lay and clerical, are seen flocking to the mess-room. The whites sit at the upper end of the table, but beyond the special privilege of tea, all fare alike, chiefly on vegetables: yams or sweet potatoes, and carrots or vegetable marrows, as may suit the season, with plenty of biscuit for more ambitious teeth, and plenty of milk to wash it down. Soon afterwards comes school for an hour and a half. Then work for the boys and men, planting yams, reaping wheat, mowing oats, fencing, carting, building, as the call may be, only no caste distinction or ordering about; it is not go and do that, but come and do this, whether the leader be an ordained clergyman, a white farm bailiff, or a white carpenter. This is noteworthy, and your readers will gain no clear idea of the Mission if they do not seize this point, for it is no matter of mere detail, but one of principle. The system is not that of the ship or the regiment, of the farm or the manufactory of the old country, but essentially of the family. It is not the officer or master saying "Go" but the father or the brother saying "Come." And to this, I firmly believe, is the hearty cheerful following and merry work of the blacks chiefly due. At 1 P.M. is dinner, much the same as breakfast. Meat, though not unknown, is the weak point of the Mission dietary. In the afternoon, work. At 6, tea. In the evening, class again for an hour or two; this evening class being sometimes a singing lesson, heartily enjoyed by the teacher. I forget precisely when the boys have to prepare matter arising out of the lessons they have received viva voce.

'There are evening prayers, and bed-time is early. Noteworthy are the happy conjunctions of perfect discipline with perfect jollity, the marvellous attainment of a happy familiarity which does not "breed contempt."

'I presume I need scarcely say to your readers that besides education in reading, writing, and arithmetic, through the medium of the Mota language, instruction in the Holy Scriptures and the most careful explanations of their meaning and mutual relation, forms a main part of the teaching given. The men and boys of the senior classes take notes; notes not by order expressly to be inspected, but, so to say, private notes for the aid of their memories; and from the translation given to me by Bishop Patteson of some of these, I should say that few, if any, of the senior class of an English Sunday School could give anything like so close, and sometimes philosophical, an explanation of Scripture, and that sometimes in remarkably few words.

'There remains to be noticed one most effectual means of doing good. After evening school, the Bishop, his clergy, and his aides, retire mostly into their own rooms. Then, quietly and shyly, on this night or the other night, one or two, three or four of the more intelligent of the black boys steal silently up to the Bishop's side, and by fits and starts, slowly, often painfully, tell their feelings, state their difficulties, ask for help, and, I believe, with God's blessing, rarely fail to find it. They are not gushing as negroes, but shy as Englishmen; we Englishmen ought, indeed, to have a fellow-feeling for these poor black boys and help them with all our hearts.

'Such is the routine for five of the six work days. Saturday is whole holiday, and all hands go to fish if the sea permits; if not, to play rounders or what not. Merry lads they are, as ever gladdened an English playground.

'On Sunday, the early Chapel is omitted. The full Liturgy is divided into two services—I forget the laws—and a kind of sermon in Mota is given; and in the afternoon, the Bishop, or one of the ordained members of the Mission, usually goes down to the town to relieve Mr. Nobbs in his service for the Pitcairners.

'As regards the manual work of the station, this general principle is observed—women for washing and house-work; the men for planting and out-of-door work; but no one, white or black, is to be too grand to do his share. The Bishop's share, indeed, is to study and investigate and compare the languages and necessary translations, but no one is to be above manual labour. No one, because he is a white man, is to say, "Here, black fellow, come and clean my boots." "Here, black people, believe that I have come to give you a treasure of inestimable price. Meantime, work for me, am I not your superior? Can I not give you money, calico, what not?"

'This Christian democracy, if I may so call it, has worked well in the long run.'

This observer does seem to have entered well into the spirit of the place; and there can be no doubt that the plan and organisation of the Mission had by this time been well tested and both found practicable, and, as at present worked, more than ordinarily successful. The college was in full working order, with a staff of clergy, all save one formed under the Bishop, one native deacon and two teachers living with their wives in a population that was fast becoming moulded by the influence of Christianity, many more being trained up, and several more islands in course of gradual preparation by the same process as was further advanced in Mota.

Such were the achievements which could be thankfully recounted by the end of 1869.

CHAPTER XII. THE LAST EIGHTEEN MONTHS. 1870-1871.

The prosperous days of every life pass away at last. Suffering and sorrow, failure and reverse are sure to await all who live out anything like their term of years, and the missionary is perhaps more liable than other men to meet with a great disappointment. 'Success but signifies vicissitude,' and looking at the history of the growth of the Church, it is impossible not to observe that almost in all cases, immediately upon any extensive progress, there has followed what seems like a strong effort of the Evil One at its frustration, either by external persecution, reaction of heathenism, or, most fatally and frequently during the last 300 years, from the reckless misdoings of unscrupulous sailors and colonists. The West Indies, Japan, America, all have the same shameful tale to tell—what wonder if the same shadow were to be cast over the Isles of the South?

It is one of the misfortunes, perhaps the temptations of this modern world, that two of its chief necessaries, sugar and cotton, require a climate too hot for the labour of men who have intelligence enough to grow and export them on a large scale, and who are therefore compelled, as they consider, to employ the forced toil of races able to endure heat. The Australian colony of Queensland is unfit to produce wheat, but well able to grow sugar, and the islands of Fiji, which the natives have implored England to annex, have become the resort of numerous planters and speculators. There were 300 white inhabitants in the latter at the time of the visit of the 'Curacoa' in 1865. In 1871 the numbers were from 5,000 to 6,000. Large sheep farms have been laid out, and sugar plantations established.

South Sea Islanders are found to have much of the negro toughness and docility, and, as has been seen, when away from their homes they are easily amenable, and generally pleasant in manner, and intelligent. Often too they have a spirit of enterprise, which makes them willing to leave home, or some feud with a neighbour renders it convenient. Thus the earlier planters did not find it difficult to procure willing labourers, chiefly from those southern New Hebrides, Anaiteum, Tanna, Erromango, &c., which were already accustomed to intercourse with sandal-wood traders, had resident Scottish or London missionaries, and might have a fair understanding of what they were undertaking.

The Fiji islanders themselves had been converted by Wesleyan Missionaries, and these, while the numbers of imported labourers were small, did not think ill of the system, since it provided the islanders with their great need, work, and might give them habits of industry. But in the years 1868 and 1869 the demand began, both in Queensland and Fiji, to increase beyond what could be supplied by willing labour, and the premium, £8 a head, on an able-bodied black, was sufficient to tempt the masters of small craft to obtain the desired article by all possible means. Neither in the colony nor in Fiji were the planters desirous of obtaining workers by foul means, but labour they must have, and they were willing to pay for it. Queensland, anxious to free herself from any imputation of slave-hunting, has drawn up a set of regulations, requiring a regular contract to be made with the natives before they are shipped, for so many years, engaging that they shall receive wages, and be sent home again at the end of the specified time. No one denies that when once the labourer has arrived, these rules are carried out; he is well fed, kindly treated, not over worked, and at the end of three or five years sent home again with the property he has earned.

A recent traveller has argued that this is all that can be desired, and that no true friend of the poor islander can object to his being taught industry and civilisation. Complaints are all 'missionary exaggeration,' that easy term for disposing of all defence of the dark races, and as to the difficulty of making a man, whose language is not understood, understand the terms of a contract—why, we continually sign legal documents we do not understand! Perhaps not, but we do understand enough not to find ourselves bound to five years' labour when we thought we were selling yams, or taking a pleasure trip. And we have some means of ascertaining the signification of such documents, and of obtaining redress if we have been deceived.

As to the boasted civilisation, a sugar plantation has not been found a very advanced school for the American or West Indian negro, and as a matter of fact, the islander who has fulfilled his term and comes home, bringing tobacco, clothes, and fire-arms, only becomes a more dangerous and licentious savage than he was in his simplicity. It is absolutely impossible, even if the planters wished it, to give any instruction to these poor fellows, so scattered are the settlements, so various the languages on each, and to send a man home with guns and gunpowder, and no touch of Christian teaching, is surely suicidal policy.

Yet, as long as the natives went in any degree willingly, though the Missionaries might deplore their so doing for the men's own sakes, and for that of their islands, it was only like a clergyman at home seeing his lads engage themselves to some occupation more undesirable than they knew. Therefore, the only thing that has been entreated for by all the missions of every denomination alike in the South Seas, has been such sufficient supervision of the labour traffic as may prevent deceit or violence from being used.

For, in the years 1869 and 1870, if not before, the captains of the labour ships, finding that a sufficient supply of willing natives could not be procured, had begun to cajole them on board. When they went to trade, they were thrust under hatches, and carried off, and if the Southern New Hebrides became exhausted, and the labour ships entered on those seas where the 'Southern Cross' was a welcome visitor, these captains sometimes told the men that 'the Bishop gave no pipes and tobacco, he was bad, they had better hold with them.' Or else 'the Bishop could not come himself, but had sent this vessel to fetch them.' Sometimes even a figure was placed on deck dressed in a black coat, with a book in his hand, according to the sailors' notion of a missionary, to induce the natives to come on deck, and there they were clapped under hatches and carried off.

In 1870, H.M.S. 'Rosario,' Captain Palmer, brought one of these vessels, the 'Daphne,' into Sydney, where the master was tried for acts of violence, but a conviction could not be procured, and, as will be seen in the correspondence, Bishop Patteson did not regret the failure, as he was anxious that ships of a fair size, with respectable owners, should not be deterred from the traffic, since the more it became a smuggling, unrecognised business, the worse and more unscrupulous men would be employed in it.

But decoying without violence began to fail; the natives were becoming too cautious, so the canoes were upset, and the men picked up while struggling in the water. If they tried to resist, they were shot at, and all endeavours at a rescue were met with the use of firearms.

They were thus swept off in such numbers, that small islands lost almost all their able-bodied inhabitants, and were in danger of famine for want of their workers. Also, the Fiji planters, thinking to make the men happier by bringing their wives, desired that this might be done, but it was not easy to make out the married couples, nor did the crews trouble themselves to do so, but took any woman they could lay hands on. Husbands pursued to save the wives, and were shot down, and a deadly spirit of hatred and terror against all that was white was aroused.

There is a still lower depth of atrocity, but as far as enquiry of the Government at Sydney can make out, unconnected with labour traffic, but with the tortoise-shell trade. Skulls, it will be remembered, were the ornament of old Iri's house at Bauro, and skulls are still the trophies in the more savage islands. It seems that some of the traders in tortoise-shell are in the habit of assisting their clients by conveying them in their vessels in pursuit of heads. There is no evidence that they actually do the work of slaughter themselves, though suspicion is strong, but these are the 'kill-kill' vessels in the patois of the Pacific, while the kidnappers are the 'snatch-snatch.' Both together, these causes were working up the islanders to a perilous pitch of suspicion and exasperation during the years 1870, 1871, and thus were destroying many of the best hopes of the fruit of the toils of all these years. But the full extent of the mischief was still unknown in Norfolk Island, when in the midst of the Bishop's plans for the expedition of 1870 came the illness from which he never wholly recovered.

Already he had often felt and spoken of himself as an elderly man. Most men of a year or two past forty are at the most vigorous period of their existence, generally indeed with the really individual and effective work of their lives before them, having hitherto been only serving their apprenticeship; but Coleridge Patteson had begun his task while in early youth, and had been obliged to bear at once responsibility and active toil in no ordinary degree. Few have had to be at once head of a college, sole tutor and steward, as well as primary schoolmaster all at once, or afterwards united these charges with those of Bishop, examining chaplain and theological professor, with the interludes of voyages which involved intense anxiety and watchfulness, as well as the hardships of those unrestful nights in native huts, and the exhaustion of the tropical climate. No wonder then that he was already as one whose work was well-nigh done, and to whom rest was near. And though the entrance into that rest was by a sudden stroke, it was one that mercifully spared the sufferings of a protracted illness, and even if his friends pause to claim for it the actual honours (on earth) of martyrdom, yet it was no doubt such a death as he was most willing to die, full in his Master's service— such a death as all can be thankful to think of. And for the like-minded young man who shared his death, only with more of the bitterness thereof, the spirit in which he went forth may best be seen in part of a letter written in the January of 1870, just after his Ordination:—

'The right way must be to have a general idea of what to aim at, and to make for the goal by what seem, as you go, the best ways, not to go on a course you fixed to yourself before starting without having seen it. It is so easy for people to hold theories, and excellent ones too, of the way to manage or deal with the native races, but the worst is that when you come to work the theory, the native race will never be found what it ought to be for properly carrying it out. I am quite sure that nothing is to be done in a hurry; a good and zealous man in ignorance and haste might do more harm in one year than could be remedied in ten. I would not root out a single superstition until I had something better to put in its place, lest if all the weeds were rooted up, what had before been fertile should become desert, barren, disbelieving in anything. Is not the right way to plant the true seed and nourish it that it may take root, and out-grow and choke the weeds? My objection to Mission reports has always been that the readers want to hear of "progress," and the writers are thus tempted to write of it, and may they not, without knowing it, be at times hasty that they may seem to be progressing? People expect too much. Those do so who see the results of Mission work, who are engaged in it; those do so who send them. We have the precious seed to sow, and must sow it when and where we can, but we must not always be looking out to reap what we have sown. We shall do that "in due time" if we "faint not." Because missionary work looks like a failure, it does not follow that it is.

'Our Saviour, the first of all Christian Missionaries, was thirty years of His life preparing and being prepared for His work. Three years He spake as never man spake, and did not His work at that time look a failure? He made no mistakes either in what He taught or the way of teaching it, and He succeeded, though not to the eyes of men. Should not we be contented with success like His? And with how much less ought we not to be contented! So! The wonder is that by our means any result is accomplished at all.'

These are remarkable words for a young man of twenty-seven, full of life, health, and vigour, and go far to prove the early ripening of a spirit chastened in hopes, even while all was bright.

In the latter part of February, Bishop Patteson, after about six days of warning, was prostrated by a very severe attack of internal inflammation, and for three days —from the 20th to the 22nd—was in considerable danger as well as suffering. Mr. Nobbs's medical knowledge seems, humanly speaking, to have brought him through, and on the 28th, when an opportunity occurred of sending letters, he was able to write a note to his brother and sisters—weak and shattered-looking writing indeed, but telling all that needed to be told, and finishing with 'in a few days (D.V.) I may be quite well;' then in a postscript: 'Our most merciful Father, Redeemer and Sanctifier is merciful indeed. There was a time when I felt drawing near the dark valley, and I thought of Father, Mother, of Uncle Frank, and our little ones, Frankie and Dolly,'—a brother and sister who had died in early infancy.

But it was not the Divine will that he should be well in a few days. Day after day he continued feeble; and suffering much, though not so acutely as in the first attack, Mr. Nobbs continued to attend him, and the treatment was approved afterwards by the physicians consulted. All the clergy took their part in nursing, and the Melanesian youths in turn watched him day and night. He did not leave his room till the beginning of April, and then was only equal to the exertion of preparing two lads for Baptism and a few more for Confirmation. On Easter Sunday he was able to baptize the first mentioned, and confirm the others; and, the 'Southern Cross' having by this time arrived for the regular voyage, he embarked in her to obtain further advice at Auckland.

Lady Martin, his kind and tender hostess and nurse, thus describes his arrival:—

'We had heard of his illness from himself and others, and of his being out of danger in the middle of March. We were therefore much surprised when the "Southern Cross," which had sailed a fortnight before for Norfolk Island, came into the harbour on the morning of the 25th of April, and anchored in our bay with the Bishop's flag flying. We went down to the beach with anxious hearts to receive the dear invalid, and were greatly shocked at his appearance. His beard, which he had allowed to grow since his illness, and his hair were streaked with grey; his complexion was very dark, and his frame was bowed like an old man's.

'The Captain and Mr. Bice almost carried him up the hill to our house. He was very thankful to be on shore, and spoke cheerfully about the improvement he had made on the voyage. It was not very apparent to us who had not seen him for two years. Even then he was looking worn and ill, but still was a young active man. He seemed now quite a wreck. For the first fortnight his faithful attendant Malagona slept in his room, and was ready at all hours to wait upon his beloved Bishop. Day by day he used to sit by the fire in an easy chair, too weak to move or to attend to reading. He got up very early, being tired of bed. His books and papers were all brought out, but he did little but doze.'

Yet, in his despatch of the 2nd of May, where the manuscript is as firm, clear, and beautiful as ever, only somewhat less minute, he says that he had improved wonderfully on the voyage, though he adds that the doctor told him, 'At an office, they would insure your life at fifty, instead of forty-three years of age.'

Dr. Goldsboro had, on examination, discovered a chronic ailment, not likely, with care and treatment, to be dangerous to life, but forbidding active exertion or horse exercise, and warning him that a sudden jar or slip or fall on rugged ground would probably bring on acute inflammation, which might prove fatal after hours of suffering.

After, in the above-mentioned letter, communicating his exact state, he adds: —'The pain has been at times very severe, and yet I can't tell you of the very great happiness and actual enjoyment of many of those sleepless nights; when, perhaps at 2 A.M., I felt the pain subsiding, and prayer for rest, if it were His will, was changed into thanksgiving for the relief; then, as the fire flickered, came restful, peaceful, happy thoughts, mingled with much, I trust, heart-felt sorrow and remorse. And Psalms seemed to have a new meaning, and prayers to be so real, and somehow there was a sense of a very near Presence, and I felt almost sorry when it was 5.30, and I got up, and my kind Melanesian nurse made me my morning cup of weak tea, so good to the dry, furred tongue.

'Well, that is all past and gone; and now the hope and prayer is, that when my time is really come, I may be better prepared to go.

'Sir William and Lady Martin are pretty well; and I am in clover here, getting real rest, and gaining ground pretty well. I have all confidence in the prudence of the other missionaries and leave the work thankfully in their hands, knowing well Whose work it is, and to Whose guidance and protection we all trust.'

On the 9th, in a letter sent by a different route, he adds:—

'So I think it will come to my doing my work on Norfolk Island just as usual, with only occasional inconvenience or discomfort. But I think I shall have to forego some of the more risky and adventurous part of the work in the islands. This is all right. It is a sign that the time is come for me to delegate it to others. I don't mean that I shall not take the voyages, and stop about on the islands (D.V.) as before. But I must do it all more carefully, and avoid much that of old I never thought about. Yet I think it will not, as a matter of fact, much interfere with my work.

'I have, you understand, no pain now, only some discomfort. The fact that I can't do things, move about, &c., like a sound healthy person is not a trial. The relief from pain, the *resty* feeling, is such a blessing and enjoyment that I don't seem, as yet at all events, to care about the other.'

So of that restful state Lady Martin says: 'Indeed it was a most happy time to us, and I think on the whole to him. It was a new state of things to keep him without any pricks of conscience or restlessness on his part. He liked to have a quiet half-hour by the fire at night; and before I left him I used to put his books near him: his Bible, his Hebrew Psalter, his father's copy of Bishop Andrewes. Sometimes I would linger for a few minutes to talk about his past illness. He used to dwell specially on his dear father's nearness to him at that time. He spoke once or twice with a reverent holy awe and joy of sleepless nights, when thoughts of God had filled his soul and sustained him.

'His face, always beautiful from the unworldly purity of its expression, was really as the face of an angel while he spoke of these things and of the love and kindness he had received. He seemed to have been standing on the very brink of the river, and it was yet doubtful whether he was to abide with us. Now, looking back, we can see how mercifully God was dealing with His servant. A time of quiet and of preparation for death given to him apart from the hurry of his daily life, then a few months of active service, and then the crown.

'At the end of a fortnight (?—you must please to rectify dates) the "Southern Cross" sailed again, with Mr. Bice and Malagona on board; when, just as we were expecting she would have reached Norfolk Island, she was driving back into the harbour.'

The following letter to the Bishop of Lichfield gives an account of her peril:—

'Taurarua: May 11, 1870.

'My dear Bishop,—I have to tell you of another great mercy. The "Southern Cross" left Auckland on May 3—fair wind and fine weather.

'On May 5 she was within 185 miles of Norfolk Island.

'Then came on a fearful gale from the east and northeast to north-west. They were hove-to for three days, everything battened down; port boat and davits carried away by a sea; after a while the starboard boat dashed to pieces.

'Malagona, my nurse at Norfolk Island, who was brought up for a treat, was thrown completely across the cabin by one lurch, when she seemed almost settling down. It was dark. The water in the cabin, which had come through the dead-light, showed a little phosphoric glimmer. "Brother," he said to Bice, "are we dying?" "I don't know; it seems like it. We are in God's hands." "Yes, I know."

'Mr. (Captain) Jacobs was calm and self-possessed. He even behaved excellently. Once, all on deck were washed into the lee scuppers, and one man washed overboard; but he held a rope, and with it and the recoil was borne in again upon the deck. Lowest barometer, 28° 65'! We were startled yesterday at about 4 P.M. with the news of the reappearance of the vessel. I think that some £30 and the replacing the boats will pay damages, but one doesn't think of that.

'We hope to get, at all events, one ready-made boat, so as to cause no delay. The good people at Norfolk Island will be anxious if the vessel does not reappear soon.

'Auckland, June 6th—"Southern Cross" could not sail till May 23. If I am not found by them at Norfolk Island on their return, they are to come on for me. I hope to make a two months' cruise.

'General health quite well, no pain for weeks past. Dr. Goldsboro' says I shall be better in a hot climate; but he won't let me out of his hands yet.

'I really think I shall do very well by-and-by.

'Your very affectionate
'J. C. PATTESON.'

'The repairs took some time (continues Lady Martin). The delay must have been very trying to the Bishop in his weak state, as it threw out all the plans for the winter voyage; but he showed no signs of fretfulness or of a restless desire to go himself to see after matters. The winter was unusually cold after the vessel sailed again; and I used to wonder sometimes whether he lay awake listening to the wind that howled in gusts round the house; he may have, but certainly there was always a look of unruffled calm and peace on his face when we met in the morning.

'Tis enough that Thou shouldst care Why should I the burden bear?

'Our dear friend mended very slowly. It was more than a month before he could bear even to be driven up to Bishop's Court to receive the Holy Communion in the private Chapel, and some time longer before he could sit through the Sunday services. I cannot be sure whether he went first on Ascension Day. His own letters may inform you. I only remember how thankful and happy he was to be able to get there. He had felt the loss of the frequent Communions in which he could join all through his illness.'

He was making a real step towards recovery, and by the 10th of June he was able to go and stay at St. Sepulchre's parsonage with Mr. Dudley, and attend the gathering at the Bishop of Auckland's Chapel on St. Barnabas Day; but the calm enjoyment and soothing indifference which seems so often a privilege of the weakness of recovery was broken by fuller tidings respecting the labour traffic that imperilled his work. A schooner had come in from Fate with from fifteen to twenty natives from that and other islands to work in flax mills; and a little later a letter arrived from his correspondent in Fiji, showing to what an extent the immigration thither had come, and how large a proportion of the young men working in the sugar plantations had been decoyed from home on false pretences.

This was the point, as far as at the time appeared in New Zealand. If violence had then begun, no very flagrant instances were known; and the Bishop was not at all averse to the employment of natives, well knowing how great an agent in improvement is civilisation. But to have them carried off without understanding what they were about, and then set to hard labour, was quite a different thing.

'The difficulty is (he writes) to prove in a court of law what everyone acknowledges to be the case, viz., that the natives of the islands are inveigled on board these vessels by divers means, then put under the hatches and sold, ignorant of their destination or future employment, and without any promises of being returned home.

'It comes to this, though of course it is denied by the planters and the Queensland Government, which is concerned in keeping up the trade.

'There will always be some islanders who from a roving nature, or from a necessity of escaping retaliation for some injury done by them, or from mere curiosity, will paddle off to a ship and go on board. But they can't understand the white men: they are tempted below to look at some presents, or, if the vessel be at anchor, are allowed to sleep on board. Then, in the one case, the hatches are clapped on; in the other, sail is made in the night, and so they are taken off to a labour of which they know nothing, among people of whom they know nothing!

'It is the regulation rather than the suppression of the employment of native labourers that I advocate. There is no reason why some of these islanders should not go to a plantation under proper regulations. My notion is that—

'1. A few vessels should be licensed for the purpose of conveying these islanders backwards and forwards.

'2. That such vessels should be in charge of fit persons, heavily bound to observe certain rules, and punishable summarily for violating them.

'3. That the missionaries, wherever they be situated, should be informed of the names of the vessels thus licensed, of the sailing masters, &c.

'4. That all other vessels engaged in the trade should be treated as pirates, and confiscated summarily when caught.

'5. That a small man-of-war, commanded by a man fit for such work, should cruise among the islands from which islanders are being taken.

'6. That special legislative enactments should be passed enabling the Sydney

Court to deal with the matter equitably.

'Something of this kind is the best plan I can suggest.

'It is right and good that the "Galatea" should undertake such work; and yet we want a little tender to the "Galatea" rather than the big vessel, as I think my experience of large vessels is that there is too much of routine; and great delay is occasioned by the difficulty of turning a great ship round, and you can't work near the shore, and even if chasing a little vessel which could be caught at once in the open sea, you may be dodged by her among islands. Yet the sense of the country is expressed very well by sending "Captain Edinburgh" himself to cruise between New Caledonia, Fiji, and the Kingsmill Islands, for the suppression of the illegal deportation of natives. So reads the despatch which the Governor showed me the other day. He asked me to give such information as might be useful to the "Galatea."'

With the Governor, Sir George Bowen, an old Oxford friend, Bishop Patteson spent several days, and submitted to him a memorial to Government, on the subject, both at home and in Queensland, stating the regulations, as above expressed.

The 'Rosario,' Captain Palmer, had actually captured the 'Daphne,' a vessel engaged in capturing natives, and brought her into Sydney, where the master was tried; but though there was no doubt of the outrage, it was not possible to obtain a conviction; and a Fiji planter whom the Bishop met in Auckland told him that the seizure of the 'Daphne' would merely lead to the exclusion of the better class of men from the trade, and that it would not stop the demand for native labourers. It would always pay to 'run' cargoes of natives into the many islets of Fiji; and they would be smuggled into the plantations. And there the government was almost necessarily by the whip. 'I can't talk to them,' said the planter; 'I can only point to what they are to do; and if they are lazy, I whip them.'

It was no wonder that Mr. Dudley thought the Bishop depressed; and, moreover, he over-exerted himself, walking a mile and a half one day, and preaching in the little Church of St. Sepulchre's. He longed to return to St. Barnabas, but was in no state to rough it in a common little sailing vessel, so he waited on. 'I am very lazy,' he says: 'I can't do much work. Sir William and I read Hebrew, and discuss many questions in which his opinion is most valuable. I have business letters to write, e.g., about the deportation of islanders and about a clergyman whom the Melbourne people are helping to go to Fiji.... This is perhaps a good trial for me, to be sitting lazily here and thinking of others at work!'

This was written about the middle of July, when the convalescent had regained much more strength, and could walk into town, or stand to read and write according to his favourite custom, as well as thoroughly enjoy conversations with his hosts at Taurarua.

'I never saw (observes Lady Martin) a larger charity united to a more living faith. He knew in Whom he believed; and this unclouded confidence seemed to enable him to be gentle and discriminating in his judgments on those whose minds are clouded with doubt.

'It was pleasant to see how at this time his mind went back to the interests which he had laid aside for years. He liked to hear bits of Handel, and other old masters, and would go back to recollections of foreign travels and of his enthusiasm for music and art as freshly and brightly as he had done in the first days of our acquaintance. But this was only in the "gloaming" or late in the evening when he was resting in his easy chair.

'At the end of July we were expecting a young relation and his bride to spend a week with us before returning to England, and we gave the Bishop the option of going to Bishop's Court for the time, where he was always warmly welcomed. Some years before, he would certainly have slipped away from the chatter and bustle; but now he decided to remain with us, and throw himself into the small interests around, in a way which touched and delighted the young couple greatly. He put away his natural shrinking from society and his student ways, and was willing to enjoy everything as it came. We had a curious instance at this time of the real difficulty the Bishop felt about writing sermons. He had not attempted to preach, save at Mr. Dudley's Church; but a week or two before he left us, Archdeacon Maunsell came to beg of him to preach at St. Mary's, where he had often taken service formerly. He promised to do so without any apparent hesitation, and said afterwards to us that he could not refuse such a request. So on Wednesday he began to prepare a sermon. He was sitting each morning in the room where I was at work, and he talked to me from time to time of the thoughts that were in his mind. The subject was all that was implied in the words, "I have called thee by thy name," the personal knowledge, interest, &c.; and I was rejoicing in the treat in store, when, to my dismay, I saw sheet after sheet, which had been written in his neat, clear hand as though the thoughts flowed on without effort, flung into the fire. "I can't write," was said again and again, and the work put by for another day. At last, on Saturday morning, he walked up to the parsonage to make his excuses. Happily Dr. Maunsell would not let him off, so on Sunday the Bishop, without any notes or sermon, spoke to us out of the fulness of his heart about the Mission work, of its encouragements and its difficulties. He described, in a way that none can ever forget who heard the plaintive tones of his voice and saw his worn face that day, what it was to be alone on an island for weeks, surrounded by noisy heathen, and the comfort and strength gained then by the thought that we who have the full privileges of Christian worship and communion were remembering such in our prayers.

'Our young friends sailed on Sunday, August 7; and we expected the Bishop to sail the next day, but the winds were foul and boisterous, and we had him with us till Friday morning, the 12th. Those last days were very happy ones. His thoughts went back to Melanesia and to his work; and every evening we drew him to tell of adventures and perils, and to describe the islands to us in a way he had scarcely ever done before. I think it was partly to please our Maori maiden, who sat by his side on a footstool in the twilight, plying him with questions with so much lively natural interest that he warmed up in return. Generally, he shrank into himself, and became reserved at once if pressed to tell of his own doings. He spoke one evening quite openly about his dislike to ship life. We were laughing at some remembrance of the Bishop of Lichfield's satisfaction when once afloat; and he burst into an expression of wonder, how anyone could go to sea for pleasure. I asked him what he disliked in particular, and he answered, Everything. That he always felt dizzy, headachy, and unable to read with comfort; the food was greasy, and there was a general sense of dirt and discomfort. As the time drew nigh for sailing, he talked a good deal about the rapidly growing evil of the labour trade. He grew very depressed one day, and spoke quite despondingly of the future prospects of the Mission. He told us of one island, Vanua Lava, I think, where, a few years ago, 300 men used to assemble on the beach to welcome him. Now, only thirty or forty were left. He saw that if the trade went on at the same rate as it had been doing for the last year or two, many islands would be depopulated, and everywhere he must expect to meet with suspicion or open ill will.'

'The next morning the cloud had rolled away, and he was ready to go forth in faith to do the work appointed him, leaving the result in God's hands. We accompanied him to the boat on Friday morning. Bishop and Mrs. Cowie came down, and one or two of the clergy, and his two English boys who were to go with him.

'It was a lovely morning. We rejoiced to see how much he had improved in his health during his stay. He had been very good and tractable about taking nourishment, and certainly looked and was all the better for generous diet. He had almost grown stout, and walked upright and briskly. Sir William parted with him on the beach, where we have had so many partings; and I meant to do so too, but a friend had brought another boat, and invited me to come, so I gladly went off to the "Southern Cross," which was lying about half-a-mile off. The Cowies were very anxious to see the vessel, and the Bishop showed them all about. I was anxious to go down to his cabin, and arrange in safe nooks comforts for his use on the voyage. In half an hour the vessel was ready to sail. One last grasp of the hand, one loving smile, and we parted—never to meet again on earth.'

So far this kind and much-loved friend! And to this I cannot but add an extract from the letter she wrote to his sisters immediately after the parting, since it adds another touch to the character now ripened:—

'I think you are a little mistaken in your notion that your brother would feel no interest in your home doings. He has quite passed out of that early stage when the mind can dwell on nothing but its own sphere of work. He takes a lively interest in all that is going on at home, specially in Church matters, and came back quite refreshed from Bishop's Court with all that Bishop Cowie had told him.

'What he would really dread in England would be the being lionised, and being compelled to speak and preach here, there, and everywhere. And yet he would have no power to say nay. But the cold would shrivel him up, and society—dinners, table talk—would bore him, and he would pine for his warmth and his books. Not a bit the less does he dearly love you all.'

The brother and sisters knew it, and forebore to harass him with remonstrances, but resigned themselves to the knowledge that nothing would bring him home save absolute disqualification for his mission.

His own last letter from Taurarua dwells upon the enjoyment of his conversations with Sir William Martin and Bishop Cowie; and then goes into details of a vision of obtaining young English boys to whom a good education would be a boon, bringing them up at St. Barnabas, and then, if they turned out fit for the Mission there, they would be prepared—if not, they would have had the benefit of the schooling.

Meantime the 'Southern Cross,' with three of the clergy, had made the voyage according to minute directions from the Bishop. Mr. Atkin made his yearly visit to Bauro. He says:—

'I hardly expected that when we came back we should have found the peace still unbroken between Wango and Hane, but it is. Though not very good friends, they are still at peace. In the chief's house I was presented with a piece of pork, about two pounds, and a dish of tauma (their favourite), a pudding made of yams, nuts, and cocoa-nut milk, and cooked by steaming. Fortunately, good manners allowed me to take it away. Before we left the village, it took two women to carry our provisions. A little boy came back with us, to stay with Taki. The two boys who ought to have come last year are very anxious to do so still.

'July 12th.—We anchored the boat on the beach at Tawatana, and I went into the oka (public house) to see the tauma prepared for the feast. There were thirty-eight dishes. The largest, about four feet long, stood nearly three feet high. I tried to lift one from the ground, but could not; it must have been five hundredweight; the smallest daras held eighty or a hundred pounds. I calculated that there was at least two tons. When freshly made it is very good, but at these feasts it is always old and sour, and dripping with cocoa-nut oil. The daras, or wooden bowls, into which it is put, are almost always carved and inlaid with mother-of-pearl shell.

'There was a great crowd at the landing-place at Saa (Malanta) to meet us. Nobody knew Wate at first, but he was soon recognised. The boat was pulled up into a little river, and everything stealable taken out. We then went up to the village, passing some women crying on the way; here, as at Uleawa, crying seems to be the sign of joy, or welcome. Wate's father's new house is the best I have seen in any of these islands. It has two rooms; the drawing-room is about forty-five feet long by thirty wide, with a roof projecting about six feet outside the wall at the end and four feet at the eaves; the bed-room is about eighteen feet wide, so that the whole roof covers about seventy feet by forty. Wate's father lives like a chief of the olden time, with large property, but nothing of his own; all that he has or gets goes as soon as he gets it to his retainers.

'August 3rd.—Went to Heuru. The bwea began about ten o'clock. A bwea means a stage, but the word is used as we speak of "the stage." There is a stage in this case about three feet square, twenty feet from the ground, walled in to three feet height on three sides, with a ladder of two stout poles. On the bwea sit or stand two or three men, on either side having a bag; visitors run up the ladder, put their money or porpoise teeth into the bags if small, give it to the men if large; and, if their present is worth it, make a speech a little way down the ladder. A party from a village generally send up a spokesman, and when he has done go up in a body and give their money. Taki was orator for Waiio, and I led the party with my present of beads, which if red or white pass as money. The object of a bwea is to get money, but it may only be held on proper occasions. The occasion of this was the adoption of a Mara lad by the chief man at Heuru; to get money to pay the lad's friends he held a bwea that all his friends might help him. As he was a connection of Taki's, and Waiio is the richest of the settlements, he got great spoils from thence.... At Tawatana the young men put on petticoats of cocoa-nut leaves, and danced their graceful "mao." I had only seen it before at Norfolk Island; it is very pretty, but must be very difficult to learn; they say that not many know it. At Nora they danced another most dirty dance: all the performers were daubed from head to foot with mud, and wore masks covered with mud and ashes; the aim of the dance, as far as I could see, was to ridicule all sorts of infirmities and imbecilities, tottering, limping, staggering, and reeling, but in time and order. One man had a basket of dripping mud on his head which was streaming down his face and back all the time. A great point is that the actors should not be recognised. Mr. Brooke was likewise dropped at Florida. After this the rest of the party had gone on to Mota, where George Sarawia was found working away well at his school, plenty of attendants, and the whole place clean, well-ventilated, and well-regulated.

A watch sent out as a present to Sarawia was a delight which he could quite appreciate, and he had sent back very sensible right-minded letters. Of Bishop Patteson's voyage the history is pieced together from two letters, one to the sisters, the other to the Bishop of Lichfield. Neither was begun till September, after which they make a tolerably full diary.

'More than five weeks have passed since I left New Zealand, more than three since I left Norfolk Island. Mr. Codrington and I reached Mota on the morning of the eighth day after leaving Norfolk Island. I spent but half an hour on shore with George Sarawia and his people; sailed across to Aroa and Matlavo, where I landed eight or ten of our scholars; and came on at once to the Solomon Islands. On Sunday morning (September 4) what joy to find Mr. Atkin well and hearty!

'Mr. Brooke, who took up his abode at the village of Mboli, had with him Dudley Lankana and Richard Maru, but they were a good deal absorbed by their relations, and not so useful to him as had been hoped, though they kept out of heathen habits, and remained constant to their intention of returning.

'"Brooke," says the Bishop, "knows and speaks the one language of Anudha very well, for there is but one language, with a few dialectical varieties of course."

'A nice little house was built for him at Mboli, which I have always thought to be a very healthy place.

'The coral grit and sand runs a long way in shore under cocoa-nut groves, but there is no very dense undergrowth. The wind when easterly blows freely along and is drawn rather upon the shore there. Two miles to windward of Mboli is the good harbour of Sara, where the vessel anchored with us.

'Brooke's house was raised on poles, five feet from the ground; the floor made of neat smooth bamboos, basket-worked. He had his table and two benches, one easy cane chair, cork bed, boxes, harmonium, and plenty of food.

'Close to his house is the magnificent kiala, or boat house, about 180 feet long, 42 high, and about as many feet broad, a really grand, imposing place. Here

Brooke, in surplice, with his little band, had his Sunday services, singing hymns, and chanting Psalms, in parts, in the presence of from 150 to 300, once nearly 400 people, to whom he spoke of course, usually twice, making two sermonets.

'The island is unlike any other; much more open, much less bush, but it is not coral crag that crops out, but almost bare reddish rock, with but little soil on it, and the population, which is large, finds it hard to procure food.

'Three brothers, Takua, Savai, and Dikea, are the principal men. Local chiefs exercise some small authority in each village. Anudha, or Aunta, is properly the name of a small island, for there is no one great mainland, but many islands separated by very narrow salt-water creeks and rivers, along which a skiff may be sculled.

'Brooke has been over every part of it. His only difficulties arose from jealousy on the part of Takua and Savai, who, living at Mboli, were very wroth at his not being their tame Pakeha, at his asserting his independence, his motive in coming to teach all, and make known to all alike a common message. Especially they were indignant at his making up small parties of boys from different parts of the island, as they of course wanted to monopolise him, and through him the trade. He has evidently been firm and friendly too, keeping his temper, yet speaking out very plainly. The result, as far as bringing boys goes, is that we have now thirteen on board, including Dudley and Richard, from six different parts of the island. But so vexed was Takua, that he would not fulfil his promise of sending his two little girls.

'The fortnight spent in the Solomon Islands has been very fine; winds very light, and very little rain. We have at length got Stephen Taroniara's child, a little girl of about seven years old, Paraitaku, from the old grandmother and aunts. So, thank God, she will be brought up as a Christian child. She is a dear little thing.

'This work of Mr. Atkin and Mr. Brooke in the easterly and more north-westerly parts of the Solomon Islands respectively, is the nearest approach that has yet been made to regular missionary operations there. Our short visits in the "Southern Cross," or my short three to ten days' visits on shore are all useful as preparing the way for something more. But it is the quiet, lengthened staying for some months among these islanders that gives opportunities for knowing them and their ways. They do everything with endless talk and discussion about it; and it is only by living with, and moving about constantly among them, that any hold can be gained over them. I think that the Mission is now in a more hopeful state than ever before in these islands.

'Our parties of scholars are large. They trust quite little fellows with us, and for any length of time. True, these little fellows cannot exercise any influence for years to come; but if we take young men or lads of sixteen or eighteen years old, it needs as many years to qualify them (with heathen habits to be unlearned, and with the quickness of apprehension of new teaching already gone) for being useful among their people as would suffice for the arrival of these young children at mature age.'

Three Tikopian giants had made a visit at Mota in the course of this year, attracted by the fame of the hospitality and fertility of the place. George Sarawia had got on well with them, and tried to keep them to meet the Bishop, but one of them fell sick, and the others took him away. This was hailed as a possible opening to those two curious isles, Oanuta and Tikopia, in so far as the 'Southern Cross' work was concerned. The Bishop continues, to his former Primate:—

'On the whole, things seem to be going on favourably. The Banks Islanders are very shy now of the vessels sent to carry off men to Fiji or Queensland. They will find their way into the Solomon Islands soon. One, indeed, a cutter, has taken about twenty men from Ulava. They were all kept under hatches. We warn the people wherever we go.

'The pressing question now is how to supply our young men and women, married Christian couples, with proper occupations to prevent their acquiescing in an indolent, useless, selfish life.

'When their "education is finished," they have no profession, no need to work to obtain a livelihood for themselves, wives, and children. They can't all be clergymen, nor all even teachers in such a sense as to make it a calling and occupation.

'Some wants they have—houses fit for persons who like reading and writing, a table, a bench, a window becomes necessary. Coral lime houses would be good for them. They make and wear light clothing, they wash and cook on new principles, &c.; but these wants are soon supplied. Only a practical sense of the duty of helping others to know what they have been taught will keep them from idleness and its consequences. And how few of us, with no other safeguard against idleness, would be other than idle!

'Some, I think, may be helped by being associated with us, and with their friends of the Solomon Isles, New Hebrides, in spending some months on shore, where they would soon acquire a fair knowledge of the language, and might be of great use to less advanced friends. This would be a real work for them. Just as Mission work is the safeguard of the settled Church, so it must be the safeguard of these young native Churches.

'No doubt the Missionary spirit infused into the Samoan and Karotongan Churches kept them living and fruitful. I am trying to think upon these points.

'If the contrast be too violent between the Mission station with its daily occupations and the island life, it becomes very difficult for the natives to perpetuate the habits of the one amidst the circumstances of the other.

'The habits acquired at Norfolk Island ought to be capable of being easily transferred to the conditions of the Melanesian isles.

'They ought, I think, to wear (in the hot summer and on week days) light loose clothing, which could be worn at home; or clothing of the same shape and fit (though perhaps of warm materials) might be worn.

'The circumstances of the two places must be different, but we must minimise the difference as much as possible.

'I often think of the steady-going English family, with regular family prayers, and attendance twice at Church on Sunday, and the same people spending two months on the Continent. No opportunity is made for family prayers before the table d'hôte breakfast; and at least one part of the Sunday is spent in the Roman

Catholic Cathedral, or in a different way from the home use. And if this be so with good respectable folk among ourselves, what must be the effect of altered circumstances on our Melanesians?

'It is not easy to keep up the devotional life on shore at home, or in the islands, or on board ship with the same regularity. And where the convert must be more dependent than we ought to be on external opportunities, the difficulty is increased. So if the alteration be as little as possible, we gain something, we make it easier to our scholars to perpetuate uninterruptedly the Norfolk Island life.

'To live with them and try to show them how, on their island, to keep up the religious life unchanged amidst the changed outward circumstances is a good way, but then we can't live among them very long, and our example is so often faulty.

'Curiously do these practical difficulties make us realise that there may really be some benefit in artificial wants; and that probably the most favourable situation for the development of the human character is a climate where the necessaries of life are just sufficiently difficult of production to require steady industry, and yet that nature should not be so rigorous as to make living so hard a matter as to occupy the whole attention, and dwarf the mental faculties.'

How remarkable, is the date of the following thoughts, almost like a foreboding:

'September 19th, 10 A.M. (to the sisters).—We are drawing near Santa Cruz, about 100 miles off. How my mind is filled with hopes, not unmingled with anxiety. It is more than eleven years since we sought to make an opening here, and as yet we have no scholar. Last year, I went ashore at a large village called Taive, about seven miles from the scene of our disaster. Many canoes came to us from that spot, and we stood in quite close in the vessel, so that people swam off to us.

'They are all fighting among the various villages and neighbouring islets of the Reef Archipelago, twenty miles north of the main island. It is very difficult what to do or how to try to make a beginning. God will open a door in His own good time. Yet to see and seize on the opportunity when given is difficult. How these things make one feel more than ever the need of Divine guidance, the gift of the Spirit of Wisdom and Counsel and ghostly strength. To human eyes it seems almost hopeless. Yet other islanders were in a state almost as hopeless apparently. Only there is a something about Santa Cruz which is probably very unreal and imaginary, which seems to present unusual difficulties. In a few days, I may, by God's goodness, be writing to you again about our visit to the group. And if the time be come, may God grant us some opening, and grace to use it aright!

'At Piteni, Matama, Nupani, Analogo, I can talk somewhat to the people, who are Polynesians, and speak a dialect connected with the Maori of New Zealand. I think that the people of Indeni (the native name for Santa Cruz) are also more than half Polynesians; but I don't know a single sentence of their language properly. I can say nothing about it. They destroy and distort their organs of pronunciation by excessive use of the betel-nut and pepper leaf and lime, so that no word is articulately pronounced. It is very hard to catch the sounds they make amidst the hubbub on deck or the crowds on shore; yet I think that if we had two or three lads quietly with us at Norfolk Island, we should soon make out something.

'Don't think I am depressed by this. I only feel troubled by the sense that I frequently lose opportunities from indolence and other faults. I am quite aware that we can do very little to bring about an introduction to these islanders; and I fully believe that in some quite unexpected way, or at all events in some way brought about independently of our efforts, a work will be begun here some day, in the day when God sees it to be fit and right.

(To the Bishop of Lichfield.)

'September 27th.—Leaving Santa Cruz we came to this group from Ulava with light fair winds; left Ulava on Saturday at 6 P.M., and sighted the island, making the west side of Graciosa Bay on the next Wednesday; sea quite smooth; thermometer reached 92 degrees.

'Sunday.—Very calm, but a light breeze took us into Nukapu. A canoe came off, I made them understand that it was our day of rest, and that I would visit them atainu (to-morrow), a curious word. I gave a few presents, and we slowly sailed on.

'Monday, 6 A.M.—Off Piteni, canoe off, went ashore, low tide, got into a canoe, and so reached the beach, people well behaved, much talk of taking lads, quite well understood. The speech is (you remember) very Maori indeed. There were some nice lads, but no one came away. Four canoes from Taumaho were here, and two Piteni men came back from Taumaho while I was on shore.

'At Nukapu at 2.30 P.M. High water, went in easily over the reef by a short cut, not by our old winding narrow passage. I was greatly pleased by the people asking me on board, "Where is Bisambe?" "Here I am." "No, no, the Bisambe tuai (of old). Your mutua (father). Is he below? Why doesn't he come up with some hatchets?"

'So you see they remember you. A tall middle-aged man, Moto, said that he was with us in the boat in 1859, and he and I remembered the one-eyed man who piloted us.

'I went here also into the houses. Here is a quaint place; many things, not altogether idols, but uncanny, and feared by the people. Women danced in my honour, people gave small presents, &c., but no volunteers. I could talk with them with sufficient ease; and took my time, lying at my ease on a good mat with cane pillow, Anaiteum fashion. I told them that they had seen on board many little fellows from many islands; that they need not fear to let their children go; that I could not spend time and property in coming year by year and giving presents when they were unwilling to listen to what I said, but they only made unreal promises, put boys in the boat merely to take them out again, and so we went away atrakoi.'

There is a little weariness of spirits—not of spirit—in the contemporaneous words to the home party:—

'I don't know what to write about this voyage. You have heard all about tropical vegetation, Santa Cruz canoes, houses, customs, &c. If indeed I could draw these fellows, among whom I was lying on a mat on Monday; if you could see the fuzzy heads, stained white and red, the great shell ornaments on the arms, the round plate of shell as big as a small dinner plate hanging over the chest, the large holes in the lobes of the ears rilled with perhaps fifteen or twenty rings of tortoise-shell hung on to one another; the woven scarves and girdles stained yellow with turmeric and stamped with a black pattern: then it would make a curious sight for you; and your worthy brother, much at his ease, lying flat on his back on two or three mats, talking to the people about his great wish to take away some of the jolly little fellows to whom he was giving fish-hooks, would no doubt be very "interesting." But really all this has become so commonplace, that I can't write about it with any freshness. The volcano in this group, Tenakulu, is now active, and was a fine sight at night, though the eruption is not continuous as it was in 1859.

'October 9th—Near Ambrym [to the Bishop]. Some people from Aruas, the large western bay of Vanua Lava, had been taken by force to Queensland or Fiji. The natives simply speak of "a ship of Sydney."

'Wednesday.—Aroa and Matlavo. 'Henry Tagalana and Joanna and their baby Elizabeth, William Pasvorang and Lydia, and six others, all baptized, and four communicants among them, had spent five weeks on shore; a very nice set. Six of them lived together at Aroa, had regular morning and evening prayers, sang their hymns, and did what they could, talking to their people. Codrington went over in a canoe, and spent four days with them, much pleased. We brought three scholars for George from thence.

'Thursday, Mota.—Codrington says the time is come, in his opinion, for some steps to be taken to further the movement in Mota. Grown-up people much changed, improved, some almost to be regarded as catechumens.

'We left Mota, bringing all that were to come; indeed, we scarcely know what it is nowadays to lose a boy or man—a great blessing. There had been another visit of eleven canoes of Tikopians; friendly, though unable to converse, and promising to return again in two months.

'October 11th.—A topsail schooner in sight, between Ambrym and Paama— one of those kidnapping vessels. I have any amount of (to me) conclusive evidence of downright kidnapping. But I don't think I could prove any case in a Sydney Court. They have no names painted on some of their vessels, and the natives can't catch nor pronounce the names of the white men on board. They describe their appearance accurately, and we have more than suspicions about some of these fellows.

'The planters in Queensland and Fiji, who create the demand for labourers, say that they don't like the kidnapping any more than I do. They pay occasionally from £6 to £12 for an "imported labourer," and they don't want to have him put into their hands in a sullen irritable state of mind.'

Touching at Nengone, the Bishop saw Mr. Creagh, who had recently visited New Caledonia, whither Basset, the poor chief who had been banished to Tahiti for refusing to receive a French priest, had been allowed to return, on the Emperor Napoleon forbidding interference with Protestant missionaries or their converts.

Wadrokala and his wife and child were brought away, making up a number of 65 black passengers, besides the 60 scholars already at Norfolk Island. The weather throughout the voyage had been unusually still, with frequent calms, the sea with hardly any swell. And this had been very happy for the Bishop; but he was less well than when he had left Taurarua, and was unequal to attending the General Synod in New Zealand, far more so to another campaign in Australia, though he cherished the design of going to see after the condition of the labourers in Fiji.

He finishes his long letter to his former Primate:—

It is perhaps cowardly to say that I am thankful that I am not a clergyman in England. I am not the man even in a small parish to stand up and fight against so many many-headed monsters. I should give in, and shirk the contest. The more I pray that you may have strength to endure it. I don't think I was ever pugnacious in the way of controversy; and I am very very thankful to be out of it.'

Indeed, the tone of the references to Church matters at home had become increasingly cautious; and one long letter to Mrs. Martyn he actually tore up, lest it should do harm. His feeling more and more was to wish for patience and forbearance, and to deprecate violent words or hasty actions—looking from his hermit life upon all the present distress more as a phase of Church history that would develop into some form of good, and perhaps hardly sensible of the urgency of the struggle and defence. For peace and shelter from the strife of tongues was surely one of the compensating blessings conferred on him. But, as all his companions agree, he was never the same man again after his illness. There was a lower level of spirits and of energy, a sensitiveness to annoyances, and an indisposition to active exertion, which distressed him.

His day began as early as ever, and was mapped out as before, for classes of all kinds, Hebrew and reading; but he seldom left his room, except for Chapel and meals, being unable to take much out-door exercise. He did not see so much of his elder scholars as before, chiefly because the very large number of newer pupils made it necessary to employ them more constantly; but he never failed to give each of them some instruction for a short time every day, though with more effort, for indeed almost everything had become a burthen to him. Mr. Codrington's photograph taken at this time shows how much changed and aged he had become. The quiet in which he now lived resulted in much letter-writing, taking up correspondences that had slumbered in more busy times, as his mind flew back to old friends: though, indeed, the letters given in the preceding Memoir must not be taken by any means to represent the numbers he wrote. When he speaks of sending thirty-five by one mail, perhaps only one or two have come into my hands; and of those only such portions are of course taken as illustrate his life, work, character, and opinions without trenching on the reserve due to survivors. Thus multitudes of affectionate letters, participating in the joys and sorrows of his brother, his cousins and friends, can necessarily find no place here; though the idea of his character is hardly complete without direct evidence of the unbroken or more truly increasing sympathy he had with those whom he had not met for sixteen years, and his love for his brother's wife and children whom he had never seen.

Soon after his return to Norfolk Island came a packet with a three months' accumulation of home despatches. He read and replied in his old conversational way, with occasionally a revelation of his deep inner self:—

'I have been thinking, dear old Fan, about your words, "there would be a good deal to give and take if you came home for a time;" less perhaps now than before I was somewhat tamed by my illness. I see more of the meaning of that petition, "from all blindness of heart, from pride, vainglory, and hypocrisy; and from all uncharitableness."

'Alas! you don't know what a misspent life I looked back upon, never losing hold, God be praised, of the sure belief in His promises of pardon and acceptance in Christ. I certainly saw that a want of sympathy, an indifference to the feelings of others, want of consideration, selfishness, in short, lay at the bottom of very much that I mourned over.

'There is one thing, that I don't mention as an excuse for a fault which really does exist, but simply as a fact, viz., that being always, even now, pressed for time, I write very abruptly, and so seem to be much more positive and dogmatic than I hope, and really think, is the case. I don't remember ever writing you a letter in which I was able to write but as I would have talked out the matter under discussion in all its bearings. This arises partly from impatience, my pen won't go fast enough; but as I state shortly my opinion, without going through the reasons which lead me to adopt it, no doubt much that I say seems to be without reason, and some of it no doubt is.'

I need make no excuse for giving as much as possible of the correspondence of these last few months, when—though the manner of his actual departure was violent, there was already the shadow, as it were, of death upon him.

To Sir J. T. Coleridge the letter was:—

'December 9, 1870.

'My dearest Uncle,—How long it is since I wrote to you!... And yet it is true that I think more often of you than of anyone, except Jem, Joan and Fan. In fact, your name meets me so often in one way or another—in papers from England, and much more in books continually in use, that I could not fail to think of you if I had not the true, deep love that brings up the old familiar face and voice so often before my eyes....

'I wish I could talk with you, or rather hear you answer my many questions on so many points. I get quite bewildered sometimes. It is hard to read the signs of our times; so hard to see where charity ends and compromise begins, where the old opinion is to be stoutly maintained, and where the new mode of thought is to be accepted. I suppose there always was some little difference among divines as to "fundamentals," and no ready-made solution exists of each difficult question as it emerges.

'There is reason for that being so, because it is part of our duty and trial to exercise our own power of discretion and judgment. But so much now seems to be left to individuals, and so little is accepted on authority. In Church matters I have for years thought Synods to be the one remedy. If men meet and talk over a difficulty, there is a probability of men's understanding each other's motives, and thus preserving charity. If one-twentieth part of a diocese insists upon certain observances which nineteen-twentieths repudiate, it seems clear that the very small minority is put out of court. Yet how often the small minority contains more salt than the large majority!

'I know indeed I am speaking honestly, that I am not worthy to understand dear Mr. Keble on many points. "The secret of our Lord" is with such men, and we fail to understand him, nous autres I mean, outside the sanctuary. Yet there is, I must confess it to you, my dear uncle, a something about his book on Eucharistic Adoration which has the character to me of foreign rather than of English divinity. I don't want to be exclusive, far from it. I don't want to be Anglican versus Primitive; but yet somehow, to me, there is a something which belongs more to French or Italian than to English character about some parts of the book. It is no doubt because I can't see what to his eye was plain.'

[An account of the voyage follows as before given.] 'The islanders are beginning to find out the true character of the many small vessels cruising among them, taking away people to the plantations in Queensland, Fiji, &c. So now force is substituted for deceit. Natives are enticed on board under promises (by signs of course, for nowhere can they talk to them) of presents, tempted down below into the hold to get tomahawks, beads, biscuit, &c., then the hatches are clapped on, and they are stolen away. I have to try and write a statement about it, which is the last thing I can do properly.'

[Then the history of the weddings and baptisms.] 'There is another pleasant feature to be noticed. The older scholars, almost all of whom are Banks Islanders, talk and arrange among themselves plans for helping natives of the islands. Thus Edward Wogale, of Mota, volunteers to go to Anudha, 300 or 400 miles off, to stay there with his friend Charles Sapinamba of that island, to aid him in working among his people. Edward is older and knows more than Charles. They talk in Mota, but Edward will soon have to speak the tongue of Anudha when living there. B—— and his wife offer to go to Santa Maria, Robert Pantatun and his wife to go to Matlavo, John Nonono to go to Savo, and Andrew Lalena also. This is very comforting to me. It is bona fide giving up country and home. It is indicative of a real desire to make known the Gospel to other lands. So long as they will do this, so long I think we may have the blessed assurance that God's Holy Spirit is indeed working in their hearts. Dear fellows! It makes me very thankful.

'My clerical staff is increased by a Mr. Jackson, long a friend and supporter of the Mission....

'Atkin is a steady-going fellow, most conscientious, with a good head-piece of his own, diligent and thoughtful rather than quick. He and Bice read Hebrew daily with me, and they will have soon a very fair knowledge of it. Joe Atkin knows his Greek Testament very fairly indeed: Ellicott, Trench, Alford, Wordsworth and others are in use among us.

'I wish you could see some of these little fellows. It is, I suppose, natural that an old bachelor should have pleasure in young things about him, ready-made substitutes for children of his own. I do like them. With English children, save and except Pena, I never was at my ease, partly I think from a worse than foolish self-consciousness about so ugly a fellow not being acceptable to children. Anyhow, I don't feel shy with Melanesians; and I do like the little things about me, even the babies come to me away from almost anyone, chiefly, perhaps, because they are acquainted at a very early age with a corner of my room where dwells a tin of biscuits.

'To this day I shut up and draw into my shell when any white specimen of humanity looms in sight. How seldom do one's natural tastes coincide with one's work. And I may be deceiving myself all along. It is true that I have a very small acquaintance with men; not so very small an acquaintance with men passed from this world who live in their books; and some living authors I read—our English Commentators are almost all alive.

'I think that I read too exclusively one class of books. I am not drawn out of this particular kind of reading, which is alone really pleasant and delightful to me, by meeting with persons who discuss other matters. So I read divinity almost if not quite exclusively. I make dutiful efforts to read a bit of history or poetry, but it won't do. My relaxation is in reading some old favourite, Jackson, Hooker, Jeremy Taylor, &c. Not that I know much about them, for my real studying time is occupied in translating and teaching. And so I read these books, and others some German, occasionally (but seldom) French: Reuss, for example, and Guizot. And on the whole I read a fair amount of Hebrew; though even now it is only the narrative books that I read, so to say, rapidly and with ease.

'I wish some of our good Hebrew scholars were sound Poly- and Melanesian scholars also. I believe it to be quite true that the mode of thought of a South Sea islander resembles very closely that of a Semitic man. And their state of mental knowledge or ignorance, too. It is certainly a mistake to make the Hebrew language do the work of one of our elaborated European languages, the products of thoughts and education and literary knowledge which the Hebrew knew nothing of. A Hebrew grammar constructed on the principle of a Greek or a Latin grammar is simply a huge anachronism.

'How did the people of the time of Moses, or David, or Jeremiah think? is the first question. How did they express their thoughts? is the second. The grammar is but the mode adapted in speech for notifying and communicating thoughts. That the Jew did not think, consequently did not speak, like a European is self-evident. Where are we to find people, children in thought, keenly alive to the outer world, impressible, emotional, but devoid of the power of abstract thought, to whom long involved processes of thought and long involved sentences of speech are unknown? Consequently, the contrivances for stringing together dependent clauses don't exist. Then some wiseacre of an 18th or 19th century German writes a grammar on the assumption that a paulo-post-futurum is necessarily to be provided for the unfortunate Israelite who thought and talked child's language. Now, we Melanesians habitually think and speak such languages. I assure you the Hebrew narrative viewed from the Melanesian point of thought is wonderfully graphic and lifelike. The English version is dull and lifeless in comparison. No modern Hebrew scholar agrees with any other as to the mode of construing Hebrew. Anyone makes anything out of those unfortunately misused tenses. Delitzsch, Ewald, Gesenius, Perowne, Thrupp, Kay too, give no rule by which the scholar is to know from the grammar whether the time is past, present, or future, i.e., whether such and such a verse is a narrative of a past fact or the prophecy of a future one. It is much a matter of exegesis; but exegesis not based on grammar is worth very little.

'Really the time is not inherent in the tense at all. But that is a strong assertion, which I think I could prove, give me time and a power of writing clearly. Sir William Martin is trying to prove it.

'All languages of the South Seas are constructed on the same principle. We say, "When I get there, it will be right." But all South Sea Islanders, "I am there, and it is right." The time is given by something in the context which indicates that the speaker's mind is in past, present, or future time. "In the beginning God made" rightly, so, but not because the tense gives the past sense, for the same tense very often can't have anything to do with a past sense, but in the beginning indicates a past time.

'The doctrine of the Vaw conversive is simply a figment of so-called grammarians; language is not an artificial product, but a natural mode of expressing ideas.

'And if they assume that Hebrew has a perfect and imperfect, or past and future (for the grammars use all kinds of names), why on earth should people who have, on their showing, a past tense, use a clumsy contrivance of turning a future tense into a past, and vice versa?

'If people had remembered that language is not a trick invented and contrived by scholars at their desks, but a natural gift, simple at first, and elaborated by degrees, they could not have made such a mess.

'The truth is, I think, that such a contrivance was devised to make Hebrew do what European scholars decided it must do, these very men being ignorant of languages in a simple uncivilised form.

'But, my dear Uncle, what a prose! Only, as I think a good deal about it, you will excuse it, I know.

'Well, it is time for the weddings! The Chapel looks so pretty, and (you can't believe it) so do the girls, Emma, Eliza, and Minnie, to be married to Edwin, Mulewasawasa, Thomas. The native name is a baptismal one, nevertheless, and a good fellow he is, my head nurse in my illness.

'I can't write about politics. Then comes the astounding news of this fearful war. What am I to say to my Melanesians about it? Do these nations believe in the Gospel of peace and goodwill? Is the Sermon on the Mount a reality or not? Is such conduct a repudiation of Christianity or not? Are nations less responsible than individuals? What possible justification is there for this war? It is fearful, fearful on every ground. Oh, this mighty belauded nineteenth-century civilisation!

'Yet society has improved in some ways. Even war is not without its accompaniment of religion. And it brings out kindly sympathy and stimulates works of charity. But what a fearful responsibility lies upon the cause of the war. It is hard to acquit Louis Napoleon of being really the cause.

'There would be great pleasure in seeing all the younger ones, not equal of course to that of seeing you all; but as I get older in my ways and habits, I think that my mind goes back more to the young ones. True, I have a large family about me, 145 Melanesians here now. Yet there is the want of community of thought on some subjects, and the difficulty of perfectly easy communication with them. No Melanesian tongue is like English to me.

'I wrote a first sheet, but filled it up with mere stupid thoughts about questions of the day, not worth sending. And this long letter, badly written, too, will weary your eyes.

'I must end. My kindest love to Aunt, Mary, and all. Always, my dearest Uncle,
'Your loving and grateful Nephew,
'**J. C. PATTESON.**'

Two letters of December 12 follow; the first to Bishop Abraham.

Mrs. Palmer's picture of the brides, at the last of the weddings the Bishop so enjoyed, may be acceptable. It went to Mrs. Abraham by the same opportunity:—

'Three were married a short time before Christmas; they, with five others, were baptized on Advent Sunday. They had been here about thirteen months, and had got on very well during that time, improved in every way. I think some of them are loveable girls, and it is pleasant to see them so happy and at home here.

'They were a queer-looking set when they first came, or I suppose I thought them so.

'I got some of the older girls to give them a good wash all over in warm water, and then gave them the new clothes. They looked at me in such a curious way. They had heard of me, "Palmer's wife," from the others, but had not seen an Englishwoman before. A few days after they came, I ran into their room with my hair down, and they exclaimed with wonder "We ura ras" ("very good"), almost shouting, and then I told them to feel it, and some kissed it with gentle reverence, as though it were something very extraordinary.

'They are very kind and obliging in doing anything I want. They have to be looked after a good bit, but are very obedient. I did not imagine they would give so little trouble. They are great chatterboxes, and very noisy, but all in an innocent way. They seldom quarrel among themselves. I don't think their feelings are so strong as those of the Maoris, either of love or hate.

'I wish you could have been present at the baptism. They looked so solemn, and spoke out very distinctly. They wore white calico jackets, and the Font was prettily decorated. The whole service was impressive, and not less so our good Bishop's voice and manner. They looked very nice, and it was amusing to see how they took it. Only one could I get to look in the glass; and she said the flowers were too large: the other two only submitted to being beautified.'

I return to the Bishop's correspondence:—

'Norfolk Island: Fourth Sunday in Advent, 1870.

'My dearest Joan,—I am choosing—a strange moment to write in. It is 8.30 A.M., and in an hour I am going to the New Church, built by the Pitcairners, to ordain Mr. C. Bice, Priest. I was up as usual early this morning, and I am not well, and feeling queer, and having already read and had Morning Chapel Service, I take now this means of quieting myself. You see it is nearly three miles to the "town;"

the service will be nearly three hours; I don't quite know how I shall get through it. I thought of having the service here; but our little Chapel won't hold even our Melanesian party (80 out of 145) who attend public prayers, and of course the islanders want to see, and it is good for them to see an ordination.

'This is my first expedition to the town since I came from the islands, I shall have a horse in case I am very tired, but I would rather walk all the way if I can.

'Just now I am headachy, and seedy too; but I think it is all coming right again. I hope to have a bright happy Christmas.

'After this day's Ordination we shall number one Bishop, six Priests, and one Deacon. There are three or four Melanesians who ought soon to be ordained; and if it is possible for me to spend two or three months this next winter at Mota, I must read with George, and perhaps ordain him Priest. It troubles me much that during all these summer months there can be no administration of the Holy Communion, though there are six communicants, besides George, now living for good at Mota. There will be four or five next year taking up their abode at the neighbouring island of Aroa.

'Dear Joan! At such times as these, when one is engaged in a specially solemn work, there is much heart-searching, and I can't tell you how my conscience accuses me of such systematic selfishness during many long years. I do see it now, though only in part. I mean, I see how I was all along making self the centre, and neglecting all kinds of duties, social and others, in consequence.

'I think that self-consciousness, a terrible malady, is one's misfortune as well as one's fault. But the want of any earnest effort at correcting a fault is worse perhaps than the fault itself. And I feel such great, such very great need for amendment here. This great fault brings its punishment in part even now. I mean, there is a want of brightness, cheerfulness, elasticity of mind about the conscious man or woman. He is prone to have gloomy, narrow, sullen thoughts, to brood over fancied troubles and difficulties; because, making everything refer to and depend on self, he naturally can get none of that comfort which they enjoy whose minds naturally turn upwards for help and light.

'In this way I do suffer a good deal. My chariot-wheels often drag very heavily. I am not often in what you may call good spirits. And yet I am aware that I am writing now under the influence of a specially depressing disorder, and that I may misinterpret my real state of mind. No one ought to be happier, as far as advantages of employment in a good service, and kindness of friends, &c., can contribute to make one happy. And, on the whole, I know my life is a happy one. I am sure that I have a far larger share of happiness than falls to the lot of most people. Only I do feel very much the lack, almost the utter lack of just that grace which was so characteristic of our dear Father, that simplicity and real humility and truthfulness of character!

'Well, one doesn't often say these things to another person! But it is a relief to say them. I know the remedy quite well. It is a very simple case for the doctor to deal with; but it costs the patient just everything short of life, when you have to dig right down and cut out by the roots an evil of a whole life standing. I assure you that it is hard work, because these feelings of ours are such intangible, untractable things! It is hard to lay hold of, and mould and direct them.

'But I pray God that I may not willingly yield to these gloomy unloving feelings. As often as I look out of myself upon Him, His love and goodness, then I catch a bright gleam. I think that you will not suspect me of being in a morbid state of mind. You will say, "Poor old fellow! he was seedy and depressed when he wrote all that." And that's true, but not the whole truth. I have much need of your prayers, indeed, for grace and strength to correct faults of which I am conscious, to say nothing of unknown sin.

'The Ordination is over, a quiet solemn service. The new Church, which I had not seen, is very creditable to the people, who built it themselves. It is wooden, about thirty-six or thirty-eight feet high, will hold 500 people well.

'Mr. Nobbs preached a very good sermon. I got on very well. Singing very good. Five Priests assisting in this little place!

'Christmas Eve.—What a meaning one of my favourite hymns (xxxviii. in "Book of Praise") has, when one thinks of this awful war, how hard to realize the suffering and misery; the rage and exasperation; the pride and exaltation! How hard to be thankful enough for the blessings of peace in this little spot!

'Our Chapel is beautifully decorated. A star at the east end over the word Emmanuel, all in golden everlasting flame, with lilies and oleanders in front of young Norfolk Island pines and evergreens.

'Seven new Communicants to-morrow morning. And all things, God be praised, happy and peaceful about us. All Christmas blessings and joys to you, dear ones!

'Christmas Day, 3 P.M.—Such a happy day! Such a solemn, quiet service at 7 A.M., followed by a short joyous 11 A.M. service. Christmas Hymn, one with words set to the tune for "Hark! the herald Angels sing."

'You know we never have the Litany on Sundays, because everybody is in Chapel twice a day, and we of course have it on Wednesday and Friday, and every native Communion Sunday, i.e., every alternate Sunday; we have no Communion Service at 11 A.M. as our Communicants have been in Chapel at the 7 o'clock service; so to-day, the Lessons being short, the service, including my short service, was over by 11.20.

'Now we have a week's holiday, that is, no school; though I think it is hard work, inasmuch as the preparing plans for school lessons, rearranging classes, sketching out the work, is tiring to me.

'Then I have such heaps of letters, which do worry me. But, on the other hand, I get much quiet time for some reading, and I enjoy that more than anything. Ten of our party were in Chapel at 11 A.M. with us for the first time. You know that we don't allow everyone to come, but only those that we believe to be aware of the meaning of Prayer, and who can read, and are in a fair way to be Catechumens. All these ten will, I hope, be baptized this summer.

'We are obliged, seriously, to think of a proper Chapel. The present one is 45 ft. by 19 ft. and too small. It is only a temporary oblong room; very nice, because we have the crimson hangings, handsome sandal-wood lectern, and some good carving. But we have to cram about eighty persons into it, and on occasions (Baptisms and Confirmations, or at an Ordination) when others come, we have no room. Mr. Codrington understands these things well, and not only as an amateur archaeologist; he knows the principle of building well in stone and wood. Especially useful in this knowledge here, where we work up our own material to a great extent. Our notion—his notion rather—is to have stone foundations and solid stone buttresses to carry a light roof. Then the rest will be wood. It ought to be about sixty feet by thirty, exclusive of chancel and apse. When we get all the measurements carefully made, we shall send exact accounts of the shape and size of the windows, and suggest subjects for stained glass by Hardman, or whoever might now be the best man. I hope that it won't cost very much, £perhaps 500.

December 21st.—We have not had a fine Christmas week, heavy rain and hot winds. But the rain has done much good. The Norfolk Islanders have much influenza, but we are at present quite free from it.

'Yesterday I spent two hours in training and putting to rights my stephanotis, which now climbs over half my verandah. I have such Japanese lilies making ready to put forth their splendours. Two or three azaleas grow well. Rhododendrons won't grow well. My little pines grow well, and are about seven feet high. It is very pleasant to see the growth of these things when I return from the voyage. The "pottering about" the little gardens, the park-like paddocks, with our sheep and cattle and horses, gives me some exercise every day. I go about quietly, and very often by myself, with a book. After thinking of all kinds of things and persons, I think that my increased and increasing unwillingness to write is one proof of my not being so strong or vigorous. I can't tell you what an effort it is to me to write a business letter; and I almost dread a long effusion from anyone, because, though I like reading it, I have the thought of the labour of answering it in my mind.

'Then again, I who used to be so very talkative, am taciturn now. Occasionally, I victimize some unfortunate with a flow of language about some point of divinity, or if I get a hearer on South Sea languages, I can bore him with much satisfaction to myself. But I am so stupid about small talk. I cannot make it. When I have to try with some Norfolk Islander, e.g. it does weary me so! Mind, I don't despise it. But instead of being a relaxation, it is of all things the hardest work to me. I am very dull in that way, you know. And sometimes I think people must take me to be sullen, for I never know how to keep the talk going. Then if I do talk, I get upon some point that no one cares for, and bore everybody. So here, too, I fall back on my own set of friends, who are most tolerant of my idiosyncrasies, and on my Melanesians who don't notice them.

'Your loving Brother,

'J. C. P.'

In spite of this distaste for writing, a good many letters were sent forth during the early months of 1871, most of them the final ones to each correspondent. The next, to Miss Mackenzie, is a reply to one in which, by Bishop Wilkinson's desire, she had sought for counsel regarding the Zulu Mission, especially on questions that she knew by experience to be most difficult, i.e., of inculcating Christian modesty, and likewise on the qualifications of a native ministry:—

'Norfolk Island: Jan. 26, 1871.

'My dear Miss Mackenzie,—In addition to a very long and interesting letter of yours, I have a letter from my sister, who has just seen you at Havant, so I must lose no more time in writing.

'First, let me say that I am as sure as I can be of anything that I have not registered, that I wrote to thank you for the prints long ago. Indeed, all these many gifts of yours are specially valuable as having been once the property of your brother, of whom it seems presumptuous for me to speak, and as having actually been used in Mission work in so distant a part of the world.

'I need not say that "Thomas a Kempis," his sextant, and his pedometer, are among my few real valuables. For the use of the prints, I can't say much on my own knowledge. My classes are for the most part made up of lads and young men, teachers, or preparing for Confirmation or Holy Communion; one class, always of younger ones, being prepared for Baptism; and sometimes youths, newcomers, when we have to take in hand a new language. Those prints are not of much use, therefore, to my special classes. Most of them have passed beyond the stage of being taught by pictures, though they like to look at them. But Mrs. Palmer has been using them constantly with the girls' classes, and so with the less advanced classes throughout the school.

'One difficulty will to the end be, that by the time we can talk freely to our scholars, and they can understand their own language employed as a vehicle for religious teaching, they are not sufficiently supplied with books. True, we have translations of such parts of the Bible as quite enable us to teach all that a Christian need know and do; but I often wish for plenty of good useful little books on other subjects, and I don't see my way to this. Our own press is always at work printing translations, &c. It is not easy to write the proper kind of book in these languages, and how are they to be printed? We haven't time to print them here, and who is to correct the press elsewhere? The great fact in your letter is the account of Bishop Wilkinson's Consecration. I am heartily glad to hear of it, and I will send, if I can, now, if not, soon, an enclosure to him for you to forward. I doubt if I can help him by any means as to qualifications of candidates for Holy Orders, &c. Our work is quite in a tentative state, and I am sometimes troubled to see that this Mission is supposed to be in a more advanced state than is really the case.

'For example, the report of a man going ashore dressed as a Bishop with a Bible in his hand to entice the natives away, assumes islands to be in a state where the conventional man in white tie and black-tail coat preaches to the natives. My costume, when I go ashore, is an old Crimean shirt, a very ancient wide-awake. Not a syllable has in all probability ever been written, except in our small note-books, of the language of the island. My attention is turned to keeping the crowd in good-humour by a few simple presents of fish-hooks, beads, &c. Only at Mota is there a resident Christian; and even there, people who don't know what Mota was, and what a Melanesian island, for the most part, alas! still is, would see nothing to indicate a change for the better, except that the people are unarmed, and would be friendly and confiding in their manner to a stranger.

'I hardly know how to bring my Melanesian experience to bear upon Zululand. The immorality, infanticide, superstition, &c., seem to be as great in a Melanesian island as in any part of the heathen world. And with our many languages, it is not possible for us to-know the "slang" of the various islands.

'We must be cheery about it all. Just see what the old writers, e.g. Chrysostom, say about Christian (nominally) morals and manners at wedding feasts, and generally. Impurity is the sin, par excellence, of all unchristian people. Look at St. Paul's words to the Corinthians and others. And we must not expect, though we must aim at, and hope, and pray for much that we don't see yet.

'What opportunity will Bishop Wilkinson have for testing the practical teaching power and steady conduct of his converts?

'Many of our Melanesians have their classes here, and we can form an opinion of their available knowledge, how far they can reproduce what they know, &c. We can see, too, whether they exercise any influence over the younger ones.

'Twelve (this season) are counted as sixth form, or monitors, or whatever you please to call them. [Then ensues an account of the rotation of industrial work, &c.]

'The other day I was examining an Ysabel lad, not formally in school, but he happened to be in my room, as they are always hanging about (as you know). He knew much more than I expected: "Who taught you all this? I am very well pleased."

'"Wogale," was the answer.

'Edward Wogale is George Sarawai's own brother, volunteering now to go to Anudha (Florida), near Ysabel Island. If I see that a young man (by his written notes, little essays so to say, analysis of lessons) understands what he has been taught; and if I see (by the proficiency of his pupils) that he can reproduce and communicate this teaching to others, then one part of the question of his fitness is answered. If he has been here for years, always well conducted, and if when at home occasionally he has always behaved well and resisted temptation; and perhaps I should add, if he is respectably married, or about to be married, to a decent Christian girl, then we may hope that the matter of moral fitness may be hopefully settled. Assuming this, and thank God, I believe I may assume that it is the case with several here now, as soon as a Deacon is required in any place that he is willing to work in, I should not hesitate to ordain him; but I can't specify exactly what his qualifications ought to be, because I can't undertake to settle the difficult question of what constitutes absolutely essential teaching for a Christian, i.e., the doctrine of fundamentals. Practically one can settle it; and that quite as well as in England, where there is, and must be any amount of inequality in the attainments and earnestness of the candidates, and where no examination can secure the fitness or even the mental capacity of the minister.

'I say to myself, "Here is an island or a part of an island from which we have had a good many scholars. Some married ones are going back to live permanently. They are Christians, and some are Communicants. They wish to do what they can to get the young ones about them for regular school and to talk to the older people. They all have and can use their Prayer-books. The people are friendly. Is there one among them of whom I can (humanly speaking) feel sure that, by God's blessing, he will lead a good life among them, and that he can and will teach them faithfully the elements of Christian truth and practice? If we all agree that there is such a one, why not ordain him?"

'But I want to see people recognising the office of Deacon as something very distinct indeed from that of the Priest. It is a very different matter indeed, when we come to talk about candidates for Priest's orders.

'Again, look at the missionary clergy of old times. No doubt in mediaeval times so much stress was laid upon the mere perfunctory performance of the ministerial act, as apart from careful teaching of the meaning and purport of the act, that the mediaeval missionary is so far not a very safe model for us to imitate.

'But I suppose that multitudes of men did good work who could no more comprehend nor write out the result of lessons that Edward, Henry, Edmund, Robert and twenty others here are writing out, than our English peasant can comprehend a learned theological treatise.

'And we must consider the qualifications of one's native clergy in relation to the work that they have to do. They have not to teach theology to educated Christians, but to make known the elements of Gospel truth to ignorant heathen people. If they can state clearly and forcibly the very primary leading fundamental truths of the Gospel, and live as simple-minded humble Christians, that is enough indeed.

'Perhaps this is as likely to make the Bishop understand my notions on the subject as any more detailed account of the course of instruction. I really have not time to copy out some ten or twelve pages of some older lad's note-book. I think you would be satisfied with their work. I don't mean, of course, the mere writing, which is almost always excellent, but there is a ready apprehension of the meaning of any point clearly put before them, which is very satisfactory. I am now thinking of the twenty or thirty best among our 145 scholars. This is a confused, almost unintelligible scrawl; but I am busy, and not very fresh for work.

'Yours very truly,
'J. C. PATTESON.'

A letter to Bishop Abraham was in hand at the same time, full of replies to the information in one newly received from this much valued friend. After deploring an attack of illness from which Mrs. Abraham had been suffering, comes the remark—

'You know what one always feels, that one can't be unhappy about good people, whatever happens to them. I do so enjoy your talk about Church works in England. It makes the modern phraseology intelligible. I know now what is meant by "missions" and "missioners" and "retreats."

'I was thinking lately of George Herbert at Hereford, as I read the four sermons which Vaughan lately preached there, one on the Atonement, which I liked very much indeed. The Cathedral has been beautifully restored, has it not? Then, I think of you in York Minster on November 20, with that good text from Psalm xcvi. I read your letter on Tuesday; on which day our morning Psalms in Chapel are always chanted, xcv., xcvi., xcvii. The application seems very natural, but to work out those applications is difficult. The more I read sermons, and I read a good many, the more I wonder how men can write them!

'Mind, I will gladly pay Charley ten shillings a sermon, if he will copy it out for me. It will do the boy good. Dear old Tutor used to fag me to write copies of the Bishop's long New Zealand letters, as I wrote a decent hand then. Don't I remember a long one from Anaiteum, and how I wondered where on earth or sea Anaiteum could be!

'I want to hear men talk on these matters (the Eucharistic question) who represent the view that is least familiar to me. And then I feel, when it comes to a point of Greek criticism, sad regret and almost remorse at my old idleness and foolish waste of time when I might have made myself a decent scholar. I cram up passages, instead of applying a scholarly habit of mind to the examination of them. And now too, it is harder than ever to correct bad habits of inattention, inaccuracy, &c. I am almost too weary oftentimes to do my work anyhow, much less can I make an effort to improve my way of doing it. But I must be content, thankful to get on somehow or other, and to be able to teach the fellows something.

'It is quite curious to see how often one is baffled in one's attempts to put oneself en rapport with the Melanesian mind. If one can manage it, they really show one that they know a good deal, not merely by heart, or as matter of memory, that is worth little; but they show that they can think. But often they seem utterly stupid and lost, and one is perplexed to know what their difficulty can possibly be. One thing is clear, that they have little faculty of generalization. As you know, they seldom have a name for their island, but only names for each tiny headland, and bay, and village. The name for the island you must learn from the inhabitants of another island who view the one whose name you are seeking as one because, being distant, it must appear to them in its oneness, not in its many various parts. Just so, they find it very difficult to classify any ideas under general heads. Ask for details, and you get a whole list of them. Ask for general principles, and only a few can answer.

'For example, it is not easy to make them see how all temptations to sin were overcome in the three representative assaults made upon Him in the wilderness; how love is the fulfilling of the Law; or how the violation of one Commandment is the violation (of the principle) of all.

'Then they have much difficulty (from shyness partly, and a want of teaching when young) in expressing themselves. They really know much that only skilful questioning, much more skilful than mine, can get out of them. It wants—all teaching does—a man with lots of animal spirits, health, pluck, vigour, &c. Every year I find it more difficult.'

To another of the New Zealand friends who had returned to England there was a letter on Jan. 31:—

'My dear Mr. Lloyd,—I must send you a line, though I have little to say. And I should be very sorry if we did not correspond with some attempt at regularity.

'What can one think of long without the mind running off to France? What a wonderful story it is! Only Old Testament language can describe it, only a Prophet can moralise upon it. It is too dreadful in its suddenness and extent. One fears that vice and luxury and ungodliness have destroyed whatever of chivalry and patriotism there once was in the French character. To think that this is the country of St. Louis and Bayard! The Empire seems almost systematically to have completed the demoralisation of the people. There is nothing left to appeal to, nothing on which to rally. It is an awful thing to see such judgments passing before our very eyes. So fearful a humiliation may do something yet for the French people, but I dread even worse news. It nearly came the other day to a repetition of the old Danton and Robespierre days.

'Here we are going on happily.... I would give something to spend a quiet Sunday with you in your old Church. How pleasant to have an old Church.

'Always yours affectionately,
'J. C. PATTESON.'

My own last letter came at the same time:—

'Norfolk Island: February 16th, 1871.

'My dear Cousin,—I must not leave your letter of last October without an instalment of an answer, though this is only a chance opportunity of sending letters by a whaler, and I have only ten minutes.

'Your account of the Southampton Congress is a regular picture. I think I can see the Bishops of Winton, Sarum, and Oxon; and all that you say by way of comment on what is going off in the Church at home interests me exceedingly. You can't think what a treat your letters are.

'You see Mr. Codrington is the only one of my age, and (so to say) education here, and so to commune with one who thinks much on these matters, which of course have the deepest interest for me, is very pleasant and useful. On this account I do so value the Bishop of Salisbury's letters, and it is so very kind of him to write to me in the midst of the overwhelming occupations of an English diocese.

'I don't think you have mentioned Dr. Vaughan. I read his books with much interest. He doesn't belong to the Keble theology; but he seems to me to be a thoughtful, useful, and eminently practical writer. He seems to know what men are thinking of, and to grapple with their difficulties. I am pleased with a little book, by Canon Norris, "Key to the New Testament": the work of a man who has read a good deal, and thought much.

'He condenses into a 2s. 6d. book the work of years.

'You are all alive now, trying to work up your parochial schools to "efficiency" mark—rather you were doing so, for I think there was only time allowed up to December 31, 1870. I hope that the efforts were successful. At such times one wishes to see great noble gifts, men of great riches giving their £10,000 to a common fund. Then I remember that the claims and calls are so numerous in England, that very wealthy men can hardly give in that way.

'Certainly I am spared the temptation myself of seeing the luxury and extravagance which must tempt one to feel hard and bitter, I should fear. We go on quietly and happily. You know our school is large. Thank God, we are all well, save dear old Fisher, who met with a sad boating accident last week. A coil of the boat raft caught his ankle as the strain was suddenly tightened by a rather heavy sea, and literally tore the front part of his foot completely off, besides dislocating and fracturing the ankle-bone. He bears the pain well, and he is doing very well; but there may be latent tetanus, and I shall not feel easy for ten days more yet.

'His smile was pleasant, and his grasp of the hand was an indication of his faith and trust, as he answered my remark, "You know Fisher, He does nothing without a reason: you remember our talk about the sparrows and the hairs of our heads."

'"I know," was all he said; but the look was a whole volume....

'Your Charlotte is Fisher's wife, you know, and a worthy good creature she is. Poor old Fisher, the first time I saw tears on his cheeks was when his wife met him being carried up, and I took her to him.

'The mail goes. Your affectionate Cousin,

'J. C. PATTESON.'

It may as well be here mentioned that Fisher Pantatun escaped tetanus, lived to have his limb amputated by a medical man, who has since come to reside at Norfolk Island, and that he has been further provided with a wooden leg, to the extreme wonder and admiration of his countrymen at Mota, where he has since joined the Christian community.

The home letter, finished the last, had been begun before the first, on Feb. 11, 'My birthday,' as the Bishop writes, adding:—'How as time goes on we think more and more of him and miss him. Especially now in these times, with so many difficult questions distressing and perplexing men, his wise calm judgment would have been such a strength and support. You know I have all his letters since I left England, and he never missed a mail. And now it is nearly ten years since he passed away from this world. What would he say to us all? What would he think of all that has taken place in the interval? Thank God, he would certainly rejoice in seeing all his children loving each other more and more as they grow older and learn from experience the blessedness and infrequency of such a thoroughly united, happy set of brothers and sisters. Why, you have never missed a single mail in all these sixteen years; and I know, in spite of occasional differences of opinion, that there is really more than ever of mutual love, and much more of mutual esteem than ever. There is no blessing like this. And it is a special and unusual blessing. And surely, next to God, we owe it to our dear parents, and perhaps especially to him who was the one to live on as we grew up into men and women. What should I have done out here without a perfect trust in you three, and without your letters and loving remembrances in boxes, &c.? I fancy that I should have broken down altogether, or else have hardened (more than I have become) to the soft and restful influences of the home life. I see some people really alone in these countries, really expatriated. Now I never feel that; partly because I have your letters, partly because I have the knowledge that, if ever I did have to go to England, I should find all the old family love, only intensified and deepened. I can tell you that the consciousness of all this is a great help, and carries one along famously. And then the hope of meeting by-and-by and for ever!'

'True to the kindred points of heaven and home.' Surely such loyalty of heart, making a living influence of parents so long in their graves, has been seldom, at least, put on record, though maybe it often and often has existed.

Again, on March 8:—'Such a fit came over me yesterday of old memories. I was reading a bit of Wordsworth (the poet).

I remembered dear dear Uncle Frank telling me how Wordsworth came over to Ottery, and called on him, and how he felt so honoured; and so I felt on thinking of him, and the old (pet) names, and most of all, of course, of Father and Mother, I seemed to see them all with unusual clearness. Then I read one of the two little notes I had from Mr. Keble, which live in my "Christian Year," and so I went on dreaming and thinking.

'Yes, if by His mercy I may indeed be brought to the home where they dwell! But as the power of keen enjoyment of this world was never mine, as it is given to bright healthy creatures with eyes and teeth and limbs sound and firm, so I try to remember dear Father's words, that "he did not mean that he was fit to go because there was little that he cared to stop here for." And I don't feel morbid like, only with a diminished capacity for enjoying things here. Of the mere animal pleasures, eating and drinking are a serious trouble. My eyes don't allow me to look about much, and I walk with "unshowing eye turned towards the earth." I don't converse with ease; there is the feeling of difficulty in framing words. I prefer to be alone and silent. If I must talk, I like the English tongue least of all. Melanesia doesn't have such combinations of consonants and harsh sounds as our vernacular rejoices in. If I speak loud, as in preaching, I am pretty clear still; but I can't read at all properly now without real awkwardness.

'I am delighted with Shairp's "Essays" that Pena sent me. He has the very nature to make him capable of appreciating the best and most thoughtful writers, especially those who have a thoughtful spirit of piety in them. He gives me many a very happy quiet hour. I wish such a book had come in my way while I was young. I more than ever regret that Mr. Keble's "Praelectiones" was never translated into English. I am sure that I have neglected poetry all my life for want of some guide to the appreciation and criticism of it, and that I am the worse for it. If you don't use Uncle Sam's "Biographia Literaria," and "Literary Remains," I should much like to have them.

'Do you, Fan, care to have any of my German books? I have, indeed, scarce any but theological ones. But no one else reads German here, and I read none but the divinity; and, indeed, I almost wish I had them in translations, for the sake of the English type and paper. My eyes don't like the German type at all.

'Moreover, now (it was not so years ago), all that is worth reading in their language is in a good serviceable English dress, and passed, moreover, through the minds of clear English thinkers—and the Germans are such wordy, clumsy, involved writers. A man need not be a German scholar to be well acquainted with all useful German theology. Döllinger is almost the only clear, plain writer I know among them. Dorner, the great Lutheran divine, gives you about two pages and a half of close print for a single sentence—awful work, worse than my English!... But I know that if I read less, and thought more, it would be better. Only it is such hard work thinking, and I am so lazy! I was amused at hearing, through another lad, of Edward Wogale's remark, "This helping in translation" (a revisal of the "Acts" in Mota) "is such hard work!" "Yes, my boy, brain work takes it out of you." I wish I had Jem's power of writing reports, condensing evidence into clear reliable statements. Lawyers get that power; while we Clergymen are careless and inaccurate, because, as old Lord Campbell said, "there is no reply to our sermons."

'What would I give to have been well drilled in grammar, and made an accurate scholar in old days! Ottery School and Eton didn't do much for me in that way, though of course the fault was chiefly in myself.

'But most of all, I think that I regret the real loss to us Eton boys of the weekly help that Winchester, Rugby, and Harrow boys had from Moberly, Arnold, and Vaughan in their sermons! I really think that might have helped to keep us out of harm!

'It is now 4.30 P.M., calm and hot. Such a tiger-lily on my table, and the pretty delicate achimenes, and the stephanotis climbing up the verandah, and a bignonia by its side, with honeysuckle all over the steps, and jessamine all over the two water-tanks at the angle of the verandah. The Melanesians have, I think, twenty-nine flower gardens, and they bring the flowers, &c.—lots of flowers, and the oleanders are a sight! Some azaleas are doing well, verbenas, hibiscus of all kinds. Roses and, alas! clove carnations, and stocks, and many of the dear old cottage things won't grow well. Scarlet passion flowers and splendid Japanese lilies of perfect white or pink or spotted. The golden one I have not yet dared to buy. They are most beautiful. I like both the red and the yellow tritoma; we have both. But I don't think we have the perfume of the English flowers, and I miss the clover and buttercup. And what would I give for an old-fashioned cabbage rose, as big as a saucer, and for fresh violets, which grow here but have little scent, and lilies of the valley! Still more, fancy seeing a Devonshire bank in spring, with primroses and daisies, or meadows with cowslip and clover and buttercups, and hearing thrushes and blackbirds and larks and cuckoos, and seeing trout rise to the flies on the water! There is much exaggeration in second-rate books about tropical vegetation. You are really much better off than we are. No trees equal English oaks, beeches, and elms, and chestnuts; and with very little expense and some care, you have any flowers you like, growing out of doors or in a greenhouse. You can make a warmer climate, and we can't a colder one. But we have plenty to look at for all that. There, what a nice hour I have spent in chatting with you!'

This same dreamy kind of 'chat,' full of the past, and of quiet meditation over the present, reminding one of Bunyan's Pilgrims in the Land of Beulah, continues at intervals through the sheets written while waiting for the 'Southern Cross.' Here is a note (March 14) of the teaching:—

'I am working at the Miracles with the second set, and I am able to venture upon serious questions, viz. the connection between sin and physical infirmity or sickness, the Demoniacs, the power of working miracles as essential to the Second Adam, in whom the prerogative of the Man (the ideal man according to the idea of his original condition) was restored. Then we go pretty closely into detail on each miracle, and try to work away till we reach a general principle or law.

'With another class I am making a kind of Commentary on St. Luke. With a third, trying to draw out in full the meaning of the Lord's Prayer. With a fourth, Old Testament history. It is often very interesting; but, apart from all sham, I am a very poor teacher. I can discourse, or talk with equals, but I can't teach. So I don't do justice to these or any other pupils I may chance to have. But they learn something among us all.'

He speaks of himself as being remarkably well and free from the discomforts of illness during the months of March and April: and these letters show perfect peace and serenity of spirit; but his silence and inadequacy for 'small talk' were felt like depression or melancholy by some of his white companions, and he always seemed to feel it difficult to rouse himself. To sit and study his Hebrew Isaiah with Delitzsch's comment was his chief pleasure; and on his birthday, April 1, Easter Eve, and the ensuing holy days, he read over all his Father's letters to him, and dwelt, in the remarks to his sisters, upon their wisdom and tenderness.

Mr. Codrington says: 'Before starting on the voyage he had confirmed some candidates in the Church in town: on which occasion he seemed to rouse himself with difficulty for the walk, and would go by himself; but he was roused again by the service, and gave a spirited and eloquent address, and came back, after a hearty meal and lively conversation, much refreshed in mind and body. This was on Palm Sunday. On Easter Day he held his last confirmation of three girls and two Solomon Island boys.

Then came the 'Southern Cross,' bringing with her from New Zealand a box with numerous books and other treasures, the pillow that the old Bishop of Exeter was leaning on when he died; a photograph, from the Bishop of Salisbury, of his Cathedral, and among the gifts for the younger Melanesians, a large Noah's ark, which elicited great shouts of delight.

'Well! [after mentioning the articles in order] all these things, and still more the thought of the pains taken and the many loving feelings engaged in getting them together, will help me much during the coming months. All the little unexpected things are so many little signs of the care and love you always have for me, and that is more than their own value, after all. I always feel it solemn to go off on these voyages. We have had such mercies. Fisher is doing quite well, getting about on crutches; and that is the only hospital case we have had during the whole summer.'

Then follows:—

'April 27th.—We start in a few hours (D.V.). The weather is better. You have my thoughts and hopes and prayers. I am really pretty well: and though often distressed by the thought of past sins and present ones, yet I have a firm trust in God's mercy through Christ, and a reasonable hope that the Holy Spirit is guiding and influencing me. What more can I say to make you think contentedly and cheerfully about me? God bless you all!'

So the last voyage was begun. The plan was much the same as usual. On the way to Mota, the Bishop landed on Whitsuntide Island, and there was told that what the people called a 'thief ship' had carried off some of their people. Star Island was found nearly depopulated. On May 16, the Bishop, with Mr. Bice and their scholars, landed at Mota, and the 'Southern Cross' went on with Mr. Brooke to

Florida, where he found that the 'Snatch-snatch' vessels, as they were there called, had carried off fifty men. They had gone on board to trade, but were instantly clapped under hatches, while tobacco and a hatchet were thrown to their friends in the canoe. Some canoes had been upset by a noose from the vessel, then a gun was fired, and while the natives tried to swim away, a boat was lowered, which picked up the swimmers, and carried them off. One man named Lave, who jumped overboard and escaped, had had two fingers held up to him, which he supposed to mean two months, but which did mean two years.

It was plain that enticing having failed, violence was being resorted to; and Mr. Brooke was left to an anxious sojourn, while Mr. Atkin returned to Mota on his way to his own special charge at Bauro. He says, on June 9:—

'The Bishop had just come back from a week's journeying with William in his boat. They had been to Santa Maria, Vanua Lava, and Saddle Island; the weather was bad, but the Bishop, although he is tired, does not think he is any the worse for his knocking about. He is not at all well; he is in low spirits, and has lost almost all his energy. He said, while talking about the deportation of islanders to Fiji, that he didn't know what was to be done; all this time had been spent in preparing teachers qualified to teach their own people, but now when the teachers were provided, all the people were taken away. The extent to which the carrying off of the natives has gone is startling. It certainly is time for us to think what is to be done next. I do not think that it is an exaggerated estimate, others would say it is under the mark, that one half the population of the Banks Islands over ten years of age have been taken away. I am trying not to expect anything about the Solomon Islands before we are there, but we have heard that several vessels have cargoes from there. If the people have escaped a little longer for their wildness, it will not be for long.

'The Bishop still remained at Mota, while I went back to the Solomon Islanders. The cliffs of Mota, and perhaps the intelligence of the people, had comparatively protected it, though Port Patteson had become a station of the "labour ships." The village of Kohimarama was not a disappointment.'

Bishop Patteson proceeds:—

'Things are very different. I think that we may, without danger, baptize a great many infants and quite young children—so many parents are actually seeking Christian teaching themselves, or willing to give their children to be taught. I think that some adults, married men, may possibly be baptized. I should think that not less than forty or fifty are daily being taught twice a day, as a distinct set of Catechumens. Besides this, some of the women seem to be in earnest.

'About two hours and a half are spent daily by me with about twenty-three grown-up men. They come, too, at all hours, in small parties, two or three, to tell their thoughts and feelings, how they are beginning to pray, what they say, what they wish and hope, &c.

'There is more indication than I ever saw here before of a "movement," a distinct advance, towards Christianity. The distinction between passively listening to our teaching, and accepting it as God's Word and acting upon it, seems to be clearly felt. I speak strongly and habitually about the necessity of baptism. "He that believeth, and is baptized" &c. Independently of the doctrinal truth about baptism, the call to the heathen man to take some step, to enter into some engagement, to ally himself with a body of Christian believers by some distinct act of his own, needing careful preparation, &c., has a meaning and a value incalculably great.

"'Yes, JESUS is to us all a source of pardon, light, and life, all these treasures are in Him. But he distributes these gifts by His Spirit in His appointed ways. You can't understand or receive the Gospel with a heart clinging to your old ways. And you can't remake your hearts. He must do it, and this is His way of doing it. You must be born again. You must be made new men."

'But why write all this, which is so commonplace?

'I feel more than ever the need of very simple, very short services for ignorant Catechumens.

'They used to throng our morning and evening prayer, perhaps 130 being present, for about that number attend our daily school; but they could not understand one sentence in ten of the Common Prayer-book. And it is bad for people to accustom themselves to a "formal" service. So I have stopped that. We baptized people have our regular service and at the end of my school, held in the dark, 7-8.30 P.M., in the verandah, we kneel down, and I pray extempore, touching the points which have formed the lesson.

'I don't like teaching these adults who can't read a form of private prayer. I try to make them understand that to wish earnestly is to pray; that they must put what they wish for clearly before their own minds, and then pray to God for it, through Christ. But I must try to supply progressive lessons for the Catechumens and others, with short prayers to be read by the teacher at the end (and beginning, too, perhaps) of the lesson. Much must depend on the individual teacher's unction and force.

'Well, I hope and trust to be able to tell you two months hence of some of these people being baptized. Only three adults have been baptized here on the island, and all three were dying.

'It is very comforting to think that all of us have been engaged in this Mota work, Dudley, and Mr. Pritt, and Mr. Kerr, too, and all our present staff have had much to do with it. Especially I think now of three young men, all married, who came to me lately, saying, "All these years (an interval of six or seven years) we have been thinking now and then about what we heard years ago, when we were with you in New Zealand for a few months." They are now thoroughly in earnest, as far as I can judge, and their wives, as I hope, move along with them. How one old set must have influenced them a long time ago. Bice, who speaks Mota very well, was very energetic during his fortnight here. He is now gone on with Mr. Brooke and Mr. Atkin that he may see the work in the Solomon Isles. I meant to go; but there seemed to be a special reason why I should stay here just now, vessels seeking labourers for Fiji and Queensland are very frequently calling at these islands.

'Mr. Thurston, late Acting Consul at Fiji, was with me the day before yesterday. He has taken a very proper view of this labour question; and he assures me that the great majority of the Fiji planters are very anxious that there should be no kidnapping, no unfair treatment of the islanders. I have engaged to go to Fiji (D.V.) at the end of my island work, i.e., on my return to Norfolk Island, probably about the end of September. I shall go there in the "Southern Cross," send her on to her summer quarters in New Zealand, and get from Fiji to New Zealand, after six or eight weeks in Fiji, in some vessel or other. There are about 4,000 or 5,000 white people in Fiji, mostly Church of England people, but (as I suppose) not very clearly understanding what is really meant by that designation. It is assumed that I am to act as their Bishop; and I ought to have been there before. But really a competent man might work these islands into a Bishopric before long.

'We must try to follow these islanders into Fiji or Queensland. But how to do it? On a plantation of, say, one hundred labourers, you may find natives of eight or ten islands. How can we supply teachers at the rate of one for every fifteen or twenty people? And there are some 6,000 or 7,000 islanders already on the Fiji plantations, and I suppose as many in Queensland.

'Some one knowing several languages, and continually itinerating from one plantation to another, might do something; but I don't think a native clergyman could do that. He must move about among white people continually in the boats, &c. I ought to do it; but I think my day has gone by for that kind of thing.

'I hope to judge of all this by-and-by. It might end in my dividing my year into Melanesian work as of old, and Melanesian work in Fiji, combined with the attempt to organise the white Church of England community, and only a month or two's work in Norfolk Island. To do this I must be in pretty good health. I may soon find out the limit of my powers of work, and then confine myself to whatever I find I can do with some degree of usefulness. We ought to make no attempt to proselytise among the Fiji natives, who have been evangelised by the Wesleyans. But there is work among our Western Pacific imported islanders and the white people.

'Norfolk Island could be quite well managed without me. Mr. Codrington could take that entirely into his own hands. I might spend a month or two there, and confirm Melanesians and Norfolk Islanders, and quietly fall into a less responsible position and be a moveable clergyman in Fiji or anywhere else, as long as my strength lasts.

'Norfolk Island certainly was rather my resting-place. But I think I am becoming more and more indifferent to that kind of thing. A tropical climate suits me, and Fiji is healthy—no ague. Dysentery is the chief trouble there. These are notions, flying thoughts, most likely never to be fully realised. Indeed, who can say what may befall me?'

Never to be fully realised! No. He, who in broken health so freely and simply sacrificed in will his cherished nook of rest on earth for a life so trying and distasteful, was very near the 'Rest that remaineth for the people of God.'

On June 26, the first public baptism in Mota took place, of one man, the Bishop and Sarawia in surplices in front of their verandah, the people standing round; but unfortunately it was a very wet day, and the rush of rain drowned the voices, as the Bishop made his convert Wilgan renounce individually and by name individual evil fashions of heathenism, just as St. Boniface made the Germans forsake Thor and Odin by name. There were twenty-five more nearly ready, and a coral-lime building was finished, 'like a cob wall, only white plaster instead of red mud,' says the Devonshire man. It was the first Church of Mota, again reminding us of the many 'white churches' of our ancestors; and on the 25th of June at 7 A.M., the first Holy Eucharist was celebrated there. It is also the place of private prayer for the Christians and Catechumens of Kohimarama.

The weather was exceedingly bad, drenching rain continually, yet the Bishop continued unusually well. His heart might well be cheered, when, on that Sunday evening in the dark, he was thus accosted:—

'I have for days been watching for a chance of speaking to you alone! Always so many people about you. My heart is so full, so hot every word goes into it, deep deep. The old life seems a dream. Everything seems to be new. When a month ago I followed you out of the Said Goro, you said that if I wanted to know the meaning and power of this teaching, I must pray! And I tried to pray, and it becomes easier as every day I pray as I go about, and in the morning and evening; and I don't know how to pray as I ought, but my heart is light, and I know it's all true, and my mind is made up, and I have been wanting to tell you, and so is Sogoivnowut, and we four talk together, and all want to be baptized.'

This man had spent one season at St. John's, seven years before; but on his return home had gone back to the ordinary island life, until at last the good seed was beginning to take root.

The next Sunday, the 2nd of July, ninety-seven children were baptized, at four villages, chosen as centres to which the adjacent ones could bring their children. It was again a wet day, but the rain held up at the first two places. The people stood or sat in a great half-circle, from which the eldest children, four or five years old, walked out in a most orderly manner, the lesser ones were carried up by their parents, and out of the whole ninety-seven only four cried! The people all behaved admirably, and made not a sound. At the last two places there was a deluge of rain; but as sickness prevailed in them, it was not thought well to defer the Baptism.

'It was a day full of thankful and anxious feelings. I was too tired, and too much concerned with details of arrangements, new names, &c., to feel the more contemplative devotional part of the whole day's services till the evening. Then, for I could not sleep for some hours, it came on me; and I thought of the old times too, the dear Bishop's early visits, my own fourteen years' acquaintance with this place, the care taken by many friends, past and present members of the Mission. The Sunday Collects as we call them, St. Michael's, All Saints', Saint Simon and St. Jude's calmed me, and my Sunday prayer, (that beautiful prayer in the Ordination of Priests, 'Almighty God and Heavenly Father,' slightly altered) was very full of meaning. So, thank God, one great step has been taken, a great responsibility indeed, but I trust not rashly undertaken.'

On July 4 the 'Southern Cross' returned, and the cruise among the New Hebrides was commenced. Mr. Bice was left to make a fortnight's visit at Leper's Island; and the Bishop, going on to Mai, found only three men on the beach, where there used to be hundreds, and was advised not to go to Tariko, as there had been fighting.

At Ambrym there was a schooner with Mr. Thurston on board, and fifty-five natives for Fiji. On the north coast was the 'Isabella,' with twenty-five for Queensland. The master gave Captain Jacob his credentials to show to the Bishop, and said the Bishop might come on board and talk to the people, so as to be convinced they came willingly, but weighed anchor immediately after, and gave no opportunity; and one man who stood on the rail calling out 'Pishopa, Pishopa,' was dragged back.

Mr. Bice was picked up again on the 17th, having been unmolested during his visit; but two of the 'Lepers,' who had been at Espiritu Santo, had brought back a fearful story that a small two-masted vessel had there been mastered by the natives, and the crew killed and eaten in revenge for the slaughter of some men of their own by another ship's company some time back.

On the voyage he wrote to the Bishop of Lichfield:—

'Off Tariko. Sloop: July 8, 1871.

'My dear Bishop,—Towards the end of April I left Norfolk Island, and after a six days' passage reached Mota. I called at Ambrym (dropping three boys) at three places; at Whitsuntide; at Leper's Island, dropping seven boys; Aurora, two places; Santa Maria, where I left B——, and so to Mota on the day before Ascension Day, and sent the vessel back at once to Norfolk Island for the Solomon Island scholars. All our Aroa and Matlavo party wished to spend Ascension Day with us; and after Holy Communion they went across with Commodore William Pasvorang in a good whale boat, which I brought down on the deck of the schooner, and which Willy looks after at Aroa. We want it for keeping up a visitation of the group.

'Bice, ordained Priest last Christmas, was with me. We found George and all well, George very steady and much respected. Charles Woleg, Benjamin Vassil and James Neropa, all going on well. The wives have done less than I hoped; true, they all had children to look after, yet they might have done more with the women. [Then as before about the movement.]

'After a week I went off in the boat, leaving Bice at Kohimarama, the Mota station. I went to B—— first at the north-east part of the island; back to Tarasagi (north-east point); sailed round to Lakona, our old Cock Sparrow Point, where B —— and I selected one or two boys to stay with him at Tarasagi. Thence we sailed to Avreas Bay, the great bay of Vanua Lava, B—— going back to Tarasagi by land. Heavy sea and rain; reached land in the dark 8 P.M., thankful to be safe on shore.

'On to Aroa, where I spent two days; Willie and Edwin doing what they can. Twenty children at school; but the island is almost depopulated, some seven hundred gone to Brisbane and Fiji. I did not go to Uvaparapara; the weather was bad, I was not well, and I expected the "Southern Cross" from Norfolk Island. Next day, after just a week's trip in the boat, I got to Mota; and the next day the "Southern Cross" arrived with Joe Atkin and Brooke and some twenty-four Solomon Islanders, many of them pressing to stay at Norfolk Island, where about eighty scholars in all are under the charge of Codrington, Palmer, and Jackson.

'I sent Bice on in the "Southern Cross," as he ought to see something of his brethren's work in the north and west. I had just a month at Mota, very interesting.

'I hope to spend three weeks more at Mota, if this New Hebrides trip is safely accomplished, and to baptize the rest of the children, and probably some ten or fifteen adults. All seem thoroughly in earnest. Some of the first scholars, who for years have seemed indifferent, are now among my class of thirty-three adults. It would be too long a story to tell you of their frequent private conversations, their stories, their private prayers, their expressions of earnest thankfulness that they are being led into the light.

'Some of the women, wives of the men, are hopeful. George's old mother said to me, "My boys are gone; George, Woleg, Wogale—Lehna died a Christian; Wowetaraka (the first-born) is going. I must follow. I listen to it all, and believe it all. When you think fit, I must join you," i.e. be baptized.

'It is very comforting that all the old party from the beginning are directly (of course indirectly also) connected with this movement. Some of those most in earnest now came under the influence of the early workers, Dudley, Mr. Pritt, &c.

'We need this comfort.

'From Mota some thirty or more have gone or been taken away, but the other islands are almost depopulated. Mr. Thurston, late Acting Consul in Fiji, was at Mota the other day seeking labourers. He says that about 3,000 natives from Tanna and Uvaparapara are now in Fiji, and Queensland has almost as many.

'He admits that much kidnapping goes on. He, with all his advantages of personal acquaintance with the people and with native interpreters on board, could only get about thirty. Another, Captain Weston, a respectable man who would not kidnap, cruised for some weeks, and left for Fiji without a single native on board. How then do others obtain seventy or one hundred more?

'But the majority of the Fiji settlers, I am assured, do not like these kidnapping practices, and would prefer some honest way of obtaining men. Indeed, many natives go voluntarily.

'In the Solomon Isles a steamer has been at Savo and other places, trying to get men.

'Three or four of these vessels called at Mota while I was there. On one day three were in sight. They told me they were shot at at Whitsuntide, Sta. Maria, Vanua Lava, &c. And, indeed, I am obliged to be very careful, more so than at any time; and here, in the North Hebrides, I never know what may happen, though of course in many places they know me.

'We are now at our maximum point of dispersion: Brooke at Anudha, J. Atkin at or near San Cristoval, Gr. Sarawia at Mota, B—— at Santa Maria, Bice at Leper's Island, Codrington at Norfolk Island, I on board "Southern Cross."

'Leper's Island is very pleasant; I longed to stay there. All the people wanting to come with us, and already discriminating between us and the other white visitors, who seem to have had little or no success there.

'July 21st.—At anchor, Lakona, west side of Santa Maria. Pleasant to be quietly at anchor on our old "shooting ground." We anchored for a day and a night at Ambrym, near the east point, very safe and comfortable place. Nine lads from five villages are on board. I bought about three and a half tons of yams there. Anchored again at the end of Whitsuntide, where I am thankful to say we have at last received two lads, one a very pleasant-looking fellow. That sad year of the dysentery, 1862, when Tanau died and Tarivai was so ill, two out of only three scholars from the island, made them always unwilling to give up lads.

'Next day at Leper's Island. Anchored a night off Wehurigi, the east end of the high land, the centre part of the island.

'Bice was quite feted by the people. We brought away three old and twelve new scholars, refusing the unpromising old scholars. There is, I hope, a sufficient opening now at Ambrym and Leper's Island to justify my assigning these islands to Jackson and Bice respectively.

'Our plan now is to take very few people indeed from the Banks Islands to Norfolk Island, as they have a permanent school and resident clergyman at Mota. The lads who may turn out clever and competent teachers are taken to Norfolk Island, none others.

'We must take our large parties from islands where there is as yet no permanent teacher: Ambrym, Leper's Island, the Solomon Islands.

'Meanwhile the traders are infesting these islands, as Captain Jacobs says, "like mosquitoes." Three vessels anchored at Mai during the day I was there. Three different vessels were at Ambrym. To-day I saw four, three anchored together near the north-east side of Santa Maria. B—— saw six yesterday.

'The people now refuse to go in them, they are much exasperated at their people being kept away so long. Sad scenes are occurring. Several white men have been killed, boats' crews cut off, vessels wrecked.

'We shall hear more of such doings; and really I can't blame the islanders. They are perfectly friendly to friends; though there is much suspicion shown even towards us, where we are not well known.

'As far as I can speak of my own plans, I hope to stay at Mota for a time, till the "Southern Cross" returns from Norfolk Island; then go to the Solomon Islands; return by way of Santa Cruz and probably Tikopia, to Mota; thence to Norfolk Island; thence probably to New Zealand, to take the steamer for Fiji. We have no chart on board of Fiji; and I don't think it right to run the risk of getting somehow to Levuka with only the general chart of the South Pacific, so I must go, as I think, to New Zealand, and either take the steamer or procure charts, and perhaps take Mr. Tilly as pilot. I don't like it; it will be very cold; but then I shall (D.V.) see our dear Taurarua friends, the good Bishop and others, and get advice about my Fiji movements. The Church of England folk there regard me as their Bishop, I understand; and the Bishops of Sydney and Melbourne assume this to be the fitting course. A really able energetic man might do much there, and, in five years, would be Bishop of Levuka.

'This is all of Melanesia and myself; but you will like to have this scrawl read to you.

'How I think of you as I cruise about the old familiar places, and think that you would like to have another trip, and see the old scenes with here and there, thank God, some little changes for the better. Best love, my dear dear Bishop, to Mrs. Selwyn, William and John.

'Your very affectionate
'J. C. PATTESON.'

About forty, old scholars and new, had been collected and brought back to Mota; where, after landing the Bishop, Captain Jacobs sailed back to Norfolk Island, carrying with him the last letters that were to be received and read as from a living man. All that follow only came in after the telegram which announced that the hand that had written them was resting beneath the Pacific waters. But this was not until it had been granted to him to gather in his harvest in Mota, as will be seen:—

'Mota: July 31, 1871.

'My dearest Sisters,—You will be glad to know that on my return hither after three weeks' absence, I found no diminution of strong earnest feeling among the people. George Sarawia had, indeed, been unable to do very much in the way of teaching 60 or 90 men and women, but he had done his best, and the 100 younger people were going on with their schooling regularly. I at once told the people that those who wished to be baptized must let me know; and out of some 30 or 40 who are all, I think, in earnest, 15, and some few women are to be baptized next Sunday. These will be the first grown-up people, save John Wilgan, baptized in Mota, except a few when in an almost dying state. They think and speak much of the fact that so many of their children have been baptized, they wish to belong to the same set. But I believe them all to be fairly well instructed in the great elementary truths. They can't read; all the teaching is oral, no objection in my eyes. It may be dangerous to admit it, but I am convinced that all that we can do is to elevate some few of the most intelligent islanders well, so that they can teach others, and be content with careful oral teaching for the rest. How few persons even among ourselves know how to use a book! And these poor fellows, for I can only except a percentage of our scholars, have not so completely mastered the mechanical difficulty of reading as to leave their minds free for examination of the meaning and sense of what they read. I don't undervalue a good education, as you know. But I feel that but few of these islanders can ever be book-learned; and I would sooner see them content to be taught plain truths by qualified persons than puzzling themselves to no purpose by the doubtful use of their little learning. You know that I don't want to act the Romish Priest amongst them. I don't want to domineer at all. And I do teach reading and writing to all who come into our regular school, and I make them read passages to verify my teaching. At the same time, I feel that the Protestant complaint of "shutting up the Bible from the laity," is the complaint of educated persons, able to read, think, and reflect.

'The main difficulty is, of course, to secure a supply of really competent teachers. George, Edward, Henry, Robert, and some three or four others are trustworthy. I comfort myself by thinking that a great many of the mediaeval Clergy certainly did not know as much nor teach as well.

'Yesterday I baptized 41 more children and infants on again an unpropitious day.

I was obliged to leave 42 to be baptized at some future time. The rain poured down. The people will bring them over to-morrow. The whole number of infants and children will amount to 230 or more, of adults to perhaps 25 or 30. You will pray earnestly for them that they may lead the rest of their lives "according to this beginning."

'There is much talk, something more than talk, I think, about putting up a large church-house here, on this side of the island (north-west side) and of a school-house, for church also, on the south-east side.

'We have all heavy coughs and colds; and I have had two or three very disturbed nights, owing to the illness of one of the many babies. The little thing howls all night.

'All our means of housing people are exhausted. People flock here for the sake of being taught. Four new houses have been built, three are being built. We shall have a large Christian village here soon, I hope and trust. At present every place is crammed, and 25 or 30 sleep on the verandah. The little cooking house holds somehow or other about 24 boys; they pack close, not being burdened with clothes and four-posters. I sleep on a table, people under and around it. I am very well, barring this heavy cold and almost total loss of voice for a few hours in the morning and evening.

'August 1st.—Very tired 7 A.M., Prayers 7.20-8.20, school 8.20-10; baptized 55 infants and young children. Now it is past 1; a boisterous day, though as yet no rain. I had a cup of cocoa at 6.30, and at 10.30 a plate of rice and a couple of eggs, nice clean fare. The weather is against me, so cold, wet, and so boisterous. I got a good night though, for I sent Mrs. Rhoda and her squalling baby to another house, and so slept quietly.

'I am sorry that teaching is so irksome to me. I am, in a sense, at it all day. But there is so much to be done, and the people, worthy souls, have no idea that one can ever be tired. After I was laid down on my table, with my air-pillow under my head and my plaid over me, I woke up from a doze to find the worthy Tanoagnene sitting with his face towards me, waiting for a talk about the rather comprehensive subject of Baptism.

'And at all odd times I ought to be teaching George and others how to teach, the hardest work of all. I think what a life a real pedagogue must have of it. There is so much variety with me, so much change and holiday, and so much that has its special interest.

'The "Southern Cross" has been gone a week. I hope they have not this kind of weather. If they have, they are getting a good knocking about, and they number about 55 on board.

'August 6th.—To-day there is no rain, for the first time for weeks. It blew a heavy gale all night, and had done so with heavy rain for some days before.

'At 8 A.M. to-day I baptized 14 grown men, one an old bald man, and another with a son of sixteen or so, five women and six lads, taught entirely in George's school. Afterwards, at a different service, 7 infants and little children were baptized. 238 + 5 who have died have now been baptized since the beginning of July. To-day's service was very comforting. I pray and trust that these grown-up men and women may be kept steadfast to their profession. It is a great blessing that I could think it right to take this step. You will, I know, pray for them; their position is necessarily a difficult one.

'It is 2 P.M., and I feel tired: the crowds are gone, though little fellows are as usual sitting all round one. I tell them I can't talk; I must sit quietly, with Charlotte Yonge's "Pupils of St. John the Divine." Dear me, what advantage young folks have nowadays, though indeed the dangers of these times far outweigh those of our young days.

'I suppose Lightfoot's "Commentaries" hardly come in your way. They are critical and learned on the Greek of St. Paul's Epistles. But there are dissertations which may be read by the English reader. He seems to me to be a very valuable man, well fitted by his learning, and moderation, and impartiality, and uncontroversial temper to do much good. His sympathies with the modern school of thought are, I fancy, beyond me.

'There is no doubt that Matthew Arnold says much that is true of the narrowness, bigotry, and jealous un-Christian temper of Puritanism; and I suppose no one doubts that they do misrepresent the true doctrine of Christianity, both by their exclusive devotion to one side only of the teaching of the Bible, and by their misconception of their own favourite portions of Scripture. The doctrine of the Atonement was never in ancient times, I believe, drawn out in the form in which Luther, Calvin, Wesley, and others have lately stated it.

'The fact of the Atonement through the Death of Christ was always clearly stated; the manner, the "why," the "how" man's Redemption and Reconciliation to God is thus brought about, was not taught, if at all, after the Protestant fashion.

'Oxenham's "History of the Catholic Doctrine of the Atonement" is a fairly-written statement of what was formerly held and taught. Such words as "substitution," "satisfaction," with all the ideas introduced into the subject from the use of illustrations, e.g. of criminals acquitted, debts discharged, have perplexed it perhaps, rather than explained, what must be beyond explanation.

'The ultra-Calvinistic view becomes in the mind and language of the hot-headed ignorant fanatic a denial of God's Unity. "The merciful Son appeasing the wrath of the angry Father" is language which implies two Wills, two Counsels in the Divine Mind (compare with this John iii. 16).

I suppose that an irreverent man, being partly disgusted with the popular theology, having no scruples about putting aside Inspiration, &c., and conceiving that he himself is an adequate representative of the nineteenth century's intelligence, and that the nineteenth century's intelligence is most profound and infallible, sets to work to demolish what is distasteful to himself, and what the unerring criticism of the day rejects, correcting St. Paul's mistakes, patronising him whenever he is fortunate enough to receive the approbation of the great thinkers of our day, and so constructs a vague "human" religion out of the Christianity which he criticises, eliminating all that lies beyond the speculative range of the mind, and that demands assent by its own authority as God's Revelation. I don't know how to state briefly what I mean.

'I think I can understand that this temper of mind is very prevalent in England now, and that I can partly trace the growth of it. Moreover, I feel that to ignore, despise, or denounce it, will do no good.

'As a matter of fact, thousands of educated men are thinking on these great matters as our fathers did not think of them. Simplicity of belief is a great gift; but then the teaching submitted to such simple believers ought to be true, otherwise the simple belief leads them into error. How much that common Protestant writers and preachers teach is not true! Perhaps some of their teaching is untrue absolutely, but it is certainly untrue relatively, because they do not hold the "proportion of the faith," and by excluding some truths and presenting others in an extravagant form they distort the whole body of truth.

'But when a man not only points out some of the popular errors, but claims to correct St. Paul when he Judaizes, and to do a little judicious Hellenizing for an inspired Apostle, one may well distrust the nineteenth century tone and spirit.

'I do really and seriously think that a great and reverently-minded man, conscious of the limits of human reason—a man like Butler—would find his true and proper task now in presenting Christian teaching in an unconventional form, stripped of much error that the terms which we all employ when speaking doctrine seem unavoidably to carry with them.

'Such a man might ask, "What do you mean by your theory of Substitution, Satisfaction, &c.?" "Where do you find it?" "Prove it logically from the Bible." "Show that the early Church held it."

'Butler, as you know, reproved the curiosity of men who sought to find out the manner of the Atonement. "I do not find," he says, "that it is declared in the Scriptures." He believed the fact, of course, as his very soul's treasure. "Our ignorance," he says, "is the proper answer to such enquiries."

'At the same time, no one now can do, it seems, what another Butler might do, viz., deal with the Bible as the best of the nineteenth-century men wish to hear a divine deal with it. He would never make mere assertions. He would never state as a proved truth, to be presented to a congregation's acceptance, a statement or a doctrine which really equalled only an opinion of Wesley or any other human teacher. He would never make arbitrary quotations from Scripture, and try to prove points by illogical reasoning, and unduly pressing texts which a more careful collation of MSS. has shown to be at least doubtful. And by fairness and learning he would win or conciliate right-minded men of the critical school. What offends these men is the cool reckless way in which so many preachers make the most audacious statements, wholly unsupported by any sound learning and logical reasoning. A man makes a statement, quotes a text or two, which he doesn't even know to be capable of at least one interpretation different from that which he gives to it; and so the critical hearer is disgusted, and no wonder.

'One gain of this critical spirit is, that it makes all of us Clergy more circumspect in what we say, and many a man looks at his Greek Testament nowadays, and at a good Commentary too, before he ventures to quote a text which formerly would have done duty in its English dress and passed muster among an uncritical congregation. Nowadays every clergyman knows that there are probably men in his congregation who know their Bible better than he does, and as practical lawyers, men of business, &c., are more than his match at an argument. It offends such men to have a shallow-minded preacher taking for granted the very points that he ought to prove, giving a sentence from some divine of his school as if it settled the question without further reference even to the Bible.

'This critical spirit becomes very easily captious; and a man needn't be unbelieving because he doesn't like to be credulous. Campbell's book on the Atonement is very hard, chiefly because the man writes such unintelligible English. I think Shairp in his "Essays," gives a good critique as far as it goes on the philosophical and religious manner of our day.

'Alexander Knox says somewhere in his correspondence with Bishop Jebb that he couldn't understand the Protestant theory of Justification. And it does seem to be often stated as if the terms employed in describing a mere transaction could adequately convey the true power and meaning of a Divine mystery.

'But I only puzzle you, I dare say, and certainly I am liable to the charge of not writing intelligible English. I can tell you I am glad enough that I am not called on to preach on these subjects after the fashion that a preacher in England must go to work.

'It is a cool thing to say, but I do believe that what half our English congregations want is just the plain simple teaching that our Melanesians get, only the English congregations wouldn't stand it.'

A letter to Arthur Coleridge is of the same date:—

'Mota Island: August 6, 1871—

'My dear Arthur,—I have had a busy day, having baptized thirty-two persons, of whom twenty-five are adults; and then the crowd, the incessant talking, teaching, and the anxious feeling which attend any step of so much importance as the Baptism from heathenism. Fourteen of the men are married, two are elderly, several are middle-aged, five women are among the number. I believe that God's spirit is indeed working in the hearts of these people. Some twelve or thirteen years have passed, and only now have I felt that I could take the step of baptizing the infants and young children here, the parents promising that they shall be sent to school as they grow up. About 200 young children have during the past month been baptized: things seem hopeful. It is very happy work; and I get on pretty well, often very tired, but that doesn't matter.

'I could wish all my good friends were here, that those who have been enabled to contribute to this end might see for themselves something of the long hoped for beginning of a new state of things in this little island.

'August 11.—In a little more than a month 248 persons have been baptized here, twenty-five of them adults, the rest infants and young children. I am very sorry to think that I must leave them soon, for I expect the "Southern Cross" in a few days; and I must go to the Solomon Islands, from them to Santa Cruz Island, and so to Norfolk Island, calling here on the way. Then I am off to the Fiji Islands for, I suppose, a month or six weeks. There are some 6,000 or 7,000 white people there, and it is assumed by them and the Church people in this part of the world that I must be regarded as their Bishop. Very soon a separate Bishop ought to be at work there, and I shall probably have to make some arrangement with the settlers. Then, on the other hand, I want to look into the question of South Sea Islanders who are taken to the Fiji plantations.

'How far I can really examine into the matter, I hardly know. But many of the settlers invite me to consider the matter with them.

'I believe that for the most part the islanders receive good treatment when on the plantations, but I know that many of them are taken away from their islands by unfair means.

'The settlers are only indirectly responsible for this. The traders and sailing masters of the vessels who take away the islanders are the most culpable. But the demand creates the supply.

'Among all my multifarious occupations here, I have not much time for reading; I am never alone night or day. I sleep on a table, with some twelve or more fellows around me; and all day long people are about me, in and out of school hours. But I have read, for the third time I think, Lightfoot's "Galatians"—and I am looking forward to receiving his book on the Ephesians. He doesn't lay himself out to do exactly the work that Bishop Ellicott has done so excellently, and his dissertations are perhaps the most valuable part of his work. He will gain the ear of the men of this generation, rather than Ellicott; he sympathises more with modern modes of thought, and is less rigid than Ellicott. But he seems very firm on all the most essential and primary points, and I am indeed thankful for such a man. I don't find much time for difficult reading; I go on quietly, Hebrew, &c. I have many good books on both Old and New Testaments, English and German, and some French, e.g. Keuss and Guizot.

'I like to hear something of what this restless speculative scientific generation is thinking and doing. But I can't read with much pleasure the fragmentary review literature of the day. The "Cornhill" and that class of books I can't stand, and sketchy writings. The best specimens of light reading I have seen of late are Charlotte Yonge's "Pupils of St. John the Divine," and Guizot's "St. Louis," excellent.

'I did read, for it was put on board, Disraeli's novel. I was on my back sea-sick for four days; what utter rubbish! clever nonsense! And I have read Mr. Arnold's "St. Paul and Protestantism." He says some clever things about the Puritan mind, no doubt. But what a painful book it is: can't he see that he is reducing all that the spirit of a man must needs rest on to the level of human criticism? simply eliminating from the writings of the Apostles, and I suppose from the words of the Saviour, all that is properly and strictly Divine.—[Then follows much that has been before given.]—How [winding up thus] thankful I am that I am far away from the noise and worry of this sceptical yet earnest age!

'There is something hazy about your friend Davis's writings. I know some of his publications, and sympathise to a very considerable extent with him. But I can't be sure that I always understand him: that school has a language of its own, and I am not so far initiated as to follow.

'I can't understand Maurice, much as I respect him. It is simply wasting my time and my brains to attempt to read him; he has great thoughts, and he makes them intelligible to people less stupid than me, and many writers whom I like and understand have taken their ideas from him; but I cannot understand him. And I think many of his men have his faults. At least I am so conceited as to think it is not all my fault.

'Do you know two little books by Norris, Canon of Bristol, "Key to the Gospel History," and a Manual on the Catechism?

'They are well worth reading, indeed I should almost say studying, so as to mould the teaching of your young ones upon them.

'How you would be amused could you see the figures and scenes which surround me here! To-day about 140 men, women, lads and girls are working voluntarily here, clearing and fencing the gardens, and digging the holes for the yams, and they do this to help us in the school; we have two pigs killed, and give them a bit of a feast. The feeling is very friendly. A sculptor might study them to great advantage, though clothing is becoming common here now. Our thirty-four baptized adults and our sixteen or twenty old scholars wear decent clothing, of course.

'Well, I must leave off.

'I think very often of you, your wife and children, and, indeed, of you all. It would be very nice to spend a few weeks with you, but I should not get on well in your climate.

'The heat seems to suit me better, and I am pretty well here. Indeed I am better than I have been for more than a year, though I have a good deal of discomfort.

'Good-bye, dear Arthur. How often I think of your dear dear Father.

'Your affectionate Cousin,

'J. C. PATTESON.'

To the sisters, the journal continues—recording, on August 14, the Baptism of twelve men and women the day before, the Communion of sixteen at 7 A.M., the presence of fifty-six baptized persons at morning service. More than 100 were working away the ensuing day in preparing yam gardens for Kohimarama, while two pigs were stewing in native ovens to feast them afterwards; and the Bishop was planting cocoa-nut trees and sowing flower seeds, or trying experiments with a machine for condensing water, in his moments of relaxation, which were few, though he was fairly well, and very happy, as no one can doubt on reading this:—

'Lots of jolly little children, and many of them know me quite well and are not a bit shy. They are often very sad-looking objects, and as they don't get regularly washed, they often have large sores and abscesses, poor little things. But there are many others—clean-skinned, reddish brown, black-eyed, merry little souls among them. The colour of the people is just what Titian and the Venetian painters delighted in, the colour of their own weather-beaten Venetian boatmen, glowing warm rich colour. White folks look as if they were bleached and had all the colour washed out of them.

'Some of the Solomon Islanders are black, and some of the New Hebrides people glossy and smooth and strong-looking; but here you seldom see any very dark people, and there are some who have the yellow, almost olive complexion of the South European. Many of the women are tattooed from head to foot, a regular network of a bluish inlaid pattern. It is not so common with the men, rather I ought to say very unusual with them, though many have their bodies marked pretty freely.'

On the 17th sixteen more adults were baptized, elderly men, whose sons had been baptized in New Zealand coming in, and enemies resigning deadly feuds.

The work in Mota is best summed up in this last letter to Bishop Abraham, begun the day after what proved the final farewell to the flock there, for the 'Southern Cross' came in on the 19th, and the last voyage was at once commenced:—

'"Southern Cross": Sunday, August 20, 1871.

'My dear dear Friends,—Yesterday the "Southern Cross" came to me at Mota, twenty-seven days after leaving that island for Norfolk Island with some fifty Melanesians on board under charge of Bice.

'Into what a new world your many kind affectionate letters take me! And how good it must be for me to be taught to think more than I, alas! usually do, about the trials and sorrows of others.

'I have had such a seven weeks at Mota, broken by a three weeks' course in the New Hebrides, into two portions of three and four weeks.

'Last year we said in our Report, that the time seemed to be come when we should seek to move the people in Mota to do more than assent to the truth of our words and the blessings promised in the Gospel, when we should urge them to appropriate to themselves those blessings, by abandoning their ignorant heathen ways, and embracing Christianity.

'That time has come in the good Providence of God, in answer to His all-prevailing Intercession, and hastened (who can doubt it?) by the prayers of the faithful everywhere—your Whit-Sunday thoughts and prayers, your daily thoughts and prayers, all contributing to bring about a blessed change indeed in the little island.

'In these two months I have baptized 289 persons in Mota, 231 children and infants, seventeen of the lads and boys at Kohimarama, George Sarawia's school, and forty-one grown and almost all married men and women.

'I have tried to proceed cautiously and to act only when I had every human probability of a personal conviction and sincere desire to embrace Christian teaching and to lead a Christian life. I think the adult candidates were all competently instructed in the great truths.

'I feel satisfied of their earnestness, and I think it looks like a stable, permanent work. Yet I need not tell you how my old text is ever in my mind, "Thine heart shall fear, and be enlarged." Now more than ever are your prayers needed for dear old George Sarawia and his infant Church.

'I never had such an experience before. It is something quite new to me. Classes regularly, morning and evening, and all day parties coming to talk and ask questions, some bringing a wife or child, some a brother, some a friend. We were 150 sleeping on the Mission premises, houses being put up all round by people coming from a distance.

'Scarce a moment's rest, but the work so interesting and absorbing, that I could scarcely feel weariness. The weather for six out of the seven weeks was very rainy and bad generally; but I am and was well, very well—not very strong, yet walking to Gatava and back, five or six miles, on slippery and wet paths, and schooling and talking all day.

'The actual services were somewhat striking. The behaviour of the people reverent and quiet during the infants' and children's baptisms; and remarkably so during the baptisms of adults.

'You can understand the drift of my teaching: trying to keep to the great main truths, so as not to perplex their minds with a multiplicity of new thoughts.

'I think that I shall have to stay a few days at Mota on my return (D.V.) from Solomon and Santa Cruz Islands, as there are still many Catechumens.

'I am half disposed to ordain George Priest on my return (D.V.) Yet on the whole I think it may be better to wait till another year. But I am balancing considerations. Should any delay occur from my incapacity to go to Mota, which I don't at all anticipate, it would be a serious thing to leave such a work in the hands of a Deacon, e.g. ten communicants are permanent dwellers now in Mota; and I really believe that George, though not learned, is in all essentials quite a fit person to be ordained Priest. This growth of the work, owing, no doubt, much to him, is a proof of God's blessing on him.

'I pray God that this may be a little gleam of light to cheer you, dear friends, on your far more toilsome and darksome path. It is a little indeed in one sense; yet to me, who know the insufficiency of the human agency, it is a proof indeed that the Gospel is dunamis Theou eis soterian.

'I can hardly realize it all yet. It is good to be called away from it for a month or two. I often wished that Codrington, Palmer, and the rest could be with me: it seemed selfish to be witnessing by myself all this great happiness—that almost visible victory over powers of darkness.

'There is little excitement, no impulsive vehement outpouring of feeling. People come and say, "I do see the evil of the old life; I do believe in what you teach us. I feel in my heart new desires, new wishes, new hopes. The old life has become hateful to me; the new life is full of joy. But it is so mawa (weighty), I am afraid. What if after making these promises I go back?"

"What do you doubt—God's power and love, or your own weakness?"

"'I don't doubt His power and love; but I am afraid."

"'Afraid of what?'" "'Of falling away."

"'Doesn't He promise His help to those who need it?"

"'Yes, I know that." "'Do you pray?"

"'I don't know how to pray properly, but I and my wife say—God, make our hearts light. Take away the darkness. We believe that you love us because you sent JESUS to become a Man and die for us, but we can't understand it all. Make us fit to be baptized."

"'If you really long to lead a new life, and pray to God to strengthen you, come in faith, without doubting."

'Evening by evening my school with the baptized men and women is the saying by heart (at first sentence by sentence after me, now they know them well) the General Confession, which they are taught to use in the singular number, as a private prayer, the Lord's Prayer, the Creed, the ten Commandments (a short version). They are learning the Te Deum. They use a short prayer for grace to keep their baptismal vows.

'I think that they know fairly well the simpler meaning of these various compendiums of Prayer, Faith and Duty. But why enter into details? You know all about it. And, indeed, you have all had your large share, so to say, in bringing about this happy change.

'And then I turn from all this little secluded work to the thoughts of England and France, the Church at home, &c....

'I have now read the "Guardian's" account of the civil war in France. There is nothing like it to be read of, except in the Old Testament perhaps. It is like the taking of Jerusalem.

'It is an awful thing! most awful! I never read anything like it. Will they ever learn to be humble? I don't suppose that even now they admit their sins to have brought this chastening on them. It is hard to say this without indulging a Pharisaic spirit, but I don't mean to palliate our national sins by exaggerating theirs. Yet I hardly think any mob but a French or Irish mob could have done what these men did.

'And what will be the result? Will it check the tendency to Republicanism? Will Governments unite to put down the many-headed monster? Will they take a lesson from the fate of Paris and France? Of course Republicanism is not the same thing as Communism. But where are we to look for the good effects of Republicanism?

'August 22nd.—The seventh anniversary of dear Fisher's death. May God grant us this year a blessing at Santa Cruz!

'Your affectionate

'J. C. PATTESON.'

The last letter to the beloved sister Fanny opened with the date of her never-forgotten birthday, the 27th of August, though it was carried on during the following weeks; and in the meantime Mr. Atkin, Stephen, Joseph and the rest were called for from Wango, in Bauro, where they had had a fairly peaceable stay, in spite of a visit from a labour traffic vessel, called the 'Emma Bell,' with twenty-nine natives under hatches, and, alas! on her way for more. After picking the Bauro party up, the Bishop wrote to the elder Mr. Atkin:—

'Wango Bay (at anchor): August 25, 1871.

'My dear Mr. Atkin,—You may imagine my joy at finding Joe looking really well when we reached this part of the world on the 23rd. I thought him looking unwell when he spent an hour or two with me at Mota, about ten weeks since, and I begged him to be careful, to use quinine freely, &c. He is certainly looking now far better than he was then, and he says that he feels quite well and strong. There is the more reason to be thankful for this, because the weather has been very rough, and rain has been falling continually. I had the same weather in the Banks Islands; scarcely a day for weeks without heavy rain. Here the sandy soil soon becomes dry again, it does not retain the moisture, and so far it has the advantage over the very tenacious clayey soil of Mota.

'Nearly all the time of the people here has been spent—wasted, perhaps, we should say—in making preparations for a great feast: so that Joe found it very hard to gain the attention of the people, when he tried to point out to them better things to think of than pigs, native money, tobacco and pipes. Such advance as has been made is rather in the direction of gaining the confidence and good-will of the people all about, and in becoming very popular among all the young folks. Nearly all the young people would come away with him, if the elders would allow them to do so. I have no doubt that much more has been really effected than is apparent to us now. Words have been said that have not been lost, and seed sown that will spring up some day. Just as at Mota, now, after some twelve or thirteen years, we first see the result in the movement now going on there, so it will be, by God's goodness, some day here. There at Mota the good example of George Sarawia, the collective result of the teaching of many years, and the steady conduct, with one exception, of the returned scholars, have now been blessed by God to the conversion of many of the people. We no longer hesitate to baptize infants and young children, for the parents engage to send them to school when they grow up, and are themselves receiving instruction in a really earnest spirit.

'Many, too, of those who have for some time abandoned the old ways, but yet did not distinctly accept the new teaching, have now felt the "power of the Gospel;" and though many candidates are still under probation, and I sought to act with caution, and to do all that lay in my power to make them perceive the exceeding solemnity of being baptized, the weighty promises, the great responsibility, yet I thought it right to baptize not less than forty-one grown men and women, besides seventeen lads of George's school, about whom there could be no hesitation. It has, indeed, been a very remarkable season there. I spent seven weeks broken by a New Hebrides trip of three weeks' duration into two periods of three and four weeks. Bice was with me for the first three weeks; and with a good many of our scholars turned into teachers here, we three (Bice, George, and I) kept up very vigorous school: a continual talking, questioning, &c., about religion, were always going on day and night. Many young children and infants were baptized, about 240 in all + 41 + 17.

'You will, I am sure, pray more than ever for George and all these converts to Christianity, that they may be strengthened and guarded against all evil, and live lives worthy of their profession. We hope to spend two or three days there on our return (D.V.); and if so, Joe will write you his impressions. Meanwhile, I tell him what I fully believe, that no one hearty effort of his to benefit these poor people is thrown away. Already they allow us to take boys, and perhaps this very day we may go off with two young girls also. And all this will result in some great change for the better some day.

'You will want to hear a word about myself. I am much better, partly I confess owing to the warmth of the climate, which certainly agrees with me. I may feel less well as we draw by-and-by to the south once more.

'I can't take strong exercise, and that is a privation. It did me good, and I feel the want of it; but I am much better than I was a year or ten months ago, and I do my work very fairly, and get about better than I expected. Remember me kindly to Mrs. Atkin and Mary, and believe me to be

'Your very sincere Friend,

'J. C. PATTESON.'

Mr. Brooke and Edward Wogale had had a far more trying sojourn at Florida.

'Wogale suffered much from his eyes; and the labour ships were frequently on the coast—all the three varieties: the fairly conducted one with a Government agent on board; the "Snatch-snatch," which only inveigled, but did not kill without necessity; and the "Kill-kill," which absolutely came head-hunting. It was a dreary eleven weeks.

'On July 11, a "Sydney vessel," as the natives called it, was on the west of the island, and nine natives were reported to Mr Brooke as having been killed, and with so much evidence that he had no doubt on the subject.

'On the 13th Takua came to him to say the "Kill-kill" vessel had anchored four miles off. What was he to do?

'"How was it you and Bisope came first, and then these slaughterers? Do you send them?"

'Mr. Brooke advised them to remain on shore; but if the strangers landed and wanted to kill or burn them, to fight for their lives. "Your words are the words of a chief," said Takua.

'This ship, however, sailed away; but on August 13 another came, much like the "Southern Cross," and canoes went out to her, in one of them Dudley Lankona. These returned safely, but without selling their fruit; and Dudley related that the men said, "Bishop and Brooke were bad, but they themselves were good, and had pipes and tobacco for those who would go with them."

'These, however, went away without doing them harm, only warning them that another vessel which was becalmed near at hand was a "killer," and the people were so uneasy about her that Mr. Brooke went on board, and was taken by the captain for a maker of cocoa-nut oil. He was a Scotchman, from Tanna, where he had settled, and was in search of labourers; a good-natured friendly kind of person on the whole, though regarding natives as creatures for capture.

'"If I get a chance to carry a lot of them off," he said, "I'll do it; but killing is not my creed."

'Mr. Brooke hinted that the natives might attack him, and he pointed to six muskets. "That's only a few of them. Let them come. We'll give it them pretty strong."

'He was rather taken aback when he found that he was talking to a clergyman. "Well, wherever you go nowadays there's missionaries. Who would have thought you'd got so far down?"

'And he looked with regret at Mr. Brooke's party of natives in their canoes, and observed, "Ah! my fine fellows, if your friend was not here I'd have the whole lot of you: what a haul!"

'He said the other ship was from Queensland, and had a Government agent on board, of whom he spoke with evident awe.

'On Mr. Brooke's return, Takua and Dikea were furbishing up old guns which some incautious person on board the "Curacoa" had given them, and they were disappointed to find that there could be no attack on the vessel.'

She, however, was scarcely gone before, at the other end of the island, Vara, four out of five men were killed by a boat's crew. The survivor, Sorova, told Mr. Brooke that he and one companion had gone out in one canoe, and three more in another, to a vessel that lay near the shore. He saw four blacks in her, as he thought Ysabel men. A white man came down from the boat, and sat in the bow of Sorova's canoe, but presently stood up and capsized both canoes, catching at Sorova's belt, which broke, and the poor fellow was thus enabled to get away, and shelter himself under the stern of the canoe, till he could strike out for land; but he saw a boat come round from the other side of the ship, with four men—whether whites or light-coloured islanders was not clear—but they proceeded to beat his companions with oars, then to fall on them with tomahawks, and finally cut off their heads, which were taken on board, and their bodies thrown to the sharks.

These men evidently belonged to that lowest and most horrible class of men-stealers, who propitiate the chiefs by assisting them in head-hunting.

Of course the island was full of rage, and on the 26th again another brig was in sight. Spite of warning, desire to trade induced five men to put off in a canoe. Two boats came down, and placed themselves on either side. Mr. Brooke could not watch, but a fierce shout arose from the crowd on shore, they rushed to the great canoe house, and a war fleet was launched, Dikea standing up in the foremost, with a long ebony spear in his hand. Fortunately they were too late: the boats were hauled up, and the brig went off at full sail. Whether the five were killed or carried captive is not clear.

The whole place was full of wailing. Revenge was all the cry. 'Let not their pigs be killed,' said Takua; 'we will give them to Bisope, he shall avenge us.' His brother Dikea broke out: 'My humour is bad because Bisope does not take us about in his vessel to kill-kill these people!'

When, two days later, the 'Southern Cross' was unmistakeably in sight, Takua said, 'Let Bisope only bring a man-of-war, and get me vengeance on my adversaries, and I shall be exalted like—like—like our Father above!'

The residence of Mr. Brooke in the island, and the testimony of their own countrymen to the way of life in Norfolk Island, had taught the Floridians to separate the Bishop from their foes; but it could scarcely be thus in places where confidence in him had not been established.

The Bishop meanwhile wrote on:—

'The New Zealand Bishops have sent me a kind letter, a round robin, urging me to go to England; but they are ignorant of two things:— 1st, that I am already much better; 2nd, that I should not derive the benefit generally to my spirits, &c. from a visit to England as they would, and take it for granted that I should do so.

'They use only one other argument, viz., that I must rest after some years' work. That is not so. I don't feel the pressure of work for a very simple reason, viz., that I don't attempt to work as I used to do.

'But just now, it is quite clear that I must not go, unless there were a very obvious necessity for it. For, 1st, Mota needs all the help we can give; 2nd, several Melanesians are coming on rapidly to the state when they ought to be ordained; 3rd, we are about to start (D.V.) new stations at Ambrym, Leper's Island, and Savo; 4th, the school is so large that we want "all hands" to work it; 5th, I must go to Fiji, and watch both Fiji and Queensland; 6th, after the 1872 voyage, we shall need, as I think, to sell this vessel, and have another new one built in Auckland. The funds will need careful nursing for this. But I will really not be foolish. If I have a return of the bad symptoms, I will go to Dr. Goldsboro', and if he advises it strongly, will go to England.

'The deportation of natives is going on to a very great extent here, as in the New Hebrides and Banks Islands. Means of all kinds are employed: sinking canoes and capturing the natives, enticing men on board, and getting them below, and then securing hatches and imprisoning them. Natives are retaliating. Lately, two or three vessels have been taken and all hands killed, besides boats' crews shot at continually. A man called on me at Mota the other day, who said that five out of seven in the boat were struck by arrows a few days before. The arrows were not poisoned, but one man was very ill. It makes even our work rather hazardous, except where we are thoroughly well known. I hear that a vessel has gone to Santa Cruz, and I must be very cautious there, for there has been some disturbance almost to a certainty.

'Whatever regulations the Government of Queensland or the Consul of Fiji may make, they can't restrain the traders from employing unlawful means to get hold of the natives. And I know that many of these men are utterly unscrupulous. But I can't get proofs that are sufficient to obtain a verdict in a court of law.

'Some islands are almost depopulated; and I dread the return of these "labourers," when they are brought back. They bring guns and other things, which enable them to carry out with impunity all kinds of rascality. They learn nothing that can influence them for good. They are like squatters in the bush, coming into the town to have their fling. These poor fellows come back to run riot, steal men's wives, shoot, fight, and use their newly acquired possessions to carry out more vigorously all heathen practices.

'September 3rd.—At anchor: Savo Island: Sunday. The experiment of anchoring at Sara (Florida) and this place answers well. The decks were crowded and crammed; but the people behaved very well, barring the picking up of everything they could lay hands upon, as is natural to many persons whose education has been neglected.

'Yesterday I took Wadrokala (of Nengone) to the village here, where he is to live with some of our old scholars from these parts, and try to begin a good work among the people. He has four baptized friends, a married couple being two, and three other very good lads, to start with. It was a long and very hot walk. A year ago I could not have got through it. I was tired, but not over-tired.

'And now we have had Holy Communion; and this afternoon we take our party on shore: Wadrokala's wife Carry, and Jemima, their daughter of eight or nine. There is no fighting or quarrelling here now. I know all the people, so I leave them with good hope.'

On the 7th, Joseph Atkin began a letter as follows:—

'Our Bishop is much improved in health and strength. His stay at Mota has put new life into him again; the whole island is becoming Christian.

'The Bishop is now very strong and clear about establishing permanent schools on the islands; I fear in almost too great a hurry. The great requisite for a school is a native teacher; and generally, if not always, a teacher ought, as George was at Mota, to be well supported by a little band of native converts, who, if their teaching, in the common use of the word, is not much, can, by their consistent lives, preach a continual sermon, that all who see may understand. What is the use of preaching an eloquent sermon on truth to a people who do not know what it means, or purity of which they have never dreamt? Their ears take in the words, they sound very pleasant, and they go away again to their sin; and the preacher is surprised that they can do so. I do not forget the power of the Spirit to change men's hearts, but do not expect the Holy Spirit to work with you as He never worked with anyone else, but rather as He always has worked with others.... If in looking into the history of Missions, you find no heathen people has been even nominally and professionally Christianised within, say, ten or fifteen years, why not be content to set to work to try that the conversion of those to whom you are sent may be as thorough and real as possible in that time, and not to fret at being unable to hurry the work some years?'....

This letter too was destined never to be finished, though it was continued later, as will be seen.

The Bishop's next letter is dated—

'September 16th.—Off the Santa Cruz group, some twenty miles distant. To-morrow, being Sunday, we stay quietly some way off the islands; and on Monday (D.V.) we go to Nukapu, and perhaps to Piteni too, wind permitting. You can enter into my thoughts, how I pray God that if it be His will, and if it be the appointed time, He may enable us in His own way to begin some little work among these very wild but vigorous energetic islanders. I am fully alive to the probability that some outrage has been committed here by one or more vessels. The master of the vessel that Atkin saw did not deny his intention of taking away from these or from any other islands any men or boys he could induce to come on board. I am quite aware that we may be exposed to considerable risk on this account. I trust that all may be well; that if it be His will that any trouble should come upon us, dear Joseph Atkin, his father and mother's only son, may be spared. But I don't think there is very much cause for fear; first, because at these small reef islands they know me pretty well, though they don't understand as yet our object in coming to them, and they may very easily connect us white people with the other white people who have been ill-using them; second, last year I was on shore at Nukapu and Piteni for some time, and I can talk somewhat with the people; third, I think that if any violence has been used to the natives of the north face of the large island, Santa Cruz, I shall hear of it from these inhabitants of the small islets to the north, Nukapu, and Piteni, and so be forewarned.

'If any violence has been used, it will make it impossible for us to go thither now. It would simply be provoking retaliation. One must say, as Newman of the New Dogma, that the progress of truth and religion is delayed, no one can say how long. It is very sad. But the Evil One everywhere and always stirs up opposition and hindrance to every attempt to do good. And we are not so sorely tried in this way as many others.'

Contrary winds—or rather a calm, with such light wind as there was, contrary—kept the vessel from approaching the island for four days more, while the volcano made every night brilliant, and the untiring pen ran on with affectionate responses to all that the last home packet had contained, and then proceeded to public interests:—

'Then the great matters you write about—the great social and religious crisis in England now. Moreover, who can estimate the effect of this German and French war upon the social state of Europe? Possibly a temporary violent suppression in North Germany of Republican principles, a reaction, an attempt to use the neutrality of England as a focus for political agitation. And then the extravagant luxury side by side with degrading poverty! It is a sad picture; and you who have to contemplate it have many trials and troubles that are in one sense far away from me.

'September 19th.—Here we are becalmed; for three days we have scarcely made ten miles in the direction we want to go. It is not prudent to go near the large island, unless we have a good breeze, and can get away from the fleets of canoes if we see reason for so doing. We may have one hundred and fifty canoes around us, and perhaps sixty or eighty strong men on deck, as we had last year; and this year we have good reason for fearing that labour vessels have been here. Many of the people here would distinguish between us and them; but it is quite uncertain, for we can't talk to the people of the large island, and can't therefore explain our object in so doing. 'Yesterday, being becalmed, a large canoe, passing (for there was occasionally a light air from the north) from Nupani to Santa Cruz, came near us. It could not get away, and the "Southern Cross" could not get near it. So we went to it in the boat. I can talk to these Nupani people, and we had a pleasant visit. They knew my name directly, and were quite at ease the moment they were satisfied it was the Bishop. They will advertise us, I dare say, and say a good word for us, and we gave them presents, &c.

'I shall be thankful if this visit ends favourably, and oh! how thankful if we obtain any lads. It seems so sad to leave this fine people year after year in ignorance and darkness, but He knows and cares for them more than we do. 'The sun is nearly vertical; thermometer 91°, and 88° at night; I am lazy, but not otherwise affected by it, and spend my day having some, about an hour's, school, and in writing and reading.

'I think that the Education question has been more satisfactorily settled than I dared to hope a year ago. A religious, as opposed to an irreligious education has been advisedly chosen by the country, and denominationalism (what a word!) as against secularism. Well, that's not much from a Christian country; but it isn't the choice of an anti-Christian, or even of a country indifferent to Christianity.

'Mrs. Abraham and Pena have sent me Shairp's little book on "Religion and

Culture." It is capital; and if you knew the man you would not wonder at his writing such sensible, thoughtful books. He is one of the most "loveable" beings I ever knew. His good wholesome teaching is about the best antidote I have seen to much of the poison circulating about in magazines and alluring ignorant, unsound people with the specious name of philosophy. And he is always fair, and credits his opponents with all that can possibly be imagined to extenuate the injury they are doing by their false and faithless teaching.'

Here the letter suddenly ceases. No doubt this last sentence had given the last impulse towards addressing the old Balliol friend above named, now Principal of St. Andrew's, in the following:—

'"Southern Cross" Mission Schooner,

'In the Santa Cruz Group, S.W. Pacific: September 19.

'My dear Principal,—You won't remember my name, and it is not likely that you can know anything about me, but I must write you a line and thank you for writing your two books (for I have but two) on "Studies on Poetry and Philosophy," and "Religion and Culture."

'The "Moral Dynamic" and the latter book are indeed the very books I have longed to see; books that one can put with confidence and satisfaction into the hands of men, young and old, in these stirring and dangerous times.

'Then it did me good to be recalled to old scenes and to dream of old faces.

'I was almost a freshman when you came up to keep your M.A. term; and as I knew some of the men you knew, you kindly, as I well remember, gave me the benefit of it. As John Coleridge's cousin and the acquaintance of John Keate, Cumin, Palmer, and dear James Eiddell, I came to know men whom otherwise I could not have known, and of these how many there still are that I have thought of and cared for ever since!

'You must have thought of Riddell, dear James Riddell, when you wrote the words in p. 76 of your book on "Religion and Culture": "We have known such." Yes, there was indeed about him a beauty of character that is very very rare. Sellar is in the north somewhere, I think I have seen Essays by him on Lucretius.

'I think that he is Professor at some University. I am ashamed to know so little about him. Should you see him, pray remember me most kindly to him. As year after year passes on, it is very pleasant to think there are men on the other side of the world that I can with a certainty count upon as friends.

'I find it difficult to read much of what is worth reading nowadays, and I have little taste for magazines, &c., I confess.

'But I know enough of what is working in men's minds in Europe to be heartily thankful for such thoughtful wholesome teaching as yours.

'Indeed, you are doing a good work, and I pray God it may be abundantly blessed.

'I remain, my dear Friend,

'Very sincerely yours,

'**J. C. PATTESON.**'

This is the last letter apparently finished and signed!

To the Bishop of Lichfield the long journal-letter says:—

'Tenakulu (the volcano) was fine last night, but not so fine as on that night we saw it together. But it was very solemn to look at it, and think how puny all man's works are in comparison with this little volcano. What is all the bombardment of Paris to those masses of fire and hundreds of tons of rock cast out into the sea? "If He do but touch the hills, they shall smoke."

'And now what will the next few days bring forth? It may be God's will that the opening for the Gospel may be given to us now. Sometimes I feel as if I were almost too importunate in my longings for some beginning here; and I try not to be impatient, and to wait His good time, knowing that it will come when it is the fulness of time. Then, again, I am tempted to think, "If not soon, if not now, the trading vessels will make it almost impossible, as men think, to obtain any opening here." But I am on the whole hopeful, though sometimes faint-hearted.

'To day's First Lesson has a good verse: Haggai, ii. 4;1 and there is Psalm xci. also.'

Then follows a good deal about further plans, and need of men; ending with the decision that the present 'Southern Cross' ought to be sold, and that a new one could be built at Auckland for £2,000, which the Bishop thought he could obtain in New Zealand and Australia.

'Yet now be strong, O Zerubbabel, saith the Lord; and be strong, O Joshua, son of Josedech, the high priest; and be strong, all ye people of the land, saith the Lord, and work: for I am with you, saith the Lord of hosts.'

A much smaller additional vessel would be useful; and he merrily says:—

'You don't know an amiable millionaire, with a nice quick yacht from 70 to 120 tons, to be given away, and sent out to Auckland free of expense, I suppose.

'We must give up all idea of our Chapel for a time, but we can do without it. And a vessel is necessary.'

The last of this letter is on Delitzsch and Biblical criticism, but too much mixed up with other persons' private affairs for quotation.

Reading Hebrew with Mr. Atkin, or studying Isaiah alone, had been the special recreation throughout the voyage.

His scholar Edward Wogale has given a touch of that last morning of the 20th:

—

'And as we were going to that island where he died, but were still in the open sea, he schooled us continually upon Luke ii. iii. up to vi., but he left off with us with his death. And he preached to us continually at Prayers in the morning, every day, and every evening on the Acts of the Apostles, and he spoke as far as to the seventh chapter, and then we reached that island. And he had spoken admirably and very strongly indeed to us, about the death of Stephen, and then he went up ashore on that island Nukapu.'

That island Nukapu lay with the blue waves breaking over the circling reef, the white line of coral sand, the trees coming down to it; and in the glowing sun of September 20, the equatorial midsummer eve, four canoes were seen hovering about the reef, as the 'Southern Cross' tried to make for the islet.

Mr. Brooke says that this lingering had seemed to intensify the Bishop's prayer and anxiety for these poor people; and, thinking that the unusual movements of the vessel puzzled the people in the canoes, and that they might be afraid to approach, he desired that at 11.30 A.M. the boat should be lowered, and entered it with Mr. Atkin, Stephen Taroniara, James Minipa, and John Nonono. He sat in the stern sheets, and called back to Mr. Brooke: "Tell the captain I may have to go ashore.' Then he waited to collect more things as presents to take on shore, and pulled towards the canoes; But they did not come to meet the boat, and seemed undecided whether to pull away or not. The people recognized the Bishop; and when he offered to go on shore they assented, and the boat went on to a part of the reef about two miles from the island, and there met two more canoes, making six in all. The natives were very anxious that they should haul the boat up on the reef, the tide being too low for her to cross it, but, when this was not consented to, two men proposed to take the Bishop into their boat.

It will be remembered that he had always found the entering one of their canoes a sure way of disarming suspicion, and he at once complied. Mr. Atkin afterwards said he thought he caught the word 'Tabu,' as if in warning, and saw a basket with yams and other fruits presented; and those acquainted with the customs of the Polynesians—the race to which these islanders belonged—say that this is sometimes done that an intended victim may unconsciously touch something tabu, and thus may become a lawful subject for a blow, and someone may have tried to warn him.

There was a delay of about twenty minutes; and then two canoes went with the one containing the Bishop, the two chiefs, Moto and Taula, who had before been so friendly to him, being in them. The tide was so low that it was necessary to wade over the reef, and drag the canoes across to the deeper lagoon within. The boat's crew could not follow; but they could see the Bishop land on the beach, and there lost sight of him.

The boat had been about half-an-hour drifting about in company with the canoes, and there had been some attempt at talk, when suddenly, at about ten yards off, without any warning, a man stood up in one of them, and calling out, 'Have you anything like this?' shot off one of the yard-long arrows, and his companions in the other two canoes began shooting as quickly as possible, calling out, as they aimed, 'This for New Zealand man! This for Bauro man! This for Mota man!' The boat was pulled back rapidly, and was soon out of range, but not before three out of the four had been struck; James only escaped by throwing himself back on the seat, while an arrow had nailed John's cap to his head, Mr. Atkin had one in his left shoulder, and poor Stephen lay in the bottom of the boat, 'trussed,' as Mr. Brooke described it, with six arrows in the chest and shoulders.

It was about two hours since they had left the ship when they reached it again: and Mr. Atkin said, 'We are all hurt? as they were helped on board; but no sooner had the arrow-head, formed of human bone, and acutely sharp, been extracted, than he insisted on going back to find his Bishop. He alone knew the way by which the reef could be crossed in the now rising tide, so that his presence was necessary. Meantime Mr. Brooke extracted as best he might the arrows from poor Stephen.

'We two Bisope,' said the poor fellow, meaning that he shared the same fate as the Bishop.

As Joseph Wate, a lad of fifteen, Mr. Atkin's Malanta godson and pupil, wrote afterwards, 'Joe said to me and Sapi, "We are going to look for the Bishop, are you two afraid?"

'"No, why should I be afraid?"

'"Very well, you two go and get food for yourselves, and bring a beaker full of water for us all, for we shall have to lie on our oars a long time to-day."'

The others who pulled the boat were Charles Sapinamba, a sailor, and Mr. Bongarde, the mate, who carried a pistol, for the first time in the records of the 'Southern Cross.'

They had long to wait till the tide was high enough to carry them across the reef, and they could see people on shore, at whom they gazed anxiously with a glass.

About half-past four it became possible to cross the reef, and then two canoes rowed towards them: one cast off the other and went back; the other, with a heap in the middle, drifted towards them, and they rowed towards it.

'But' (says Wate), 'when we came near we two were afraid, and I said to Joe, "If there is a man inside to attack us, when he rises up, we shall see him."'

Then the mate took up his pistol, but the sailor said, 'Those are the Bishop's shoes.'

As they came up with it, and lifted the bundle wrapped in matting into the boat, a shout or yell arose from the shore. Wate says four canoes put off in pursuit; but the others think their only object was to secure the now empty canoe as it drifted away. The boat came alongside, and two words passed, 'The body!' Then it was lifted up, and laid across the skylight, rolled in the native mat, which was secured at the head and feet. The placid smile was still on the face; there was a palm leaf fastened over the breast, and when the mat was opened there were five wounds, no more.

The strange mysterious beauty, as it may be called, of these circumstances almost makes one feel as if this were the legend of a martyr of the Primitive Church; but the fact is literally true, and can be interpreted, though probably no account will ever be obtained from the actors in the scene.

The wounds were, one evidently given with a club, which had shattered the right side of the skull at the back, and probably was the first, and had destroyed life instantly, and almost painlessly; another stroke of some sharp weapon had cloven the top of the head; the body was also pierced in one place; and there were two arrow wounds in the legs, but apparently not shot at the living man, but stuck in after his fall, and after he had been stripped, for the clothing was gone, all but the boots and socks. In the front of the cocoa-nut palm, there were five knots made in the long leaflets. All this is an almost certain indication that his death was the vengeance for five of the natives. 'Blood for blood' is a sacred law, almost of nature, wherever Christianity has not prevailed, and a whole tribe is held responsible for the crime of one. Five men in Fiji are known to have been stolen from Nukapu; and probably their families believed them to have been killed, and believed themselves to be performing a sacred duty when they dipped their weapons in the blood of the Bisope, whom they did not know well enough to understand that he was their protector. Nay, it is likely that there had been some such discussion as had saved him before at Mai from suffering for Petere's death; and, indeed, one party seem to have wished to keep him from landing, and to have thus solemnly and reverently treated his body.

Even when the tidings came in the brief uncircumstantial telegram, there were none of those who loved and revered him who did not feel that such was the death he always looked for, and that he had willingly given his life. There was peace in the thought even while hearts trembled with dread of hearing of accompanying horrors; and when the full story arrived, showing how far more painless his death had been than had he lived on to suffer from his broken health, and how wonderfully the unconscious heathen had marked him with emblems so sacred in our eyes, there was thankfulness and joy even to the bereaved at home.

The sweet calm smile preached peace to the mourners who had lost his guiding spirit, but they could not look on it long. The next morning, St. Matthew's Day, the body of John Coleridge Patteson was committed to the waters of the Pacific, his 'son after the faith,' Joseph Atkin, reading the Burial Service.

Mr. Atkin afterwards wrote to his mother. He had written to his father the day before; but the substance of his letter has been given in the narrative:—

'September 21, 1871.

'My dear Mother,—We have had a terrible loss, such a blow that we cannot at all realise it. Our Bishop is dead; killed by the natives at Nukapu yesterday. We got the body, and buried it this morning. He was alone on shore, and none of us saw it done. We were attacked in the boat too, and Stephen so badly wounded that I am afraid there is small hope of his recovery. John and I have arrow wounds, but not severe. Our poor boys seem quite awe-stricken. Captain Jacobs is very much cut up. Brooke, although not at all well, has quite devoted himself to the wounded, and so has less time to think about it all.

'It would only be selfish to wish him back. He has gone to his rest, dying, as he lived, in his Master's service.

'It seems a shocking way to die; but I can say from experience that it is far more to hear of than to suffer. In whatever way so peaceful a life as his is ended, his end is peace. There was no sign of fear or pain on his face—just the look that he used to have when asleep, patient and a little wearied. "What a stroke his death will be to hundreds!" What his Mission will do without him, God only knows Who has taken him away. His ways are not as our ways. Seeing people taken away, when, as we think, they are almost necessary to do God's work on earth, makes one think that we often think and talk too much about Christian work. What God requires is Christian men. He does not need the work, only gives it to form or perfect the character of the men whom He sends to do it.

'Stephen is in great pain at times to-night; one of the arrows seems to have entered his lungs, and it is broken in, too deep to be got out. John is wounded in the right shoulder, I in the left. We are both maimed for the time; but, if it were not for the fear of poison, the wounds would not be worth noticing. I do not expect any bad consequences, but they are possible. What would make me cling to life more than anything else is the thought of you at home; but if it be God's will that I am to die, I know He will enable you to bear it, and bring good for you out of it.

'Saturday, 23rd.—We are all doing well. Stephen keeps up his strength, sleeps well, and has no long attacks of pain. We have had good breezes yesterday and to-day—very welcome it is, but the motion makes writing too much labour. Brooke and Edward Wogale are both unwell—ague, I believe, with both of them; and Brooke's nerves are upset. He has slept most of to-day, and will probably be the better for it.'....

His private journal adds:—

'September 21st.—Buried the Bishop in the morning. The wounded all doing well, but Stephen in pain occasionally. Calm day, passed over a reef in the morning, about eighteen miles north of Nukapu, nine fathoms on it. Thermometer ninety-one degrees yesterday and to-day. Began writing home at night. Began reading Miss Yonge's "Chaplet of Pearls."

'Friday, 22nd.—A light breeze came up in the evening, which freshened through the night, and carried us past Tenakulu. Stephen doing very well, had a good night, and has very little pain to-day. A breeze through the day, much cooler. I am dressing my shoulder with brine. Read some sermons of Vaughan's, preached at Doncaster during Passion Week.

'Saturday, 23rd.—Breeze through the day. A few showers of rain. Brooke and Wogale down with ague; gave Wogale ipecacuanha and quinine afterwards. Read Mota prayers in evening. All wounds going on well. Finished "Chaplet of Pearls," and wrote a little.

'Sunday, 24th.—This morning the wind went round to N.E. and N. and then died away. We were 55 miles W. of the Torres Islands at noon. Brooke took English and Mota morning Prayers. I celebrated Holy Communion afterwards. John came into cabin; I went out to Stephen.

'Brooke and Wogale both better, but B—— quite weak.'

During that Celebration, while administering the Sacred Elements, Mr. Atkin's tongue stumbled and hesitated over some of the words.

Then the Mota men looked at one another, and knew what would follow.

He knew it himself too, and called to Joseph Wate, his own special pupil, saying (as the lad wrote to Mr. Atkin the elder), 'Stephen and I again are going to follow the Bishop, and they of your country—! Who is to speak to them?'

'I do not know.'

Then he said again, 'It is all right. Don't grieve about it, because they did not do this thing of themselves, but God allowed them to do it. It is very good, because God would have it so, because He only looks after us, and He understands about us, and now He wills to take away us two, and it is well.'

There was much more for that strong young frame to undergo before the vigorous life could depart. The loss was to be borne. The head of the Mission, who had gone through long sickness, and lain at the gates of the grave so long, died almost painlessly: his followers had deeply to drink of the cup of agony. The night between the 26th and 27th was terrible, the whole nervous system being jerked and strained to pieces, and he wandered too much to send any message home; 'I lost my wits since they shot me,' he said. Towards morning he almost leapt from his berth on the floor, crying 'Good-bye.'

Mr. Brooke asked if he would have a little Sal volatile.

'No.'

'A little brandy?'

'No.'

'Do you want anything?'

'I want nothing but to die.'

Those were his last words. He lay convulsed on a mattress on the floor for about an hour longer, and was released on the morning of the 29th.

Stephen, with an arrow wound in the lungs, and several more of these wounds in the chest, could hardly have lived, even without the terrible tetanus. He had spent his time in reading his Mota Gospel and Prayer-book, praying and speaking earnestly to the other men on board, before the full agony came on. He was a tall, large, powerfully framed man; and the struggles were violent before he too sank into rest on the morning of the 28th, all the time most assiduously nursed by Joseph Wate. On St. Michael's Day, these two teachers of poor Bauro received at the same time their funeral at sea.

John Coleridge Patteson was forty-four years and a half old.

Joseph Atkin, twenty-nine.

Stephen Taroniara probably twenty-five—as he was about eighteen when he joined the Mission in 1864. His little girl will be brought up at Norfolk Island; his wife Tara, to whom he had been married only just before his voyage, became consumptive, and died January, 1873, only twenty minutes after her Baptism. As one of the scholars said, "Had the songs of the angels for joy of her being made a child of God finished before they were again singing to welcome her an inheritor of the kingdom of heaven?"

John Nonono showed no symptoms of tetanus, but was landed at Mota to recover under more favourable circumstances than the crowded cabin could afford.

Calms and baffling winds made the return to this island trying and difficult, and Mota was not reached till the 4th of October. George Sarawia was still perfectly satisfactory; and his community, on the whole, going on hopefully. Want of provisions, which Mota could not supply, made the stay very brief; and after obtaining the necessary supplies at Aurora, the 'Southern Cross' brought her sad tidings to Norfolk Island on the 17th. That day Mrs. Palmer wrote:—

'On Monday afternoon, 15th, Mr. Codrington went for a ride to the other side of the island, and there espied the schooner, eight miles off. He rode home quickly, and soon the shouting and racing of the boys told us that the vessel had come. They were all at arrowroot-making. Never, I think, had the whole party, English and natives, seemed in higher spirits. Mr. Bice walked to the settlement, to see if she was far in enough to land that night; we asked him to call and tell us on his way home.

'Next morning Mr. Bice rode down to see if it really was the schooner, and was back to breakfast, all thinking we should soon see them come up.

'Mr. Codrington and Mr. Bice got their horses ready to ride down, and I got the rooms ready, when, in an hour, a Norfolk Island boy rode up to say the flag was half-mast high.'

'We told the boys and girls something was wrong, to stop their joyous shouting and laughing; and then I waited till Mr. Jackson returned, and all he could say was, "Only Brooke has come!"'

What more shall I tell? Comments on such a life and such a death are superfluous; and to repeat the testimonies of friends, outpourings of grief, and utterances in sermons is but to weaken the impression of the reality!

There is pain too in telling the further fate of Nukapu. H.M.S. 'Rosario,' Commander Markham, then cruising in the Southern Pacific, touched at Norfolk Island, and Captain Markham undertook at once to go to the island and make enquiries.

A protest was drawn up and signed by all the members of the Mission against any attempt to punish the natives for the murder; and Captain Markham, a kind, humane, and conscientious man, as no one can doubt, promised that nothing of the kind should be attempted.

But the natives could not but expect retaliation for what they had done. There was no interpreter. They knew nothing of flags of truce; and when they saw a boat approaching, full of white men, armed, what could they apprehend but vengeance for 'Bisope'? So they discharged a volley of arrows, and a sergeant of marines was killed. This was an attack on the British flag, and it was severely chastised with British firearms. It is very much to be doubted whether Nukapu will ever understand that her natives were shot, not for killing the Bishop, but for firing on the British flag. For the present the way is closed, and we can only echo Fisher Young's sigh, 'Poor Santa Cruz people!'

Bishop Patteson's will bequeathed his whole inheritance to the Melanesian Mission, and appointed that the senior Priest should take charge of it until another Bishop should be chosen.

The Rev. Robert Codrington, therefore, took the management, though refusing the Episcopate; and considering the peculiar qualifications needful for a Melanesian Bishop, which can only be tested by actual experiment on physical as well as moral and spiritual abilities, it has, up to the present moment (May 1873), been thought better to leave the See vacant, obtaining episcopal aid from the Bishop of Auckland.

But this implies no slackness nor falling off in the Mission. By God's good providence, Coleridge Patteson had so matured his system that it could work without him. Mr. Codrington and the other clergy make their periodic voyages in the 'Southern Cross.' Kohimarama flourishes under George Sarawia, who was ordained Priest at Auckland on St. Barnabas Day, 1873. Bishop Cowie has paid a visit to Norfolk Island, and ordained as Deacons, Edward Wogale, Robert Pantatun, Henry Tagalana, to work in Mota, Santa Maria, and Ara. Joseph Wate remains the chief teacher of the lads from Bauro; but there is much to be done before the work in that island can be carried on. The people there seem peculiarly devoid of earnestness; and it is remarkable that though they were among the first visited, and their scholars the very earliest favourites, Stephen has been the only one whose Christianity seems to have been substantial. But the sight of his patient endurance had the same effect on those who were with him in the ship as Walter Hotaswol's exhortations had had on himself, and several of them began in earnest to prepare for Baptism.

The English staff of the Mission has been recruited by the Rev. John R. Selwyn, and the Rev. John Still, as well as by Mr. Kenny from New Zealand. And there is good hope that 'He who hath begun a good work will perform it unto the day of the Lord.'

As to the crimes connected with the murder, the Queen herself directed the attention of Parliament to it in her Speech at the commencement of the Session of 1872. The Admiralty do what in them lies to keep watch over the labour vessels by means of Queen's ships; and in Queensland, regulations are made; in Fiji, the British Consul endeavours to examine the newly arrived, whether they have been taken away by force. But it may be feared that it will not be possible entirely to prevent atrocities over so wide a range; though if, as Bishop Patteson suggested, all vessels unregistered, and not committed to trustworthy masters, were liable to be seized and confiscated, much of the shameless deceit and horrible skull-hunting would be prevented.

Perhaps the fittest conclusion to the Bishop's history will be the words written by Henry Tagalana, translated literally by Mr. Codrington:—

'As he taught, he confirmed his word with his good life among us, as we all know; and also that he perfectly well helped anyone who might be unhappy about anything, and spoke comfort to him about it; and about his character and conduct, they are consistent with the law of God. He gave the evidence of it in his practice, for he did nothing carelessly, lest he should make anyone stumble and turn from the good way; and again he did nothing to gain anything for himself alone, but he sought what he might keep others with, and then he worked with it: and the reason was his pitifulness and his love. And again, he did not despise anyone, nor reject anyone with scorn; whether it were a white or a black person he thought them all as one, and he loved them all alike.'

'He loved them all alike!' That was the secret of John Coleridge Patteson's history and his labours.

Need more be said of him? Surely the simple islander's summary of his character is the honour he would prefer.

Printed in Great Britain
by Amazon